Going Nuclear:
Nuclear Proliferation and International Security
in the 21st Century

International Security Readers

Strategy and Nuclear Deterrence (1984)

Military Strategy and the Origins of the First World War (1985)

Conventional Forces and American Defense Policy (1986)

The Star Wars Controversy (1986)

Naval Strategy and National Security (1988)

Military Strategy and the Origins of the First World War,
revised and expanded edition (1991)

—published by Princeton University Press

Soviet Military Policy (1989)

Conventional Forces and American Defense Policy, revised edition (1989)

Nuclear Diplomacy and Crisis Management (1990)

The Cold War and After: Prospects for Peace (1991)

America's Strategy in a Changing World (1992)

The Cold War and After: Prospects for Peace, expanded edition (1993)

Global Dangers: Changing Dimensions of International Security (1995)

The Perils of Anarchy: Contemporary Realism and International Security (1995)

Debating the Democratic Peace (1996)

East Asian Security (1996)

Nationalism and Ethnic Conflict (1997)

America's Strategic Choices (1997)

Theories of War and Peace (1998)

America's Strategic Choices, revised edition (2000)

Rational Choice and Security Studies: Stephen Walt and His Critics (2000)

The Rise of China (2000)

Nationalism and Ethnic Conflict, revised edition (2001)

Offense, Defense, and War (2004)

New Global Dangers: Changing Dimensions of International Security (2004)

Primacy and Its Discontents: American Power and International Stability (2009)

*Going Nuclear: Nuclear Proliferation and International Security in the
21st Century* (2010)

—published by The MIT Press

Going Nuclear
Nuclear Proliferation and International Security in the 21st Century

AN *International Security* READER

EDITED BY
Michael E. Brown
Owen R. Coté Jr.
Sean M. Lynn-Jones
and Steven E. Miller

THE MIT PRESS
CAMBRIDGE, MASSACHUSETTS
LONDON, ENGLAND

The contents of this book were first published in *International Security* (ISSN 0162-2889), a publication of the MIT Press under the sponsorship of the Belfer Center for Science and International Affairs at Harvard University. Copyright in each of the following articles is owned jointly by the President and Fellows of Harvard College and of the Massachusetts Institute of Technology.

Scott D. Sagan, "Why Do States Build Nuclear Weapons? Three Models in Search of a Bomb," 21:3 (Winter 1996/97); Etel Solingen, "The Political Economy of Nuclear Restraint," 19:2 (Fall 1994); William C. Potter and Gaukhar Mukhatzhanova, "Divining Nuclear Intentions: A Review Essay," 33:1 (Summer 2008); Matthew Fuhrmann, "Spreading Temptation: Proliferation and Peaceful Nuclear Cooperation Agreements," 34:1 (Summer 2009); Sumit Ganguly, "India's Pathway to Pokhran II: The Prospects and Sources of New Delhi's Nuclear Weapons Program," 23:4 (Spring 1999); Samina Ahmed, "Pakistan's Nuclear Weapons Program: Turning Points and Nuclear Choices," 23:4 (Spring 1999); Sumit Ganguly, "Nuclear Stability in South Asia," 33:2 (Fall 2008); S. Paul Kapur, "Ten Years of Instability in a Nuclear South Asia," 33:2 (Fall 2008); Peter Liberman, "The Rise and Fall of the South African Bomb," 26:2 (Fall 2001); Ariel E. Levite, "Never Say Never Again: Nuclear Reversal Revisited," 27:3 (Winter 2002/03); Chaim Braun and Christopher F. Chyba, "Proliferation Rings: New Challenges to the Nuclear Nonproliferation Regime," 29:2 (Fall 2004); Alexander H. Montgomery, "Ringing in Proliferation: How to Dismantle an Atomic Bomb Network," 30:2 (Fall 2005); Whitney Raas and Austin Long, "Osirak Redux? Assessing Israeli Capabilities to Destroy Iranian Nuclear Facilities," 31:4 (Spring 2007).

Selection, preface, and Matthew Bunn, "Nuclear Terrorism: A Strategy for Prevention," copyright © 2010 by the President and Fellows of Harvard College and of the Massachusetts Institute of Technology.

Library of Congress Cataloging-in-Publication Data

Going nuclear : nuclear proliferation and international security in the 21st century / edited by Michael E. Brown...[et al.].
    p. cm. — (International security readers)
  Includes bibliographical references.
  ISBN 978-0-262-52466-7 (pbk. : alk. paper)
  1. Nuclear nonproliferation. 2. Security, International. 3. International relations. I. Brown, Michael E.
  JZ5675.N8386 2010
  327.1'747—dc22
                                    2009034753

10 9 8 7 6 5 4 3 2

Contents

The Contributors

MICHAEL E. BROWN is Dean of the Elliott School of International Affairs and Professor of International Affairs and Political Science at the George Washington University.

OWEN R. COTÉ JR. is Co-Editor of *International Security* and Associate Director of the Security Studies Program at the Massachusetts Institute of Technology.

SEAN M. LYNN-JONES is Co-Editor of *International Security* and a research associate at the Belfer Center for Science and International Affairs, John F. Kennedy School of Government, Harvard University.

STEVEN E. MILLER is Editor-in-Chief of *International Security*, Co–Principal Investigator, Project on Managing the Atom, and Director of the International Security Program at the Belfer Center for Science and International Affairs, John F. Kennedy School of Government, Harvard University.

SAMINA AHMED is South Asia Project Director at the International Crisis Group.

CHAIM BRAUN is Consulting Professor at the Center for International Security and Cooperation, Freeman Spogli Institute for International Studies, Stanford University.

MATTHEW BUNN is Associate Professor of Public Policy at the Harvard Kennedy School; Co–Principal Investigator, Project on Managing the Atom, and Co–Principal Investigator, Energy Research, Development, Demonstration, and Deployment Policy Project at the Belfer Center for Science and International Affairs, John F. Kennedy School of Government, Harvard University.

CHRISTOPHER F. CHYBA is Professor of Astrophysical Sciences and International Affairs and Director of the Program on Science and Global Security at the Woodrow Wilson School of Public and International Affairs, Princeton University.

MATTHEW FUHRMANN is Assistant Professor of Political Science at the University of South Carolina and is also an Associate with the Project on Managing the Atom at the Belfer Center for Science and International Affairs.

SUMIT GANGULY holds the Rabindranath Tagore Chair in Indian Cultures and Civilizations at Indiana University in Bloomington.

S. PAUL KAPUR is Associate Professor in the Department of National Security Affairs at the U.S. Naval Postgraduate School and a Faculty Affiliate at Stanford University's Center for International Security and Cooperation.

ARIEL E. LEVITE is Senior Associate in the Nonproliferation Program at the Carnegie Endowment for International Peace.

PETER LIBERMAN is Professor of Political Science at Queens College.

AUSTIN LONG is a Ph.D. candidate in Political Science and a member of the Security Studies Program at the Massachusetts Institute of Technology.

ALEXANDER H. MONTGOMERY is Assistant Professor of Political Science at Reed College.

GAUKHAR MUKHATZHANOVA is a research associate at the James Martin Center for Nonproliferation Studies at the Monterey Institute of International Studies.

WILLIAM C. POTTER is Sam Nunn and Richard Lugar Professor of Nonproliferation Studies and Director of the James Martin Center for Nonproliferation Studies at the Monterey Institute of International Studies.

WHITNEY RAAS is an analyst at the Center for Naval Analyses.

SCOTT D. SAGAN is Professor of Political Science and Co-Director of the Center for International Security and Cooperation, Freeman Spogli Institute for International Studies, Stanford University.

ETEL SOLINGEN is Professor of Political Science at the University of California, Irvine.

Acknowledgments

The editors gratefully acknowledge the assistance that has made this book possible. A deep debt is owed to all those at the Belfer Center for Science and International Affairs, Harvard University, who have played an editorial role at *International Security*. Special thanks go to Diane McCree and Katherine Bartel for their invaluable help in preparing this volume for publication.

Preface | *Sean M. Lynn-Jones*

The spread of nuclear weapons is an important issue in the theory and practice of international relations. The most fundamental reason why scholars and analysts study nuclear proliferation is that the spread of nuclear weapons may increase the likelihood of nuclear war. Although there has been a vigorous debate between nuclear optimists and nuclear pessimists over whether nuclear proliferation increases the risk of war,[1] most analysts and policymakers have worried that war—including nuclear war—will become more likely as more states go nuclear.

There are many reasons to think that the spread of nuclear weapons will make it more likely that such weapons will be used. If more states have nuclear weapons, the probability that one leader will decide to use them may increase. Even if rational decisionmakers are likely to be deterred by the threat of nuclear retaliation, the possibility of inadvertent or accidental use remains.

The spread of nuclear weapons also increases the probability of theft of nuclear materials. Even if nuclear weapons have a stabilizing effect on relations between states, terrorist groups may be able to steal nuclear materials or nuclear bombs and then detonate a nuclear weapon in a major city, killing hundreds of thousands. Such concerns existed before the terrorist attacks of September 11, 2001, but have become more acute since. As more states acquire nuclear weapons, there will probably be more opportunities for theft by terrorists.

A state's quest for nuclear weapons can be a source of conflict even when such efforts are terminated, unsuccessful, or incomplete. A state that fears that an adversary is developing nuclear weapons may launch preventive attacks against its adversary's nuclear facilities. Israel bombed the nuclear reactor at Osirak, Iraq, in 1981 and attacked an apparent nuclear facility in Syria in 2007. The United States made plans to strike North Korean nuclear facilities in 1994. Many analysts believe that Israel or the United States might attack sites related to Iran's nuclear program.[2] In extreme cases, a state may respond to concern over the nuclear program of a hostile state by launching a full-scale war. The 2003 U.S. invasion of Iraq was at least partially motivated by U.S. fears that Iraq was developing nuclear weapons.

Concern over nuclear proliferation is likely to increase in the coming years. Many observers believe that the spread of nuclear weapons to one or two more

---

1. The classic contribution to the optimism-pessimism debate remains Scott D. Sagan and Kenneth N. Waltz, *The Spread of Nuclear Weapons: A Debate Renewed* (New York: W.W. Norton, 2002).
2. See Whitney Raas and Austin Long, "Osirak Redux? Assessing Israeli Capabilities to Destroy Iranian Nuclear Facilities," in this volume.

states will trigger a wave of new nuclear states. More states may turn to nuclear power to meet their energy needs as other sources of energy become more costly or undesirable because they emit carbon that contributes to global climate change. As more nuclear reactors are built, the world's stock of nuclear expertise and fissionable materials is likely to grow.

Because most analysts and policymakers have feared the consequences of nuclear proliferation, states have attempted to limit the spread of nuclear weapons. The centerpiece of international efforts to limit nuclear proliferation is the Nuclear Nonproliferation Treaty (NPT), which was signed in 1968 and extended indefinitely in 1995. The NPT requires that states without nuclear weapons not seek them and that states with nuclear weapons not transfer them. It recognizes that states without nuclear weapons have a right to the peaceful use of nuclear energy, provided that they accept safeguards overseen by the International Atomic Energy Agency (IAEA). The NPT's Article 6 also requires nuclear weapon states to attempt to reduce or even eliminate their nuclear arsenals.

In addition to the NPT, many states—particularly the United States—have pursued additional policies to prevent the spread of nuclear weapons. These policies have included diplomatic and economic pressure on potential proliferants, as well as restrictions on the transfer of technologies required for the production and delivery of nuclear weapons.

The essays in this book focus on two questions. First, why do states want nuclear weapons? Second, what can be done to prevent or slow the spread of nuclear weapons? Although several essays also consider the effects of nuclear proliferation—particularly in South Asia—this volume is primarily about understanding and preventing the spread of nuclear weapons.

The essays in the volume—and the broader literature on nuclear proliferation—include several explanations for states' nuclear decisions. What motivates them to devote resources to acquiring nuclear materials, technologies, and knowledge and combining them to build bombs?

First, many analysts and scholars argue that states seek nuclear weapons because such weapons can enable them to counter threats to their security. For a state that faces conventional military threats, nuclear weapons can be used to deter attacks. Nuclear weapons also may be the best means of deterring attacks with nuclear weapons. This explanation of nuclear proliferation suggests that states will be less likely to go nuclear—and may even dismantle their nuclear weapons—if they are relatively secure or become more secure.

Second, other analysts and scholars focus on domestic instead of international explanations for nuclear proliferation. They argue that external security threats often matter less than internal organizational dynamics. For example, the nuclear scientists and engineers in a country often will have a vested interest in maximizing the resources devoted to their programs. They may be able to lobby for increased funding for expanded programs that at least create the capability to build nuclear weapons. In other cases, nuclear decisions may be driven by public opinion. An unpopular leader may try to enhance his or her standing with the public by, for example, testing a nuclear weapon.

Third, international norms may constrain or encourage nuclear proliferation. If nuclear weapons are seen as legitimate weapons that confer status and prestige on states that possess them, states may be more likely to seek them. On the other hand, if nuclear weapons are regarded as illegitimate and there is a strong norm against acquiring them, fewer states are likely to pursue the nuclear option. Many observers believe that the NPT has encouraged the development of a strong international norm against acquisition of nuclear weapons.

Fourth, external incentives, including norms, may interact with domestic factors. States that seek nuclear weapons may face economic sanctions or a cutoff of foreign aid. Whether a state is sensitive to these external incentives and disincentives may depend on its internal political economy, its integration into world markets, and its domestic structure.

Finally, some analysts argue that states with access to sophisticated nuclear technology—including the knowledge and facilities vital to a civilian nuclear power program—are more likely to acquire nuclear weapons. Although this argument is not "technological determinism," because it does not hold that all states with nuclear technology inevitably develop nuclear weapons, it suggests that proliferation policies should pay attention to the "supply side" of nonproliferation and do more to restrict the spread of nuclear technologies and knowledge.

The essays in this volume assess the importance of each of these factors in shaping the nuclear decisions of France, India, Israel, North Korea, Pakistan, South Africa, Sweden, and many other states that have (or have not) become nuclear weapons states.

The second major question examined in this book is how to prevent nuclear proliferation. In many cases, the policies chosen to limit proliferation reflect an understanding of proliferation's causes. If states seek nuclear weapons because they want to enhance their security, the logical nonproliferation policies include pledges by major powers to defend vulnerable states, and commitments not to use nuclear weapons against nonnuclear weapons states. If a particular domestic interest group is driving a country's quest for nuclear weapons, external support for other groups may be the best way to prevent proliferation. Strengthening the norm against nuclear weapons and nuclear proliferation (e.g., by reaffirming the NPT and reducing the nuclear arsenals of nuclear weapons states) may affect the political calculations of many states that might otherwise consider acquiring nuclear weapons. The NPT and other aspects of the existing nuclear nonproliferation regime include many elements of these policies.

Understanding and preventing nuclear proliferation must begin with an examination of why states acquire nuclear weapons. The first section of this volume thus features essays that attempt to explain why states build the bomb. The four essays in this section present and assess alternative theories.

Scott Sagan, in "Why Do States Build Nuclear Weapons? Three Models in Search of a Bomb," challenges the conventional wisdom that countries seek nuclear weapons when facing a security threat that they cannot meet with nonnuclear forces. He examines three alternative theoretical frameworks for explaining why states develop nuclear weapons. The first is the "security model," which embraces the conventional wisdom that states seek nuclear weapons to provide security against foreign threats. The second, the "domestic politics model," holds that nuclear weapons programs are often used to advance domestic political and bureaucratic interests. The third is the "norms model," which argues that a state's policies toward nuclear weapons often symbolize its modernity and identity.

Sagan finds that each theory can explain some cases. The security model's central premise is that states acquire nuclear weapons because they are threatened by the nuclear arsenals of other states. Nuclear proliferation is therefore "a strategic chain reaction." The Soviet Union developed nuclear weapons because it feared the U.S. nuclear monopoly after the nuclear attacks on Hiroshima and Nagasaki. Britain and France responded to the Soviet threat by acquiring nuclear forces. China was initially threatened by the United States and later by the Soviet Union, giving it a double impetus to build its own bomb. India responded to China's nuclear weapons with its own nuclear program, which in turn provoked Pakistan to seek the bomb.

The security model explains nuclear restraint as a response to the reduction of threats. By this logic, South Africa, for example, could dismantle its small nuclear arsenal in 1991, because it was no longer threatened by the Soviet Union and it had negotiated settlements of regional issues in Angola and

Namibia. Similarly, Argentina and Brazil ended their nascent nuclear programs when they realized that they did not pose a threat to each other. The security model also argues that the former Soviet republics Belarus, Kazakhstan, and Ukraine could relinquish the nuclear weapons on their territory because they did not see Russia as a military threat.

Sagan notes that the security model has several policy implications. First, the United States should continue to guarantee the security of its allies, which otherwise might be tempted to seek nuclear weapons. Second, the United States should support the NPT, because that treaty reduces incentives to develop nuclear weapons by reassuring countries that their neighbors will not develop them. Sagan points out, however, that the realist logic that underpins the security model also implies that nuclear proliferation can be slowed, but not prevented. The inherent insecurity of international politics and chain-reaction dynamics make it inevitable that more states will want nuclear weapons.

Is the security model valid? Although it seems plausible, Sagan argues that decisionmakers often have a vested interest in claiming that they opted to develop nuclear weapons in response to threats. Such policies appear to be rational attempts to pursue the national interest. Moreover, it is almost always possible to identify some threat that existed before a state decided to seek nuclear weapons. Looking inside the "black box of decision-making" may reveal other motives for building the bomb.

The domestic politics model recognizes that acquiring nuclear weapons often serves the interests of various domestic groups: a state's nuclear energy establishment; units within the armed forces; and politicians in states where the public supports nuclear weapons. Sagan recognizes that there are no good general theories of domestic politics and foreign policy; he argues that bureaucrats and weapons scientists with an interest in starting or expanding a nuclear weapons program often can manipulate information and threat perceptions. Whereas the security model emphasizes the importance of threats as causes of nuclear programs, the domestic politics model regards threats as "windows of opportunity through which parochial interests can jump."

Sagan examines how the domestic politics model explains the nuclear decisions of India and South Africa. India did not respond to China's 1964 nuclear test by initiating a nuclear weapons program. Instead, a prolonged bureaucratic battle ensued, in which some groups argued for nuclear weapons and others favored global nuclear disarmament. India eventually conducted a "peaceful" nuclear test in 1974. It is unclear whether security concerns or domestic-political considerations drove India to develop nuclear weapons, but the nuclear test immediately boosted the political standing of an unpopular government.[3]

South Africa's decision to start and then terminate a nuclear weapons program also can be explained by looking at domestic political factors. South Africa initiated its nuclear program in 1971, long before Cuban forces intervened in the Angolan civil war. The program may have been intended to produce peaceful nuclear explosions for use in South African mining operations. The first nuclear devices were produced by South Africa's nuclear establishment without consulting the South African military. South Africa decided to dismantle its nuclear weapons before the Cold War ended and the external threat to South Africa diminished. The decision apparently reflected concern that the weapons would be controlled by a black successor government.[4]

Domestic political factors also may have played a role in the decisions of Argentina and Brazil not to develop nuclear weapons in the 1980s. Neither country saw a reduction in external security threats. On the contrary, Argentina may have had more incentives to develop nuclear weapons after its 1982 military defeat by Great Britain, a nuclear power. Yet Argentina and Brazil apparently decided to eschew nuclear weapons because they were ruled by liberalizing coalitions that did not want to jeopardize access to international markets.[5]

The domestic politics model suggests that the United States needs a diverse array of policy instruments to limit nuclear proliferation. Foreign aid should be made conditional on reductions in military budgets. The United States could provide accurate estimates of the costs of nuclear weapons programs. Encouraging strict civilian control of the military might prevent secret nuclear programs. The United States also could provide alternative sources of employment for nuclear scientists and others who might participate in nuclear programs. The NPT should be viewed as an instrument to empower domestic actors who oppose nuclear weapons programs. The United States and other nuclear powers should attempt to limit and reduce their nuclear arsenals so that advocates of nuclear weapons in other countries cannot justify nuclear programs by accusing the nuclear powers of failing to live up to their NPT obligations.

---

3. See Sumit Ganguly, "India's Pathway to Pokhran II: The Prospects and Sources of New Delhi's Nuclear Weapons Program," in this volume for a different interpretation of India's nuclear decisions.
4. See also Peter Liberman, "The Rise and Fall of the South African Bomb," in this volume.
5. For a more complete discussion of Argentina and Brazil and the role of liberalizing coalitions, see Etel Solingen, "The Political Economy of Nuclear Restraint," in this volume.

The norms model holds that states make decisions about nuclear weapons on the basis of norms and beliefs about legitimate international behavior. Nuclear weapons are symbols of a state's identity, not instruments of national security. Whether a state seeks or shuns nuclear weapons may depend on prevailing international norms. International regimes and the positions of the leading powers influence beliefs about what behavior is legitimate and responsible. Nuclear norms have changed over time. The NPT itself contributed to the emergence of norms against nuclear weapons. The cases of France and Ukraine reflect the changes in nuclear norms since the 1950s.

According to the norms theory, France pursued nuclear weapons because it believed that having the bomb would symbolize France's status as a great power. Nuclear weapons would endow France with grandeur even after it had lost its colonial empire and slipped from the ranks of the leading conventional military powers. France began to pursue nuclear weapons even before its confrontation with the nuclear Soviet Union in the 1956 Suez crisis. For French President Charles de Gaulle, the atomic bomb was primarily a symbol of French prestige and independence, not a strategic deterrent.

In contrast to France, Ukraine decided to relinquish the nuclear arsenal it inherited from the Soviet Union after the Soviet Union collapsed in 1991. This decision is at odds with the security model's emphasis on how states rely on nuclear weapons to respond to threats. Ukraine's renunciation of nuclear weapons was initially linked to its quest for independence. Ukraine sought international support for its secession from the Soviet Union by proclaiming that it would be a nonnuclear neutral state. It did not want to be regarded as a "rogue" state that violated the norm of nonproliferation. U.S. policies that made economic support for Ukraine conditional on denuclearization also played a role.

The norms model generates policy prescriptions that sometimes contradict policies derived from other models and that may be difficult for the United States to implement. For example, U.S. threats to use nuclear weapons to defend nonnuclear allies that might otherwise seek their own nuclear arsenals are in conflict with NPT norms against possessing or using nuclear weapons. In other cases, however, the United States could follow the norms model by offering alternative sources of prestige to potential nuclear powers. For example, countries could be offered permanent UN Security Council membership only if they renounced nuclear weapons. More generally, the norms model suggests that the United States should reaffirm its commitment to global nuclear disarmament and reduce its nuclear forces in accordance with Article 6 of the NPT.

Sagan concludes that further research is necessary to determine when each of the three models applies. He also observes that the United States eventually will have to face the contradictions among the policies implied by each of the three models. If the United States hopes to prevent nuclear proliferation by enhancing the norms against nuclear possession and use, it will have to abandon its nuclear first-use doctrine and wean its allies away from nuclear guarantees.[6]

One way for states to exercise nuclear restraint and not develop nuclear weapons is to participate in a regional regime. Why do some states join regional nuclear regimes? Etel Solingen, in "The Political Economy of Nuclear Restraint," argues that "ruling coalitions pursuing economic liberalization" are more likely to embrace regional regimes that limit nuclear proliferation.[7]

Solingen argues that neorealist theories that explain nuclear choices as a response to security concerns are inadequate, because such theories do not explain the wide range of behavior across countries and across time. Variations in the level of vulnerability do not correlate with variations in nuclear policies. Israel, South Africa, South Korea, and Taiwan are vulnerable to conventional attacks, yet all but Israel have renounced nuclear weapons. When one regional state acquires or seeks nuclear weapons, the others do not necessarily follow. The certainty—or uncertainty—of security guarantees often does not influence nuclear decisions. Such guarantees played no role in the decisions of Argentina, Brazil, Egypt, and South Africa to abandon their quests for nuclear weapons.

Propositions derived from hypotheses about the "democratic peace" offer an alternative to the neorealist approach to explaining nuclearization and denuclearization.[8] The logic of the democratic peace suggests that democracies will not rely on nuclear weapons for their security against other democracies, but they may resort to nuclear deterrence against threats from nondemocracies.

---

6. Sagan now advocates a U.S. no-first-use policy. See Scott D. Sagan, "The Case for No First Use," *Survival*, Vol. 51, No. 3 (June–July 2009), pp. 163–182.
7. For additional discussion of Solingen's arguments, see William C. Potter and Gaukhar Mukhatzhanova, "Divining Nuclear Intentions: A Review Essay," in this volume.
8. The "democratic peace" argument holds that democracies rarely, if ever, go to war with one another. There is a huge body of literature on this topic. For representative works that offer different perspectives, see Bruce Russett, *Grasping the Democratic Peace: Principles for a Post–Cold War World* (Princeton, N.J.: Princeton University Press, 1993); Michael E. Brown, Sean M. Lynn-Jones, and Steven E. Miller, *Debating the Democratic Peace* (Cambridge, Mass.: MIT Press, 1996); and Sebastian Rosato, "The Flawed Logic of Democratic Peace Theory," *American Political Science Review*, Vol. 97, No. 4 (November 2003), pp. 585–602.

Democratic political systems are also supposed to have more credibility, transparency, and predictability than their authoritarian counterparts. These characteristics may make democracies more likely to join nuclear regimes.

Solingen argues that the factors that account for the apparent peace among democracies may not explain whether or not democracies join nuclear regimes. In most cases, including the NPT and the Treaty of Tlatelolco in Latin America, international regimes consist of democracies and nondemocracies. Solingen writes, "Political freedom thus seems neither necessary nor sufficient for the emergence of a nuclear regime." She also suggests that the democratic peace primarily has been a peace among advanced industrial democracies. Lessons from the experience of such countries may not apply to less stable emerging democracies.

Solingen contends that states with ruling coalitions that are pursuing economic liberalization are more likely to join regional nuclear regimes than states governed by inward-looking nationalists. In her view, "economic liberalization implies a reduction of state control over markets and of barriers to trade, and expansion of private economic transactions and foreign investment, and the privatization of public sector enterprises." Liberalizing coalitions recognize that maintaining ambiguous nuclear intentions or cheating on NPT commitments can jeopardize access to foreign technology, capital, and markets. Such coalitions also may want to limit the power of domestic nuclear industrial complexes and other bureaucracies that oppose economic liberalization and openness.

Liberalizing coalitions generally include large banks and industrial complexes, smaller firms that produce exports, and highly skilled workers. The members of these coalitions rely heavily on the global economy and seek good relations with the major powers that control international economic regimes and institutions. They therefore prefer nuclear restraint, which makes good relations with leading international states and regimes more likely. Domestically, liberalizing coalitions also oppose the expansion of state power and unproductive investments. Denuclearization can help such coalitions to limit the power of secret or semi-secret state bureaucracies engaged in nuclear weapons programs.

On the other hand, inward-looking nationalist coalitions include state enterprises and their employees, unskilled workers, small businesses, firms that produce goods that compete with imports, and politicians who control state enterprises and rely on them as a source of patronage. These coalitions derive limited benefits from participating in the international economy and may resent international economic regimes that, for example, demand unwelcome adjustment policies. In the Middle East and South Asia, these coalitions often include religious extremists who also resent foreign investment and the policies of the International Monetary Fund (IMF).

In many cases, states are governed by mixed coalitions that pursue industrialization strategies that combine liberalizing and inward-looking policies. Solingen notes that the domestic political determinants of which coalition comes to power are important, but they are beyond the scope of this essay. She points out that both types of coalitions may or may not be democratically elected.

Solingen assesses how domestic coalitions have influenced policies toward nuclear weapons and regional nuclear regimes in four cases: the Korean Peninsula; India-Pakistan; the Middle East; and Argentina and Brazil.

The two Koreas provide clear support for Solingen's argument. South Korea's liberalization coalition pursued economic development by increasing its integration into the world economy. In the 1970s it recognized that seeking nuclear weapons would undermine this strategy and thus ratified the NPT in 1975. North Korea, in contrast, is essentially an ideal-type of a state ruled by an inward-looking nationalist coalition. For Pyongyang, the pursuit of nuclear weapons is a symbol of national independence. North Korea's nuclear policies have strong support from its military establishment.[9]

The nuclear policies of India and Pakistan reflect the presence or absence of liberalizing coalitions in the governing circles of each country. After independence, India adopted an inward-looking economic policy and sought to distance itself from international economic regimes. It rejected nonproliferation and exploded a nuclear device in 1974. In Pakistan President Zulfikar Ali Bhutto adopted a similar inward-looking strategy and also pursued the bomb. In the 1970s, 1980s, and early 1990s, tentative steps toward liberalization in both countries coincided with limited efforts at nuclear cooperation. In each country, however, inward-looking nationalist coalitions reasserted themselves, rejected or limited economic liberalization, and continued or expanded nuclear programs.

In the Middle East, liberalizing coalitions that have sought greater engagement in the international economy have supported the NPT and called for a

---

9. Solingen wrote her essay before North Korea's nuclear ambitions were clear, but events since 1994 appear to confirm her argument about the domestic support for North Korea's nuclear program.

Nuclear-Weapon-Free Zone (NWFZ) in the region. Egypt—especially under President Anwar al-Sadat—is a prime example. Radical Islamic political blocs have pursued the opposite approach, rejecting ties to the international economy and pursuing nuclear programs, as exemplified by Iran. Under Saddam Hussein, Iraq was a clear example of an inward-looking, nationalist, militarized state. It rejected economic liberalization and sought nuclear weapons. Israel is a more ambiguous case. Although Israel's liberalizing Labor-led coalitions sometimes endorsed an NWFZ in the Middle East, the continued threat from Arab states that refused to recognize Israel made it impossible for them to renounce nuclear weapons. Likud-led coalitions tended to embrace economic nationalism, but they did not take a position on the NWFZ issue.

The nuclear policies of Argentina and Brazil reflect the complex evolution of their domestic coalitions and attitudes toward economic liberalization. In the late 1940s and early 1950s, both countries embraced national populism and opposed free trade and international economic institutions. Each began a nuclear program during this period. In subsequent decades, liberalizing coalitions sometimes gained strength under military and civilian governments, but liberalizing forces were never strong enough to end each country's quest for nuclear weapons. At the end of the 1980s, both countries responded to economic crises by adopting economic liberalization. In 1990 Argentina and Brazil began a process of nuclear cooperation that included mutual renunciation of nuclear weapons, mutual verification and inspection procedures, and support for an updated version of the Tlatelolco treaty.

Solingen concludes that the character of domestic coalitions can explain policies toward nuclear weapons in many different regions and security environments. Only liberalizing coalitions have embraced denuclearization and regional nuclear regimes. International institutions can and should encourage and support liberalizing coalitions. The IMF and other institutions should avoid imposing harsh structural adjustment programs that could weaken liberalizing coalitions. Such institutions also should consult more effectively with liberalizing coalitions in developing countries and be more sensitive to the domestic political needs of those coalitions. The nuclear members of the NPT should bolster support for the nonproliferation regime by reducing their nuclear arsenals, as required by Article 6 of the treaty.

Since the beginning of the nuclear age, many analysts have predicted that nuclear weapons will spread quickly. In "Divining Nuclear Intentions: A Review Essay," William Potter and Gaukhar Mukhatzhanova explore why nuclear proliferation has been less rapid than expected and question the prevailing view that many states will seek nuclear weapons. They assess two important recent books that offer explanations for why states do or do not decide to acquire nuclear weapons: Jacques Hymans's *The Psychology of Nuclear Proliferation: Identity, Emotions, and Foreign Policy* and Etel Solingen's *Nuclear Logics: Alternative Paths in East Asia and the Middle East*. Hymans and Solingen both reject the conventional wisdom that security fears drive states to go nuclear.

Hymans argues that few national leaders desire nuclear weapons. Most are reluctant to take the risky and revolutionary decision to build and deploy nuclear weapons. Those who want to acquire a nuclear arsenal are likely to be "oppositional nationalists" who regard the external world as extremely hostile and believe their own countries are superior to others. Fortunately, such leaders are rare.

Solingen argues that regimes that seek economic growth through outward-looking policies and integration into the world economy are less likely to seek nuclear weapons than those that rely on inward-looking policies.[10] Thus changes in the external security environment may have little impact on nuclear decisions. Changes in domestic political coalitions matter much more. Solingen's explanation sheds new light on Japan's decision to renounce nuclear weapons, which others have attributed to the legacy of Hiroshima and Nagasaki or to Japan's reliance on the U.S. nuclear umbrella.

Potter and Mukhatzhanova praise the books by Hymans and Solingen as models of "theoretical sophistication, methodological rigor, focused comparative analysis involving original field research, and attention to hypothesis testing." They note that Hymans focuses on individual decisionmakers, whereas Solingen emphasizes the role of broad political coalitions. More important, Hymans emphasizes the role of emotions such as pride and fear. Solingen, on the other hand, sees nuclear decisions as rational calculations that take into account internal and external costs and benefits. Hymans suggests that nuclear decisions are hard to reverse. Solingen recognizes that states may alter their nuclear policies if domestic or regional circumstances change.

Potter and Mukhatzhanova commend Hymans for providing new insights into cases in which countries have sought nuclear weapons, including Argentina, France, and India. They admire the quality of Solingen's case studies, but question whether her theory of liberalizing coalitions can explain

---

10. For an elaboration of this argument, see Solingen, "The Political Economy of Nuclear Restraint," in this volume.

Israel's quest for the bomb, which seems to reflect security-related neorealist logic.

Hymans and Solingen find that three prominent theories of international relations that have been applied to nuclear proliferation—neorealism, neoliberal institutionalism, and constructivism—explain little about states' nuclear decisions.

Potter and Mukhatzhanova recall that scholarly and governmental analyses have been predicting rapid nuclear proliferation for decades. In the 1950s and 1960s, Canada, Italy, Japan, Sweden, Switzerland, and West Germany were all identified as states on the verge of going nuclear. Many analysts expected that India's 1974 "peaceful nuclear explosion" would trigger a cascade of nuclear proliferation.

The books by Hymans and Solingen provide a useful corrective to this tradition of alarmism. Hymans indicates that leadership intentions may matter more than whether a potential proliferator is a "rogue" state. He also questions the "domino theory" of proliferation on the grounds that states' decisions to go nuclear "are not highly contingent on what other states decide." In general, he doubts that states seek the bomb as a deterrent or as a source of status. He also questions claims that the interests of domestic groups drive states to pursue nuclear weapons, as well as the argument that the international nonproliferation regime prevents proliferation. Although Potter and Mukhatzhanova contend that some of Hymans's arguments need to be qualified, they acknowledge that Hymans casts much doubt on the conventional pessimism about the spread of nuclear weapons.

Solingen is also mildly optimistic that the world is not on the verge of a wave of nuclear proliferation. She, like Hymans, sees little evidence of proliferation chain reactions. States make decisions based on their own domestic and international interests, and those interests vary from state to state. Solingen, however, is concerned that regional or global dynamics—such as a global economic downturn—could undermine liberalizing coalitions and accelerate proliferation.

Potter and Mukhatzhanova conclude by enumerating four policy implications of the books by Hymans and Solingen. First, Hymans's book points to the need to pay attention to public leadership statements, which may offer a better guide to nuclear intentions than restricted human and signals intelligence. Second, Hymans and Solingen reveal the importance of developing counterintuitive explanations for nuclear decisions and subjecting all explanations to rigorous empirical tests. For example, both authors find that security guarantees do little to curtail states' nuclear ambitions. They provide evidence for this claim, which deserves further serious examination. Third, Hymans and Solingen demonstrate that assertions that nuclear capacity leads to nuclear weapons acquisition are greatly exaggerated. Although they offer different explanations, they agree that there is no technological imperative to develop nuclear weapons. Hymans calls attention to the need to focus on the national identity conceptions of leaders, not just their latent technical capabilities to develop nuclear weapons. Solingen suggests that analysts consider regional perspectives on liberalization, as well as the global political and economic rewards for states that exercise nuclear restraint. Finally, the books by Hymans and Solingen are an important reminder that classified forecasts of nuclear proliferation are not necessarily better than analyses by scholars using open sources.

The next essay in this volume assesses one hypothesis about the sources of nuclear proliferation: the argument that countries that receive civilian nuclear assistance are more likely to develop nuclear weapons. In "Spreading Temptation: Proliferation and Peaceful Nuclear Cooperation Agreements," Matthew Fuhrmann finds that "all types of civilian assistance raise the risks of proliferation." He notes that this finding contradicts the conventional wisdom that states go nuclear when they believe that they need the bomb, not when they have the technical capacity to start a nuclear weapons program.[11]

Fuhrmann calls for shifting focus from demand-side to supply-side explanations of proliferation. Unlike other recent studies of the supply side of proliferation, he argues that all forms of atomic assistance—not just sensitive assistance such as providing weapons-grade fissile material—make nuclear proliferation more likely. He points out that weapons-related nuclear technologies have dual uses and thus can be employed for civilian purposes. Uranium enrichment facilities can produce fuel for nuclear reactors or fissile material for nuclear bombs. Similarly, civilian nuclear cooperation spreads knowledge that can be used to develop nuclear weapons. For example, familiarity with handling radioactive materials can be developed in a civilian program and used in a weapons program.

Fuhrmann develops and tests four hypotheses about the connection between peaceful nuclear cooperation and the spread of nuclear weapons. First, states that receive civilian nuclear assistance become more likely to begin nu-

---

11. The other essays in this volume, for example, consider explanations for proliferation such as perceived security needs, a desire for international status and prestige, and pressure from domestic interest groups.

clear weapons programs, because such assistance reduces the costs of such programs and makes their leaders more confident about developing a bomb. Second, states that receive civilian nuclear assistance and find themselves in a deteriorating security environment are more likely to develop nuclear weapons. Third, peaceful nuclear cooperation makes it more likely that a country will successfully build nuclear weapons, because civilian nuclear assistance helps states to produce fissile material and establishes a technical knowledge base. Fourth, countries that receive civilian nuclear assistance and experience a worsening security environment are especially likely to succeed in developing nuclear weapons.

Fuhrmann briefly examines three cases that show how civilian nuclear assistance influenced nuclear decisionmaking. In South Africa, U.S. peaceful nuclear assistance contributed to the start of that country's nuclear weapons program. The United States constructed a reactor, provided highly enriched uranium, and trained scientists. South Africa's atomic energy complex made technological progress and its scientists acquired political influence, enabling them to lobby successfully for a nuclear weapons program. Israel was able to assemble a nuclear weapon much faster because France assisted in reprocessing and Norway, the United Kingdom, and the United States supplied heavy water. North Korea received technical assistance and a research reactor from the Soviet Union in the 1950s and 1960s. It subsequently used the knowledge it acquired to develop and test a nuclear device.

Fuhrmann devotes more attention to the important cases of India and Pakistan. India built its first research reactor in 1955 with designs supplied by Britain. In 1956 Canada agreed to supply a research reactor. The United States provided heavy water and trained Indian nuclear scientists. In the 1960s, further U.S. and Canadian assistance included another reactor, uranium, and a reprocessing plant that could extract plutonium from spent nuclear fuel. This assistance gave India the capability to pursue a nuclear weapons program, a fact recognized and emphasized during the 1950s and 1960s by Homi Bhabha, chairman of the Indian Atomic Energy Commission. Even though India faced economic hardships, Bhabha was able to argue that the country had the technical base to produce nuclear weapons at relatively low cost. India thus began a nuclear program in 1964. Security threats from China played a role in this decision, but so did foreign nuclear assistance.

Pakistan acquired a research reactor in the 1950s. The United States and Canada supplied uranium and heavy water. European countries provided additional assistance in the 1960s and 1970s. The United States and European countries also trained Pakistani personnel. Pakistan initiated its nuclear weapons program after its defeat by India in 1971. India's 1974 test of a nuclear device gave further impetus to the program. The Pakistan Atomic Energy Commission was confident that it had the nuclear knowledge to produce a bomb. While working in the Netherlands, a Pakistani metallurgist, Abdul Qadeer (A.Q.) Khan, stole blueprints for centrifuges that could be used to enrich uranium. Pakistan constructed enrichment facilities and was able to assemble at least one nuclear bomb by 1987. The training and assistance that Pakistan's scientists received enabled them to use the technology and material acquired from abroad.

Fuhrmann tests his four hypotheses quantitatively using a data set that includes all nuclear cooperation agreements signed from 1945 to 2000. His statistical analysis also finds that other factors, including industrial capacity and membership in the NPT, affect proliferation, but civilian nuclear assistance is "consistently salient" in explaining why states start nuclear weapons programs and ultimately build a bomb. States that receive nuclear assistance are 360 percent more likely to acquire nuclear weapons. States that receive assistance and are involved in frequent militarized disputes are 750 percent more likely to build the bomb. Fuhrmann notes that 80 percent of the countries that initiated a nuclear weapons program had received civilian nuclear assistance and that from 1955 to 2000 every country that started a nuclear program had first received civilian assistance. The effect of civilian nuclear assistance is significant even when confounding variables are taken into account.

One potential criticism of Fuhrmann's argument is that states seek civilian nuclear assistance after they have already decided to pursue nuclear weapons. If this is the general pattern, civilian assistance would not be a cause of states' decisions to go nuclear. Fuhrmann attempts to address this endogeneity issue with a two-stage probit least squares model, and the results are consistent with his general findings.

The main implication of Fuhrmann's findings is that nuclear states and the international community need to reconsider policies that encourage civilian nuclear assistance. Such policies have been in place since U.S. President Dwight Eisenhower proclaimed the goal of "atoms for peace" in 1953. The International Atomic Energy Agency (IAEA) and the NPT regime are designed to facilitate peaceful nuclear cooperation while inhibiting the spread of nuclear weapons. Fuhrmann does not dispute that illicit nuclear transfers can contribute to nuclear proliferation, but he emphasizes that legal commerce also poses significant risks.[12] Fuhrmann recommends that countries provide more resources to the IAEA so that it can monitor nuclear facilities and implement safeguards agreements more effectively. Nuclear suppliers also need to limit nuclear exports, especially to countries that face security threats. He calls for further research on why nuclear suppliers provide civilian nuclear assistance.

The first section of this volume considers the causes of nuclear proliferation. The next section of essays focuses on the causes and the effects of nuclear proliferation in South Asia, where India and Pakistan have acquired nuclear weapons. Why did these two countries eventually decide to build the bomb? How has their acquisition of nuclear capabilities influenced their relationship? Does the experience of nuclear South Asia confirm or refute existing theories, beliefs, and predictions about nuclear proliferation?

In "India's Pathway to Pokhran II: The Prospects and Sources of New Delhi's Nuclear Weapons Program," Sumit Ganguly examines India's decision to become a nuclear power. India had exploded a "peaceful" nuclear device in 1974, but then adopted an ambiguous policy toward nuclear weapons until 1998, when it tested five nuclear devices and became a nuclear weapons state.

Ganguly traces the evolution of India's nuclear program through five phases. Phase one of the program began when Indian physicist Homi Bhabha persuaded Prime Minister Jawaharlal Nehru of the importance of atomic energy research. Nehru opposed nuclear weapons but allowed Bhabha to develop India's nuclear infrastructure. China's defeat of India in the 1962 Sino-Indian border war revealed the folly of India's conciliatory policy toward China and probably stimulated India to consider developing a nuclear arsenal.

The second phase of India's nuclear program began after China's October 1964 nuclear test. China's test prompted India to consider developing a nuclear deterrent. Bhabha and Indian strategists articulated the advantages of nuclear deterrence, but Nehru remained opposed to nuclear weapons. In the mid-1960s Indian political leaders continued to debate whether to seek nuclear weapons. Many senior figures in the Congress Party rejected going nuclear on moral grounds. At the same time, India tried unsuccessfully to obtain nuclear guarantees from the Soviet Union, the United Kingdom, and the United States.

---

12. For discussions of illicit nuclear rings, see Chaim Braun and Christopher F. Chyba, "Proliferation Rings: New Challenges to the Nuclear Nonproliferation Regime"; and Alexander H. Montgomery, "Ringing in Proliferation: How to Dismantle an Atomic Bomb Network," both in this volume.

India initially was active in drafting the NPT, but after the 1965 Indo-Pakistani war, it stopped supporting the NPT and did not sign the treaty.

Phase three of India's nuclear program was marked by its May 1974 test of a "peaceful" nuclear device. Prior to the test, India had failed to obtain security guarantees and had reoriented its foreign policy away from moral principles and nonalignment and toward traditional statecraft. After the 1971 war with Pakistan, Prime Minister Indira Gandhi tilted toward the Soviet Union and eventually authorized India's first nuclear test. Although external factors increased India's motivation to seek nuclear weapons, the test was timed to boost Prime Minister Gandhi's domestic popularity. After the test, the United States and other Western states restricted nuclear cooperation with India and adopted other measures to limit proliferation more generally.

In its fourth phase, which began in the late 1970s and lasted through the 1980s, India's nuclear program initially made relatively little progress. Cooperation with the Soviet Union reduced India's security fears. Indira Gandhi's Congress Party faced domestic opposition and was voted out of office from 1977 to 1980. After the United States increased its military and economic aid to Pakistan following the Soviet invasion of Afghanistan in 1979, India became increasingly concerned about the threat from Pakistan. India's concerns increased as Pakistan supported insurgents in Indian-controlled Kashmir. In the 1980s, India also became aware that Pakistan had the capability to develop nuclear weapons. India continued to expand its own capabilities—including ballistic missiles—for an effective nuclear deterrent.

The fifth phase of India's nuclear program began when the Indo-Soviet security relationship collapsed with the disintegration of the Soviet Union in 1991. India opposed the 1995 extension of the NPT and the 1996 Comprehensive Test Ban Treaty. When the United States resumed military assistance to Pakistan, India was on the verge of conducting a nuclear test. U.S. reconnaissance satellites detected the preparations, however, and the United States was able to persuade India to cancel the planned test. In 1998 elections, the nationalist Bharatiya Janata Party (BJP) emerged as India's largest parliamentary party and formed a governing coalition. The BJP favored making India a nuclear power, a stance that had widespread military, scientific, and public support. Pakistan's April 1998 missile tests were sufficient to trigger India's decision to conduct its May 1998 nuclear tests.

On the basis of the historical record, Ganguly argues that three factors explain India's decision to test nuclear weapons in 1998. First, over the years India had accumulated the capability to build nuclear weapons. Second,

Indian leaders made a series of political decisions that fitfully advanced the nuclear program even in the absence of a commitment to develop nuclear weapons. Third, perceived security threats from Pakistan and China and the absence of superpower security guarantees accelerated India's nuclear program.[13]

Ganguly rejects prominent alternative explanations, many of which pay too little attention to the security imperatives that contributed to India's decision to develop nuclear weapons. In particular, he criticizes claims that attribute India's nuclear choice entirely to the 1998 electoral success of the BJP. Although the BJP clearly supported nuclear weapons, it could pursue this option only because India's previous governments had developed an enormous nuclear infrastructure. Nor was the BJP alone in perceiving a growing threat from Pakistan and China.

Ganguly finds little evidence to support claims that the 1974 and 1998 Indian nuclear tests were intended to bolster the domestic standing of the ruling party. Even if the 1974 test temporarily bolstered Indira Gandhi's popularity, electoral and political motivations cannot explain India's long-term investments in nuclear capabilities.

Ganguly also questions claims that India's nuclear tests were intended to enhance India's international status and prestige, arguing that if India had been most concerned with its ebbing prestige, the tests would have come at the end of the Cold War, when India's place in the international order was particularly uncertain.

Finally, Ganguly rebuts the argument that India sought nuclear weapons because leading members of its nuclear scientific-bureaucratic establishment fostered the mythology that nuclear weapons would enhance India's security, even if they could not prove this proposition. Ganguly contends that the nuclear establishment was not unified in its fervor for nuclear weapons and that ultimate authority remained in the hands of India's political leaders.

Ganguly concludes by noting that India must now consider what sort of doctrine to adopt for its nuclear forces. He also recommends that India begin discussions with China and Pakistan about stabilizing the region and avoiding a regional arms race.

---

13. Other analysts dispute Ganguly's claims that India's security fears were key reasons why India acquired nuclear weapons. See the letter by Rodney Jones, as well as Ganguly's response, in "Correspondence: Debating New Delhi's Nuclear Decision," *International Security*, Vol. 24, No. 4 (Spring 2000), pp. 181–189. Jones attributes India's nuclear test to "an elite interest group's subjective drive for international esteem and for national assertion in great power politics." Ibid., p. 186.

In "Pakistan's Nuclear Weapons Program: Turning Points and Nuclear Choices," Samina Ahmed traces the evolution of Pakistan's quest to become a nuclear power and discusses the implications of the 1998 nuclear tests.

Ahmed puts Pakistan's nuclear program in context by noting that since independence Pakistan has regarded India as the prime threat to its security. Pakistan's military has controlled its security policy, which has been based on external alliances against India. During the 1950s the United States became Pakistan's main ally. U.S. support enabled Pakistan's military to strengthen its domestic position and to build up its conventional forces. Pakistan did not initially consider acquiring nuclear weapons, but in 1957 the Pakistan Atomic Energy Commission (PAEC) was established and the country began to develop a nuclear infrastructure.

Pakistan began to explore the nuclear option after it failed to expand its control over Kashmir in its 1965 war with India. The United States banned military assistance to both countries after the war, tipping the conventional balance in favor of India. Foreign Minister Zulfikar Ali Bhutto, who had previously been minister for atomic energy, argued that Pakistan should develop nuclear weapons. In 1966 he declared that "even if Pakistanis have to eat grass, we will make the bomb" if India went nuclear. Like India, Pakistan refused to sign the NPT.

After Pakistan's defeat by India in the 1971 war with India, Bhutto became Pakistan's leader and initiated a nuclear weapons program. India's 1974 nuclear test gave added impetus to the program, which was headed by A.Q. Khan but also relied on the nuclear infrastructure and scientists of the PAEC. Bhutto sought to purchase from France a reprocessing plant that could enrich plutonium, claiming that Pakistan was pursuing a civilian nuclear power program. The United States became suspicious, urged Pakistan to abandon its quest for reprocessing technology, and then persuaded France to cancel the sale. The U.S. Congress also voted to cut off U.S. aid to countries that imported unsafeguarded enrichment or reprocessing technology. In 1977 Bhutto was deposed in a military coup led by Gen. Mohammed Zia-ul-Haq and then hanged in 1979. While in prison, Bhutto accused U.S. Secretary of State Henry Kissinger of threatening to have him eliminated if he did not give up Pakistan's quest for nuclear weapons. This accusation resonated with the Pakistani public, who came to associate nuclear weapons with Pakistan's national sovereignty and prestige.

The Zia military regime that had removed Bhutto invoked the Indian threat and Pakistan's nuclear program in order to maintain domestic support. Zia oversaw a clandestine and overt quest for uranium enrichment technology. China provided significant assistance, including weapons-grade uranium and help with uranium enrichment. In 1977 and 1979, the United States imposed sanctions on Pakistan to curb Pakistan's nuclear program.

After the 1979 Soviet invasion of Afghanistan, the United States needed Pakistan as an ally and waived sanctions in return for Pakistan's cooperation. Ronald Reagan's administration looked the other way as Pakistan continued to develop its nuclear infrastructure. The United States sold Pakistan F-16 aircraft, which could deliver nuclear weapons. In 1988, when Zia was killed in a midair explosion, Pakistan was on the threshold of becoming a nuclear state. Pakistan acknowledged that it had a nuclear weapons program and unofficially disclosed that it could build nuclear weapons.

After Zia's death, Pakistan's military continued to control nuclear policy, even though civilian rule returned to the country. The alternating civilian governments of Benazir Bhutto and Nawaz Sharif depended on the goodwill of the military and realized that they could not change Pakistan's nuclear policy. During this period, Pakistan also developed ballistic missiles that could deliver nuclear weapons. When the Cold War ended and the United States no longer needed Pakistan's support in fighting Soviet forces in Afghanistan, U.S. pressure on Pakistan to curtail its nuclear program increased. Nevertheless, the Pakistani military calculated that it could withstand U.S. sanctions and enhanced its nuclear production capabilities. Pakistan also resorted to implicit nuclear threats against India as Indo-Pakistani tension over Pakistan's support of insurgents in Kashmir grew. Bill Clinton's administration adopted a more flexible posture on U.S. sanctions against Pakistan, which convinced Pakistan's policymakers that the United States was willing to accept Pakistan's de facto nuclear status.

The April 1998 electoral victory of the BJP in India ended a tentative rapprochement between India and Pakistan and set the stage for both countries' May 1998 nuclear tests. Pakistan's military decided to test its Ghauri ballistic missile in April 1998. India responded by testing nuclear weapons, thereby carrying out the BJP's electoral promise. After an internal debate between proponents of overt weaponization and those who favored continued nuclear ambiguity, Pakistan decided to test nuclear weapons, which was the strong preference of the military. The absence of a strong international response to India's tests helped to convince Pakistani decisionmakers that Pakistan would not be punished heavily for its tests. After both countries had tested nuclear weapons, however, international concern about a nuclear arms race in South

Asia grew. The United States imposed sanctions that significantly damaged Pakistan's economy and exacerbated regional and ethnic schisms in Pakistan.

Ahmed, writing in early 1999, correctly predicted that the military would respond to Pakistan's economic turmoil by staging a coup to remove the civilian government of Prime Minister Sharif. (The coup took place in October 1999.) She recommended that the United States and other influential actors send clear signals of their resolve to roll back nuclear proliferation in South Asia. The strategic situation changed fundamentally after the terrorist attacks of September 11, 2001, however, and regional nuclearization continued.

In the next two essays, Sumit Ganguly and Paul Kapur assess the first decade of open nuclear rivalry in South Asia. They reach opposite conclusions about the impact of nuclear weapons on South Asian security.

In "Nuclear Stability in South Asia," Ganguly contends that "nuclear weapons have reduced the risk of full-scale war in the region and have therefore contributed to strategic stability." Nuclear deterrence in South Asia will remain robust unless India deploys viable defenses against ballistic missiles.

Ganguly starts by summarizing the pessimistic perspective on proliferation in general. He notes that organization theorists claim that organizational pathologies create risks in new nuclear states. Organization theory suggests that the rigid routines and parochial interests of professional militaries may cause deterrence failures. Firm civilian control over the military may limit this risk, but such control is not always present in new nuclear states. Other pessimists point to the "stability/instability paradox" and argue that nuclear deterrence may make South Asia safe for lower-level conventional wars, which could nonetheless escalate as a result of misjudgments and misperceptions. A variation of this argument holds that Pakistan will take greater risks and provoke India because it believes its nuclear arsenal deters large-scale Indian retaliation. A low-level conflict could escalate if India shows less restraint than Pakistan expects.

Ganguly next examines the history of repeated Indo-Pakistani conflicts since 1947–48. The two countries have gone to war in 1947–48, 1965, 1971, and 1999. With the exception of the 1971 conflict, all the wars were over Kashmir, which is central to the identity of both states. Pakistan claims Muslim-majority Kashmir because it sees itself a homeland for South Asia's Muslims. India wants to retain Kashmir because including it in India reaffirms India's secular ideology. In all these conflicts, India and Pakistan pursued limited aims and exercised military restraint.

India and Pakistan also have been involved in many crises. Three of the most recent include the Brasstacks crisis of 1987, the 1990 crisis over Pakistan's support for insurgents in Kashmir, and the 1999 Kargil crisis, which qualifies as a war due to the extent of the fighting and number of battle deaths. In the Brasstacks crisis, India and Pakistan conducted military exercises at a time when Pakistan's support for insurgents in the border Indian state of Punjab had increased Indo-Pakistani tensions. Pakistan may have issued a veiled nuclear threat. The crisis was resolved with the aid of U.S. and Soviet diplomatic intervention. The 1990 crisis arose when Pakistan deployed military units near the Indian border after completing an exercise. At the same time, an uprising in Kashmir grew with the support of Pakistan, causing India to strengthen its forces in Kashmir. Concerned by bellicose rhetoric emanating from New Delhi and Islamabad and aware that India and Pakistan were pursuing nuclear weapons, the United States dispatched Deputy National Security Adviser Robert Gates on a diplomatic mission that contributed to a resolution of the crisis. The 1999 Kargil crisis/war was the first to take place after India and Pakistan became overt nuclear weapons states. For reasons that remain unclear, Pakistani forces crossed the Line of Control and occupied positions in the mountains near Kargil. After several months of difficult fighting and U.S. diplomacy, India recaptured most of the occupied territory and Pakistan withdrew its forces. Ganguly argues that the conflict did not escalate because Indian leaders were aware of the possibility of nuclear war and thus exercised restraint.

India and Pakistan experienced more crises in 2001–02, as insurgents supported by Pakistan staged terrorist attacks on the Jammu and Kashmir State Assembly building in October 2001 and on the Indian parliament building in December of that year. India demanded that Pakistan take action against terrorist groups operating from Pakistan and deployed large forces near the Pakistani border. In May 2002, tensions increased after insurgents attacked an Indian military base in Kashmir and killed many wives and children of Indian soldiers. War seemed imminent at the end of May, when India shifted more forces to its border with Pakistan. Under diplomatic pressure from the United States and other countries, Pakistan appeared to limit its support for the Kashmiri insurgency in June and war was averted. Ganguly argues that India again did not initiate a major attack against Pakistan in 2002 because nuclear deterrence worked.

Ganguly recognizes that possession of nuclear weapons may have emboldened Pakistan to take greater risks and to support insurgents in Kashmir more actively, but he notes that Pakistan may have acted in this manner even without nuclear weapons. The end of the Cold War enabled Pakistan—and insurgents—to turn their attention from Afghanistan to Kashmir. The insurgency also expanded in response to India's poor administration of Kashmir, which was unrelated to Pakistan's pursuit of nuclear weapons.

In Ganguly's view, nuclear weapons imposed much greater restraint on India's military operations. Indian aircraft, for example, were ordered not to cross the Line of Control. India's behavior in 1999 and 2002 was much more restrained than in the 1965 war, in which India launched an attack into Pakistani Punjab.

Ganguly concludes that efforts to persuade India and Pakistan to abandon their nuclear arsenals are futile. The United States and other major powers should instead help Pakistan to protect its nuclear weapons from theft, sabotage, or unauthorized use; urge India to adhere to its plans to maintain a minimum deterrence capability; and promote a peace process in Kashmir.

In "Ten Years of Instability in a Nuclear South Asia," Paul Kapur offers a different perspective on Indo-Pakistani nuclear relations. He argues that nuclear weapons have destabilized the South Asian security environment in two ways. First, they have encouraged aggressive Pakistani behavior. Nuclear deterrence shields Pakistan from the risk of significant retaliation for its aggressive actions. At the same time, the prospect of nuclear war attracts international attention to Pakistan's dispute with India. Second, Indo-Pakistani crises since 1998 have driven India to adopt a more aggressive and dangerous conventional military posture that could increase the risk of future wars. Kapur supports these arguments with evidence from three phases of Indo-Pakistani relations since the 1998 nuclear tests.

In the first phase, from 1998 to 2002, Pakistan took advantage of its ability to deter Indian retaliation to initiate low-intensity conflicts that provoked confrontations with India. In the 1998–99 Kargil crisis, Pakistani forces infiltrated Indian-controlled Kashmir and occupied positions inside the Line of Control before eventually being dislodged by an Indian offensive. These conflicts were not resolved because of the presence of nuclear weapons. Instead, Kapur argues, diplomatic calculations and conventional military factors motivated each country to avoid war. India did not cross the Line of Control because it feared that it would lose the support of world public opinion if it did so. In any event, Indian forces were able to repel the Pakistani forces without crossing the Line of Control. On the basis of the historical record and interviews with Pakistani strategic analysts and political leaders, including Benazir Bhutto and President Musharraf, Kapur concludes that Pakistan's acquisition of nuclear weapons facilitated each crisis by enabling Pakistan to challenge India without fear of catastrophic Indian retaliation.

The second phase of Indo-Pakistani relations in a nuclear South Asia began in 2002 and ended in 2008. These years were marked by less tension and fewer crises than 1998–2002, but nuclear weapons were not responsible for this stability. Kapur argues that Pakistan has reduced its support for Islamic militants and insurgents in Kashmir because of U.S. pressure in the aftermath of the September 11, 2001, terrorist attacks. India has attempted to improve relations with Pakistan because it wants to focus on promoting domestic economic growth.

The third phase, which began in 2008, may feature increased instability in South Asia. Nuclear weapons may continue to encourage provocative behavior by Pakistan. India's emerging conventional military doctrine, formulated to respond to Pakistani provocations, may cause further destabilization. India has started to develop a "Cold Start" doctrine, which calls for Indian forces to mobilize quickly and then launch large-scale attacks into Pakistan.[14] This new doctrine may intensify the regional security dilemma and make escalation more likely in any future Indo-Pakistani war.

Kapur concludes that the "nuclear proliferation optimists" have been wrong about South Asia. He further argues that the implications of Pakistan's experience with nuclear weapons include the possibility that Iran will also adopt risky policies that undermine regional stability if it acquires nuclear weapons.

Most analyses of nuclear proliferation focus on understanding and preventing the initial acquisition of nuclear weapons. In some cases, however, states that already have the bomb may decide to give it up and once again become nonnuclear states. Persuading nuclear weapons states to abandon their nuclear arsenals permanently is thus a potentially important nonproliferation policy. The essays in the third section explore the phenomenon of nuclear reversal.

Peter Liberman examines the most prominent case of nuclear reversal: South Africa. In "The Rise and Fall of the South African Bomb," he considers three explanations for why South Africa built and then dismantled nuclear weapons. The first explanation holds that changing external security threats motivated South Africa's nuclear decisions. The second attributes South African policies to domestic and bureaucratic politics, particularly the influence of the coun-

---

14. For a detailed analysis of this doctrine, see Walter C. Ladwig III, "A Cold Start for Hot Wars? The Indian Army's New Limited War Doctrine," *International Security*, Vol. 32, No. 3 (Winter 2007/08), pp. 158–190.

try's nuclear research complex and armaments agency. The final explanation includes international incentives other than security, including norms, rewards, and sanctions. Liberman recounts the history of South Africa's nuclear weapons program and concludes that no single factor explains South Africa's decisions.

South Africa's civilian nuclear research program evolved into a weapons program in the mid-1970s, at approximately the same time as South Africa's external threat environment deteriorated. The program ostensibly aimed to develop a capability for peaceful nuclear explosions that might be used for digging harbors and oil storage cavities. Although the precise date is uncertain, between 1974 and 1977 South Africa's political leaders decided to build nuclear weapons. Two nuclear devices were completed in 1978 and 1979. There were six and a half bombs in the arsenal by 1989. South Africa's nuclear strategy consisted of maintaining a covert nuclear capability that would be disclosed to Western nations if Soviet or Soviet-backed forces threatened to invade South Africa or Namibia. If the Western nations doubted the existence of South Africa's bomb, a weapon would be detonated over the ocean. The goal of the strategy was to induce Western countries to intervene on behalf of South Africa. South African strategists disagreed over whether nuclear weapons actually should be used in war, because nuclear use might invite Soviet retaliation that would destroy South Africa.

Liberman argues that South Africa's decision to pursue nuclear weapons appears to have been motivated by external security threats. In the mid-1970s, a Marxist regime came to power in Angola after the Portuguese withdrew from what had been their colony. Cuban troops intervened to support that regime against its opponents in the Angolan civil war. World pressure against South Africa on the issues of apartheid and South Africa's occupation of Namibia grew. Although South Africa did not face local adversaries with nuclear weapons, its leaders feared Soviet-backed aggression, even if chances of a Soviet or Cuban invasion were remote. Security factors also seem to explain subsequent South African nuclear decisions. For example, when Cuban troops advanced into southern Angola and clashed with South African forces in 1987–88, South Africa reopened its Kalahari nuclear test site. Nevertheless, South Africa did not develop a coherent nuclear strategy, which suggests that security concerns were not the only factors shaping South Africa's nuclear decisions.

Liberman argues that the organizational interests and influence of South Africa's Atomic Energy Board (AEB) contributed to the growth of South Africa's nuclear program. The AEB's nuclear scientists had considerable expertise and prestige. They were able to persuade key decsionmakers to support the program, which was shrouded in secrecy and therefore difficult to criticize. The South African military was not enthusiastic about nuclear weapons, but Liberman suggests that military descriptions of the external threat to South Africa helped to build support for a South African nuclear arsenal.

External pressure had relatively little impact on South Africa's nuclear program. Although many international embargoes and boycotts were imposed on South Africa during the 1970s, the country was able to continue its nuclear program. Threats of even more serious sanctions or a rupture in diplomatic relations dissuaded South Africa from actually testing a nuclear device and becoming an overt nuclear power. Liberman argues that the South African government had many of the characteristics of a nationalist inward-looking coalition and thus would be expected to pay little heed to international pressures.

In 1991 South Africa became the only nuclear state to dismantle its entire arsenal.[15] South Africa's policy changed after F.W. de Klerk became president in 1989. De Klerk believed that having nuclear weapons would make it harder for South Africa to gain international acceptance.

Liberman points out that South Africa's decision to give up the bomb followed a reduction in external threats to South Africa. In 1988 and 1989, the Soviet Union moderated its foreign policy and reduced aid to Angola, Mozambique, and the African National Congress. Negotiations led to the withdrawal of Cuban and South African forces from Angola and independence for Namibia. Liberman argues, however, that these changes in the security environment may not have caused South Africa to dismantle its nuclear weapons. Such weapons may no longer have been deemed essential to meet extreme threats to South Africa's security, but they did not make South Africa less secure.

In Liberman's view, South Africa's decision to relinquish the bomb undermines organizational theories, because such theories predict that organizations will not give up their autonomy and missions, let alone dissolve themselves. The decision reflected de Klerk's policy preferences, not the influence of advisers or the heads of powerful bureaucracies. Liberman regards the South Africa case as a triumph of presidential leadership over organizational politics.

---

15. The former Soviet republics of Belarus, Kazakhstan, and Ukraine had nuclear weapons on their territory when they became independent in 1991, but they did not build these weapons and had limited control over them before they were removed to Russian territory.

Liberman argues that South Africa's increased sensitivity to international pressure was a key factor in bringing about the end of South Africa's nuclear weapons program. De Klerk wanted to end apartheid, gain international acceptance, and remove sanctions. He thought that destroying South Africa's nuclear weapons and joining the NPT would win Western political and economic support for his efforts to transform South Africa's domestic political system. Liberman observes that South Africa's nuclear disarmament is consistent with Solingen's theory about liberalization and nuclear restraint.

Liberman concludes that the organizational politics theory best explains the growth of South Africa's latent nuclear capability, but it does not account for the decisions to build and then dismantle nuclear weapons. Changes in South Africa's security environment appear to provide partial explanations for South African nuclear decisions, but they were not sufficient to provide strong explanations. International pressure and liberalization within South Africa also account for some changes in policy.[16] Liberman notes that alternative U.S. policies might have discouraged South Africa's acquisition of nuclear weapons. The United States could have provided security guarantees, found ways to employ South Africa's nuclear scientists in civilian research, or imposed harsher sanctions. The U.S. policy of negotiating the withdrawal of Cuban troops from Angola was successful in helping to create the conditions for South African denuclearization.

In "Never Say Never Again: Nuclear Reversal Revisited," Ariel Levite examines all the cases of nuclear reversal, which he defines as "the phenomenon in which states embark on a path leading to nuclear weapons acquisition but subsequently reverse course, though not necessarily abandoning altogether their nuclear ambitions." He identifies about twenty states that fall into this category.

Levite acknowledges that it is very difficult to analyze nuclear reversal, because nuclear programs and decisions often remain secret. Countries that want to keep open the option of resuming a terminated nuclear program are particularly likely to maintain such secrecy. Other countries may refuse to disclose the details of abandoned programs because they fear the domestic or international

---

16. For different perspectives on the factors that influenced South Africa's nuclear decisions, see the letter by Helen E. Purkitt and Stephen F. Burgess, and the reply by Peter Liberman, in "Correspondence: South Africa's Nuclear Decisions," *International Security*, Vol. 27, No. 1 (Summer 2002), pp. 186–194. Purkitt and Burgess suggest that Liberman overlooks psychological factors, such as the Afrikaner nationalist mentality of South Africa's leaders, as well as the role of U.S. pressure on South Africa.

political repercussions of revealing that they once pursued a nuclear option. There are other motives for secrecy, as well. In some cases, states may want to create the impression that they are on the threshold of having a nuclear capability. In others, states may use the belief that they might seek nuclear weapons to gain bargaining leverage as they attempt to extract security commitments from other states.

Levite notes that previous studies have identified several factors that cause nuclear reversal: changes in a state's external security situation; changes in the state's domestic regime; and changes in systemic incentives, such as the emergence of new norms.[17] He argues that no single explanation accounts for nuclear reversal.

Levite introduces the concept of "nuclear hedging," which he defines as "a national strategy of maintaining, or at least appearing to maintain, a viable option for the relatively rapid acquisition of nuclear weapons." He argues that some cases of nuclear reversal should be classified as examples of nuclear hedging, because states that sign the NPT and appear to renounce nuclear weapons may do so only because they can retain a latent nuclear capability. Levite cites Japan's nuclear policy as a prominent example of nuclear hedging.[18]

Like other contributors to this volume, Levite argues that external security threats play an important role in state's nuclear choices. He recognizes, however, that other factors, including domestic regime change and external incentives, play a particularly important role in the process of nuclear reversal. These factors often must be combined with changes in the security environment to bring about nuclear reversal.

Levite finds that the process of nuclear reversal often involves one or more of the following characteristics. First, nuclear programs tend to "fizzle out" instead of being shut down abruptly and completely. (South Africa is a key exception, as discussed by Peter Liberman in his contribution to this volume.) Second, states do not have a clear objective when they begin to contemplate nuclear reversal. Third, states do not assume that reversal is permanent.

Levite argues that the United States has played a critical role in persuading countries to abandon their nuclear programs or to at least adopt a posture of

---

17. The factors are similar to those identified as causes of proliferation in many of the essays in this volume.
18. For further discussion of Japan's nuclear program, see Llewelyn Hughes, "Why Japan Will Not Go Nuclear (Yet): International and Domestic Constraints on the Nuclearization of Japan," *International Security,* Vol. 31, No. 4 (Spring 2007), pp. 67–96.

nuclear hedging. The United States has provided security guarantees, threatened to cut off or provide aid, revealed details about states' nuclear programs, encouraged regime change, and attempted to influence domestic debates over nuclear weapons. In many cases, including Argentina, Australia, Brazil, Egypt, Japan, NATO members, South Africa, South Korea, and Taiwan, these U.S. policies have been at least somewhat successful. In others, such as India, North Korea, and Pakistan, the United States has been much less successful.

Levite concludes that three factors help to persuade nuclear aspirants to switch to a posture of nuclear reversal or hedging: (1) a change in domestic perceptions of the utility of having nuclear weapons; (2) U.S. efforts to address a country's security concerns and requirements; and (3) U.S.-led attempts to prevent a country from acquiring nuclear weapons. The United States and other countries will not always succeed, as the case of Pakistan shows, but a sustained effort to address security concerns and to influence the domestic debate between proponents and opponents of nuclear weapons often can create the conditions for nuclear reversal or at least nuclear hedging.

Most of the preceding essays in this volume have analyzed the causes and, to some extent, the consequences of decisions to go nuclear. The essays in the final section focus on nuclear proliferation issues that have become prominent since the 1990s. Each assesses an important contemporary proliferation problem and makes policy recommendations.

Even before the September 11, 2001, terrorist attacks, many analysts regarded nuclear terrorism as a major threat.[19] Matthew Bunn, in "Nuclear Terrorism: A Strategy for Prevention," assesses the risk that terrorists will acquire and use a nuclear bomb, examines existing programs to reduce that risk, and recommends a comprehensive strategy "to ensure that every nuclear weapon and every stock of potential bomb material worldwide is secured against the kinds of threats terrorists and criminals have demonstrated they can pose."

Bunn identifies many factors that increase the risk of nuclear terrorism. Although most terrorists do not want nuclear weapons, al-Qaida has made no secret of its desire to acquire nuclear weapons for use against the United States. A sophisticated terrorist group could build a nuclear bomb if it had the nuclear

---

19. See, for example, Graham T. Allison, Owen R. Coté Jr., Richard A. Falkenrath, and Steven E. Miller, *Avoiding Nuclear Anarchy: Containing the Threat of Loose Russian Nuclear Weapons and Fissile Material* (Cambridge, Mass.: MIT Press, 1996); and Richard A. Falkenrath, Robert D. Newman, and Bradley A. Thayer, *America's Achilles' Heel: Nuclear, Biological, and Chemical Terrorism and Covert Attack* (Cambridge, Mass.: MIT Press, 1998).

material, which could be stolen from any one of multiple facilities in many countries. Nuclear materials—and nuclear weapons—are particularly vulnerable to theft in Pakistan and Russia. Terrorists also could steal highly enriched uranium from many research reactors around the world. Some thefts have been detected already. Once they have stolen or built a nuclear bomb, terrorists probably would be able to smuggle it into the United States, where even a small blast in a U.S. city would have catastrophic consequences.

The good news is that there is no clear evidence that terrorists have yet acquired a nuclear bomb or the material required to make one. Terrorist groups would face many daunting technical challenges as they attempted to build a bomb. Even former al-Qaida members and other Islamist writers question the morality of detonating a nuclear weapon. Nuclear security at sites in Russia and elsewhere is improving, which makes it less likely that terrorists will be able to steal nuclear materials.

Existing programs have improved nuclear security and have made it harder for terrorists to steal nuclear weapons or nuclear materials. Bunn approvingly notes that security upgrades have been completed for most nuclear warhead sites and nuclear materials buildings in Russia and the other former Soviet republics, although it is not clear whether these measures will be adequate or permanent. Much less has been done to secure research reactors in other countries. Efforts to improve nuclear security in China, India, and Pakistan remain secret or minimal. The Global Threat Reduction Initiative (GTRI) has made progress in removing material from vulnerable sites and converting reactors to use low-enriched uranium that cannot be used for nuclear weapons, but much more needs to be done. There are also no global standards for what should be done to make nuclear materials secure.

Bunn outlines a comprehensive strategy for preventing nuclear terrorism. The four key elements of his approach are (1) securing and reducing nuclear stockpiles; (2) countering terrorist nuclear plots; (3) preventing and deterring state transfers of nuclear weapons or materials to terrorists; and (4) interdicting nuclear smuggling. Complacency, secrecy, political disputes, and bureaucratic obstacles all threaten to prevent successful implementation of this strategy. The United States will need to forge global cooperation and build a sense of urgency to prevent nuclear terrorism. It also should fulfill its own arms reduction obligations, organize and fund its organizations devoted to preventing nuclear terrorism, and improve its nuclear security. Finally, the United States must prepare for the worst and develop plans for responding to a nuclear terrorist attack on American soil.

The next two essays examine a relatively new issue: the growth of illicit networks of states and nonstate actors that exchange information and materials that could be used in nuclear weapons programs.[20] Such networks appear to be an important new threat to the nonproliferation regime, but the magnitude of the threat and the best way to respond are open to debate.

In "Proliferation Rings: New Challenges to the Nuclear Nonproliferation Regime," Chaim Braun and Christopher Chyba examine how potential nuclear states trade or sell nuclear technologies, nuclear information, and delivery systems such as ballistic missiles. They argue that proliferation rings of third world nations threaten to undermine the nuclear nonproliferation regime, and recommend policies to address this important problem.

Braun and Chyba find ample evidence of significant interactions among the nuclear and ballistic missile programs of North Korea, Iran, Pakistan, and Libya. Pakistan has provided North Korea centrifuges and blueprints for uranium enrichment in return for plans for ballistic missiles. Pakistani nuclear scientist A.Q. Khan appears to have been involved in this arrangement, as well as a much larger illicit network that procured and sold nuclear technologies and information to Iran, Libya, and other countries. Iran appears to be developing a nuclear weapons program and has received assistance from China, North Korea, and Russia. It may have helped North Korea's uranium enrichment efforts in return for engines for its ballistic missiles. These illicit networks could provide the technology and designs that would enable states to reduce the time required to obtain nuclear weapons and the necessary delivery systems. They also could enable terrorists to gain access to nuclear technologies.

Braun and Chyba believe that many of these transfers are intended to serve strategic requirements. Pakistan, for example, needed a less vulnerable delivery system that could strike targets in India. It therefore was interested in bartering for North Korean missiles.

The existing nonproliferation regime could be improved to address the threat posed by illicit proliferation networks. Braun and Chyba recommend taking steps to prevent or at least detect theft or smuggling of fissile material that could be used to build nuclear bombs,[21] providing inducements for ratification of the IAEA's Additional Protocol, and strengthening export con-

---

20. For a discussion of North Korea's role in these illicit networks, see Sheena Chestnut, "Illicit Activity and Proliferation: North Korean Smuggling Networks," *International Security*, Vol. 32, No. 1 (Summer 2007), pp. 80–111.
21. For a comprehensive discussion of this issue, see Matthew Bunn, "Nuclear Terrorism: A Strategy for Prevention," in this volume.

trol regimes. These steps are only incremental improvements to the existing nonproliferation regime, however, and they will not address all the challenges posed by proliferation rings.

In 2003–04, the George W. Bush administration and Director General Mohammed ElBaradei offered proposals to prevent the spread of nuclear technologies and materials. President Bush initiated the Proliferation Security Initiative (PSI) in 2003. The PSI consists of countries that have pledged to interdict shipments of missiles, chemical and biological agents, and nuclear components through their territories. This approach depends on having good intelligence about suspect shipments. The initiative may not allow for the detection or interdiction of small shipments.

Director General ElBaradei's October 2003 proposals include establishing multilateral control over facilities that produce separated plutonium or highly enriched uranium; converting existing highly enriched uranium facilities to low-enriched uranium; considering multinational approaches to spent fuel and radioactive waste disposal; pursuing a Fissile Material Cutoff Treaty; increasing adherence to the Additional Protocol; prohibiting withdrawal from the NPT; and universalizing the export control system. These steps could make it more difficult for a country to construct an illicit nuclear program and also might limit proliferation rings involved in exporting nuclear weapons–related material. Braun and Chyba note, however, that nonnuclear states might not be eager to accept the limitations on their sovereignty that ElBaradei's proposals would impose.

President Bush offered many additional proposals in February 2004. Most of them did not call for new treaties to limit exports of sensitive nuclear materials, but instead relied on the cooperation of coalitions of the willing. The United States did, however, take the lead in proposing what became UN Security Council Resolution 1540 in April 2004. This resolution requires states to "prohibit any non-State actor to manufacture, acquire, possess, develop, transport, transfer, or use nuclear, chemical, or biological weapons and their means of delivery." The resolution also requires all states to control supplies of nuclear material and to take steps to prevent illicit trafficking.

Braun and Chyba recommend several new initiatives that would build on Security Council Resolution 1540 and the Bush and ElBaradei proposals. For example, nuclear exports would be permitted only to countries that have concluded Additional Protocol agreements with the IAEA and are honoring those commitments. They also argue that supply-side restrictions will be insufficient to control nuclear proliferation. Globalization will ensure that nuclear weapons–relevant technologies—some of which have civilian applications—and knowledge will spread. Demand-side measures, such as security guarantees and the threat of economic sanctions, will continue to be necessary.

Braun and Chyba also recommend new initiatives that would ensure that the nonproliferation regime was regarded as equitable by nonnuclear states. They call for an Energy Security Initiative that would offer energy-related benefits to states that accept the burdens of the Additional Protocol and other export controls. Such countries could, for example, lease subsidized fuel for their nuclear reactors or even receive assistance with their nonnuclear energy programs. They also recommend that nuclear weapons states, including those that have not ratified the NPT, support a Fissile Material Cutoff Treaty (FMCT). Such a treaty would demonstrate that nuclear weapons states were willing to accept limits on their activities and contribute to nonproliferation by placing a cap on the production of nuclear weapons material. Finally, the United States should revise its nuclear posture to make clear that its policies do not emphasize attacks on states without nuclear weapons or preventive attacks on states suspected of seeking nuclear weapons.

In "Ringing in Proliferation: How to Dismantle an Atomic Bomb Network," Alexander Montgomery offers a different perspective on proliferation networks. He argues that the danger posed by such networks has been exaggerated. He coins the term "proliferation determinism" to describe some of the alarmist reactions to the combination of illicit networks and "rogue" states, and disputes claims that illicit networks have accelerated the pace of proliferation, that rogue states are determined to build the bomb, and that proliferation rings are so decentralized that they can be controlled only with universal measures, if at all. He suggests that proliferation determinists—many of whom were in the George W. Bush administration—should abandon their harsh rhetoric and determination to overthrow the regimes of potential proliferators such as Iran and North Korea. Montgomery recommends using the full range of potential incentives and disincentives to prevent states from going nuclear, identifying and targeting the hubs of proliferation rings, and negotiating directly with "rogue" states.

Montgomery argues that proliferation networks have not enabled potential nuclear proliferants to make rapid technological progress toward acquiring a bomb. Despite the apparent assistance of illicit networks, Iran, Libya, and North Korea all made slow progress in their quest to produce large quantities of fissionable material.

Montgomery also argues that there is no relationship between regime type and the propensity to proliferate. He notes that France, India, Israel, the United Kingdom, and the United States are all democracies and all acquired (or are thought to have acquired) nuclear weapons. Many states that have abandoned their quest for nuclear weapons did so without experiencing regime change: Libya is the most obvious recent example.[22]

According to Montgomery, existing ballistic missile and nuclear proliferation networks tend to have a hub-and-spokes structure, which makes them easier to shut down than decentralized networks. North Korea and Pakistan are the principal hubs in the networks. Montgomery contends that the networks have this type of structure because building nuclear weapons requires much "tacit knowledge," and this sort of knowledge "must be learned through trial and error, potentially under the direct tutelage of someone who has already learned it." Only the central hubs in the networks can provide the expertise "to train new proliferants in constructing and operating equipment."

Montgomery calls for the United States to end its policy of attempting to overthrow the regimes of potential nuclear weapons states such as Iran and North Korea. Attempting to isolate or contain potential proliferants is also likely to fail or backfire. A U.S. strategy of "proliferation pragmatism" would balance threats of force with offers of diplomatic incentives and economic benefits. Montgomery advocates applying tailored incentives and disincentives to Iran, North Korea, and Pakistan to roll back the proliferation networks those states have created "before they form a network of ties so dense that it will be impossible to pull apart."

Iran's apparent interest in acquiring nuclear weapons provoked much concern and diplomatic activity in the first decade of the twenty-first century. In "Osirak Redux? Assessing Israeli Capabilities to Destroy Iranian Nuclear Facilities," Whitney Raas and Austin Long examine whether Israel could successfully attack and destroy Iran's nuclear facilities, much as it did when it bombed the Iraqi nuclear reactor at Osirak in 1981.[23] Their essay offers an important analysis of the problems and prospects of using military force to stop nuclear proliferation, as well as an overview of Iran's nuclear program and Israel's capabilities to launch an airstrike against it.

---

22. For an analysis of why Libya ended its nuclear program and ceased to be a "rogue" state, see Bruce W. Jentleson and Christopher A. Whytock, "Who 'Won' Libya? The Force-Diplomacy Debate and Its Implications for Theory and Policy," *International Security*, Vol. 30, No. 3 (Winter 2005/06), pp. 47–86.
23. Israel also attacked and destroyed a site that may have contained a nuclear reactor in Syria on September 6, 2007.

Raas and Long point out that Iran's nuclear complex includes multiple sites throughout the country. Iran has argued that its nuclear facilities are elements of a civilian nuclear power program that will generate energy to meet Iran's future needs. Iran is developing uranium enrichment capabilities that could produce weapons-grade uranium, as well as a plutonium reactor and facilities to reprocess spent fuel and extract plutonium. Iran's nuclear facilities include the reactor at Bushehr, uranium mines, uranium conversion and enrichment plants, a fuel fabrication plant, and a heavy-water production facility. Iran is building heavy water reactors. There are probably additional clandestine facilities, but Raas and Long doubt that Iran has an entire covert parallel nuclear program.[24]

If Israel wanted to delay Iran's ability to build nuclear weapons, it would probably target three critical facilities: (1) the uranium conversion facility in Isfahan; (2) the uranium enrichment facility at Natanz; and (3) a heavy water plant and plutonium reactors being built at Arak. The uranium conversion and enrichment facilities are the most important for producing highly enriched uranium for nuclear weapons. Raas and Long do not think Israel would launch airstrikes against the Bushehr reactor, because it is not vital to Iran's quest for nuclear weapons. If Israel decided to attack the reactor, it could do so with sea-launched cruise missiles.

Since the 1981 Osirak raid, the Israeli Air Force has acquired precision-guided penetrating munitions that enable it to destroy hardened targets such as Iran's underground facilities at Natanz. Israel's bombs would have less difficulty destroying the facility at Isfahan and the reactor at Arak. Raas and Long estimate that no more than twenty-four 5,000-pound bombs and twenty-four 2,000-pound bombs would be necessary.

Israel would probably use F-15 and F-16 aircraft with external fuel tanks to attack targets in Iran. Although Iran has some surface-to-air missiles and fighter aircraft, many of its weapons systems are old and may lack spare parts. Israel has some of the same missiles in its arsenal and would have developed effective countermeasures. Iran also lacks an integrated air defense system.

Raas and Long suggest that Israeli aircraft could use three possible routes on their way to targets in Iran: (1) north over the Mediterranean Sea and then across Turkey to Iran; (2) southeast and then along the Jordan–Saudi Arabia border and then across Iraq; (3) southeast and then along the Saudi-Iraq border and then north over the Persian Gulf. All three routes pose operational and

---

24. In September 2009 it was revealed that Iran had an additional uranium enrichment plant.

diplomatic challenges, but all are feasible. Israel would have to decide, for example, whether it preferred to risk facing hostile fire over Jordan or Saudi Arabia or to create a diplomatic crisis with Turkey.

Regardless of the route chosen to fly to Iran, if the Israeli force consisted of fifty strike aircraft, a sufficient number almost certainly would arrive at each target and drop their bombs. Iranian air defenses would have to shoot down approximately 40 percent of the Israeli planes to prevent the attackers from delivering enough ordnance. It is highly unlikely that Iran would be able to achieve attrition rates even close to that level. On the first day of the 1973 Yom Kippur War, the heavy attrition suffered by Israeli aircraft did not exceed 8 percent. The attrition rate for the 1986 U.S. raid on Libya—a mission similar to a potential Israeli attack on Iran—was only 4 percent. Even if Iran shot down more Israeli planes than expected and others malfunctioned, the remaining aircraft would be able to inflict significant damage on Iran's nuclear facilities.

Raas and Long conclude that Israel has the capability "to destroy even well-hardened targets in Iraq with some degree of confidence." More generally, their analysis suggests that precision-guided weapons can be an important counterproliferation tool, provided that intelligence on the location of nuclear facilities is available. They note, however, that any military attack on Iran may involve a "day after" problem: Iran would probably strike back at Israel or the United States. Counterproliferation policy should not rely on military actions alone.

The essays in this volume do not address every topic related to nuclear nonproliferation. Many important issues, such as international efforts to prevent North Korea from becoming a nuclear weapons state, continue to emerge and evolve. Other countries will almost certainly consider acquiring nuclear weapons. We hope that the essays collected here offer enduring insights into why states seek nuclear weapons and how the international community can strengthen the existing nonproliferation regime.

Part I:
Why States Build the Bomb

Why Do States Build Nuclear Weapons?

Scott D. Sagan

Three Models in Search of a Bomb

Why do states build nuclear weapons? Having an accurate answer to this question is critically important both for predicting the long-term future of international security and for current foreign policy efforts to prevent the spread of nuclear weapons. Yet given the importance of this central proliferation puzzle, it is surprising how little sustained attention has been devoted to examining and comparing alternative answers.

This lack of critical attention is not due to a lack of information: there is now a large literature on nuclear decision-making inside the states that have developed nuclear weapons and a smaller, but still significant, set of case studies of states' decisions to refrain from developing nuclear weapons. Instead, the inattention appears to have been caused by the emergence of a near-consensus that the answer is obvious. Many U.S. policymakers and most international relations scholars have a clear and simple answer to the proliferation puzzle: states will seek to develop nuclear weapons when they face a significant military threat to their security that cannot be met through alternative means; if they do not face such threats, they will willingly remain non-nuclear states.[1]

Scott D. Sagan is Associate Professor of Political Science and a faculty associate of the Center for International Security and Arms Control at Stanford University.

I greatly benefited from discussions about earlier drafts of this article at seminars at the Aspen Strategy Group, the Institute for Defense Analysis, the Lawrence Livermore National Laboratory, the Monterey Institute of International Studies, the Olin Institute for Strategic Studies, and the Stockholm International Peace Research Institute. For especially detailed comments and criticisms, I thank Itty Abraham, Eric Arnett, Michael Barletta, George Bunn, Colin Elman, Miriam Fendius Elman, Peter Feaver, Harald Müller, George Perkovich, Jessica Stern, and Bradley Thayer. Benjamin Olding and Nora Bensahel provided excellent research assistance. Support for this research was provided by the W. Alton Jones Foundation and the Institute for Defense Analysis.

1. Among policymakers, John Deutsch presents the most unadorned summary of the basic argument that "the fundamental motivation to seek a weapon is the perception that national security will be improved." John M. Deutsch, "The New Nuclear Threat," *Foreign Affairs*, Vol. 71, No. 41 (Fall 1992), pp. 124–125. Also see George Shultz, "Preventing the Proliferation of Nuclear Weapons," *Department of State Bulletin*, Vol. 84, No. 2093 (December 1984), pp. 17–21. For examples of the dominant paradigm among scholars, see Michael M. May, "Nuclear Weapons Supply and Demand," *American Scientist*, Vol. 82, No. 6 (November–December 1994), pp. 526–537; Bradley A. Thayer, "The Causes of Nuclear Proliferation and the Nonproliferation Regime," *Security Studies*, Vol. 4, No. 3 (Spring 1995), pp. 463–519; Benjamin Frankel, "The Brooding Shadow: Systemic Incentives and Nuclear Weapons Proliferation," and Richard K. Betts, "Paranoids, Pygmies, Pariahs, and Nonproliferation Revisited," both in Zachary S. Davis and Benjamin Frankel, eds. *The Prolifer-*

International Security, Vol. 21, No. 3 (Winter 1996/97), pp. 54–86
© 1996 by the President and Fellows of Harvard College and the Massachusetts Institute of Technology.

The central purpose of this article is to challenge this conventional wisdom about nuclear proliferation. I argue that the consensus view, focusing on national security considerations as the cause of proliferation, is dangerously inadequate because nuclear weapons programs also serve other, more parochial and less obvious objectives. Nuclear weapons, like other weapons, are more than tools of national security; they are political objects of considerable importance in domestic debates and internal bureaucratic struggles and can also serve as international normative symbols of modernity and identity.

The body of this article examines three alternative theoretical frameworks—what I call "models" in the very informal sense of the term—about why states decide to build or refrain from developing nuclear weapons: "the security model," according to which states build nuclear weapons to increase national security against foreign threats, especially nuclear threats; "the domestic politics model," which envisions nuclear weapons as political tools used to advance parochial domestic and bureaucratic interests; and "the norms model," under which nuclear weapons decisions are made because weapons acquisition, or restraint in weapons development, provides an important normative symbol of a state's modernity and identity. Although many of the ideas underlying these models exist in the vast case-study and proliferation-policy literatures, they have not been adequately analyzed, nor placed in a comparative theoretical framework, nor properly evaluated against empirical evidence. When I discuss these models, therefore, I compare their theoretical conceptions of the causes of weapons development, present alternative interpretations of the history of some major proliferation decisions, and contrast the models' implications for nonproliferation policy. The article concludes with an outline of a research agenda for future proliferation studies and an examination of the policy dilemmas produced by the existence of these three proliferation models.

It is important to recognize from the start that the nuclear proliferation problem will be a critical problem in international security for the foreseeable future. Despite the successful 1995 agreement to have a permanent extension of the Nuclear Nonproliferation Treaty (NPT), there will be continuing NPT review conferences assessing the implementation of the treaty every five years; each member state can legally withdraw from the treaty, under the "supreme national interest" clause, if it gives three months notice; and many new states

ation Puzzle, special issue of *Security Studies,* Vol. 2, No, 3/4 (Spring/Summer 1993), pp. 37–38 and pp. 100–124; and David Gompert, Kenneth Watman, amd Dean Wilkening, "Nuclear First Use Revisited," *Survival,* Vol. 37, No. 3 (Autumn 1995), p. 39.

can be expected to develop a "latent nuclear weapons capability" over the coming decade. Indeed, some fifty-seven states now operate or are constructing nuclear power or research reactors, and it has been estimated that about thirty countries today have the necessary industrial infrastructure and scientific expertise to build nuclear weapons on a crash basis if they chose to do so.[2] The NPT encourages this long-term trend by promoting the development of power reactors in exchange for the imposition of safeguards on the resulting nuclear materials. This suggests that while most attention concerning proliferation in the immediate-term has appropriately focused on controlling nuclear materials in the former Soviet Union and preventing the small number of active proliferators (such as Iraq, Iran, Libya, and North Korea) that currently appear to have vigorous nuclear weapons programs from getting the bomb, the longer-term and enduring proliferation problem will be ensuring that the larger and continually growing number of latent nuclear states maintain their non-nuclear weapons status. This underscores the policy importance of addressing the sources of the political *demand* for nuclear weapons, rather than focusing primarily on efforts to safeguard existing stockpiles of nuclear materials and to restrict the *supply* of specific weapons technology from the "haves" to the "have-nots."

If my arguments and evidence concerning the three models of proliferation are correct, however, any future demand-side nonproliferation strategy will face inherent contradictions. For, in contrast to the views of scholars who claim that a traditional realist theory focusing on security threats explains all cases of proliferation and nuclear restraint,[3] I believe that the historical record suggests that each theory explains some past cases quite well and others quite poorly. Unfortunately, since the theories provide different and often contradictory lessons for U.S. nonproliferation policy, this suggests that policies designed to address one future proliferation problem will exacerbate others. As I discuss in more detail below, particularly severe tensions are likely to emerge in the future between U.S. extended deterrence policies designed to address security

---

2. See Steve Fetter, "Verifying Nuclear Disarmament," Occasional Paper No. 29, Henry L. Stimson Center, Washington, D.C., October 1996, p. 38; and "Affiliations and Nuclear Activities of 172 NPT Parties," *Arms Control Today*, Vol. 25, No. 2 (March 1995), pp. 33–36. For earlier pioneering efforts to assess nuclear weapons latent capability and demand, see Stephen M. Meyer, *The Dynamics of Nuclear Proliferation* (Chicago: University of Chicago Press, 1984); and William C. Potter, *Nuclear Power and Nonproliferation* (Cambridge, Mass: Oelgeschlager, Gunn and Hain, 1982).
3. For example, May, "Nuclear Weapons Supply and Demand"; Thayer, "The Causes of Nuclear Proliferation and the Nonproliferation Regime"; and Frankel, "The Brooding Shadow: Systemic Incentives and Nuclear Weapons Proliferation."

concerns of potential proliferators and U.S. NPT policies designed to maintain and enhance international norms against nuclear use and acquisition.

The Security Model: Nuclear Weapons and International Threats

According to neorealist theory in political science, states exist in an anarchical international system and must therefore rely on self-help to protect their sovereignty and national security.[4] Because of the enormous destructive power of nuclear weapons, any state that seeks to maintain its national security must balance against any rival state that develops nuclear weapons by gaining access to a nuclear deterrent itself. This can produce two policies. First, strong states do what they can: they can pursue a form of internal balancing by adopting the costly, but self-sufficient, policy of developing their own nuclear weapons. Second, weak states do what they must: they can join a balancing alliance with a nuclear power, utilizing a promise of nuclear retaliation by that ally as a means of extended deterrence. For such states, acquiring a nuclear ally may be the only option available, but the policy inevitably raises questions about the credibility of extended deterrence guarantees, since the nuclear power would also fear retaliation if it responded to an attack on its ally.

Although nuclear weapons could also be developed to serve either as deterrents against overwhelming conventional military threats or as coercive tools to compel changes in the status quo, the simple focus on states' responses to emerging nuclear threats is the most common and most parsimonious explanation for nuclear weapons proliferation.[5] George Shultz once nicely summarized the argument: "Proliferation begets proliferation."[6] Every time one state develops nuclear weapons to balance against its main rival, it also creates a

---

4. The seminal text of neorealism remains Kenneth N. Waltz, *Theory of International Politics* (New York: Random House, 1979). Also see Kenneth N. Waltz, "The Origins of War in Neorealist Theory," in Robert I. Rotberg and Theodore K. Rabb, eds., *The Origin and Prevention of Major Wars* (New York: Cambridge University Press, 1989), pp. 39–52; and Robert O. Keohane, ed., *Neorealism and Its Critics* (New York: Columbia University Press, 1986).

5. The Israeli, and possibly the Pakistani, nuclear weapons decisions might be the best examples of defensive responses to conventional security threats; Iraq, and possibly North Korea, might be the best examples of the offensive coercive threat motivation. On the status quo bias in neorealist theory in general, see Randall L. Schweller, "Bandwagoning for Profit: Bringing the Revisionist State Back In," *International Security*, Vol. 19, No. 1 (Summer 1994), pp. 72–107, and Richard Rosecrance and Arthur A. Stein, eds., *The Domestic Bases of Grand Strategy* (Ithaca, N.Y.: Cornell University Press, 1993).

6. Shultz, "Preventing the Proliferation of Nuclear Weapons," p. 18.

nuclear threat to another state in the region, which then has to initiate its own nuclear weapons program to maintain its national security.

From this perspective, one can envision the history of nuclear proliferation as a strategic chain reaction. During World War II, none of the major belligerents was certain that the development of nuclear weapons was possible, but all knew that other states were already or could soon be working to build the bomb. This fundamental fear was the central impetus for the United States, British, German, Soviet, and Japanese nuclear weapons programs. The United States developed atomic weapons first, not because it had any greater demand for the atomic bomb than these other powers but, rather, because the United States invested more heavily in the program and made the right set of technological and organizational choices.[7]

After August 1945, the Soviet Union's program was reinvigorated because the U.S. atomic attacks on Hiroshima and Nagasaki demonstrated that nuclear weapons were technically possible, and the emerging Cold War meant that a Soviet bomb was a strategic imperative. From the realist perspective, the Soviet response was perfectly predictable. Josef Stalin's reported request to Igor Kurchatov and B.L. Yannikov in August 1945 appears like a textbook example of realist logic:

A single demand of you comrades. . . . Provide us with atomic weapons in the shortest possible time. You know that Hiroshima has shaken the whole world. The balance has been destroyed. Provide the bomb—it will remove a great danger from us.[8]

The nuclear weapons decisions of other states can also be explained within the same framework. London and Paris are seen to have built nuclear weapons because of the growing Soviet military threat and the inherent reduction in the credibility of the U.S. nuclear guarantee to NATO allies once the Soviet Union was able to threaten retaliation against the United States.[9] China developed the bomb because Beijing was threatened with possible nuclear attack by the United States at the end of the Korean War and again during the Taiwan Straits

---

7. On the genesis of the atomic programs in World War II, see McGeorge Bundy, *Danger and Survival: Choices about the Bomb in the First Fifty Years* (New York: Random House, 1988) pp. 3–53; and Richard Rhodes, *The Making of the Atomic Bomb* (New York: Simon and Schuster, 1986).

8. A. Lavrent'yeva in "Stroiteli novogo mira," *V mire knig*, No. 9 (1970), in David Holloway, *The Soviet Union and the Arms Race* (New Haven, Conn.: Yale University Press, 1980), p. 20, also quoted in Thayer, "The Causes of Nuclear Proliferation," p. 487.

9. Important sources on the British case include Margaret Gowing, *Britain and Atomic Energy, 1939–1945* (London: Macmillan, 1964); Margaret Gowing, *Independence and Deterrence: Britain and Atomic Energy 1945–1952*, vols. 1 and 2 (London: Macmillan, 1974); and Andrew Pierre, *Nuclear Pol-*

crises in the mid-1950s. Not only did Moscow prove to be an irresolute nuclear ally in the 1950s, but the emergence of hostility in Sino-Soviet relations in the 1960s further encouraged Beijing to develop, in Avery Goldstein's phrase, the "robust and affordable security" of nuclear weapons, since the border clashes "again exposed the limited value of China's conventional deterrent."[10]

After China developed the bomb in 1964, India, which had just fought a war with China in 1962, was bound to follow suit. India's strategic response to the Chinese test came a decade later, when their Atomic Energy Commission successfully completed the long research and development process required to construct and detonate what was called a "peaceful nuclear explosion" (PNE) in May 1974. According to realist logic, India has maintained an ambiguous nuclear posture since that time—building sufficient nuclear materials and components for a moderate-sized nuclear arsenal, but not testing or deploying weapons into the field—in a clever strategic effort to deter the Chinese, while simultaneously not encouraging nuclear weapons programs in other neighboring states.[11] After the Indian explosion, however, the nascent Pakistani weapons program had to move forward according to the realist view: facing a recently hostile neighbor with both nuclear weapons and conventional military superiority, it was inevitable that the government in Islamabad would seek to produce a nuclear weapon as quickly as possible.[12]

---

itics: The British Experience with an Independent Strategic Force, 1939–1970 (London: Oxford University Press, 1972). On the French case, see Lawrence Scheinman, *Atomic Energy Policy in France Under the Fourth Republic* (Princeton, N.J.: Princeton University Press, 1965) and Wilfred L. Kohl, *French Nuclear Diplomacy* (Princeton, N.J.: Princeton University Press, 1971).

10. Avery Goldstein, "Robust and Affordable Security: Some Lessons from the Second-Ranking Powers During the Cold War," *Journal of Strategic Studies*, Vol. 15, No. 4 (December 1992), p. 494. The seminal source on the Chinese weapons program, which emphasizes the importance of U.S. nuclear threats in the 1950s, is John W. Lewis and Xue Litai, *China Builds the Bomb* (Stanford, Calif.: Stanford University Press, 1988).

11. Recent estimates of the number of weapons India could deploy on short notice range from 25 to 105. See Mitchell Reiss, *Bridled Ambition: Why Countries Constrain Their Nuclear Capabilities* (Washington, D.C.: Woodrow Wilson Center Press, 1995), p. 185; Leonard S. Spector and Mark G. McDonough, *Tracking Nuclear Proliferation* (Washington, D.C.: Carnegie Endowment for International Peace, 1995), p. 89; and Eric Arnett, "Implications of the Comprehensive Test Ban," in Eric Arnett, ed., *Nuclear Weapons after the Comprehensive Test Ban* (Oxford: Oxford University Press, 1996), p. 13. Important sources on the Indian nuclear program include Ashok Kapur, *India's Nuclear Option: Atomic Diplomacy and Decision Making* (New York: Praeger, 1976); Brahma Chellaney, "South Asia's Passage to Nuclear Power," *International Security*, Vol. 16, No. 1 (Summer 1991), pp. 43–72; and T. T. Poulose, ed., *Perspectives of India's Nuclear Policy* (New Delhi: Young Asia Publications, 1978).

12. Valuable sources on Pakistan's program include Ziba Moshaver, *Nuclear Weapons Proliferation in the Indian Subcontinent* (Basingstoke, U.K.: Macmillan, 1991) and Ashok Kapur, *Pakistan's Nuclear Development* (New York: Croom Helm, 1987).

EXPLAINING NUCLEAR RESTRAINT

Given the strong deterrent capabilities of nuclear weapons, why would any state give up such powerful sources of security? The major recent cases of nuclear weapons restraint can also be viewed through the lens provided by the security model if one assumes that external security threats can radically change or be reevaluated. The case of South Africa has most often been analyzed in this light, with the new security threats that emerged in the mid-1970s seen as the cause of South Africa's bomb program and the end of these threats in the late 1980s as the cause of its policy reversal. As President F.W. de Klerk explained in his speech to Parliament in March 1993, the Pretoria government saw a growing "Soviet expansionist threat to southern Africa"; "the buildup of the Cuban forces in Angola from 1975 onwards reinforced the perception that a deterrent was necessary, as did South Africa's relative international isolation and the fact that it could not rely on outside assistance should it be attacked."[13] Six atomic weapons were therefore constructed, but were stored disassembled in a secret location, between 1980 and 1989, when the program was halted. The South African nuclear strategy during this period was designed to use the bomb both as a deterrent against the Soviets and as a tool of blackmail against the United States. If Soviet or Soviet-supported military forces directly threatened South Africa, the regime reportedly planned to announce that it had a small arsenal of nuclear weapons, dramatically testing one or more of the weapons if necessary by dropping them from aircraft over the ocean, hoping that such a test would shock the United States into intervention on behalf of the Pretoria regime.[14]

South Africa destroyed its small nuclear weapons arsenal in 1991, the theory suggests, because of the radical reduction in the external security threats to the regime. By 1989, the risk of a Soviet-led or sponsored attack on South Africa was virtually eliminated. President de Klerk cited three specific changes in military threats in his speech to Parliament: a cease-fire had been negotiated in

---

13. F. W. de Klerk, March 24, 1993 address to the South African parliament as transcribed in Foreign Broadcast Information Service (FBIS), JPRS-TND-93-009, (March 29, 1993), p. 1 (henceforth cited as de Klerk, "Address to Parliament.") For analyses that focus largely on security threats as the cause of the program, see Darryl Howlett and John Simpson, "Nuclearization and Denuclearization in South Africa," *Survival*, Vol. 35, No. 3 (Autumn 1993), pp. 154–173; and J.W. de Villers, Roger Jardine, and Mitchell Reiss, "Why South Africa Gave up the Bomb," *Foreign Affairs*, Vol. 72, No. 5 (November/December 1993), pp. 98–109. For a more detailed and more balanced perspective see Reiss, *Bridled Ambition*, pp. 7–44.

14. Military planners nonetheless developed nuclear target lists in their contingency military plans and research was conducted on development of the hydrogen bomb until 1985. See Reiss, *Bridled Ambition*, p. 16.

Angola; the tripartite agreement granted independence to Namibia in 1988; and most dramatically, "the Cold War had come to an end."[15]

Although the details change in different cases, the basic security model has also been used to explain other examples of nuclear restraint. For example, both Argentina and Brazil refused to complete the steps necessary to join the Latin American nuclear weapons-free zone (NWFZ) and began active programs in the 1970s that could eventually have produced nuclear weapons; however, their 1990 joint declaration of plans to abandon their programs is seen as the natural result of the recognition that the two states, which had not fought a war against one another since 1828, posed no fundamental security threat to each other.[16] Similarly, it has been argued that the non-Russian former states of the Soviet Union that were "born nuclear"—Ukraine, Kazakhstan, and Belarus—decided to give up their arsenals because of a mixture of two realist model arguments: their long-standing close ties to Moscow meant that these states did not perceive Russia as a major military threat to their security and sovereignty, and increased U.S. security guarantees to these states made their possession of nuclear weapons less necessary.[17] In short, from a realist's perspective, nuclear restraint is caused by the absence of the fundamental military threats that produce positive proliferation decisions.

POLICY IMPLICATIONS OF THE SECURITY MODEL

Several basic predictions and prescriptions flow naturally from the logic of the security model. First, since states that face nuclear adversaries will eventually develop their own arsenals unless credible alliance guarantees with a nuclear power exist, the maintenance of U.S. nuclear commitments to key allies, in-

---

15. See de Klerk, "Address to Parliament," p. 2.

16. Thayer, "The Causes of Nuclear Proliferation," p. 497; and May, "Nuclear Weapons Supply and Demand," pp. 534–535. For analyses of the Argentine-Brazilian decision, see Monica Serrano, "Brazil and Argentina," in Mitchell Reiss and Robert S. Litwak, eds. *Nuclear Proliferation After the Cold War* (Washington, D.C.: Woodrow Wilson Center Press, 1994), pp. 231–255; Jose Goldemberg and Harold A. Feiveson, "Denuclearization in Argentina and Brazil," *Arms Control Today*, Vol. 24, No. 2 (March 1994), pp. 10–14; Reiss, *Bridled Ambition*, pp. 45–88; and John R. Redick, Julio C. Carasales, and Paulo S. Wrobel, "Nuclear Rapprochement: Argentina, Brazil, and the Nonproliferation Regime," *Washington Quarterly*, Vol. 18, No. 1 (Winter 1995), pp. 107–122.

17. Sherman Garnett writes, for example, that "for many Ukrainian citizens—not just the ethnic Russians—it is difficult to conceive of Russia as an enemy to be deterred with nuclear weapons." Sherman W. Garnett, "Ukraine's Decision to Join the NPT," *Arms Control Today*, Vol. 25, No. 1 (January 1995), p. 8. Garnett also maintains that "the role that security assurances played in the creation of a framework for Ukrainian denuclearization is obvious. They were of immense importance." Sherman W. Garnett, "The Role of Security Assurances in Ukrainian Denuclearization," in Virginia Foran, ed., *Missed Opportunities?: The Role of Security Assurances in Nuclear Non-Proliferation* (Washington, D.C.: Carnegie Endowment for International Peace, forthcoming 1997).

cluding some form of continued first-use policy, is considered crucial.[18] Other efforts to enhance the security of potential proliferators—such as confidence-building measures or "negative security assurances" that the nuclear states will not use their weapons against non-nuclear states—can also be helpful in the short-run, but will likely not be effective in the long-term given the inherent suspicions of potential rivals produced by the anarchic international system.

Under the security model's logic, the NPT is seen as an institution permitting non-nuclear states to overcome a collective action problem. Each state would prefer to become the only nuclear weapons power in its region, but since that is an unlikely outcome if it develops a nuclear arsenal, it is willing to refrain from proliferation if, and only if, its neighbors remain non-nuclear. The treaty permits such states to exercise restraint with increased confidence that their neighbors will follow suit, or at a minimum, that they will receive sufficient advance warning if a break-out from the treaty is coming. It follows, from this logic, that other elements of the NPT regime should be considered far less important: specifically, the commitments that the United States and other nuclear states made under Article VI of the treaty—that the nuclear powers will pursue "negotiations in good faith on measures relating to cessation of the nuclear arms race at an early date and to nuclear disarmament"—are merely sops to public opinion in non-nuclear countries. The degree to which the nuclear states follow through on these Article VI commitments will not significantly influence the actual behavior of non-nuclear states, since it will not change their security status.

Under realist logic, however, U.S. nonproliferation policy can only slow down, not eliminate, the future spread of nuclear weapons. Efforts to slow down the process may of course be useful, but they will eventually be countered by two very strong structural forces that create an inexorable momentum toward a world of numerous nuclear weapons states. First, the end of the Cold War creates a more uncertain multipolar world in which U.S. nuclear guarantees will be considered increasingly less reliable; second, each time one state develops nuclear weapons, it will increase the strategic incentives for neighboring states to follow suit.[19]

---

18. See Lewis Dunn, *Controlling the Bomb* (New Haven, Conn.: Yale University Press, 1982); May, "Nuclear Weapons Supply and Demand," p. 535; and Frankel, "The Brooding Shadow," pp. 47–54.
19. See Kenneth N. Waltz, "The Emerging Structure of International Politics," *International Security*, Vol. 18, No. 2 (Fall 1993), pp. 44–79; and John J. Mearsheimer, "Back to the Future: Instability in Europe after the Cold War," *International Security*, Vol. 15, No. 1 (Summer 1990), pp. 5–56.

PROBLEMS AND EVIDENCE

What's wrong with this picture? The security model is parsimonious; the resulting history is conceptually clear; and the theory fits our intuitive belief that important events in history (like the development of a nuclear weapon) must have equally important causes (like national security). A major problem exists, however, concerning the evidence, for the realist history depends primarily on first, the statements of motivation by the key decision-makers, who have a vested interest in explaining that the choices they made served the national interest; and second, a correlation in time between the emergence of a plausible security threat and a decision to develop nuclear weapons. Indeed, an all too common intellectual strategy in the literature is to observe a nuclear weapons decision and then work backwards, attempting to find the national security threat that "must" have caused the decision. Similarly, scholars too often observe a state decision not to have nuclear weapons and then work backwards to find the change in the international environment that "must" have led the government to believe that threats to national security were radically decreasing.

These problems suggest that a more serious analysis would open up the black box of decision-making and examine in more detail how governments actually made their nuclear decisions. Any rigorous attempt to evaluate the security model of proliferation, moreover, also requires an effort to develop alternative explanations, and to assess whether they provide more or less compelling explanations for proliferation decisions. The following sections therefore develop a domestic politics model and a norms model of proliferation and evaluate the explanations that flow from their logic, versus the security model's arguments offered above, for some important cases of both nuclear proliferation and nuclear restraint.

The Domestic Politics Model: Nuclear Pork and Parochial Interests

A second model of nuclear weapons proliferation focuses on the domestic actors who encourage or discourage governments from pursuing the bomb. Whether or not the acquisition of nuclear weapons serves the national interests of a state, it is likely to serve the parochial bureaucratic or political interests of at least some individual actors within the state. Three kinds of actors commonly appear in historical case-studies of proliferation: the state's nuclear energy establishment (which includes officials in state-run laboratories as well as civilian reactor facilities); important units within the professional military (often within the air force, though sometimes in navy bureaucracies interested in nuclear propulsion); and politicians in states in which individual parties or the mass public strongly favor nuclear weapons acquisition. When such actors form coalitions that are strong enough to control the government's decision-making process—either through their direct political power or indirectly through their control of information—nuclear weapons programs are likely to thrive.

Unfortunately, there is no well-developed domestic political theory of nuclear weapons proliferation that identifies the conditions under which such coalitions are formed and become powerful enough to produce their preferred outcomes.[20] The basic logic of this approach, however, has been strongly influenced by the literature on bureaucratic politics and the social construction of technology concerning military procurement in the United States and the Soviet Union during the Cold War.[21] In this literature, bureaucratic actors are not seen as passive recipients of top-down political decisions; instead, they create the conditions that favor weapons acquisition by encouraging extreme perceptions of foreign threats, promoting supportive politicians, and actively lobbying for increased defense spending. This bottom-up view focuses on the formation of domestic coalitions within the scientific-military-industrial complex. The initial ideas for individual weapons innovations are often developed inside state laboratories, where scientists favor military innovation simply because it is technically exciting and keeps money and prestige flowing to their laboratories. Such scientists are then able to find, or even create, sponsors in the professional military whose bureaucratic interests and specific military responsibilities lead them also to favor the particular weapons system. Finally, such a coalition builds broader political support within the executive or legislative branches by shaping perceptions about the costs and benefits of weapons programs.

Realists recognize that domestic political actors have parochial interests, of

---

20. This is a serious weakness shared by many domestic-level theories in international relations, not just theories of proliferation. On this issue, see Ethan B. Kapstein, "Is Realism Dead? The Domestic Sources of International Politics," *International Organization*, Vol. 49, No. 4 (Autumn 1995), pp. 751–774.
21. The best examples of this literature include Morton H. Halperin, *Bureaucratic Politics and Foreign Policy* (Washington, D.C.: The Brookings Institution, 1974); Matthew Evangelista, *Innovation and the Arms Race: How the United States and Soviet Union Develop New Military Technologies* (Ithaca, N.Y.: Cornell University Press, 1988); and Donald MacKenzie, *Inventing Accuracy: A Historical Sociology of Nuclear Missile Guidance* (Cambridge, Mass.: MIT Press, 1990). For a valuable effort to apply insights from the literature on social construction of technology to proliferation problems, see Steven Flank, "Exploding the Black Box: The Historical Sociology of Nuclear Proliferation," *Security Studies*, Vol. 3, No. 2 (Winter 1993/94), pp. 259–294.

course, but argue that such interests have only a marginal influence on crucial national security issues. The outcome of bureaucratic battles, for example, may well determine whether a state builds 500 or 1000 ICBMs or emphasizes submarines or strategic bombers in its nuclear arsenal; but a strong consensus among domestic actors will soon emerge about the need to respond in kind when a potential adversary acquires nuclear weapons. In contrast, from this domestic politics perspective, nuclear weapons programs are not obvious or inevitable solutions to international security problems; instead, nuclear weapons programs are solutions looking for a problem to which to attach themselves so as to justify their existence. Potential threats to a state's security certainly exist in the international system, but in this model, international threats are seen as being more malleable and more subject to interpretation, and can therefore produce a variety of responses from domestic actors. Security threats are therefore not the central cause of weapons decisions according to this model: they are merely windows of opportunity through which parochial interests can jump.

PROLIFERATION REVISITED: ADDRESSING THE INDIA PUZZLE
The historical case that most strongly fits the domestic politics model is the Indian nuclear weapons experience. In contrast to the brief realist's account outlined above, a closer look at the history of the Indian program reveals that there was no consensus among officials in New Delhi that it was necessary to have a nuclear deterrent as a response to the 1964 Chinese nuclear test. If that had been the case, according to realist logic, one of two events would likely have occurred. First, a crash weapons program could have been initiated; there is no evidence that such an emergency program was started, however, and indeed, given the relatively advanced state of Indian nuclear energy at the time, such an effort could have produced a nuclear weapon by the mid-to-late 1960s, relatively soon after the Chinese test, instead of in 1974.[22] Second, leaders in New Delhi could have made a concerted effort to acquire nuclear guarantees from the United States, the Soviet Union, or other nuclear powers. Indian officials, however, did not adopt a consistent policy to pursue security guarantees: in diplomatic discussions after the Chinese test, officials rejected the idea

22. In 1963, U.S. intelligence agencies estimated that India could test a nuclear weapon in four to five years (1967 or 1968). By 1965, U.S. estimates were that it would take one to three years additional years. See Peter R. Lavoy, "Nuclear Myths and the Causes of Proliferation," in Davis and Frankel, *The Proliferation Puzzle*, p. 202; and George Bunn, *Arms Control by Committee: Managing Negotiations with the Russians* (Stanford, Calif.: Stanford University Press, 1992), p. 68.

of bilateral guarantees because they would not conform with India's non-aligned status, refused to consider foreign bases in India to support a nuclear commitment, and publicly questioned whether any multilateral or bilateral guarantee could possibly be considered credible.[23]

Instead of producing a united Indian effort to acquire a nuclear deterrent, the Chinese nuclear test produced a prolonged bureaucratic battle, fought inside the New Delhi political elite and nuclear energy establishment, between actors who wanted India to develop a nuclear weapons capability as soon as possible and other actors who opposed an Indian bomb and supported global nuclear disarmament and later Indian membership in the NPT. Soon after the Chinese nuclear test, for example, Prime Minister Lal Bahadur Shastri argued against developing an Indian atomic arsenal, in part because the estimated costs ($42–84 million) were deemed excessive; Homi Bhabba, the head of the Atomic Energy Commission (AEC), however, loudly lobbied for the development of nuclear weapons capability, claiming that India could develop a bomb in 18 months and that an arsenal of 50 atomic bombs would cost less than $21 million (a figure that excluded the construction of reactors, separation plants, and the opportunity costs of diverting scientists from development projects).[24] Although Shastri continued to oppose weapons development and rebuked legislators in congressional debates for quoting Bhabba's excessively optimistic cost estimates, he compromised with the pro-bomb members of the Congress party and the AEC leadership, agreeing to create a classified project to develop an ability to detonate a PNE within 6 months of any final political decision.[25] However, even this compromise was short-lived, as Bhabha's successor at the AEC, Vikram Sarabhai, opposed the development of any Indian nuclear explosives, whether they were called PNEs or bombs, and ordered a halt to the PNE preparation program.[26]

After Sarabhai's death in 1971, the pro-bomb scientists in the AEC began to

23. See A.G. Noorani, "India's Quest for a Nuclear Guarantee," *Asian Survey*, Vol. 7, No. 7 (July 1967), pp. 490–502.

24. Frank E. Couper, "Indian Party Conflict on the Issue of Atomic Weapons," *Journal of Developing Areas*, Vol. 3, No. 2 (January 1969), pp. 192–193. Also see Lavoy, "Nuclear Myths and the Causes of Proliferation," p. 201.

25. See Shyam Bhatia, *India's Nuclear Bomb* (Ghaziabad: Vikas Publishing House, 1979), pp. 120–122. The director of the PNE study later wrote that "getting the Prime Minister to agree to this venture must have required great persuasion, as Shastriji was opposed to the idea of atomic explosions of any kind." Raja Ramanna, *Years of Pilgrimage: An Autobiography* (New Delhi: Viking, 1991), p. 74.

26. See Kapur, *India's Nuclear Option*, p. 195; Mitchell Reiss, *Without the Bomb: The Politics of Nuclear Nonproliferation* (New York: Columbia University Press, 1988), p. 221 and p. 325 (note 42); and Ramanna, *Years of Pilgrimage*, p. 75.

lobby Prime Minister Indira Gandhi, and developed an alliance with defense laboratories whose participation was needed to fabricate the explosive lenses for a nuclear test.[27] Unfortunately, firm evidence on why Gandhi decided to approve the scientists' recommendation to build and test a "peaceful" Indian nuclear device does not exist: indeed, even nuclear scientists who pushed for the May 1974 test now acknowledge that it is impossible to know whether Gandhi was primarily responding to domestic motives, since she neither asked questions at the critical secret meetings in early 1974 nor explained why she approved their PNE recommendations.[28] A number of observations about the decision, however, do suggest that addressing domestic political concerns, rather than countering international security threats, were paramount. First, it is important to recognize that the decision was made by Prime Minister Gandhi, with the advice of a very small circle of personal advisers and scientists from the nuclear establishment. Senior defense and foreign affairs officials in India were not involved in the initial decision to prepare the nuclear device, nor in the final decision to test it: the military services were not asked how nuclear weapons would affect their war plans and military doctrines; the Defense Minister was reportedly informed of, but not consulted about, the final test decision only 10 days before the May 18 explosion; the Foreign Minister was merely given a 48-hour notice of the detonation.[29] This pattern suggests that security arguments were of secondary importance, and at a minimum, were not thoroughly analyzed or debated before the nuclear test. Second, the subsequent absence of a systematic program for either nuclear weapons or PNE development and testing, and New Delhi's lack of preparedness for Canada's immediate termination of nuclear assistance, suggest that the decision was taken quickly, even in haste, and thus may have focused more on immediate political concerns rather than on longer-term security or energy interests.

Third, it is important to recognize that domestic support for the Gandhi government had fallen to an all-time low in late 1973 and early 1974 due to a prolonged and severe domestic recession, the eruption of large-scale riots in a

---

27. Ramanna, *Years of Pilgrimage*, p. 89.
28. See George Perkovich, "Indian Nuclear Decision-Making and the 1974 PNE," unpublished manuscript, W. Alton Jones Foundation, Charlottesville, Va., 1996, p. 15; and Ramanna, *Years of Pilgrimage*, p. 89.
29. See Neil H.A. Joeck, *Nuclear Proliferation and National Security in India and Pakistan*, unpublished dissertation, UCLA, 1986, p. 229; and Kapur, *India's Nuclear Option*, p. 198. One former Indian Defense Secretary, K.B. Lall, has stated that the chairman of the chiefs of staff, the defense minister, and the defense secretary were not involved in the planning and argued therefore that "[the test] did not arise out of the Defense Ministry or on security grounds" since "if it was a defense project, there should have been some discussion." Lall interview quoted in Joeck, *Nuclear Proliferation and National Security*, p. 229.

number of regions, and the lingering effects of the splintering of the ruling Congress Party. From a domestic politics perspective, it would be highly surprising for a politician with such problems to resist what she knew was a major opportunity to increase her standing in public opinion polls and to defuse an issue about which she had been criticized by her domestic opponents.[30] Indeed, the domestic consequences of the test were very rewarding: the nuclear detonation occurred during the government's unprecedented crackdown on the striking railroad workers and contributed to a major increase in support for the Gandhi government. Indian public opinion polls taken in June 1974 reported, for example, that a full 91 percent of the adult literate population knew about the explosion and 90 percent of those individuals answered in the affirmative when asked if they were "personally proud of this achievement." The overall result was that public support for Mrs. Gandhi increased by one-third in the month after the nuclear test according to the Indian Institute of Public Opinion, leading the Institute to conclude that "both she [Gandhi] and the Congress Party have been restored to the nation's confidence."[31]

These arguments linking decision-making processes and domestic results to potential causes of proliferation clearly do not prove that the domestic politics model provides the correct explanation of the Indian case. But they do constitute stronger evidence than what has been offered in the literature to support a security model explanation, and provide an answer to what is otherwise the very puzzling occurrence of a state (India) *not* developing the bomb for ten years after one rival (China) tested a weapon, and then changing its proliferation policy and developing and testing a weapon less than three years after it attacked and dismembered its other rival state (Pakistan). In light of the domestic politics model, the unusual nature of Indian nuclear weapons policy since the 1974 test also becomes more understandable; it appears less like a calculated strategy of nuclear ambiguity and more like a political rationalization for latent military capabilities developed for other reasons. Finally, from the domestic model's perspective, the 1974 test and subsequent building of

---

30. Although Gandhi denied, in a later interview, that domestic concerns influenced her 1974 decision, she did acknowledge that the nuclear test "would have been useful for elections." See Rodney W. Jones, "India," in Jozef Goldblat, ed., *Non-Proliferation: the Why and the Wherefore* (London: Taylor and Francis, 1985), p. 114.

31. The Institute's analysis was that the increase was the result of both "the demonstration of India's atomic capability and the decisive action on the Railway strike," though the data outlined above suggests that more emphasis should be placed on the weapons test. See "The Prime Minister's Popularity: June 1974," and "Indian Public Opinion and the Railway Strike," in *Monthly Public Opinion Surveys* (Indian Institute of Public Opinion), Vol. 19, No. 8 (May 1974), pp. 5–6 and pp. 7–11; and "Public Opinion on India's Nuclear Device," *Monthly Public Opinion Surveys*, Vol. 19, No. 9 (June 1974), Blue Supplement, pp. III–IV.

significantly greater nuclear weapons capabilities are not seen as proud symbols of the success of an Indian national security program; instead, they are symbols of the failure of the Indian civilian nuclear power industry, which was forced to form an alliance with the pro-bomb lobby to justify its existence and funding after its failure to avoid cost overruns and prevent safety problems in its domestic energy program.[32]

DEVELOPMENT AND DENUCLEARIZATION: SOUTH AFRICA REVISITED

From the domestic model's perspective, one would expect that reversals of weapons decisions occur not when external threats are diminished, but rather when there are major internal political changes. There are a number of reasons why purely internal changes could produce restraint: a new government has an opportunity to change course more easily because it can blame failed policies of the previous regime; actors with parochial interests in favor of weapons programs may lose internal struggles to newly empowered actors with other interests; and the outgoing government may fear that the incoming government would not be a reliable custodian over nuclear weapons. It is important to note, however, that each of these domestic pathways to restraint can be relatively independent of changes in international security threats.

A quite different interpretation of the South African weapons program emerges when one reexamines the history with a focus on domestic political interests rather than national security. For example, President de Klerk's public explanation for the program stressed that it was caused by the need to deter "a Soviet expansionist threat to Southern Africa," especially after Cuban military forces intervened in Angola in October 1975. Yet the preliminary research needed to develop nuclear devices was started inside South Africa's Atomic Energy Board in 1971, on the independent authority of the Minister of Mines; a non-nuclear scale model of a gun-type explosive device was secretly tested in May 1974; and later in 1974, after the results of this test were known, Prime Minister John Voster approved plans to construct a small number of explosive devices and to build a secret testing site in the Kalahari desert.[33] Such evidence strongly supports the claims of South African scientists that the nuclear pro-

32. For a detailed analysis, see Itty Abraham's *Atomic Energy and the Making of the Indian State*, unpublished manuscript, Center for International Security and Arms Control, Stanford University, 1996; and Itty Abraham, "India's 'Strategic Enclave': Civilian Scientists and Military Technologies," *Armed Forces and Society*, Vol. 18, No. 2 (Winter 1992), pp. 231–252.

33. See the chronology in Reiss, *Bridled Ambition*, p. 8 and p. 27; and Waldo Stumpf, "South Africa's Nuclear Weapons Program: From Deterrence to Dismantlement," *Arms Control Today*, Vol. 25, No. 10 (December 1995/January 1996), p. 4. Also see David Fischer, "South Africa," in Mitchell

gram was originally designed to produce PNEs, and was championed within the government by the South African nuclear power and mining industries to enhance their standing in international scientific circles and to be utilized in mining situations.[34]

This explanation for the origin of the nuclear program helps in turn to explain South African nuclear doctrine, which otherwise appears so strange, as a *post hoc* development used to exploit devices that were originally developed for other purposes. (Testing a nuclear device in the event of a Soviet invasion might, after all, *reduce* the likelihood of U.S. intervention and would raise great risks of the use of Soviet nuclear weapons.) Senior officials in the program have stated, for example, that the military was not consulted about the bomb design and that operational considerations, such as the size and weight of the devices, were not taken into account.[35] As a result, the first South African nuclear device was actually too large to be deliverable by an aircraft and had to be redesigned because it did not meet the safety and reliability standards set by Armscor, the engineering organization run by the South African military, which took over the nuclear program in 1978.[36]

The timing and details of actions concerning the decision to dismantle and destroy the existing bomb stockpile also suggest that domestic political considerations were critical. In September 1989, de Klerk was elected president and immediately requested a high-level report on the possibility of dismantling the existing six nuclear devices. It is important to note that this request came before the Cold War was unambiguously over (the Berlin Wall fell in November 1989), and that de Klerk's action was considered by officials in South Africa as a sign that he had already decided to abandon the weapons program. Although possible concerns about who would inherit nuclear weapons are rarely discussed in the public rationales for the dismantlement decision, the de Klerk government's actions spoke more loudly than its words: the weapons components were dismantled *before* IAEA inspections could be held to verify the activities, and all the nuclear program's plans, history of decisions, and approval and design documents were burned prior to the public announcement of

Reiss and Robert S. Litwak, eds., *Nuclear Proliferation After the Cold War* (Washington, D.C.: Woodrow Wilson Center Press, 1994), p. 208; and David Albright, "South Africa's Secret Nuclear Weapons," *ISIS Report* (Washington, D.C.: Institute for Science and International Security, May 1994), pp. 6–8.

34. See Mark Hibbs, "South Africa's Secret Nuclear Program: From a PNE to a Deterrent," *Nuclear Fuel*, May 10, 1993, pp. 3–6; and Stumpf, "South Africa's Nuclear Weapons Program," p. 4.

35. See Reiss, *Bridled Ambitions*, p. 12.

36. Albright, "South Africa's Secret Nuclear Weapons," p. 10.

the program's existence. This was a highly unusual step and strongly suggests that fear of ANC control of nuclear weapons (and perhaps also concern about possible seizure by white extremists) was critical in the decision.[37]

Domestic politics can also be seen as playing critical roles in other cases of nuclear restraint. In Argentina and Brazil, for example, the key change explaining the shift from nuclear competition to cooperative restraint in the 1980s could not have been a major reduction of security threats, since there was no such reduction. Indeed, a traditional realist view would predict that the experience of the 1982 Falklands/Malvinas War—in which Argentina was defeated by a nuclear power, Great Britain—would have strongly encouraged Argentina's nuclear ambitions. Instead, the important change was the emergence of liberalizing domestic regimes in both states, governments supported by coalitions of actors—such as banks, export-oriented firms, and state monetary agencies—who value unimpeded access to international markets and oppose economically unproductive defense and energy enterprises. Nuclear programs that were run as fiefdoms and served the interests of the atomic industry bureaucrats and the military were therefore abandoned by new civilian regimes with strong support of liberalizing coalitions.[38]

POLICY IMPLICATIONS OF THE DOMESTIC POLITICS MODEL
With respect to U.S. nonproliferation policy, a domestic politics approach both cautions modest expectations about U.S. influence and calls for a broader set of diplomatic efforts. Modest expectations are in order, since the key factors that influence decisions are domestic in origin and therefore largely outside the control of U.S. policy. Nevertheless, a more diverse set of tools could be useful to help create and empower domestic coalitions that oppose the development or maintenance of nuclear arsenals.

A variety of activities could be included in such a domestic-focused nonproliferation strategy. International financial institutions are already demanding that cuts in military expenditures be included in conditionality packages

---

37. A rare public hint that concerns about domestic stability played a role in the decision is the acknowledgment by the head of the Atomic Energy Corporation that the government discussed issuing an immediate announcement revealing the existence of the weapons and thus permitting the IAEA to dismantle them because "the state of the country's internal political transformation was not considered conducive to such an announcement at the time." See Stumpf, "South Africa's Nuclear Weapons Program," p. 7.
38. The best analysis is Etel Solingen, "The Political Economy of Nuclear Restraint," *International Security*, Vol. 19, No. 2 (Fall 1994), pp. 126–169.

for aid recipients. More direct conditionality linkages to nuclear programs—such as deducting the estimated budget of any suspect research and development program from IMF or U.S. loans to a country—could heighten domestic opposition to such programs.[39] Providing technical information and intellectual ammunition for domestic actors—by encouraging more accurate estimates of the economic and environmental costs of nuclear weapons programs and highlighting the risks of nuclear accidents[40]—could bring new members into anti-proliferation coalitions. In addition, efforts to encourage strict civilian control of the military, through educational and organizational reforms, could be productive, especially in states in which the military has the capability to create secret nuclear programs (like Brazil in the 1980s) to serve their parochial interests. Finally, U.S. attempts to provide alternative sources of employment and prestige to domestic actors who might otherwise find weapons programs attractive could decrease nuclear incentives. To the degree that professional military organizations are supporting nuclear proliferation, encouraging their involvement in other military activities (such as Pakistani participation in peacekeeping operations or the Argentine Navy's role in the Persian Gulf) could decrease such support. Where the key actors are laboratory officials and scientists, assistance in non-nuclear research and development programs (as in the current U.S.-Russian "lab-to-lab" program) could decrease personal and organizational incentives for weapons research.

A different perspective on the role of the NPT also emerges from the domestic politics model. The NPT regime is not just a device to increase states' confidence about the limits of their potential adversaries' nuclear programs; it is also a tool that can help to empower domestic actors who are opposed to nuclear weapons development. The NPT negotiations and review conferences create a well-placed elite in the foreign and defense ministries with considerable bureaucratic and personal interests in maintaining the regime. The IAEA creates monitoring capabilities and enforcement incentives against unregulated activities within a state's own nuclear power organizations. The network

---

39. Etel Solingen, *The Domestic Sources of Nuclear Postures,* Institute of Global Conflict and Cooperation, Policy Paper No. 8, October 1994, p. 11.
40. On these costs and risks, see Kathleen C. Bailey, ed., *Weapons of Mass Destruction: Costs Versus Benefits* (New Delhi: Manohar Publishers, 1994); Stephen I. Schwartz, "Four Trillion and Counting," *Bulletin of the Atomic Scientists,* Vol. 51, No. 6 (November/December 1995); Bruce G. Blair, *The Logic of Accidental Nuclear War* (Washington, D.C.: The Brookings Institution, 1993); and Scott D. Sagan, *The Limits of Safety: Organizations, Accidents, and Nuclear Weapons* (Princeton, N.J.: Princeton University Press, 1993).

of non-governmental organizations built around the treaty supports similar anti-proliferation pressure groups in each state.

According to this model, the U.S. commitment under Article VI to work for the eventual elimination of nuclear weapons is important because of the impact that the behavior of the United States and other nuclear powers can have on the domestic debates in non-nuclear states. Whether or not the United States originally signed Article VI merely to placate domestic opinion in non-nuclear states is not important; what is important is that the loss of this pacifying tool could influence outcomes in potential proliferators. In future debates inside such states, the arguments of anti-nuclear actors—that nuclear weapons programs do not serve the interests of their states—can be more easily countered by pro-bomb actors whenever they can point to specific actions of the nuclear powers, such as refusals to ban nuclear tests or the maintenance of nuclear first-use doctrines, that highlight these states' continued reliance on nuclear deterrence.

The Norms Model: Nuclear Symbols and State Identity

A third model focuses on norms concerning weapons acquisition, seeing nuclear decisions as serving important symbolic functions—both shaping and reflecting a state's identity. According to this perspective, state behavior is determined not by leaders' cold calculations about the national security interests or their parochial bureaucratic interests, but rather by deeper norms and shared beliefs about what actions are legitimate and appropriate in international relations.

Given the importance of the subject, and the large normative literature in ethics and law concerning the use of nuclear weapons, it is surprising that so little attention has been paid to "nuclear symbolism" and the development of international norms concerning the acquisition of nuclear weapons.[41] Sociologists and political scientists have studied the emergence and influence of international norms in other substantive areas, however, and their insights can lead

---

41. On nuclear ethics, see Joseph S. Nye, Jr., *Nuclear Ethics* (New York: Free Press, 1986); and Steven P. Lee, *Morality, Prudence, and Nuclear Weapons* (New York: Cambridge University Press, 1993). For a recent analysis of legal restraints on the use of nuclear weapons, see Nicholas Rostow, "The World Health Organization, the International Court of Justice, and Nuclear Weapons," *Yale Journal of International Law*, Vol. 20, No. 1 (Winter 1995), pp. 151–185. For a rare analysis of the symbolism of nuclear weapons, see Robert Jervis, "The Symbolic Nature of Nuclear Politics," in Jervis, *The Meaning of the Nuclear Revolution* (Ithaca, N.Y.: Cornell University Press, 1989), pp. 174–225.

to a valuable alternative perspective on proliferation. Within sociology, the "new institutionalism" literature suggests that modern organizations and institutions often come to resemble each other (what is called institutional isomorphism) not because of competitive selection or rational learning but because institutions mimic each other.[42] These scholars emphasize the importance of roles, routines, and rituals: individuals and organizations may well have "interests," but such interests are shaped by the social roles actors are asked to play, are pursued according to habits and routines as much as through reasoned decisions, and are embedded in a social environment that promotes certain structures and behaviors as rational and legitimate and denigrates others as irrational and primitive.

From this sociological perspective, military organizations and their weapons can therefore be envisioned as serving functions similar to those of flags, airlines, and Olympic teams: they are part of what modern states believe they have to possess to be legitimate, modern states. Air Malawi, Royal Nepal Airlines, and Air Myanmar were not created because they are cost-effective means of transport nor because domestic pressure groups pushed for their development, but rather because government leaders believed that a national airline is something that modern states have to have to be modern states. Very small and poor states, without a significant number of scientists, nevertheless have official government-sponsored science boards. From a new institutionalist perspective, such similarities are not the result of functional logic (actions designed to serve either international or domestic goals); they are the product of shared beliefs about what is legitimate and modern behavior.[43]

Within political science, a related literature has evolved concerning the development and spread of norms within international regimes. Although this norms perspective has rarely been applied to the proliferation problem, schol-

---

42. Among the most important sources are the essays collected in Walter W. Powell and Paul J. DiMaggio, eds., *The New Institutionalism in Organizational Analysis* (Chicago: University of Chicago Press, 1991); and John W. Meyer and W. Richard Scott, *Organizational Environments: Ritual and Rationality*, 2nd ed. (Newbury Park, Calif.: Sage Publications, 1992).

43. See Marc C. Suchman and Dana P. Eyre, "Military Procurement as Rational Myth: Notes on the Social Construction of Weapons Proliferation," *Sociological Forum*, Vol. 7, No. 1 (March 1992), pp. 137–161; Martha Finnemore, "International Organizations as Teachers of Norms: UNESCO and Science Policy," *International Organization*, Vol. 47, No. 4 (Autumn 1993), pp. 565–598; Francisco O. Ramirez and John Boli, "Global Patterns of Educational Institutionalization," in George M. Thomas, John W. Meyer, Francisco O. Ramirez, and John Boli, eds., *Institutional Structure: Constituting State, Society, and the Individual* (Newbury Park, Calif.: Sage Publications, 1987), pp. 150–172. For an excellent survey and critique, see Martha Finnemore, "Norms, Culture, and World Politics: Insights from Sociology's Institutionalism," *International Organization*, Vol. 50, No. 2 (Spring 1996), pp. 325–348.

ars have studied such important phenomena as the global spread of anti-colonialism, the abolition of the African slave trade, the near-total elimination of piracy at sea, and constraints against the use of chemical weapons.[44] There is a diverse set of ideas emerging in this field, producing a valuable debate about the role of global norms, but not a well-developed theory about their causal influence. Still, as one would expect of political scientists, coercion and power are seen to play a more important role in spreading norms than is the case in the sociologists' literature. Normative pressures may begin with the actions of entrepreneurial non-state actors, but their beliefs only have significant influence once powerful state actors join the cause. Religious and liberal opposition to slavery, for example, was clearly important in fueling American and British leaders' preferences in the nineteenth century, but such views would not easily have become an international norm without the bayonets of the Army of the Potomac at Gettysburg or the ships of the British Navy patrolling the high seas between Africa and Brazil.[45] Similarly, normative beliefs about chemical weapons were important in creating legal restrictions against their use in war; yet, the norm was significantly reenforced at critical moments by the fear of retaliation-in-kind and by the availability of other weapons that were believed by military leaders to be more effective on the battlefield.[46]

The sociologists' arguments highlight the possibility that nuclear weapons programs serve symbolic functions reflecting leaders' perceptions of appropriate and modern behavior. The political science literature reminds us, however,

---

44. For rare applications of the norms perspective to proliferation, see Harald Müller, "The Internationalization of Principles, Norms, and Rules by Governments: The Case of Security Regimes," in Volker Rittberger, ed., *Regime Theory and International Relations* (Oxford: Clarendon Press, 1995), pp. 361–390; and Müller, "Maintaining Non-Nuclear Weapon Status," in Regina Cowen Karp, ed., *Security With Nuclear Weapons?* (New York: Oxford University Press, 1991), pp. 301–339. Also see Robert H. Jackson, "The Weight of Ideas in Decolonization: Normative Change in International Relations," in Judith Goldstein and Robert O. Keohane, eds., *Ideas and Foreign Policy* (Ithaca, N.Y.: Cornell University Press, 1993), pp. 111–138; Neta C. Crawford, "Decolonization as an International Norm," in Laura W. Reed and Carl Kaysen, eds., *Emerging Norms of Justified Intervention* (Cambridge, Mass.: American Academy of Arts and Sciences, 1993), pp. 37–61; Ethan A. Nadelmann, "Global Prohibition Regimes: The Evolution of Norms in International Society," *International Organization*, Vol. 44, No. 4 (Autumn 1990), pp. 479–526; and Richard Price, "A Genealogy of the Chemical Weapons Taboo," *International Organization*, Vol. 49, No. 1 (Winter 1995), pp. 73–104.
45. Ethan Nadelman, who stresses this point about power, also adds, however, that "even among the laggards, indeed especially among the laggards, the consciousness of being perceived as primitive and deviant surely weighed heavily in the decisions of local rulers to do away with slavery." Nadelman, "Global Prohibition Regimes," p. 497.
46. See Price, "A Genealogy of the Chemical Weapons Taboo"; and Jeffrey Legro, *Cooperation Under Fire: Anglo-German Restraint During World War II* (Ithaca, N.Y.: Cornell University Press, 1995), pp. 144–216.

that such symbols are often contested and that the resulting norms are spread by power and coercion, and not by the strength of ideas alone. Both insights usefully illuminate the nuclear proliferation phenomenon. Existing norms concerning the non-acquisition of nuclear weapons (such as those embedded in the NPT) could not have been created without the strong support of the most powerful states in the international system, who believed that the norms served their narrow political interests. Yet, once that effort was successful, these norms shaped states' identities and expectations and even powerful actors became constrained by the norms they had created.[47] The history of nuclear proliferation is particularly interesting in this regard because a major discontinuity—a shift in nuclear norms—has emerged as the result of the NPT regime.

Although many individual case studies of nuclear weapons decisions mention the belief that nuclear acquisition will enhance the international prestige of the state, such prestige has been viewed simply as a reasonable, though diffuse, means used to enhance the state's international influence and security. What is missing from these analyses is an understanding of why and how actions are granted symbolic meaning: why are some nuclear weapons acts considered prestigious, while others produce opprobrium, and how do such beliefs change over time? Why, for example, was nuclear testing deemed prestigious and legitimate in the 1960s, but is today considered illegitimate and irresponsible? An understanding of the NPT regime is critical here, for it appears to have shifted the norm concerning what acts grant prestige and legitimacy from the 1960s notion of joining "the nuclear club" to the 1990s concept of joining "the club of the nations adhering to the NPT." Moreover, the salience of the norms that were made explicit in the NPT treaty has shifted over time. These arguments are perhaps best supported by contrasting two cases—the French decision to build and test nuclear weapons and the Ukrainian decision to give up its nuclear arsenal—in which perceptions of legitimacy and prestige appear to have had a major influence, albeit with very different outcomes.

PROLIFERATION REVISITED: FRENCH GRANDEUR AND WEAPONS POLICY

According to realist theory, the French decision to develop nuclear weapons has a very simple explanation: in the 1950s, the Soviet Union was a grave mili-

---

47. For an excellent analysis of how such a process can work in other contexts, see Michael Byers, "Custom, Power, and the Power of Rules," *Michigan Journal of International Law*, Vol. 17, No. 1 (Fall 1995), pp. 109–180.

tary threat to French national security, and the best alternative to building an independent arsenal—reliance on the United States's nuclear guarantee to NATO—was ruled out after the Soviet development of a secure second strike capability reduced the credibility of any U.S. nuclear first-use threats. According to this explanation, the need for a French arsenal was driven home by the 1956 Suez Crisis, when Paris was forced to withdraw its military intervention forces after a nuclear threat from Russia and under U.S. economic pressure. "The Suez humiliation of 1956 was decisive," writes David Yost. "It was felt that a nuclear weapons capability would reduce France's dependence on the U.S. and her vulnerability to Soviet blackmail."[48] The central realist argument for French nuclear weapons was clearly expressed in the rhetorical question Charles de Gaulle posed to Dwight Eisenhower in 1959: "Will they [future U.S. presidents] take the risk of devastating American cities so that Berlin, Brussels and Paris might remain free?"[49]

This explanation of French nuclear policy, however, does not stand up very well against either existing evidence or logic. Indeed, the two most critical decisions initiating the weapons program—Prime Minister Mendes-France's December 1954 decision to start a secret nuclear weapons research program inside the Commissariat à l'énergie atomique (CEA) and the May 1955 authorization by the Ministry of Defense for funds to be transferred to the CEA for the development of a prototype weapon—predated the 1956 Suez Crisis.[50] In addition, as Lawrence Scheinman has argued, it is by no means clear why French leaders would think that the traumatic Suez experience could have been avoided if there had been an independent French nuclear arsenal, since Great Britain had also been forced to withdraw from the intervention in Egypt under U.S. and Soviet pressure, despite its possession of nuclear weapons.[51] A simple exercise in comparative logic also raises doubts about the security model. If the critical cause of proliferation in France was the lack of credibility of U.S. nuclear guarantees given the growing Soviet threat in the mid-1950s, why then did other nuclear-capable states in Europe, faced with similar security threats at the time, not also develop nuclear weapons?[52] If one even briefly examines

48. David S. Yost, "France's Deterrent Posture and Security in Europe, Part I: Capabilities and Doctrine," Adelphi Paper No. 194 (London: International Institute for Strategic Studies [IISS], Winter 1984/85), p. 4. Also see Kohl, *French Nuclear Diplomacy*, p. 36.
49. Jean Lacouture, *De Gaulle: The Ruler 1945–1970* (New York: W.W. Norton, 1993), p. 421, as quoted in Thayer, "The Causes of Nuclear Proliferation," p. 489.
50. See Bertrand Goldschmidt, *The Atomic Complex* (La Grange Park, Ill.: American Nuclear Society, 1982), p. 131; and Scheinman, *Atomic Energy Policy in France Under the Fourth Republic*, pp. 120–122.
51. Scheinman, *Atomic Energy Policy in France Under the Fourth Republic*, pp. 171–173.
52. The British acquisition of nuclear weapons in 1952 predated the Soviet development of a secure second-strike capability.

the list of all the nuclear-capable states in Europe that were both threatened by Soviet military power and had reasons to doubt the credibility of the U.S. first-use pledge, France appears alone on the nuclear proliferation side of the ledger; West Germany, the Netherlands, Italy, Switzerland, Belgium, Norway, and Sweden were all on the nuclear restraint side. This presents a puzzle for the security model, since the Soviet Union's conventional and nuclear threat to most of these states' security was at least as great as the Soviet threat to France; the American nuclear guarantee should not have been not considered more credible by those states that had been U.S. enemies or neutrals in World War II, compared to France, a U.S. ally of long standing, and one which the United States had strongly aided once it entered the war in 1941.

A stronger explanation for the French decision to build nuclear weapons emerges when one focuses on French leaders' perceptions of the bomb's symbolic significance. The belief that nuclear power and nuclear weapons were deeply linked to a state's position in the international system was present as early as 1951, when the first French Five-Year Plan was put forward with its stated purpose being "to ensure that in 10 years' time France will still be an important country."[53] France emerged from World War II in an unusual position: it was a liberated victor whose military capabilities and international standing were not at all comparable to the power and status it had before the war. It should therefore not be surprising that the governments of both the Fourth and the Fifth Republics vigorously explored alternative means to return France to its historical great power status.[54] After the war, the initial French effort to restore its tarnished prestige focused on the fight to hold onto an overseas empire, yet as Michel Martin has nicely put it, "as the curtain was drawn over colonial domination, it became clear that the country's *grandeur* had to be nourished from other sources."[55]

After 1958, the Algerian crisis contributed greatly to Charles de Gaulle's obsession with nuclear weapons as the source of French *grandeur* and independence. In contrast, de Gaulle appeared less concerned about whether French nuclear forces could provide adequate deterrence against the Soviet military

---

53. The document is quoted in Goldschmidt, *The Atomic Complex*, p. 126.
54. For detailed analyses of the French nuclear weapons decision which focus attention on political prestige as the central source of policy, see Scheinman, *Atomic Energy Policy in France Under the Fourth Republic;* and Kohl, *French Nuclear Diplomacy.* Also see Bundy, *Danger and Survival*, pp. 472–487, 499–503.
55. Michel L. Martin, *Warriors to Managers: The French Military Establishment Since 1945* (Chapel Hill, N.C.: University of North Carolina Press, 1981), p. 21.

threat. For example, during both the Berlin crisis of 1958 (before the 1960 French nuclear weapons test) and the 1962 Cuban crisis (after the test, but before French nuclear forces were operational), de Gaulle expressed great confidence that the Soviets would not risk an attack on NATO Europe.[56] Wilfred Kohl also reports on a revealing incident in which a French military strategist sent de Gaulle a copy of a book on French nuclear doctrine and de Gaulle replied, "thanking the man for his interesting analysis of strategic questions, but stressing that for him the central and clearly the only important issue was: 'Will France remain France?'"[57] For de Gaulle, the atomic bomb was a dramatic symbol of French independence and was thus needed for France to continue to be seen, by itself and others, as a great power. He confided to President Dwight Eisenhower in 1959:

A France without world responsibility would be unworthy of herself, especially in the eyes of Frenchmen. It is for this reason that she disapproves of NATO, which denies her a share in decision-making and which is confined to Europe. It is for this reason too that she intends to provide herself with an atomic armament. Only in this way can our defense and foreign policy be independent, which we prize above everything else.[58]

When the French nuclear weapons arsenal is viewed as primarily serving symbolic functions, a number of puzzling aspects of the history of French atomic policy become more understandable. The repeated Gaullist declarations that French nuclear weapons should have world-wide capabilities and must be aimed in all directions (*"tous azimuts"*) are seen, not as the product of security threats that came from all directions, but rather because only such a policy could be logically consistent with global *grandeur* and independence. Similarly, the French strategic doctrine of "proportional deterrence" against the Soviet Union during the Cold War—threatening more limited destruction in a retaliatory strike than did the United States under its targeting doctrine— is seen as being produced, not by France's geographical position or limited economic resources, but rather because deterrence of the Soviet Union was a justification, and never the primary purpose of its arsenal. Finally, the profound French reluctance to stop nuclear testing in the mid-1990s is seen as be-

---

56. See Philip H. Gordon, "Charles de Gaulle and the Nuclear Revolution," *Security Studies*, Vol. 5, No. 1 (Autumn 1995), pp. 129–130.
57. Kohl, *French Nuclear Diplomacy*, p. 150, quoted in Bundy, *Danger and Survival*, p. 502.
58. Charles de Gaulle, *Memoirs of Hope: Renewal and Endeavor* (New York: Simon and Schuster, 1971), p. 209 (emphasis in the original), quoted in Yost, *France's Deterrent Posture and Security in Europe*, pp. 13–14.

ing produced, not only by the stated concerns about weapons modernization and warhead safety, but also because weapons tests were perceived by Parisian leaders as potent symbols of French identity and status as a great power.

RESTRAINT REVISITED: THE NPT AND THE UKRAINE CASE

Stark contrasts exist between French nuclear decisions in the 1950s and Ukrainian nuclear decisions in the 1990s. When the Soviet Union collapsed in 1991, an independent Ukraine was "born nuclear" with more than 4,000 nuclear weapons on or under its soil. In November 1994, however, the Rada in Kiev voted overwhelmingly to join the NPT as a non-nuclear state, and all weapons were removed from Ukrainian territory by June 1996.

This decision to give up a nuclear arsenal is puzzling from the realist perspective: a number of prominent realist scholars, after all, maintained that given the history of Russian expansionist behavior and continuing tensions over the Crimea and the treatment of Russian minorities, Ukraine's independence was seriously threatened, and further argued that nuclear weapons were the only rational solution to this security threat.[59] The disarmament decision is also puzzling from a traditional domestic politics perspective. Despite the tragic consequences of the Chernobyl accident, public opinion polls in Ukraine showed rapidly growing support for keeping nuclear weapons in 1992 and 1993: polls showed support for an independent arsenal increasing from 18 percent in May 1992 to 36 percent in March 1993, to as much as 45 percent in the summer of 1993.[60] In addition, well-known retired military officers, such as Rada member General Volodomyr Tolubko, vigorously lobbied to maintain an arsenal and senior political leaders, most importantly Prime Minister (then President) Leonid Kuchma, came from the Soviet missile-building industry and would not therefore be expected to take an anti-nuclear position.[61]

An understanding of Ukraine's decision to eliminate its nuclear arsenal requires that more attention be focused on the role that emerging NPT nonproliferation norms played in four critical ways. First, Ukrainian politicians

---

59. See John J. Mearsheimer, "The Case for a Ukrainian Nuclear Deterrent," *Foreign Affairs*, Vol. 72, No. 3 (Summer 1993), pp. 50–66; and Barry R. Posen, "The Security Dilemma and Ethnic Conflict," *Survival*, Vol. 35, No. 1 (Spring 1993), pp. 44–45.
60. See William C. Potter, "The Politics of Nuclear Renunciation: The Cases of Belarus, Kazakhstan, and Ukraine," Henry L. Stimson Center, Occasional Paper No. 22, April 1995, p. 49.
61. For a detailed analysis see Bohdan Nahaylo, "The Shaping of Ukrainian Attitudes Toward Nuclear Arms," *RFE/RL (Radio Free Europe/Radio Liberty) Research Report*, Vol. 2, No. 8 (February 19, 1993), pp. 21–45.

initially adopted anti-nuclear positions as a way of buttressing Kiev's claims to national sovereignty. In one of its first efforts to assert an independent foreign policy from Moscow, Ukraine tried to accede to the NPT as a non-nuclear state in early 1990, attempting to use NPT membership as a way of separating itself from the Soviet Union.[62] In July 1990, this policy was underscored when the parliament in Kiev issued its Declaration of Sovereignty. Embedded in declarations about Ukraine's right to participate as a full member in all agreements concerning "international peace and security" was the proclamation that Ukraine would "become a neutral state that does not participate in military blocs and that adheres to three non-nuclear principles: not to maintain, produce, or acquire nuclear weapons." This extraordinary statement was an expedient designed to buttress Kiev's claim to independence from the Soviet Union, rather than a blueprint laying out Ukraine's long-term strategy: indeed, it was adopted by a vote of 355–4, without extensive debate, by the parliament in which conservative communists (many of whom would later take pro-nuclear positions) still held the majority of seats.[63] Nevertheless, the declaration placed the onus of reneging on an international commitment on the politicians and scholars who afterwards called for keeping an arsenal, and it is revealing that even many of the more hawkish analysts thereafter defensively advocated keeping the arsenal on a temporary basis until other sources of security could be found.[64] Second, although Ukrainian officials continued to be interested in enhancing the state's international prestige, the strength of the NPT regime created a history in which the most recent examples of new or potential nuclear states were so-called "rogue states" such as North Korea, Iran, and Iraq. This was hardly a nuclear club whose new members would receive international prestige, and during the debate in Kiev, numerous pro-NPT Ukrainian officials insisted that renunciation of nuclear weapons was now the best route to enhance Ukraine's international standing.[65] Third, economic pressures were clearly critical to the Ukrainian decision: the United States and NATO allies encouraged Kiev to give up the arsenal not by convincing officials that nuclear weapons could never serve as a military deterrent against Moscow, but by persuading them that not following the NPT norm would result in

62. Potter, "The Politics of Nuclear Renunciation," p. 19.
63. See Nahaylo, "The Shaping of Ukrainian Attitudes," pp. 21–22.
64. Potter, "The Politics of Nuclear Renunciation," pp. 21–23; and Nahaylo, "The Shaping of Ukrainian Attitudes."
65. See Potter, "The Politics of Nuclear Renunciation," p. 44; and Garnett, "Ukraine's Decision to Join the NPT," p. 12.

very negative economic consequences.[66] It is important to recognize, however, that the ability to coordinate such activities, and credibly to threaten collective sanctions and promised inducements for disarmament, were significantly heightened by the existence of the NPT norm against the creation of new nuclear weapons states. Fourth, the Kiev government and the Ukrainian public could more easily accept the economic inducements offered by the United States—such as Nunn-Lugar payments to help transport and destroy the weapons—with the belief that they were enabling Ukraine to keep an international commitment.

As with all counterfactuals, it is impossible to assess with certainty whether Ukraine would have made the same decision had the NPT norms not been in existence. Still, it is valuable to try to imagine how much more difficult a disarmament outcome would have been in the absence of the NPT and its twenty-five year history. Without the NPT, a policy of keeping a nuclear arsenal would have placed Ukraine in the category of France and China; instead, it placed Ukraine in the company of dissenters like India and Pakistan and pariahs like Iraq and North Korea. International threats to eliminate economic aid and suspend political ties would be less credible, since individual states would be more likely to defect from an agreement. Finally, without the NPT norm, U.S. dismantlement assistance would have been seen in Kiev as the crass purchase of Ukrainian weapons by a foreign government, instead of being viewed as friendly assistance to help Kiev implement an international agreement.

POLICY IMPLICATIONS OF THE NORMS MODEL

If the norms model of proliferation is correct, the key U.S. policy challenges are to recognize that such norms can have a strong influence on other states' nuclear weapons policy, and to adjust U.S. policies to increase the likelihood that norms will push others toward policies that also serve U.S. interests. Recognizing the possibility that norms can influence other states' behavior in complex ways should not be difficult. After all, the norms of the NPT have already influenced U.S. nuclear weapons policy in ways that few scholars or policymakers predicted ahead of time: in January 1995, for example, the Clinton administration abandoned the long-standing U.S. position that the Comprehensive Test Ban Treaty (CTBT) must include an automatic escape clause per-

---

66. An excellent analysis of U.S. policy appears in Garnett, "Ukraine's Decision to Join the NPT," pp. 10–12.

mitting states to withdraw from the treaty after ten years. Despite the arguments made by Pentagon officials that such a clause was necessary to protect U.S. security, the administration accepted the possibility of a permanent CTBT because senior decision-makers became convinced that the U.S. position was considered illegitimate by non-nuclear NPT members, due to the Article VI commitment to eventual disarmament, and might thereby jeopardize the effort to negotiate a permanent extension of the NPT treaty.[67]

Adjusting U.S. nuclear policies in the future to reenforce emerging nonproliferation norms will be difficult, however, because many of the recommended policies derived from the norms perspective directly contradict recommendations derived from the other models. Focusing on NPT norms raises especially severe concerns about how existing U.S. nuclear first-use doctrine influences potential proliferators' perceptions of the legitimacy or illegitimacy of nuclear weapons possession and use.[68] To the degree that such first-use policies create beliefs that nuclear threats are what great powers do, they will become desired symbols for states that aspire to that status. The norms argument against U.S. nuclear first-use doctrine, however, contradicts the policy advice derived from the security model, which stresses the need for continued nuclear guarantees for U.S. allies. Similarly, the norms perspective suggests that current U.S. government efforts to maintain the threat of first use of nuclear weapons to deter the use of biological or chemical weapons would have a negative impact on the nuclear nonproliferation regime.[69] Leaders of non-nuclear states are much less likely to consider their own acquisition of nuclear weapons to deter adversaries with chemical and biological weapons illegitimate and ill-advised if the greatest conventional military power in the world can not refrain from making such threats.

Other possible policy initiatives are less problematic. For example, if norms concerning prestige are important, then it would be valuable for the United States to encourage the development of other sources of international prestige

---

67. Douglas Jehl, "U.S. in New Pledge on Atom Test Ban," *New York Times,* January 31, 1995, p. 1; Dunbar Lockwood, "U.S. Drops CTB 'Early Out' Plan; Test Moratorium May Be Permanent," *Arms Control Today,* Vol. 25, No. 2 (March 1995), p. 27.
68. On this issue, see Barry M. Blechman and Cathleen S. Fisher, "Phase Out the Bomb," *Foreign Policy,* No. 97 (Winter 1994–95), pp. 79–95; and Wolfgang K.H. Panofsky and George Bunn, "The Doctrine of the Nuclear-Weapons States and the Future of Non-Proliferation," *Arms Control Today,* Vol. 24, No. 6 (July/August 1994), pp. 3–9.
69. For contrasting views on this policy, see George Bunn, "Expanding Nuclear Options: Is the U.S. Negating its Non-Use Pledges?" *Arms Control Today,* Vol. 26, No. 4 (May/June 1996), pp. 7–10; and Gompert, Watman, and Wilkening, "Nuclear First Use Revisited."

for current or potential proliferators. Thus, a policy that made permanent UN Security Council membership for Japan, Germany, and India conditional upon the maintenance of non-nuclear status under the NPT might further remove nuclear weapons possession from considerations of international prestige.

Finally, the norms model produces a more optimistic vision of the potential future of nonproliferation. Norms are sticky: individual and group beliefs about appropriate behavior change slowly, and over time norms can become rules embedded in domestic institutions.[70] In the short run, therefore, norms can be a brake on nuclear chain reactions: in contrast to more pessimistic realist predictions that "proliferation begets proliferation," the norms model suggests that such nuclear reactions to emerging security threats can be avoided or at least delayed because of normative constraints. The long-term future of the NPT regime is also viewed with more optimism, for the model envisions the possibility of a gradual emergence of a norm against all nuclear weapons possession. The development of such a norm may well have been inadvertent in the sense that the United States did not take its Article VI commitment to work in good faith for complete nuclear disarmament seriously, for quite understandable reasons, during the Cold War. But to the degree that other states believe that such commitments are real and legitimate, their perceptions that the United States is backsliding away from Article VI will influence their behavior over time. This emphasis on emerging norms therefore highlights the need for the nuclear powers to reaffirm their commitments to global nuclear disarmament, and suggests that it is essential that the U.S. and other governments develop a public, long-term strategy for the eventual elimination of nuclear weapons.[71] The norms model can not, of course, predict whether such efforts will ever resolve the classic risks of nuclear disarmament: that states can break treaty obligations in crises, that small arsenals produce strategic instabilities, and that adequate verification of complete dismantlement is exceedingly difficult. But the model does predict that there will be severe costs involved if

---

70. For useful discussions, see Abram Chayes and Antonia Handler Chayes, *The New Sovereignty: Compliance with International Regulatory Agreements* (Cambridge, Mass.: Harvard University Press, 1995); and Andrew P. Cortell and James W. Davis Jr., "How Do International Institutions Matter?: The Domestic Impact of International Rules and Norms," *International Studies Quarterly*, Vol. 40, No. 4 (December 1996), pp. 451–478.

71. For important efforts to rethink the elimination issue, see "An Evolving U.S. Nuclear Posture," Report of the Steering Committee of the Project on Eliminating Weapons of Mass Destruction, Henry L. Stimson Center, Washington, D.C., December 1995; and Donald MacKenzie and Graham Spinardi, "Tacit Knowledge, Weapons Design, and the Uninvention of Nuclear Weapons," *American Journal of Sociology*, Vol. 101, No. 1 (July 1995), pp. 44–100.

the nuclear powers are seen to have failed to make significant progress toward nuclear disarmament.

Conclusions: Causal Complexity and Policy Tradeoffs

The ideas and evidence presented in this article suggest that the widely held security model explanation for nuclear proliferation decisions is inadequate. A realist might well respond to this argument by asserting that evidence is always ambiguous in complex historical events, and that I underestimate foreign threats and thus provide a poor measure of the effects of security concerns on decision-makers. Moreover, it could be argued that the best theories are those that explain the largest number of cases and that the largest number of positive nuclear weapons decisions in the past (the United States, the Soviet Union, China, Israel, Pakistan) and the majority of the most pressing proliferation cases today (Iraq, Libya, and possibly North Korea and Iran) appear to be best explained by the basic security model.

I have no quarrel with the argument that the largest number of past and even current active proliferant cases are best explained by the security model. But the evidence presented above strongly suggests that multicausality, rather than measurement error, lies at the heart of the nuclear proliferation problem. Nuclear weapons proliferation and nuclear restraint have occurred in the past, and can occur in the future, for more than one reason: different historical cases are best explained by different causal models.

If this central argument is correct, it has important implications for future scholarship on proliferation as well as for U.S. nonproliferation policy. The challenge for scholars is not to produce increasing numbers of detailed, but atheoretical, case studies of states' nuclear proliferation and restraint decisions; it is to produce theory-driven comparative studies to help determine the conditions under which different causal forces produced similar outcomes. Predicting the future based on such an understanding of the past will still be problematic, since the conditions that produced the past proliferation outcomes may themselves be subject to change. But future scholarship focusing on how different governments assess the nuclear potential and intention of neighbors, on why pro-bomb and anti-bomb domestic coalitions form and gain influence, and on when and how NPT norms about legitimate behavior constrain statesmen will be extremely important.

For policymakers, the existence of three different reasons why states develop nuclear weapons suggests that no single policy can ameliorate all future proliferation problems. Fortunately, some of the policy recommendations derived from the models are quite compatible: for example, many of the diplomatic tools suggested by the domestic politics model, which attempts to reduce the power of individual parochial interests in favor of nuclear weapons, would not interfere with simultaneous efforts to address states' security concerns. Similarly, efforts to enhance the international status of some non-nuclear states need not either undercut deterrence or promote pro-nuclear advocates in those countries.

Unfortunately, other important recommendations from different models are more contradictory. Most importantly, a security-oriented strategy of maintaining a major role for U.S. nuclear guarantees to restrain proliferation among allies will eventually create strong tensions with a norms-oriented strategy seeking to delegitimize nuclear weapons use and acquisition. The final outcome of these alternative strategies, of course, is not under the control of the United States, as leaders of potential proliferators will decide for themselves whether to pursue or reject nuclear weapons programs. Yet U.S. policy will not be without influence, and intelligent decisions will not emerge if we refuse to recognize that painful tradeoffs are appearing on the horizon. U.S. decisionmakers will eventually have to choose between the difficult non-proliferation task of weaning allies away from nuclear guarantees without producing new nuclear states, and the equally difficult task of maintaining a norm against nuclear proliferation without the U.S. government facing up to its logical final consequence.

The Political Economy of Nuclear Restraint

Etel Solingen

The choice between establishing a regional nuclear regime and maintaining an ambiguous nuclear status among the second tier or would-be nuclear powers is at the heart of debates about global security in the aftermath of the Cold War era.[1] The study of nuclear postures of regional powers (beyond the original five nuclear states) in the last three decades has traditionally emphasized their external security concerns. Such emphasis provided a powerful tool to explain the pursuit of a nuclear deterrent by countries like South Korea, Israel, and Taiwan, on the basis of legitimate existential fears. However, while their security concerns have been more or less constant for over thirty years, the nuclear postures of some of these countries have shifted over time. The external security context in and of itself is not enough, therefore, to advance our knowledge about why these states embraced different instruments, at different times, for coping with such fears.

More recently, the notion that the democratic nature of states explains their reluctance to wage wars against their democratic brethren (but not against others) has become central to theoretical endeavors in international relations theory. The explosion of studies on the relationship between liberal democracy and peace has not yet included a systematic extension to the study of nonproliferation, but it is often asserted that democratization will have a benign effect on denuclearization. However, this apparent connection may be

Etel Solingen is Assistant Professor of Political Science at the University of California, Irvine.

For their helpful comments I would like to thank Harry Eckstein, Ted Hopf, Miles Kahler, Robert R. Kaufman, Timur Kuran, Stephen Krasner, Peter Lavoy, Pat Morgan, Kongdan Oh, Mark Petracca, Jim Ray, Richard Rosecrance, Wayne Sandholtz, Susan Shirk, Jack Snyder, Dorothy Solinger, Jessica Stern, Alec Stone, and two anonymous reviewers for *International Security*.

1. Regimes involve mutual policy adjustments through a joint process of coordination and collaboration leading to the establishment of binding principles, rules, and decision-making procedures. See Stephen D. Krasner, *International Regimes* (Ithaca, N.Y.: Cornell University Press, 1983); Friedrich Kratochwil and John G. Ruggie, "International Organization: A State of the Art on an Art of the State," *International Organization*, Vol. 40, No. 4 (Autumn 1986), pp. 753–776; Stephan Haggard and Beth A. Simmons, "Theories of International Regimes," *International Organization*, Vol. 41, No. 3 (Summer 1987), pp. 491–517; Oran R. Young, *International Cooperation* (Ithaca, N.Y.: Cornell University Press, 1989); and John G. Ruggie, "Multilateralism: The Anatomy of an Institution," *International Organization*, Vol. 46, No. 3 (Summer 1992), pp. 561–598.

International Security, Vol. 19, No. 2 (Fall 1994), pp. 126–169
© 1994 by the President and Fellows of Harvard College and the Massachusetts Institute of Technology.

less solid than we might like to expect: I argue that examining the economic component of domestic liberalization in the different regional contexts may bring us closer to identifying an important engine of regime creation. In particular, ruling coalitions pursuing economic liberalization seem more likely to embrace regional nuclear regimes than their inward-looking, nationalist, and radical-confessional counterparts.[2]

I do not suggest that security considerations are irrelevant to nuclear postures. Rather, I suggest an interpretation for why different states choose—over time—different portfolios to cope with their respective security concerns. My emphasis is more on explaining a favorable disposition to enter regime-like arrangements in nuclear matters than on listing incentives to procure nuclear weapons, as in the classical tradition of nonproliferation scholarship. Moreover, my argument is only relevant to would-be or second-tier nuclear powers—"fence-sitters"—whose choices have taken place at a different world-time than that of the great powers.[3] Finally, although I refer to nuclear-weapons-free-zones (NWFZ) as the ultimate form of a regional nuclear regime, there may be other points "along the Pareto frontier" that might help avoid the dangers of nuclearization.[4]

The next section summarizes the strengths and weaknesses of two alternative ways of conceptualizing the choices of "fence-sitters": neorealism and liberal-democratic theories of peace. I then explore the link between the nature of domestic political coalitions (liberalizing versus nationalist-confessional) to regional nuclear postures. The following section examines the argument in light

2. I am aggregating under the "nationalist" rubric an eclectic group that often colludes in challenging different aspects of liberalizing agendas. Not all elements are present everywhere and their relative strength varies across states and regions. The confessional category includes radical ethnic or religious groups that are commonly labelled "fundamentalist." Because of some uneasiness with this last term—among some scholars of Islam, for instance—I use the terms radical or extreme confessionalism instead.
3. "Fence-sitters" are undecided states reluctant to commit themselves fully and effectively to a denuclearizing regime (it is important to differentiate between a formal commitment, such as Iraq's ratification of the NPT, and an *effective* one). Such states can wait to make the ultimate declaratory political stand while sitting on various types of fences (some with basements), holding different levels of nuclear capabilities. The term "fence-sitting" thus: 1) refers to effective international political postures, not military status; 2) can accommodate an array of countries that are often attributed different ranges of capabilities, intentions, and formal commitments; and c) seems preferable to an older term—"nth countries"—which often evokes the image of a compulsive, irrevocable march towards the emergence of the next "n." See Etel Solingen, "The Domestic Sources of Nuclear Postures: 'Fence-sitting' in the Post–Cold War Era," *IGCC Policy Paper No. 8* (University of California, Institute on Global Conflict and Cooperation, San Diego, 1994).
4. See Stephen D. Krasner, "Global Communications and National Power: Life on the Pareto Frontier," *World Politics*, Vol. 43, No. 3 (April 1991), pp. 336–366.

of evidence from South Asia, the Korean peninsula, the Middle East, and the Southern Cone of Latin America. It is followed by a section exploring the impact of international institutional forces on the stability of domestic coalitions and on their effectiveness in pursuing nuclear cooperation. The last section lays out the implications of this perspective for conceptualizing international-domestic linkages, and suggests ways in which the framework may be applied to further our understanding of how regional security regimes emerge.

Competing Perspectives on the Sources of Fence-Sitting

Neorealism and liberal-democratic theories of peace provide two alternate ways of viewing the choices made by would-be nuclear powers.

NEOREALISM

The point of departure of neorealist perspectives is that in an anarchic world states strive through self-help to increase their power relative to that of other states, in a zero-sum context, to secure their survival. This structure compels states to secure a balance-of-power equilibrium, and nuclear weapons can do the job by increasing security for all, and by generating caution, rough equality, and a clarity of relative power.[5] Regimes, in this view, are anomalies of international life and their occurrence ought not to be expected anyway. Where they emerge, they are no more than an epiphenomenon of deeper forces in world politics, that is, of power distribution. *Prima facie,* this perspective provides an intuitive entry into the kind of thinking that might have attracted many of these regional powers to the nuclear fence.[6] Yet, several logical and empirical problems afflict this theoretical approach.

A general weakness of neorealism in explaining nuclear choices is its inconclusiveness. States indeed hope to reduce their external vulnerability yet, under a given structure, such an objective leaves room for a wide range of means.

5. John J. Mearsheimer, "Back to the Future: Instability in Europe After the Cold War," *International Security,* Vol. 15, No. 1 (Summer 1990), pp. 5–56. The classic statement is Kenneth N. Waltz, *The Spread of Nuclear Weapons: More May Be Better,* Adelphi Paper No. 171 (London: International Institute for Strategic Studies [IISS], 1981). For a comprehensive overview and critique of this literature see Etel Solingen, "The Domestic Sources of International Regimes: The Evolution of Nuclear Ambiguity in the Middle East," *International Studies Quarterly,* Vol. 38, No. 4 (June 1994).
6. Moreover, competition in the realm of security explains almost singlehandedly the decisions of the original five nuclear weapon states in the decade following World War II. As the introduction makes clear, the focus in this article is on second-tier states that weighed their nuclear postures against a different "world-time," characterized by a highly integrated global economy and an integrating multilateral institutional foundation.

A regional power with fears for its survival may opt for any of a number of different solutions to alleviate them, from a full-fledged declaration of nuclear capabilities to their total renunciation (to avoid escalation and instability, or to induce the other side to accept regional denuclearization). Consider, as an example of this variability of responses, India's test of a nuclear device and rejection of a regional nuclear regime; Israel's abstention from testing (but its warning that it would never be "second" in a regional nuclear race), while developing greater receptivity over time to a nuclear-weapons-free-zone (NWFZ); South Korea's, South Africa's, Egypt's, and Taiwan's unilateral ratification and implementation of the Nuclear Non-proliferation Treaty (NPT), after tinkering with a weapons program; and Pakistan's new openness to NPT and NWFZ solutions after dedicated efforts to acquire a nuclear deterrent. Moreover, not only have different states chosen contrasting portfolios, but almost all have shifted their postures throughout the years. Taiwan, South Korea, Egypt and, more recently, South Africa, Brazil, and Argentina each overturned an ambiguous nuclear status by entering international commitments for effective denuclearization. The pursuit of security simply does not tell us enough about differences across space nor changes over time.

In the extensive, mostly descriptive, literature on the choices of fence-sitters, one finds three main structural explanations of such differences.[7] The first explanation points to variance in vulnerability to massive conventional attacks. Thus, the more acutely vulnerable, such as Israel, Taiwan, South Korea, and (some have argued) South Africa, could be expected to be less likely to renounce a nuclear deterrent.[8] However, the last three of these four countries have done precisely that. A second explanation addresses the impact on its regional adversaries of one regional power's acquisition, or pursuit of, a nuclear option. However, the activities of a nuclear "pioneer" did not invariably lead to matching capabilities among adversaries. Egypt, South Korea, Taiwan (and even some African states) were suspected of harboring such designs to one degree or another but, in the end, all renounced that path. A third explanation traces these differences or, more particularly, the decision to forgo a nuclear deterrent, to the willingness of a hegemon to provide fence-sitters with protection. Many analysts interpret the behavior of South Korea and Taiwan—under

7. See Waltz, *The Spread of Nuclear Weapons: More May Be Better.*
8. Robert E. Harkavy, "Pariah States and Nuclear Proliferation," in George H. Quester, ed., *Nuclear Proliferation: Breaking the Chain,* Special Issue of *International Organization,* Vol. 35, No. 1 (Winter 1981), pp. 135–163.

U.S. tutelage—in this light.[9] But hegemonic protection does not seem to be either necessary or sufficient for a turnabout in nuclear postures. Such guarantees of protection played no role in the decisions of Egypt, Argentina, Brazil, or South Africa to reverse ambiguous nuclear stances, while the security commitments of superpowers were insufficient to persuade North Korea, Iraq, Pakistan, or Israel to effectively abandon nuclear weapons programs. Moreover, the U.S. commitment to Taiwan, said to have convinced it not to go nuclear, became questionable following the normalization of relations with the P.R.C. and the abrogation of the Washington-Taipei mutual security treaty.

In sum, the valuable insights we gain from a structural perspective are offset by its deficiencies. A state's structural context helps identify potential sources of nuclear postures, but does not account parsimoniously for the great variation encountered across countries and throughout time. Diverse responses came about under comparable and quite stable regional security threats, and against a common global-historical background characterized by three constants: a bipolar world, unrelenting pressure from the respective hegemons (the United States and the Soviet Union) for eschewing nuclear weapons, and a global normative structure squarely opposed to the horizontal proliferation of such weapons. Shifts in overt substantive postures and signals of internal differences over the virtues and costs of alternative nuclear paths suggest that, at the very least, the consequences of, and solutions to, similar security predicaments are not universally consistent. Exclusively structural analyses offer limited ground for inter-regional comparisons beyond general truisms, such as arguing that the security context is more fragile in the Middle East than in Latin America. But that reality did not prevent Brazil and Argentina from nurturing weapons capabilities for over two decades. Indeed, two contrasting security contexts—the Middle East and the Southern Cone—had similar outcomes: regional powers embracing ambiguous nuclear postures and unwilling to commit to safeguarded denuclearization. In the end, studies that focus exclusively on structural explanations either cast the argument in nonfalsifiable terms, or explain variation away through brief references to domestic considerations or to a rough-and-tumble bureaucratic-politics account.[10]

---

9. See, for instance, Harkavy, "Pariah States"; and Lewis A. Dunn, *Controlling the Bomb* (New Haven, Conn.: Yale University Press, 1982).

10. A related problem is evident in the widespread disagreement among experts about actual or perceived "levels of vulnerability" (the most common formulation of the independent variable). There may be more agreement on the Israeli and South Korean situation than on India, South Africa, or North Korea. The bottom line is that an elusive independent variable undermines efforts to operationalize it without resorting to internal factors.

One cannot, therefore, understand differences in hegemonic effectiveness without studying the domestic political conditions that make certain states more receptive to external persuasion than others. The lack of a rigorous examination of the domestic sources of nuclear postures among fence-sitters is particularly puzzling in light of the lessons from the U.S.-Soviet experience, where domestic processes acquired paramount importance in explaining arms control negotiations and eventual steps toward dramatic, if incomplete, nuclear reductions. Yet, the nonproliferation literature has largely resisted analytical inroads such as those that Matthew Evangelista and Jack Snyder applied to the study of major powers. Neither has it explored the links between security and trade strategies.[11] There seems to be an emerging concern with domestic considerations, but mostly in the context of democratization and its likely impact on the nuclear evolution of regions.

LIBERAL-DEMOCRATIC THEORIES OF COOPERATION

Different hypotheses seek to explain the "democratic peace" or why liberal democracies are not likely to wage wars amongst themselves, and why they are at least as likely as others to engage non-democratic partners in armed conflict.[12] However, there has been no systematic attempt to extend these hypotheses to account for cooperative or non-cooperative behavior in the nuclear realm. What follows is an effort to (1) summarize, from the extant literature, a list of complementary institutional, perceptual, and normative explanations of why democracies cooperate, and (2) to expand these hypotheses to specify potential nuclear outcomes.

A first set of explanations relates the "democratic peace" to domestic legitimacy and accountability, to democracy's built-in institutional checks and balances, and to the basic norm of peaceful resolution of disputes. Following a Kantian conception of citizens' consent, the assumption is that the legitimacy granted by the domestic public of one liberal democracy to the elected representatives of another has a moderating effect away from violent solutions.[13]

---

11. Matthew Evangelista, *Innovation and the Arms Race: How the United States and the Soviet Union Develop New Military Technologies* (Ithaca, N.Y.: Cornell University Press, 1988); Jack Snyder, *Myths of Empire: Domestic Politics and International Ambition* (Ithaca, N.Y.: Cornell University Press, 1991). Earlier studies include Samuel P. Huntington, *The Common Defense* (New York: Columbia University Press, 1961); and James R. Kurth, "A Widening Gyre: The Logic of American Weapons Procurement," *Public Policy*, Vol. 19, No. 3 (Summer 1971), pp. 373–404. On the links between security and trade strategies, see, for instance, Richard Rosecrance, *The Rise of the Trading State* (New York: Basic Rooks, 1986).
12. See Bruce Russett, *Grasping the Democratic Peace: Principles for a Post–Cold War World* (Princeton, N.J.: Princeton University Press, 1993).
13. Michael W. Doyle, "Kant, Liberal Legacies, and Foreign Affairs," Parts I and II, *Philosophy and*

Moreover, free speech, electoral cycles, and the public policy process act as re-straints on the ability of democratic leaders to pursue extreme policies toward fellow democracies.[14] Similarly, the normative rejection of violent behavior at home is extended to cover citizens of other democracies.

How do we apply this reasoning to gauge the potential behavior of demo-cratic dyads regarding nuclear weapons? One might extrapolate it to suggest that democratic dyads would be likely to shy away from basing their mutual security on nuclear weapons, which entail the most violent and extreme form of protection. Nuclear deterrence cannot preclude some measure of risk; even a low probability of deterrence failure leaves the door open to complete devas-tation. Such risk would be particularly intolerable in the context of a relation-ship between fellow democracies, which is rarely characterized by the kind of hostility apparent in mixed dyads. Dyads in which a democracy faces a non-democratic rival can be expected to behave differently than a democratic dyad. Abhorrence of authoritarianism and its lack of popular accountability could encourage a democracy to deter non-democratic adversaries through nuclear weapons, as in Western deterrence strategy against the Warsaw Pact.[15] The au-thoritarianism and praetorianism of an adversary can cancel the moderating effects of institutional checks and balances in a democracy that faces it.[16] The fear that a non-democratic rival with a concentrated monopoly of political power and with praetorian domestic structures could hold a democracy hos-tage through nuclear threats might raise the threshold of tolerance for risk among citizens and leaders of that democracy. Where a democracy suspects an asymmetry in risk-aversion or propensity to go to war, it will arguably be more

---

Public Affairs, Vol. 12, Nos. 3–4 (Summer, Fall 1983); Doyle, "Liberalism and World Politics," *Ameri-can Political Science Review*, Vol. 80, No. 4 (December 1986), pp. 1151–1170; and Stephen Van Evera, "Primed for Peace: Europe After the Cold War," in Sean Lynn-Jones, ed., *The Cold War and After: Prospects for Peace* (Cambridge, Mass.: MIT Press, 1991), pp. 193–243.

14. Bruce Bueno de Mesquita and David Lalman, *War and Reason* (New Haven: Yale University Press, 1992); and Carol R. Ember, Melvin Ember, and Bruce M. Russett, "Peace Between Participa-tory Polities," *World Politics*, Vol. 44, No. 4 (July 1992), p. 576. According to Kant, the public will hesitate to start wars because of the heavy costs which they themselves would have to bear. See Doyle, "Liberalism and World Politics," p. 1160; and Joseph Schumpeter, *Imperialism and Social Classes* (Cleveland: World Publishing Company, 1955), pp. 64–98.

15. This argument might explain the development of an Israeli nuclear deterrent. However, a 1986 public opinion poll found two-thirds of the Israeli public opposing the use of nuclear weapons un-der any circumstances. Asher Arian, Ilan Talmud, and Tamar Hermann, *National Security and Pub-lic Opinion in Israel* (Boulder: Westview, 1988), p. 96. Similarly, democratic South Korea does not appear to be responding to North Korean nuclear behavior with a nuclear deterrent of its own (discussed below).

16. On practorianism, see Jack Snyder, "Averting Anarchy in the New Europe," in Lynn-Jones, *The Cold War and After*, pp. 104–140. On the distrust of liberal states for their nonliberal counterparts, see Doyle, "Kant."

willing to contemplate extreme solutions, such as nuclear weapons, for its security predicament.

A second, related, set of explanations for the "democratic peace" points to the credibility, transparency, and predictability of democratic systems. Democracies are respectful of the rule of law and appear to undertake more credible and durable commitments, which strengthens their reputation as predictable partners.[17] Moreover, democracies are information-rich societies where knowledge about the internal evaluations of a policy or of the intensity of the preferences reinforces mutual credibility, enhancing the propensity to cooperate.[18] Maximizing information is of particular importance in the creation of security regimes, where the risks of error and deception can be catastrophic.[19] How would these conditions influence the nuclear behavior of democratic dyads? One might expect that by minimizing fears of deception (which underlie classical prisoners' dilemmas), mutual credibility and transparency would strengthen their propensity to accept mutual nuclear disarmament. In contrast, problems of uncertainty over ratification and implementation would be exacerbated for mixed or non-democratic dyads, because procedures cannot easily be followed. Asymmetric levels of transparency could lower the incentives of democracies to join a nuclear regime, because potential assaults on its stipulations by non-democratic would-be partners are harder to foresee (given more secretive and informal institutional procedures).[20] Stable democracies bind successive governments to international agreements, whereas non-democratic regimes might be replaced by challengers capable of reneging on international commitments to maintain legitimacy at home.[21] Thus, under the conditions of lack of transparency, severe uncertainty, and low credibility characteristic of mixed or non-democratic dyads, one can expect greater reluctance to embrace nuclear disarmament.

This overview enables us to extract some preliminary conclusions and sug-

---

17. Doyle, "Kant"; and Kurt T. Gaubatz, "Democratic States and Commitment in International Relations," paper presented at the annual meeting of the American Political Science Association, Chicago, September 3–6, 1992. On democratic dyads and alliances see Randolph M. Siverson and Julian Emmons, "Birds of a Feather: Democratic Political Systems and Alliance Choices in the Twentieth Century," *Journal of Conflict Resolution*, Vol. 35, No. 2 (June 1991), pp. 285–306.
18. Robert O. Keohane, *After Hegemony: Cooperation and Discord in the World Political Economy* (Princeton, N.J.: Princeton University Press, 1984), p. 95; see Bueno de Mesquita and Lalman, *War and Reason*.
19. Robert Jervis, "From Balance to Concert: A Study of International Security Cooperation," in Kenneth A. Oye, ed., *Cooperation under Anarchy* (Princeton, N.J.: Princeton University Press, 1986).
20. Keohane, *After Hegemony*, pp. 93–95.
21. In fact, authoritarian rulers may enter an agreement and defect soon after, as Saddam Hussein's recanting of his earlier acceptance of some cease-fire stipulations demonstrates.

gest some obvious limitations.[22] The expectation is that (1) nuclear regimes based on the principle of disarmament might be more likely where all potential partners share like-minded democratic political systems; and that (2) asymmetric and non-democratic dyads might be more prone to maintain ambiguity or outright deterrence postures.[23] In other words, both democracies and non-democracies discount the value of future nuclear cooperation with non-democracies.

This seemingly reasonable, albeit speculative, extension of democratic theories of cooperation to explain the behavior of fence-sitters exposes some problems of logical inference and empirical fit. First, more research is required to assess whether or not the same mechanisms explaining the "absence of war" among liberal democracies are useful in explaining nuclear cooperation. After all, democracies do engage in conflict with other democracies, short of war.[24] Second, the expectation that non-democracies would be less transparent and credible in their commitments and less reliable on ratification is often postulated, but very seldom explained or tested: it is more of a premise than a hypothesis. Third, the empirical evidence contradicts the notion that regimes, including nuclear ones, are less likely to emerge between mixed or non-democratic dyads. In fact, most international regimes in every issue-area emerged out of compromises among a wide variety of political systems. The global nuclear nonproliferation regime is a case in point.[25] At the regional level, democratic administrations in Pakistan and in India failed to agree to mutual denuclearization, while military dictatorships in Brazil and Argentina

---

22. Additional propositions linking the democratic nature of states to cooperation might be logically extended to account for nuclear behavior. For instance, states sharing an open political system develop high levels of formal and informal communication, which lowers the cost of forming a regime (Keohane, *After Hegemony*, pp. 95–97). Openness allows the "trans-governmental networks" of democratic dyads to share information on their respective domestic conditions, thus facilitating transnational logrolling of support for a regime. Mixed or authoritarian dyads, in contrast, are likely to engage in more contained communication patterns in efforts to protect the autonomy of decision-making from outside interference. The efforts necessary to improve mutual communication raise the costs of creating a regime, particularly one involving mutual disarmament.
23. Such postures may include elements of cooperation, as with U.S.-Soviet arms control agreements, but have a built-in rationale for developing unilateral advantages.
24. Zeev Maoz and Nasrin Abdolali, "Regime Type and International Conflict, 1816–1976," *Journal of Conflict Resolution*, Vol. 33, No. 1 (March 1989), pp. 3–36. Democracies do not necessarily engage in "better" behavior toward one another, even when they do not fight wars. Harvey Starr, "Why Don't Democracies Fight One Another? Evaluating the Theory-Findings Feedback Loop," *The Jerusalem Journal of International Relations*, Vol. 14, No. 4 (1992), pp. 41–59.
25. Joseph S. Nye, Jr., "Maintaining a Nonproliferation Regime," in Quester, *Nuclear Proliferation*, pp. 15–38.

set in motion bilateral nuclear cooperation in 1980. A highly mixed and politically quite unstable group of Latin American states signed the Treaty of Tlatelolco in 1968, establishing a NWFZ. On the Korean peninsula, a relic of Cold War authoritarianism and a democratizing (but far from genuinely democratic) South began negotiations over a system of reciprocal inspections in 1991, a process that is now derailed. In the Middle East a mixed lot is negotiating regional arms control, including weapons of mass destruction, in the context of the multilateral peace process. Moreover, the diffusion of democracy might be expected to mitigate Israeli concerns with the credibility and reliability of its non-democratic neighbors; however, where radical Islamic forces are its bearers, democratization may not bode well for a security regime, given these forces' advocacy of total and final wars against infidels generally, and against Israel in particular.[26] Political freedom thus seems neither necessary nor sufficient for the emergence of a nuclear regime.

Perhaps the most severe problem lies in inferring the potential nuclear behavior of fence-sitters, without qualifications, from the experience of advanced industrialized democracies,[27] from whose history the democratic predisposition to avoid wars and build regimes with fellow democracies is overwhelmingly drawn. First is the question of the extent to which democratic stability, far more abundant among industrialized states, plays a critical role in explaining the "zone of peace" these states have created.[28] Lack of democratic stability might thus anticipate why the emergence of "zones of peace" in Third World regions would be more tentative and piecemeal, particularly on nuclear matters. Second is the possibility that economic liberalism, rather than democracy, may be more useful in explaining nuclear cooperation, a hypothesis I explore in the remainder of this paper.

Economic Liberalization, Political Coalitions, and Nuclear Preferences

The type of domestic political system does not explain why fence-sitters shift their nuclear postures and join international and regional nuclear regimes;

---

26. See Timothy D. Sisk, *Islam and Democracy* (Washington, D.C.: United States Institute of Peace, 1992); Safa Haeri, "Saudi Arabia: A warning to the King," *Middle East International*, June 14, 1991, p. 11.
27. Of first-tier nuclear powers, it might be argued that the three democracies in that group (the United States, France, and Britain) went nuclear to confront bitter non-democratic rivals (fascism first, communism later).
28. See Doyle, "Kant," p. 213; and Russett, *Grasping the Democratic Peace.*

therefore a more disaggregated analysis of domestic determinants of nuclear cooperation, and particularly of the role of economic liberalization and of the political coalitions that sustain it, are required.[29] I suggest that ruling coalitions pursuing economic liberalization are more likely to embrace regional nuclear regimes than their inward-looking, nationalist, and radical-confessional counterparts.

This hypothesis is based on two main assumptions: first, the kinds of ties binding actors (groups, sectors, parties, institutions) to economic and other international processes affect their conceptions of interests.[30] Such ties influence actors' definitions of what trade-offs are desirable or tolerable. For example, a state's decision to maintain ambiguity in nuclear intentions (e.g., by refusing full-scope safeguards or by cheating on NPT commitments) has involved, since the 1970s, a series of trade-offs: access to international markets, capital, investments, and technology has been curtailed, directly and indirectly.[31] Such trade-offs create domestic coalitions favoring or rejecting such linkages: groups that might otherwise pay little attention to their country's nuclear posture become more attentive to the elements of the international bargain. Groups interested in importing highly sophisticated computers, for example, might not be concerned with their country's refusal to commit unambiguously to renounce nuclear weapons, if such refusal had no direct implications for their access to external resources. Interested actors both respond to, and anticipate, international constraints.[32]

Second, nuclear postures are not merely a response to international constraints: the domestic consequences of alternative nuclear paths are no less important to political actors and coalitions. For instance, the political effects of doing away with nuclear ambiguity often includes the weakening of state bureaucracies and industrial complexes that constitute an impediment to eco-

---

29. On trading states and cooperation, see Rosecrance, *Trading State*. On domestic coalitions and cooperation, see Jack Snyder, "International Leverage on Soviet Domestic Change," *World Politics*, Vol. 42, No. 1 (October 1989), pp. 1–30. "Economic freedom" is central, but is not the focus of Rudolph Rummel's analysis in "Libertarianism and International Violence," *Journal of Conflict Resolution*, Vol. 27, No. 1 (March 1983), pp. 27–71.
30. Peter Gourevitch, "The Second Image Reversed: The International Sources of Domestic Politics," *International Organization*, Vol. 32, No. 4 (Autumn 1978), pp. 881–911.
31. Initially the United States applied these measures unilaterally, particularly through the Symington amendment (1976) and the U.S. Non-proliferation Act (1979). Multilateral mechanisms soon followed, such as the Nuclear Suppliers Group organized in 1977, now including over twenty-seven states.
32. Peter F. Cowhey, "'States' and 'Politics' in American Foreign Policy," in John S. Odell and Thomas D. Willett, eds., *International Trade Policies—Gains from Exchange between Economics and Political Science* (Ann Arbor: University of Michigan Press), pp. 225–252.

nomic rationalization.[33] Conversely, denuclearization tends to be part of a broader program of domestic reform that strengthens market-oriented forces and the political entrepreneurs and central economic institutions promoting their development. This has clearly been the case in Argentina and Brazil, where multibillion dollar nuclear investments undertaken in the 1970s became primary casualties of the contraction of state activities in the 1980s and 1990s.

Thus, two basic types of coalition—one advocating economic liberalization, the other opposing it—may develop contrasting perspectives on both the domestic and international consequences of alternative nuclear paths.

LIBERALIZING COALITIONS

The interests of political coalitions favoring economic liberalization are generally internationalist; that is, they require openness to global market and institutional forces.[34] A policy of economic liberalization implies a reduction of state control over markets and of barriers to trade, an expansion of private economic transactions and foreign investment, and the privatization of public sector enterprises. Different liberalizing coalitions emphasize different aspects of economic liberalization, depending on their interest in specific issues, such as expanding exports, deregulating financial flows, opening the domestic market to foreign goods and investment, and reducing state entrepreneurial activities. Their selective and gradual agenda of economic liberalization explains why the adjective "liberalizing" is more appropriate than "liberal"; the state often plays a powerful role in steering this process. Political liberalization— reduction of state monopoly over political life—is not an immediate requirement for economic liberalization, at least during its initial phase.[35]

For the most part, the pillars of liberalizing coalitions are liquid-asset holders and export-oriented firms—including large banking and industrial complexes capable of surviving without state protection—and state monetary

---

33. The loss of ambiguity involves greater transparency in budgetary allocations leading to leaner nuclear bureaucracies and industrial complexes. Bloated nuclear-industrial complexes have come to symbolize the excesses of state expansion among virtually all fence-sitters.

34. Robert R. Kaufman, "Liberalization and Democratization in South America: Perspectives from the 1970s," in Guillermo O'Donnell, Philippe C. Schmitter, and Laurence Whitehead, eds., *Transitions from Authoritarian Rule* (Baltimore: Johns Hopkins University Press, 1986), pp. 85–107; and Barbara Stallings, "International Influence on Economic Policy: Debt, Stabilization, and Structural Reform," in Stephan Haggard and Robert R. Kaufman, eds., *The Politics of Economic Adjustment* (Princeton: Princeton University Press, 1992), p. 53.

35. Peter H. Smith, "Crisis and Democracy in Latin America," *World Politics*, Vol. 43, No. 4 (July 1991), pp. 608–634; and Miles Kahler, "Liberalization and Foreign Policy" (unpublished ms. for Social Science Research Council project, "Liberalization and Foreign Policy," University of California at San Diego, 1992).

agencies.[36] They tend to be more receptive to structural adjustment policies, and opposed to external confrontations with the international financial and investing community.[37] The ability of big business (locally and foreign-owned) to influence domestic investment patterns and to move capital abroad gives them an important voice in shaping domestic and external adjustment policy.[38] Smaller firms engaged in exports or supplying internationalized enterprises can also be part of these coalitions, along with the highly-skilled labor force associated with these firms. Public and private managerial, technical, scientific, educational, information, and service-oriented professional groups, which might be called "symbolic analysts," similarly tend to be oriented towards an open global economic and knowledge system.[39]

The economic orientation of such coalitions, which strive to maximize their gains from international economic exchange, makes them more likely to be receptive to compromise nuclear postures that do not endanger their interests. These coalitions rely extensively on the global economy and on the political support of major powers within regimes and institutions involved in managing international economic relations. A policy of nuclear disarmament enhances their status with international institutions and powerful states, who associate these coalitions with the promise of democracy, rationalization, and regional cooperation. Related domestic considerations reinforce these coalitions' opposition to large-scale, ambiguous and unbounded nuclear programs: such programs often contribute to the ailments afflicting these countries' domestic political economy, such as the expansion of state power, the maintenance of unproductive and inflation-inducing military investments, and the perpetuation of rent-seeking patterns.[40] In other words, liberalizing coalitions

36. On this "bankers' alliance," see Sylvia Maxfield, *Governing Capital: International Finance and Mexican Politics* (Ithaca, N.Y.: Cornell University Press, 1990). On why firms with strong international ties oppose protection, see Helen Milner, "Trading Places: Industries for Free Trade," *World Politics*, Vol. 40, No. 3 (April 1988), pp. 350–376.
37. Structural adjustment is "a set of measures designed to make the economy competitive." It often includes currency devaluation, deficit reduction, de-indexing of wages, reduction in consumer subsidies, price deregulation, and tariff reductions. Adam Przeworski, *Democracy and the Market: Political and Economic Reforms in Eastern Europe and Latin America* (Cambridge: Cambridge University Press, 1991), p. 144; Joan Nelson, *Fragile Coalitions: The Politics of Economic Adjustment* (New Brunswick, N.J.: Transaction, 1989).
38. See Robert W. Cox, "Social Forces, States, and World Orders: Beyond International Relations Theory," in Robert O. Keohane, ed., *Neorealism and Its Critics* (New York: Columbia University Press, 1986), pp. 204–254.
39. On "symbolic analysts" see Robert Reich, *The Work of Nations* (New York: Knopf, 1991).
40. Rent-seeking refers to the unproductive economic activities of groups that seek transfers of wealth under the aegis of the state. See J.M. Buchanan, R.D. Tollison, and G. Tullock, eds., *Toward a Theory of the Rent-Seeking Society* (College Station: Texas A & M University Press, 1980), p. 4. De-

do not merely trade away the right to have "the bomb" for the right to make money; they perceive little inherent benefit in a policy of nuclear ambiguity for both domestic and international reasons. For such coalitions, denuclearization is quite compatible with an agenda of liberalizing the economy and reining in adversarial political forces at home. A restrained nuclear posture can secure certain international economic, financial, and political benefits—such as debt relief, export markets, technology transfer, food imports, aid, and investments—that can be used to maintain or broaden domestic political support and to strengthen the domestic institutional framework underpinning economic liberalization. In sum, cooperative regimes in the economic and security realms are mutually reinforcing; they spell transparency, predictability, a good reputation, and the blessing of the international community. They also help carry out domestic policies largely in line with these coalitions' political and economic preferences.

INWARD-LOOKING, NATIONALIST, AND RADICAL-CONFESSIONAL COALITIONS

The distributional consequences of economic liberalization also create coalitions that oppose liberalization. Such coalitions often reject orthodox stabilization plans imposed by the International Monetary Fund (IMF) and other financial institutions, and favor a more expansionist course.[41] These inward-looking coalitions include popular sectors comprising unskilled blue-collar workers, white-collar and other state employees, and small businesses; firms that compete with imports and that have close ties to the state and domestic markets; underemployed intelligentsia, and politicians who fear the dismantling of state enterprises and the consequent erosion of their basis of political patronage.[42] They may also include arms-importing military establishments, which are often adversely affected by adjustment programs.[43]

---

bunking the conventional wisdom that nuclear weapons are universally cheap, see Steven E. Miller, "The Case Against a Ukrainian Nuclear Deterrent," *Foreign Affairs*, Vol. 72, No. 3 (Summer 1993), pp. 67–80. A nuclear weapons program was expected to require three-fourths of the entire outlay of India's proposed Fourth Five-Year Plan. See Mitchell Reiss, *Without the Bomb* (New York: Columbia University Press, 1988), p. 213.

41. Stabilization involves short-term measures to slow down inflation and reduce balance-of-payments and government deficits. Przeworski, *Democracy and the Market*, p. 144.

42. Valeriana Kallab and Richard E. Feinberg, eds., *Fragile Coalitions: The Politics of Economic Adjustment* (New Brunswick, N.J.: Transaction, 1989); and Robert R. Kaufman, "Domestic Determinants of Stabilization and Adjustment Choices," in Bruce M. Russett, Harvey Starr, and Richard Stoll, eds., *Choices in World Politics: Sovereignty and Interdependence* (New York: W.H. Freeman, 1989), pp. 261–282.

43. Yahya M. Sadowski, *Scuds or Butter? The Political Economy of Arms Control in the Middle East* (Washington, D.C.: The Brookings Institution, 1993), p. 32.

In the Middle East and South Asia, nationalist coalitions often attract extremist religious movements. Such movements thrive on popular resentment over adjustment policies they regard as externally-imposed, reliance on foreign investment, and the "Western" principles and norms embodied in most international regimes.[44] The material basis for opposing internationalization and liberalization may be particularly strong where import-substituting and state-based industrial interests are powerful. In other cases religious or ideological components may be the driving force. Very often these two tend to reinforce each other. Leaders of these logrolled coalitions of rent-seeking economic interests and militant religious, ethnic, or cultural groups rely heavily on what Jack Snyder labels mythmaking; that is, they sell myths that justify the allocation of state resources to the wide array of interests backing an inward-looking strategy.[45] Their rejection of global markets and institutions is echoed in their adversarial regional postures. In the extreme form of nationalist coalitions, such as the one that supported Saddam Hussein, nuclear weapons often play a central (and more open) role in the call for final, "redeeming" solutions. Many such inward-looking, state-oriented (rather than market-oriented) economic leaderships, whether democratic or otherwise—such as North Korea, India, Iraq, Libya, and Cuba, and even Brazil and Argentina—long resisted external pressures for joining or complying with the global nonproliferation regime or any regional alternative to it.

Summing up the argument so far: the political impact (at home and abroad) of transcending nuclear ambiguity is positive for liberalizing coalitions, which pursue an export-oriented and internationalist grand strategy of industrialization, and negative for nationalist coalitions, which pursue an inward-looking industrialization strategy.[46]

---

44. Timur Kuran, "Fundamentalisms and the Economy," in Martin E. Marty and R. Scott Appleby, eds., *Fundamentalisms and the State: Remaking Polities, Economies and Militance* (Chicago: The University of Chicago Press, 1993), pp. 289–301; Emile Sahliyeh, *Religious Resurgence and Politics in the Contemporary World* (New York: State University of New York Press, 1990); J.L. Esposito, *Islam and Politics* (Syracuse University Press, 1991); and Alan Richards and John Waterbury, *A Political Economy of the Middle East: State, Class, and Economic Development* (Boulder, Colo.: Westview, 1990).

45. Snyder, *Myths of Empire*, p. 17. On chauvinist mythmaking as a hallmark of nationalism, see Stephen Van Evera, "Hypotheses on Nationalism and War," *International Security*, Vol. 18, No. 4 (Spring 1994), pp. 5–39.

46. Such strategies not only determine a country's relation to the global political economy but also the internal allocation of resources among groups and institutions. On grand strategy as an economic, political, and military means-ends chain designed to achieve security, see Barry R. Posen, *The Sources of Military Doctrine: France, Britain, and Germany between the World Wars* (Ithaca, N.Y.: Cornell University Press, 1984); Paul Kennedy, ed., *Grand Strategies in War and Peace* (New Haven, Conn.: Yale University Press, 1991); and Richard Rosecrance and Arthur A. Stein, eds., *The Domes-*

The foregoing analysis of the relationship between political-economic strategies and nuclear postures suggests a pattern, not an infallible rule. Thus, domestic coalitions in an industrializing state may be strongly supportive of their country's integration within the international economy, while resisting other (political, security, environmental, human rights) global regimes; China is an example. However, international tolerance for attempts by ruling coalitions to disaggregate a state's allegiance to emerging global arrangements ("we will trade as freely as we repress and pollute") may be rapidly declining. The commitment to international regimes is becoming increasingly indivisible. Nuclear postures have become nested in a broader context of global (primarily economic) relations that create certain mutual expectations. The international community expects adherence to nonproliferation principles, while fence-sitters expect to share in the benefits of international economic interdependence.

Coalitions of one type or the other come to power through electoral means, where democratic institutions are in place, or through more or less coercive methods, often in alliance with the military. At times, a rough parity in the competition between these two basic kinds of coalition precludes the adoption of a clear-cut strategy concerning international economic, nuclear, and other regimes, as in Argentina during much of the postwar era. At other times, one coalition is able to impose a relatively unchallenged path, as with South Korea, Taiwan, and other East Asian countries. Most often, however, industrialization strategies incorporate different mixes of inward and outward-looking instruments, and vary in the extent to which it is state officials or rather powerful societal forces that dominate the definition and implementation of strategy. This point underscores the need to understand differences between the ideal-types of coalitions outlined above and the more nuanced versions in the real world.

Political institutions affect when and how certain coalitions of interests can prevail.[47] There is considerable variation in the way in which the preferences of different coalitions are aggregated. For instance, incipient democratization and electoral trial-runs provided new opportunities for nationalist-confessional coalitions in the Middle East. These opportunities were quickly shut down where

---

tic Bases of Grand Strategy (Ithaca, N.Y.: Cornell University Press, 1993). For a more detailed elaboration of the connections between coalition type and security postures, see Etel Solingen, "Democracy, Economic Reform, and Emerging Regional Orders," in David Lake and Patrick Morgan, eds., Reconceptualizing Regional Relations (unpublished ms., University of California, 1994).

47. Peter A. Gourevitch, Politics in Hard Times: Comparative Responses to International Economic Crises (Ithaca, N.Y.: Cornell University Press, 1986).

the military perceived them to weaken its institutional viability and strength, as in Algeria in 1993. In Israel, proportional representation has precluded the emergence of a single dominant coalition. Understanding the domestic determinants of different coalitions' success in gaining or maintaining power is an important question in itself, but not a task that can be undertaken here.

The Empirical Record Across Nuclear Regions

This section examines the impact of coalition type on the nature of nuclear postures in four regions. Reasons of space preclude a more detailed historical account.

THE KOREAN PENINSULA

South Korea provides a classic example of a liberalizing coalition implementing a nuclear policy compatible with its fundamental interests and grand strategy of industrialization. Following a relatively brief import-substitution phase, state bureaucrats guided the country's integration in the global economy, leaning on foreign markets, loans, technology, and investments.[48] To embrace a nuclear deterrent, which the leadership considered doing in 1971, would have threatened that strategy and, consequently, the regime's viability.[49] Thus, the coalition backing the Park regime responded to U.S. threats of a major break in bilateral economic relations by cancelling the incipient weapons program and ratifying the NPT in 1975.[50] For a regime taking cues from a strong military establishment, this shift in nuclear posture makes the triumph of political-economic considerations in defining the country's survival strategy even more remarkable.[51] By the 1980s South Korea's export-oriented coalition included

---

48. See Frederic C. Deyo, ed., *The Political Economy of the New Asian Industrialism* (Ithaca, N.Y.: Cornell University Press, 1987); and Stephan Haggard, *Pathways from the Periphery: The Politics of Growth in the Newly Industrializing Countries* (Ithaca, N.Y.: Cornell University Press, 1990).

49. Export-oriented firms were critically dependent on primarily U.S. and Japanese investors, loans, and markets. Moreover, in an oil-dependent economy, the promise of plentiful nuclear energy from Western-supplied power plants to fuel heavy industry and intermediary sectors was at risk if nonproliferation commitments were not maintained. Reiss, *Without the Bomb*, pp. 78–108. On the 1973 oil crisis as a threat to South Korea's industrialization strategy, see Anne O. Krueger, *Political Economy of Policy Reform in Developing Countries* (Cambridge, Mass.: MIT Press, 1993), p. 125.

50. Stephen M. Meyer, *The Dynamics of Nuclear Proliferation* (Chicago: University of Chicago Press, 1984), pp. 125–127; Leonard S. Spector with Jacqueline R. Smith, *Nuclear Ambitions* (Boulder: Westview, 1990), pp. 118–137.

51. See Peter Hayes, *International Missile Trade and the Two Koreas, Program for Nonproliferation Studies* (Monterey Institute of International Studies Working Paper No. 1, March 1993), p. 22. The case of Taiwan bears many similarities to that of South Korea and has also become an exemplar of

virtually all segments of business and labor.[52] At the end of the decade this co-alition was actively pursuing a NWFZ, despite South Korea's unquestionable technical and industrial capacity to "beat" North Korea in a conventional or nuclear arms race.[53] Despite a North Korean threat to turn Seoul into a "sea of fire," there seems to be little popular and governmental support for a South Korean nuclear deterrent, and few in the South believe the North would ever use an atomic weapon.[54]

No doubt hegemonic protection (that is, U.S. tactical nuclear weapons) was an important consideration in weighing denuclearization, but one should not exaggerate its impact. In the aftermath of Vietnam, the Nixon Doctrine, and the normalization of relations with Beijing, the South Korean leadership had reason to question the robustness of U.S. security guarantees.[55] The prospects of U.S. economic sanctions were even more troubling for a leadership that was acutely aware of U.S. contributions to the country's internal political stability and, in essence, to the regime's survival. The potential for disrupting an average annual rate of growth of over 10 percent and for domestic political turmoil was a powerful threat to reckon with.

The North Korean case approaches the inward-looking, nationalist coalition ideal-type as closely as any real case can. Self-reliance and the cult of the leadership became central political instruments of mythmaking, somewhat like a secular version of radical confessionalism. Nuclear weapons (or ambiguity about their possession) became the ultimate expression of national independence *(juche)* and technical achievement that the regime could wield as evidence of its own viability; this was particularly critical once the South's economic vigor became apparent.[56] An independent and ambiguous stand on nuclear matters was thus an important ingredient in the North's political-economic grand strategy of self-reliance, and one with high payoffs for soothing a restive military and nuclear establishment and its nationalist allies in the bureaucracy.[57] The United States and North Korea's former Soviet protector coerced it

a trading state's grand strategy. On the ruling coalition, see Deyo, *New Asian Industrialism*. On Taiwan's nuclear shifts, see Dunn, *Controlling the Bomb*, pp. 56–57.

52. Haggard and Kaufman, *The Politics*, p. 334.

53. Harkavy, "Pariah States," p. 144; Andrew Mack, "North Korea and the Bomb," *Foreign Policy*, No. 83 (Summer 1991), pp. 92, 96–97.

54. Andrew Pollack, "Nuclear Fears? Noodle Sales Say No," *New York Times*, May 9, 1994, p. A7.

55. Reiss, *Without the Bomb*, pp. 80–85.

56. James Cotton, "North Korea's Nuclear Ambitions," in *Asia's International Role in the Post–Cold War Era*, Adelphi Paper No. 275, Part I (London: IISS, 1993), pp. 94–106.

57. Paul Bracken, "Nuclear Weapons and State Survival in North Korea," *Survival*, Vol. 34, No. 3 (Autumn 1992), pp. 137–153.

into ratifying the NPT in 1985, an event that, tellingly, followed a feeble North Korean attempt at economic liberalization. However, giving new meaning to the difference between formal and effective commitments to nonproliferation principles, North Korea continued to reject full-scope IAEA inspections *de facto*, even after the United States had removed tactical nuclear weapons from South Korea in 1991. This outcome highlights the difficulty of reducing North Korea's behavior, as paranoiac as it may seem, exclusively to security concerns.[58] What compelled the North Korean leadership to drag its feet on the nuclear issue was the fact that U.S., South Korean, Japanese, and multilateral promises of improved economic ties did not materialize.[59] With this, the regime's expectation of preventing its own collapse, by relying on economic reforms, evaporated. In the absence of tangible international commitments to provide economic aid to North Korea, the incipient liberalizing forces in North Korea lost out to the hard-liners in the military and nuclear establishment. By March 1993 North Korea announced its intention to withdraw from the NPT, unleashing an international crisis. Despite the efforts of very powerful strategic allies and very powerful strategic adversaries, North Korea was not persuaded to relinquish nuclear aspirations for an extended period of time. Domestic receptivity is an important intervening factor in the relationship between hegemonic assertion and fence-sitters' responses.

INDIA-PAKISTAN

The coalition shaping economic and industrial policy in India's post-independence era embraced a classical import-substitution model of industrialization, aimed at avoiding vulnerability to international markets and economic institutions.[60] It strongly criticized international regimes as constructs of Western powers, opposed the nonproliferation regime as the crowning example of neocolonialism, and conspicuously exploded a nuclear device in 1974. Advocates of an Indian nuclear deterrent pointed to China's nuclear status as a convenient justification for their position, despite China's clear "no first use" policy.

---

58. For a well-argued case on the centrality of regime survival and on the incompleteness (at best) and incorrectness (at worst) of the external security interpretation of North Korea's behavior, see Cotton, "North Korea." On the struggle between moderates and hard-liners in North Korea, see Selig S. Harrison, "Three Myths May Foil Progress," *New York Times*, June 24, 1994, p. A11.
59. Michael J. Mazarr, "Lessons of the North Korean Crisis," *Arms Control Today*, July/August 1993, p. 9.
60. Joseph M. Grieco, *Between Dependency and Autonomy: India's Experience with the International Computer Industry* (Los Angeles: University of California Press, 1984); and Dennis J. Encarnation, *Dislodging Multinationals* (Ithaca, N.Y.: Cornell University Press, 1989).

A group of Congress Party officials favored nuclear weapons for domestic political reasons (polls indicated majority support for such weapons), to counteract the party's responsibility for India's defeat by China in 1962.[61] A similar overall inward-looking strategy at first characterized Pakistan under democratically-elected Zulfiqar Ali Bhutto, a populist who pursued nuclear weapons and discussed the merits of an "Islamic bomb."[62] President-General Zia ul-Haq maintained a patronage system and used Islam as a source of national identity, but sought greater reliance on the West; political survival required straddling antagonistic nuclear postures, or the maintenance of ambiguity.[63]

India took initial steps at economic liberalization under the Janata government (1977–80), one far less friendly than any of its predecessors to state-centered inward-looking policies in general and to the nuclear-industrial complex in particular. Prime Minister Morarji Desai vehemently opposed India's nuclear weapons program.[64] Subsequent incipient Indian and Pakistani efforts at liberalizing their domestic markets and foreign trade during the 1980s coincided with a modest attempt by Indian Prime Minister Rajiv Gandhi and Pakistani Prime Minister Benazir Bhutto to initiate nuclear cooperation.[65] But in India, liberalization (including lowering of some import barriers) encountered heavy opposition from beneficiaries of the old model, bent on keeping international economic institutions and foreign investment at arms' length. Business groups, state central financial agencies, and the professional middle class supported the relaxation of state controls, but many opposed lowering trade barri-

---

61. Reiss, *Without the Bomb*, pp. 204–246. On how external crises strengthened the Congress party ruling coalition and the opposition to denuclearization, see Ashok Kapur, "Nuclear Scientists and the State: The Nehru and Post-Nehru Years," in Etel Solingen, ed., *Scientists and the State: Domestic Structures and the International Context* (Ann Arbor: University of Michigan Press, 1994).
62. Dunn, *Controlling the Bomb*, p. 44; Brahma Chellaney, "Regional Proliferation: Issues and Challenges," in Stephen P. Cohen, ed., *Nuclear Proliferation in South Asia* (Boulder, Colo.: Westview, 1991), p. 313; on Bhutto's political strategy see Stanley Wolpert, *Zulfi Bhutto of Pakistan: His Life and Times* (New York: Oxford University Press, 1993).
63. Cohen, *Nuclear Proliferation*, pp. 9–10. On Zia's proposals for mutual denuclearization, see Robert G. Wirsing, *Pakistan's Security under Zia, 1977–1988* (New York: St. Martin's, 1991), pp. 98–101.
64. G.G. Mirchandani and P.K.S. Namboodiri, *Nuclear India* (New Delhi: Vision, 1981) p. 159; Reiss, *Without the Bomb*, pp. 209 and 235. On India's nuclear restraint in those years, see Dunn, *Controlling the Bomb*, p. 47. On the preference of foreign-oriented Indian elites for denuclearizing India, see Kapur, "India," p. 215.
65. India and Pakistan signed an agreement not to attack each other's nuclear facilities in late 1988. On Benazir Bhutto's effort to stop weapons-grade uranium production, see David Albright, "India and Pakistan's Nuclear Arms Race: Out of the Closet but not in the Street," *Arms Control Today*, June 1993, p. 15. On Rajiv Gandhi's liberalizing agenda and its unraveling, see Atul Kohli, "The Politics of Economic Liberalization in India," in Ezra N. Suleiman and John Waterbury, eds., *The Political Economy of Public Sector Reform and Privatization* (Boulder, Colo.: Westview, 1991), pp. 364–388.

ers. The rank and file in the Congress party, public sector employees, the intelligentsia, which is mostly state-employed, and some rural sectors (known as "middle peasants") rejected all efforts at liberalization, internal and external. Nationalist, inward-looking constituencies, including the technical and entrepreneurial military-industrial complex, were increasingly under attack, but not yet retreating.[66]

India's government under P.V. Narasimha Rao represents a stronger attempt at economic liberalization; it has shaken subsidized sectors and state-owned industries, actively pursued European Community, Japanese, and U.S. investments and World Bank and IMF loans, and allowed Finance Minister Manmohan Singh to rechart not only India's economic course, but its foreign policy as well.[67] Very early in its tenure, and following a strong electoral showing by the opposition Bharatiya Janata Party (BJP), Rao's minority government did not embrace a 1991 Pakistani overture for a NWFZ, but neither did it reject the offer completely, and it agreed to exchange information with Pakistan on the location of their respective nuclear facilities.[68] The Pakistani proposals notably followed the November 1990 ascendancy of Prime Minister Nawaz Sharif, whose trademark was an emphasis on free markets, economic liberalization, foreign investment, and international financial aid; urban business, commercial, and professional groups backed this strategy.[69] A representative of industrial interests, Sharif publicly rejected the label "fundamentalist" and lamented the political energy invested in debates over Islamization "while the world is marching fast to meet the challenges [of] the twenty-first century."[70] Yet Sharif, like his predecessor Benazir Bhutto, proved to be too willing to undertake public projects with high political payoffs, which helped bankrupt Pakistan.[71] With the ousting of Prime Minister Sharif, former World Bank vice

66. See Kapur, "India."
67. Edward A. Gargan, "India Seems Adrift in Changed World," *New York Times*, January 2, 1992.
68. *PPNN Newsbrief* (University of Southampton: Programme for Promoting Nuclear Non-Proliferation [PPNN]), Winter 1991–92, p. 3. On pressures from the opposition to prevent Rao from concessions in the nuclear field, see John F. Burns, "India Resists Plan to Curb Nuclear Arms," *New York Times*, May 15, 1994, p. 8.
69. In July 1991 Pakistan expressed interest in signing the NPT unilaterally (without India doing so) if the United States would reinstate aid cut off under the Pressler Amendment. *Eye on Supply* (Monterey Institute of International Studies), No. 6 (Spring 1992), p. 11. On the freezing of Pakistan's weapons program in 1991, see Albright, "India and Pakistan," p. 14. On Japan's 1992 witholding of loans and investments on the basis of concerns with Pakistan's nuclear program, see "N-controversy delays $400m Japanese loan," *The Nation*, December 22, 1992, p. 2.
70. Ann E. Mayer, "The Fundamentalist Impact on Law, Politics, and Constitutions in Iran, Pakistan, and the Sudan," in Marty and Appleby, *Fundamentalisms and the State*, p. 131.
71. Edward A. Gargan, "After Political Tumult, Pakistan Holds a National Election," *New York Times*, June 6, 1993, p. A7.

president Moeen Qureshi challenged the power of entrenched elites during his brief transitional administration, giving the Central Bank new powers to control government deficits while he attempted to freeze nuclear activities.[72] The policies of Sharif and Qureshi of attracting foreign loans and investments required a dramatic reduction of defense spending, which antagonized segments of the Pakistani military.[73] The second administration of Benazir Bhutto, re-elected in October 1993, rejected Qureshi's reforms and remained responsive to feudal landowners, the bureaucracy, and the army; it also pledged to protect Pakistan's nuclear program.[74]

The platform of India's main opposition party, the radical-confessional Hindu BJP, combines calls to ban foreign loans, investments, and imports with a call to build and deploy nuclear weapons.[75] Cashing in on widespread popular resentment against the West, both for its economic success and for imposing a nuclear cartel, the BJP also enjoys increasing support from import-competing industries such as food processing, automobile manufacturing, banking, and communications. The party thus expressly rejects a wide range of "Western" regimes, from the NPT, to GATT, the World Bank, and IMF-imposed restructuring plans, to the policies of international development agencies that favor population control and the eradication of illiteracy. Many of these positions were echoed by Pakistan's militant Islamic party Jamaat-i-Islami, which challenged what it regards as the Westernized policies of the Sharif coalition.[76] President Ghulam Isaq Khan, representing the nationalist political camp, was thought to support efforts to produce a nuclear weapon, and to have refused to allow elected politicians to negotiate over nuclear matters.[77] The relative

---

72. *PPNN Newsbrief*, Third Quarter 1993, p. 19.
73. Not necessarily advocates of an open deterrent, the militaries in India and Pakistan surely benefit from an ambiguous posture that is more likely to ensure continued budgetary support than is a program of denuclearization. On support of dual use technologies within the scientific-industrial complex, see Kapur, "India," p. 214.
74. Edward A. Gargan, "Bhutto Standing by Nuclear Program," *New York Times*, October 21, 1993, p. A9.
75. *New York Times*, January 24, 1993. On BJP leader Lal Krishna Advani's statement that India will go nuclear when BJP comes to power, see *PPNN Newsbrief*, Second Quarter 1993, p. 14. On the historical support of nuclear weapons by the ultranationalist Jana Sangh Party and the People's Socialist Party, see Reiss, *Without the Bomb*, p. 323.
76. On the party's political basis, see Mumtaz Ahmad, "Islamic Fundamentalism in South Asia: The Jamaat-i-Islami and the Tablighi Jamaat of South Asia," in Martin E. Marty and R. Scott Appleby, eds., *Fundamentalisms Observed* (Chicago: University of Chicago Press, 1991), pp. 457–530.
77. Edward A. Gargan, "A Talk with Bhutto: Is Her Sure Touch Slipping?" *New York Times*, June 19, 1993. In February 1992 Foreign Minister Shahryar Khan announced that Pakistan had the components to assemble such weapon. John J. Schulz, "Riding the Nuclear Tiger: The Search for Security in South Asia," *Arms Control Today*, June 1993, p. 5. On Benazir Bhutto's statement that the military had kept her in the dark with respect to the nuclear program, see "N-controversy," *The Nation*, p. 2.

strength of competing radical nationalist-confessional coalitions is bound to play a key role in shaping the Kashmir crisis and South Asia's nuclear future.

THE MIDDLE EAST

Current ruling coalitions in the Middle East comprise oil-exporting industries in the Gulf and the Arabian peninsula; tourist-based, commercial-agriculture, and *munfatihun* ("openers") economies in Egypt and Jordan; high-tech export oriented industrialists in Israel; and influential Sunni merchants in Damascus.[78] These coalitions advocate openness to international markets, investments, and tourism; cooperative relations with international financial institutions; and support for the Arab-Israeli peace process. Most have ratified the NPT and have consistently advanced NWFZ proposals at UN fora.[79] Leading exemplars of such coalitions—Iran under the shah and Egypt under President Sadat—played entrepreneurial roles in organizing support for a NWFZ. This behavior does not merely imply a passive acceptance of security concessions in exchange for economic advantages, as opponents of liberalizing coalitions often argue. The domestic consequences of cooperative regional postures have positive attractions for advocates of reform. They help the coalition politically, in coping with the socioeconomic havoc left by declining oil prices, bloated bureaucracies and economic mismanagement, overpopulation, militarization, and foreign-policy adventurism.[80] *Infitah* (economic liberalization) was at the heart of a grand strategy for a new, triumphant Egypt, introduced at a time of scarce resources and dwindling state revenues.[81] It required foreign capital, financial assistance, and Western technology, as well as a commitment to private capitalist accumulation, all of which secured the backing of a powerful coalition of business interests and technocrats. *Infitah* played an important role in persuading President Sadat to negotiate an unprecedented peace treaty with Israel.[82] The Camp David agreements, in turn, marginalized the domestic op-

---

78. On the *munfatihun*, who facilitate exchanges with a global market, see John Waterbury, *The Egypt of Nasser and Sadat: The Political Economy of Two Regimes* (Princeton, N.J.: Princeton University Press, 1983); on economic elites, Leonard Binder, *Islamic Liberalism: A Critique of Development Ideologies* (Chicago: University of Chicago Press, 1988); on the rising power of civilian technocrats and politicians implementing economic liberalization in Syria, see Sadowski, *Scuds or Butter?* p. 35.
79. Israel has not signed the NPT but has supported the idea of a NWFZ at the UN, particularly since 1980. On this and other aspects of Israel's nuclear postures, see Solingen, "The Domestic Sources."
80. Sadowski, *Scuds or Butter?*
81. Michael N. Barnett, *Confronting the Costs of War: Military Power, State, and Society in Egypt and Israel* (Princeton, N.J.: Princeton University Press, 1992), pp. 128–129.
82. Janice G. Stein, "Deterrence and Reassurance," in Philip E. Tetlock, Jo L. Husbands, Robert Jer-

position to Sadat's regional politics, even if it radicalized the Islamic fringes. It is quite suggestive that *infitah* was launched in 1974, the same year Egypt first proposed, with Iran, a NWFZ.[83]

Different strains of radical Islamic challenger offer themselves as an alternative to liberalizing coalitions. Islamic blocs include "bourgeois fractions, some rural agrarian capitalists, notables and estate-owners, and the virtually proletarianized members of the state-employed petit-bourgeoisie, the underemployed intelligentsia, and the large student population."[84] These blocs propose a new political economy that, for the most part, appears incompatible with a regional nuclear regime. Opposition to liberalizing coalitions often involves a rejection of ties to the international economy and its perceived associated scourges: inequality, corruption, unemployment, and enslaving indebtedness.[85] In addition, militant Islamic political movements promote a new social order that is not receptive to the idea of a comprehensive peace settlement, let alone a regional nuclear regime.[86] The domestic political appeal of these movements increases primarily with their ability to satisfy popular socioeconomic and educational needs, and in some cases, with calls for extreme "redeeming" solutions.[87] However, the ability of such radical coalitions to

vis, Paul C. Stern, Charles Tilly, eds., *Behavior, Society, and Nuclear War*, Vol. 2 (New York: Oxford University Press, 1991). For a dissenting view on Egypt's motives, see Shibley Telhami, *Power and Leadership in International Bargaining: The Path to the Camp David Accords* (New York: Columbia University Press, 1990). Among other things, *infitah* increased Egypt's dependence on foreign loans, raising the debt burden from $1.64 billion in 1970 to $10 billion in 1978. See Barnett, *Confronting the Costs of War*, p. 222. See also Robert Springborg, *Mubarak's Egypt* (Boulder, Colo.: Westview, 1989).

83. Sadowski, *Scuds or Butter?* p. 41. In 1974 Egypt was also ready to accept full-scope safeguards following the U.S. proposal to supply nuclear reactors to Egypt and Israel. Pro-Soviet Nasserites like Ali Sabri, Ahmed Sidki, and Hasnein Haikal continued advocating nuclear weapons. See Amos Perlmutter, Michael Handel, and Uri Bar-Joseph, *Two Minutes Over Baghdad* (London: Vallentine, Mitchell, 1982), p. 33; Fuad Jabber, *Israel and Nuclear Weapons* (London: IISS/Chatto and Windus, 1971), p. 141. On the shift from an inward-looking Nasserite developmental strategy into an accumulation and growth model see Waterbury, *The Egypt of Nasser and Sadat;* and Barnett, *Confronting the Costs of War.*

84. Binder, *Islamic Liberalism*, pp. 357–358; Springborg, *Mubarak's Egypt*, pp. 63–69.

85. Kuran, "The Economic Impact"; Sahliyeh, *Religious Resurgence.*

86. On nuclear weapons in the Muslim world as redemptive anti-colonial tools, see Ali Mazrui, "The Political Culture of War and Nuclear Proliferation: A Third World Perspective," in Hugh C. Dyer and Leon Mangasarian, eds., *The Study of International Relations* (London: Macmillan, 1989). See also Pervez Hoodbhoy, "Myth-Building: The 'Islamic' Bomb," *The Bulletin of the Atomic Scientists,* June 1993, pp. 42–49.

87. See Mary-Jane Deeb, "Militant Islam and the Politics of Redemption," *Annals,* American Academy of Political and Social Sciences, Vol. 524 (November 1992), pp. 52–65. On the lack of evidence that Islamic economics has made Muslim economies more just, equal, productive, or innovative, see Timur Kuran, "Fundamentalist Economics and The Economic Roots of Fundamentalism: Policy Prescriptions for a Liberal Society," in Martin E. Marty and R. Scott Appleby, eds., *Funda-*

"deliver" on the warfare *(jihad)* side, by investing in military infrastructure, is limited by their need to secure welfare and redistribution. These tasks are much harder to fulfill without preserving the export-oriented *rentier* state and, therefore, preserving extensive ties to the world economy.[88]

Radical Islamic movements are not an ideological monolith; their political-economy themes vary, as do their approaches to the West.[89] Moderate Islamic movements do exist, even if their influence in Middle East politics has so far been somewhat limited.[90] Some of these movements are less concerned with military buildups and exotic weapons than with the socioeconomic transformation of their societies. Such differences are neglected if one focuses only on the behavior of the two Islamic Republics in existence, Iran and Sudan, and on the political platforms of militant movements. These do not bode well for compromising solutions to regional security predicaments. Likewise, the most forceful message of the radical Islamic bloc in the 1993 Jordanian elections was opposition to an Arab-Israeli peace settlement, relegating the rejection of IMF-induced economic reform to a secondary theme.

IRAN. The shah is credited with embarking on a large-scale nuclear energy program and an interest in nuclear weapons has even been imputed to him; yet his regime pioneered a Middle East NWFZ.[91] Following the Islamic revolution in 1979, Iran discontinued its active role in promoting a NWFZ. The emerging Islamic Republic of Iran acquired many of the characteristics of the radical-confessional inward-looking ideal-type, expressing contempt for principles of diplomatic extraterritoriality, individual freedoms, and anti-terrorism, and executing a national redistribution of wealth from the private to the public sector.[92] Although an NPT signatory, Iran is suspected of pursuing a weapons program, an accusation President Hashemi Rafsanjani has denied.[93] However,

---

mentalisms and Public Policy (Chicago: University of Chicago Press, forthcoming 1995) 88. Hazem Beblawi and Giacomo Luciani, *Nation, State and Integration in the Arab World*, Vol. 2: *The Rentier State* (London: Croom Helm, 1987).

88. Hazem Beblawi and Giacomo Luciani, *Nation, State and Integration in the Arab World*, Vol. 2: *The Rentier State* (London: Croom Helm, 1987).

89. Leon T. Hadar, "What Green Peril?" *Foreign Affairs*, Vol. 27, No. 2 (Spring 1993), pp. 27–42; Sisk, *Islam and Democracy*, p. 35; Kuran, "Fundamentalist Economics."

90. Salame argues that, in practice, moderates and militants alike play a political game that mutually reinforces their bargaining power. See Ghassan Salame, "Islam and the West," *Foreign Policy*, Vol. 90 (Spring 1993), pp. 22–37; and G. Hossein Razi, "Legitimacy, Religion, and Nationalism in the Middle East," *American Political Science Review*, Vol. 84, No. 1 (March 1990), pp. 69–92.

91. M. Karem, *A Nuclear-Weapon-Free-Zone in the Middle East: Problems and Prospects* (New York: Greenwood, 1988), p. 103. On the Shah's supposed intentions, see Dunn, *Controlling the Bomb*, p. 63.

92. Sisk, *Islam and Democracy*, pp. 3–32.

93. *PPNN Newsbrief* (Winter 1992), p. 15.

Vice-president Sayed Ayatollah Mohajerani argued in 1992 that "we, the Muslims, must cooperate to produce an atomic bomb, regardless of UN efforts to prevent proliferation."[94] Although mention of Iran's "moderate" wing often raises incredulity, outward-looking undercurrents do appear to be alive, if not well. Teheran's *Bazari* (bazaar) merchants and moneylenders have backed President Rafsanjani's attempts at reform and at reducing state control over the economy. Their gradually increasing control of the 270-seat Parliament could consolidate their struggle for domestic political dominance.[95] They call for privatization of an extensive network of state-run factories and power plants, and are stepping up pressures for increased trade with Europe and Asia and for a utilitarian—as opposed to an ideological—approach to foreign policy. The unresolved contest between liberalizing and radical Islamic blocs may help explain the unclear and unstable nature of Iran's nuclear postures in the past decade.

IRAQ. Iraq's Ba'athist regime approximates the inward-looking, state-based, nationalizing, militarized ideal-type rather well. Saddam Hussein's more recent use of Islam is an ideological ornamentation with occasional political payoffs; it does not alter—in fact, reinforces—the basic rejection of economic liberalism that Ba'athism embraced in the first place. His regime's survival can be traced to a combination of repressive controls, involving abominable human rights abuses and successful redistributive policies.[96] The entrenched combined power of state enterprise bureaucracies, import-substituting interests, and their respective beneficiaries among the professional, construction, and working class may have been responsible for preventing change beyond a limited, tentative effort at economic liberalization.[97] The external expression of this domestic model was a formal rejection of the international economic order and of the Camp David peace agreements, a reliance on the Soviet Union, advocacy of nonalignment, and a "hawkish" position within the Organization of Petroleum Exporting Countries (OPEC). Iraq's nuclear program represented a

94. Hoodbhoy, "Myth-Building," p. 43.
95. Sadowski, *Scuds or Butter?* p. 63; *New York Times*, January 31, 1993, p. 6.
96. Phebe Marr, *The Modern History of Iraq* (Boulder, Colo.: Westview, 1985); and Yousef A. Ahmad, "The Dialectics of Domestic Environment and Role Performance: The Foreign Policy of Iraq," in Baghat Korany and Ali E. Hillal Dessouki, eds., *The Foreign Policy of Arab States* (Boulder, Colo.: Westview, 1991), pp. 186–215. On the historical relationship between inward-looking nationalist populist regimes (Syria, Iraq, Libya, and Egypt in the 1950s and 1960s) and the active pursuit of nuclear weapons, see Solingen, "The Domestic Sources."
97. On *infitah* in Iraq see Richards and Waterbury, *A Political Economy of the Middle East*, pp. 255–257. The Iraqi state accounted for over 80 percent of gross domestic product, in infrastructure, manufacturing, trade, and services.

crowning symbol of the interests and wherewithal of this ruling coalition emphasizing self-reliance. The activities of the UN Special Commission on Iraqi disarmament have neutralized a substantial portion of that program, in an unusual case of forced denuclearization. Genuine Iraqi openness to any regional cooperation—nuclear or otherwise—may have to await a new leadership that reflects the interests of a coalition oriented to global trade, investments, and to the emerging international institutional order.

ISRAEL. Israel's developmental strategy in the immediate post-independence era combined statism and import-substitution with some dependence on foreign capital and agricultural exports.[98] Despite a general political and economic orientation toward the West, Israel developed high mistrust of international institutions, where Third World majorities could automatically endorse Arab positions regardless of substantive merit. It is assumed that a small group around Prime Minister Ben-Gurion, who embodied statism *(Mamlachtiut)*, developed the foundations of a nuclear weapons program in the 1950s and 1960s, never acknowledging its existence.[99] The ambiguous nature of this program relieved a succession of precarious, unwieldy ruling coalitions from the need to debate a program about which little agreement could be found.[100]

External and especially alliance considerations and their impact on domestic constituencies played an important role in the way in which different coalition members defined their positions on nuclear weapons. For instance, in the 1950s the leadership of the Mapam and Ahdut Avoda parties (both politically powerful within Israel's General Federation of Labor, Histadrut) forcefully rejected nuclear deterrence; the policy would have threatened not only relations with the Soviet Union, but also the anti-nuclear feelings of the pro-Soviet constituencies on which these two parties relied.[101] Leading members of the larg-

98. Incoming soft loans and grants, however, had few political and military strings attached, which allowed state agencies high allocative autonomy. Barnett, *Confronting the Costs of War*, p. 231.
99. Robert E. Harkavy, *Spectre of a Middle Eastern Holocaust: The Strategic and Diplomatic Implications of the Israeli Nuclear Weapons Program*, University of Denver Graduate School of International Studies, Monograph Series in World Affairs, Vol. 14, Book 4 (1977); Shai Feldman, *Israeli Nuclear Deterrence* (New York: Columbia University Press, 1982); Louis René Beres, ed., *Security or Armageddon* (Lexington, Mass.: Lexington Books, 1986); Shlomo Aronson, *The Politics and Strategy of Nuclear Weapons in the Middle East* (Albany: State University of New York Press, 1992). Ben-Gurion's statism emphasized autonomous state interests and the state's obligation to provide all required services to its citizens. See Michael Shalev, *Labor and the Political Economy in Israel* (Oxford, U.K.: Oxford University Press, 1992).
100. Solingen, "The Domestic Sources of Regimes"; Naomi Chazan, "The Domestic Foundations of Israeli Foreign Policy," in Judith Kipper and Harold H. Saunders, eds., *The Middle East in Global Perspective* (Boulder, Colo.: Westview, 1991), pp. 82–126.
101. See *Ha'aretz*, March 14, 1962; Yair Evron, "Israel and the Atom: The Uses and Misuses of Am-

est bloc in the Labor coalition (Mapai) similarly opposed reliance on nuclear deterrence. In the late 1960s, Prime Minister (and previously Finance Minister) Levy Eshkol and Finance Minister Pinhas Sapir conceived an incipient policy of economic liberalization aimed at promoting export-led and high-tech industrialization. By that time, not only did dependence on foreign capital leap, but donors (including the United States) applied much more restrictive conditions than those characterizing earlier discretionary capital inflows. As Michael Barnett argues, the Israeli state at that time became "more beholden to foreign actors to stabilize its financial life."[102] Mapai's leaders were not about to endanger the nascent domestic strategy or its external underpinnings (international markets and a political alliance with the West) by being unresponsive to U.S. concerns over Israel's nuclear designs. Eshkol is credited with attempts to rein in Israel's nuclear program.[103] The political windfalls of such steps for Eshkol's Mapai faction included weakening a program that, since Ben-Gurion, had access to unsupervised budgetary sources.

In the last decade two basic modalities have come to characterize Israeli coalition politics. On the one hand, Labor-led coalitions tend to attract support from the urban professional and middle class, from high-tech industrialists, highly-skilled labor, and export-oriented cooperative agriculture. It was Labor's Shimon Peres who designed and implemented the economic reform and currency stabilization plan of the mid-1980s, albeit in the context of a government of national unity with Likud. Labor coalitions (which include smaller secular left-of-center parties) are more receptive to international institutions, territorial compromise, regional regimes, and arms control agreements. With the exception of Ben Gurion and his group (which eventually formed a new party, Rafi) during the 1950s, most of the Labor party has traditionally opposed reliance on nuclear deterrence. Many influential Labor leaders have favored a NWFZ.[104] Prime Minister Yitzhak Rabin declared in 1974, in response to Defense Minister Moshe Dayan's call for nuclear weapons: "Attempts to rely on

---

biguity, 1957–1967," *Orbis*, Vol. 17, No. 4 (Winter 1974), p. 1330; and Yigal Allon, *Betachbulot milhama* (Tel Aviv: Hakibutz Hameuchad, 1990), p. 91.

102. Barnett, *Confronting the Costs of War*, p. 233.

103. Ephraim Inbar, "Israel and Nuclear Weapons since October 1973," in Bercs, *Security or Armageddon*, p. 62; Simha Flaphan, "Nuclear Power in the Middle East," *New Outlook*, July 1974, pp. 46–54.

104. Inbar, "Israel and Nuclear Weapons," pp. 61–78. The Committee for Denuclearization of the Middle East was headed by a prominent Knesset member from Labor (Mapai), Eliezer Livne, and had good access to prominent Labor figures. Avner Cohen, "Nuclear Weapons, Opacity, and Israeli Democracy," in Avner Yaniv, ed., *National Security and Democracy in Israel* (Boulder, Colo.: Lynne Rienner, 1993), pp. 205–207 and p. 224.

mystical weapons are negative trends."[105] In 1975 Foreign Minister Yigal Allon (of the Ahdut Avoda party) proposed direct negotiations over a regional NWFZ at the UN General Assembly. By 1980 Israel was voting in favor of the Egyptian NWFZ proposal, submitted regularly to the UN since 1974. Yet, in the context (until very recently) of a rigid Arab refusal to recognize the existence of the state of Israel, let alone its security concerns, any attempt by Labor to endorse a unilateral denuclearization was politically prohibitive.

On the other hand, populist Likud-led coalitions, a bloc that in Israel's early years represented free-enterprise liberalism, are now more susceptible to demands from nationalist economic interests (including small business, blue-collar and underemployed workers, development towns, and West Bank and Gaza settlers) and from the orthodox, including some radical religious and nationalist constituencies. They tend to be more dismissive of international institutions and untrusting of their objectives, and to use the myth of self-reliance to gather political support from an array of economic and ideological groups, most of which reject a territorial compromise with Palestinians.[106] Menachem Begin's Likud government bombed Iraq's Osirak reactor in 1981 (in a pre-elections period), against the opposition of important Labor leaders who, sensitive to the response of allies and institutions like the International Atomic Energy Agency, sought more time for diplomacy.[107] Although prominent Likud leaders are associated with opposition to a NWFZ, the party has no declared policy on this issue.[108] Overall, Likud and its more natural coalition partners on the right are more responsive to nationalist policies and economic constituencies, and distrustful of international institutions and regional cooperation.

Labor's political comeback in 1992 foreshadows greater Israeli willingness to

---

105. Inbar, "Israel and Nuclear Weapons," p. 64. Moshe Dayan later joined a Likud government.
106. Yahoshafat Harkabi, *Israel's Fateful Hour* (New York: Harper and Row, 1988); Ephraim Inbar, *War and Peace in Israeli Politics* (Boulder: Lynne Rienner, 1991), p. 105. On the proclivity of this public to regard the threat of war as much more probable than peace, see A. Arian, I. Talmud, and T. Hermann, *National Security and Public Opinion in Israel* (Boulder, Colo.: Westview, 1988), p. 72.
107. Perlmutter, *Two Minutes*, pp. 80–81; and Inbar, *War and Peace*, p. 105. The Chief of Staff at the time was Rafael Eitan, who went on to create a new political party with high ideological affinity to Likud.
108. On the position of Ariel Sharon, Yuval Ne'eman, and Rafael Eitan, see Y. Nimrod, "Arms Control or Arms Race?" *New Outlook*, September/October 1991, pp. 15–18; and Uri Bar Joseph, "The Hidden Debate: The Formation of Nuclear Doctrines in the Middle East," *The Journal of Strategic Studies*, Vol. 5, No. 2 (June 1982), pp. 205–227. Supporters of Likud and its rightist allies justify the use of nuclear weapons by a larger margin (46 and 57 percent respectively) than the electorate of Labor and its partners (43 and 36 respectively); Arian, et al., *National Security*, p. 72.

embrace a regime, and eventually a NWFZ. First, the Labor coalition has led, rather than followed, public opinion in matters of national security; it presented the public with a *fait accompli* in the form of the September 1993 Declaration of Principles recognizing the Palestine Liberation Organization. A 3:2 margin of voter approval followed. Moreover, the Labor coalition is more sensitive to Israel's international standing, and to the domestic political and economic consequences of such status.[109] A recent statement by Deputy Foreign Minister Yossi Beilin summarizes the aims of Labor diplomacy: "to use the new situation in order to become a more welcome member of the international club."[110] The coalition emphasizes the exigencies of economic survival, privatization, and international competitiveness as well as the futility of technological fixes as the solution to Israel's security dilemma.[111] This approach threatens the rents and political influence of military-industrial groups and state bureaucracies, while expanding the opportunities for civilian-oriented private entrepreneurship and the power and autonomy of economic agencies such as the Central Bank.[112]

The future of Israel's alleged nuclear arsenal is on the agenda of the Arms Control Group in the multilateral peace negotiations, although there is disagreement whether non-conventional weapons should be discussed at the outset or at the end of the process.[113] It is doubtful that representatives from the Labor government can politically afford to agree to any arrangements on the nuclear issue prior to the achievement of a comprehensive peace settlement and to the resolution of outstanding problems with Iran and Iraq. There is a strong proclivity among Labor leaders and their core supporters to do away

---

109. As a reward for the Rabin government's more flexible positions in the Middle East peace talks, even prior to September 1993, the United States approved $10 billion in loan guarantees for investments in infrastructure and jobs, a program that may help solidify Labor's position as the core of future coalitions. Likud had chosen to retain an intractable position in the peace negotiations at the expense of economic gains. The issue of the loan guarantees reaffirms the need to transcend neorealist interpretations of state behavior. Moreover, Labor's flexible positions were far from externally imposed; the loan approval was a windfall for a policy that Labor supported anyway.
110. Quoted in Eric Silver, *Financial Times*, December 7, 1992.
111. The inability to prevent Iraqi Scud missiles from landing on Tel Aviv (or on the Negev desert, where the Dimona nuclear center is located), and the internal threat posed by the *intifada* increased popular receptivity to political solutions to Israel's security predicament.
112. On pressures for conversion to civilian industries, see Aharon Klieman and Reuven Pedatzur, *Rearming Israel: Defense Procurement Through the 1990s* (Boulder, Colo.: Westview, 1991), pp. 222–225.
113. See generally Geoffrey Kemp, *The Control of the Middle East Arms Race* (New York: Carnegie Endowment for International Peace, 1991).

with most barriers to effective regional cooperation.[114] However, the need to secure swing votes (potentially attracted to Labor and its political allies in all but their security postures) may require caution on the question of tradeoffs for peace, and in the rate at which they are delivered. On the other hand, Egypt and other incumbent coalitions in the region may be unlikely to obtain popular ratification of a comprehensive peace settlement that omits the curtailment of Israel's nuclear capabilities, at least at some point in the future. The successful completion and implementation of such a settlement will deflate the myth-making potential of radical-confessional groups on both sides. Despite promising developments, the concluding chapter of the Middle East's NWFZ has yet to be written.

ARGENTINA AND BRAZIL

The presidency of Juan D. Perón in Argentina epitomized the national populist economic model that vied for control of the state for half a century.[115] It involved a coalition of national small and medium-sized firms involved in import-substitution industrialization, state firms producing the required infrastructural inputs, and popular sectors represented in the central trade union organization (the General Labor Confederation). The external expression of national populism was a challenge to free trade and the unpredictability of the international market, and also a rejection of foreign borrowing and investment as well as membership in the IMF and the World Bank. Perón actively pursued nuclear capabilities in the early 1950s, and announced the country's mastery of fusion technology in 1953, on the basis of a false claim by expatriate Austrian physicist Ronald Richter, who managed Argentina's nuclear program at the time.[116] The origins of a well-funded nuclear program in Argentina are thus deeply rooted in the national populism of the Perón era; such origins endowed the program with the myth of self-reliance.

After the military coup of 1955 deposed Perón, a tripartite division of state industrial assets among Argentina's armed services allowed the navy to shelter the nuclear program during an unstable succession of mostly military regimes. This succession was notable for alternating stop-go economic and

114. In answering a question posed by Chancellor Helmut Kohl, Foreign Minister Shimon Peres declared that Israel would sign on to regional denuclearization "the day after" a comprehensive peace settlement is signed; *National Public Radio*, October 8, 1993.
115. Kathryn Sikkink, *Ideas and Institutions; Developmentalism in Brazil and Argentina* (Ithaca, N.Y.: Cornell University Press, 1991).
116. Mario Mariscotti, *El Secreto Atómico de Huemul* (Buenos Aires: Sudamericana-Planeta, 1987).

industrial policy cycles, reflecting the inability of either coalition—the one supporting liberalization, the other opposing it—to prevail politically for a sustained period of time. Attempts at liberalization, as with President Arturo Frondizi's acceptance of an IMF stabilization plan and of foreign exploitation of Argentina's oil reserves, coincided with attempts in the 1960s to curtail the nuclear program and reduce its autonomy. The military administration of Videla in 1976, strongly influenced by Economic Minister Martínez de Hoz and his orthodox policies, challenged the costly nationalist-mercantilist orientation of the nuclear program, the bloated and inefficient state sector and noncompetitive national private industry. Although privatization and dwindling governmental expenditures threatened the nuclear program, the navy was able to defend it throughout the 1970s and 1980s. Martínez de Hoz was ousted, and no coalition supporting widespread liberal economic reforms was strong enough to implement them until the early 1990s.

In Brazil, the administration of Getulio Vargas in the early 1950s evoked many of the same elements of national populism as in Argentina under Perón. Restrictions on foreign investment led to a refusal by the World Bank to finance the Vargas strategy of industrialization, or that of his successors, until 1964. In the nuclear realm this policy was expressed in the regime's attempt to develop independent national nuclear capabilities as early as the 1950s.[117] In 1952 President Vargas approved directives to the National Security Council demanding "specific compensations" in the form of transfer of technical know-how on plant construction, and delivery of equipment and materials for chemical treatment, in exchange for any sale of uranium or thorium to the United States. Admiral Alvaro Alberto, the director of the National Research Council (CNPq), attempted to purchase three ultracentrifuge systems for uranium enrichment from Bonn in 1954. That year interim President Café Filho, who succeeded Vargas and launched a policy to attract foreign investments, dismissed Alberto and allowed the United States to take over the monopoly on uranium research and extraction for a period of two years.

The old pro-Vargas coalition supported the ascendancy of President Kubitschek in 1955, while anti-statist groups and supporters of free trade opposed it. The Kubitschek coalition resisted IMF stabilization programs that

---

117. Regina L. de Morel, *Ciencia e Estado: A política científica no Brasil* (Sao Paulo: T.A. Queiroz, 1979). On the political economy of the nuclear sector in Brazil and Argentina, see Etel Solingen, *Industrial Policy, Technology, and International Bargaining: Designing Nuclear Industries in Argentina and Brazil* (Stanford: Stanford University Press, forthcoming 1995).

threatened its power basis. In 1956 President Kubitschek appointed a parliamentary commission of inquiry into nuclear policy following a denunciation of "improper" U.S. influences exerted upon the administration of President Café Filho. The commission's report urged the pursuit of independent nuclear capabilities and the creation of a National Atomic Energy Commission (CNEN), directly answerable to the president of the republic. With the ascension of a new national-populist team in 1961, President Quadros reaffirmed a nationalist nuclear policy, based on natural uranium (which granted Brazil fuel independence), a policy in tune with the broader developmental priorities that characterized his short presidency. Quadros' successor João Goulart (1961–63) maintained the emphasis on national nuclear capabilities and approved a Nuclear Energy Law subordinating the Nuclear Energy Commission directly to the presidency, as a way to increase its bureaucratic independence.

Unlike the nationalist inward-looking coalitions backing Argentina's President Perón and Brazil's Presidents Quadros and Goulart, the military regimes that intervened in Brazil and Argentina since the 1960s shifted—without abandoning import-substitution altogether—to greater reliance on foreign direct investment, industrial exports, and indebted industrialization.[118] This strategy required stronger economic ties with the United States, Western Europe, Japan, and international financial institutions. Although formally headed by repressive military rulers with some constituencies that favored nuclear weapons, these coalitions of technocrats, industrialists, and bankers maintained considerable control over economic policy. They were thus able to resist pressures (such as that of Peronist legislator Quiroz) for a nuclear posture that could trigger international penalties or other restrictions on technology transfer. Throughout these years, characterized by a hybrid model of secondary import-substitution and closer trade and financial links to the international system, nuclear policy revealed two main features. On the one hand, both Brazil and Argentina continued their longstanding rejection of the NPT as a discriminatory tool of nuclear powers, and their resistance to making the regional Tlatelolco NWFZ effective on their territory. On the other hand, they refrained from developing nuclear weapons and from threatening to do so.[119] The beginnings of moderate nuclear cooperation can be traced to the late 1970s and,

---

118. On indebted industrialization, see Jeffry A. Frieden, *Debt, Development, and Democracy* (Princeton, N.J.: Princeton University Press, 1991).
119. Daniel Poneman, "Nuclear Proliferation Prospects for Argentina," *Orbis*, Vol. 27, No. 4 (Winter 1984), pp. 853–880. On the evolution of these postures, see John R. Redick, "Argentina-Brazil Nuclear Non-Proliferation Initiatives," *PPNN*, No. 3 (January 1994).

more specifically, to the 1980 agreements signed in Foz do Iguaçu by Presidents-General Videla of Argentina and Figueiredo of Brazil.

In the mid-1980s, Brazil's President José Sarney implemented a nationalist-populist mixture of domestic heterodoxy and anti-IMF policy that led eventually to Brazil's 1987 debt moratorium. In an attempt to maintain both business and popular support, President Raúl Alfonsín defined a heterodox adjustment policy in Argentina, relying on neither the old radical Peronist populism nor the radical orthodox rhetoric of the military's policy under Videla, while preserving a cooperative stance with international creditors. The new democratic administrations, neither of which was prepared to adopt orthodox liberal medicine for their countries' economic ailments, proceeded with a moderate pace, but no real breakthrough, in both economic liberalization and nuclear cooperation. In Brazil, sections of the military continued to develop a "parallel program" with weapons applications, even after attempts, through the Constitution drafted in 1988, to place all nuclear activities under democratic control.[120]

By the late 1980s, drops in real wages, price freezes, and tax reforms alienated Sarney's popular constituencies, forcing Brazil to turn to an IMF-style orthodox stabilization package. The Argentine government was at this time particularly careful to provide strong reassurance to its banking and industrial firms, in light of populist challenges to the state during the late 1980s.[121] At the end of the decade, both President Fernando Collor de Mello of Brazil and President Carlos S. Meném of Argentina supported shock economic programs unambiguously committed to effective economic liberalization and structural adjustment. The liberalizing Meném revolution reduced a Weimar-style inflation level to single digits, balanced the budget, privatized many public services, and attracted an avalanche of foreign investment. The external dimension of these policies included not only an unprecedented embrace of liberal trade rules but also of other international regimes, including missile control.[122] Following his election, President Collor was equally committed to liberalizing Brazil's economy, a policy that won him an approval rating of close to 90 percent in early 1990. By November of 1990 Brazil and Argentina agreed

---

120. Ruth Stanley, "Cooperation and Control: The New Approach to Nuclear Non-proliferation in Argentina and Brazil," *Arms Control*, Vol. 13, No. 2 (September 1992), pp. 191–213.
121. Kaufman, "Domestic Determinants," p. 278.
122. This shift included, for instance, Argentine naval participation in the Gulf War and a severance of membership in the Nonaligned Movement. Roberto Russell, ed., *La política exterior Argentina en el nuevo orden mundial* (Buenos Aires: Facultad Latinoamericana de Ciencias Sociales, 1992).

explicitly, for the first time, to renounce nuclear weapons and to establish mutual verification and inspection procedures, which were ultimately approved in December 1991.[123] The two countries also expressed their intention to put into effect an updated version of the regional Tlatelolco Treaty, and Brazil's President Collor closed down presumed nuclear weapons test sites. After over 35 years of unassailed navy control, Argentina's nuclear program was now at the mercy of President Meném's director of planning, whose major goal was the privatization of nuclear activities. Aided by advisors from large Argentine corporations and joint ventures, the Meném administration neutralized the program's sensitive nuclear facilities.[124] Meném has gone as far as expressing unilateral readiness to ratify the NPT by the time of the 1995 Extension and Review Conference.[125]

In Brazil, following Collor's resignation in 1992 over a corruption scandal, his successor Itamar Franco began wooing a nationalist and military constituency, attacking international financial institutions and their domestic "allies," and endorsing statements on Brazil's sovereignty in nuclear matters.[126] However, nationalist forces failed to prevent Brazil's House of Deputies, under heavy pressure from the Foreign and Economic Ministries, from approving the mutual inspection agreements with Argentina in late 1993.[127] The Senate is expected to follow suit. Brazil's opposition to NPT ratification may well be explained as a side-payment to the nationalist camp, including portions of the military.

Lessons and Implications

This cross-regional analysis suggests that the political-economic nature of domestic coalitions and the choice of nuclear postures are related. I suggest that this relationship can be traced to the type of industrialization strategy these coalitions embrace. Liberalizing coalitions strive to maximize their gains from international economic exchange. Their receptivity to compromising regional

---

123. On how ensuring a favorable economic and investment climate underpinned the agreement, see Stanley, "Cooperation," p. 207.
124. Joint Publications Research Service (Arlington, Va.: Foreign Broadcast information Service), August 21, 1991, p. 5.
125. Redick, "Argentina-Brazil," p. 4.
126. Scott Tollefson, *Memorandum* (Monterey: Naval Postgraduate School, 1992).
127. Redick, "Argentina-Brazil," pp. 1–3.

nuclear postures secures them access to international economic regimes and the political support of major powers; denuclearization is also quite compatible with the domestic agenda of liberalizing the economy and reining in adversarial political forces and institutions. In contrast, nationalist and radical-confessional coalitions logroll economic interests and militant groups that regard nuclear weapons as a useful political tool, to rally opposition to global markets and regimes and to the settlement of regional conflicts. As with most propositions about the sources of state behavior, however, the argument suggests no more than a probabilistic relationship.

These assumptions help explain the behavior of states operating a) in different regional security contexts; b) with different associations with hegemonic powers; and c) over time, throughout a historical succession of alternating coalition-types. The Middle East, the Korean peninsula, and South Asia offered a natural quasi-experimental ground to examine the impact of different political regimes, controlling for the intensity of the security dilemma and the presence of hegemons providing protection. Under comparable regional structural contexts we would have expected to find similar responses, but we do not. And under disparate security-related conditions—compare the Southern Cone with the Middle East, the Korean peninsula, or South Asia—some states embraced similar policies of nuclear ambiguity for lengthy periods of time. A wide variety of domestic political regime types (democratic and otherwise) converged in cooperative practices, despite expectations from the theories connecting democracy and cooperation.

The cross-regional and longitudinal analysis suggests that where liberalizing coalitions had the upper hand, nuclear policy shifted towards more cooperative nuclear postures. Nationalist-confessional coalitions, in contrast, shied away from any commitments for effective denuclearization. Moreover, where the domestic interests potentially affected by external sanctions were most concentrated and coherent, and less challenged domestically, as in South Korea and Taiwan, the shift in nuclear policy was relatively swift. The stronger the coalition supporting economic liberalization grew, the more clear-cut the departure from nuclear ambiguity was (even where the security context deteriorated, as in the Korean peninsula). This is illustrated by Argentina's commitment to the full-scope safeguards regime in the early 1990s, following the consolidation of political forces supporting economic liberalization. It is also clear from the example of South Africa's acceptance of NPT arrangements in 1991, even as it disclosed past attempts to produce a bomb. In another example, Spain endorsed the NPT when a liberalizing coalition eager to join the

European Community was able to put the inward-looking, nationalist policies of the Franco era behind it.

In contrast, the weaker the liberalizing coalitions—as was the case historically in India and Israel, Argentina until the early 1990s, and Iran today—the more politically constrained they were in curbing nuclear programs. Weak liberalizing coalitions are often less able to defend themselves from the accusation of selling out; their very weakness also renders them more dependent on additional domestic partners. Liberalizing coalitions walk a tightrope to sustain their legitimacy: they must not only deliver on their promises but also preserve fluid external ties while avoiding the appearance of foreign subordination.[128] Such conditions may help explain the hesitation of the Rao government in India to promise effective denuclearization, or Brazil's initial wariness under Itamar Franco to implement it.

Of all states beyond the original five that have considered a nuclear option in the last three decades, not one endorsed a NWFZ under a nationalist coalition. Only liberalizing coalitions undertook effective commitments to denuclearization. The North Korean case may offer fresh insights into the process by which economic liberalization, coalition survival, and nuclear postures become entangled. There are indications that the same political forces staunchly opposed to economic liberalization are using the nuclear issue to stave off the end of the present regime.[129]

What are the more general implications for theories of international cooperation and regimes? First, the approach suggested here points to a more precise link between economic liberalism and the probability of cooperation than general theories of interdependence have postulated.[130] Rather than assuming that the expanded domestic welfare resulting from free trade fosters cooperative preferences, it suggests that where free-trade coalitions prevail, their interests at home and abroad dictate compatible security regimes. The gains from trade need not be highly concentrated nor contribute to widespread societal welfare, at least in the short term, to have this effect. Moreover, cooperation does not depend on the extent of economic interdependence between or among the re-

---

128. Miles Kahler, "International Financial Institutions and the Politics of Adjustment," in Kallab and Feinberg, *Fragile Coalitions;* Kaufman, "Domestic Determinants."
129. Bracken, "Nuclear Weapons"; Cotton, "North Korea."
130. The classic formulations include Richard Cooper, *The Economics of Interdependence: Economic Policy in the Atlantic Community* (New York: Columbia University Press, 1968); Robert O. Keohane and Joseph S. Nye, Jr., eds., *Power and Interdependence: World Politics in Transition* (Boston: Little, Brown, 1977); and Rosecrance, *Rise of the Trading State.*

gional participants in a regime. Finally, my argument is more specific about whose absolute gains matter in the analysis of cooperation: the gains that matter are those of particular coalitions.

Second, this last point places more constraints on purely neorealist formulations beyond those discussed above. The preferences, domestic and international, of domestic ruling coalitions matter a great deal. These coalitions evaluate costs and benefits with an eye to strengthening their political standing at home, and they define the balance between the costs (if any) of nuclear cooperation and the overall gains from participating in global regimes. To say that once these coalitions embrace an internationalist strategy of industrialization they become more sensitive to pressures from powerful states and international institutions is not the same as arguing that foreign pressures or inducements singlehandedly, and invariably, account for the outcome. Such pressures were a constant for most of the Cold War era, yet they cannot settle the puzzle of why they triggered a regime-oriented behavior at certain times and not others, and among certain states, and not others. The accession of contending domestic coalitions provides a more powerful predictor of such dynamics and variability. Identifying the domestic conditions underlying behavioral shifts takes us several steps beyond structural explanations in understanding how external and internal factors interact to produce changes in nuclear postures. The next section explores this interaction by analyzing how international institutions can strengthen different coalitions over others.

INTERNATIONAL INSTITUTIONS: SECOND ORDER EFFECTS AND "REVERSE CONDITIONALITY"

How do international institutions affect the domestic balance of power between coalitions, and thus, as a second-order effect, their respective nuclear postures?[131] As allies of liberalizing coalitions, the international institutions that provide credit (World Bank, IMF, private banks) and define the terms of trade and investment (GATT, regional common markets) can play an important role in the political longevity of these coalitions.[132] Imposing harsh and widespread structural adjustments can undermine these coalitions' legitimacy and survival, and weaken their capacity to gather support for regional security

---

131. I subsume the influence of powerful states within the operation of international institutions, because such influence is increasingly likely to be exerted through multilateral mechanisms in the future. See Ruggie, "Multilateralism"; Solingen, "Fence-sitting."
132. On how external economic threats can undermine the influence of weakly institutionalized liberal coalitions, see Snyder, "International Leverage."

regimes. The failures of some liberalizing coalitions in the Arab world (and of the international institutions within which their interests are embedded) to bring about a genuine socio-economic transformation in the region has provided fertile soil for the rise of radical Islamic challengers. To prevent further erosion of popular support for liberalizing coalitions, international economic regimes must encourage domestic redistribution.[133] Tight conditionality arrangements have been ineffective anyway, whereas securing a stable political environment improves the borrowers' ability to attract investments, repay debts, and stem authoritarian challenges.[134] The IMF and the World Bank could return to their true call by lending for economic development, stabilization, and recovery, rather than helping debtors pay their debts to big banks.[135]

In other words, the survival of liberalizing coalitions requires that the benefits from a cooperative nuclear posture—in trade, investments, removal from export control lists, debt-relief, and aid—be distributed more broadly, beyond just the concentrated interests which sustain these coalitions. Providing resources, compensatory payments, and relief from the pressures of international competition can weaken domestic opposition to liberalization and pragmatism. Such efforts may build on a wave of growing popular awareness of the opportunity costs of arms races.[136] Furthermore, a shift in the style of foreign institutional intervention toward effective consultation over domestic political needs, and more active participation of developing countries in the decisionmaking process within international institutions, can deflate nationalist resentment.[137] Such an approach may help these institutions tame extreme views and foster a form of liberalism, even one attentive to moderate confessional aspirations, that would view regional and international regimes positively.[138] The other side of this coin, of course, is the power of liberalizing

---

133. On the social costs of economic adjustment, see Joan M. Nelson, "Poverty, Equity, and the Politics of Adjustment," in Haggard and Kaufman, *The Politics,* pp. 221–269. On the negative effects of neoliberal economic reform on democratic institutions, see Adam Przeworski, "The Neoliberal Fallacy," *Journal of Democracy,* Vol. 3, No. 3 (July 1992), pp. 45–59. On economic decline as leading to the rise of militant Islam, see Deeb, "Militant Islam," p. 53.

134. Nelson, *Fragile Coalitions;* and Stephan Haggard and Robert R. Kaufman, "Economic Adjustment in New Democracies," in Kallab and Feinberg, *Fragile Coalitions,* pp. 57–76. On the positive effects of income equality, education, and welfare on economic growth, see Przeworski, "The Neoliberal Fallacy."

135. On the collusion between IMF officials and the big private banks see Jeffrey Sachs, "Robbin' Hoods: How the Big Banks Spell Debt 'Relief'," *The New Republic* (1989).

136. Sadowski, *Scuds or Butter?* p. 78. On compensatory payments see Nelson, *Fragile Coalitions.*

137. Kahler, "International Financial Institutions."

138. See Binder, *Islamic Liberalism.*

coalitions to "use" the threat from nationalists and radical-confessional movements to extract concessions from their international partners and to alleviate the conditions for continued credit and investment. This "reverse conditionality" will continue to be part of the bargaining strategies of struggling liberalizing coalitions in the future.

International institutions can strengthen the hands of certain domestic institutions at the expense of others. For example, externally-induced structural adjustment efforts often threaten military-industrial complexes while strengthening those in charge of reform (particularly finance ministries, central banks, and export-promotion bureaus). Similarly, international pressures for human rights standards empower the domestic groups responsible for monitoring compliance, at the expense of repressive agencies. Environmental regimes endow local institutional networks with the ability, backed by unprecedented legal powers, to challenge certain industrial activities such as nuclear energy production. The resulting coalitional balances are more likely to reinforce openness and receptivity to nuclear regimes than the coalitions and institutions they are replacing.[139] Interests opposed to nuclear weapons could become more concentrated (and therefore, more attractive partners for logrolling) than those that favor them.

Finally, the fact that international regimes strengthen the influence of the most powerful countries that created them is not lost on developing countries, particularly fence-sitters, or on those in transition to market-oriented economies. If such regimes continue to be regarded as an instrument for control of the less powerful, their legitimacy could be eroded. But this can be ameliorated if their injunctions are universally binding, especially where they require the elimination of nuclear arsenals, as required by Article VI of the Nonproliferation Treaty.

Conclusions

In this article I offer a framework for understanding the domestic sources of regime creation by outlining how contending coalitions affect nuclear postures.[140] The growing attention to domestic factors has mostly been directed at

---

139. On how the institutional setting can favor the emergence of some coalitions over others, see Snyder, *Myths of Empire.*
140. On the inattention to domestic politics in regime theory see Charles Lipson, "International Cooperation in Economic and Security Affairs," *World Politics,* Vol. 37, No. 1 (October 1984), pp. 1–23; Oye, *Cooperation Under Anarchy;* Haggard and Simmons, "Theories of International Regimes";

understanding the structure of interests within a specific issue area to explain cooperation (or its absence) in that same area,[141] but understanding outcomes in the security arena requires a broader consideration of how political-economic strategies affect security choices.[142] Such an approach helps specify what early neoliberal-institutionalism left unexplained: where the preference to cooperate comes from. By relying on a single analytical category, this approach transcends the practice of nonproliferation studies of explaining each country or region through a list of individualized peculiarities.

The evidence points to an association between strategies of industrialization and nuclear postures that is worthy of both theoretical and policy-making consideration. Understanding this association may prove an effective means of moving beyond extant scholarship and conventional wisdoms that have become more convention than truth. The findings suggest that the credibility of commitments by fence-sitters may be more affected by what kind of domestic political-economic coalition underwrites them than by the institutional constraints of democracy. Where these coalitions rely for their domestic political survival on an open economic system, they will not only be more susceptible to international inducements to cooperate but will favor denuclearization for its domestic effects as well. State structures influence the fate of different coalitions and, in turn, are changed by them; states are both the agents of liberalization and the victims of it. The performance of coalitions varies with the nature and strength of technocratic agencies on the one hand, and of rent-seeking actors and their challengers on the other. Exploring how this variation accounts for different paths to regional denuclearization may be a logical next step. Additional research may also enable us to understand thresholds, lags, and sequences in the process by which developmental grand strategies and nuclear postures become linked.

Because international institutions bankroll free-trade coalitions, they are a great source of strength for such coalitions, as repositories of side-payment "currency," and at the same time a potential Achilles heel, a symbol of curtailed sovereignty. Thus, these institutions must calibrate their performance to enable cooperative coalitions to mobilize societal resources in support of nu-

---

and Helen Milner, "International Theories of Cooperation among Nations: Strengths and Weaknesses," *World Politics*, Vol. 44, No. 3 (April 1992), pp. 466–496.

141. Oye, *Cooperation Under Anarchy*.

142. See, for instance, Ali E. Hillal Dessouki, "Dilemmas of Security and Development in the Arab World: Aspects of the Linkage," in Baghat Korany, Paul Noble and Rex Brynen, eds., *The Many Faces of National Security in the Arab World* (New York: St. Martin's Press, 1993), p. 79.

clear regimes.[143] Imposing heavy burdens on such coalitions may result in their "involuntary defection," or in their inability to deliver because of low prospects for domestic ratification.[144] Understanding the impact of international processes on the strength of domestic coalitions is not equivalent to reducing the politics of these countries to external forces. As the international political economy literature suggests, different coalitions have chosen contrasting grand strategies of industrialization (integrative or inward-looking) under similar international circumstances.

Finally, economic liberalization appears to require democratization if it is to be sustained over the long term.[145] In that sense, it may well be that many regional partners negotiating nuclear regimes, now and in the future, are and will be democratic. Yet both democracy and nuclear cooperation could still be an outcome of economic liberalism. Exploring further the extent to which political freedom will be necessary or sufficient for the emergence and maintenance of regional nuclear regimes is a compelling task for a social science theory sensitive to the construction of a more peaceful global order.

---

143. This might be relevant for the emerging Eurasian nuclear regime. Ukraine, Belarus, and Kazakhstan, unlike the cases reviewed here, acquired overt nuclear status at birth, rather than contemplating their acquisition.
144. The term is Robert D. Putnam's in "Diplomacy and Domestic Politics," *International Organization*, Vol. 42, No. 3 (Summer 1988), pp. 427–459.
145. The Middle East and China appear to require longer lags than previously thought. For a more nuanced interpretation of the political consequences of economic adjustment, see Haggard and Kaufman, "Economic Adjustments."

Divining Nuclear Intentions

A Review Essay

William C. Potter and Gaukhar Mukhatzhanova

Jacques E.C. Hymans, *The Psychology of Nuclear Proliferation: Identity, Emotions, and Foreign Policy* (New York: Cambridge University Press, 2006)

Etel Solingen, *Nuclear Logics: Alternative Paths in East Asia and the Middle East* (Princeton, N.J.: Princeton University Press, 2007)

For much of the nuclear age, academic experts, intelligence analysts, and public commentators periodically have forecast rapid bursts of proliferation, which have failed to materialize. Central to their prognoses, often imbued with the imagery and metaphors of nuclear dominoes and proliferation chains, has been the assumption that one state's nuclearization is likely to trigger decisions by other states to "go nuclear" in quick succession. Today the proliferation metaphors of choice are "nuclear cascade" and "tipping point," but the implication is the same—we are on the cusp of rapid, large-scale nuclear weapons spread. It is with some justification, therefore, that the study of proliferation has been labeled "the sky-is-still-falling profession."[1]

Although proliferation projections abound, few of them are founded on, or even informed by, empirical research and theory.[2] This deficiency, though regrettable, is understandable given the small body of theoretically or empiri-

William C. Potter is Sam Nunn and Richard Lugar Professor of Nonproliferation Studies and Director of the James Martin Center for Nonproliferation Studies at the Monterey Institute of International Studies. Gaukhar Mukhatzhanova is Research Associate at the James Martin Center.

---

1. William M. Arkin, "The Sky-Is-Still-Falling Profession," *Bulletin of the Atomic Scientists*, Vol. 50, No. 2 (March/April 1994), p. 64.
2. An early, notable exception to this general tendency is Stephen M. Meyer, *The Dynamics of Nuclear Proliferation* (Chicago: University of Chicago Press, 1984). Although not primarily oriented toward forecasting, a number of unpublished dissertations on nonproliferation themes display an admirable mix of empirical research and theory. See, in particular, Tanya Ogilvie-White, "Theorizing Nuclear Weapons Proliferation: Understanding the Nuclear Politics of India, South Africa, and Ukraine," University of Southampton, 1998; James J. Walsh, "Bombs Unbuilt: Power, Ideas, and Institutions in International Politics," Massachusetts Institute of Technology, 2001; Maria Rost Rublee, "Persuasion, Social Conformity, and Identification: Constructivist Explanations for Non-Nuclear States in a Nuclear World," George Washington University, 2004; Alexander H. Montgomery, "Social Action, Rogue Reaction: U.S. Post–Cold War Nuclear Counterproliferation Strategies," Stanford University, 2005; Karthika Sasikumar, "Regimes at Work: The Nonproliferation Order and Indian Nuclear Policy," Cornell University, 2006; and Matthew H. Kroenig, "The Enemy of My Enemy Is My Customer: Why States Provide Sensitive Nuclear Assistance," University of California, Berkeley, 2007. Several recent quantitative studies also are noteworthy for their attentiveness

---

International Security, Vol. 33, No. 1 (Summer 2008), pp. 139–169

cally grounded research on forecasting proliferation developments, and the underdeveloped state of theory on nonproliferation and nuclear decisionmaking more generally. Also contributing to this knowledge deficit is the stunted development of social science research on foreign policy–oriented forecasting and the emphasis on post hoc explanations, rather than predictions on the part of the more sophisticated frameworks and models of nuclear decisionmaking.

Two important exceptions to this general paucity of nonproliferation theory with predictive value are recent books by Jacques Hymans, *The Psychology of Nuclear Proliferation: Identity, Emotions, and Foreign Policy*, and Etel Solingen, *Nuclear Logics: Alternative Paths in East Asia and the Middle East*.[3] These studies merit careful attention because of their solid grounding in comparative field research and social science theory, their challenges to prevailing conceptions about the sources of nuclear weapons decisions, and their promise for predicting proliferation developments. As such, they go well beyond the influential but historically oriented explanatory frameworks developed by scholars such as Peter Lavoy, Ariel Levite, T.V. Paul, Scott Sagan, and James Walsh.[4] Although the approaches advanced by Hymans and Solingen have their own limitations, these two books represent the cutting edge of nonproliferation research and should be of great interest to both policy practitioners and scholars. In particular, a careful review of their studies sheds new insights into why past predictions of rapid proliferation have proved faulty, why the current alarm over impending proliferation doom is largely without merit, and why we should not count on single theories of international relations—at least in their

---

to empiricism and theory in exploring proliferation determinants. See Sonali Singh and Christopher R. Way, "The Correlates of Nuclear Proliferation," *Journal of Conflict Resolution*, Vol. 48, No. 6 (December 2004), pp. 859–885; Christopher R. Way and Karthika Sasikumar, "Leaders and Laggards: When and Why Do Countries Sign the NPT?" REGIS Working Paper, No. 16 (Montreal: University of Montreal/McGill University, November 2004), presented at the annual meeting of the American Political Science Association, Washington, D.C., September 1–4, 2005; and Dong-Joon Jo and Erik Gartzke, "Determinants of Nuclear Weapons Proliferation," *Journal of Conflict Resolution*, Vol. 51, No. 1 (February 2007), pp. 167–194.

3. Jacques E.C. Hymans, *The Psychology of Nuclear Proliferation: Identity, Emotions, and Foreign Policy* (New York: Cambridge University Press, 2006); and Etel Solingen, *Nuclear Logics: Alternative Paths in East Asia and the Middle East* (Princeton, N.J.: Princeton University Press, 2007). Further references to these volumes appear parenthetically in the text.

4. See, for example, Peter R. Lavoy, "Nuclear Myths and the Causes of Nuclear Proliferation," in Zachary S. Davis and Benjamin Frankel, eds., *The Proliferation Puzzle: Why Nuclear Weapons Spread and What Results* (London: Frank Cass, 1993), pp. 192–212; Ariel E. Levite, "Never Say Never Again: Nuclear Reversal Revisited," *International Security*, Vol. 27, No. 3 (Winter 2002/03), pp. 59–88; T.V. Paul, *Power versus Prudence: Why Nations Forgo Nuclear Weapons* (Montreal: McGill-Queen's University Press, 2000); Scott D. Sagan, "Why Do States Build Nuclear Weapons? Three Models in Search of a Bomb," *International Security*, Vol. 21, No. 3 (Winter 1996/97), pp. 54–86; and Walsh, "Bombs Unbuilt."

current state—to offer much guidance in explaining or predicting the dynamics of nuclear weapons spread.

This review essay begins with an analysis of the basic premises and overarching theses of Hymans and Solingen, and illustrates their approaches with references to several specific cases of nuclear decisionmaking. We then compare their works in terms of methodology, theoretical orientation, and insights about the process by which nuclear decisions are taken and the possibility for altering their outcomes. Special attention is given to those areas in which Hymans and Solingen depart significantly from prevailing assumptions in the international relations literature about the sources of nuclear proliferation decisions and the implications of these departures for divining nuclear weapons intentions. This discussion entails an assessment of the relative strengths and limitations of major schools of international relations theory as they pertain to nuclear renunciation and proliferation choices.

We next provide an overview and analysis of illustrative, past proliferation predictions by both government and academic analysts, and the assumptions underlying these estimates. Various reasons for past forecasting failures are identified, including a fixation on capabilities and security drivers, inattention to the domestic context in which nuclear decisions are made, disinterest in hypothesis testing or comparative analyses, and reliance on faulty analogies such as nuclear proliferation dominoes and chains. The theory-driven comparative case studies employed by Hymans and Solingen, we argue, provide a useful corrective to these traditional tendencies and help explain why one state's nuclear weapons preference is unlikely to be highly contingent on what other states decide.

Finally, we consider the policy implications of Hymans's and Solingen's work with respect to forecasting proliferation developments. In particular, we suggest how policy practitioners might exploit the authors' methods and insights to explain the sources of nuclear proliferation and improve predictions about states' nuclear ambitions.

The Role of Individuals and Ruling Coalitions

Hymans and Solingen join a long list of international relations scholars who have sought to probe the "proliferation puzzle" about why some states choose to acquire nuclear weapons, why a subset of these states reverse course and abandon their pursuit, and why others never initiate the quest.[5] They are not

---

5. As Tanya Ogilvie-White points out, the word "puzzle" has been used to connote a variety of

the first analysts to explore the discrepancy between the popular foreboding of a "nuclear-armed crowd" and the reality of an international arena largely devoid of nuclear weapons possessors.[6] More than most, however, they offer compelling and original explanations for the enormous gap between states' technical potential and actual weapons acquisition, and, more important, when and where one may expect weapons pursuit and restraint.

OPPOSITIONAL NATIONALISTS' LOOK INTO THE ABYSS
The more extreme position of the two authors is staked out by Hymans, for whom the real proliferation puzzle is not why there are so few nuclear weapons possessors, but why there are any at all (p. 8). Hymans finds the major international relations paradigms—realism, institutionalism, and constructivism—of limited utility in explaining the slow pace of proliferation and those rare instances of its occurrence. The answer to the puzzle, he believes, has to do primarily with the lack of motivation on the part of nearly all state leaders. Put simply, he argues, nonproliferation restraint stems less from external efforts to stop states from going nuclear, and more from "the hearts of state leaders themselves" (p. 7). Contrary to conventional wisdom, he maintains, few national political figures have either the desire or certitude to go nuclear (p. 8). According to Hymans, although the nonproliferation regime may have many virtues, the appearance of its success in containing proliferation results mainly from the fact "that few state leaders have desired the things it prohibits" (ibid.). A major determinant of this reticence to pursue nuclear weapons, Hymans explains, is the revolutionary nature of a decision to acquire them, which is recognized as such by all top decisionmakers. Only leaders who possess a deep-seated "national identity conception" (NIC) of a particular type will acutely perceive the need for the bomb and have the exceptional willpower to take that extraordinary step (p. 12).

Leaders who see their nations in starkly "us against them" terms are labeled "oppositional," in contrast to those "sportsmanlike" leaders who see the world in a less dichotomous light. Leaders who regard their nations as equal or superior to the external "other" are referred to as "nationalists," while those who

---

proliferation issues, involving both causes and effects. Ogilvie-White, "Is There a Theory of Nuclear Proliferation? An Analysis of the Contemporary Debate," *Nonproliferation Review*, Vol. 4, No. 1 (Fall 1996), p. 43. See also Davis and Frankel, *The Proliferation Puzzle*; and Walsh, "Bombs Unbuilt." We focus on the causes.
6. The phrase was coined by Albert Wohlstetter in *Moving toward Life in a Nuclear Armed Crowd? Final Report to the U.S. Arms Control and Disarmament Agency* (Los Angeles, Calif.: Pan Heuristics, 1976).

have a lower regard for their nations' international standing are known as "subalterns." This matrix yields four ideal-type NICs: sportsmanlike nationalists, sportsmanlike subalterns, oppositional nationalists, and oppositional subalterns. The requisite NIC profile for a weapons proliferator, according to Hymans, is an "oppositional nationalist" who combines intense enmity toward an external rival and intense pride in his/her own state's ability to challenge the external foe. Oppositional nationalism, he argues, thrives on the explosive mixture of fear and pride, emotions that link national identities with foreign policy choices. It is an emotional cocktail in which fear inflates perceived threats and pride inspires confidence in the ability to achieve amazing feats if a nation exerts itself—a view reminiscent of Ali Bhutto's famous pledge that Pakistan would acquire nuclear weapons even if its people had to eat grass.

For oppositional nationalist leaders, "the decision to acquire nuclear weapons is not only a means to the end of getting them; it is also an end in itself, a matter of self-expression" (p. 13). As a consequence, Hymans posits, decisions to go nuclear are likely to be made hastily and without considerable vetting or input from others. Stripped to its essence, the book's argument is twofold, although, as we discuss below, only the first proposition is thoroughly explored: (1) only oppositional nationalists push for the bomb; and (2) oppositional nationalist leaders are rare. Three other types of leaders are expected to show varying degrees of interest in security guarantees, nuclear weapons, and nuclear technology, but not go for the bomb itself.

Unlike most analysts who probe the causes of nuclear proliferation, Hymans proposes a method to test his theory empirically. It involves the use of content analysis of leaders' major speeches to determine their NIC profiles. These profiles are then compared to nuclear decisionmaking behavior in four countries with very different geographic locations, political systems, and nuclear status. Two of those countries—France and India—opted for the bomb, whereas Argentina and Australia decided against it.

Australia is an interesting test case for Hymans's theory as it periodically contemplated the idea of an independent nuclear deterrent but ultimately chose not to pursue one. Both the degree of interest in nuclear weapons and the decision to renounce a nuclear option, Hymans postulates, were largely unrelated to changes in the perceived external security environment or the state of the international nonproliferation regime. Rather, he argues, Australia's nuclear posture must be understood in terms of the NICs of different prime ministers. Consistent with this thesis, he finds that the only time Australia actively sought to acquire an independent nuclear capability was when it was led by John Gorton (1968–71), the one Australian prime minister between 1949 and 1975 to fit the oppositional nationalist NIC profile. According to Hymans, Gorton believed that Australia was both entitled to and capable of developing a nuclear deterrent. He therefore insisted that Australia remain outside the Nuclear Nonproliferation Treaty (NPT) while seeking to develop indigenous uranium enrichment and plutonium reprocessing capabilities (pp. 126–129).

Significantly, Gorton's nuclear orientation was not based on the perception of a more hostile international security environment than those of his predecessors. Indeed, if anything, Prime Minister Robert Menzies (1949–66) viewed the world in more threatening terms, especially following the Chinese nuclear test in 1964. Unlike Gorton, however, Menzies' NIC profile was that of an oppositional subaltern who was far more inclined to seek protection through assurances from "great and powerful friends" in the West than through an independent nuclear deterrent (pp. 115–117).

According to Hymans, Gorton's efforts to launch a nuclear weapons program ultimately were stymied by his shaky hold on power and bureaucratic opposition from the Atomic Energy Commission (pp. 130–133). When Gorton's government fell and he was replaced by Gough Whitlam—a sportsmanlike subaltern—Australia predictably (from Hymans's perspective) soon adopted a new nuclear posture, renounced nuclear weapons, and ratified the NPT.

"IT'S THE ECONOMY, STUPID": THE POLITICS OF REGIME SURVIVAL

Solingen, like Hymans, challenges conventional wisdom about why states acquire or renounce nuclear weapons. In nine in-depth case studies, she discerns that nuclear weapons programs are driven more by concerns about regime survival than by state insecurity. Although she also focuses on subnational dynamics to understand the nuclear outcomes, the crucial explanatory variable for her is the domestic political survival model preferred by the ruling coalition. Solingen distinguishes between outward-looking regimes that derive domestic legitimacy from ensuring economic growth through global integration and inward-oriented ones that employ import-substituting models favoring extreme nationalism and autarky. Different orientations toward the global political economy and its associated economic, political, and security institutions, she argues, have direct implications for the nuclear choices that are taken.[7]

---

7. The thesis in *Nuclear Logics* is an extension and refinement of the argument advanced in Solingen, "The Political Economy of Nuclear Restraint," *International Security,* Vol. 19, No. 2 (Fall 1994), pp. 126–169.

On the one hand, for example, nuclear weapons programs are seen as less likely to emerge when the domestic political landscape is sympathetic to economic openness, trade liberalization, foreign investment, and international economic integration. Alternatively, dominant political coalitions dependent on inward-looking bases of support and hostility to integration into the global political economy are more likely to pursue nuclear weapons programs. Two important implications follow from this thesis: (1) policies toward nuclear weapons acquisition or forbearance within states may be relatively immune to changes in the external security environment; and (2) nuclear policies within states may vary significantly over time as domestic economic and political conditions change even when the external security landscape remains relatively constant.

To test her model, Solingen conducts a series of comparative case studies across two regions that have taken divergent nuclear paths.[8] Her analyses, unlike those of Hymans, do not employ quantitative measures of any variables, but are structured in nature and comparative in orientation. They also are remarkable for the systematic manner in which they provide an assessment of each country's nuclear choices in terms of alternative "nuclear logics": neorealism, neoliberal institutionalism, constructivism, democratic peace, and domestic politics.

Perhaps the most startling findings pertain to Japan, whose nuclear renunciation decision Solingen carefully analyzes through the prisms of competing paradigms. Contrary to conventional wisdom, she challenges the notion that Japan's nuclear restraint can be explained primarily in terms of the U.S. nuclear umbrella or due to a persistent "nuclear allergy." She also finds that NPT considerations played a marginal role in Japan's decision to remain nonnuclear. Far more important than security and regime factors, Solingen argues, were domestic political considerations related to Japan's place in the global political economy.

According to Solingen, a major problem with security/structural power-based explanations of Japan's nuclear posture is their indeterminate nature. In other words, the same factors can be cited to explain Japan's pursuit and renunciation of nuclear weapons (p. 63). In fact, her study finds neither evidence of significant U.S. coercion of Japan to remain nonnuclear nor a strong demand on the part of the Japanese public for nuclear weapons.

Solingen's analysis also finds the absence of a close correspondence between

---

8. Solingen's case studies are Egypt, Iran, Iraq, Israel, Japan, Libya, North Korea, South Korea, and Taiwan.

the ebb and flow of a "nuclear taboo" among the Japanese populace and the nonproliferation policies pursued by Tokyo over time. What was decisive in determining Japan's nonnuclear status, she argues, was the adoption of the "Yoshida model" of development that required "a strong economic infrastructure, manufacturing capabilities . . . and swimming with (not against) the great tide of market forces" (p. 70). From this perspective, Japan's Liberal Democratic Party's hold on power was contingent on securing Japan's place in the global economy, an objective incompatible with the pursuit of nuclear weapons. As such, the decision to renounce nuclear weapons preceded the negotiation of the NPT.

The Two Models: Exploring Differences and Similarities

The books by Hymans and Solingen share a number of important features, including rejection of conventional wisdom regarding the sources of nuclear proliferation and a common focus on subsystemic determinants of state nuclear weapons policies. They also display a combination of theoretical sophistication, methodological rigor, focused comparative analysis involving original field research, and attention to hypothesis testing rarely found in the nonproliferation literature.[9] In addition, both books are distinguished by their authors' efforts to explore the policy implications of their findings, some of which converge rather closely, including skepticism about the impact of the NPT in stemming nuclear weapons spread. Despite these significant similarities, the books diverge in important respects. These pertain to the precise research questions under review, the methodology and level of analysis employed, the time frame under study, the generalizability of the findings, the authors' comfort level with multicausality, and their optimism with respect to the future pace and scope of proliferation.

Both Hymans and Solingen address the general question of why nations decide to proliferate or exercise proliferation restraint. A careful reading of their books, however, suggests a significant difference in focus regarding the principal outcome variable under consideration. For Hymans, the primary focus is both precise and narrow—it is the leader's "yes-no" decision to go nuclear. What, he seeks to determine, drives some state leaders to desire the bomb and launch a nuclear weapons program? Although Hymans sometimes departs from this fixation on an individual decision to explore the broader issue of

---

9. The only comparable work on the same theme is the Ph.D. dissertation by James J. Walsh, "Bombs Unbuilt," which unfortunately has never been published and is not widely cited.

why states obtain nuclear weapons, the state's capacity to move from the leader's decision to initiate a weapons program to its implementation and conclusion is a secondary consideration (pp. 44–46).

In contrast, the nuclear puzzle for Solingen is one of process and product. She is less precise than Hymans in specifying the primary dependent (outcome) variable, but it is apparent from her introduction and subsequent analysis that she is interested in understanding both why some states proliferate yet others do not, and how the preferences of political elites are translated into national policy. Her usage of the terms "nuclearization" to connote movement toward nuclear weapons acquisition and "denuclearization" to mean nuclear weapons renunciation, however, is not always consistent and, on occasion, can be confusing (p. 301). For example, when she speaks of the evolution of the Middle East "toward nuclearization," it implies a degree of nuclear weapons acquisition that does not correspond to reality (p. 27). Similarly, a discussion of the role of security guarantees in nuclear renunciation decisions is not advanced by lumping together as "denuclearized" such states as Egypt (which once sought nuclear weapons), South Africa (which once assembled nuclear weapons), Argentina (which, at a minimum, had acquired many of the requisites for a nuclear weapons program), and Jordan (whose nuclear program consists of uranium ore reserves) (p. 27). More generally, one may question the utility of her terminology for distinguishing between a country's latent nuclear weapons capability and its intentions.

THE NATURE OF NUCLEAR DECISIONS

In addition to asking somewhat different research questions, Hymans and Solingen also provide different answers to a common question: What is the nature of the decision to acquire nuclear weapons? To some extent, the divergence of views is a function of the alternative levels of analysis they employ: a focus by Hymans on individual leaders and by Solingen on political coalitions. More significant, however, is the differential importance they attribute to emotion and rationality. For Hymans, the choice of nuclear weapons is a revolutionary decision that is beyond "a reasonable cost-benefit calculation" (p. 10). Defined by the NIC in the leader's mind and driven by intense emotions of pride and fear, the decision is made in haste and without careful consideration of consequences. Hymans suggests, however, that less revolutionary nuclear decisions are more prone to cost-benefit analysis and less susceptible to the influence of emotion. These include decisions involving the pursuit of nuclear technology, membership in the NPT, and acquisition of security assurances. An important policy implication of the distinction Hymans draws between the sources of nuclear weapons decisions and those of ancillary programs is that a state's pursuit of sensitive fuel-cycle technology and nuclear "hedging" may not correspond to intent to acquire nuclear weapons.

In marked contrast to Hymans's emphasis on nonrational considerations for the "big" nuclear decision, Solingen argues that the decision to pursue nuclear weapons is in almost all instances the result of a careful, rational calculation that reflects the domestic survival interests of the ruling coalition.[10] In its emphasis on rational choice, Solingen's decisionmaking model resembles that of neoliberal institutionalism, except that for her the choice is for the benefit of the domestic regime rather than the state. It also is not dependent on the existence of an international nonproliferation regime. We offer a more in-depth discussion of how Solingen's and Hymans's models compare to neoliberal institutionalism and other leading paradigms in the next section.

The two authors also differ in their views of the stability or durability of choice regarding nuclear weapons. In Hymans's individual leader-centric world, which is not limited to a particular time period, the desire for the bomb is deeply entrenched in the identity conception of the leader and, as such, is unlikely to undergo change. In this respect, Muammar Qaddhafi's readiness to reverse course and abandon the Libyan nuclear weapons program he previously had initiated would appear to constitute an interesting challenge to Hymans's thesis, but it is not addressed. Although Hymans acknowledges that the leader's decision may founder in the implementation phase, he argues that even though "it may be hard to make a nuclear decision, . . . once that decision has been made, for both institutional and psychological reasons it is also hard—though not impossible—to unmake it" (p. 45).

The situation is more dynamic in Solingen's model, in which nuclear decisions are based on ongoing cost-benefit calculations by the ruling coalition. Her model, which she suggests may not be applicable to nuclear decisions in pre-NPT "world time," implies the lack of "linear or irreversible trajectories . . . in either direction" (p. 285).[11] In other words, nuclear decisions may be reversed if circumstances change and cost-benefit considerations determine that the pursuit (or disavowal) of nuclear weapons no longer serves the ruling coalition's interests. Although not insensitive to the force of institutional con-

10. A possible exception to this rule, which is not explained in detail, is a situation in which the state (as opposed to the regime) faces an extreme threat to its survival.
11. In her book Solingen is careful to delimit the time frame under consideration to the post-1968 period. She discusses the concept of "world time" in "Nuclear Logics: Why Some Do and Others Don't (Proliferate): Implications for Proliferation Chains," paper presented at the Workshop on Forecasting Proliferation Developments, Washington, D.C., September 27, 2007.

straints on nuclear choice, Solingen's dynamic model highlights the potential for policy change even in a country such as Japan, often regarded as the bedrock of nuclear abstinence. An important factor bearing on the stability of policy, she suggests, is the regional environment—a dimension less central to Hymans's paradigm. A change in the predominance of a particular political-economic model in a region, Solingen argues, can influence the nuclear choices of other ruling coalitions in the same geographical area, a topic we return to in the section dealing with proliferation forecasting.

One of the great virtues of Hymans's writing is an approach that leaves little to the imagination. Where many authors might hedge their argument or hesitate to follow it to its logical conclusion, he unabashedly pushes it as far as possible. This tendency often serves him well, but on occasion leads him to discount the influence of plausible alternative explanations. Thus, although effective in challenging the explanatory power of unitary state actor models and those that focus exclusively on security drivers or status considerations, Hymans's preferred model would be bolstered if it allowed for and better explained the impact of the surrounding security and political environment on the emergence of oppositional nationalists.

Solingen tends to be more circumspect than Hymans in touting the departure of her theory from prior paradigms. She also is more comfortable with multicausal and multilevel explanations for nuclear decisions in which her approach provides another piece of a multidimensional puzzle. Indeed, a key contribution of her work is its success in bridging the gap between comparative politics' and international relations' treatments of nuclear proliferation.[12] As she candidly acknowledges, models of political survival are only ideal types and should be thought of as heuristic devices to better understand complex reality. As such, they offer a key to unlocking a country's nuclear logic, but are unlikely to fit precisely in all cases.[13] This caution in overestimating the effects of any single causal variable is admirable and facilitates her incorporation of insights from alternative theories as she probes past nuclear choices. The greater complexity of her model, however, also provides a major challenge in its application for predictive purposes.

---

12. We are grateful to Scott Sagan for highlighting this contribution. Sagan, personal correspondence with authors, October 8, 2007.
13. Solingen elaborated on this point in a short paper about her book's approach in which she writes, "Balance of power, norms, and institutions may be more relevant than political survival in some cases than in others." See Solingen, "Nuclear Logics: Why Some Do and Others Don't (Proliferate)," p. 7.

NEW INSIGHTS ON THE USUAL SUSPECTS

In addition to making an important contribution to the development of non-proliferation theory, the empirically grounded books by Hymans and Solingen provide many new and useful insights into specific cases of nuclear decision-making. Hymans's seamless mix of quantitative and qualitative analysis and his familiarity with primary sources in each of his four country studies enables him to convincingly advance a number of provocative arguments. In the French case study, he offers new evidence to challenge the view that decisions leading to the bomb were incremental, taken by a small number of secondary government officials under the principal administration of the Commissariat à l'Energie Atomique.[14] His focus on the oppositional nationalist NICs of John Gorton and Atal Bihari Vajpayee and their determined pursuit of nuclear weapons for Australia and India also nicely supplements and modifies the pioneering work on the nuclear choices of the "land down under" and the "smiling Buddha" previously undertaken by James Walsh and George Perkovich, respectively.[15]

Hymans's treatment of Indian decisionmaking is provocative and centers to a large extent on the nature of India's 1974 "peaceful nuclear explosion" (PNE) and its near test of 1995. Hymans argues that although India possessed the capability to go nuclear for decades, it took the decision of Vajpayee, an oppositional nationalist leader, to finally cross that threshold. The 1974 PNE, Hymans maintains, was exactly that—a peaceful demonstration by the sportsmanlike nationalist Indira Gandhi that India could master the most complex technology but did not want nuclear weapons (pp. 183–188). Even if one accepts that problematic interpretation, one is hard pressed to employ Hymans's theory to account for the readiness of the Congress Party, led by a sportsmanlike nationalist, to conduct a nuclear test in 1995. According to a number of leading analysts, Prime Minister Narasimha Rao decided to abandon the planned test after the United States became aware of it and informed him that economic sanctions would have to be imposed on India in accordance with U.S. legislation—a decision process more closely in line with Solingen's thesis.[16] Hymans acknowledges the challenge to his theory posed by the 1995

---

14. This view is most closely associated with Lawrence Scheinman, *Atomic Energy Policy in France under the Fourth Republic* (Princeton, N.J.: Princeton University Press, 1965).

15. See Walsh, "Bombs Unbuilt"; Jim Walsh, "Surprise Down Under: The Secret History of Australia's Nuclear Ambitions," *Nonproliferation Review*, Vol. 5, No. 1 (Fall 1997), pp. 1–20; and George Perkovich, *India's Nuclear Bomb: The Impact on Global Proliferation* (Berkeley: University of California Press, 1999).

16. Perkovich, *India's Nuclear Bomb*, p. 370; Sumit Ganguly, "India's Pathway to Pokhran II: The Prospects and Sources of New Delhi's Nuclear Weapons Program," *International Security*, Vol. 23,

case, but contends that Prime Minister Rao decided against going nuclear before the United States found out about such plans (pp. 193–195). Finally, Hymans completely discounts the role of prominent nuclear scientists who consistently tried to pressure Rao and the subsequent United Front government into conducting the test.[17]

Hymans's most original and controversial interpretation, and the one with the greatest potential policy implications, concerns Argentina. Rejecting conventional wisdom about a failed but dedicated quest by Argentina to acquire nuclear weapons, he presents evidence that Argentina's behavior—though at times consistent with the pursuit of nuclear weapons—in fact was never motivated by nuclear weapons ambitions. In addition, he suggests that the more the United States pushed Argentina to adopt explicit nonproliferation commitments, the more Argentina pushed back, even embracing economically irrational policies, but ones not driven by nuclear weapons ambitions (pp. 141–170). If correct, and we are not in a position to evaluate all of his evidence, Hymans may have proved the danger of automatically attributing nuclear weapons intentions to states that eschew the NPT, embark on economically dubious nuclear energy projects that have dual civilian-military applications, and strongly resist international efforts by nuclear weapons states to modify their behavior.

As noted earlier, Solingen bases her thesis on the comparison of different nuclear paths taken by two regions traditionally on the list of prime proliferation suspects. Although all of her nine case studies are of high quality, they do not always devote adequate attention to alternative "nuclear logics," and, on occasion, the evidence that is presented appears at odds with the conclusions that are drawn. Solingen's case study of Israel is most bothersome in this regard and does not represent a convincing illustration of the power of the domestic political survival model. For example, her detailed account of the bureaucratic battles and changes among the ruling Israeli parties does not persuasively demonstrate the linkage between these actors' preferred economic models and their stance regarding nuclear weapons. In fact, the evidence Solingen presents tends to support both a neorealist argument that nuclear weapons were pursued for security reasons and the institutionalist argument that it was not in Israel's rational interest to join an international treaty that

---

No. 4 (Spring 1999), p. 168; and Neil Joeck, personal communication with authors, February 15, 2008. Perkovich makes a less definitive conclusion about Rao's rationale, writing that while the prime minister "was willing in principal to authorize tests, he had not made up his mind that they were in India's interest." Perkovich, *India's Nuclear Bomb*, p. 370.
17. See Perkovich, *India's Nuclear Bomb*, pp. 353–377.

could not significantly ease its legitimate concerns about threats from regional adversaries.[18]

One may also question if Solingen's exceptionally fine examination of Japan's nuclear decisionmaking is as supportive of her preferred domestic politics model as she purports. Although her chapter on Japan is the strongest in the book in terms of thoroughly applying alternative approaches to divine nuclear intentions, it is not necessarily the best example of the power of her domestic survival thesis. As she herself observes, Japan's nuclear restraint was overdetermined by a variety of factors and can be, at least in part, explained by each of the leading theories (p. 80).

International Relations Theory and the Sources of Nuclear Proliferation

Having discussed the arguments and cases presented by Hymans and Solingen, we now examine more closely how their premises regarding nuclear predilections build on and depart from those of leading international relations theories. Here, we are mainly interested in contrasting their relative explanatory and predictive powers with the approaches favored by Hymans and Solingen.[19] For purposes of this comparative assessment, we focus primarily on theories often referred to as neorealism, neoliberal institutionalism, and constructivism.[20]

One of the major problems in distilling useful, future-oriented information from the enormous body of literature on nuclear proliferation that has been produced during the past half century is the extent to which it is largely speculative and contradictory in its insights. Contributing to this Rashomon effect is a lack of agreement about what constitutes nuclear proliferation, the appropriate level of analysis for study, the importance to be attached to a multitude of

18. Solingen, *Nuclear Logics*, p. 194, makes the argument that Israel had reason to doubt the impartiality of the International Atomic Energy Agency and to mistrust international institutions dominated by states opposed to it.

19. Important prior critiques include Ogilvie-White, "Is There a Theory of Nuclear Proliferation?"; Sagan, "Why Do States Build Nuclear Weapons?"; and Jacques E.C. Hymans, "Theories of Nuclear Proliferation: The State of the Field," *Nonproliferation Review*, Vol. 13, No. 3 (November 2006), pp. 455–465. Solingen's book under review also provides a thorough critique of many international relations theories.

20. Although one could legitimately identify a larger set of influential paradigms, including many variations of neorealism, their inclusion in the comparative assessment would not significantly alter our conclusions. We have not sought to include a number of important conceptual frameworks such as those advanced by Sagan and Lavoy, which in some respects more closely resemble the orientation of Hymans and Solingen but lack predictive power.

plausible proliferation determinants, and how best to penetrate the veil of secrecy surrounding nuclear decisions.[21]

NEOREALISM

Much of the thinking about nuclear proliferation has been informed by realist perspectives, which assume that states are unitary actors that seek nuclear weapons because their security—precarious in an anarchic world—demands it. From a classical realist perspective, the quest for nuclear weapons is a rational form of self-help designed to maximize power.[22] Neorealism embraces the same basic assumptions as classical realism, but it is more attentive to the impact of structural differences in the international system on the occurrence of war and peace.[23] Applied to the proliferation arena, neorealism offers an elegant and simple explanation for why and when nations would go nuclear. In its view, regime type, domestic politics, and personalities are of no consequence, and all that really matters is an understanding of the balancing dynamic in which one state's pursuit of nuclear weapons begets another.[24] Employing this logic, John Mearsheimer, Stephen Van Evera, and Benjamin Frankel, among others, thought it likely that the decline of bipolarity after the end of the Cold War would generate a new spate of proliferators, including countries such as Germany, Japan, and Ukraine.[25] Taken to its logical conclusion, unadulterated neorealism predicts a lengthy nuclear proliferation chain that extends to as many states as have access to technical know-how and material to build nuclear weapons.

One is hard pressed to find commonalities in the assumptions underlying

---

21. For a review of the early literature on proliferation determinants, see William C. Potter, *Nuclear Power and Nonproliferation: An Interdisciplinary Perspective* (Cambridge, Mass.: Oelgeschlager, Gunn, and Hain, 1982), pp. 131–196.

22. Elegant in its simplicity, classical realism affords a powerful means to circumvent the problem of nuclear secrecy and the need to collect difficult-to-obtain data through in-country research. For its most influential exponent, see Hans J. Morgenthau, *Politics among Nations: The Struggle for Power and Peace* (New York: Alfred A. Knopf, 1948).

23. The seminal work in neorealism is by Kenneth N. Waltz, *Theory of International Politics* (New York: Random House, 1979).

24. In his penetrating critique of neorealist models, Sagan depicts the alleged process as follows: "Every time one state develops nuclear weapons to balance against its main rival, it also creates a nuclear threat to another state in the region, which then has to initiate its own nuclear weapons program to maintain its national security." Sagan, "Why Do States Build Nuclear Weapons?" p. 58.

25. See, for example, John J. Mearsheimer, "Back to the Future: Instability in Europe after the Cold War," *International Security*, Vol. 15, No. 1 (Summer 1990), pp. 5–56; John J. Mearsheimer, "The Case for a Ukrainian Nuclear Deterrent," *Foreign Affairs*, Vol. 72, No. 3 (Summer 1993), pp. 50–66; Stephen Van Evera, "Primed for Peace: Europe after the Cold War," *International Security*, Vol. 15, No. 3 (Winter 1990/91), pp. 7–57; and Benjamin Frankel, "The Brooding Shadow: Systemic Incentives and Nuclear Weapons Proliferation," in Davis and Frankel, *The Proliferation Puzzle*, pp. 37–78.

neorealism (or any variant of realism) and those advanced by Hymans.[26] Although he probably appreciates the clarity and parsimony of realist theory, which in some ways resembles his own razor-sharp and unambiguous formulations, Hymans rejects out of hand the realist fixation on systemic explanations of nuclear weapons behavior. His research on the nuclear policies of Argentina, Australia, France, and India finds that structural analyses favored by neorealists are unable to explain why, when, and how these four countries adopted their nuclear postures. In stark contrast to neorealist assumptions about the inconsequential nature of subsystemic factors in divining state nuclear behavior, for Hymans, one cannot begin to explain or anticipate proliferation outcomes without reference to national leaders and the correct identification of their national identity conceptions. Hymans acknowledges that three of the leaders in the four countries under review in his book—Pierre Mendès-France of France, John Gorton of Australia, and Atal Bihari Vajpayee of India—did regard nuclear weapons as useful for purposes of deterrence. He rejects the thesis, however, that nations are predisposed to pursue nuclear weapons for that purpose given that his case studies yield a variety of national leaders who rejected this outlook despite facing similar external threats.

Solingen also is skeptical of the explanatory and predictive power of neorealism. Like Hymans, she identifies numerous occasions in which neorealist premises fail to account for nuclear behavior. Looking at nine East Asian and Middle Eastern countries, Solingen finds too many "dogs that didn't bark"— or states that faced acute security vulnerabilities but refrained from acquiring nuclear weapons. These include Egypt, Japan, South Korea, and Taiwan. Moreover, even if one invokes the role of alliances to explain these anomalies, as do some offshoots of realism, she finds little empirical support for the premise.[27] "U.S. and Soviet commitments to client states (North Korea, Iraq, Israel, and Pakistan) did not lead these states to renounce nuclear weapons," she observes (p. 25).[28] "Nor did the absence of security guarantees play any role in the decisions by Egypt (1971), Libya, South Africa, Argentina, or Brazil to reverse nuclear ambitions" (p. 25). In addition, Solingen finds neorealism to be conceptually deficient in both its underspecification of key variables such as

---

26. One possible exception is the focus of neoclassical realism on state capacity and a similar emphasis by Hymans on state structure and managerial capacity in his more recent unpublished work.

27. T.V. Paul, an exponent of "prudential realism," argues that superpower security guarantees are the key explanation for why typical realist forecasts of proliferation failed to materialize.

28. Her inclusion of Israel in this category is questionable, as Israel did not possess security guarantees from the United States or any other nuclear weapons state when it decided to pursue an independent nuclear weapons program.

balancing, which impedes hypothesis testing, and its overestimation of the influence of state security on nuclear decisions to the neglect of regime security—the centerpiece of her preferred model of domestic political survival.[29]

NEOLIBERAL INSTITUTIONALISM

Neoliberal institutionalism—an alternative paradigm to neorealism—shares many basic neorealist assumptions about the pursuit by state actors of rational self-interest in an anarchic international system. Neoliberal institutionalists, however, ascribe a much greater role to economics and are far more optimistic about the possibilities for mitigating security dilemmas and accomplishing long-term cooperation among states.[30] The key to achieving cooperative outcomes, they argue, is the creation of international institutions that facilitate information sharing about others' capabilities and intentions, mediate conflict, and monitor (and on occasion even enforce) regime compliance.[31] By extension, a neoliberal institutionalist might be expected to argue that countries join nonproliferation institutions to address immediate and projected security concerns or to derive economic benefits such as access to peaceful nuclear energy. Although intuitively plausible, in practice, this proposition tends to be more implied than rigorously tested, and relatively few studies have sought to demonstrate the influence of nonproliferation institutions on nuclear weapons restraint.[32]

---

29. Neoclassical realism seeks to compensate for this shortcoming by employing both systemic-level and national (unit)-level analysis. For neoclassical realists, state actions are defined not only by the structure of the international system and the state's relative position in it, but also by its capacity to extract resources and support from within the state—so-called state power. Although neoclassical realism has yet to be applied to nonproliferation, the approach has the potential to help explain different nuclear outcomes in countries facing similar security threats. Natasha Bajema is conducting dissertation research on the subject at the Fletcher School of Law and Diplomacy at Tufts University. For a useful introduction to neoclassical realism, see Gideon Rose, "Neoclassical Realism and Theories of Foreign Policy," *World Politics,* Vol. 51, No. 1 (October 1998), pp. 144–172. A more recent treatment is provided by Jeffrey W. Taliaferro, "State Building for Future Wars: Neoclassical Realism and the Resource-Extractive State," *Security Studies,* Vol. 15, No. 3 (July–September 2006), pp. 464–495.

30. Robert O. Keohane, *After Hegemony: Cooperation and Discord in the World Political Economy* (Princeton, N.J.: Princeton University Press, 1984); and Robert Axelrod and Robert O. Keohane, "Achieving Cooperation under Anarchy: Strategies and Institutions," *World Politics,* Vol. 38, No. 1 (October 1985), pp. 226–254.

31. See, for example, Peter Alexis Gourevitch, "The Governance Problem in International Relations," in David A. Lake and Robert Powell, eds., *Strategic Choice and International Relations* (Princeton, N.J.: Princeton University Press, 1999), pp. 137–164; and John Gerard Ruggie, *Constructing the World Polity: Essays on International Institutionalization* (New York: Routledge, 1998).

32. Some support for the thesis is provided by Mitchell Reiss, who is not a self-described neoliberal institutionalist. See, for example, Reiss, *Without the Bomb: The Politics of Nuclear*

Hymans is not altogether unsympathetic to the argument made most forcefully by institutionalists that the nonproliferation regime has played a useful role in dampening proliferation tendencies. He is skeptical, however, of the assumption that the regime has caused states that otherwise would have acquired nuclear weapons to abandon their pursuit. Among the counterarguments he mounts is that were the regime to have played this significant role, one might have expected rampant proliferation prior to its emergence in the mid-1970s as a widely subscribed to international treaty. In fact, though, there was a large gap at this time between states that were capable of going nuclear and those that actually did so.[33]

In addition, Hymans believes that if the regime performed the key role attributed to it by neoliberal institutionalism, it should have created far more stable and durable expectations among states than he regards to be the case. Instead, as he points out, fears about the regime's stability and survival have been common throughout its existence, which undermines the argument that states refrained from going nuclear because of their reliance on the NPT and other states' compliance.[34] In this regard, Hymans appears to confuse the popular perspective of "the sky-is-falling" pundits with a minority view among NPT members that the nonproliferation regime is about to collapse.

Solingen's critique of neoliberal institutionalism parallels that of Hymans. Thus, although crediting the paradigm for focusing attention on the nonproliferation regime as a potentially powerful force for nuclear restraint, she remains unconvinced that it actually has played a more significant role in shaping states' nuclear decisions than have considerations of security, norms, or domestic politics. In most cases, she finds that decisions to remain nonnuclear were made prior to, rather than as a consequence of, the decision to ratify the NPT. This was the case, she argues, for Japan, South Korea, and Taiwan. In addition, the NPT did not prevent Iran, Iraq, Libya, and North Korea from pursuing nuclear weapons subsequent to their membership in the

---

Nonproliferation (New York: Columbia University Press, 1988); and Reiss, *Bridled Ambition: Why Countries Constrain Their Nuclear Capabilities* (Washington, D.C.: Woodrow Wilson Center Press, 1995). See also William C. Potter, "The Politics of Nuclear Renunciation: The Cases of Belarus, Kazakhstan, and Ukraine," Occasional Paper, No. 22 (Washington, D.C.: Henry L. Stimson Center, April 1995).

33. Hymans does not comment on why, according to his own chart (p. 4), the gap between nuclear-capable and nuclear-armed states increased sharply during the 1965–70 period, precisely when the NPT was negotiated, signed, and entered into force.

34. Questions about the NPT's survivability, for example, were raised as early as in the 1970s, both before and after the first NPT review conference. A particularly insightful analysis of the challenges facing the NPT during its first decade is provided by William Epstein, *The Last Chance: Nuclear Proliferation and Arms Control* (New York: Free Press, 1976), pp. 244–258.

nonproliferation regime. Among the nine countries she examines, only the nuclear behavior of Egypt and Israel (an NPT outlier) corresponds to institutionalist expectations, and even these states' nuclear choices, she contends, cannot be adequately explained without reference to domestic politics.

CONSTRUCTIVISM

Constructivist theory, which emphasizes the evolution and impact of international norms on state behavior, represents a further progression away from realist assumptions. Although accepting the existence of anarchy and the pivotal role of states in the international system, constructivists view anarchy in cultural rather than materialist terms. As its most influential exponent explains, "Anarchy is what states make of it."[35] As such, even "power politics" can be tempered by human practice.[36] Under appropriate conditions, adherents to constructivism maintain, institutions and norms may evolve that are hospitable to the emergence of normative prohibitions against nuclear weapons possession and use.[37] According to this perspective, for example, the international nonproliferation regime has its roots in the antinuclear sentiment that developed following the bombings of Hiroshima and Nagasaki.[38] Some constructivists also attach considerable importance to the role of subnational factors in shaping the institutionalization of the nuclear taboo, including the role of organizational actors and individual leaders, or "norm entrepreneurs."[39] By directing attention to considerations of social reality other than those of a purely materialistic nature, constructivists expand the range of explanations for nuclear weapons abstinence. Most important, they demonstrate the potential impact of the international social environment in depressing demand for nuclear weapons.[40] Typically, however, they provide little guidance about when and where to expect normative factors to prevail.

---

35. Alexander Wendt, "Anarchy Is What States Make of It: The Social Construction of Power Politics," *International Organization*, Vol. 46, No. 2 (Spring 1992), pp. 391–425; and Alexander Wendt, *Social Theory of International Politics* (Cambridge: Cambridge University Press, 1999).
36. Martha Finnemore and Kathryn Sikkink, "International Norm Dynamics and Political Change," *International Organization*, Vol. 52, No. 4 (Autumn 1998), pp. 887–917; Peter J. Katzenstein, ed., *The Culture of National Security: Norms and Identity in World Politics* (New York: Columbia University Press, 1996); and John Gerard Ruggie, "What Makes the World Hang Together? Neo-utilitarianism and the Social Constructivist Challenge," *International Organization*, Vol. 52, No. 4 (Autumn 1998), pp. 855–885.
37. See Katzenstein, *The Culture of National Security*.
38. Nina Tannenwald, "Stigmatizing the Bomb: Origins of the Nuclear Taboo," *International Security*, Vol. 29, No. 4 (Spring 2005), pp. 5–49.
39. Ibid., pp. 29–30; and Finnemore and Sikkink, "International Norm Dynamics and Political Change."
40. Rublee, "Persuasion, Social Conformity, and Identification."

Hymans does not devote much attention in his book to a direct refutation of constructivist precepts. This reticence is understandable, as his own theoretical focus on the causal power of ideas (including identities, perceptions, and emotions) is very much in the constructivist tradition, as is his concentration on the demand side for the bomb. Unlike most constructivist studies, however, Hymans's approach stresses neither the dampening effect on proliferation tendencies of broad trends in international norms nor the corresponding constraints that may follow from societal pressures. Rather, his is an individual-level approach that derives both its explanatory and predictive power by focusing attention on "deviant" oppositional nationalist leaders whose combination of fear and pride propel them down the nuclear weapons path. Those who wanted the bomb, such as Australia's Gorton and India's Vajpayee, he argues, "would not let nonproliferation norms stand in the way of their objective" (p. 215).

Although Solingen is respectful of the constructivist insight that institutions such as the NPT both reflect and influence the collective identities of its members, thereby altering member beliefs regarding the desirability of nuclear weapons, she finds little concrete evidence in her case studies that antinuclear weapons acquisition norms significantly influenced key nuclear renunciation or proliferation decisions. As discussed earlier, Solingen's conclusion is most striking with respect to Japan. Although acknowledging the presence of institutional and normative restraints, she is more impressed by Japan's "pragmatic pacifism."[41] She sees similar pragmatic rather than normative considerations at work in the nuclear forbearance displayed by South Korea and Taiwan, and finds little evidence that nonproliferation norms have taken root in any of the countries she reviews from the Middle East.

Solingen regards constructivist analysis of nuclear proliferation to be deficient in systematically examining how, why, and to what extent norms condemning nuclear weapons development have diffused internationally, and in accounting for the parallel emergence of competing norms that value nuclear weapons. Nevertheless, she believes that constructivist approaches, if applied with more methodological rigor, could help sort out the relative influence on states' nuclear behavior of socialization effects and those resulting from hegemonic coercion and rational nuclear learning (pp. 270–271).

---

41. Solingen, *Nuclear Logics*, p. 268, quotes Mike Mochizuki, "Japan's Drift Away from Pacific Policy," *Los Angeles Times*, September 22, 2006, on how "Japan's pacifism has always been pragmatic."

PREDICTING PROLIFERATION: BACK TO THE FUTURE

Today it is hard to find an analyst or commentator on nuclear proliferation who is not pessimistic about the future. It is nearly as difficult to find one who predicts the future without reference to metaphors such as proliferation chains, cascades, dominoes, waves, avalanches, and tipping points.[42] The lead author of this essay also has been guilty of the same tendency, and initially named an ongoing research project on forecasting proliferation he directs "21st Century Nuclear Proliferation Chains and Trigger Events." As both authors proceeded with research on the project, however, and particularly after reading the books by Hymans and Solingen, we became convinced that the metaphor is inappropriate and misleading, as it implies a process of nuclear decisionmaking and a pace of nuclear weapons spread that are unlikely to transpire.

The current alarm about life in a nuclear-armed crowd has many historical antecedents and can be found in classified National Intelligence Estimates (NIEs) as well as in scholarly analyses. The 1957 NIE, for example, identified a list of ten leading nuclear weapons candidates, including Canada, Japan, and Sweden.[43] Sweden, it predicted, was "likely to produce its first weapons in about 1961," while it was estimated that Japan would "probably seek to develop weapons production programs within the next decade."[44] In one of the

---

42. For works that speak of chains or chain-style dynamics, see, for example, Graham Allison, "A Cascade of Nuclear Proliferation," *International Herald Tribune,* December 17, 2004; Kofi Annan, "A More Secure World: The Future of the United Nations," speech delivered at the Munich Conference on Security Policy, Munich, Germany, February 13, 2005; Kurt M. Campbell, Robert J. Einhorn, and Mitchell B. Reiss, eds., *The Nuclear Tipping Point: Why States Reconsider Their Nuclear Choices* (Washington, D.C.: Brookings Institution Press, 2004); Ashton B. Carter, Gordon Oehler, Michael Anastasios, Robert Monroe, Keith B. Payne, Robert Pfaltzgraff, William Schneider, and William Van Cleave, "Report on Discouraging a Cascade of Nuclear Weapons States" (Washington, D.C.: International Security Advisory Board, U.S. Department of State, October 19, 2007); Joseph Cirincione, "Asian Nuclear Reaction Chain," *Foreign Policy,* No. 118 (Spring 2000), pp. 120–136; Patrick Clawson, "Nuclear Proliferation in the Middle East: Who Is Next after Iran?" in Henri D. Sokolski, ed., *Taming the Next Set of Strategic Weapons Threats* (Carlisle, Pa.: Strategic Studies Institute, U.S. Army War College, 2006), pp. 27–39; James Clay Moltz, "Future Nuclear Proliferation Scenarios in Northeast Asia," *Nonproliferation Review,* Vol. 13, No. 3 (November 2006), pp. 591–604; and George Tenet, quoted in Mitchell B. Reiss, "The Nuclear Tipping Point: Prospects for a World of Many Nuclear States," in Campbell, Einhorn and Reiss, *The Nuclear Tipping Point,* p. 4.
43. "Weapons Production in Fourth Countries: Likelihood and Consequences," National Intelligence Estimate, No. 100-6-57 (Washington, D.C.: National Security Archive, June 18, 1957).
44. Ibid., p. 1. Interestingly, the same NIE concluded that "the chances now appear at least even that Japan will undertake the initial steps in a nuclear weapons production program within five years," but that the Chinese communists will be reluctant to divert resources "urgently needed for basic economic development" and therefore "will develop a nuclear weapons program only gradually." Ibid., pp. 6–7.

most famous forecasts, President John Kennedy in 1963 expressed a nightmarish vision of a future world with fifteen, twenty, or twenty-five nuclear weapons powers.[45]

A number of the earliest scholarly projections of proliferation also tended to exaggerate the pace of nuclear weapons spread. A flurry of studies between 1958 and 1962, for example, focused on the "Nth Country Problem" and identified as many as twelve candidates capable of going nuclear in the near future.[46] Canada, West Germany, Italy, Japan, Sweden, and Switzerland were among the states most frequently picked as near-term proliferators.

The "peaceful nuclear explosion" by India in 1974 was seen by many analysts of the time as a body blow to the young NPT that would set in motion a new wave of proliferation. Although the anticipated domino effect did not transpire, the Indian test did precipitate a marked increase in scholarship on proliferation, including an innovative study developed around the concept—now in vogue—of proliferation chains. Rarely cited by today's experts, the 1976 monograph on *Trends in Nuclear Proliferation, 1975–1995*, by Lewis Dunn and Herman Kahn, set forth fifteen scenarios for nuclear weapons spread, each based on the assumption that one state's acquisition of nuclear weapons would prompt several other states to follow suit, which in turn would trigger a succession of additional nuclearization decisions.[47] Although lacking any single theoretical underpinning and accepting of the notion that proliferation decisions are likely to be attributed to security needs, the Dunn-Kahn model rejected the exclusive focus by realists on security drivers and sought to probe

---

45. See "Why the U.S. Keeps Talking," *Time*, March 29, 1963, http://www.time.com/time/magazine/article/0,9171,896717,00.html?iid?chix-sphere. Oddly, the NIE for the same year estimated that no more than "eight countries, in addition to France, had the physical and financial resources to develop an operational nuclear capability (weapons and means of delivery) over the next decade." See Directorate of Central Intelligence, "Likelihood and Consequences of a Proliferation of Nuclear Weapons Systems," National Intelligence Estimate, No. 4-63 (Washington D.C.: National Security Archive, June 28, 1963). The countries in question were Canada, China, India, Israel, Italy, Japan, Sweden, and West Germany.
46. See, for example, Howard Simons, "World-Wide Capabilities for Production and Control of Nuclear Weapons," *Daedalus*, Vol. 88, No. 3 (Summer 1959), pp. 385–409; Christopher Hohenemser, "The Nth Country Problem Today," in Seymour Melman, ed., *Disarmament: Its Politics and Economics* (Boston: American Academy of Arts and Sciences, 1962); and Oskar Morgenstern, "The Nth Country Problem," *Fortune*, March 1961, p. 136.
47. Lewis A. Dunn and Herman Kahn, *Trends in Nuclear Proliferation, 1975–1995*, Final Report to the U.S. Arms Control and Disarmament Agency (Washington, D.C.: Hudson Institute, May 15, 1976). The earliest usage of the proliferation chain metaphor of which we are aware is by Sir John Cockcroft, who in 1968 expressed concern about the "likelihood of a chain reaction in which the acquisition of nuclear weapons by one country would provoke other nations to follow suit." See Cockroft, "The Perils of Nuclear Proliferation," in Nigel Calder, ed., *Unless Peace Comes* (New York: Viking, 1968), p. 37, quoted in Walsh, "Bombs Unbuilt," p. 5.

beneath the rhetoric to identify the possible presence of other pressures and constraints.

To their credit, Dunn and Kahn got many things right and advanced the study of proliferation. Their forecasts, however, were almost without exception wildly off the mark. Why, one may inquire, were their pessimistic projections about nuclear weapons spread—and those of their past and subsequent counterparts in the intelligence community—so often divorced from reality? Although Hymans and Solingen appear not to have been familiar with the research by Dunn and Kahn on proliferation trends at the time of their books' publications, their national leadership and domestic political survival models offer considerable insight into that dimension of the proliferation puzzle.[48]

THE FOUR MYTHS OF NUCLEAR PROLIFERATION

Hymans is keenly aware of the deficiency of past proliferation projections, which he attributes in large part to the "tendency to use the growth of nuclear capabilities, stances toward the non-proliferation regime, and a general 'roguishness' of the state as proxies for nuclear weapons intentions" (p. 217). Such intentions, he believes, cannot be discerned without reference to leadership national identity conceptions, a focus that appears to have been absent to date in intelligence analyses devoted to forecasting proliferation.[49]

Hymans is equally critical of the popular notion that "the 'domino theory' of the twenty-first century may well be nuclear."[50] As he points out, the new domino theory, like its discredited Cold War predecessor, assumes an oversimplified view about why and how decisions to acquire nuclear weapons are taken.[51] Leaders' nuclear preferences, he maintains, "are not highly contingent on what other states decide," and, therefore, "proliferation tomorrow will probably remain as rare as proliferation today, with no single instance of proliferation causing a cascade of nuclear weapons states" (p. 225). In addition, he argues, the domino thesis embraces "an exceedingly dark picture of world trends by lumping the truly dangerous leaders together with the merely self-

---

48. Solingen does cite Lewis Dunn's 1982 book, *Controlling the Bomb* (New Haven, Conn.: Yale University Press), which includes a number of the earlier insights from Dunn and Kahn, *Trends in Nuclear Proliferation*.

49. The limited number of declassified NIEs precludes a more definitive statement on this point, but there is no evidence of their use in the nine NIEs we have examined for the years 1957, 1958, 1960, 1961, 1963, 1964, 1966, 1974, and 2007.

50. George Tenet, quoted in Hymans, *The Psychology of Nuclear Proliferation*, p. 208.

51. For a fascinating discussion of the use (and misuse) of metaphors (including dominoes) in foreign policy decisionmaking, see Yuen Foon Khong, *Analogies at War: Korea, Munich, Dien Bien Phu, and the Vietnam Decisions* (Princeton, N.J.: Princeton University Press, 1992).

assertive ones," and equating interest in nuclear technology with weapons intent (pp. 208–209). Dire proliferation forecasts, both past and present, Hymans believes, flow from four myths regarding nuclear decisonmaking: (1) states want the bomb as a deterrent; (2) states seek the bomb as a "ticket to international status"; (3) states go for the bomb because of the interests of domestic groups; and (4) the international regime protects the world from a flood of new nuclear weapons states (pp. 208–216). Each of these assumptions is faulty, Hymans contends, because of its fundamental neglect of the decisive role played by individual leaders in nuclear matters.

As discussed earlier, Hymans argues that the need for a nuclear deterrent is entirely in the eye of the beholder—a leader with an oppositional nationalist NIC. By the same token, just because some leaders seek to achieve international prestige through acquisition of the bomb, it does not mean that other leaders "necessarily view the bomb as the right ticket to punch": witness the case of several decades of Argentine leaders, as well as the Indian Nehruvians (pp. 211–212). The case of Egypt under Anwar al-Sadat, though not discussed by Hymans, also seems to fit this category.

Hymans's focus on the individual level of analysis leads him to discount bureaucratic political explanations for nuclear postures, as well. Central to his argument is the assumption that decisions to acquire nuclear weapons are taken "without the considerable vetting that political scientists typically assume precedes most important states choices" (p. 13). As such, although he is prepared to credit nuclear energy bureaucracies as playing a supporting role in the efforts by Australia, France, and India to go nuclear, he does not observe their influence to be a determining factor in root nuclear decisions by national leaders. Moreover, contrary to a central premise of Solingen's model of domestic political survival, Hymans finds little evidence in his case studies of leaders pursuing nuclear weapons to advance their political interests (p. 213). For example, he argues, the 1998 nuclear tests in India were as risky domestically for Vajpayee as they were internationally (p. 214).

Most provocatively, Hymans invokes an individual-centric mode of analysis to challenge the necessity and utility of a strong international nonproliferation regime. As discussed in a preceding section, he finds no evidence that the NPT regime prevented any of the leaders who desired nuclear weapons from pursuing them.

FOUR MYTHS: THE CAVEATS

As noted earlier, Hymans is more willing than many to state his argument in unambiguous terms and to pursue it as far as logically possible. Though admirable in illuminating his position, this intrepid approach also makes him more vulnerable to charges of overinterpreting ambiguous information, overlooking inconvenient alternative explanations, and overstating his conclusions. Although we are sympathetic to most of his myth-busting arguments, several caveats are in order.

First, Hymans is too quick to dismiss the possibility of multicausality. This tendency leads him to discount the potential influence of both systemic- and national-level determinants on the emergence of leaders with different NIC types. To what extent, for example, can one account for the rise or demise of oppositional nationalists due to the behavior (nuclear or otherwise) of other states? More generally, it would be useful for predictive purposes to know the frequency distribution of oppositional nationalists and other NIC types in different kinds of regimes and under different international conditions. Although Hymans acknowledges that "different cultures may be more or less congenial environments for the development of certain types of NICs," he provides no clues about which cultural or societal attributes are likely to be most conducive to the emergence of oppositional nationalists (p. 29). It is tempting, however, to draw on Solingen's findings about the differences in nuclear weapons proclivity in the Middle East and East Asia and to combine these findings with Hymans's national identity conception model to posit a link between a region's history, culture, and political-economic orientation and the emergence of leaders with particular NICs.

In addition, although Hymans implies that oppositional nationalists are a rarity among national leaders, it is unclear how uncommon they are relative to other NIC types. Knowledge of this information could be particularly valuable for forecasting purposes given Hymans's innovative attempt to link NIC type to a variety of nuclear policy preferences, including not only pursuit of nuclear weapons but support for the nonproliferation regime, efforts to achieve nuclear technology autonomy, and interest in superpower nuclear guarantees (p. 38, table 2.2).

A second caveat is Hymans's premature dismissal of the force of domestic political and bureaucratic factors as both pressures for, and constraints on, nuclear weapons choices. Although Hymans presents new information consistent with a minimalist interpretation of bureaucratic determinants in his examination of nuclear decisions by Mendès-France and Vajpayee, the evidence is much less conclusive in the Australian case, and appears to be at odds with conventional wisdom about nuclear decisionmaking in a number of other cases. Prime Minister Gorton, for example, may have decided early on that Australia should acquire nuclear weapons, but in fact was repeatedly frustrated in his pursuit of them by his cabinet. Hymans's depiction of Gorton's efforts "to sneak a nuclear weapons program into existence" past traditional opposition in the government and to try "mightily to jumpstart a nuclear weapons program while never daring to speak its name" fits poorly with a model in which the national leader is portrayed as exercising decisive or nearly undiluted power over nuclear weapons decisions (pp. 130, 133).

An additional cautionary note is in order regarding Hymans's portrayal of the limited effect of the international nonproliferation regime on nuclear weapons spread. One problem with his argument is that the case studies he undertakes are ill suited to test rigorously the proposition. France acquired nuclear weapons well before the negotiation of the most important element of the regime—the NPT; Gorton's flirtation with nuclear weapons also began prior to the entry into force of the treaty; and Indian leaders of almost every political stripe and national identity conception shared a profound antipathy for a treaty-based regime that treated India as a second-class citizen whether or not it possessed nuclear weapons. For Hymans (or Solingen) to demonstrate that the NPT and its associated nonproliferation regime elements play a minor role in forestalling nuclear weapons spread, he (she) must marshal evidence from a much broader set of countries in the post-NPT period.

DOMESTIC POLITICAL SURVIVAL IN A REGIONAL CONTEXT
Solingen, like Hymans, is wary of predicting rampant weapons spread and finds little evidence in her case studies to suggest the existence of a proliferation dynamic that resembles nuclear chains. Her guarded optimism about the near-term nuclear future follows logically from her decisionmaking paradigm, which emphasizes the manner in which the external environment is filtered through the lens of domestic political coalitions. These political groupings, it is assumed, typically will make rational choices based on their calculation of regime (rather than state) benefits. These decisions, moreover, are apt to vary significantly from state to state and regime to regime. As a consequence, one state's decision to withdraw from the NPT, launch a nuclear weapons program, and even test a nuclear device need not lead to a similar response in other states.

Solingen is more cautious than Hymans, however, in rejecting the possibility of proliferation chains per se, because of the importance she attaches to regional dynamics and nuclear neighborhoods. A widely subscribed to nonproliferation norm in the region may have a reinforcing effect on the nuclear calculus of individual states. Likewise, regional predominance of inward-looking models and a propensity for nuclear weapons adventurism may lead states that, for political and economic reasons, would have preferred nuclear weapons abstinence to tilt toward the regional center of (proliferation) gravity. Thus, a state with an outward-looking ruling coalition may pursue nuclear weapons should these outward-oriented elites perceive extreme external threats and calculate that the political benefits of economic integration and nuclear restraint no longer outweigh those of going nuclear. Although Solingen does not elaborate on this scenario, she does express concern about the potential impact of severe global shocks, such as a worldwide economic downturn, on the resilience of outward-looking political coalitions. Such shocks, she worries, might lead to "domestic evolutions away from internationalizing trajectories," particularly in East Asia, and might somehow "encourage nuclear dominos" (pp. 288–289).[52] The manner in which this hypothetical proliferation process would unfold, however, is not explained, and the domino metaphor does not appear to be consistent with any of the actual decisionmaking processes she depicts in her case studies.[53]

The thrust of Solingen's argument, and that of Hymans, provides good reasons to be skeptical of forecasts involving rapid proliferation, especially in the near term. Although the two authors disagree about the relative influence of single individuals and political coalitions on nuclear decisions, they agree that proliferation decisions are heavily contingent on the right combination of domestic factors, be it the presence of a leader with an appropriate national identity conception or an inward-looking regime whose political interests are served by pursuit of nuclear weapons. The nuclear weapons behavior of other states at best plays an indirect and typically secondary role in influencing their own nuclear weapons choices. The two books thus provide a useful corrective to the simplistic, overly mechanistic, and all too commonly expressed view that we are near a tipping point at which a single new entrant to the nuclear club could trigger a proliferation epidemic, chain, or avalanche.

Policy Implications

The overall record of proliferation prognoses by government intelligence analysts and political science scholars alike instills little confidence that the international community will receive early warning about emerging nuclear

---

52. See also Solingen's reference to the "possible nuclear domino effect or 'breakout' in East Asia" should Japan go nuclear. Solingen, *Nuclear Logics*, p. 260.
53. Solingen is particularly effective in critiquing neorealist notions of "reactive proliferation" in her analysis of Egyptian nuclear decisionmaking. Ibid., p. 244.

weapons threats. Repeatedly, both communities have failed to anticipate significant nuclear weapons developments in a timely fashion or, in some instances, have missed them altogether. Examples of proliferation surprises include the first Soviet and Indian nuclear explosions, the initiation and successful development of Israeli nuclear weapons, the timing of India's second and Pakistan's first nuclear tests, the rise and demise of Iraq's nuclear activities, and the nature and scope of North Korea's nuclear weapons ambitions.[54] Illustrative of the second variety of forecasting failure—total ignorance—was the failure by U.S. intelligence to detect the revival of Yugoslavia's covert nuclear weapons program in 1974 and its growth over the next fourteen years, an intelligence blind spot apparently shared by the Soviet government.[55]

Just as government and academic experts often have missed significant proliferation activities, they also frequently have exaggerated the scope and pace of nuclear weapons proliferation. For reasons described in the preceding section, many current proliferation prognoses appear destined to repeat this phenomenon of "crying wolf." The books by Hymans and Solingen do not provide simple or foolproof antidotes to the current proliferation forecasting malaise. They do, however, offer promising new insights and tools to assist policy practitioners in avoiding common errors and making better-informed estimates of nuclear proliferation futures.

One of the most important implications for forecasting proliferation to be drawn from Hymans's book is the danger of reliance on highly restricted and sensitive human and signals intelligence to the neglect of careful analysis of public leadership statements.[56] Relevant to this point is Senator Patrick Moynihan's admonition to U.S. officials following the 1998 Indian nuclear weapons test—"Learn to read."[57] As the comparative case studies of Hymans

---

54. For an extended discussion of these intelligence failures and some more successful estimates, see Jeffrey T. Richelson, *Spying on the Bomb: American Nuclear Intelligence from Nazi Germany to Iran and North Korea* (New York: W.W. Norton, 2006).
55. For an analysis of this period as well as the initial phase of the Yugoslav program between the late 1940s and early 1960s, with which U.S. intelligence was slightly familiar, see William C. Potter, Djuro Miljanić, and Ivo Slaus, "Tito's Nuclear Legacy," *Bulletin of the Atomic Scientists*, Vol. 56, No. 2 (March/April 2000), pp. 63–70. According to Ambassador Roland Timerbaev, the Soviet government also appears to have been oblivious to Tito's nuclear weapons ambitions. Personal communication by Potter with Timerbaev, April 29, 1998. See also Roland Timerbaev, *Rossiya i yadernoye nerasprostraneniye, 1945–1968* [Russia and nuclear nonproliferation, 1945–1968] (Moscow: Nauka, 1999).
56. Hymans, *The Psychology of Nuclear Proliferation*, p. 217, points to early declarations by Gorton of his nuclear ambitions before the Australian Senate.
57. Quoted in ibid. Moynihan's admonition is somewhat ironic given the total surprise he experienced fourteen years earlier as U.S. ambassador to India at the time of the first Indian nuclear detonation. See Richelson, *Spying on the Bomb*, p. 233.

and Solingen also demonstrate, there is no good substitute for extended in-country research and use of primary-source materials. Finally, the "learn to read" dictum for intelligence analysts also might usefully apply to English-language, open-source nuclear trade journals such as *Nucleonics Week, Nuclear Fuel, Nuclear Engineering International, and Nuclear News*—expensive and rela-tively esoteric publications, but extremely valuable sources of information on nuclear commerce often overlooked in the past by intelligence personnel pre-cisely because they were unclassified.[58]

A second implication for forecasting suggested by Hymans's and Solingen's research is that despite the limited predictive power of a number of leading in-ternational relations paradigms, theory may be valuable in directing attention to counterintuitive explanations regarding proliferation dynamics. Although Hymans and Solingen disagree about what constitutes the most powerful theory in this respect, they share skepticism about conventional wisdom and a readiness to subject their preferred approaches to empirical testing.[59] This hypothesis-testing orientation and skepticism about prevailing views often has been unwelcome in the intelligence community, whose organizational culture is ill disposed to the vetting and acknowledgment of past mistakes.

One counterintuitive proposition highlighted by the work of Hymans and Solingen and deserving particular attention by U.S. policymakers with re-sponsibility for nonproliferation policy asserts the limited value of security guarantees in forestalling nuclear weapons ambitions. Although the evidence presented by Hymans and Solingen is by no means conclusive and ignores some relevant counterexamples, their parallel conclusions drawn from differ-ent theoretical perspectives and based on a variety of case studies cannot be dismissed out of hand and suggest the need to examine more closely a number of often asserted but infrequently tested causal relationships involving the im-pact of alliances on nuclear weapons restraint.

The books by Hymans and Solingen also offer important insights of great relevance to proliferation forecasting involving the murky area of nuclear

---

58. It would be an interesting exercise to compare the timeliness and accuracy of the last twenty years of NIEs with the published analyses of *Nuclear Fuel* and *Nucleonics Week* reporter Mark Hibbs, whose news reports about the nuclear weapons–related activities of both state and nonstate actors often appear to be better informed than those of U.S. government spokespersons. For an ac-count of Hibbs's reporting, see William Langewiesche, *The Atomic Bazaar: The Rise of the Nuclear Poor* (New York: Farrar, Straus and Giroux, 2007).

59. This open-mindedness is more apparent in Solingen's book, but it also is reflected in the subse-quent writing of Hymans. See, for example, Hymans, "Individuals, Institutions, and Nuclear Choices: A Theoretical Framework and Research Agenda," paper presented at the Workshop on Forecasting Proliferation Developments.

weapons latency and the relationship among technical capabilities, leadership and political coalition motivations, and nuclear weapons choices. Again, the authors offer competing explanations about the primacy of emotions or politics, but both demonstrate conclusively the fallacy of the "technological imperative," and the limited utility of nuclear capacity as a predictor of nuclear weapons acquisition.[60] Hymans's thesis, because of its great clarity and parsimony, and because it is supported by well-developed content analysis techniques, is essentially available on the shelf and ready for use today by those who would like to estimate the nuclear weapons proclivities of Mahmoud Ahmadinejad, Hugo Chávez, and Aleksandr Lukashenko. It also begs to be tested against a much larger body of past would-be proliferators such as Saddam Hussein, Muammar Qaddhafi, and Josef Broz Tito. Hymans's approach may prove deficient and require major revisions or abandonment altogether, but it certainly merits experimentation for forecasting purposes.

Although more complex and therefore more difficult to apply in making prognoses, Solingen's model of domestic survival also has potential for estimating which of the many countries with "virtual" or "near virtual" nuclear arsenals will move to translate these latent capabilities into actual weapons stockpiles, under what circumstances they will choose to do so, and the likely impact of sanctions and inducements in altering their choices. Her comparative analyses, for example, suggest the importance of regional dynamics in shaping proliferation trends and the potential for shared perspectives toward the global economy to modify or reinforce the preferences of ruling coalitions regarding nuclear weapons. Her study also implies that a significant change globally in the political economic reward structure for states adhering to stringent nonproliferation behavior could alter how ruling coalitions assess the costs and benefits of nuclear restraint. Although she does not directly relate this argument to the pending U.S.-India nuclear deal, one could imagine that perceived rewards in the form of nuclear trade with a non-NPT party might contribute to a reassessment by outward-looking elites of the costs of pursuing nuclear weapons.

Finally, the books by Hymans and Solingen offer a useful corrective to the assumption, especially pronounced among those in the intelligence community, that a high correlation exists between that which is classified and that which is true or important. This assumption underlies a tendency on the part

---

60. See also Jo and Gartzke, "Determinants of Nuclear Proliferation," for a recent quantitative analysis of the relationship between "latent nuclear weapons production capability" and nuclear weapons programs.

of those in government to dismiss the attempts at policy-oriented analysis by those in academe. Although much of the future-oriented nonproliferation literature over the past half century provides grounds for this perspective, the overall record of government forecasts is hardly better. Taken together, an overconfidence in often inaccurate predictions by government proliferation analysts and scholars alike lends credence to the "empty suit" fallacy popularized by Nassim Taleb in his book *The Black Swan* and based in part on research by Philip Tetlock.[61] According to this fallacy, experts are no more likely than others to predict certain kinds of events. As Tetlock demonstrates, however, these same experts are far more likely to have confidence in their predictions, to discount dissonant data, and to defend conditional forecasts long after they should have been abandoned.[62] The books by Hymans and Solingen do not enable us to avoid the empty suit fallacy when it comes to divining nuclear ambitions, but they provide us with a set of mirrors to better see how well the suit fits and what alterations are needed.

61. Nassim Nicholas Taleb, *The Black Swan: The Impact of the Highly Improbable* (New York: Random House, 2007); and Philip E. Tetlock, "Theory-Driven Reasoning about Plausible Pasts and Probable Futures in World Politics: Are We Prisoners of Our Preconceptions?" *American Journal of Political Science,* Vol. 43, No. 2 (April 1999), pp. 335–366.
62. Tetlock, "Theory-Driven Reasoning about Plausible Pasts and Probable Futures in World Politics," p. 335.

Spreading Temptation

| Matthew Fuhrmann

Proliferation and Peaceful Nuclear Cooperation Agreements

$\mathbf{P}$eaceful nuclear cooperation—the transfer of nuclear technology, materials, or knowledge from one state to another for peaceful purposes—has figured prominently in international politics since the dawn of the atomic age.[1] During an address before the United Nations General Assembly in December 1953, U.S. President Dwight Eisenhower encouraged the nuclear suppliers to promote international peace and prosperity by sharing their technology and know-how.[2] Since this "atoms for peace" speech, countries have signed more than 2,000 bilateral civilian nuclear cooperation agreements (NCAs) pledging to exchange nuclear technology, materials, or knowledge for peaceful purposes.[3] Recently, NCAs have been signed at an increasingly rapid rate, as countries look for solutions to global climate change and for assistance in combating energy shortages and high oil prices. For example, since coming to office in May 2007, French President Nicolas Sarkozy has signed NCAs with a plethora of states seeking to begin or revive civilian nuclear programs, including Algeria, Jordan, Libya, Qatar, the United Arab Emirates, and Vietnam.

This article examines the relationship between peaceful nuclear cooperation and nuclear weapons proliferation. Specifically, it explores whether countries receiving civilian nuclear aid over time are more likely to initiate weapons programs and build the bomb. The conventional wisdom is that civilian nuclear cooperation does not lead to proliferation. Most scholars argue that nuclear weapons spread when states have a demand for the bomb—not when they have the technical capacity to proliferate.[4] Those who recognize the im-

Matthew Fuhrmann is Assistant Professor of Political Science at the University of South Carolina.

The author thanks Hassan Abbas, Katherine Barbieri, Kyle Beardsley, Gary Bertsch, Matthew Bunn, Jonathan Caverley, Erica Chenoweth, Alexander Downes, Erik Gartzke, John Holdren, Matthew Kroenig, Quan Li, Martin Malin, Vipin Narang, Negeen Pegahi, Etel Solingen, Harvey Starr, Dominic Tierney, Jaroslav Tir, and participants in research seminars at Harvard University and the University of South Carolina for useful comments. All data for replication and the online appendix are available at http://people.cas.sc.edu/fuhrmann.

1. I use the terms "peaceful nuclear cooperation," "civilian nuclear cooperation," and "nuclear assistance" interchangeably throughout this article.
2. Dwight D. Eisenhower, "Address by Mr. Dwight D. Eisenhower, President of the United States of America, to the 470th Plenary Meeting of the United Nations General Assembly," December 8, 1953, http://www.iaea.org/About/history_speech.html.
3. See Matthew Fuhrmann, "Taking a Walk on the Supply Side: The Determinants of Civilian Nuclear Cooperation," *Journal of Conflict Resolution*, Vol. 53, No. 2 (April 2009), pp. 181–208.
4. See, for example, George H. Quester, *The Politics of Nuclear Proliferation* (Baltimore, Md.: Johns

International Security, Vol. 34, No. 1 (Summer 2009), pp. 7–41
© 2009 by the President and Fellows of Harvard College and the Massachusetts Institute of Technology.

portance of the supply side of proliferation argue that certain types of nuclear assistance enable countries to build nuclear weapons but that others are innocuous or even positive from a nonproliferation standpoint. Nuclear suppliers, for instance, generally restrict the sale of uranium enrichment or plutonium reprocessing facilities because these can be used directly to produce fissile material for a bomb, but suppliers routinely build research or power reactors in other countries and train foreign scientists.[5] A recent study finds that countries receiving enrichment and reprocessing facilities, bomb designs, or significant quantities of weapons-grade fissile material are more likely to acquire the bomb.[6] The implication of this research is that other forms of atomic assistance do not lead to the spread of nuclear weapons.

This article argues that the conventional wisdom is wrong—and dangerous. All types of civilian nuclear assistance raise the risks of proliferation. Peaceful nuclear cooperation and proliferation are causally connected because of the dual-use nature of nuclear technology and know-how.[7] Civilian cooperation provides technology and materials necessary for a nuclear weapons program and helps to establish expertise in matters relevant to building the bomb. I develop four hypotheses based on this general insight. First, receiving civilian nuclear assistance over time increases the likelihood that states will begin nuclear weapons programs because it reduces the expected costs of such a campaign and inspires greater confidence among leaders that the bomb could be successfully developed. Second, militarized disputes with other countries condition the effect of civilian nuclear assistance on program initiation. The likelihood that nuclear assistance causes countries to begin weapons programs increases as their security environments worsen. Third, peaceful aid increases

Hopkins University Press, 1973); Etel Solingen, "The Political Economy of Nuclear Restraint," *International Security*, Vol. 19, No. 2 (Fall 1994), pp. 126–169; Mitchell Reiss, *Bridled Ambition: Why Countries Constrain Their Nuclear Capabilities* (Washington, D.C.: Woodrow Wilson Center Press, 1995); Scott D. Sagan, "Why Do States Build Nuclear Weapons? Three Models in Search of a Bomb," *International Security*, Vol. 21, No. 3 (Winter 1996/97), pp. 54–86; T.V. Paul, *Power versus Prudence: Why Nations Forgo Nuclear Weapons* (Montreal: McGill-Queens University Press, 2000); Jacques E.C. Hymans, *The Psychology of Nuclear Proliferation: Identity, Emotions, and Foreign Policy* (Cambridge: Cambridge University Press, 2006); and Etel Solingen, *Nuclear Logics: Contrasting Paths in East Asia and the Middle East* (Princeton, N.J.: Princeton University Press, 2007).

5. See, for example, Office of the Press Secretary, "Statement by Bush on Nonproliferation of Nuclear Weapons Treaty" (Washington, D.C.: White House, July 1, 2008), http://www.america.gov/st/texttrans-english/2008/July/20080701141025eaifas0.9588587.html. The guidelines of the Nuclear Suppliers Group, an informal organization of countries designed to harmonize nuclear export policies, explicitly discourage the supply of enrichment or reprocessing facilities.

6. Matthew Kroenig, "Importing the Bomb: Sensitive Nuclear Assistance and Nuclear Proliferation," *Journal of Conflict Resolution*, Vol. 53, No. 2 (April 2009), pp. 161–180.

7. On the dual-use dilemma, see Matthew Fuhrmann, "Exporting Mass Destruction: The Determinants of Dual-Use Trade," *Journal of Peace Research*, Vol. 45, No. 5 (September 2008), pp. 633–652.

the probability that countries will successfully build nuclear weapons. Fourth, this is especially true when a country's security environment deteriorates.

To test these hypotheses, I produced a data set on civilian nuclear assistance based on the coding of all NCAs signed from 1945 to 2000.[8] A combination of qualitative and quantitative analysis yields support for my arguments, even when controlling for the other variables thought to influence proliferation. The results from my statistical analysis indicate that other factors, such as industrial capacity and membership in the nuclear Nonproliferation Treaty (NPT), also have significant effects on proliferation. But peaceful cooperation is among the few variables that is consistently salient in explaining both nuclear weapons program onset and weapons acquisition.

The conclusions reached in this article should raise concern among policymakers in the United States and abroad. For more than fifty years, the international community has behaved as though peaceful atomic assistance could serve as an effective arms control policy. The United Nations established the International Atomic Energy Agency (IAEA) in 1957 to help bring nuclear energy to countries around the world and establish a system of safeguards to ensure that countries did not use peaceful assistance for military purposes.[9] A decade later, Eisenhower's notion of "atoms for peace" was codified in the NPT, which obligates signatories to forgo nuclear weapons in exchange for access to nuclear technology for peaceful purposes. The findings in this article reveal that efforts to promote the spread of nuclear technology for peaceful use have largely backfired. Given that a nuclear energy renaissance looms on the horizon, the United States and other supplier countries should reevaluate their export practices.

Previous research has noted that illicit proliferation networks operated by "rogue" states can contribute to nuclear proliferation.[10] Most infamously, the Pakistan-based Abdul Qadeer (A.Q.) Khan network served as a "Wal-Mart for

---

8. I end the analysis in 2000 because of data restrictions. More than 2,000 agreements were signed during this period. These efforts build on James F. Keeley's work and are described in more detail below. See Keeley, "A List of Bilateral Civilian Nuclear Cooperation Agreements," University of Calgary, 2003.

9. See Leonard Weiss, "Atoms for Peace," *Bulletin of the Atomic Scientists*, Vol. 59, No. 6 (November–December 2003), p. 40.

10. See, for example, Chaim Braun and Christopher F. Chyba, "Proliferation Rings: New Challenges to the Nuclear Nonproliferation Regime," *International Security*, Vol. 29, No. 2 (Fall 2004), pp. 5–49; Alexander H. Montgomery, "Ringing in Proliferation: How to Dismantle an Atomic Bomb Network," *International Security*, Vol. 30, No. 2 (Fall 2005), pp. 153–187; Sheena Chestnut, "Illicit Activity and Proliferation: North Korean Smuggling Networks," *International Security*, Vol. 32, No. 1 (Summer 2007), pp. 80–111; and Gordon Corera, *Shopping for Bombs: Nuclear Proliferation, Global Insecurity, and the Rise and Fall of the A.Q. Khan Network* (Oxford: Oxford University Press, 2006).

proliferators," selling weapons-relevant technology to Iran, North Korea, and Pakistan, and possibly other countries.[11] This article does not dispute that illicit commercial activities conducted by second-tier suppliers can facilitate the spread of nuclear weapons. Rather, it demonstrates that legal nuclear commerce conducted under the auspices of the NPT can also have damaging effects for national and international security.

The next section offers an overview of the existing research on the causes of nuclear proliferation. In subsequent sections, I lay out my hypotheses linking peaceful nuclear cooperation and proliferation. I then draw from several cases to illustrate the plausibility of my argument and describe how civilian nuclear cooperation can contribute to the spread of nuclear weapons. Next I describe the statistical tests used to evaluate the hypotheses and discuss the results. I conclude by summarizing the article's findings, underscoring the contributions of this study, and offering directions for future research.

Why Do States Pursue Nuclear Weapons?

There is a rich literature on why states pursue nuclear weapons. In recent years this scholarship has turned its attention toward factors influencing a country's demand for nuclear weapons and has treated technological considerations as a secondary concern. For example, Scott Sagan argues that scholars and practitioners should focus on "addressing the sources of the political *demand* for nuclear weapons, rather than focusing primarily on efforts to safeguard existing stockpiles of nuclear materials and to restrict the *supply* of specific weapons technology from the 'haves' to the 'have-nots.'"[12] The extant literature identifies a number of demand-side considerations that are salient in explaining nuclear proliferation, including: a state's security environment, international norms, domestic politics, and intangible or symbolic motivations.[13] These studies are often dismissive of supply-side approaches because several countries—most notably Germany and Japan—have the technical capacity to build nuclear bombs but have chosen not to do so. This critique fails to

11. IAEA Director-General Mohamed ElBaradei compared the Khan network to Walmart. See especially Corera, *Shopping for Bombs*.
12. Sagan, "Why Do States Build Nuclear Weapons?" p. 56 (emphasis in original).
13. Quester, *The Politics of Nuclear Proliferation*; Richard K. Betts, "Paranoids, Pygmies, Pariahs, and Nonproliferation," *Foreign Policy*, No. 26 (Spring 1977), pp. 157–183; Sagan, "Why Do States Build Nuclear Weapons?"; Hymans, *The Psychology of Nuclear Proliferation*; William Epstein, "Why States Go—and Don't Go—Nuclear," *Annals of the American Academy of Political and Social Science*, Vol. 430 (March 1977), pp. 16–28; Lewis A. Dunn and Herman Kahn, *Trends in Nuclear Proliferation, 1975–1995: Projections, Problems, and Policy Options* (Washington, D.C.: Hudson Institute, 1976); Ashok Kapur, *International Nuclear Proliferation: Multilateral Diplomacy and Regional Aspects* (New York: Praeger, 1979); and Solingen, *Nuclear Logics*.

consider, however, that technology-based arguments are probabilistic, not deterministic.[14]

Recent research focuses on the supply side of nuclear proliferation. This author has examined why states transfer dual-use technology that could be employed to build weapons of mass destruction and why countries export nuclear technology, materials, and know-how for peaceful purposes.[15] Matthew Kroenig has analyzed reasons why states provide "sensitive" nuclear assistance to help other countries to build nuclear weapons.[16] Other quantitative studies examine the links between technical capacity and the spread of nuclear weapons.[17] These studies have found that indicators of economic capacity, such as a state's gross domestic product (GDP) and the nuclear-related resources it possesses, are correlated with weapons proliferation. Despite its many contributions, this work has not adequately addressed the links between civilian nuclear cooperation and weapons proliferation. In particular, it fails to sufficiently test the argument that the diffusion of knowledge and technology makes proliferation more likely. Dong-Joon Jo and Erik Gartzke include a variable in their model measuring the natural log of the number of years between 1938 and time t, which allows the authors to test the systemic effects of diffusion, but diffusion does not occur equally across all states.[18] Kroenig examines the relationship between nuclear assistance and proliferation more directly, although he does not explore how peaceful aid can encourage countries to pursue nuclear weapons.[19] He also does not examine how strategic factors such as militarized interstate disputes could interact with nuclear assistance. Kroenig argues that only certain sensitive nuclear assistance helps countries acquire the bomb.[20] This type of aid makes up a mere fraction of all nuclear assistance,

---

14. For more on this point, see Sonali Singh and Christopher R. Way, "The Correlates of Nuclear Proliferation: A Quantitative Test," *Journal of Conflict Resolution*, Vol. 48, No. 6 (December 2004), pp. 859–885.
15. Fuhrmann, "Exporting Mass Destruction"; and Fuhrmann, "Taking a Walk on the Supply Side."
16. Matthew Kroenig, "Exporting the Bomb: Why States Provide Sensitive Nuclear Assistance," *American Political Science Review*, Vol. 103, No. 1 (February 2009), pp. 113–133.
17. See Singh and Way, "The Correlates of Nuclear Proliferation"; Dong-Joon Jo and Erik Gartzke, "Determinants of Nuclear Weapons Proliferation," *Journal of Conflict Resolution*, Vol. 51, No. 1 (February 2007), pp. 167–194; and Kroenig, "Importing the Bomb." For an earlier study, see Stephen M. Meyer, *The Dynamics of Nuclear Proliferation* (Chicago: University of Chicago Press, 1984).
18. Jo and Gartzke, "The Determinants of Nuclear Weapons Proliferation." For example, a state that receives a significant amount of civilian nuclear assistance (e.g., India) will experience a great deal of diffusion, whereas a state that receives no assistance (e.g., Lebanon) will not experience the same effects.
19. Kroenig, "Importing the Bomb."
20. He defines "sensitive nuclear assistance" as assistance in the design and construction of nuclear weapons, the supply of weapons-grade fissile material, or assistance in building uranium enrichment or plutonium reprocessing facilities.

however. Of the more than 2,000 bilateral civilian nuclear cooperation agreements signed from 1945 to 2000, only 14 (less than 0.7 percent) meet Kroenig's definition of sensitive assistance. I argue that the relationship between nuclear aid and atomic weapons is much broader. All forms of atomic assistance—whether it involves training scientists, supplying reactors, or building fuel fabrication facilities—raise the likelihood that nuclear weapons will spread.

Civilian Nuclear Cooperation and the Bomb

Decades ago scholars offered a "technological momentum" hypothesis, suggesting that countries are more likely to pursue nuclear weapons once they obtain civilian nuclear technology and expertise.[21] The logic driving this hypothesis is that the accumulation of nuclear technology and knowledge leads to incremental advances in the field of nuclear engineering that ultimately makes progress toward developing a nuclear weapons capability before a formal decision to build the bomb is made.[22] John Holdren illustrates this argument well when he states that the proliferation of nuclear power represents the spread of an "attractive nuisance."[23] This logic highlights the relationship between the peaceful and military uses of the atom, but it underplays the political dimensions of proliferation.[24]

Peaceful nuclear cooperation and nuclear weapons are related in two key respects. First, all technology and materials linked to a nuclear weapons program have legitimate civilian applications. For example, uranium enrichment and plutonium reprocessing facilities have dual uses because they can produce fuel for power reactors or fissile material for nuclear weapons. Second, civilian nuclear cooperation increases knowledge in nuclear-related matters. This knowledge can then be applied to weapons-related endeavors. Civilian nu-

---

21. Lawrence Scheinman, *Atomic Energy Policy in France under the Fourth Republic* (Princeton, N.J.: Princeton University Press, 1965); Dunn and Kahn, *Trends in Nuclear Proliferation;* Richard N. Rosecrance, *The Dispersion of Nuclear Weapons: Strategy and Politics* (New York: Columbia University Press, 1964); and William C. Potter, *Nuclear Power and Nonproliferation: An Interdisciplinary Perspective* (Cambridge, Mass.: Oelgeschlager, Gunn, and Hain, 1982).
22. Potter, *Nuclear Power and Nonproliferation;* John Holdren, "Nuclear Power and Nuclear Weapons: The Connection Is Dangerous," *Bulletin of the Atomic Scientists,* Vol. 39, No. 1 (January 1983), pp. 40–45; Roberta Wohlstetter, "U.S. Peaceful Aid and the Indian Bomb," in Albert Wohlstetter, Victor Gilinsky, Robert Gillette, and Roberta Wohlstetter, *Nuclear Policies: Fuel without the Bomb* (Cambridge, Mass.: Ballinger, 1978), pp. 57–72; and Peter Lavoy, "Nuclear Myths and the Causes of Nuclear Proliferation," in Zachary S. Davis and Benjamin Frankel, eds., *The Proliferation Puzzle: Why Nuclear Weapons Spread (and What Results)* (Portland, Ore.: Frank Cass, 1993), pp. 192–212.
23. Holdren, "Nuclear Power and Nuclear Weapons," p. 42.
24. Meyer, *The Dynamics of Nuclear Proliferation;* Matthew Bunn, "Realist, Idealist, and Integrative Approaches to Proliferation Policy," Harvard University, 2003.

clear programs necessitate familiarity with the handling of radioactive materials, processes for fuel fabrication and materials having chemical or nuclear properties, and the operation and function of reactors and electronic control systems. They also provide experience in other crucial fields, such as metallurgy and neutronics.[25] These experiences offer "a technology base upon which a nuclear weapon program could draw."[26]

These linkages suggest that peaceful nuclear assistance reduces the expected costs of a weapons program, making it more likely that a decision to begin such a program will be made. Considerable political and economic costs—such as international sanctions, diplomatic isolation, and strained relationships with allies—can accompany nuclear weapons programs.[27] Leaders may be reluctant to take on these burdens unless they believe that a weapons campaign could succeed relatively quickly.[28] As Stephen Meyer argues, "When the financial and resource demands of [beginning a weapons program] become less burdensome, states might opt to proceed . . . under a balance of incentives and disincentives that traditionally might have been perceived as insufficient for a proliferation decision."[29]

Sometimes, nuclear assistance can cause leaders to initiate nuclear weapons programs in the absence of a compelling security threat. This usually happens when scientists and other members of atomic energy commissions convince the political leadership that producing a nuclear weapon is technologically possible and can be done with relatively limited costs.[30] Scientists do not always push leaders down the nuclear path, but in many cases they do.[31] Leaders are persuaded by this lobbying because they are keenly aware that the quicker the bomb can be developed, the less likely other national priorities will suffer.

Although nuclear assistance occasionally produces bomb programs in the

25. Donald MacKenzie and Graham Spinardi, "Tacit Knowledge, Weapons Design, and the Uninvention of Nuclear Weapons," *American Journal of Sociology*, Vol. 101, No. 1 (July 1995), pp. 44–99.
26. U.S. Congress, United States Office of Technology Assessment, *Technologies Underlying Weapons of Mass Destruction* (Washington, D.C.: U.S. Government Printing Office, December 1993), No. OTA-BP-ISC-115, p. 153.
27. See, for example, Solingen, *Nuclear Logics*.
28. Ted Greenwood, Harold A. Feiveson, and Theodore B. Taylor, *Nuclear Proliferation: Motivations, Capabilities, and Strategies for Control* (New York: McGraw-Hill, 1977), p. 150.
29. Meyer, *The Dynamics of Nuclear Proliferation*, p. 143.
30. Peter Liberman, "The Rise and Fall of the South African Bomb," *International Security*, Vol. 26, No. 2 (Fall 2001), pp. 45–86; Lavoy, "Nuclear Myths and the Causes of Nuclear Proliferation"; Matthew Bunn, "Civilian Nuclear Energy and Nuclear Weapons Programs: The Record," working draft, Belfer Center for Science and International Affairs, Harvard University, June 29, 2001.
31. In Germany and Brazil, for example, scientists lobbied leaders not to develop the bomb. I thank Etel Solingen for this insight.

absence of a security threat, the relationship between such assistance and pro-liferation is usually more nuanced. Countries that have received considerable assistance are especially likely to initiate bomb programs when threats arise because they have greater demand for the strategic advantages that nuclear weapons offer.[32] In other words, peaceful nuclear assistance typically condi-tions the effect that a security environment has on a state's political decision to begin a weapons program. A state that suffers a defeat in war or feels threat-ened for another reason is unlikely to initiate a program if it lacks a developed civilian nuclear program. Without the technical base in place, it is too costly to venture down the weapons path. This explains, in part, why Saudi Arabia has yet to begin a nuclear weapons program even though it faces considerable se-curity threats.[33] Likewise, countries are unlikely to nuclearize—even if they have accumulated significant amounts of assistance—if they do not face secu-rity threats. On the other hand, initiation of a weapons program is more likely in states that operate in dangerous security environments and possess peaceful nuclear facilities and a cadre of trained scientists and technicians.

There are also strong theoretical reasons to suggest the existence of a rela-tionship between civilian nuclear cooperation and the acquisition of nuclear weapons. Given the links described above, civilian nuclear energy cooperation can aid nuclear weapons production by providing the technology and items necessary to produce fissile material.[34] This is noteworthy because fissile mate-rial production is the most difficult step in building the bomb.[35] Cooperation also establishes a technical knowledge base that permits advances in nuclear explosives and related fields, ultimately facilitating bomb production. Occa-sionally, technical capacity alone causes states to produce the bomb. But just as all states receiving nuclear aid do not begin weapons programs, every country that acquires assistance does not assemble bombs. Security threats, which pro-

---

32. On the strategic benefits of the bomb, see Thomas C. Schelling, *The Strategy of Conflict* (Cam-bridge, Mass.: Harvard University Press, 1960); Bruce Bueno de Mesquita and William H. Riker, "An Assessment of the Merits of Selective Nuclear Proliferation," *Journal of Conflict Resolution*, Vol. 26, No. 2 (June 1982), pp. 283–306; Robert Powell, *Nuclear Deterrence Theory: The Search for Credibil-ity* (Cambridge: Cambridge University Press, 1990); Erik Gartzke and Dong-Joon Jo, "Bargaining, Nuclear Proliferation, and International Disputes," *Journal of Conflict Resolution*, Vol. 53, No. 2 (April 2009), pp. 209–233; Michael Horowitz, "The Spread of Nuclear Weapons and International Conflict: Does Experience Matter?" *Journal of Conflict Resolution*, Vol. 53, No. 2 (April 2009), pp. 234–257; Robert Rauchhaus, "Evaluating the Nuclear Peace Hypothesis: A Quantitative Ap-proach," *Journal of Conflict Resolution*, Vol. 53, No. 2 (April 2009), pp. 258–277; and Kyle Beardsley and Victor Asal, "Winning with the Bomb," *Journal of Conflict Resolution*, Vol. 53, No. 2 (April 2009), pp. 278–301.
33. Singh and Way include Saudi Arabia on a list of "Dogs That Did Not Bark." Singh and Way, "The Correlates of Nuclear Proliferation."
34. Bunn, "Civilian Nuclear Energy and Nuclear Weapons Programs."
35. Joseph Cirincione, Jon B. Wolfsthal, and Miriam Rajkumar, *Deadly Arsenals: Nuclear, Biological, and Chemical Threats* (Washington, D.C.: Carnegie Endowment for International Peace, 2005).

vide the political motivation to build the bomb, coupled with atomic aid are a recipe for the acquisition of nuclear weapons.

Four hypotheses flow from this logic:

Hypothesis 1: Countries receiving peaceful nuclear assistance are more likely to begin nuclear weapons programs.

Hypothesis 2: Countries receiving peaceful nuclear assistance are more likely to begin nuclear weapons programs when a security threat arises.

Hypothesis 3: Countries receiving peaceful nuclear assistance are more likely to acquire nuclear weapons.

Hypothesis 4: Countries facing security threats and receiving peaceful nuclear assistance are more likely to acquire weapons.

Below I apply these hypotheses to several cases to show how peaceful nuclear cooperation can lead to proliferation.

Case Studies

In this section I briefly discuss why my argument is salient in explaining nuclear decisionmaking in three proliferation cases. Then I examine two cases in more detail: (1) India's decision to begin a weapons program in 1964, and (2) Pakistan's acquisition of the bomb in 1987. The qualitative evidence shows that nuclear assistance can lead to proliferation—especially when combined with security threats. After discussing these cases, I turn to the statistical analysis.

The South African experience illustrates how peaceful nuclear assistance can contribute to the onset of a weapons program in the absence of a security threat. U.S. assistance to South Africa's peaceful nuclear program, which began in July 1957, had a salient effect on that country's decision to begin a nuclear weapons program. U.S. aid included the construction of a nuclear research reactor in Pelindaba, the supply of highly enriched uranium, and the training of nuclear scientists. This cooperation led to significant technological advancements and provided key scientists in the South African atomic energy complex with tremendous political influence.[36] Particularly significant was the president of the Atomic Energy Corporation, A.J. "Ampie" Roux, who reportedly quipped, "I can ask [the South African] government for anything I want and I'll get it."[37] Indeed, Roux convinced Prime Minister John Vorster to fund construction of a pilot uranium enrichment plant in 1968, despite the latter's

---

36. See David Albright, "South Africa and the Affordable Bomb," *Bulletin of the Atomic Scientists,* Vol. 50, No. 4 (July/August 1994), pp. 37–47.
37. Quoted in Liberman, "The Rise and Fall of the South African Bomb," p. 64.

concerns about the costs of such a program.[38] In the 1970s Roux then lobbied the prime minister to develop nuclear bombs on the grounds that doing so was technologically feasible.[39] Vorster decided to authorize a nuclear weapons program in part because he recognized that South Africa's civil nuclear infrastructure would permit the quick and successful development of these weapons. As Mitchell Reiss notes, "With the [civilian nuclear] capability already in place, the subsequent decision to build nuclear weapons was made that much easier."[40] This logic is especially compelling in light of revelations from recently declassified documents that security motivations—particularly the need for a deterrent against a Soviet-supported attack from Angola or Mozambique— had little role in influencing the onset of South Africa's weapons program.[41] Because the nuclear program could not have developed as it did without U.S. assistance beginning in the late 1950s, this short narrative exemplifies how peaceful nuclear cooperation can enable proliferation decisions.

Evidence from two other cases also reveals that peaceful nuclear cooperation can enable acquisition of the bomb. French reprocessing aid to Israel between 1958 and 1965 enhanced Israel's ability to assemble a nuclear weapon much quicker than it would have been able to through solely indigenous means.[42] But this assistance alone was insufficient for Israel to cross the nuclear threshold. Heavy water supplied by Norway, the United Kingdom, and the United States also facilitated Israel's acquisition of nuclear weapons.[43] Gary Milhollin highlights the importance of foreign-supplied heavy water for Israel's weapons program when he notes that "the reactor at Dimona is Israel's only means of making plutonium, and plutonium is Israel's primary nuclear weapon material. When Dimona opened in 1963 . . . Israel was producing heavy water only in laboratory quantities. Therefore, it was physically impossible to start Dimona without U.S. or Norwegian heavy water."[44]

I argued above that the knowledge acquired from peaceful nuclear coopera-

38. Verne Harris, Sello Hatang, and Peter Liberman, "Unveiling South Africa's Nuclear Past," *Journal of Southern African Studies*, Vol. 30, No. 3 (September 2004), pp. 457–476; and Reiss, *Bridled Ambition*, p. 29.
39. Waldo Stumpf, "South Africa's Nuclear Weapons Program: From Deterrence to Dismantlement," *Arms Control Today*, Vol. 25, No. 10 (December/January 1995/96), p. 4; and Liberman, "The Rise and Fall of the South African Bomb."
40. Reiss, *Bridled Ambition*, p. 29.
41. Harris, Hatang, and Liberman, "Unveiling South Africa's Nuclear Past."
42. Kroenig, "Importing the Bomb"; and Avner Cohen, *Israel and the Bomb* (New York: Columbia University Press, 1998).
43. Gary Milhollin, "Heavy Water Cheaters," *Foreign Policy*, Vol. 69 (Winter 1987/88), pp. 100–119; Astrid Forlan, "Norway's Nuclear Odyssey: From Optimistic Proponent to Nonproliferator," *Nonproliferation Review*, Vol. 4, No. 2 (Winter 1997), pp. 1–16; and "UK Helped Israel Get Nuclear Bomb," *BBC News*, August 4, 2005, http://news.bbc.co.uk/2/hi/uk_news/4743987.stm.
44. Milhollin, "Heavy Water Cheaters," p. 105.

tion also plays a major role in enabling countries to manufacture nuclear bombs.[45] The North Korean case illuminates this point. The Soviet Union trained North Korean nuclear scientists beginning in the late 1950s and completed construction of a research reactor at Yongbyon in 1965. This technical aid provided a base of knowledge in nuclear matters sufficient to help the North Koreans build an "experimental nuclear installation" in the 1980s.[46] Pyongyang employed this facility to produce plutonium, which it then used to explode a nuclear bomb in October 2006.[47] As the case studies presented below make clear, this experience is not atypical.

THE ORIGINS OF INDIA'S NUCLEAR WEAPONS PROGRAM, 1964

In 1955 India built its first research reactor using British-supplied designs. This facility, known as the Apsara research reactor, became operational in 1956 using enriched uranium fuel also supplied by the United Kingdom. In April 1956 Canada agreed to supply India with a 40-megawatt research reactor known as the Canada-India-United States research reactor (CIRUS). The CIRUS reactor was built as part of the Colombo Plan, a developmental aid program for countries of South Asia modeled after the Marshall Plan.[48] It was intended to help the Indians develop their knowledge in nuclear engineering.[49] The United States provided heavy water to moderate the CIRUS reactor, enabling it to begin operating in 1960. In addition, beginning in 1955, it invited 1,104 Indian nuclear scientists to train at the Argonne Laboratory School of Nuclear Science and Engineering, among other facilities.[50]

U.S. and Canadian assistance continued in the 1960s. In April 1961 India began construction of a reprocessing plant designed to extract plutonium from spent nuclear fuel. This facility, named Phoenix, was designed in part by an American firm, Vitro International, and based on declassified U.S. plans for reprocessing using the PUREX method.[51] In 1964 Canada agreed to assist India in developing its first power reactor, known as Rajasthan Atomic Power Plant (RAPP-1), and supply one-half of the initial uranium fuel charge. This assistance enabled India to obtain "detailed design data, including plans and work-

45. Bunn, "Civilian Energy Programs and Nuclear Weapons Programs."
46. Alexander Zhebin, "A Political History of Soviet-North Korean Nuclear Cooperation," in James Clay Moltz and Alexander Y. Mansourov, eds., *The North Korean Nuclear Program: Security, Strategy, and New Perspectives from Russia* (New York: Routledge, 2000), pp. 27–40.
47. Faye Flam, "American Scientists Explain North Korean Nuclear Test," *Philadelphia Inquirer,* October 10, 2006.
48. Shyam Bhatia, *India's Nuclear Bomb* (Ghaziabad, India: Vikas, 1979).
49. Duane Bratt, *The Politics of CANDU Exports* (Toronto: University of Toronto Press, 2006), p. 89.
50. George Perkovich, *India's Nuclear Bomb: The Impact on Global Proliferation* (Berkeley: University of California Press, 1999), p. 30.
51. Ibid., p. 64.

ing drawings regarding the design and construction of nuclear power stations of the heavy water type."[52] Canada additionally agreed to provide one-half of the initial uranium fuel charge for the Rajasthan reactor. In December 1966 it agreed to offer assistance in the design and construction of a second nuclear power reactor at Rajasthan (RAPP-2). At the same time, the United States agreed to supply plutonium to India for research purposes.[53]

These transfers were highly consequential for India's civilian nuclear program. In the 1950s and 1960s, India could not have developed a nuclear program in the absence of foreign assistance.[54] Peaceful nuclear assistance also spurred India's decision to begin a nuclear weapons program. To begin, it decreased the expected costs of obtaining the bomb and increased the likelihood that one could be produced relatively quickly. The training and technology that India received had applications for both peaceful and military programs. Key Indian decisionmakers were well aware of this. In September 1956 Homi Bhabha, the chairman of the Indian Atomic Energy Commission, argued that countries can easily use know-how and experiences obtained through peaceful programs to develop a separate military program.[55] Bhabha expressed a similar opinion in January 1964 when he indicated that "any knowledge of operating a reactor for peaceful purposes can be employed later for operating a reactor for military purposes."[56] Prime Minister Jawaharlal Nehru was equally aware that nuclear assistance could serve both peaceful and military programs, and he expressed this belief publicly on several occasions.[57] By 1964 U.S. and Canadian peaceful nuclear assistance had yielded results that would have important implications for India's civilian and military nuclear programs. In June of that year, the first spent fuel from the Canadian-supplied CIRUS reactor was delivered to the reprocessing plant at Trombay. This meant that India would soon separate plutonium for the first time. Plutonium can be used to power certain types of nuclear reactors, but it is also an important component of nuclear weapons. Using this plutonium in a nuclear weapon, however, would have broken New Delhi's prior commitments that it would use technology and training provided by Canada and the United States

52. "India Profile: Nuclear Chronology, 1960–1964" (Monterey, Calif.: Center for Nonproliferation Studies, Monterey Institute for International Studies, August 2003), http://www.nti.org/e_research/profiles/India/Nuclear/2296_2346.html.
53. Bratt, *The Politics of CANDU Exports*.
54. Wohlstetter, "U.S. Peaceful Aid and the Indian Bomb."
55. Perkovich, *India's Nuclear Bomb*, p. 29.
56. Homi J. Bhabha, "The Implications of a Wider Dispersal of Military Power for World Security and the Problem of Safeguards," proceedings of the Twelfth Pugwash Conference on Science and World Affairs, January 27–February 1, 1964, Udaipur, India, pp. 78–79.
57. See, for example, Ashok Kapur, *India's Nuclear Option: Atomic Diplomacy and Decisionmaking* (New York: Praeger, 1976), p. 193.

only for peaceful purposes. Nevertheless, developments in the civilian sector had a salient effect on Prime Minister Lal Bahadur Shastri's decisionmaking.

Shastri was highly sensitive to the expected costs of a nuclear weapons program because India faced economic hardship and massive food shortages during his tenure. He was initially reluctant to initiate a weapons program because this would force New Delhi to abandon plans for economic development and divert substantial resources away from other domestic programs.[58] These sentiments were captured in an editorial published in the *Statesman* in August 1964: "Both bomb production and effective delivery could be secured if the price is paid for it in terms of economic deprivation. But no responsible person has suggested that the object is worth that price."[59]

Fears that the bomb would be technically too difficult to produce and would command substantial resources initially led Shastri to oppose beginning a nuclear weapons program. But Bhabha relentlessly lobbied the prime minister in asserting that the bomb could be produced with relative ease due to developments in India's civilian nuclear program. In October 1964 Bhabha proclaimed that India could acquire a nuclear bomb within eighteen months of a political decision to develop it and that a 10-kiloton blast would cost only $350,000.[60] These estimates were overly optimistic because India would not acquire weapons-usable plutonium until 1965 (even though the spent fuel was loaded into the reprocessing facility in June 1964), and it lacked a reliable bomb design.[61] But these challenges were overlooked, in part because Bhabha had an extraordinary amount of power, and information relevant to the nuclear program was so tightly guarded that others did not have a chance to question his assertions. Eventually, Bhabha convinced Shastri that a bomb could be built relatively quickly without diverting substantial resources away from development programs. This argument was especially compelling because the country's rivalry with China provided strategic incentives to build the bomb.[62]

On November 27, 1964, after meeting with Bhabha, Shastri officially endorsed a nuclear weapons program. This decision, which marked the official beginning of the Indian program, resulted from the combination of foreign nuclear assistance and security threats emanating from China. But the former factor played an especially crucial and underappreciated role.

58. K. Rangaswami, "Leaders Reject Demand for Atom Bomb," *Hindu*, November 9, 1964.
59. Quoted in Perkovich, *India's Nuclear Bomb*, p. 65.
60. Ibid., p. 65.
61. Ibid., p. 71.
62. Brahma Chellaney, "India," in Mitchell Reiss and Robert S. Litwak, eds., *Nuclear Proliferation after the Cold War* (Washington, D.C.: Woodrow Wilson Center Press, 1994), pp. 165–190; Kapur, *India's Nuclear Option;* and Ashok Kapur, *Pokhran and Beyond: India's Nuclear Behaviour* (Oxford: Oxford University Press, 2001).

PAKISTAN'S BOMB ACQUISITION, 1987

Pakistan's civilian nuclear program began in the 1950s with the help of foreign assistance. In August 1955 the United States signed a nuclear cooperation agreement with Pakistan that led to the construction of a small research reactor at the Pakistan Institute of Nuclear Science and Technology (PINSTECH) and the supply of highly enriched uranium to fuel it. The PINSTECH reactor, which began operation in 1963, was used to provide training to Pakistani technicians, produce isotopes, and conduct neutron physics experiments.[63] In the 1960s Canada signed a nuclear cooperation agreement with Pakistan allowing the Canadians to build the Karachi Nuclear Power Plant and supply heavy water and uranium to fuel the reactor. This reactor began operation in 1972. Canada also helped Pakistan develop a fuel fabrication facility at Chasma in the late 1970s.[64] Western European suppliers offered considerable amounts of assistance to Pakistan as well. The United Kingdom, for example, provided hot cells capable of separating plutonium on a laboratory scale.[65] Similarly, Belgium and France assisted Pakistan in developing the "New Laboratories" at PINSTECH to reprocess spent nuclear fuel.[66] Brussels also provided Islamabad with a heavy water production facility that came online at Multan in 1980.[67] Paris agreed in 1976 to supply a large-scale reprocessing center at Chasma, but it suspended this deal in 1978.[68]

In addition to transferring these materials and technology, many suppliers provided substantial know-how to Pakistan.[69] For instance, the United States trained promising young scientists from Pakistan at Argonne National Laboratory just outside of Chicago between 1955 and 1961.[70] These scientists were trained in the design and construction of nuclear reactors, the handling of radioactive materials, chemistry and metallurgy, and other peaceful applications of atomic energy.[71] The United Kingdom, Belgium, and other countries in Western Europe provided similar training to Pakistani personnel.[72]

---

63. Central Intelligence Agency, "Pakistan's Nuclear Program," National Intelligence Estimate, April 26, 1978.
64. Ashok Kapur, *Pakistan's Nuclear Development* (London: Croom Helm, 1987), p. 75.
65. Given its size, this facility was not well suited to producing plutonium for bombs. Ibid., p. 156.
66. U.S. Department of State, "The Pakistani Nuclear Program," briefing paper, June 23, 1983.
67. Andrew Koch and Jennifer Topping, "Pakistan's Nuclear-Related Facilities," fact sheet (Monterey, Calif.: Center for Nonproliferation Studies, Monterey Institute of International Studies, 1997), http://cns.miis.edu/reports/pdfs/9707paki.pdf.
68. U.S. Department of State, "Apprehensions Regarding Pakistan's Nuclear Intentions," memorandum of conversation, September 3, 1975.
69. Central Intelligence Agency, "Pakistan's Nuclear Program."
70. *International Institute of Nuclear Science and Engineering Classbook* (Argonne, Ill.: Argonne National Laboratory, 1961).
71. Argonne National Laboratory, "International School Focused on Peaceful Uses of Nuclear Energy" (Washington, D.C.: U.S. Department of Energy, October 12, 1996), http://www.anl.gov/Media_Center/News/History/news961012.html.
72. Shahid-Ur Rehman, *Long Road to Chagai* (Islamabad: Print Wise, 1999), pp. 36–37.

After Pakistan suffered a humiliating defeat at the hands of India in the 1971 Indo-Pakistani War, it initiated a nuclear weapons program. Islamabad redoubled its efforts to acquire nuclear weapons after India tested a nuclear explosive device in May 1974.[73] Prime Minister Zulfikar Ali Bhutto famously proclaimed that all Pakistani citizens would "eat grass or leaves, even go hungry" to develop the bomb for Pakistan to counter the Indian nuclear threat.[74] When Bhutto initiated the program, he planned to develop reactors and reprocessing centers to produce plutonium for nuclear weapons. The prime minister tapped Munir Ahmad Khan, the chairman of the Pakistan Atomic Energy Commission (PAEC), to implement this plan. Khan was one of the Pakistanis trained at Argonne National Laboratory more than a decade earlier.[75] Not only did Khan personally benefit from that training, but as chairman of the PAEC, he was able to share his expertise with others once he returned to Pakistan. Others who received training abroad were also able to share their experiences with Pakistani scientists. This accumulation of nuclear know-how enabled Pakistan to develop a technical base that was "equally adept" to India's scientific abilities in the early 1970s.[76] It also increased the PAEC's confidence that it could deliver the bomb for Pakistan.[77]

Bhutto and Khan believed that Pakistan could use facilities built for peaceful purposes to develop nuclear weapons—just as India would do in 1974.[78] But ultimately, Islamabad chose a slightly different path, focusing instead on the uranium route to the bomb. The history of Pakistan's enrichment program is well known.[79] In September 1974 a young metallurgist named A.Q. Khan wrote a letter to Prime Minister Bhutto offering to help Pakistan build the bomb.[80] Khan had been working in the Netherlands for a subcontractor of the European enrichment consortium URENCO. While employed by URENCO, he stole sensitive information dealing with centrifuge technology that could be used to enrich uranium. At the end of 1975, he suddenly left the

---

73. See, for example, Kapur, *Pakistan's Nuclear Development;* Corera, *Shopping for Bombs;* and Hassan Abbas, "Causes That Led to Nuclear Proliferation from Pakistan to Iran, Libya, and North Korea," Fletcher School of Law and Diplomacy, Tufts University, 2008.
74. Bhutto made this statement as defense minister in the 1960s. Mitchell B. Reiss, "The Nuclear Tipping Point: Prospects for a World of Many Nuclear Weapons States," in Kurt M. Campbell, Robert J. Einhorn, and Reiss, eds., *The Nuclear Tipping Point: Why States Reconsider Their Nuclear Choices* (Washington, D.C.: Brookings Institution Press, 2004), p. 6.
75. Walter Kato, interview by author, Cambridge, Massachusetts, November 20, 2008. Dr. Kato was personally involved in the training that took place at Argonne National Laboratory.
76. Kapur, *Pakistan's Nuclear Development,* p. 169.
77. See ibid., p. 136.
78. See ibid., p. 169; and Central Intelligence Agency, "Pakistan's Nuclear Program."
79. See especially Corera, *Shopping for Bombs.*
80. Michael Laufer, "A.Q. Khan Nuclear Chronology, *Nonproliferation Issue Brief,* Vol. 8, No. 8 (Washington, D.C.: Carnegie Endowment for International Peace, September 7, 2005), http://www.carnegieendowment.org/static/npp/Khan_Chronology.pdf.

Netherlands and returned to Pakistan with stolen blueprints for centrifuges and a Rolodex containing information on 100 companies that supplied enrichment technology.[81]

Pakistan used this information to purchase subcomponents from abroad and to construct covert enrichment facilities dedicated to a nuclear bomb program.[82] As a result of Khan's activities, Pakistan had virtually everything it needed to build a centrifuge enrichment plant as early as 1979.[83] With this equipment in hand, Pakistan began to construct enrichment facilities at Sihala and Kahuta using stolen blueprints.[84] In the end, highly enriched uranium produced at these plants enabled Islamabad to assemble at least one bomb by 1987 and conduct nuclear tests eleven years later.[85]

Pakistan was able to master sophisticated enrichment technology and produce highly enriched uranium for nuclear weapons because of the peaceful assistance it received beginning in the mid-1950s. Islamabad was able to draw on training provided by the United States, Canada, and West European countries to construct and operate the enrichment centers at Sihala and Kahuta. Pakistani scientists received training in uranium metallurgy—the physical and chemical behavior of uranium and its alloys. Expertise in metallurgy is vital to enriching uranium using the gas centrifuge method. Without this know-how, Islamabad would not have known what to do with the technology and materials it procured from abroad. As a developing country, Pakistan could not have obtained the requisite expertise solely through indigenous means. Munir Kahn underscored the significance of foreign assistance:

I have no place from which to draw talented scientists and engineers to work in our nuclear establishment. We don't have a training system for the kind of cadres we need. But, if we can get France or somebody else to come and create a broad nuclear infrastructure, and build these plants and these laboratories, I will train hundreds of my people in ways that otherwise they would never be able to be trained. And with that training, and with the blueprints and the

81. Ibid.
82. James M. Markham, "Bonn Checks Report of Smuggling of Atomic Technology to Pakistan," *New York Times*, May 5, 1987; Corera, *Shopping for Bombs*, p. 23; and Shelby McNichols, "Chronology of Pakistani Nuclear Development" (Monterey, Calif.: Center for Nonproliferation Studies, Monterey Institute of International Studies, July 2000).
83. Corera, *Shopping for Bombs*, p. 27.
84. Ibid., p. 22.
85. David Albright and Kevin O'Neill, "ISIS Technical Assessment: Pakistan's Stock of Weapon-Grade Uranium" (Washington, D.C.: Institute for Science and International Security, June 1998), http://www.isis-online.org/publications/southasia/ta-pak060198.html; Christopher Clary, "Dr. Khan's Nuclear WalMart," *Disarmament Diplomacy*, No. 76 (March/April 2004); David Albright and Mark Hibbs, "Pakistan's Bomb: Out of the Closet," *Bulletin of the Atomic Scientists*, Vol. 48 (July/August 1992), p. 39; Corera, *Shopping for Bombs*, p. 49; and Kapur, *Pakistan's Nuclear Development*, p. 208.

other things that we'd get along the way, then we could set up separate plants that would not be under safeguards, that would not be built with direct foreign assistance, but I would not have the people who could do that. If I don't get the cooperation, I can't train the people to run a weapons program.[86]

Samar Mubarakmand, who headed the team of scientists that orchestrated Pakistan's 1998 nuclear tests, expressed similar sentiments.[87] He suggested that any country can procure dual-use equipment relevant to a weapons program, but states cannot build the bomb "unless there is a human resource available . . . which understands [nuclear-related] work to such an extent that it is able to develop and raise this program from zero to 100% all by itself."[88] He added that countries such as Libya were unable to develop the bomb because they lacked what Pakistan had: the requisite knowledge base. Between 1970 and 2003, Libya attempted to procure nuclear weapons–relevant technology on the black market but was never able to develop the bomb.

Statistical Tests

Given that every empirical approach has drawbacks, a multimethod assessment of my theory can inspire greater confidence in the findings presented in this article.[89] The case study analysis above provides rich descriptions of my argument and illustrates that the causal processes operate as expected in actual instances of proliferation.[90] Statistical analysis allows me to minimize the risks of selection bias and determine the average effect of independent variables on proliferation aims and outcomes.[91] Additionally, it permits me to control for confounding variables and to show that peaceful nuclear cooperation—and not some other factor—explains nuclear proliferation. This is especially important because proliferation is a complicated process, and there is rarely only one factor that explains why nuclear weapons spread.[92]

For the statistical analysis, I use a data set compiled by Sonali Singh and

---

86. Quoted in George Perkovich, "Nuclear Power and Nuclear Weapons in India, Pakistan, and Iran," in Paul Leventhal, Sharon Tanzer, and Steven Dolley, eds., *Nuclear Power and the Spread of Nuclear Weapons: Can We Have One without the Other?* (Washington, D.C.: Brassey's, 2002), p. 194.
87. Samar Mubarakmand, *Capital Talk Special*, Geo-TV, May 3, 2004, http://www.pakdef.info/forum/showthread.php?t+9214.
88. Ibid.
89. For a similar discussion, see Alexander B. Downes, *Targeting Civilians in War* (Ithaca, N.Y.: Cornell University Press, 2008), pp. 40–41.
90. See, for example, Alexander L. George and Andrew Bennett, *Case Studies and Theory Development in the Social Sciences* (Cambridge, Mass.: MIT Press, 2005).
91. Will H. Moore, "Synthesis v. Purity and Large-N Studies: How Might We Assess the Gap between Promise and Performance?" *Human Rights and Human Welfare*, Vol. 6 (2006), pp. 89–97.
92. Sagan, "Why Do States Build Nuclear Weapons?"

Christopher Way to identify the determinants of nuclear proliferation.[93] I adopt a standard time-series cross-sectional data structure for the period 1945 to 2000, and the unit of analysis is the country (monad) year. For my analysis of nuclear weapons program onset, a country exits the data set once it initiates a weapons acquisition campaign. Similarly, for my analysis of nuclear weapons acquisition, a country exits the data set once it obtains at least one nuclear bomb.

DEPENDENT VARIABLES

To analyze nuclear proliferation, I coded two dependent variables, both of which are dichotomous. The first is coded 1 if the country initiated a nuclear weapons program in year t and 0 otherwise. The second is coded 1 if the country acquired nuclear weapons in year t and 0 otherwise. To create these variables, I consulted a list of nuclear proliferation dates compiled by Singh and Way.[94]

EXPLANATORY VARIABLES

I hypothesized above that the accumulation of civilian nuclear assistance makes states more likely both to begin nuclear weapons programs and to acquire such weapons—especially when security threats are also present. To operationalize civilian nuclear assistance, I collected and coded new data on NCAs signed from 1945 to 2000. NCAs are an appropriate independent variable for this analysis because they must be in place in virtually all cases before the exchange of nuclear technology, materials, or knowledge can take place. These agreements typically lead to the construction of a nuclear power or research reactor, the supply of fissile materials (e.g., plutonium or enriched uranium), the export of fissile material production facilities, or the training of scientists and technicians. Related agreements that are not classified as NCAs include: (1) agreements that are explicitly defense related; (2) financial agreements; (3) agricultural or industrial agreements unrelated to nuclear power; (4) agreements dealing with the leasing of nuclear material; and (5) liability agreements.

To produce these data, I consulted a list compiled by James Keeley of more than 2,000 NCAs.[95] Figure 1 plots the number of NCAs signed from 1950 to

---

93. Singh and Way, "The Correlates of Nuclear Proliferation."
94. Ibid.
95. See Keeley, "A List of Bilateral Civilian Nuclear Cooperation Agreements." I conducted further research on all of the agreements in Keeley's list to ensure that I included only deals that actually provide the basis for the exchange of nuclear technology, materials, or knowledge. Additionally, Keeley included some NCAs that are simply amendments to earlier agreements, and

Figure 1. Total Number of Nuclear Cooperation Agreements Signed, 1950–2000

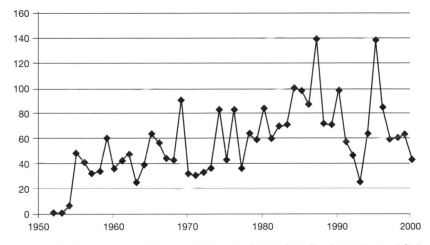

SOURCES: Matthew Fuhrmann, "Taking a Walk on the Supply Side: The Determinants of Civilian Nuclear Cooperation," *Journal of Conflict Resolution,* Vol. 53, No. 2 (April 2009), pp. 181–208; and James F. Keeley, "A List of Bilateral Civilian Nuclear Cooperation Agreements," University of Calgary, 2003.

2000. The figure shows a general increase in the number of NCAs over time, which is explained by the emergence of a greater number of capable nuclear suppliers. The number has fluctuated slightly, with peaks in the late 1980s and the mid-1990s. The first NCA was signed in 1952, after which the average number of agreements signed each year was 58.

I created an independent variable that measures the aggregate number of NCAs that a state signed in a given year entitling it to nuclear technology, materials, or knowledge from another country.[96] If a state signed an NCA but only supplied—and did not receive—nuclear assistance as part of the terms of the deal, then this would not be captured by the nuclear cooperation agreements variable. Table 1 lists the thirty countries that received the most nuclear assistance via these agreements from 1945 to 2000.[97]

do not authorize the supply of additional nuclear technology, materials, or know-how. I excluded these agreements from the coding of the independent variable.

96. Sometimes there is a delay between the time an NCA is signed and the time that nuclear technology, materials, or know-how are actually transferred. To account for this possibility, I lag the independent variables five years, so that if a state signed an agreement in 1975, it would not "count" until 1980. I estimate all models using this alternate coding of the variable, and the results are the same.

97. Some of these countries are included in my sample for only a limited number of years because

Table 1. Top Recipients of Nuclear Cooperation Agreements, 1945–2000

Country	Total Number of Agreements
United States	396
France	221
Germany	171
Russia	136
United Kingdom	133
Japan	122
Italy	112
Belgium	93
Argentina	92
Netherlands	80
Canada	77
Brazil	70
Spain	70
Switzerland	68
Luxembourg	63
Sweden	56
Denmark	55
China	53
South Korea	49
India	39
Ireland	36
Romania	35
Portugal	33
Czechoslovakia (1945–91)	30
Greece	30
Egypt	29
Finland	29
Poland	28
Australia	25
Indonesia	22

NOTE: summary statistics: N = 186; mean = 15.34; minimum = 0; maximum = 396

To operationalize security threats, I created a variable measuring the five-year moving average of the number of militarized interstate disputes (MIDs) per year in which a country was involved. This variable is based on version 3.0 of the Correlates of War's MID data set.[98] I coded a third variable that interacts these two measures to test for the conditional effect of nuclear cooperation on proliferation.

states are removed once they pursue or acquire nuclear weapons. The first NCA was not signed until 1952.
98. Faten Ghosn, Glenn Palmer, and Stuart A. Bremer, "The MID3 Data Set, 1993–2001: Procedures, Coding Rules, and Description," *Conflict Management and Peace Science*, Vol. 21, No. 2 (2004), pp. 133–154.

CONTROL VARIABLES

I controlled for other factors thought to affect proliferation.[99] To control for technological capacity, I included a variable measuring a country's GDP per capita and a squared term of this measure to allow for the possible curvilinear relationship between economic development and the pursuit of nuclear weapons.[100] To measure a state's industrial capacity, I included a dichotomous variable that is coded 1 if it produced steel domestically and had an electricity-generating capacity greater than 5,000 megawatts and 0 otherwise. I included a dichotomous variable that is coded 1 if the state was involved in at least one enduring rivalry as an additional proxy for a state's security environment.[101] A dichotomous variable that is coded 1 if a state shared a defense pact with one of the nuclear-capable great powers and 0 otherwise is also included because security guarantees of this magnitude could reduce states' incentives to develop their own nuclear weapons.[102]

There are a number of "internal determinants" that could affect incentives to proliferate. I included two variables related to democracy. The first measures the country's score on the Polity IV scale.[103] The second variable, which measures whether a state is democratizing, calculates movement toward democracy over a five-year span by subtracting a state's Polity score in year t-5 from its Polity score in year t. To control for a state's exposure to the global economy, I included a variable measuring the ratio of exports plus imports as a share of GDP.[104] I also included a measure of trade liberalization that mirrors the democratization measure described above.

For the sake of robustness, I included one variable that Singh and Way excluded from their model.[105] I created a dichotomous variable and coded it 1 if the state signed the NPT in year t and 0 otherwise. NPT membership could be

---

99. These are generally the same variables used by Singh and Way, "The Correlates of Nuclear Proliferation."

100. See ibid., p. 868.

101. Singh and Way code this variable based on D. Scott Bennett's 1998 list of rivalries. See Bennett, "Integrating and Testing Models of Rivalry Duration," *American Journal of Political Science,* Vol. 42, No. 4 (October 1998), pp. 1200–1232.

102. Singh and Way rely on version 3.0 of the Correlates of War alliance data set to code this variable. Douglas M. Gibler and Meredith Reid Sarkees, "Measuring Alliances: The Correlates of War Formal Interstate Alliance Dataset," *Journal of Peace Research,* Vol. 41, No. 2 (March 2004), pp. 211–222.

103. The Polity IV data are based on a 21-point scale that measures the relative openness of political institutions. See Monty G. Marshall and Keith Jaggers, "Polity IV Project: Political Regime Characteristics and Transitions, 1800–2002," http://www.systemicpeace.org/polity/polity4.htm.

104. Singh and Way take their GDP data from version 6.1 of the Penn World Tables. A. Heston, R. Summers, and B. Aten, *Penn World Table* (Philadelphia: Center for International Comparisons, University of Pennsylvania, 2002), ver. 6.1.

105. See Singh and Way, "The Correlates of Nuclear Proliferation."

salient in explaining decisions to proliferate because states make legal pledges not to pursue nuclear weapons when they sign this treaty.

METHODS OF ANALYSIS

I used probit regression analysis to estimate the effect of independent variables on nuclear weapons program onset and bomb acquisition. Given that the proliferation outcomes analyzed here occurred relatively infrequently, I also used rare events logit to estimate the effect of independent variables on nuclear weapons program onset and nuclear weapons acquisition.[106] This estimator is appropriate when the dependent variable has thousands of times fewer 1's than 0's. I used clustering over states to control for heteroskedastic error variance. To control for possible temporal dependence in the data, I also included a variable to count the number of years that passed without a country pursuing nuclear weapons or acquiring the bomb.[107] Finally, I lagged all independent variables one year behind the dependent variable to control for possible simultaneity bias.

Results of the Statistical Tests

Before moving to the multivariate analysis, I considered cross tabulations of nuclear cooperation agreements against nuclear weapons program onset and nuclear weapons acquisition. The results are presented in tables 2 and 3. These simple cross tabulations underscore that proliferation is a relatively rare event. Decisions to begin weapons program occur in fifteen of the observations in the sample (0.22 percent), and bomb acquisition occurs in nine observations in the sample (0.13 percent). Even though proliferation occurs infrequently, these cross tabulations show that nuclear cooperation strongly influences whether countries will go down the nuclear path. Participation in at least one nuclear cooperation agreement increases the likelihood of beginning a bomb program by about 500 percent. The combination of militarized conflict and nuclear assistance has an even larger substantive effect on program onset. Experiencing both of these phenomenon increases the probability of initiating

---

106. Gary King and Langche Zeng, "Logistic Regression in Rare Events Data," *Political Analysis*, Vol. 9, No 2 (February 2001), pp. 137–163. I also use a Cox proportional hazard model to estimate all models, and the results are virtually identical. I do not list the Cox results because of space constraints.

107. Nathaniel Beck, Jonathan N. Katz, and Richard Tucker, "Taking Time Seriously: Time-Series-Cross-Section Analysis with a Binary Dependent Variable," *American Journal of Political Science*, Vol. 42, No. 4 (October 1998), pp. 1260–1288. Cubic splines are not included because proliferation outcomes cannot recur; once a country begins a program or acquires the bomb, it is removed from the sample.

Table 2. Nuclear Cooperation, Militarized Disputes, and Nuclear Weapons Program Onset, 1945–2000

		Civilian Nuclear Cooperation			Civilian Nuclear Cooperation and Militarized Disputes		
		No	Yes	Total	No	Yes	Total
Nuclear weapons program onset	No	4,066 (99.93%)	2,865 (99.58%)	6,931 (99.78%)	5,080 (99.92%)	1,851 (99.41%)	6,931 (99.78%)
	Yes	3 (0.07%)	12 (0.42%)	15 (0.22%)	4 (0.08%)	11 (0.59%)	15 (0.22%)
	Total	4,069 (100%)	2,877 (100%)	6,946 (100%)	5,084 (100%)	1,862 (100%)	6,946 (100%)

Pearson Chi2(1) = 9.22, Pr = 0.002   Pearson Chi2(1) = 16.59, Pr < 0.0001

Table 3. Nuclear Cooperation, Militarized Disputes, and Nuclear Weapons Acquisition, 1945–2000

		Civilian Nuclear Cooperation			Civilian Nuclear Cooperation and Militarized Disputes		
		No	Yes	Total	No	Yes	Total
Nuclear weapons program onset	No	4,077 (99.95%)	3,050 (99.77%)	7,127 (99.87%)	5,099 (99.96%)	2,028 (99.66%)	7,127 (99.78%)
	Yes	2 (0.05%)	7 (0.23%)	9 (0.13%)	2 (0.04%)	7 (0.34%)	9 (0.13%)
	Total	4,079 (100%)	3,057 (100%)	7,136 (100%)	5,101 (100%)	2,035 (100%)	7,136 (100%)

Pearson Chi2(1) = 4.49, Pr = 0.034   Pearson Chi2(1) = 10.73, Pr = 0.0001

a weapons program by about 638 percent. This simple analysis emphasizes that these relationships are not deterministic. Although countries that receive peaceful assistance were more likely to begin weapons programs, the majority of countries that benefit from such aid do not proliferate. It is also noteworthy that 80 percent of the countries that began programs did so after receiving civilian aid. The four countries that initiated nuclear weapon programs without receiving such assistance—France, the Soviet Union, the United Kingdom, and the United States—did so in the 1940s and early 1950s when peaceful nuclear cooperation was not an option. From 1955 to 2000, no country began a nuclear weapons program without first receiving civilian assistance. This suggests that after the early days of the atomic age, nuclear aid became a necessary condition for launching a nuclear weapons program.

Table 4. Determinants of Nuclear Weapons Proliferation, 1945–2000

Atomic Assistance	Model 1	Model 2	Model 3	Model 4	Model 5	Model 6	Model 7	Model 8
Peaceful nuclear cooperation	0.023***	0.062***	0.016**	0.049***	0.019***	0.055***	0.004	0.014
	(0.009)	(0.023)	(0.007)	(0.018)	(0.006)	(0.020)	(0.011)	(0.033)
Militarized disputes	0.152***	0.286***	0.132***	0.265***	0.107**	0.206	0.069*	0.155
	(0.040)	(0.095)	(0.030)	(0.066)	(0.047)	(0.126)	(0.041)	(0.121)
Peaceful nuclear cooperation × militarized disputes			0.025**	0.057***			0.013**	0.024**
			(0.010)	(0.022)			(0.006)	(0.011)
Control Variables								
Nuclear protection	0.085	0.105	0.043	0.005	−0.297	−0.544	−0.340	−0.693
	(0.264)	(0.742)	(0.274)	(0.775)	(0.348)	(1.042)	(0.360)	(1.121)
Nuclear Nonproliferation Treaty	−1.040**	−2.375*	−1.168**	−2.642*				
	(0.463)	(1.286)	(0.536)	(1.435)				
Democracy	−0.000	0.007	−0.006	−0.008	0.016	0.025	0.010	0.011
	(0.016)	(0.045)	(0.016)	(0.042)	(0.016)	(0.053)	(0.017)	(0.055)

Democratization	-0.014 (0.022)	-0.034 (0.065)	-0.015 (0.024)	-0.036 (0.075)	-0.036 (0.035)	-0.079 (0.103)	-0.036 (0.040)	-0.099 (0.127)
Economic openness	0.002 (0.005)	0.008 (0.013)	0.001 (0.005)	0.008 (0.015)	0.003 (0.003)	0.014 (0.012)	0.003 (0.003)	0.015 (0.009)
Liberalization	-0.001 (0.006)	-0.004 (0.017)	0.003 (0.006)	0.019 (0.017)	0.005 (0.004)	0.040*** (0.012)	0.005 (0.003)	0.036*** (0.011)
GDP per capita	0.000* (0.000)	0.000 (0.000)	0.000** (0.000)	0.001 (0.000)	0.000 (0.000)	0.000 (0.000)	0.000 (0.000)	0.000 (0.000)
GDP per capita squared	-0.000*** (0.000)	-0.000* (0.000)	-0.000*** (0.000)	-0.000** (0.000)	-0.000*** (0.000)	-0.000 (0.000)	-0.000** (0.000)	-0.000 (0.000)
Industrial capacity threshold	0.874*** (0.334)	2.150** (0.875)	0.878*** (0.340)	2.219*** (0.861)	1.259*** (0.233)	2.666** (1.056)	1.268*** (0.248)	2.867*** (1.099)
Rivalry	0.909*** (0.317)	2.385** (0.975)	0.758*** (0.286)	1.863** (0.816)	0.884** (0.394)	1.977 (1.286)	0.769* (0.404)	1.638 (1.323)
No proliferation years	0.012 (0.009)	0.031 (0.026)	0.007 (0.009)	0.015 (0.026)	-0.017** (0.008)	-0.038 (0.024)	-0.021** (0.009)	-0.049* (0.026)
Constant	-4.510*** (0.459)	-9.280*** (1.195)	-4.417*** (0.430)	-9.097*** (1.067)	-4.431*** (0.481)	-8.787*** (1.433)	-4.232*** (0.461)	-8.155*** (1.264)
Observations	5,511	5,511	5,511	5,511	5,702	5,702	5,702	5,702

NOTE: Robust standard errors in parentheses; *significant at 0.10; **significant at 0.05; ***significant at 0.01. GDP = gross domestic product.

Similar patterns emerged between nuclear assistance and weapons acquisition. Nuclear aid increases the likelihood of acquiring the bomb by about 360 percent; the combination of atomic assistance and militarized disputes increases the probability of building nuclear weapons by 750 percent. The relationship between nuclear assistance and weapons acquisition is also probabilistic—not deterministic—because not all countries that receive aid cross the nuclear threshold. Table 3 indicates that atomic assistance was not always a necessary condition for bomb acquisition, although the vast majority of all proliferators did receive help. Seventy-eight percent of the countries that produced the bomb received some assistance, and no country acquired weapons without receiving aid from 1953 to 2000.

To explore the role of possible confounding variables, I turn now to the multivariate analysis. Table 4 presents the initial results from the multivariate statistical analysis. The odd-numbered models were estimated using probit, and the even-numbered models were estimated using rare events logit. In models 1–4, the dependent variable is weapons program onset. Models 1 and 2 exclude the interaction term and allow me to evaluate whether peaceful nuclear assistance affects decisions to begin bomb programs independent of the security environment. Models 3 and 4 include the interaction term and enable me to evaluate the conditional effect of atomic assistance on the initiation of nuclear weapons campaigns. In models 5–8 the dependent variable is acquisition. Models 5–6 exclude the interaction term, allowing me to evaluate the unconditional effect of nuclear aid on bomb development. Models 7 and 8 include the interaction term, so I can assess the conditional effect of atomic assistance on a country successfully building nuclear weapons.

The results show that peaceful nuclear assistance continues to contribute to both nuclear weapons program onset and bomb acquisition, even when accounting for confounding variables. In models 1–2 the coefficient on the variable measuring the cumulative amount of atomic assistance a country has received is positive and highly statistically significant.[108] This indicates that, on average, countries receiving nuclear aid are more likely to initiate bomb programs. The substantive effect of this variable is also strong. Raising the value of the NCA variable from its mean (6.69) to one standard deviation above the mean (22.72) increases the likelihood of beginning a weapons program by 185 percent.[109] The findings in table 4 reveal a similar relationship be-

---

108. One could argue that there is a threshold effect involving NCAs whereby making a few agreements increases the risk of proliferation but many agreements make states more likely to foreswear the bomb. To test for this, I add a squared term of the NCA variable to the models displayed in table 4. This does not affect the results.
109. These calculations are based on the results from model 2.

tween atomic assistance and bomb acquisition. As shown in models 5–6, the coefficient on the variable measuring the number of NCAs a country has signed is positive and highly significant, indicating that countries receiving peaceful nuclear aid are more likely to build the bomb. Increasing the NCA variable from its mean to one standard deviation above the mean raises the probability that a country will build nuclear weapons by 243 percent.[110]

Does peaceful nuclear assistance have an especially strong effect on proliferation when countries also face security threats? Because I use an interaction term to test this part of my argument, it is not possible to evaluate this effect based solely on the information presented in table 4. The appropriate way to interpret interaction terms is to graph the marginal effect of atomic assistance and the corresponding standard errors across the full range of the militarized interstate dispute variable.[111] If zero is included in the confidence interval, then atomic assistance does not have a statistically significant effect on proliferation at that particular level of conflict. Figures 2 and 3 allow me to evaluate how the combination of atomic aid and militarized conflict affect proliferation.

Figure 2 plots the marginal effect of nuclear aid on weapons program onset as the number of militarized disputes rises.[112] It is difficult to see in the figure, but atomic assistance has a statistically significant effect on weapons programs across all levels of conflict because zero is never included in the confidence interval. At low levels of conflict, increases in peaceful nuclear assistance have relatively small substantive effects on the likelihood of bomb program onset. But as the security environment worsens, the substantive effect of atomic assistance on initiating a bomb program is magnified.

The probability that an average country experiencing six militarized disputes will develop the bomb rises from 0.000936 to 0.0902 when the country receives increases in atomic aid.[113] This indicates that countries are highly unlikely to begin weapons programs in the absence of such assistance—even if they face security threats. But if threats are present and states receive additional atomic assistance, the likelihood of beginning a bomb program spikes dramatically. If that same country were to be involved in twelve militarized disputes in one year, increases in nuclear assistance would raise the probability of program initiation from 0.0625 to 0.737, an increase of 1,078 percent. If an

110. These calculations are based on the results from model 6.
111. Thomas Brambor, William Roberts Clark, and Matt Golder, "Understanding Interaction Models: Improving Empirical Analyses," *Political Analysis*, Vol. 14, No. 1 (Winter 2006), pp. 63 82.
112. Figure 2 is based on the results in model 3. To calculate the marginal effects, I increase the value of the peaceful nuclear cooperation variable from its mean to one-half standard deviation above the mean.
113. To calculate these figures, I set all other variables at their mean.

Figure 2. Marginal Effect of Nuclear Assistance on Weapons Program Onset as Number of Disputes Increases

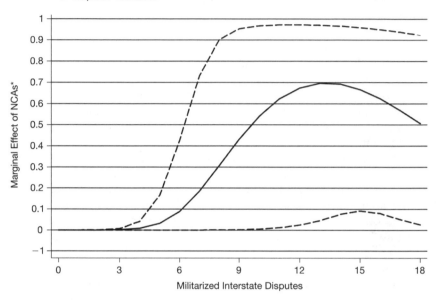

*NCAs = nuclear cooperation agreements

average country that experiences eighteen militarized disputes in a year receives additional atomic assistance, the likelihood that it will begin a weapons program rises from 0.426 to 0.933, an increase of 119 percent. Note that at high levels of conflict, the probability of weapons program onset approaches 1 with increases in peaceful aid, but countries that face numerous security threats are also likely to proliferate in the absence of assistance. Consequently, increases in nuclear assistance yield smaller rises in the probability of proliferation at high levels of conflict. This is why the marginal effect displayed in figure 2 declines slightly after about thirteen disputes.

Figure 3 illustrates the conditional effect of nuclear aid on weapons acquisition as the number of disputes rises.[114] Nuclear assistance does not have a statistically significant effect on acquisition when countries experience an average of zero militarized disputes, because zero is included in the confidence inter-

---

114. Figure 3 is based on the results in model 7.

Figure 3. Marginal Effect of Nuclear Assistance on Weapons Acquisition as Number of Disputes Increases

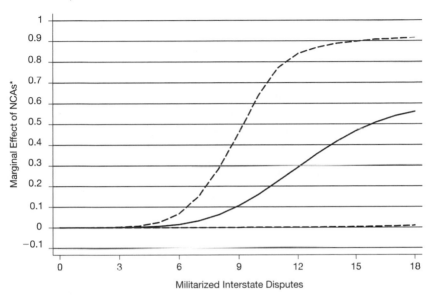

Militarized Interstate Disputes

*NCAs = nuclear cooperation agreements

val. For all other levels of conflict, atomic assistance has a statistically significant effect. If countries experience an average of one militarized dispute, the substantive effect of atomic aid is modest. Increases in peaceful assistance raise the probability of bomb acquisition from 0.0000165 to 0.0000122, an increase of 43 percent. For an average state experiencing six disputes, receiving nuclear aid raises the probability it will acquire nuclear weapons more substantially, from 0.000504 to 0.00202. If that same state were to experience twelve disputes in a year, the probability of acquisition would rise from 0.0144 to 0.306, an increase of 2,031 percent. Likewise, receiving atomic assistance and experiencing eighteen conflicts increases the probability of bomb development by 511 percent, from 0.110 to 0.671. These results indicate that, on average, countries that receive atomic assistance are more likely to proliferate—especially when security threats arise.

Turning to the control variables, the coefficient on the variable measuring whether a state shares a military alliance with a nuclear-armed power is statistically insignificant in all eight models, suggesting that nuclear protection has no effect on whether a country pursues the bomb or successfully builds it. The coefficients on the variables measuring whether a country is democratic or is democratizing are also statistically insignificant, indicating that regime type has little effect on proliferation aims and outcomes. Many policymakers assume that proliferation is a problem caused by "rogue" or undemocratic states. Although some autocratic states such as North Korea have proliferated in recent years, on average democracy is less salient in explaining the spread of nuclear weapons than the conventional wisdom suggests. The results also fail to support the argument that trade dependence influences nuclear proliferation. The coefficients on the variables measuring trade dependence and liberalization are not statistically significant in models 1–4, meaning that these factors have no effect on states' decisions to build the bomb. Economic openness also has an insignificant effect on bomb acquisition. But interestingly, liberalization has a positive and statistically significant effect in models 6 and 8, indicating that liberalizing states are more likely to cross the nuclear threshold. Future research should explore whether these results may be due to imperfect measurement of these concepts.

Some of the control variables do behave as expected. The coefficient on the variable measuring whether a country has signed the NPT is negative and statistically significant in models 1–4, indicating that countries making nonproliferation commitments are less likely to initiate bomb programs. Substantively, NPT membership reduces the likelihood that a country will begin a nuclear weapons program by more than 90 percent. For statistical reasons, it was necessary to exclude the NPT variable from models 5–8.[115] The coefficient on the variable measuring whether a country is involved in a rivalry is positive and statistically significant across models 1–4, but it is insignificant in models 6 and 8. Likewise, the GDP variables have statistically significant effects in models 1 and 3, but these results are sensitive to model specification. Industrial capacity has a positive and statistically significant effect in all eight models, indicating that countries with high industrial capabilities are more likely to begin weapons programs and successfully build the bomb. This is the only variable other than the factors operationalizing my argument that has a statistically significant effect across model specifications. Having adequate industrial capacity increases the probability of program initiation from 0.00000226 to 0.000105 and the probability of acquisition from 0.000487 to 0.000804.

To further assess the robustness of my findings, I conducted a sensitivity analysis. I used a new estimator to account for possible endogeneity and an alternate coding for the dependent variable. In addition, I excluded "sensitive"

---

115. The NPT variable is not included in the acquisition analysis because it predicts failure perfectly. This poses problems for standard statistical techniques.

nuclear cooperation agreements from the coding of my key independent variable. For space considerations, I discuss only briefly the results of these robustness checks. Detailed discussions of the results and procedures, as well as all of the tables displaying the statistical results, are available in an online appendix.[116]

ENDOGENEITY

My argument is that the accumulation of nuclear cooperation agreements encourages states to begin nuclear weapons programs and that receiving atomic aid ultimately enables states to acquire nuclear weapons. But it is also possible that states seek nuclear assistance when they are pursuing nuclear weapons.[117] Thus, nuclear cooperation may be endogenous to nuclear weapons pursuit.

One standard approach to address the endogeneity issue is to lag the independent variables one year behind the dependent variable.[118] I adopted this approach in the analysis presented above. As an additional way to address this issue, I estimated two endogenous equations simultaneously. The first equation represents the total number of nuclear cooperation agreements a state has made in a particular year, and the second estimates the likelihood that it is pursuing nuclear weapons. As was the case above, the proliferation equation parallels the work of Singh and Way.[119] The nuclear cooperation equation that I employed is based on a recent study of the causes of atomic assistance.[120] To estimate these equations simultaneously, I used a technique originally developed by G.S. Maddala and practically implemented by Omar Keshk.[121] This method is designed for simultaneous equation models where one of the endogenous variables is continuous and the other is dichotomous, which is precisely the nature of the variables in this analysis. The two-stage estimation technique generates instruments for each of the endogenous variables and then substitutes them in the respective structural equations. The first equation (with the continuous variable) is estimated using ordinary least squares, and the second (with the dichotomous variable) is estimated using probit.[122]

---

116. See data section, http://people.cas.sc.edu/fuhrmann.
117. See Fuhrmann, "Taking a Walk on the Supply Side."
118. See, for example, Erik Gartzke and Quan Li, "Measure for Measure: Concept Operationalization and the Trade Interdependence-Conflict Debate," *Journal of Peace Research*, Vol. 40, No. 5 (September 2003), pp. 553–571.
119. Singh and Way, "The Correlates of Nuclear Proliferation."
120. Fuhrmann, "Taking a Walk on the Supply Side."
121. G.S. Maddala, *Limited-Dependent and Qualitative Variables in Econometrics* (Cambridge: Cambridge University Press, 1986); and Omar Keshk, "CDSIMEQ: A Program to Implement Two-Stage Probit Least Squares," *Stata Journal*, Vol. 3, No. 2 (June 2003), pp. 157–167.
122. For other work in political science that uses this approach, see Omar M.G. Keshk, Brian M. Pollins, and Rafael Reuveny, "Trade Still Follows the Flag: The Primacy of Politics in a Simulta-

The results of the two-stage probit least squares model that addresses the simultaneity issue are generally consistent with the findings presented above.[123] Most important, nuclear cooperation has a positive and statistically significant effect on nuclear weapons pursuit. This result is robust to alternate model specifications.[124]

DEPENDENT VARIABLE CODING

It is often difficult to determine the year that a country begins a nuclear weapons program or acquires the bomb, given the secrecy that surrounds such military endeavors. As a result, there is some disagreement among scholars on the dates that certain countries began to proliferate. To explore whether my results are sensitive to proliferation codings, I used an alternate set of proliferators and dates compiled by Jo and Gartzke.[125] Estimating the same models displayed above but with the alternate proliferation dates also does not affect the results relating to my argument.

REMOVAL OF SENSITIVE AGREEMENTS

Recent research finds that countries receiving certain "sensitive" nuclear assistance are more likely to acquire nuclear weapons.[126] For the reasons I argued above, the relationship between nuclear assistance and proliferation is broader. Training in nuclear engineering, the supply of research or power reactors, and

---

neous Model of Interdependence and Armed Conflict," *Journal of Politics*, Vol. 66, No. 4 (November 2004), pp. 1155–1179; Hyung Min Kim and David L. Rousseau, "The Classical Liberals Were Half Right (or Half Wrong): New Tests of the 'Liberal Peace,' 1960–88," *Journal of Peace Research*, Vol. 42, No. 5 (September 2005), pp. 523–543; and Cameron Thies, "Of Rules, Rebels, and Revenue: State Capacity, Civil War Onset, and Primary Commodities," paper presented at the Pan-European Conference on International Relations, Torino, Italy, September 12–15, 2007.

123. I did not include the interaction term in the simultaneous equations model. It is possible to include interaction terms in such models by calculating the predicted value of the endogenous variable (peaceful nuclear cooperation), interacting this predicted variable with the exogenous variable (militarized disputes), estimating the second equation. This approach is problematic, however, because it does not appropriately correct the standard errors. See Jeffrey M. Wooldridge, *Introductory Econometrics: A Modern Approach* (New York: South-Western College, 2000), pp. 501–528.

124. One of the weaknesses of simultaneous equations models is that the independent variables in the first equation should be exogenous. In other words, they should be unrelated to the dependent variable in the second equation. In international relations, it is difficult for scholars to meet this assumption when using simultaneous equations models. For instance, international trade and militarized conflict are endogenous variables because trade suppresses conflict but conflict also reduces trade. This is why some scholars use the same estimator applied in this article to examine the trade-conflict nexus. But many of the correlates of trade—such as the distance between two countries—are also correlated with conflict. See Keshk, Pollins, and Reuveny, "Trade Still Follows the Flag." The best I can do to address this issue is to reestimate the models while excluding the variables in the first equation that are clearly related to nuclear proliferation. This alteration does not change my core findings.

125. Jo and Gartzke, "Determinants of Nuclear Weapons Proliferation."

126. Kroenig, "Importing the Bomb."

the transfer of certain nuclear materials also affect proliferation. To test whether my results may be driven by a few sensitive deals, I excluded them from the coding of my independent variable. This type of sensitive agreement is extremely rare, so this change resulted in the removal of a small number of agreements. I then estimated all models displayed in table 4 with this alternate coding of the independent variable. The findings relevant to my argument are generally unaltered when sensitive agreements are excluded from my coding of atomic assistance.[127]

Conclusion

Aided by a new data set, this article systematically explored the relationship between civilian nuclear cooperation and nuclear proliferation. It argued that civilian assistance and weapons proliferation are linked because the former leads to the supply of technology and materials that have applications for nuclear energy and nuclear weapons, and because civilian assistance establishes an indigenous base of knowledge in nuclear matters that could be useful for a weapons program. These linkages reduce the expected costs of a nuclear weapons program, making states more likely to begin such a campaign when they have accumulated peaceful assistance—especially when a crisis or security threat arises. Similarly, countries receiving civilian aid are more likely to acquire nuclear bombs because important technological hurdles are lowered.

The analysis conducted in this article lends support for these arguments, even when controlling for the other variables believed to influence proliferation. Other factors are also strong predictors of proliferation, but peaceful nuclear cooperation is one of the more salient variables in explaining why atomic weapons spread. Thus, this article suggests that students of proliferation should take greater stock of civilian nuclear assistance. This is particularly true given that the links between the peaceful and military uses of the atom appear broader than previously believed. Even seemingly "innocuous" nuclear cooperation such as providing training to nuclear scientists or supplying power/research reactors can produce deleterious effects. There is no such thing as "proliferation-proof" atomic assistance.

Since the early days of the atomic age, policymakers have attempted to pro-

---

127. In a related robustness check unreported here, I removed the sensitive agreements from my independent variable and included a separate dichotomous variable that is coded 1 beginning in the first year a state received sensitive nuclear assistance. I then reestimated all of the models displayed in table 4. The results still show that atomic assistance has a strong effect on both stages of nuclear proliferation. The only noteworthy difference is that at high levels of conflict (more than seven militarized disputes per year), nuclear assistance loses its statistical significance. But it is unclear that sensitive aid explains why this happens. The dummy variable measuring only sensitive nuclear assistance did not attain conventional levels of statistical significance in any of the models.

mote the peaceful uses of nuclear energy. These initiatives were based, at least in part, on the belief that spreading technology would make states less likely to want nuclear weapons. This analysis reveals that "atoms for peace" policies have, on average, facilitated—not constrained—nuclear proliferation. Atoms for peace become atoms for war. From a nonproliferation standpoint, this is a troubling conclusion that carries tremendous policy implications, especially given the looming renaissance in nuclear power. The global nuclear market-place is more active today than it has been in at least twenty years. Countries in Latin America, Southeast Asia, the Middle East, and Africa have expressed a desire to begin or revive civilian nuclear programs. And many of them are receiving assistance in developing such programs from France, Japan, Russia, the United States, and other capable suppliers.

This article suggests that proliferation will occur as the nuclear renaissance unfolds. But there are measures policymakers can implement to reduce the risks that accompany the spread of nuclear technology. After all, as former U.S. senator and nonproliferation advocate Sam Nunn frequently argues, policy-makers are in the business of "risk reduction," not "risk elimination." To reiter-ate a point made previously, most instances of civilian assistance do not result in proliferation, and there is little reason to expect deterministic links between these two phenomena. Thus, swift and meaningful action by the international community might be able to reverse past trends. In particular, countries should provide additional resources to the IAEA. Safeguards agreements im-plemented by the IAEA allow it to monitor nuclear facilities to ensure that they are used strictly for peaceful purposes. But the agency is grossly underfunded. IAEA Director-General Mohamed ElBaradei recently stated that the agency's budget "does not by any stretch of the imagination meet our basic, essential re-quirements," and "our ability to carry out our essential functions is being chipped away."[128] This is troubling because the rise in demand for nuclear en-ergy will increase the IAEA's requirements for safeguards and inspections. Countries must ensure that the agency has adequate resources to fulfill its mis-sion. It would also be prudent to consider ways that the IAEA's mission could be expanded to further decrease the likelihood that civilian nuclear coopera-tion will aid weapons acquisition.

Additionally, nuclear suppliers should adopt responsible export practices and avoid the temptation to sacrifice long-term nonproliferation objectives in pursuit of short-term economic or political gains. They should be espe-cially cautious when supplying technology or know-how to countries that

---

128. Quoted in Paul Kerr, "ElBaradei: IAEA Budget Problems Dangerous," *Arms Control Today*, Vol. 37, No. 6 (July/August 2007), http://www.armscontrol.org/act/2007_07-08/IAEABudget.

face significant security threats. Many of the countries currently beginning or expanding their civilian nuclear programs are in the Middle East—the world's most dangerous region. Algeria, Jordan, Libya, Saudi Arabia, and the United Arab Emirates have all received pledges of support from at least one supplier country since 2006. None of these countries currently intends to build nuclear weapons. But that could change if Iran crosses the nuclear threshold or if Israel conducts an atomic test and reverses its policy of opacity. One of the important conclusions of this article is that the combination of atomic assistance and security threats is a recipe for the spread of nuclear weapons. Suppliers such as France and the United States, therefore, should rethink their offers of atomic assistance to states in the Middle East and other dangerous regions.

There is still more work to be done to advance scholarly understanding of the relationship between peaceful nuclear cooperation and proliferation. Future research should examine illicit nuclear trade and explore how it relates to peaceful nuclear assistance. It would be productive to analyze additional cases of licit and illicit nuclear commerce to confirm or invalidate the propositions advanced in this article. Additional case studies that examine why some countries receiving peaceful assistance pursue the bomb whereas others do not would be particularly welcome because they might reveal useful policy recommendations for how to promote nuclear energy while minimizing proliferation risks.

This study also raises an interesting puzzle: Why do suppliers provide civilian assistance? If countries generally want to limit the spread of nuclear weapons and if nuclear cooperation agreements lead to proliferation, then it seems puzzling that supplier states would engage in civilian nuclear cooperation. Recent research suggests that countries ignore proliferation risks in pursuit of strategic or economic benefits.[129] For example, France's recent NCAs with Saudi Arabia and the United Arab Emirates are motivated in part by a desire to obtain assurances on the supply of oil. Another possibility is that countries offer assistance to intentionally spread the bomb and constrain other countries.[130] Additional work examining suppliers' motivations would be welcome, as it could shed further light on how and why nuclear weapons spread.

---

129. Fuhrmann, "Taking a Walk on the Supply Side."
130. Kroenig, "Exporting the Bomb."

Part II:
The Sources and Consequences of Nuclear
Proliferation in South Asia

India's Pathway to Pokhran II

Sumit Ganguly

The Prospects and Sources of New Delhi's Nuclear Weapons Program

On May 11 and 13, 1998, India set off five nuclear devices at its test site in Pokhran in the northwestern Indian state of Rajasthan—its first such tests in twenty-four years. The initial test had been carried out at the same site on May 18, 1974. Not unexpectedly, as in 1974 much of the world community, including the majority of the great powers, unequivocally condemned the Indian tests.[1] The coalition national government, dominated by the jingoistic Bharatiya Janata Party (BJP), knew that significant international pressures would be brought to bear upon India once it breached this important threshold. Yet the BJP chose to disregard the likely adverse consequences and departed from India's post-1974 "nuclear option" policy, which had reserved for India the right to weaponize its nuclear capabilities but had not overtly declared its weapons capability. National governments of varying political persuasions had adhered to this strategy for more than two decades.

A number of seemingly compelling possibilities have been offered to explain India's dramatic departure from its policy of nuclear restraint. None, however, constitutes a complete explanation. Yet each offers useful insights into the forces that led to the Indian nuclear tests. One explanation holds that the chauvinistic BJP-led government conducted the tests to demonstrate both its own virility to the Indian populace and India's military prowess to the rest of the world. A second argument suggests that the BJP conducted the tests to cement its links with contentious parliamentary allies. A third argument contends that

Sumit Ganguly is a Professor of Political Science at Hunter College and the Graduate School of the City University of New York. During the spring 1999 term, he will be a Visiting Professor of Government and South Asian Studies at the University of Texas at Austin.

The author would like to thank Stephen P. Cohen, Ted Greenwood, Robert L. Hardgrave, Jr., Traci Nagle, Andrew Polsky, and Jack Snyder for their comments. He is also grateful for the assistance of Rahul Mukherji in the preparation of this article. Research support was provided by the United States Institute of Peace.

1. For a compendium of official reactions to the 1998 Indian and Pakistani nuclear tests, see "India and Pakistan Nuclear Tests: Details and International Reaction," *Disarmament Diplomacy*, No. 20 (May 1998), pp. 1–20. A small debate has arisen over the number and quality of both the Indian and Pakistani tests. See Robert Lee Hotz, "Tests Were Exaggerated by India and Pakistan," *International Herald Tribune*, September 17, 1998, p. 1; and Raj Chengappa, "Is India's H-Bomb a Dud?" *India Today International*, October 12, 1998, pp. 22–28.

International Security, Vol. 23, No. 4 (Spring 1999), pp. 148–177

these tests were designed to bolster India's prestige in the international system. A fourth argument focuses on the role of key Indian scientists in endowing nuclear weapons with mythical significance.

My analysis draws upon components of the various proffered explanations and seeks to develop them in a historically contextualized fashion. I argue in this article that three factors impelled India toward its 1998 nuclear tests: fifty years of critical political choices, influenced by ideology and the imperatives of statecraft; fitful scientific advances in India's nuclear infrastructure; and an increased perception of threat from China and Pakistan since the end of the Cold War.

The debates and decisions pertaining to India's nuclear weapons program can be divided into five distinct phases, each of which brought the country closer to the May 1998 tests. The first phase began with the creation of India's Atomic Energy Commission (AEC) in 1948; the Chinese nuclear test in 1964 marked the beginning of the second phase; the third comprises the buildup and execution of India's first nuclear test, in 1974; the fourth began in the aftermath of that test; and the fifth brought India from the collapse of the Soviet Union in 1991 to the tests in 1998. At each of these stages and, more important, at each of the crucial points where decisions were made to take India closer to nuclear weapons status, the three factors outlined above can explain India's nuclear decisions.[2] India's perceptions of external threats and the reactions of the great powers to its security concerns played a fundamental role in driving the nuclear program. Segments of the scientific community within India, at these critical junctures, not only enabled but encouraged the program's development. Finally, the most critical element involved the political choices made by the Indian national leadership. A sixth section assesses a number of proffered explanations for the Indian tests and discusses the prospects for regional stability.

Phase One: The Origins of India's Nuclear Program

The Indian nuclear program in a sense predates India's independence from the British Empire in 1947. The civilian program can be traced to the work of the Indian physicist Homi J. Bhaba, who had studied with the eminent nuclear scientist Lord Ernest Rutherford at Cambridge University in the 1930s. Upon his return to India, Bhaba persuaded one of India's industrial giants, the Tata fam-

---

2. India's quest for great power status also, in some measure, contributed to the nuclear tests. But this explanation has received inordinate emphasis, especially in the Western press, to the neglect of other, more compelling explanations. See, for example, Pankaj Mishra, "A New Nuclear India?" *New York Review of Books*, June 25, 1998, pp. 55–64.

ily, to contribute money toward the creation of a center for the study of nuclear physics. The Tata Institute for Fundamental Research opened in Bombay in 1945. After India's independence, Bhaba convinced India's first prime minister, Jawaharlal Nehru, of the signal importance of atomic energy research in enabling India to build an industrial base and to tackle the overwhelming problems of entrenched poverty. Bhaba's views impressed Nehru, who had a fundamentally scientific demeanor.[3] From the outset the Indian atomic energy establishment, under the direction of the prime minister, enjoyed a high degree of autonomy and was largely shielded from public scrutiny.[4] Bhaba, as the first head of the Department of Atomic Energy, created on August 3, 1954, worked zealously to preserve the organizational autonomy of India's nuclear energy estate. Shortly after India's independence, the AEC had been established under the Department of Scientific Research, and, in accordance with India's strategy of economic self-reliance, every effort was made to keep the program indigenous. Perforce India had to obtain some assistance in reactor design from the United Kingdom and from Canada.

Publicly, Nehru opposed the development of nuclear weapons, a position that accorded with his deep-seated opposition to the use of force to resolve international disputes.[5] This conviction, in part, stemmed from the Gandhian legacy of the Indian nationalist movement. Nehru's aversion to nuclear weapons also drew from his fundamental fear of the militarization of Indian society.[6] Additionally, his opposition was an outgrowth of his firm beliefs about the role of the use of military force in world affairs.[7] Nehru believed that military spending was, at best, a necessary evil.[8]

---

3. On this point, see Leonard Beaton and John Maddox, *The Spread of Nuclear Weapons* (New York: Praeger, 1962), p. 136.
4. For particularly strident criticisms of the lack of accountability in the Indian nuclear program, see David Brown, *Nuclear Power in India: A Comparative Analysis* (London: Allen and Unwin, 1983).
5. There has been some speculation during the last decade that, despite his public stance, Nehru wanted to keep India's weapons option open. On Nehru's ambivalence toward nuclear weapons, see Peter Lavoy, "Learning to Live with the Bomb? India and Nuclear Weapons, 1947–74," Ph.D. dissertation, University of California, 1997, especially pp. 153–158.
6. Stephen P. Cohen, *The Indian Army* (Berkeley: University of California Press, 1967).
7. Western commentators have often commented on Nehru's willingness to use force in Kashmir in 1947–48 and subsequently in Goa in 1960. These charges of hypocrisy are largely polemical. The Kashmir war involved the defense of a besieged state. In the Goan case all negotiated attempts to induce the Portuguese to withdraw peacefully from their anachronistic colonial enclave failed. Only under these conditions did Nehru authorize the use of force. The literature on Kashmir's accession to India and the subsequent war is voluminous; for a dispassionate account, see H.V. Hodson, *The Great Divide* (Karachi: Oxford University Press, 1985). For a particularly thoughtful account of the Goa question and India's resort to force, see Arthur Rubinoff, *India's Use of Force in Goa* (Bombay: Popular Prakashan, 1971).
8. Even a quick perusal of his many writings reveals the depth of these convictions. See, for example, Jawaharlal Nehru, *The Discovery of India* (New Delhi: Oxford University Press, 1995).

As prime minister, Nehru enunciated a policy of nonalignment, principally to distance India from the superpower struggle. Both the Western and Soviet blocs derided this doctrine, especially when it was inconsistently applied. Nevertheless, Nehru refused to be swayed. He spoke out vigorously against the growing nuclear arsenals of both superpowers and sought to reduce international tensions in various parts of the world.[9]

Despite his public opposition to nuclear weapons, Nehru granted Bhaba a free hand in the development of India's nuclear infrastructure. Meanwhile, he sought to lay the necessary foundations should a political decision to acquire nuclear weapons be made. In pursuit of this end, Bhaba worked inexorably toward a complete mastery of the nuclear fuel cycle and toward a completely indigenous production process. As early as 1958, Bhaba had a conversation with the British physicist and defense adviser Lord P.M.S. Blackett about his interest in the acquisition of nuclear weapons.[10] Four years later, India's disastrous war with China likely reinforced Bhaba's interest in pursuing the nuclear weapons option.[11]

THE 1962 SINO-INDIAN BORDER WAR AND ITS AFTERMATH
A turning point in the Indian foreign policy establishment's attitude toward defense spending came in the aftermath of the Sino-Indian border war of October 1962. After invading India along the Himalayan border, the Chinese People's Liberation Army routed the ill-equipped and ill-prepared Indian army and came to occupy some 14,000 square miles of Indian territory. Worse still, the Chinese declared a unilateral cease-fire after achieving their territorial objectives, thereby humiliating Nehru and the Indian political leadership.[12] The significance of this war on India's foreign and security policymakers cannot be underestimated. The Chinese attack fundamentally called into question Nehru's varied attempts to court the Chinese and to bring China into the comity of nations: he had expressed the mildest condemnation of the harsh Chinese occupation of Tibet in 1950; had readily ceded India's extraterritorial

9. For a discussion of the philosophical origins of nonalignment and the quest for an alternative world order, see A.P. Rana, *The Imperatives of Nonalignment* (Delhi: Macmillan, 1976). For a discussion of the practice of nonalignment and Nehru's attempt to defuse international tensions in a neighboring region, see D.R. Sardesai, *Indian Foreign Policy in Cambodia, Laos, and Vietnam, 1947–1964* (Berkeley: University of California Press, 1968).
10. See Shyam Bhatia, *India's Nuclear Bomb* (Ghaziabad, India: Vikas, 1979), p. 114.
11. For a discussion of Bhaba's concerns about Chinese capabilities and intentions, see Incoming Telegram, U.S. Department of State, November 14, 1964, available in file "Nuclear Proliferation: India-Pakistan," National Security Archive, Washington, D.C.
12. On this point, see Steven Hoffman, *India and the China Crisis* (Berkeley: University of California Press, 1990).

privileges in Tibet, inherited from the British colonial period, in 1952; and had championed China's entry into the United Nations (UN). Through these measures Nehru had hoped to avoid a conflict with China, which he knew would compel him to increase defense spending. The border war forced Nehru to reappraise his strategy and his most cherished ideals.

Phase Two: The Chinese Test at Lop Nor

The second phase of India's nuclear program started shortly after the first Chinese nuclear test at Lop Nor on October 16, 1964.[13] Following that test, segments of India's political and scientific establishments evinced a greater interest in acquiring nuclear weapons.

By this time Bhaba had begun to articulate the politico-military significance of nuclear weapons: "Nuclear weapons coupled with an adequate delivery system can enable a State to destroy more or less totally the cities, industry, and all-important targets in another State. It is then largely irrelevant whether the State so attacked has greater destructive power at its command. With the help of nuclear weapons, therefore, a State can acquire what we may call a position of absolute deterrence even against another having a many times greater destructive power under its control."[14]

Bhaba's stance toward nuclear deterrence would find many adherents and some critics in India in the wake of the Chinese test. To no one's surprise, the news of the test released a firestorm of controversy across India. China's acquisition of nuclear weapons in the aftermath of the 1962 Sino-Indian border war dealt a further blow to India's national security. Sisir Gupta, one of India's ablest diplomats, spelled out the concerns of most Indian strategists: ". . . without using its nuclear weapons and without unleashing the kind of war which would be regarded in the West as the crossing of the provocation-threshold, China may subject a non-nuclear India to periodic blackmail, weaken its people's spirit of resistance and self-confidence, and thus achieve without a war its major political and military objectives in Asia."[15] Minoo Masani, a leader of the small, pro-Western Swatantra Party, expressed the fears of many of India's leaders: "The Chinese explosion cannot be ignored; it cannot be written off; it

---

13. John Wilson Lewis and Xue Litai, *China Builds the Bomb* (Stanford, Calif.: Stanford University Press, 1988).
14. H.J. Bhaba, "Safeguards and the Dissemination of Military Power," paper presented at the Twelfth Pugwash Conference on Science and World Affairs, Geneva, January 27–February 1, 1964.
15. Sisir Gupta, "The Indian Dilemma," in Alastair Buchan, ed., *A World of Nuclear Powers?* (Englewood Cliffs, N.J.: Prentice-Hall, 1966), pp. 55–67, at p. 62.

cannot be played down; it is of major significance. We are the country for which it has the most immediate importance."[16]

Masani and other opposition members rebuked the government for not undertaking a more thorough review of the changed security situation on the subcontinent following the Chinese test and for not developing an appropriate response. The Bharatiya Jana Sangh (the forerunner to the BJP) condemned India's policy of nuclear abstinence.[17] Even normally progovernment newspapers questioned the leadership's seeming complacency in the wake of the Chinese nuclear tests.[18]

Nehru, however, remained publicly opposed to the development of nuclear weapons. Nine days before his death, in a television interview in New York on May 18, 1964, he stated, "We are determined not to use weapons for war purposes. We do not make atom bombs. I do not think we will."[19] His defense minister, Y.B. Chavan, however, felt compelled to reaffirm India's commitment to the modernization of its conventional forces in the wake of the Chinese test.[20]

THE QUEST FOR A NUCLEAR GUARANTEE
In December 1964 at a press conference in London, Prime Minister Lal Bahadur Shastri revealed India's efforts to obtain a nuclear guarantee from the nuclear weapons states.[21] He pursued this course even though a number of Indian politicians, including some within the ruling Congress Party, feared that it would compromise their country's nonalignment stance.

At the same time, political analysts with close connections to the government argued that India's credentials for boosting the nuclear disarmament agenda could be strengthened if the country refrained from developing nu-

---

16. Quoted in *Lok Sabha Debates* 35, November 16–27, 1964 (New Delhi: Lok Sabha Secretariat, 1964), pp. 1239–1240.
17. A representative sample is Eskayji (pseudonym), "Why India Must Have the Bomb," *Organizer* (India), December 28, 1964, p. 5.
18. Editorial, "Time for Rethinking," *Hindustan Standard* (Delhi), October 20, 1964, p. 4.
19. Quoted in G.G. Mirchandani, *India's Nuclear Dilemma* (New Delhi: Popular Book Services, 1968), p. 23.
20. "New Strategy on Defence: Impact of Chinese Atomic Test," *Statesman* (Calcutta), October 20, 1964, p. 1; and Express News Service, "Chavan Urges a Look at the Bomb from Defence Angle: Chinese Threat Not Yet Over," *Indian Express* (Delhi), December 1, 1964, p. 1. See also Incoming Telegram, U.S. Department of State, October 27, 1968, available in file "Nuclear Proliferation: India-Pakistan," National Security Archive, Washington, D.C.
21. On the basis of the limited sources in the public domain, it appears that India's quest for a nuclear guarantee was poorly executed. It is hard to discern what exactly the Indian leadership had in mind when it sought to acquire such a guarantee from the great powers. For a discussion of India's attempts to obtain a nuclear guarantee, see A.G. Noorani, "India's Quest for a Nuclear Guarantee," *Asian Survey*, Vol. 7, No. 7 (July 1967), pp. 490–502.

clear weapons even in the face of potential aggression by a nuclear-armed adversary.[22] These sentiments were first aired in a vigorous debate that took place at the All India Congress Committee (AICC) meeting between January 7 and 9, 1965. In the aftermath of the Chinese tests a number of Congress Party members of parliament favored dropping India's rigid stance on questions of disarmament. They forcefully and repeatedly called for a reorientation of India's foreign policy in light of the new perceived threat from China. However, the Congress leadership refused to address their central demand—a fundamental shift in India's nuclear policy—contending that the prohibitive costs of embarking on a nuclear weapons program, India's historic commitment to a nuclear-free world, its belief in Gandhian principles, and misgivings about alienating world opinion undermined the case for the acquisition of a nuclear weapons option.[23] In effect, the AICC chose to defer the question of acquiring nuclear weapons.[24] Interestingly, several individuals upbraided Homi Bhaba at this conference for a recent public statement in which he had spelled out the potential economic costs of developing a modest nuclear force for India.[25]

These sentiments, which rallied against a drastic shift in India's security policy, were again expressed, despite continuing dissension, at the next meeting of the AICC, held on January 8, 1966.[26] The arguments for rejecting the call to nuclear arms were made mostly along moral and ethical lines. One of the more prominent critics of nuclear weapons, senior Congress politician Morarji Desai, led the charge against the proponents of a shift in India's nuclear policies. Desai argued that India should not jettison its moral objections to nuclear weapons at the first sign of danger. At the same time, Prime Minister Shastri argued that the superpowers could not afford to be indifferent to India's plight in the face of a nuclear threat from China; however, he did not completely forswear the nuclear option. Some evidence shows that Shastri allowed Bhaba to work toward reducing the time needed to develop nuclear explosives.[27] He

---

22. Some flavor of the strategic debate within India can be gathered from R.K. Nehru, "The Challenge of the Chinese Bomb," *India Quarterly* (1965), pp. 3–14.
23. Shastri's concerns about the economic burden of pursuing a nuclear weapons program were entirely understandable: he had inherited an unenviable economy legacy. See Michael Brecher, *Nehru's Mantle: The Politics of Succession in India* (New York: Praeger, 1966), pp. 138–150.
24. Thomas W. Graham, "Nuclear Deterrence, Arms Control, and Confidence-Building Measures in South Asia," in Eric H. Arnett, ed., *New Perspectives for a Changing World Order* (Washington, D.C.: American Association for the Advancement of Science, 1991), p. 127.
25. Special Correspondent, "AICC Split on Atomic Issue," *Statesman* (Delhi), November 8, 1964, p. 1.
26. K. Rangaswami, "Atom Bomb to Meet China's Threat: Vigorous Support in AICC for Independent Deterrent," *Hindu* (Madras), January 8, 1965, p. 3.
27. Albert Wohlstetter, Victor Gilinsky, Robert Gillette, and Roberta Wohlstetter, *Nuclear Policies: Fuel without the Bomb* (Cambridge, Mass.: Ballinger, 1978), p. 58.

concluded that, for the present term, India should strengthen its conventional forces to defend itself against a possible Chinese attack.[28]

Amid these debates, Shastri dispatched Sardar Swaran Singh, his foreign minister, to ascertain the views of the United States, the Soviet Union, and the United Kingdom on India's request for a nuclear guarantee. Swaran Singh's initial assessment suggested that the requisite guarantees would materialize. Subsequently, however, during a debate on May 10, 1965, in the Lok Sabha (the lower house of the Indian parliament), he admitted that the nuclear weapons states had ultimately failed to provide any such guarantees.

APPROACHES TO A NONPROLIFERATION TREATY

During this period the United States and the Soviet Union, exercised by the Chinese nuclear tests, sought to forge a multilateral treaty to stop the further spread of nuclear weapons.[29] Accordingly, in November 1965 the UN Political Committee adopted a resolution detailing the guidelines for a treaty on nuclear nonproliferation. The Indian delegation to the UN had played a key role in drafting the central provisions of the text, which embodied two principles of special significance to India's concerns. First, the draft treaty specified a balance of mutual responsibilities and obligations on the part of the nuclear and nonnuclear powers. It offered the nonnuclear states access to peaceful nuclear technology in return for their agreement not to obtain or develop nuclear weapons. Second, the draft indicated that the attempts to promote nonproliferation would be merely a first step toward the ultimate goal of universal nuclear disarmament. As discussions on the proposed treaty progressed, India added another qualification: nonnuclear states should be able to carry out "peaceful nuclear explosions."[30] The United States firmly opposed this last proposal on the grounds that no meaningful distinction could be made between "peaceful" and "nonpeaceful" nuclear explosions.[31] The various Indian delegations to the Eighteen Nation Disarmament Conference (ENDC) in Geneva in April and June 1965 nevertheless continued to press this distinction.[32] As the proposed treaty started to take shape, Indian diplomats outside

28. See, for example, Express News Service, "The Bomb to Loom Large at AICC Meet," *Indian Express* (New Delhi), January 5, 1965, p. 4.
29. John Simpson and Anthony G. McGrew, eds., *The International Nuclear Non-Proliferation System: Challenges and Choices* (New York: St. Martin's, 1984).
30. Ashok Kapur, "India's Nuclear Politics and Policy: Janata Party's Evolving Stance," in T.T. Poulose, ed., *Perspectives of India's Nuclear Policy* (New Delhi: Young Asia Publications, 1978), p. 172.
31. For a useful discussion, see Mirchandani, *India's Nuclear Dilemma*, pp. 121–150.
32. Ashok Kapur, *India's Nuclear Option: Atomic Diplomacy and Decision Making* (New York: Praeger, 1976).

the ambit of the ENDC again raised the question of nuclear guarantees for nonnuclear powers but to little avail.[33]

THE 1965 INDO-PAKISTANI WAR

A second Indo-Pakistani war over Kashmir broke out, in September 1965. During this conflict China provided diplomatic support for Pakistan and threatened to open a second front along India's Himalayan border.[34] Although this crude ultimatum was never carried out, Indian decisionmakers, still reeling from the debacle of 1962, took the Chinese warnings seriously and maintained a high level of alert along the Himalayan border. The war ended in a stalemate. As the United States was unwilling to involve itself in promoting an Indo-Pakistani postwar accord, the Soviets stepped in, helping negotiate a settlement in January 1966 at the then-Soviet Central Asian city of Tashkent. Under the terms of the Tashkent agreement the two sides agreed to return to the status quo ante.

Just before the war ended a hundred members of the Lok Sabha wrote to Prime Minister Shastri calling for India to exercise the nuclear weapons option.[35] Amid the growing public and political pressure, Shastri revealed a slight shift in the government's public pronouncements on nuclear weapons. The pressures confronting Shastri were genuine; India faced the possibility of a two-front war.

While answering a question asked in the Rajya Sabha (the upper house of the Indian parliament), Shastri stated that if the Chinese perfected their nuclear delivery systems India would be forced to reconsider its nuclear policies.[36] During this period India's apprehensions continued to mount as increasing evidence emerged about China's growing nuclear capabilities.[37]

Shastri died in January 1966 shortly after negotiating the postwar accord with Pakistan. His successor, Nehru's daughter, Indira Gandhi, continued the quest for a nuclear guarantee from the major powers against a future Chinese threat. To this end, she dispatched a distinguished senior bureaucrat, Laxmi Kant Jha, to Moscow and Washington, D.C., in April 1967 to discuss the possibility of a guarantee designed to deter a possible Chinese attack. Despite India's pleas the United States would only offer a guarantee that included

33. Mirchandani, *India's Nuclear Dilemma*, p. 139.
34. For a description and analysis of the three Indo-Pakistani wars, see Sumit Ganguly, *The Origins of War in South Asia: The Indo-Pakistani Conflicts since 1947*, 2d ed. (Boulder, Colo.: Westview, 1994).
35. "Time for A-Bomb—Say 100 M.P.'s," *Indian Express*, September 23, 1965, p. 1.
36. Lal Bahadur Shastri, "If China Develops Nuclear Weapons India Will Have to Consider What to Do," *India News* (Washington, D.C.), December 3, 1965, p. 4.
37. See, for example, Hanson W. Baldwin, "China's Atomic Potential," *New York Times*, March 15, 1966, p. 3.

significant qualifications. Among other matters, the guarantee would not have had the force of law because it would not be formally ratified by the U.S. Senate.[38] The Soviets were even less forthcoming. At best, they were prepared to make a joint declaration under UN auspices not to employ nuclear weapons against nonnuclear powers.[39] In the event, the qualified guarantees that both sides offered failed to satisfy India's requirements.

BACK TO THE NONPROLIFERATION TREATY

The discussions under way at the ENDC to formulate a nonproliferation treaty had a significant impact on India's disarmament and security plans. The country's earlier emphasis on the pursuit of global nuclear disarmament had been based upon fundamental moral premises. Now the terms of discourse at the international level shifted markedly. This movement was clearly reflected in the positions that India adopted at various multilateral forums. Three shifts were evident in India's negotiating stance: a reduced sense of urgency about the need for international agreements in disarmament matters, a withdrawal from an active role in international arms control negotiations, and the pursuit of more traditional goals of statecraft (such as national security based upon military power, as opposed to reliance on the force of moral arguments).[40]

When the major powers agreed on a draft treaty, India was quick to register its opposition. On January 18, 1968, the Soviet Union and the United States presented identical drafts of the treaty to the ENDC. Three of the great powers—the United States, the United Kingdom, and the Soviet Union—signed the treaty on July 1, 1968. The Nuclear Nonproliferation Treaty (NPT) came into force on March 5, 1970. The government of India refused to accede to the terms of the treaty because it failed to address India's misgivings; spe-

38. Noorani, "India's Quest for a Nuclear Guarantee," pp. 498–499. Interestingly, U.S. government analysts not only were cognizant of the Chinese threat to India but also concurred that "the military security argument for an independent Indian nuclear deterrent to a Chinese attack is a particularly powerful one, given the looseness of India's collective security arrangements." See "Background Paper on Factors Which Could Influence National Decisions Concerning Acquisition of Nuclear Weapons," SECRET/NOFORN Background Paper from the Committee on Nuclear Proliferation, January 21, 1965, available in file "Nuclear Proliferation: India and Pakistan," National Security Archive, Washington, D.C.
39. Richard B. Freund, "Indian-Soviet Discussion of Nuclear Guarantees," Memorandum of Conversation, February 16, 1965, available in file "Nuclear Proliferation: India and Pakistan," National Security Archive, Washington, D.C.
40. Michael J. Sullivan, III, "Re-orientation of Indian Arms Control Policy, 1969–1971," paper presented at the annual meeting of the Pennsylvania Political Science Association, Philadelphia, April 14, 1972.

cifically, the continued nuclear abstinence of the nonnuclear states was not linked to explicit reciprocal obligations by the nuclear weapons states.[41] Although India's argument was couched in moral terms, a more pragmatic consideration—namely, keeping its nuclear weapons option open—guided its decision not to sign the treaty.[42]

Phase Three: The Road to Pokhran I

The third phase of India's nuclear program began with its first nuclear test, in May 1974. Both structural and proximate factors led up to this decision. The repeated failure of the great powers to address India's security concerns and the emergence of a different brand of political leadership within India caused important, if subtle, shifts in its nuclear policies. Prime Minister Indira Gandhi, while repeating the platitudes of nonalignment, reoriented India's foreign policy, basing it less on adherence to moral principles and more on the imperatives of statecraft. In place of her predecessors' carefully forged equidistance from the superpowers, she steadily tilted in a pro-Soviet direction, especially after significant policy differences with the United States arose in 1967 on trade, investment, and foreign aid issues.[43] Furthermore, some Indian analysts argue that U.S. pressure on India during the 1971 Indo-Pakistani War also convinced Indira Gandhi of the signal importance of developing India's military nuclear capabilities.[44]

While insisting upon India's adherence to the principles of nonalignment, Prime Minister Gandhi signed a twenty-year treaty of "peace, friendship, and cooperation" with the Soviet Union in August 1971. Article 9 of the treaty virtually included a Soviet security guarantee.[45] Although the influence of this treaty is often overlooked in Western strategic analyses of India's security, it greatly assuaged India's fears about military pressures on its borders from a recalcitrant and nuclear-armed China.

India's failure to influence the creation of a global regime that would ad-

41. Sisir Gupta, "India and Non-Proliferation: Hard Choices Ahead," *Times of India* (Delhi), January 29, 1968, p. 6.
42. K. Subrahmanyam, "India: Keeping the Option Open," in Robert M. Lawrence and Joel Larus, eds., *Nuclear Proliferation: Phase II* (Lawrence: University of Kansas Press, 1973).
43. For a discussion of the sources of discord, see Sumit Ganguly, "Of Great Expectations and Bitter Disappointments: Indo-U.S. Relations during the Johnson Administration," *Asian Affairs*, Vol. 15, No. 4 (Winter 1988–89), pp. 212–219. For an analysis of the pro-Soviet tilt, see Robert Horn, *Soviet-Indian Relations: Issues and Influence* (New York: Praeger, 1982).
44. Subrahmanyam, "India: Keeping the Option Open."
45. For an analysis of the significance of this article, see Linda Racioppi, *Soviet Policy towards South Asia since 1970* (Cambridge, U.K.: Cambridge University Press, 1994).

dress its security concerns pushed the country further down the nuclear path. Subsequent events bolstered the Indian elite's commitment to acquire nuclear weapons. In 1971 India and Pakistan became embroiled in a third war, which resulted in the breakup of the Pakistani state and the emergence of Bangladesh in place of the former East Pakistan. In the aftermath of this war India emerged as the preeminent power on the subcontinent.

In the interim, after Homi Bhaba's death in 1966, his successor, Vikram Sarabhai, continued to broaden India's nuclear infrastructure.[46] On May 25, 1970, Sarabhai in a public document spelled out the key features and goals of India's nuclear and space programs for the coming decade. Specifically, the document called for important developments in the arena of space research, including a commitment to develop rocket systems capable of placing 1,200-kilogram payloads into geosynchronous orbit, the development of flight guidance systems for rockets, and the construction of large solid-propellant blocks.[47] The discovery of uranium deposits in northern India had also helped boost India's nuclear programs.[48]

Thus at the start of the 1970s India had both the capability and the political motivation to conduct a nuclear test. The only question that remained about weaponization was the political decision to proceed based upon some assessment of the likely external costs of such a test. In an effort to bolster India's newfound political status in South Asia after its victory in the 1971 war, Indira Gandhi authorized a nuclear test. The precise timing of the test, however, had much to do with her sagging domestic popularity in the aftermath of the 1973 oil crisis induced by the Organization of Petroleum Exporting Countries.

THE FIRST NUCLEAR TEST

India carried out its first nuclear test on May 18, 1974. Billed as a "peaceful nuclear explosion," the test had a 15-kiloton yield.[49] Subsequently, Defense Minister Jagjivan Ram argued that the test had few or no military implica-

---

46. For a discussion of India's weapons-making capabilities, see Brahma Chellaney, "South Asia's Passage to Nuclear Power," *International Security*, Vol. 16, No. 1 (Summer 1991), pp. 43–72. For a more skeptical view of India's nuclear infrastructure, see Ravindra Tomar, "The Indian Nuclear Power Program: Myths and Mirages," *Asian Survey*, Vol. 20, No. 5 (May 1980), pp. 517–531.
47. Vikram Sarabhai, "India's Nuclear and Space Programs: A Design for Decade 1970–80," *Institute of Defence Studies and Analysis Journal* (Delhi), Vol. 3, No. 1 (July 1970), pp. 90–91.
48. David Gosling, "India on Way to Nuclear Independence," *Statesman* (New Delhi), November 23, 1971, p. 8.
49. The slightest doubt of the military significance of the test was effectively ruled out in October 1997 when Raja Ramanna, one of the key scientists involved in conducting the test, explicitly stated that the 1974 test was that of a nuclear weapon. See Adirupa Sengupta, "Scientist Says Bomb Was Tested in '74," *India Abroad*, October 17, 1997, p. 14.

tions and was simply part of India's ongoing attempts to harness the peaceful uses of nuclear energy.[50] The two scientists closely associated with the nuclear test, R. Chidambaram and R. Ramanna, maintained the same public posture.[51]

India's explanation of the test found few adherents abroad, however. Of the great powers, only France congratulated the Indians on their success.[52] The Chinese and Soviet reactions were muted, but critical. The United States and Canada cut off all nuclear cooperation with India. Canada accused India of having diverted nuclear materials from a Canadian-supplied reactor to make the bomb.[53] The U.S. reaction, however, was the most severe: in 1976 Congress introduced the Symington amendment to the foreign aid bill, thereby cutting off certain forms of economic and military assistance to countries that received enrichment or reprocessing equipment, materials, or technology without full-scope International Atomic Energy Agency safeguards.[54] Further restrictions soon followed under the Carter administration, which had made nonproliferation one of the key elements of its foreign policy platform. Most important, the Carter administration introduced and passed the Nuclear Nonproliferation Act, omnibus legislation designed to severely curb nuclear sales to recalcitrant nations.[55] The United States also undertook significant efforts to limit proliferation at the multilateral level, taking the lead in the formation of the London Suppliers Group, which sought to coordinate and limit the sales of sensitive and dual-use technologies to countries outside the ambit of the NPT.

The raft of legislation that the U.S. Congress passed after the Indian nuclear test significantly hobbled India's ability to further its nuclear weapons program. The sharpness of international reactions and the variety of nuclear export restrictions that the major industrial powers placed on India came as a surprise to the Indian political elite. This body of restrictive legislation also had a perverse and unintended consequence, however: it made the Indian program increasingly indigenous.

Despite the initial wave of domestic support following the test, pressing in-

---

50. On this point, see "Indian Rules Out Atomic Arms' Use," *New York Times*, May 23, 1974, p. 5.
51. R. Chidambaram and R. Ramanna, "Some Studies on India's Peaceful Nuclear Experiment," *Peaceful Nuclear Explosions IV* (Vienna: International Atomic Energy Agency, 1975).
52. "New Delhi Assailed at Parley in Geneva for Atom Explosion," *New York Times*, May 22, 1974, p. 3.
53. Robert Trumbull, "Canada Says India's Blast Violated Use of Atom Aid," *New York Times*, May 21, 1974, p. 4.
54. Brahma Chellaney, *Nuclear Proliferation: The U.S.-Indian Conflict* (New Delhi: Orient Longman, 1993), pp. 74–75.
55. For a detailed discussion, see ibid., pp. 56–66.

ternal concerns diverted the public's attention from the pursuit of a nuclear weapons option. In fact, within two years of the test Indira Gandhi had declared a "state of emergency" to avoid prosecution for a number of minor electoral violations. With her personal political survival at stake, she could ill afford to devote significant time and resources to the nuclear question.

Phase Four: A Period of Restraint

The next stage in India's nuclear program was marked by little progress in attaining nuclear weapons status, even though there was increasing public and military (and even some political) support for acquiring nuclear weapons. Two factors explain this restraint. At one level, Indira Gandhi had taken stock of the adverse international reactions to India's nuclear test. At another level, a robust Indo-Soviet strategic relationship assuaged India's security concerns.

In 1977 Indira Gandhi ended the state of emergency and called for fresh national elections. Her sycophantic advisers convinced her that she would win by a wide margin at the polls. Their expectations were completely belied when the Indian electorate turned against her and the Congress Party. An eclectic collection of political parties and leaders who had been opposed to the draconian features of the state of emergency, when personal rights and civil liberties had been dramatically curtailed, formed a coalition government.[56] Morarji Desai, a senior Gandhian and former Congress politician, assumed the prime ministership. Long an opponent of nuclear weapons, primarily on moral grounds, Desai reversed the direction of Indian nuclear planning. He even derided the potential scientific or technological benefits of "peaceful nuclear explosions" and publicly pledged that under his regime India would not conduct nuclear tests.[57]

Desai's term in office lasted only until July 1979. His anti-Congress coalition split amid conflicting ideologies and personal predilections. The caretaker regime of Prime Minister Charan Singh altered Desai's ironclad commitment not to acquire nuclear weapons, holding that the decision was a sovereign Indian prerogative. Many in New Delhi also believed that the incoming Congress government would reverse Desai's policy.[58] In January 1980, when new na-

56. For a discussion of the "state of emergency," see Henry Hart, ed., *Indira Gandhi's India: A Political System Re-Appraised* (Boulder, Colo.: Westview, 1978).
57. On this issue, see Prime Minister Morarji Desai, "Statement on Peaceful Nuclear Explosions," Rajya Sabha, July 31, 1978, Official Text (New Delhi: Press Information Bureau, Government of India).
58. Mohan Ram, "The South Asian Arms Race," *Far Eastern Economic Review,* November 16, 1979,

tional elections were held, Indira Gandhi and the Congress Party returned with a significant majority.

THE SOVIET INVASION OF AFGHANISTAN

The Soviet Union's occupation of Afghanistan in late December 1979 had important ramifications for the security of South Asia. In particular, the resulting transformation of U.S.-Pakistani relations was nothing short of dramatic. Under the Carter administration Pakistan had been scorned because of its poor human rights record and its clandestine quest to acquire nuclear weapons. Following the Soviet invasion, the Carter administration's offers of a limited arms and economic assistance package to Pakistan were dismissed by General Mohammed Zia-ul-Haq, the Pakistani military dictator, as "peanuts." In the Reagan administration, Pakistan's relations with the United States entered new territory.

General Zia managed to turn the potentially destabilizing civil war across the Afghan border to his advantage, becoming the beneficiary of significant American largesse in the process. Specifically, the Reagan administration offered his regime a package of concessionary loans and grant aid totaling $3.2 billion over five years. In return, the Pakistani regime was to give the Central Intelligence Agency a largely unrestricted hand in organizing, training, and arming the Afghan resistance. In addition, to assuage Pakistani fears of Indo-Soviet collusion, the Reagan administration agreed to sell Pakistan several squadrons of F-16 fighter jets.

India, as expected, vehemently lobbied against the sale of the F-16s to Pakistan, but with little success. Unhappy with the potential transformation of the South Asian security situation, India turned to the Soviet Union for military assistance.[59] The Soviets were extraordinarily forthcoming in providing arms at concessional rates, but at another price: India had to refrain from publicly criticizing the Soviet invasion and abstain from the UN General Assembly resolutions condemning the Soviet invasion and occupation of Afghanistan.

As the arms transfer relationship between the United States and Pakistan was renewed and India's conventional military superiority eroded, the clamor for India to exercise the nuclear weapons option resumed. Prominent newspaper commentators and security analysts argued that India needed to have a

---

pp. 38–39. For an analysis of the mounting pressures on the Indira Gandhi regime to weaponize, see Rajiv Desai, "Nuclear Shadow on Subcontinent," *Chicago Tribune*, August 17, 1981, p. 21.
59. For a discussion of the Soviet willingness to transfer advanced weaponry to India, see G.S. Bhargava, *South Asia after Afghanistan* (Lexington, Mass.: D.C. Heath, 1983).

nuclear edge over Pakistan to cope with the emerging security situation in the region. The earlier preoccupation with Chinese nuclear capabilities was redirected toward Pakistan's growing nuclear status. The argument ran along the following lines: the United States, with full knowledge of Pakistan's nuclear ambitions, was nevertheless supplying Pakistan with sophisticated weaponry and potentially nuclear-capable aircraft. Growing evidence of Chinese collusion in the Pakistani nuclear weapons program fueled Indian concerns.[60] Under these changed security circumstances India had to reevaluate its nuclear policies.[61]

ACQUIRING GREATER CAPABILITIES

In the early 1980s the clamor for the acquisition of a nuclear option grew as, ironically, U.S. sources increasingly provided evidence of Pakistan's quest for nuclear weapons and the Chinese supply of a nuclear weapons design to Pakistan.[62] India's bomb-making capabilities also expanded during this period.[63] Specifically, in February 1983 reports surfaced of India's ability to reprocess plutonium to weapons grade.[64] Also in 1983 the Defense Research and Development Organization (DRDO) was given increased funding and a new mandate, the Integrated Guided Missile Development Program (IGMDP).[65] A space scientist, A.P.J. Abdul Kalam, who had previously worked for the civilian Indian Space Research Organization, was shifted to the DRDO and placed in charge of the IGMDP.[66] Kalam's transfer to the military component of India's rocketry program was significant, because he had a personal passion for the development of indigenous ballistic missile technology.[67] Indira Gandhi's faith in Kalam's ability was not misplaced. Under his leadership the DRDO developed and successfully test-fired India's first intermediate-range ballistic missile, the Agni (the name literally means "fire") on May 22, 1989, from a test range

---

60. William E. Burrows and Robert Windrem, *Critical Mass* (New York: Simon and Schuster, 1994).
61. See, for example, Jonathan Power, "Mrs. Gandhi's Nuclear Nuances," *International Herald Tribune*, December 18, 1981, p. 5.
62. K. Subrahmanyam, "Pak Bomb in Basement," *Times of India*, November 7, 1986, p. 5.
63. Suman Dubey, "India, Keeping Its Nuclear Options Open, Monitors Arms Program in Neighboring Pakistan with Concern," *Wall Street Journal*, November 26, 1984, p. 36.
64. Clyde H. Farnsworth, "India Now Producing Plutonium of Arms Grade at Bombay Plant," *New York Times*, February 21, 1983, p. 7.
65. Significantly, these changes came about when allegations of Chinese nuclear assistance to Pakistan had gathered steam.
66. Chris Smith, *India's Ad Hoc Arsenal: Direction or Drift in Defence Policy?* (Oxford, U.K.: Oxford University Press, 1991), p. 201; and Burrows and Windrem, *Critical Mass*, pp. 372–373.
67. On this point, see Sunil Dasgupta, "A Quiet Launch," *India Today International*, June 30, 1994, p. 93.

at Chandipore in the eastern coastal state of Orissa. Since then, the DRDO has developed a panoply of short- and medium-range ballistic missiles.[68]

In the wake of Indira Gandhi's assassination in October 1984, her son, Rajiv Gandhi, assumed the prime ministership. During Rajiv's tenure in office India pursued contradictory policies on the nuclear question.[69] On the one hand, he proposed a comprehensive plan for the gradual elimination of nuclear weapons, popularly referred to as the Rajiv Gandhi Action Plan. This plan, which he presented in an address to the UN General Assembly, called for the elimination of all nuclear arsenals by the year 2010. It spelled out particular stages and targets that were to be achieved by all nuclear weapons states and imposed reciprocal restrictions on all nuclear-threshold powers.[70] It is not entirely clear whether this proposal was merely symbolic or whether it represented a serious effort by the government to reclaim its Nehruvian roots. In the event, the great powers showed scant attention to the proposal. Also during Rajiv's term, India and Pakistan reached an accord not to attack each other's nuclear facilities.[71] This treaty was not formally ratified, however, until 1991.

On the other hand, despite this renewed attempt at multilateral diplomacy and some movement on the bilateral front with Pakistan, the scientific-military establishment received a considerable boost under Rajiv. A newspaper account based upon a conversation with M.R. Srinavasan, the chairman of the AEC and a prominent Indian antinuclear activist, confirmed that India had made substantial progress toward the acquisition of a nuclear weapons capability. Specifically, the report stated that India had stockpiled between 100 and 200 kilograms of plutonium, sufficient to build between twelve and forty weapons.[72]

Furthermore, a belated realization that hortatory efforts toward encouraging multilateral disarmament were next to meaningless influenced Rajiv's decision to boost India's nuclear capabilities. K. Subrahmanyam, a key participant in many of the critical decisions of India's nuclear weapons policy, argues along these lines in a work published shortly after the 1998 Indian nuclear tests. Ac-

---

68. Smith, *India's Ad Hoc Arsenal*, pp. 199–203.
69. A particularly thoughtful discussion of the contradictions in India's *declaratory* nuclear weapons policy can be found in Bhabani Sen Gupta, "The Nuclear Option: Ambivalent Stand," *India Today International*, May 31, 1985, p. 47. See also K. Subrahmanyam, "Indian Nuclear Policy, 1964–1998: A Personal Recollection," in Jasjit Singh, ed., *Nuclear India* (New Delhi: Knowledge World, 1998), pp. 26–53.
70. Rajiv Gandhi, "Address to the Third Special Session on Disarmament," United Nations General Assembly, New York, June 9, 1988.
71. Steve Coll, "India, Pakistan Pursue Peace by Creating Nuclear Standoff," *Washington Post*, December 29, 1990, p. A13.
72. Steven R. Weisman, "India's Nuclear Energy Policy Raises New Doubts on Arms," *New York Times*, May 7, 1988, p. 1.

cording to Subrahmanyam, it was under Rajiv Gandhi that India made the decision to acquire the missiles and other technology to form an effective nuclear deterrent.[73]

Rajiv's interest in India's military modernization may have also contributed to South Asia's first nuclear crisis in 1987, in the wake of a major military exercise code-named "Brasstacks."[74] The precise dimensions of the nuclear component of this crisis remain somewhat murky.[75] It is known, however, that toward the end of the crisis, in late January 1987, Abdul Qadeer Khan, widely known as the "father" of the Pakistani nuclear program, gave an interview to a prominent Indian journalist, Kuldip Nayar. In this interview, Khan made clear to Nayar that Pakistan had succeeded in producing weapons-grade uranium.[76] There is little or no question that the Indian political leadership took Khan's claim about uranium enrichment seriously.

THE 1990 CRISIS

Within three years India became embroiled in another crisis with Pakistan—one with an obvious nuclear dimension. This crisis, unlike the 1987 Brasstacks crisis, stemmed directly from the outbreak of a secessionist, ethnoreligious insurgency in the disputed state of Jammu and Kashmir.[77] Soon Pakistani infiltrators began crossing the porous border to join forces with the Kashmiri insurgents.[78] The dramatic rise in the incidence of violence within the Kashmir valley, the principal locus of the insurgency, is widely believed to have led Indian decisionmakers to consider deep strikes into Pakistani territory to destroy insurgent training camps and sanctuaries. Pakistani intelligence sources, it is asserted, learned of India's plans and, fearing a wider invasion, placed key portions of the Pakistani air force on alert. Pakistani decisionmakers also allegedly considered resorting to the use of nuclear weapons in the event of a concerted Indian incursion into Pakistan's heartland.[79] As the crisis peaked in May

---

73. Subrahmanyam, "Indian Nuclear Policy, 1964–1998," p. 44.
74. For a detailed description and analysis of the Brasstacks crisis, see Kanti Bajpai, P.R. Chari, Pervaiz Iqbal Cheema, Stephen P. Cohen, and Sumit Ganguly, *Brasstacks and Beyond: Perception and the Management of Crisis in South Asia* (New Delhi: Manohar, 1994).
75. See Lawrence Lifshultz, "Doom Thy Neighbour," *Far Eastern Economic Review,* June 4, 1998, pp. 30–34.
76. Steven R. Weisman, "Pakistan Stiffens on Atomic Program," *New York Times,* March 22, 1987, p. A4.
77. Sumit Ganguly, "Political Mobilization and Institutional Decay: Explaining the Crisis in Kashmir," *International Security,* Vol. 21, No. 2 (Fall 1996), pp. 76–107.
78. On Pakistan's involvement in the insurgency, see Edward Desmond, "Pakistan's Hidden Hand," *Time,* July 22, 1991, p. 23; and John Ward Anderson and Kamran Khan, "Pakistan Shelters Islamic Radicals," *Washington Post,* March 8, 1995, pp. A21–A22.
79. It is not entirely clear whether the Pakistani air force squadrons were equipped with nuclear

1990, on the basis of reports from U.S. intelligence agencies, President George Bush sent Robert Gates, the deputy national security adviser, to India and Pakistan. In New Delhi Gates counseled restraint. In Islamabad he warned Pakistani decisionmakers that in every war-game scenario that the Pentagon had developed, Pakistan emerged as the loser. Consequently, he argued, it was not in Pakistan's interest to provoke India.[80]

In October President Bush invoked the Pressler amendment to the Foreign Assistance Act, stating that he could not certify to Congress that Pakistan did not possess a nuclear explosive device.[81] This conclusion led to a cutoff of the substantial U.S. economic and military assistance that had been flowing to Pakistan since the beginning of the civil war in Afghanistan.[82] Despite the cessation of aid the Pakistani nuclear program proceeded apace, and the Chinese continued to support Pakistan's efforts to acquire nuclear weapons.[83] Within the next two years Pakistani political leaders as well as diplomats openly confirmed that Pakistan had acquired the ability to manufacture a nuclear bomb.[84] These developments were carefully noted in New Delhi.

Phase Five: The Collapse of the Security Guarantee

The final phase of the Indian nuclear program started in the aftermath of the Soviet collapse in 1991, which had profound implications for India's security and foreign policies. It meant the loss of the support of a veto-wielding power in the UN on the critical question of Kashmir. It also brought to an end a highly favorable arms-transfer relationship. But most important, from the standpoint of Indian security, it resulted in the loss of a critical counterweight to the Chinese threat: the security guarantee implied in the 1971 treaty with the Soviet

weapons. The initial tocsin was sounded by Seymour Hersh in "On the Nuclear Edge," *New Yorker*, March 29, 1993, pp. 56–73. For a more temperate analysis of the crisis, see Stephen P. Cohen, "1990: South Asia's Useful Nuclear Crisis," paper presented at the annual meeting of the American Association for the Advancement of Science, Chicago, February 6–7, 1992, pp. 2–10. See also Michael Krepon and Mishi Faruqee, eds., *Conflict Prevention and Confidence-Building Measures in South Asia: The 1990 Crisis*, Occasional Paper No. 17 (Washington, D.C.: Henry L. Stimson Center, April 1994).

80. Mitchell Reiss, *Bridled Ambition: Why Countries Constrain Their Nuclear Capabilities* (Washington, D.C.: Woodrow Wilson Center Press, 1995).

81. The amendment, formally known as the International Security and Development Cooperation Act of 1985, required the president of the United States to certify that Pakistan did not possess a nuclear device.

82. Michael R. Gordon, "Nuclear Issue Slows U.S. Aid to Pakistan," *New York Times*, October 1, 1990, p. A3.

83. Steven A. Holmes, "China Denies Violating Pact by Selling Arms to Pakistan," *New York Times*, July 26, 1993, p. 6.

84. Stefan Wagstyl, "A Damaging Diversion," *Financial Times*, August 26, 1994, p. 7.

Union disintegrated with the Soviet collapse; Russia is now too debilitated to provide much reassurance to India.

THE NONPROLIFERATION TREATY RENEWAL

In 1995 the NPT came up for its twenty-five-year review. The United States, one of the principal proponents of the NPT regime, sought an "unconditional and indefinite extension" of the treaty. India, which had chosen to stay outside the NPT regime, decided not to participate in the proceedings in New York during April–May 1995 and did not even seek observer status.[85] The Indian hope was that the United States would fail to cobble together a coalition that would unconditionally and indefinitely extend the treaty. Such expectations and fears were belied, as able and relentless American diplomacy ensured the achievement of the U.S. goal.[86] After the treaty was extended, only India, Pakistan, and Israel remained outside its scope. The U.S. success came as a dramatic shock to the Indian security policy establishment, which now realized that India would come under acute pressure to sign the NPT or at least to agree to full-scope safeguards on its nuclear power plants, including those of indigenous origin.

THE BROWN AMENDMENT

In the fall of 1995 the Clinton administration sought to obtain some leverage over Pakistan to contain its quest for nuclear weapons. Specifically, the administration, in concert with Senator Hank Brown (R-Colo.), introduced legislation designed to override the provisions of the Pressler amendment. The Brown amendment allowed the provision of economic and some military assistance to Pakistan without any attached conditions. Despite vigorous opposition from senators committed to nonproliferation, the amended bill passed.[87]

THE "NEAR TEST"

The extension of the NPT and the passage of the Brown amendment, which led to a renewal of up to $368 million in U.S. military assistance to Pakistan, inevi-

---

85. India's reservations about the NPT regime can be found in Rakesh Sood, "The NPT and Beyond," paper presented at a seminar entitled "Non-Proliferation and Technology Transfer," University of Pennsylvania, October 3–6, 1993, pp. 1–20. In this paper, Sood, the director of the Disarmament and International Security Division of India's Ministry of External Affairs, traces some of the early history of the NPT negotiations and discusses the possibilities of expanding the scope of the regime to address India's concerns.
86. Lewis A. Dunn, "High Noon for the NPT," *Arms Control Today*, Vol. 25, No. 6 (July/August 1995), pp. 3–9.
87. Elaine Sciolino, "Despite Nuclear Fears, Senate Acts to Lift Pakistan Curbs," *New York Times*, September 22, 1995, p. 4.

tably provoked Indian security concerns.[88] At one level, the Indian leadership under Prime Minister Narasimha Rao feared, justifiably or not, that the renewal of American arms transfers to Pakistan would lead to a larger U.S. security relationship with Pakistan. On another level the Indians were anxious about the pressures that would be brought upon them in the wake of the extension of the NPT. Additionally, moves toward the finalization of the Comprehensive Test Ban Treaty (CTBT) were also under way at the United Nations Disarmament Conference (UNDC) in Geneva. It is reasonable to infer that the Indian government believed that its window of opportunity was rapidly closing. It is in this politico-strategic context that Prime Minister Rao permitted the preparations for carrying out a nuclear test in December 1995.[89] The test was stymied when U.S. reconnaissance satellites picked up signs of activity at the test site and, in response, the U.S. ambassador to India, Frank Wisner, prevailed upon the infamously indecisive prime minister to call off the tests.[90]

THE CTBT LOOMS

In 1996, following two years of extensive negotiations, the CTBT process gathered steam in Geneva.[91] Although India had been one of the principal sponsors of the treaty in its initial form, it had three objections to the treaty as negotiated in Geneva. First, the Indians insisted that they would accede to the treaty only if the nuclear weapons states agreed to a time-bound plan for universal nuclear disarmament. For the most part, this position was little more than a ploy; Indian policymakers knew only too well that none of the nuclear weapons states would agree to this proposition. Consequently, the inevitable failure to include such a time-bound objective would give India the option to remain outside the treaty.

The second objection stemmed from the demand of some states that the

---

88. Aziz Haniffa, "Arms for Pakistan Near Passage; India Hurt," *India Abroad,* November 3, 1995, p. 14.

89. The Indian "near test" of December 1995 decisively shows the fallacy of the "domestic imperatives" argument for the Indian tests of 1998. Obviously, the 1998 tests briefly boosted the BJP's domestic ratings. Larger security concerns propelled the BJP, however, just as they had driven the Narasimha Rao regime less than two years earlier.

90. Vipin Gupta and Frank Pabian, "Investigating the Allegations of Indian Nuclear Test Preparations in the Rajasthan Desert," *Science and Global Society* (1996), pp. 101–189. Some allegations also suggest that India toyed with another nuclear explosion in early 1982. On this issue, see Shubharrata Bhattacharya, "Another Nuclear Blast at Pokhran?" *Sunday* (Calcutta), May 12, 1982, pp. 12–14.

91. For an analysis of India's negotiating stances at the UNDC, see C. Raja Mohan, "India and the CTBT: Time to Quit," *Hindu,* June 10, 1996, p. 11. For discussions of subsequent developments, see John F. Burns, "Old Foe of Atom Arms, India Now Blocks Test Ban," *New York Times,* August 17, 1996, p. 2; and Barbara Crossette, "India Vetoes Pact to Forbid Testing of Nuclear Weapons," *New York Times,* August 21, 1996, p. A1.

treaty could come into force only after forty-four countries that had ongoing nuclear research and power facilities ratified the treaty. Again, although the argument against the "entry into force" clause was questioned on the grounds of fairness, India's interest in challenging the clause was purely pragmatic. As a state with an ongoing but largely untested nuclear weapons program, India would come under enormous pressure to accede to the CTBT.[92]

The third Indian objection was more substantive:[93] it dealt with the treaty's allowance of computer simulations of nuclear tests and hydronuclear tests. In the Indian view, the failure to close these two technological loopholes undermined the larger goal of taking steps toward the elimination of nuclear weapons. In the end, India could not block the reporting of the treaty from the UNDC to the General Assembly in New York.[94] Its efforts to modify the treaty text or to prevent its adoption by the General Assembly also proved fruitless. The treaty was passed on September 10, 1996, by an overwhelming majority of the member states.[95]

Two factors explain the Indian shift from support to rejection of the CTBT. At one level, as has already been discussed, the Indians were acutely concerned about the "entry into force" clause and the likely effects of this upon their nuclear weapons program. The other concern dealt with the spate of Chinese nuclear tests just prior to China's accession to the CTBT. The Indian strategic community correctly inferred that the Chinese were willing to accede to the treaty only because they had reached such a level of competence in their weapons development that they felt no need to test further.[96]

RETURNING TO POKHRAN

The years 1997–98 proved momentous for India in terms of its domestic politics. Within the span of one year three different governments ruled the country.[97] With the collapse of the shaky United Front coalition government in December 1997, new national elections were called for February–March 1998. In

92. Stephen W. Young, "A Test Ban Treaty That Doesn't Ban Tests," *BASIC Reports* (Washington, D.C.: British-American Security Information Council, September 23, 1996), pp. 1–2.
93. K. Subrahmanyam, "The CTBT Puzzle," *Economic Times* (Bombay), June 8, 1996, p. 5.
94. Tarun Basu, "Nation Ignores Veiled Threats, Blocks CTBT," *India Abroad*, August 23, 1996, p. 4.
95. Jim Wurst, "Comprehensive Test Ban Overwhelmingly Adopted," *Disarmament Times* (New York, September 20, 1996), p. 1. The treaty passed with 158 votes in support, 3 opposed, and 5 abstentions.
96. Seth Faison, "China Sets Off Nuclear Test, Then Announces Moratorium," *New York Times*, July 30, 1996, p. 4; and Sanjay Suri, "Chinese Test Seen behind Indian CTBT Stand," *India Abroad*, August 23, 1996, p. 8.
97. Sumit Ganguly, "India in 1997: Another Year of Turmoil," *Asian Survey*, Vol. 38, No. 2 (February 1998), pp. 126–134.

these elections, the BJP emerged as the largest single party within parliament and, with the support of a number of regional parties, it assumed power.

The BJP's election manifesto had spoken of the perceived need to "induct" nuclear weapons into India's arsenal along with a "strategic review" of India's security environment. Most Western analysts, however, had dismissed the BJP's electoral promise as bluff and bluster meant for domestic political consumption.[98] Yet a more careful perusal of the BJP's public stance toward perceived security threats from Pakistan and China, as well as its position on defense spending and nuclear weapons, should have suggested otherwise.[99] Given the BJP's hawkish proclivities and the substantial scientific, military, and public support for the nuclear program, only a triggering event was necessary to propel the BJP to break from India's long-standing policy of nuclear abstinence.

This trigger came in the form of Pakistan's test of an intermediate-range ballistic missile, code-named Ghauri, on April 6, 1998. The Ghauri, built with either Chinese or North Korean technology, has a range of 1,500 kilometers and can carry a payload of 750 kilograms. Its range would enable Pakistan to target twenty-six cities in India.[100] This new Pakistani capability reinforced prior perceptions in India about the deterioration of India's immediate security environment. For example, in 1997 even under the United Front government, the Ministry of Defense's annual report had expressed considerable misgivings about China's support for Pakistan's nuclear and ballistic missile programs as well as China's own growing ballistic missile capabilities.[101] Any remaining qualms about the wisdom of carrying out nuclear tests were set aside in the aftermath of the Ghauri test. Between May 9 and 10, 1998, Prime Minister Atal Behari Vajpayee informed key ministers and the highest-ranking bureaucrats as well as the three service chiefs of his decision to proceed with the nuclear tests.[102]

98. Tim Weiner, "Every Nation's Just Another U.S.," *New York Times*, June 7, 1998, p. 5.
99. See the section entitled "Our Nation's Security," in the BJP's 1998 election manifesto, http://bjp.org.
100. A debate has arisen about the precise sources of the technology used in the manufacture of the Ghauri. Some argue that it is of Chinese origin. Others contend that it is based on North Korean technology. Muhammad Najeeb, "After Ghauri, It Is Long-Range Ghaznavi's Turn," *India Abroad*, April 24, 1998, p. 18; Pratap Bhanu Mehta, "India: The Nuclear Politics of Self-Esteem," *Current History*, Vol. 97, No. 623 (December 1998), pp. 403–406; and Tim Weiner, "U.S. and China Helped Pakistan Build Its Bomb," *New York Times*, June 1, 1998, p. A6. For a detailed discussion and analysis of the Chinese role in supporting Pakistan's nuclear and ballistic missile programs, see Nayan Chanda et al., "The Race Is On," *Far Eastern Economic Review*, June 11, 1998, pp. 20–22.
101. Ministry of Defense, *Annual Report, 1996–1997* (New Delhi: Government of India, 1997). See also International Institute for Strategic Studies (IISS), *The Military Balance, 1997–98* (London: Oxford University Press, 1997), p. 164.
102. One could well ask why the BJP did not simply declare India to be a nuclear weapons state

It is tempting to argue that a different Indian regime would not have acted with similar alacrity to the Ghauri test. To this question there can be no definitive answer. It is well known, however, that several previous governments had made careful preparations for a nuclear test. In fact, had U.S. reconnaissance satellites not discovered India's nuclear test preparations, it is likely that Prime Minister Narasimha Rao would have given the word to proceed in 1995.

Explanations of India's Nuclear Behavior

Three factors drove India's decision to test it nuclear weapons in 1998. The first was the incremental and fitful acquisition of the capability to manufacture nuclear weapons. This process was haphazard, discontinuous, and ridden with setbacks. Nevertheless, from the outset of the civilian nuclear program, Homi Bhaba harbored aspirations to make India a nuclear weapons state. His successors moved the program along to varying degrees, depending on their personal predilections and based upon political directions from New Delhi.

Second, the fitful movement toward a nuclear weapons capacity closely followed the shifting calculations of Indian leaders, who responded to a mix of ideology (initially a force for restraint), statecraft, and domestic pressures reflecting security concerns.[103] The evolution of the nuclear program and the 1998 tests were the product of calculated political choices based upon considerations of national security. Certain regimes and specific political leaders brought definite ideas about India's national security needs to office and acted upon those beliefs and assumptions. In large part, decisions, sometimes secret or subtle, made by Indian prime ministers advanced the nuclear weapons program without a full-fledged commitment to develop weapons.

The third factor was the perception of external security threats and the absence of security guarantees from friendly nuclear states. Perceived threats from China and Pakistan repeatedly accelerated the program, with the period of the Soviet security guarantee providing an interlude.

---

without actually testing five nuclear devices. Two plausible answers can be suggested. First, India's nuclear weapons establishment would not feel that they possessed the requisite confidence in their weapons designs short of a series of tests. Second, if the press reports are accurate, one of the devices tested was thermonuclear. A thermonuclear device requires a nuclear triggering device. See Manoj Joshi, "Nuclear Shock Waves," *India Today*, May 25, 1998, pp. 12–20.

103. Ideological beliefs, on occasion, acted as forces for restraint. For example, Prime Minister Morarji Desai, a staunch Gandhian, opposed India's development of nuclear weapons. The BJP-led government that came to power in March 1998, however, included a number of individuals who believed that the acquisition of nuclear weapons was critical to India's security. On Desai's beliefs, see Kapur, *India's Nuclear Option*.

Many foreign and several Indian political commentators have dismissed the security imperatives underlying the Indian nuclear weapons program as well as the Indian tests, while privileging other explanations based on considerations of status, prestige, and the short-term exigencies of domestic politics.[104] Worse still, much of the conventional wisdom dismisses India's felt security needs and blithely asserts that India would be better off without nuclear weapons. The purveyors of this perspective, with important exceptions, had evinced little or no interest in India's security concerns prior to the nuclear tests.[105] Yet ample evidence suggests that India's security misgivings did play an important role in the evolution of the program as well as in precipitating the nuclear tests of May 1998.

Indeed, most of the explanations proffered to date for the tests are inadequate in part because they disregard one or more of the fundamental elements I have discussed. One argument suggests that the decision to carry out the tests can be directly attributed to the rise of the BJP to dominance in India's government in March 1998.[106] The argument holds that the BJP leaders, many of whom are virulently anti-Pakistani, wish to craft a strong, virile India to dominate the subcontinent. The demonstration of India's nuclear capability would send a message of India's enormous military power and prowess to its long-term adversary and recalcitrant neighbor and, in turn, would instill a degree of Pakistani restraint on the nettlesome Kashmir dispute. This argument has some merit but is nevertheless inadequate. Segments of the BJP leadership do have a profoundly chauvinistic bent and are indeed enamored of India's nuclear status. Moreover, the BJP election manifesto explicitly states that one of the party's intentions upon assuming power was to "induct nuclear weapons" into India's arsenal.[107] Yet this argument ignores two critical pieces of evi-

---

104. For an Indian feminist critique of the tests, see Madhu Kishwar, "BJP's Wargasm," *Manushi* (New Delhi), No. 106 (May–June 1998) available at <<http://www.arbornet.org:81/~radhika/manushi/issue106/wargasm.html>>. For other dissenting voices from India, see Vinod Mehta, "How a 'Tired' PM Became a 'Bold' PM," *Outlook* (New Delhi), June 8, 1998, pp. 28–29. For an extraordinarily shallow American analysis of the dynamics of Indian politics ridden with factual errors, see Peter Beinart, "The Return of the Bomb," *New Republic*, August 3, 1998, pp. 22–27. In this article, for example, the author asserts that Prime Minister Narasimha Rao attempted to revive secularism in India. In fact, he did nothing of the sort. It was during his tenure in office that Hindu fanatics destroyed the Babri mosque in Uttar Pradesh on December 6, 1992. Rao also did little to control the anti-Muslim rioting that followed in the wake of the mosque's destruction.

105. An important exception is Stephen P. Cohen, "India's Strategic Misstep," *New York Times*, June 3, 1998.

106. The pioneering study of the BJP's origins, ideology, and organization remains Bruce Graham, *Hindu Nationalism and Indian Politics: The Origins and Development of the Bharatiya Jana Sangh* (Cambridge, U.K.: Cambridge University Press, 1990). See also John Cherian, "The BJP and the Bomb," *Frontline* (Madras), April 24, 1998, pp. 4–9.

107. On this point, see the BJP's 1998 election manifesto.

dence. First, the BJP government was heir to the huge scientific-military nuclear infrastructure that previous regimes of vastly divergent political persuasions had forged. The BJP-led government could not have carried out the May tests in the absence of this well-established nuclear program. Second, this argument ignores India's perceived security threats from growing Chinese military capabilities and arms transfers to Pakistan. The most immediate provocation, of course, was Pakistan's launch in March 1998 of the Chineseassisted Ghauri missile. The only compelling feature of this argument is that it underscores the BJP's more aggressive stance on questions pertaining to national security.

A second argument holds that India's 1974 and 1998 tests were conducted to divert attention from the nation's crippling social and economic problems and to bolster the sagging fortunes of the ruling party.[108] This argument clearly has some merit if one focuses on the *timing* of the 1974 test. Prime Minister Indira Gandhi did face a number of apparently intractable domestic problems that had eroded her popularity after the 1971 war against Pakistan. Consequently, the popularity of the nuclear test did provide her a brief political respite. Nevertheless, this argument is far from unproblematic. It can explain the occurrence of a discrete event but cannot account for the long-term investments in nuclear infrastructure that enabled her to order the nuclear test. Even worse, those who resurrect this argument to account for the 1998 tests demonstrate remarkable insensitivity to the nuances of the contemporary Indian political landscape. The BJP-led government could hardly use this dramatic demonstration of India's nuclear capabilities to cement its ties with its fractious parliamentary allies. The coalition's differences stem from the quintessentially regional and parochial concerns of its members, cleavages that the nuclear decision will do little, if anything, to contain.

A third argument posits that the tests reflect India's attempt to meet its unrequited goals for prestige and status in the international system.[109] The exponents of this view hold that India has long sought and failed to find adequate recognition of its status in global affairs. Indian decisionmakers, according to this logic, feel slighted by the most powerful states in the international community despite India's size, economic potential, and civilizational heritage. The tests, it is contended, were designed to confer on India great power status. As Indians themselves have argued, it is no accident that the five permanent

108. See the argument developed about the motivations underlying the 1974 test in Scott D. Sagan, "Why Do States Build Nuclear Weapons? Three Models in Search of a Bomb," *International Security*, Vol. 21, No. 3 (Winter 1996/97), pp. 65–69. On the 1998 tests, see Mehta, "How a 'Tired' PM Became a 'Bold' PM."
109. Amitav Ghosh, "Countdown," *New Yorker*, October 26–November 2, 1998, pp. 186–197.

members of the UN Security Council possess nuclear weapons. But this argument fails to explain why previous regimes had not taken the same decision. If India's ebbing prestige had so concerned its elites, the tests should have come much earlier, especially in the waning days of the Cold War, when the country found itself adrift in the international order.[110]

A fourth argument suggests that members of the scientific-bureaucratic establishment infused nuclear weapons with an almost mythical status, because they *believed* that nuclear weapons would enhance India's security. On the other hand, they could not causally demonstrate how India's security would be greater through their acquisition.[111] As Peter Lavoy argues, "The identity, skill, and political power of the proponents of these myths . . . also play a crucial role in shaping policy."[112] This argument, however, overlooks the structure of political decisionmaking in India. There is little question that it was under the tutelage of Homi Bhaba that the foundations of India's nuclear infrastructure were put in place in the first two decades after independence. But not all of his successors shared his level of enthusiasm for the acquisition of nuclear weapons. Some willingly followed the directions of their political masters in New Delhi; others were opposed to the development of nuclear weapons and made few efforts to boost India's weapons program.[113] Thus the scientific-bureaucratic community did constitute a significant pressure group. They protected the program from an excess of scrutiny and, on occasion, sought to mythologize the significance of nuclear weapons. However, the fundamental political decisions and strategic choices remained in the hands of political leaders in New Delhi, not in those of "mythmakers" in the AEC.

Conclusion

Two key questions confront India's political leadership. First, where are India's nuclear and ballistic missile programs headed? Unfortunately, few scholars or

---

110. Sumit Ganguly, "South Asia after the Cold War," *Washington Quarterly*, Vol. 15, No. 4 (Autumn 1992), pp. 173–184.
111. Peter Lavoy, "Nuclear Myths and the Causes of Nuclear Proliferation," *Security Studies*, Vol. 2, Nos. 3/4 (Spring/Summer 1993), pp. 192–212.
112. Peter Lavoy, "South Asian Military Programs: Characteristics, Trends, Implications," paper presented at a conference entitled "The Impact of the South Asia Nuclear Crisis on the Nonproliferation Regime," Carnegie Endowment for International Peace, Washington, D.C., July 16, 1998.
113. For the views of the second chairman of the AEC, Vikram Sarabhai, about nuclear weapons and disarmament, see Sarabhai, "Security of Developing Countries," in Kamla Chowdhry, ed., *Science Policy and National Development* (New Delhi: Macmillan, 1974). For the divergent views of various AEC chairmen, see Raja Ramanna, *Years of Pilgrimage: An Autobiography* (New Delhi: Penguin, 1991).

security analysts have devoted much thought to the development of a strategic doctrine for India.[114] Only now, in the wake of the abrupt decision by the BJP government to test, have India's strategic minds begun to grapple with this difficult issue. In the absence of a clear-cut strategic doctrine, domestic scientific and technological capabilities and bureaucratic pressures are likely to drive the Indian nuclear and ballistic missile programs. Thus far, the political leadership and most sections of India's strategic community have eschewed any interest in developing a second-strike capability. Instead they have argued that a "minimum deterrent" of some thirty to forty bombs that can be delivered by air would constitute a sufficient deterrent.[115]

Second, would such a deterrent suffice against potential Chinese and Pakistani threats and contribute to stability in the region? Despite U.S. and other international pressures, for now neither India nor Pakistan is likely to eschew its nuclear weapons program. Consequently, instead of focusing upon unrealistic and chimerical goals, it may be more useful for all parties to discuss ways to bring some stability to the region. Three distinct forms of stability—strategic stability, crisis stability, and arms race stability—deserve discussion.

Strategic stability occurs when both sides are assured that each has a secure second-strike capability—that is, adequate numbers of invulnerable nuclear weapons to inflict unacceptable damage after sustaining a nuclear attack. Crisis stability exists when neither side fears a preemptive strike. And finally, arms race stability reigns when neither side has concerns that its adversaries are trying to build weapons that undermine either strategic or crisis stability.[116]

To what extent do these conditions now obtain on the subcontinent?[117] India's concerns in these three realms involve two potential adversaries, China and Pakistan. Strategic stability does exist between India and Pakistan. Neither side can be certain that its extant capabilities will enable it to carry out a decapitating first strike. Consequently, a condition of mutual vulnerability will exist. Similarly, crisis stability is also likely to endure because neither side would be confident of destroying a substantial portion of the other's forces in a preemp-

---

114. George K. Tanham, *Indian Strategic Thought: An Interpretive Essay* (Santa Monica, Calif.: RAND, 1992). For a thoughtful discussion of a possible strategic posture for India in the aftermath of the nuclear tests, see Kapil Kak, "Strategic Template for Nuclear India," *Times of India*, August 11, 1998, p. 6.

115. Raj Chengappa and Manoj Joshi, "Future Fire," *India Today International*, May 25, 1998, pp. 22–24. See also Kapil Kak, "Command and Control of Small Nuclear Arsenals," in Singh, *Nuclear India*, pp. 266–285.

116. On this point, see the discussion in Leon V. Sigal, "Warming to the Freeze," *Foreign Policy*, No. 48 (Fall 1982), pp. 54–65.

117. I am grateful to Ashley Tellis of RAND for suggesting the application of these categories to the subcontinental nuclear context. The particular interpretations developed in this article are mine, however.

tive strike. The question of arms race stability is more vexing. The growth of ballistic missile capabilities on both sides may endanger strategic or crisis stability. Consequently, one of the principal priorities of the proponents of nuclear nonproliferation should be the development of measures to ensure arms race stability. To this end, India and Pakistan need to discuss missile production and deployment issues and move toward the creation of an arms control regime.

India's conventional forces are more than a match for China's capabilities. China's substantial nuclear and ballistic missile capabilities present problems for Indian defense planners, however. The current Sino-Indian relationship fails to meet the demands of strategic stability. India does not yet possess ballistic missile capabilities to target significant Chinese military or civilian assets. China, on the other hand, can inflict unacceptable damage on India. Crisis stability may be a bit stronger in this relationship, however. Given the acute secrecy surrounding the Indian nuclear weapons program and its dispersed assets, few Chinese decisionmakers would contemplate a disarming preemptive strike. India, on the other hand, lacks the capability to similarly strike China. Finally, arms race stability between India and China is also problematic. The Chinese already possess intermediate-range ballistic missiles that can target portions of the Indian heartland.[118] India, in turn, is developing the Agni II, which would be able to reach targets in southern China. The extant Chinese capabilities and incipient Indian capabilities threaten arms race stability. Thus, once mutual recriminations about the nuclear tests subside, it is imperative that India and China start discussions in conjunction with Pakistan about future force levels, deployments, and acquisitions. Now that the nuclear genie has escaped the bottle in South Asia, an arms control regime that involves China may offer the best hope of containing the genie's reach.[119]

118. IISS, *The Military Balance, 1997–98.*

119. For a thoughtful discussion of Chinese perspectives on arms control prior to the conclusion of the CTBT negotiations and the Indian nuclear tests, see Banning N. Garrett and Bonnie S. Glaser, "Chinese Perspectives on Nuclear Arms Control," *International Security,* Vol. 20, No. 3 (Winter 1995/96), pp. 43–78.

Pakistan's Nuclear Weapons Program

Turning Points and Nuclear Choices

Samina Ahmed

$\mathbf{P}$akistan tested a series of nuclear devices on May 28 and 30, 1998, signaling the abandonment of its policy of nuclear ambiguity, which it had adopted in the 1980s.[1] Under this policy, Pakistan had neither renounced nor acquired nuclear weapons for overt weaponization. The Pakistani action was motivated primarily by similar tests conducted in India on May 11 and 13, and was taken by Pakistan's nuclear weapons decisionmaking apparatus, comprising the military and the civil bureaucracy, including nuclear scientists. Despite a rigorous debate on the pros and cons of testing, Pakistan's political leadership played only a marginal role in determining Islamabad's response. Following the tests, Pakistan laid claim to the status of a nuclear weapons state, with Prime Minister Nawaz Sharif declaring, "No matter we are recognized as a nuclear weapons power or not, we are a nuclear power."[2]

Pakistan's decision to test its nuclear capability represents a major turning point in its nuclear program. To date, however, Islamabad has given no indication that it intends to weaponize and deploy its nuclear devices and their delivery systems. Pakistani policymakers have three choices: (1) to adopt an overt nuclear weapons posture, which would involve the development, assembly, and deployment of nuclear weapons and their delivery systems; (2) to maintain the new status quo, that is, to retain an overt nuclear weapons capability without opting for deployment of nuclear weapons and their delivery systems; or (3) to roll back the nuclear weapons program and accept the international nonproliferation regime. The acceptance or rejection of any of these options will be determined, as in the past, by a number of related domestic, regional, and international variables.

Regional factors, especially Pakistan's relations with India, will continue to play a major role in determining Islamabad's nuclear course. From its incep-

---

Samina Ahmed has written extensively on South Asian nuclear proliferation. She is coeditor of Pakistan and the Bomb: Public Opinion and Nuclear Options *(Notre Dame, Ind.: University of Notre Dame Press, 1998). She is currently a Fellow at the Belfer Center for Science and International Affairs, John F. Kennedy School of Government, Harvard University.*

---

1. To date the government has provided very little technical data on the nuclear tests, and officials have contradicted one another about the number of tests conducted.
2. Quoted in "Prime Minister Links Pak-India Amity to Kashmir Solution," *News,* June 14, 1998.

International Security, Vol. 23, No. 4 (Spring 1999), pp. 178–204

tion, Pakistan's nuclear policy has been India-centric, revolving around perceptions of threat from and hostility toward India. The issue of prestige, evident in Pakistan's desire to acquire equal standing with India in nuclear weapons development, also looms large.[3] International developments and the role of influential regional and extraregional actors have also helped shape Pakistan's nuclear policy and will continue to do so. These include Pakistan's formal and informal alliances with the United States, the unraveling of this alliance relationship, Pakistan's military links with China, and the impact of the Cold War and post–Cold War environments on South Asia.

Domestic factors will also continue to play a critical role in the adoption or rejection of nuclear options. Direct or indirect authoritarian rule, weak representative governments, and an inept and divided political leadership have combined to perpetuate the military's control over security policy, including the nuclear weapons program, which the military formulates in line with its perceptions and institutional interests. The military's security policies are dictated by its traditional hostility toward, and perceptions of threat from, India, as well as its desire to acquire an adequate conventional and nuclear force to counter this threat. This interpretation of security also advances the armed forces' institutional interests by legitimizing the existence of a large standing military and a constant increase in defense expenditure. Moreover, the partnership between the armed forces and the civil bureaucracy, including its subsidiary nuclear scientific establishment, further marginalizes the role of the political leadership in the nuclear decisionmaking process.

Pakistan's decision to opt for nuclear tests in May 1998 was determined by its regional environment. This decision was adopted by the military and the civil bureaucracy with the acquiescence of the political leadership. International factors came into play later with the imposition of a sanctions regime that has created an economic crisis of unprecedented dimensions.[4] Collectively, the rise in tensions with India in the wake of the tests, international isolation, a faltering economy, and the internal balance of power will determine Pakistan's nuclear choices in the post-test South Asian environment.

---

3. According to Minister for Information Mushahid Hussain Syed, "The world community now treats Pakistan and India as equals." Quoted in "N-Tests Elevated Pakistan's Political Stature: Mushahid," *News*, June 26, 1998. See also Sandy Gordon, "Capping South Asia's Nuclear Weapons Program: A Window of Opportunity?" *Asian Survey*, Vol. 34, No. 7 (July 1994), p. 667.
4. Addressing the National Assembly on September 8, 1998, Commerce Minister Ishaq Dar admitted that Pakistan was on the verge of financial default as a result of the sanctions. Mariana Babar, "Pakistan Faces Engineered Default, Dar Tells NA," *News*, September 9, 1998.

This article traces Pakistan's nuclear history and attempts to identify the role of domestic, regional, and international variables in determining Pakistan's nuclear choices. The first four sections highlight key turning points in Pakistan's nuclear weapons program and the motivations behind its nuclear choices from 1947 until 1988. The fifth section examines the impact of a changed domestic and external environment on Pakistan's nuclear weapons program following the restoration of democracy in 1988 after eleven years of military rule. The sixth section examines events immediately leading up to May 1998 and the consequences of Pakistan's nuclear tests. The conclusion offers some observations on the future of Pakistan's nuclear weapons program.

Pakistan's Nascent Nuclear Policy

Pakistan's nuclear weapons program can be traced to Prime Minister Zulfikar Ali Bhutto's decision to pursue the nuclear weapons route in 1972 in reaction to a perceived threat from India. The India-centric bias of Pakistan's nuclear weapons policy has a much longer history, however. The events accompanying the partition of Britain's Indian Empire into two independent states in 1947 shaped Pakistan's security environment. The mass migration of Hindus and Muslims across the India-Pakistan border resulted in hundreds of thousands of casualties, differences over divided economic and military assets, and disputes over territory, including armed conflict in 1948 over the Muslim-majority state of Kashmir. Together they sowed the seeds of mistrust and hostility between the two states.[5]

Independence created a variety of political, economic, and strategic challenges for Pakistan. The policies it adopted to meet these challenges were determined by the composition of the ruling elite. Although the Muslim League had formed a government, it had a limited support base in the areas that now constituted Pakistan. The military-bureaucratic apparatus inherited from the British gained ascendancy over the political leadership as early as 1951. While the bureaucracy governed the state, the military—with the support of the pro-Western, anti-Indian civil bureaucracy—controlled security policy, choosing to rely on external alliances to counter the perceived Indian threat.

---

5. Pakistan refused to accept the accession of the Muslim-majority state of Kashmir to India, which resulted in armed conflict in 1948. India, however, succeeded in retaining control over most of the princely state's territory. India and Pakistan have since rejected each other's authority over Kashmir, and a Line of Control, instead of an international boundary, divides Indian- and Pakistani-administered Kashmir.

Pakistan's geostrategic position—contiguous to Communist China and located near the Soviet Union and West Asia—combined with its anticommunist military, made it a natural ally for the United States in its strategy of encircling the Soviet Union in the 1950s. As Pakistan joined a number of U.S.-sponsored alliances,[6] the United States became a reliable source of conventional arms, underwriting the military's belief that alliance with the West would provide Pakistan the security it needed against perceived Indian threats. U.S. military and economic assistance also allowed for the continuing expansion of the military establishment, further strengthening its standing vis-à-vis rival domestic actors.[7]

In the 1950s, as Pakistan's leadership consolidated its defense links with the West and continued to build up its conventional forces, there was little evidence of a nuclear weapons program. There was, however, interest in the peaceful uses of nuclear energy. In 1957 the Pakistan Atomic Energy Commission (PAEC) was established to train nuclear scientists and to set up a nuclear research reactor. This marked the beginnings of a nascent indigenous nuclear scientific establishment.

Rethinking the Nuclear Weapons Option

Dissatisfied with its indirect control of the government, the military took power in 1958 with the support of the civil bureaucracy. Army Chief General Mohammad Ayub Khan assumed the dual mantles of field martial and president, heading his own wing of the ruling party, the Muslim League. Under Khan's direct rule, the military formulated defense and security policies in accordance with its perceptions and institutional interests. During this period the military believed that conventional weapons were sufficient to safeguard and advance Pakistani security interests vis-à-vis India. Pakistan's nuclear program, therefore, appeared to be geared solely toward developing peaceful uses for nuclear energy. Its only research reactor, which began operations in 1965, and its natural uranium heavy-water nuclear power plant, the Karachi Nuclear Power Project, were placed under comprehensive International Atomic Energy Agency (IAEA) safeguards.

---

6. Pakistan became a member of a number of U.S. or U.S.-sponsored security alliances in the mid-1950s, including the Southeast Asia Treaty Organization and the Baghdad Pact (later renamed the Central Treaty Organization).
7. Yunas Samad, "The Military and Democracy in Pakistan," *Contemporary South Asia*, Vol. 3, No. 3 (Fall 1994), p. 190.

Official thinking about Pakistan's nuclear program began to change in the 1960s, as relations with India continued to deteriorate in a pervasive atmosphere of mutual suspicion and contempt. Domestically, the military's authority was questioned, especially in the East Wing and in Sindh, by an assertive opposition angered by the military's continued rule and lopsided economic policies that favored West Pakistani interests, particularly those of the Punjab, the military's and civil bureaucracy's traditional recruiting ground.

In a bid to divert domestic attention, the military in 1965 tried once again to oust India from Kashmir. Domestic unrest heightened, however, when the Pakistani military failed to make any substantive gains in Kashmir. Tensions increased further when it was learned that the ensuing peace treaty with India, the Tashkent agreement of 1966, included no concessions for Pakistan on Kashmir. As the regime's popularity waned, Ayub's foreign minister, Zulfikar Ali Bhutto, launched a bid for political power by publicly adopting a strident anti-India stance. Known for his deep distrust of India, Bhutto in 1958, as minister for fuel and power and minister in charge of atomic energy, had urged Ayub to begin actively exploring the nuclear weapons option. Ayub, however, had rejected Bhutto's advice on the grounds that, if Pakistan needed a nuclear weapons capability, it could buy it "off the shelf"[8] (i.e., from Pakistan's Western allies).

The 1965 war was an important turning point for Pakistan's nuclear weapons program. After the war the conventional weapons disparity between Pakistan and India began to shift in India's favor when the United States, Pakistan's main arms provider, banned the supply of weaponry to both states as punishment for the war. Pakistan's security alliances with the West, in any case, had become a casualty of U.S.-Soviet détente, which had reduced the strategic significance of Cold War allies such as Pakistan for the United States. In the mid-1960s, however, Pakistan developed closer ties with China, which soon became one of its major suppliers of conventional weapons. However, influential segments of the Pakistani military believed that the Chinese arms were neither quantitatively nor qualitatively adequate to counterbalance India's conventional arms superiority.

Foreign Minister Bhutto, rightly concluding that India was well on the road to acquiring a nuclear weapons capability, renewed his bid for a Pakistani nu-

---

8. Quoted in Samina Ahmed and David Cortright, "Going Nuclear: The Weaponization Option," in Ahmed and Cortright, eds., *Pakistan and the Bomb: Public Opinion and Nuclear Options* (Notre Dame, Ind.: University of Notre Dame Press, 1998), p. 90.

clear weapons capability to counter the perceived Indian threat. In 1966 he declared that if India acquired a nuclear bomb, "even if Pakistanis have to eat grass, we will make the bomb."[9] Bhutto's position increased Ayub's vulnerability to domestic opposition at the same time that support was growing within policymaking circles for a nuclear weapons capability. This was evident, for example, in Pakistan's refusal to sign the Nuclear Nonproliferation Treaty (NPT) in 1968, which followed India's rejection of the treaty on grounds that it was discriminatory. After Pakistan's defeat in the 1971 India-Pakistan War, the military use of nuclear power became the focal point of Pakistan's nuclear policy.

Adopting the Nuclear Weapons Option

In December 1971 Pakistan split apart when the East Wing seceded from the federation following a bloody civil conflict and a war in which India supported independence for Bangladesh. Ayub's presidential successor, Army Chief Yahya Khan, was held responsible for the debacle. He was removed by powerful factions within the military and replaced by Zulfikar Ali Bhutto, who first became president and chief martial-law administrator and then prime minister.[10] The 1971 war reinforced Pakistan's hostility toward India and its perceptions of insecurity. The leadership in Islamabad believed that the United States had failed to come to Pakistan's aid, while India had received both moral and military support from its Soviet allies.

Domestically, Bhutto faced the dual challenges of creating a new identity for a traumatized nation and salvaging the prestige of a defeated yet politically powerful military. Using nationalistic, anti-imperialist, and anti-Indian rhetoric to build popular support, Bhutto embarked on a program of expanding the size of the armed forces. And in March 1972, with the support of the military and the civil bureaucracy, he adopted a nuclear weapons program.[11] Pakistan's resolve to establish a nuclear weapons infrastructure was reinforced when In-

---

9. Cited in Zafar Iqbal Cheema, "Pakistan's Nuclear Policies: Attitudes and Postures," in P.R. Chari, Pervaiz Iqbal Cheema, and Iftekharuzzaman, eds., *Nuclear Non-Proliferation in India and Pakistan: South Asian Perspectives* (New Delhi: Monohar, 1996), p. 10.
10. Bhutto's Pakistan People's Party had won a majority of seats in West Pakistan during the 1970 general elections.
11. Bhutto's army chief, for example, declared that an Indian acquisition of nuclear weapons would mean that "we will have to beg or borrow to develop our own nuclear capability." Quoted in Leonard S. Spector, *Nuclear Proliferation Today* (Cambridge, Mass.: Ballinger, 1984), p. 34.

dia detonated a nuclear device in May 1974, another turning point that set Pakistan irrevocably along the nuclear weapons path.

Soon after the 1974 Indian explosion, Pakistan established a nuclear weapons program that was separate from the PAEC. The PAEC and the nuclear weapons program remained close, however. In fact, PAEC-trained scientists staffed the nuclear weapons establishment, and a board of senior bureaucrats coordinated their activities. The new program was headed by a metallurgical engineer, Abdul Qadeer Khan. Bhutto assigned Khan the task of enriching uranium to weapons grade. Khan had allegedly stolen the technology and blueprints for uranium enrichment while working at the Almelo ultracentrifuge uranium enrichment plant in the Netherlands.[12] In addition, the civil bureaucracy and military intelligence set up clandestine networks to acquire the necessary technology and hardware for ultra-high-speed centrifuges from Western European sources.

In 1973, however, even before the Indian nuclear test, Bhutto had opened negotiations with the French to purchase a nuclear reprocessing plant for the enrichment of plutonium, ostensibly for Pakistan's civilian energy program. Signing the deal in 1976, the Pakistani government claimed that it intended to set up a large number of nuclear power plants to help Pakistan meet its energy needs. Pakistan, however, lacked the technological and economic resources to create such a large nuclear infrastructure, making it clear to the United States that the extracted plutonium would be diverted for military purposes.

By the mid-1970s the United States had become concerned about the acquisition of nuclear weapons capabilities by hostile third world states (such as Libya), and began to rethink its approach to the transfer of nuclear technology. U.S. fears of horizontal proliferation were reinforced by India's 1974 nuclear explosion and by the impending sale of a French nuclear reprocessing plant to Pakistan.[13] Reacting to this concern, the U.S. Congress in 1976 passed the Symington amendment to the International Security Assistance and Arms Export Control Act. The amendment denied U.S. military and economic assistance to any country importing unsafeguarded enrichment or reprocessing technology.

Subsequently, the United States called upon Pakistan and France to cancel their nuclear reprocessing plant deal. Pakistan's policymakers, however, were committed to pursuing the nuclear weapons option. To counter the external

---

12. Ibid., pp. 75–76.
13. Ibid., p. 79.

pressure, the Pakistanis launched a diplomatic campaign to convince the international community of their country's peaceful nuclear intentions and to highlight its India-centric threat perceptions. At the same time, Pakistan pledged its support for regional nuclear disarmament in international forums, urging in particular the establishment of a nuclear weapons–free zone in South Asia.

Prime Minister Bhutto's close links with Libya and his use of anti-imperialist rhetoric to acquire domestic support had not endeared him to policymakers in Washington, who were even more irked by his refusal to abandon the reprocessing plant deal. In August 1976 Henry Kissinger visited Pakistan in an effort to dissuade Bhutto from acquiring the plutonium reprocessing technology. In 1977 the French succumbed to U.S. pressure and agreed to cancel the sale. Bhutto later claimed that Pakistan "was on the threshold of full nuclear capability. All we needed was the nuclear reprocessing plant."[14]

In July 1977 the military, led by Mohammed Zia-ul-Haq, ousted Prime Minister Bhutto and reimposed martial law. Domestic realities, particularly Bhutto's disregard for democratic norms, had eroded his popular base and were primarily responsible for the coup d'état. Bhutto's ouster marked another key turning point for Pakistan's nuclear weapons program. Imprisoned by Zia, Bhutto accused Kissinger of threatening to have him eliminated if he did not abandon Pakistan's nuclear weapons program.[15] For many Pakistanis, U.S. opposition to the reprocessing deal, the military coup, and Bhutto's subsequent hanging were intrinsically linked. Pakistan's nuclear weapons program became synonymous with national sovereignty and national prestige, even when it was run by the very military that had eliminated Pakistan's best-known populist politician.

Acquiring Nuclear Weapons Capability

After Bhutto's execution on April 4, 1979, domestic opposition to martial law increased. The military regime faced the dilemma of retaining its political dominance without further eroding the domestic legitimacy of the armed forces. Consequently, the military high command used the Indian threat and

14. Zulfikar Ali Bhutto, *If I Am Assassinated . . .* (New Delhi: Vikas, 1979), pp. 137–138.
15. Bhutto claimed that Kissinger had "threatened" to make "a horrible example" out of him if he did not give up the nuclear weapons program. Quoted in Stanley Wolpert, *Zulfi Bhutto of Pakistan: His Life and Times* (Oxford, U.K.: Oxford University Press, 1993), p. 273.

the acquisition of a countervailing nuclear weapons capability to generate domestic support.

The nuclear weapons program operated under the absolute control of the armed forces, while the civil bureaucracy played an active role through its subsidiary arm, the nuclear scientific establishment. In an effort to accelerate Pakistan's ability to enrich uranium to weapons-grade levels through centrifuge technology, the Zia regime established an extensive clandestine network in Western Europe. The regime also used existing loopholes in Western European legislation to openly acquire the uranium enrichment technology and equipment it needed from countries such as Germany and the Netherlands.

At this stage in Pakistan's nuclear weapons program, China became a major supplier of nuclear know-how and hardware in a bid to counter India's military capabilities. Chinese assistance included the provision of weapons-grade uranium, technical information on uranium enrichment, and help in setting up the Kahuta ultracentrifuge uranium enrichment plant, which became operational in the mid-1980s. In addition, work began on a second uranium enrichment plant, and a uranium hexaflouride plant was set up at Dera Ghazi Khan in the province of Punjab.

Pakistan continued to mask its nuclear ambitions under the guise of nuclear ambiguity to offset external pressures. During the Carter administration Pakistan's relations with the United States were tense, as Washington applied pressure—including the imposition of military and economic sanctions in September 1977 and again in April 1979—to curb Pakistan's nuclear program. To assuage external, particularly U.S., concerns, and to strengthen Pakistan's claims that its nuclear program was peaceful, the Zia regime proposed a number of regional nonproliferation measures, including simultaneous Indian and Pakistani accession to the NPT and acceptance of IAEA full-scope safeguards. These offers posed little risk to the Pakistani nuclear weapons program, however, because India had linked its nuclear policy to global disarmament and opposed any regional nonproliferation regime that excluded China.

The Soviet Union's invasion of Afghanistan in 1980 proved another crucial turning point for Pakistan's nuclear weapons program. In reaction to the Soviet military intervention, U.S. opposition to the Pakistani program began to ease and then finally disappeared as Washington again focused on Pakistan's strategic significance in the region. Soon the Zia regime was serving U.S. interests in Afghanistan. The United States, especially under the Reagan administration, waived nonproliferation sanctions against Pakistan and began providing massive military and economic assistance. As a consequence, the Pakistani military was able to greatly strengthen its control over domestic opponents.

Unwilling to alienate the Zia regime, the Reagan administration intentionally ignored the rapid growth of Pakistan's nuclear weapons infrastructure, so that it could claim that Pakistan was abiding by the nonproliferation terms set by Congress. At the same time, the administration justified the extension of military and economic assistance to Pakistan on the grounds that incentives, especially the supply of conventional weaponry, would effectively contain Pakistan's nuclear weapons program. The U.S. undersecretary of state for security assistance, science, and technology, James Buckley, for example, argued: "In place of the ineffective sanctions on Pakistan's nuclear program imposed by the past administration, we hope to address, through conventional means, the sources of insecurity that prompt a nation like Pakistan to seek a nuclear capability in the first place."[16] The Reagan administration even ignored U.S. intelligence reports in 1983 and 1984 that China provided Pakistan the design for a low-yield uranium device, based on data China had obtained during its fourth series of tests in 1964.[17]

The U.S. Congress, however, continued to express concern about the rapid progress in Pakistan's nuclear weapons capabilities. In 1985 it passed the Pakistan-specific Pressler amendment, which called for the imposition of economic and military sanctions against Pakistan unless the U.S. president could certify that Pakistan neither had nor was attempting to acquire nuclear weapons. In response, President Reagan warned the Zia regime to refrain from crossing the 5-percent uranium enrichment mark.[18] But even after Pakistan had acquired the capability to enrich uranium beyond 5-percent U235, Reagan certified that Pakistan did not have a nuclear weapons program. The U.S. supply of military and economic assistance to Pakistan, therefore, continued.[19] This assistance included the sale of F-16 fighter bombers, a potential delivery system for a future Pakistani nuclear arsenal.

By the mid-1980s Pakistan, secure in its belief that U.S. patronage would continue, abandoned the earlier claim that its nuclear program was solely for peaceful purposes.[20] Domestically, Pakistan's official acknowledgment that it

---

16. Quoted in Akhtar Ali, *Pakistan's Nuclear Dilemma: Energy and Security Dimensions* (Karachi: Economic Research Unit, 1984), p. 10. See also Mitchell Reiss, "Safeguarding the Nuclear Peace in South Asia," *Asian Survey*, Vol. 33, No. 12 (December 1993), pp. 1110–1111.
17. Spector, *Nuclear Proliferation Today*, p. 101.
18. Pakistan's KANUPP plant did not require uranium enriched beyond 3 to 5 percent U235.
19. U.S. intelligence agencies believed that Pakistan had acquired weapons-grade material, and had even cold-tested some components of its nuclear device by 1986. Leonard S. Spector with Jacqueline R. Smith, *Nuclear Ambitions: The Spread of Nuclear Weapons, 1989–1990* (Boulder, Colo.: Westview, 1990), pp. 95, 99.
20. In an interview with an Urdu-language newspaper, *Nawai-i-Waqt*, in 1984, Abdul Qadeer Khan declared that Pakistan could "efficiently enrich (weapons-grade) uranium." This represented the

had a nuclear weapons program was used with some success to legitimize the military's interventionist role as the guardian of Pakistan's national sovereignty.[21] In its relations with India, the Zia regime attempted to use nuclear ambiguity to deter any potential Indian threat by claiming that Pakistan had acquired a nuclear deterrent. For example, when war almost broke out in 1987 in the wake of a large-scale Indian military exercise (known as "Brasstacks") near the Pakistani border, which was followed by retaliatory Pakistani military maneuvers, Pakistani policymakers used a two-pronged strategy. Islamabad and New Delhi held high-level diplomatic talks to diffuse tensions, and Pakistan publicly disclosed its nuclear weapons capability.[22] By the time of General Zia's assassination in a midair explosion in August 1988, Pakistan had achieved the status of a nuclear-threshold state.

Nuclear Continuity and Domestic Change

Zia's assassination and the subsequent restoration of democracy in 1988 had little impact on Pakistani decisionmaking and control over nuclear policy, because the military retained control over defense and security policymaking.[23] Under the military's guidance and with the support of the civil bureaucracy, the nuclear weapons program continued to advance rapidly. According to Army Chief General Mirza Aslam Beg, Pakistan had acquired the ability to assemble a nuclear device by 1988.[24] After 1988 Pakistan's ballistic missile program began to expand, with Chinese assistance, in response to India's acquisition of short-range and intermediate-range nuclear-capable missiles. In 1989 Pakistan tested its short-range, nuclear-capable Hatf-I and Hatf-II ballistic missiles, with a range of 80 kilometers and 180 kilometers, respectively.[25]

Changes in the international environment, however, placed new constraints on Pakistan's nuclear weapons program. The post–Cold War environment re-

first public, albeit unofficial, acknowledgment of Pakistan's nuclear weapons capability. Quoted in Spector, *Nuclear Proliferation Today*, pp. 98–99.
21. Ali, *Pakistan's Nuclear Dilemma*, p. 62.
22. In an interview with an Indian journalist, Kuldip Nayyar, Abdul Qadeer Khan disclosed that Pakistan had the ability to assemble a nuclear weapon. Nayyar, "Pakistan Has the Bomb," *Tribune*, March 1, 1987.
23. Beg delayed the transfer of power to Benazir Bhutto after the 1988 general elections until Bhutto agreed to the military's control over defense and security matters. Samad, "The Military and Democracy," pp. 194–195.
24. General Mirza Aslam Beg (ret.), "Who Will Press the Button?" *News*, April 23, 1994.
25. Spector, *Nuclear Ambitions*, pp. 100–101, 107.

duced Pakistan's strategic significance for the United States once again. This in turn led Washington to rethink its policy of deliberately ignoring Pakistan's nuclear ambitions. Initially reluctant to use coercive means that could destabilize Pakistan's fragile democracy, the United States merely issued warnings to Pakistan to cap its production of weapons-grade uranium. In addition, presidential certifications were provided for another two years. Pakistani policymakers, unwilling to jeopardize U.S. economic assistance and military supplies, appeared to give in to U.S. pressure. In 1989 Army Chief General Beg and President Ghulam Ishaq Khan, a former bureaucrat, decided to halt the enrichment of uranium to 5-percent U235. Pakistani policymakers, however, had no intention of maintaining the freeze, because the military considered the benefits of its nuclear weapons capability to far outweigh its costs.[26]

Impatient with civilian control, General Beg used the nuclear program to adopt a more assertive profile. Publicly supporting overt weaponization, Beg accelerated the pace of the program, abandoning even the facade of consulting with the political leadership. During a visit to the United States in June 1989, for example, Zia's successor, Prime Minister Benazir Bhutto, claimed that Pakistan had restrained its nuclear weapons program and expressed shock when U.S. sources painted a different picture of the state of Pakistan's nuclear development.[27]

In August 1989 Beg dismissed Bhutto and set up a shadow military government. In 1990 general elections were held, and Nawaz Sharif became prime minister. The military, however, retained control over the nuclear program and discovered new uses for its nuclear weapons capability, including the use of nuclear diplomacy. Under the Zia regime, Pakistan had adopted a strategy of undermining Indian security through a war by proxy in Indian-administered Kashmir. By 1990 Kashmiri alienation was at its peak, and Pakistan's relations with India had deteriorated to the brink of open conflict. Pakistan, implicitly threatening to use nuclear weapons if India intervened militarily across the Line of Control in Kashmir, persuaded the United States to act as an intermediary.[28] Although it is unlikely that Pakistan would have seriously contemplated using nuclear weapons, the success of the nuclear bluff reinforced the leader-

---

26. Pakistani officials did admit that weapons cores stockpiled before 1990 had not been destroyed. Reiss, "Safeguarding the Nuclear Peace in South Asia," p. 1111.
27. Zahid Hussain, "Deliberate Nuclear Ambiguity," Ahmed and Cortright, *Pakistan and the Bomb*, pp. 38–39.
28. "Special Rack-Fitted F-16s Heading for Airfields," *Patriot*, May 26, 1990.

ship's belief in the value of nuclear weapons both as a deterrent and as a tool of diplomatic bargaining.[29]

After 1990, and again at the military's behest, Pakistan's cap on the enrichment of uranium to weapons-grade levels was removed, and its nuclear production capability was further enhanced. President George Bush responded in mid-1990 by refusing to certify that Pakistan did not possess nuclear weapons. The United States then imposed sanctions under the Pressler amendment, halting all U.S. military and economic assistance. U.S. sanctions, however, had little effect on Pakistani policymaking for several reasons. First, the military realized that the supply of preferential U.S. military and economic assistance was bound to dry up in the post–Cold War environment. Second, the Pakistanis did not believe that their economy would be seriously affected, because U.S. sanctions did not extend to loans and grants provided by international financial institutions such as the International Monetary Fund (IMF), the World Bank, and the Asian Development Bank. Third, in the absence of an international consensus on South Asian nuclear proliferation, Pakistan could approach other advanced industrialized countries for soft loans and grants as well as for the purchase of advanced weapons systems.

As Pakistan's nuclear production capabilities grew apace,[30] its nuclear rhetoric changed. Islamabad began to acknowledge publicly its ability to assemble nuclear weapons. In January 1992 Foreign Secretary Shahrayar Khan declared in an interview with the *Washington Post* that Pakistan possessed "all the elements which, if hooked together, would become a (nuclear) device."[31] This statement was meant to send a message to external actors, particularly the United States, to reaffirm Pakistan's commitment to its nuclear weapons program. Domestically, the military ensured that the elected political leadership did not challenge its nuclear preferences. In 1991 Prime Minister Nawaz Sharif favored a freeze on the enrichment of uranium in return for concessions from the United States. Sharif, however, admitted in an interview with *New York*

---

29. According to Pervez Hoodbhoy, although "the facts seem to indicate that the alleged reports of nuclear movements (in 1990) were false, the belief that Pakistan's threat of nuclear devastation stopped Indian aggression dead in its tracks has become enshrined as an article of faith." Hoodbhoy, "Pakistan's Nuclear Future," in Ahmed and Cortright, *Pakistan and the Bomb*, p. 71.
30. Pakistan's nuclear infrastructure now included a plutonium production reactor and a reprocessing facility at Khushab, both under construction with Chinese assistance.
31. Quoted in Samina Ahmed and David Cortright, "Pakistani Public Opinion and Nuclear Weapons Policy," in Ahmed and Cortright, *Pakistan and the Bomb*, pp. 3–4.

Times correspondent Barbara Crossette that he could not cap the nuclear program without the military's assent.[32]

Sharif's dependence on the continued goodwill of the military for his very survival was clearly demonstrated when he was abruptly removed in 1993 and Benazir Bhutto was put in charge of forming a new government. Thereafter, conscious of their vulnerability, all elected governments and their political opponents supported the military's preferences in all sensitive areas, including the nuclear weapons program. Given the entire political leadership's support of Pakistan's nuclear weapons policy, it was inevitable that the Pakistani public would internalize this official position.

Although Pakistani policymakers had no intention of abandoning the nuclear weapons option, they were conscious of the need to placate international opinion. They sought to do this by pledging their support for nonproliferation measures, conditional on the removal of the Indian nuclear threat. Thus Pakistan linked its approval of the NPT's indefinite extension in 1995 to India's acceptance of the treaty. In 1996 Pakistan declared that it would sign the Comprehensive Test Ban Treaty (CTBT) if India also acceded. Pakistan's use of the Indian threat heightened tensions between the two countries. In addition, the maneuverability of Pakistani policymakers was adversely affected because their declaratory nuclear policy became dependent on India's nuclear choices.

The Pakistani leadership, however, was less concerned about the negative impact of its nuclear rhetoric on India and much more concerned about persuading the United States to remove the Pressler sanctions. Pakistani officials claimed that Pakistan's legitimate security needs demanded the retention of its nuclear capability and that these discriminatory sanctions had served only to reduce Washington's leverage in its dealings with Islamabad. These arguments had some effect on U.S. thinking. The Clinton administration, for example, adopted a more flexible approach, emphasizing positive engagement and incentives to persuade both Pakistan and India to freeze their nuclear weapons programs. The new U.S. emphasis on engagement in South Asia represented another turning point in Pakistan's nuclear weapons program.

Recognizing the central role of the military in the formulation of Pakistan's nuclear policy, the Clinton administration held negotiations with the Pakistani political leadership and the military high command, offering them both military and economic incentives. In 1993 U.S. Assistant Secretary of State for

---

32. Hussain, "Deliberate Nuclear Ambiguity," p. 40.

South Asian Affairs Robin Raphel visited Pakistan. Under a onetime waiver of the Pressler amendment and in return for a cap on uranium enrichment, Raphel, on behalf of the United States, offered to deliver the twenty-eight F-16s that Pakistan had purchased before the embargo and to sell the Pakistanis military hardware.[33]

Despite Pakistan's reluctance to compromise, the United States continued to negotiate with the Pakistani military.[34] Under the Brown amendment to the 1996 Foreign Assistance Act, a onetime waiver of the Pressler amendment, the United States agreed to sell $368 million worth of military hardware to Pakistan.[35] U.S. concessions and President Bill Clinton's flexible approach were seen by Pakistani policymakers as the unraveling of U.S. resolve to halt South Asian nuclear proliferation and the acceptance of Pakistan's and India's de facto nuclear status. At a time when South Asian leaders were receiving mixed signals from the United States on horizontal proliferation, the regional nuclear equation changed drastically when India's Bharatiya Janata Party (BJP) abandoned nuclear ambiguity for a policy of overt weaponization.

The May 1998 Nuclear Tests and Their Consequences

Pakistan's relations with India improved considerably after a meeting between Prime Ministers I.K. Gujral and Nawaz Sharif at the South Asian Association for Regional Cooperation summit in Male in May 1997, in which they agreed to open a dialogue. As foreign minister, Gujral in March 1997 had adopted a policy of improving India's relations with its neighbors. Sharif, who had been a businessman before entering politics, also believed that improved relations, especially closer trade links, would benefit both India and Pakistan. He declared at one point that "we must come out of the atmosphere of confrontation, we should learn lessons from the past."[36] Subsequently, the two states agreed to hold foreign secretary–level talks in mid-1997 on a range of contentious issues, including Kashmir.

The dialogue process came to a halt, however, after the BJP's electoral vic-

---

33. U.S. Deputy Secretary of State Strobe Talbott made a similar offer the same year.
34. During a visit to the United States in 1994, Army Chief Abdul Waheed Kakar rejected a cap in return for the F-16s. Zahid Hussain, "Carrot Talk," *Newsline* (April 1994), p. 26.
35. The Senate Foreign Affairs Committee, however, refused to make another concession to the Pakistani military. Specifically, it would not resume military-to-military links under the International Military and Education Training program, proposed in the Harkin-Warner amendment to the Foreign Operation Appropriations Act in mid-1997.
36. Quoted in "Pakistan Wants Good Ties with India," *Frontier Post*, June 9, 1997.

tory in April 1998. The BJP's aversion to any compromise on the Kashmir issue and its threats to opt for an overt nuclear weapons policy were partly responsible for the deterioration in Indo-Pakistani relations. In its election manifesto, for example, the BJP had promised to "reevaluate" the nuclear policy and to "exercise the option to induct nuclear weapons."[37] Pakistan's foreign office bureaucrats, however, by insisting on the centrality of the Kashmir dispute in any future resolution of Pakistan's differences with India, were equally responsible for derailing the talks even before the dismissal of the Gujral government. Furthermore, the Pakistani military did not approve of Sharif's attempts to open negotiations with India, and the perfect opportunity to stall the dialogue was presented as the BJP, a party that is perceived in Pakistan as an anti-Muslim, Hindu-extremist organization, formed a government in New Delhi.

In April 1998 Pakistan's military high command raised the stakes in its nuclear and missile arms race with India by testing the Ghauri ballistic missile, which it claimed was nuclear-capable and had a reach of 1,500 kilometers. Pakistani policymakers declared that the threat posed by India's short-range and intermediate-range missiles had been equalized now that Pakistan had the ability to strike any major Indian city.[38] Even as the international community focused its attention on preventing a destabilizing ballistic missile race in South Asia, the BJP government decided to honor its election pledge by testing a series of nuclear devices.

India's nuclear tests surprised the international community, particularly the United States, which had not expected the BJP to follow through on its threat of overt weaponization.[39] Following the Indian tests, the United States attempted to ward off a retaliatory Pakistani response. For their part, Pakistani policymakers initially adopted a wait-and-see attitude to have time to assess the international community's response to the Indian tests. At the same time, however, they were making preparations for a retaliatory test at a site in Baluchistan.

---

37. The BJP-led coalition's National Agenda for Governance also reiterated this pledge. Savita Pande, "The Nuclear Option," *Pioneer,* February 17, 1998; and "BJP's National Agenda for Governance," *Hindu,* March 19, 1998.

38. The Pakistani government has repeatedly refuted media reports that the Ghauri was developed with technology acquired from North Korea.

39. As a result of assurances given by India during high-level meetings between Indian and U.S. officials, the United States believed that India would continue to exercise nuclear restraint. These meetings included Indian Foreign Secretary K. Ragunath's visit to the United States on April 2 and presidential envoy Bill Richardson's visit to India in early May. Jyothi Malhotra, "Days of Dialogue," *Indian Express,* May 1, 1998.

Within Pakistani policymaking circles, the tussle between supporters of overt weaponization and proponents of the official policy of nuclear ambiguity began in earnest, with both sides attempting to gain public support by using the broadcast and print media. Prime Minister Sharif, aware of Pakistan's vulnerability to economic sanctions, hesitated in opting for a retaliatory test. His cabinet, however, was divided between those who opposed nuclear tests and long-standing supporters of weaponization. Proponents included Information Minister Mushahid Hussain, who controlled the broadcast media, a powerful avenue for influencing public opinion in a country with a largely illiterate population. Foreign Minister Gohar Ayub, General Ayub Khan's son, whose resignation had been submitted but not formally accepted just weeks before the Indian nuclear tests, became the most ardent official supporter of overt weaponization, often contradicting Sharif's more cautious posture. Ayub's support for overt weaponization reflected the thinking of the armed forces, which were still in charge of the overall direction of Pakistan's nuclear policy, and where the predominant belief was that Pakistan had no choice but to test. In the words of one senior officer: "We will never be able to remove the nuclear imbalance if we do not follow suit with our own explosion."[40] Hence a tit-for-tat response was almost inevitable.

Pakistan, however, had made the decision to respond to an Indian nuclear test with a test of its own as early as 1995, when the government of Narasimha Rao decided to test India's nuclear devices. U.S. intelligence detected the Indian preparations, however, and the government, under U.S. pressure, opted not to test. In 1996, after India's intentions to test were made public, Pakistan completed its preparations for a retaliatory test at a site in the Chagai district of southwestern Baluchistan, bordering on Iran and Afghanistan.[41]

Following India's May 1998 tests, the United States sent Deputy Secretary of State Strobe Talbott to ask the Pakistanis to exercise restraint. In negotiations with Islamabad, Washington offered a series of economic and military incentives, including repeal of the Pressler amendment. At the same time, U.S. officials warned Pakistan that economic sanctions would be imposed if it tested a nuclear device.

In a telephone conversation with President Clinton, Prime Minister Sharif stressed that, given the extreme pressure he was under, his options were lim-

40. Quoted in Zahid Hussain, "The Bomb and After," *Newsline* (June 1998), p. 23.
41. According to Prime Minister Benazir Bhutto, Pakistan's preparations for test explosion were meant to deter India and to warn the West "that they had better do something to stop the Indians." Quoted in Zahid Hussain, "Laying the Groundwork," *Newsline* (June 1998), p. 24.

ited. According to Sharif, the decision "was out of my hands," implying that the final decision lay with the military high command.[42] The only way Sharif could have successfully lobbied the armed forces against overt weaponization would have been to provide tangible proof that testing would gravely harm Pakistani interests. The muted international reaction to the Indian tests, however, undermined Sharif's stand. Although the United States did impose economic and military sanctions against India under the Glenn amendment, other UN Security Council members and the Group of Eight (G-8) merely condemned the Indian tests, refusing to follow the U.S. example of punitive action.

The absence of a concerted international response tilted the internal balance in Pakistan in favor of a retaliatory test. Pakistani policymakers believed that the costs of testing would be bearable in both political and economic terms. Furthermore, they feared that a failure to test could undermine other vital Pakistani interests, particularly in Kashmir. In the wake of the Indian tests, BJP Interior Minister Lal Krishna Advani warned Pakistan that it would be "costly" and "futile" if Pakistan did not end its intervention in Kashmir, adding that India's nuclear tests had brought about a "qualitatively new stage in Indo-Pakistan relations."[43] A final factor in favor of testing was the question of prestige. Following the Indian tests, Prime Minister Atal Behari Vajpayee called upon the international community to admit India into the exclusive nuclear weapons club. For Pakistani policymakers, particularly the military, a nuclear stature less than India's was unacceptable.

Thus hostility toward India was rife in Pakistan, and public opinion was manipulated in favor of testing. On May 28 and 30, Pakistan tested its nuclear devices at Chagai and later declared that the success of the tests demonstrated its nuclear weapons capability. Addressing jubilant Pakistanis, Prime Minister Sharif announced, "Today we have settled scores with India by detonating five nuclear devices of our own." He added, "We have paid them back."[44]

Concerned about the possibility of an adverse international response, Pakistani government officials asked important foreign actors, particularly the United States, to understand Pakistan's security needs. They stressed that Pakistan had been forced to test simply to counterbalance the new threat India posed to its security. Hoping to defuse international pressure and, even optimistically, to gain some diplomatic leverage over India on the Kashmir dispute, the Pakistani government also stressed that Pakistan's and India's overt

---

42. Quoted in Michael Hirsh and John Barry, "Nuclear Jitters," *Newsweek*, June 8, 1998, p. 16.
43. Quoted in "Advani Flexes Nuclear Muscle in Kashmir," *Telegraph*, May 19, 1998.
44. Quoted in Hussain, "The Bomb and After," p. 22.

nuclear weapons status had increased the chances of an outbreak of conflict, which now could have a nuclear dimension.[45]

Pakistan's retaliatory response, however, increased international concern about the dangers posed by an overt nuclear arms race between India and Pakistan. On June 6 the UN Security Council passed a U.S.-sponsored resolution deploring the Indian and Pakistani nuclear tests. The foreign ministers of the permanent five members of the council (P-5) in Geneva unanimously condemned the nuclear tests and urged both states to exercise restraint and refrain from assembling and deploying their nuclear weapons and further developing their missile delivery systems. In addition, the P-5, the G-8, and the European Union asked Pakistan and India to join the international nonproliferation regime as nonnuclear weapons states, to sign the NPT and the CTBT without conditions, and to participate actively in negotiations on a fissile material cutoff agreement in the Conference on Disarmament.

Pakistan dismissed the international condemnation as discriminatory and unfair. Nonetheless, it faced a formidable challenge in the form of economic sanctions that were imposed in response to its tests. The immediate goal of Pakistani policymakers, therefore, was to minimize the negative impact of sanctions on their weak economy in a way that would not jeopardize Pakistan's nuclear weapons program. The Pakistani decision to test had been made in the belief that U.S. bilateral sanctions would have little adverse effect on the Pakistani economy in the absence of an international consensus for punitive action.[46] It had also been assumed that Pakistan's allies, including China and the Islamic Middle Eastern states, would help Pakistan withstand diplomatic isolation and economic pressure. Sanctions, however, seriously destabilized the fragile Pakistani economy, already in dire straits as a result of decades of mismanagement and political instability.

U.S. sanctions imposed under the Glenn amendment included opposition to nonhumanitarian credits and loans to Pakistan from international financial institutions including the World Bank, the IMF, and the Asian Development Bank. Japan, Pakistan's largest aid donor and a major trading partner, also im-

45. Urging the international community to find a solution to the Kashmir dispute, Foreign Minister Ayub warned that "with the situation so volatile and in the presence of mistrust and suspicion . . . a nuclear conflict could erupt." Quoted in Anwar Iqbal, "Pakistan Yet to React to U.S. Sanctions," *News*, June 20, 1998.
46. The decision to test was influenced by the Pakistani belief that sanctions would not last long. This was reflected in the 1998 budget, in which estimates were based on projected foreign assistance inflows of 152 billion rupees for 1998, an increase over similar inflows of 141 billion rupees in 1997. See "IMF Puts Loans to Pakistan on Hold," *Dawn*, June 17, 1998; and "Economic Experts' Views: Budget Lacks Steps to Offset Effects of Curbs," *Dawn*, June 22, 1998.

posed economic sanctions. Under U.S. sponsorship and with Japanese support, a coordinated international strategy of punitive action emerged. On June 12, 1998, the G-8 decided to defer other than humanitarian loans from these financial institutions to both Pakistan and India. In addition, European Union foreign ministers recommended a delay of nonhumanitarian loans to India and Pakistan, warning that an even harsher punitive approach could be adopted if Pakistan and India failed to demonstrate progress toward restraining their nuclear arms competition.

According to Pakistan's finance minister, Ishaq Dar, sanctions would cost Pakistan $1.5 billion annually in preferential loans and aid and $2.5 billion in foreign investment and remittances. The impact of sanctions was far more severe, however. On the first day of trading after the Pakistani tests, the Karachi stock market crashed and has since lost more than $4 billion in value. Domestic and external investment continues to decline, and the Pakistani rupee has weakened considerably. Inflation is rampant as the government attempts to deal with the widening gap in its domestic and foreign deficit by increasing the price of fuel and imposing additional direct and indirect taxes. The freezing of foreign currency accounts to prevent capital outflow has further eroded market confidence, resulting in a sharp decline in foreign remittances.

Since the 1980s Pakistan has used foreign currency inflows, including credits and loans from multilateral agencies, to finance current account deficits, which in turn has resulted in a growing external debt. To service this debt and to purchase essential commodities such as fuel and food, Pakistan has become heavily dependent on credits and loans from international financial institutions. Hence the IMF decision to defer the disbursement of payments under a $1.6 billion extended structural adjustment facility greatly aggravated Pakistan's balance-of-payments deficit. As of November 1998 Pakistan had approximately $500 million in foreign exchange reserves to service $32 billion of debt.[47]

In an attempt to divert domestic attention away from the adverse economic consequences of nuclear testing, the government has emphasized the need for national cohesion in the face of multiple external threats and pressures. It has thus condemned the international sanctions regime as a bid to undermine Pakistani sovereignty.[48] Appeals have been made to help the government resist external pressures by supporting revenue-raising schemes such as the National

---

47. "Sartaj Sees IMF Pact after Easing of Sanctions," *News*, November 8, 1998.
48. "Text of Resolution Moved in NA," *News*, June 6, 1998.

Self-Reliance Fund. The importance of Pakistan's nuclear weapons capability in neutralizing the Indian threat has been highlighted against the backdrop of increased tensions, including clashes along the Line of Control in Kashmir. These diversionary tactics, however, have failed to counter rising socioeconomic tensions in a deteriorating economic climate. As a result, political divisions along regional and ethnic lines have continued to widen.

The manner in which the May 1998 nuclear tests were conducted has contributed to increased ethnoregional tensions and schisms. Prior to the tests, an internal consensus of sorts existed on Pakistan's need for a nuclear weapons capability to counter the perceived Indian threat. The Pakistani nuclear tests and the imposition of U.S. sanctions did initially result in a rally-round-the-flag response. The immediate deterioration of the economy as a result of sanctions, however, has led to unprecedented internal debate among segments of Pakistan's civil society on the pros and cons of its overt nuclear weapons status. This debate also marks an overwhelming rejection of the government's attempt to silence dissenting views with the imposition of a state of emergency (i.e., civil martial law) following the nuclear tests, effectively depriving Pakistani citizens of their constitutionally guaranteed civil rights. The Supreme Court later upheld the state of emergency but removed all restrictions on fundamental rights.

The declaration of a state of emergency has taken the domestic debate beyond Pakistan's nuclear choices to questions of the very nature of the state. In Baluchistan, where the Pakistani nuclear tests were conducted, the ruling party, the Baluchistan National Party (BNP), and its student wing, the Baluchistan Students' Organization, have criticized Pakistan's nuclear weapons policy on the grounds that scarce resources are being diverted from developmental purposes to defense. In July 1998 the BNP government, despite an alliance with Prime Minister Sharif's Muslim League, was dismissed after losing its parliamentary majority following internal defections. BNP Chief Minister Sardar Akhtar Mengal accused the center and its intelligence agencies of having contrived his dismissal to punish his party for its opposition to Pakistan's nuclear weapons policy and, specifically, to the tests on Baluch soil.[49] In Sindh and the North West Frontier Province, the state of emergency is seen as yet an-

---

49. The Muslim League's parliamentary secretary in the National Assembly, Syed Zafar Ali Shah, claimed that Mengal's government could have arrested the scientists involved in the nuclear explosions had a state of emergency not been imposed, a charge later refuted by his own government. "Mengal Denies PML Leader's Charges," *Dawn,* June 11, 1998.

other encroachment by the Punjabi-dominated central government on provincial autonomy. Their grievances against the center have led to the forging of an alliance among the political leaderships of Sindh, the North West Frontier Province, and Baluchistan, posing a further challenge to a besieged central government presiding over an economic collapse.

Conclusion

Less concerned about the adverse domestic repercussions of testing than about the strain on the economy as a result of sanctions, and conscious of the dangers of default should the United States continue to block multilateral funding, Pakistan's leadership has begun to reevaluate its nuclear options. Despite its unwillingness to roll back the nuclear program, the military high command is also aware that Pakistan lacks the economic and technological means for full-scale weaponization and deployment. Both would require additional expenditures—for example, for the establishment of an adequate command, control, and communications infrastructure—which the country's strained economy could not possibly sustain.

Technological and material assistance from China could have helped counter some of the economic constraints on Pakistan's nuclear weapons program, but, contrary to expectations, China has not helped Pakistan break its diplomatic isolation. The Chinese have been far more critical of the Indian decision to test than that of their regional ally. However, for the Chinese, an overt nuclear arms race between two mutually hostile states in its immediate neighborhood is cause for concern. Thus China has fully supported the UN Security Council resolution condemning the Pakistani and Indian nuclear tests. In a joint statement with Russia, India's ally, China has called upon both India and Pakistan to join the NPT and the CTBT unconditionally as nonnuclear weapons powers. In a joint statement issued after summit talks, Presidents Jiang Zemin and Bill Clinton declared their resolve to work together "within the P-5, the Security Council, and other international forums to prevent an accelerating nuclear and missile arms race in South Asia and strengthen international nonproliferation efforts and the peaceful resolution of differences between India and Pakistan."[50] Chinese pledges to support efforts to restrain Pakistan's nuclear weap-

---

50. Quotation in "U.S., China Not to Target N-Weapons at Each Other," *News*, June 28, 1998; and "China Vows to Stop Missile Cooperation with Pakistan: U.S.," *News*, June 29, 1998.

ons program and to halt missile cooperation with Pakistan will inevitably impose technological constraints on Pakistan's nuclear weapons program.

Pakistan's hopes of withstanding international economic pressure through support from its Middle Eastern allies, especially Saudi Arabia, Kuwait, and the United Arab Emirates, have also proved unfounded. Apart from a $250 million loan from Kuwait, which amounted to roughly two weeks of imports, no substantial assistance has been forthcoming, despite a series of visits and personal appeals from Prime Minister Sharif. Even commercial loans from the International Islamic Bank are dependent on IMF approval.[51]

Given Pakistan's unwillingness to roll back its nuclear weapons capability, Islamabad has adopted a three-pronged strategy: (1) to acquire international recognition for its new nuclear status quo, that is, for Pakistan's inclusion into the ranks of the declared nuclear weapons states, (2) to encourage international efforts to prevent the deployment of nuclear devices and their delivery systems in South Asia, given that Pakistan lacks the economic and technological resources to match the Indian program, and (3) to convince international actors, especially the United States, to replace punitive action with a policy of engagement based on incentives. In adopting this strategy, Pakistan hopes that its nuclear weapons program will continue to grow apace, but under cover of an overt nuclear status that stops short of assembly and deployment.

The success of this strategy will depend on domestic, regional, and international factors. The response of the international community has thus far proved unsympathetic to Pakistani efforts to acquire de jure recognition for its de facto nuclear status. The P-5 have unanimously called upon Pakistan to join the NPT as a nonnuclear weapons power, dismissing Pakistan's objections to the "discriminatory" and "undemocratic" nature of the treaty.[52] The declared nuclear weapons powers are unlikely to risk an unraveling of the international nonproliferation regime as an incentive to contain the nuclear arms race in South Asia.[53]

---

51. Although on September 9 the Islamic Development Bank agreed to formally launch the Pakistan Fund, including a $1.5 billion financial package. This is a new fund established by the Islamic Development Bank. However, release of the funding is dependent on IMF approval. Special Correspondent, "IDB Agrees to Launch Pakistan Fund," *News*, September 10, 1998.

52. Hasan Akhtar, "Islamabad Calls Big Five Stance Biased," *Dawn*, June 7, 1998.

53. According to Deputy Secretary of State Strobe Talbott, modification of the NPT and CTBT to accept India and Pakistan as nuclear weapons states would constitute "an incentive for other nuclear want-to-be's to blast their way into the same status—it would be breaking the faith with the many non-nuclear would-have-been's that had the wisdom and good sense to break away from the brink." Quoted in Nayan Chanda, "Risk Management: U.S. Grapples with New Nuclear Reality," *Far Eastern Economic Review*, June 18, 1998, p. 28.

Recognizing the serious nature of the economic crisis, however, the United States has offered Pakistan certain incentives in return for progress toward nonproliferation. Thus, in its negotiations with Pakistan, Washington has offered to remove its objections to IMF loans in return for Pakistani nonproliferation pledges, including Pakistani guarantees of nondeployment of nuclear weapons and their missile delivery systems as well as nontransfer of nuclear weapons and weapons-related technology. The United States has also specifically called for Pakistan's accession to the CTBT.

Because a default on its external debt liabilities could cut off Pakistan from all sources of external finance—its credit rating has already sunk to the lowest level possible—its leaders have pledged that they would neither deploy nor transfer nuclear weapons. They have not, however, agreed to a verifiable cap. More substantive pledges have been made on the CTBT, as Pakistan has declared its willingness to sign the treaty even without Indian accession. Initially, in the post-test period Pakistan declared a moratorium on nuclear testing but warned that it could reverse its position if India took the lead in the nuclear arms race. According to an official spokesperson, "There are a number of factors which need to be analyzed, including the results of India's nuclear tests and its potential weapons capability."[54] Since then Pakistan, in parliament and in its negotiations with the United States and the UN General Assembly, has proclaimed its acceptance of the CTBT, conditional upon the easing of sanctions by the United States and other concerned international actors.[55]

On November 7, 1998, President Clinton decided on a partial lifting of sanctions against Pakistan and India, using the one-year waiver authority provided by the India-Pakistan Relief Act (also known as the Brownback amendment), which Congress passed on October 22. According to a U.S. official, sanctions have been eased because of the "concrete steps" Pakistan and India have taken "to address our nonproliferation concerns."[56] This action includes U.S support for IMF assistance to Pakistan as a onetime exception to the sanctions still in

---

54. Quoted in Anwar Iqbal, "N-Moratorium Can Be Reversed If India Provokes," *News*, June 19, 1998.

55. In his address to the UN General Assembly on September 22, Sharif declared that Pakistan would sign the CTBT before September 1999 (the first meeting of CTBT state members) "only in conditions free from coercion and pressure." Quoted in Masood Hyder, "PM Seeks Parity with India on CTBT Issue," *Dawn*, September 24, 1998; and Raja Zulfiqar, "Pakistan Ready to Adhere to the CTBT," *News*, September 24, 1998.

56. Quoted in "U.S. Partially Lifts Curbs against Pakistan, India," *News*, November 8, 1998. U.S. Export-Import Bank lending and access to loans from the Trade and Development Agency, Overseas Private Investment Corporation risk insurance cover, and international military education training have been restored to both Pakistan and India.

place. Thus the Pakistani government hopes to receive between $3.5 and $4 billion in loans from multilateral institutions and narrowly avert the danger of default in 1998–99.[57] Because sanctions on multilateral lending will otherwise remain in place, pressure on the Pakistani economy will continue to mount.[58] Pakistani decisionmakers, therefore, might be forced to consider other nonproliferation measures. The military, however, will oppose a more substantive rollback as long as it considers the nuclear weapons program essential for reasons of security and prestige.[59]

The Muslim League government, facing a resurgent opposition, unable to resolve Pakistan's pressing political and economic problems, and conscious of the high command's dismissals of previous governments, is unlikely to challenge the military's preferences. The government, for example, has rejected external pressures for reconciliation with India, using the Kashmir issue to block any progress toward a substantial dialogue, knowing that the military would oppose such a policy. Thus Prime Minister Sharif continues to stress that improved relations with India are conditional on a resolution of the Kashmir dispute, which remains the "sole root-cause of the problems and tensions in the region."[60] Ongoing secretary-level negotiations in Islamabad and New Delhi on a number of contentious issues have failed to make any progress, as Pakistani officials accuse India of attempting to "vitiate the atmosphere" by maintaining an unfair position that "grossly" damages the cause of peace in South Asia.[61]

The internal contradictions in Pakistan's power structure, therefore, continue to be primarily responsible for its nuclear choices. Should the economic crisis spiral out of control, the military could remove the Muslim League government from power by making Prime Minister Sharif the scapegoat for the adverse domestic and international repercussions of testing. In such an eventuality, the military would continue to dominate the nuclear decisionmaking process, weakening domestic constituencies who favor nuclear restraint through coer-

---

57. Shakil Sheikh, "Lifting of Sanctions to Avert Short-term Crisis, Says Sartaj," *News*, November 9, 1998.
58. According to IMF sources, Pakistan's existing annual funding gap is more than $5 billion.
59. The military's opposition to the NPT is faithfully reflected in the Sharif government. According to Foreign Minister Sartaz Aziz, Pakistan would not sign the NPT "on account of its discriminatory nature." Quoted in "CTBT Signing after Sanctions Waiver: Sartaj," *News*, October 28, 1998.
60. Shakil Sheikh, "Nawaz Hopeful of Talks on All Issues with Vajpayee," *News*, June 25, 1998.
61. Comment by a Pakistani official following the first round of negotiations in Islamabad during the first week of November. Shakil Sheikh, "Crucial Pak-India Talks Start Tomorrow," *News*, November 4, 1998.

cion and the manipulation of public opinion. Domestic imperatives will inevitably play a major role in determining the direction of Pakistan's nuclear policy. Therefore they cannot be ignored in any future international efforts to contain, let alone reverse, Pakistani nuclear proliferation. At the same time, the policies of influential actors such as the United States must also demonstrate a clear resolve to roll back and ultimately eliminate South Asian nuclear proliferation so as to avoid giving mixed signals to Pakistani policymakers.

Bilateral and multilateral economic sanctions, because they have been accompanied by tangible incentives (i.e., the resumption of multilateral lending) have succeeded in forcing an economically vulnerable Pakistan to reluctantly express its willingness to accept the CTBT. A mix of incentives and sanctions could prove equally effective in persuading Pakistan to make further nonproliferation concessions, but only if they are targeted, flexible, and multilateral.[62] Moreover, nonproliferation strategies must be formulated in a way that both influences public opinion and persuades Pakistani officials to accept nuclear restraint.

An effective nonproliferation policy should make a clear distinction between the general public and decisionmakers, because sanctions that affect the weaker segments of society without influencing the behavior of governments are countereffective in the long run. In the Pakistani context, sanctions and incentives should be used to target those institutions and officials who support a nuclear weapons option, with the aim of influencing their behavior. For example, multilateral curbs on the sale of conventional armaments could be used to target Pakistan's military establishment, which, facing economic constraints and a widening arms disparity vis-à-vis India, could begin to rethink its nuclear ambitions. At the same time, targeted incentives could include a partial forgiveness of Pakistan's mounting external debt in return for tangible progress toward nonproliferation, provided the rewards were specifically allocated to developmental activities and could not be diverted to military use. Such steps would go a long way toward strengthening domestic constituencies for peace.

A nonproliferation policy that is based on targeted sanctions and incentives needs a gestation period to affect domestic behavior. Therefore care should be taken to ensure that such policies are not changed in midstream. In the past, U.S. policies toward Pakistan failed because of tactical compromises or impa-

---

62. David Cortright and Samina Ahmed, "Sanctions: Modify 'em," *Bulletin of the Atomic Scientists*, Vol. 45, No. 5 (September 1998), pp. 22–23.

tience with the lack of immediate results. According to a U.S. official, there is little doubt that Washington's concern about a potential Pakistani economic meltdown was responsible for President Clinton's decision to ease sanctions "in a very limited, targeted way" in November 1998.[63] The United States, however, must take care that the flexibility provided by the Brownback amendment is wisely used and that the international consensus on horizontal proliferation in South Asia remains intact. In the post-test nuclear environment, when one obstacle to full-scale weaponization has already been removed, there is urgent need for consistency and patience. Should the international community ignore the penultimate goal of eliminating nuclear proliferation in South Asia, the arms race will continue unabated, threatening regional security and the lives of more than a billion people.

---

63. "U.S. Partially Lifts Curbs against Pakistan, India."

Nuclear Stability in South Asia

Sumit Ganguly

On May 11 and 13, 1998, India conducted a series of five nuclear tests. Pakistan followed with six tests of its own on May 30 and 31.[1] These tests effectively lifted the veil of opacity that had long characterized the two countries' nuclear weapons programs.[2] The reactions of the global community, led by the United States, were swift and condemnatory. Policymakers and analysts alike united in issuing harsh indictments of the tests. Their misgivings were twofold: first, they expressed grave concerns about the impact of these tests on the global nonproliferation regime; second, they argued that the tests would further destabilize an already fraught security environment in South Asia. To induce both states to eschew their nuclear weapons programs, the international community imposed a raft of bilateral and multilateral sanctions. Simultaneously, the United States embarked on a dialogue with India and Pakistan in an attempt to convince them to dismantle their nuclear weapons and ballistic missile programs and to reduce Indo-Pakistani tensions.[3]

Yet despite thirteen rounds of arduous talks, neither India nor Pakistan agreed to abandon its ongoing nuclear weapons and ballistic missile programs. Worse still for nonproliferation advocates, two crises punctuated India-Pakistan relations, in 1999 and 2001–02. Indeed, the 1999 crisis erupted into a limited war.[4]

A decade has passed since the two adversaries crossed the nuclear Rubicon.

Sumit Ganguly is a professor of political science and holds the Rabindranath Tagore Chair at Indiana University, Bloomington.

The author thanks Paul Kapur, Traci Nagle, and Praveen Swami for comments on an initial draft of this article and Manjeet Pardesi for able research assistance.

1. On their respective roads to the nuclear tests, see Sumit Ganguly, "India's Pathway to Pokhran II: The Sources and Prospects of New Delhi's Nuclear Weapons Program," *International Security,* Vol. 23, No. 4 (Spring 1999), pp. 148–177; and Samina Ahmed, "Pakistan's Nuclear Weapons Program: Turning Points and Nuclear Choices," *International Security,* Vol. 23, No. 4 (Spring 1999), pp. 178–204.
2. On the concept of opacity, see Benjamin Frankel, ed., *Opaque Nuclear Proliferation: Methodological and Policy Implications* (London: Frank Cass, 1991).
3. For details about U.S. goals in this dialogue, see Strobe Talbott, *Engaging India: Diplomacy, Democracy, and the Bomb* (Washington, D.C.: Brookings Institution Press, 2004).
4. For the origins of the war and its conduct, see Sumit Ganguly, *Conflict Unending: India-Pakistan Tensions since 1947* (New York: Columbia University Press, 2001).

International Security, Vol. 33, No. 2 (Fall 2008), pp. 45–70
© 2008 by the President and Fellows of Harvard College and the Massachusetts Institute of Technology.

Accordingly, it may be a propitious moment to take stock of the security environment in the region, especially because South Asia has witnessed much political turbulence since then—including a military coup in Pakistan in October 1999.[5] Moreover, since the dramatic terrorist attacks on the United States on September 11, 2001, the region, and in particular Pakistan and Afghanistan, has become a major focus of U.S. foreign and security policy concerns.[6]

Is South Asia the "most dangerous place on earth," as President Bill Clinton once characterized it?[7] Or has the overt nuclearization of the region dramatically reduced the possibilities of full-scale war? The preponderance of scholarship on the subject suggests that the likelihood of full-scale war with the possibility of escalation to the nuclear level has become significantly higher in the region since the nuclear tests of May 1998.[8] A smaller corpus of scholarship holds that the overt presence of nuclear weapons has contributed to strategic stability in the region.[9]

In this article I argue that, contrary to the views of the proliferation pessimists, nuclear weapons have reduced the risk of full-scale war in the region and have therefore contributed to strategic stability. I also contend that, barring India's acquisition and deployment of viable antiballistic missile capabilities, nuclear deterrence in South Asia should remain robust.[10]

The next section of this article lays out the arguments of the proliferation pessimists. Subsequent sections examine key propositions about prior wars (1947–48, 1965, 1971) and crises (1987, 1990) in the region, before discussing

---

5. Sumit Ganguly, "Pakistan's Never-Ending Story: Why the October Coup Was No Surprise," *Foreign Affairs*, Vol. 79, No. 2 (March/April 2000), pp. 2–9.

6. On the September 11, 2001, terrorist attacks on the United States, see *The 9/11 Commission Report: Final Report of the National Commission on Terrorist Attacks upon the United States* (New York: W.W. Norton, 2002). See also James F. Hoge Jr. and Gideon Rose, eds., *How Did This Happen? Terrorism and the New War* (New York: PublicAffairs, 2001).

7. President William Jefferson Clinton, as quoted in Alex Perry, "On the Brink," *Time*, May 27, 2002, http://www.time.com/time/magazine/article/0,9171,250061,00.htm.

8. On this subject, see S. Paul Kapur, *Dangerous Deterrent: Nuclear Weapons Proliferation and Conflict in South Asia* (Stanford, Calif.: Stanford University Press, 2007). See also Polly Nayak and Michael Krepon, "U.S. Crisis Management in South Asia's Twin Peaks Crisis," No. 57 (Washington, D.C.: Henry L. Stimson Center, 2006); and Mario E. Carranza, "Avoiding a Nuclear Catastrophe: Arms Control after the 2002 India-Pakistan Crisis," *International Politics*, Vol. 40, No. 3 (September 2003), pp. 313–339.

9. For arguments about nuclear stability, see Sumit Ganguly and Devin T. Hagerty, *Fearful Symmetry: India and Pakistan in the Shadow of Nuclear Weapons* (Seattle: University of Washington Press, 2005); John Arquilla, "Nuclear Weapons in South Asia: More May Be Manageable," *Comparative Strategy*, Vol. 16, No. 1 (January 1997), pp. 13–31; and David J. Karl, "Proliferation Pessimism and Emerging Nuclear Powers," *International Security*, Vol. 21, No. 3 (Winter 1996/97), pp. 87–119.

10. For a contrary formulation, see Rajesh M. Basrur, *Minimum Deterrence and Indian Nuclear Security* (Stanford, Calif.: Stanford University Press, 2006).

how the 1999 and 2001–02 crises evolved and showing that nuclear weapons were critical in preventing the escalation to full-scale war.[11] The article concludes with several policy recommendations that flow from this analysis.

The Contours of the Debate

Much of the literature on the consequences of nuclear proliferation, whether optimistic or pessimistic, whether focused on South Asia or elsewhere, is inherently deductive.[12] Proliferation pessimists, while agreeing that the dispersion of nuclear weapons is likely to contribute to greater instability, proffer different reasons for their pessimism, depending on their theoretical preferences. Organization theorists, most importantly Scott Sagan, argue that the dangers of nuclear war stem from various organizational pathologies. He points out two significant issues with regard to nascent nuclear states. First, most professional militaries tend to have inflexible routines and parochial interests that predispose them toward organizational behaviors that are conducive to deterrence failures. Second, and more pertinent, he contends, such organizational propensities can best be curtailed through tight and sustained civilian control over the military; such control, however, is unlikely to exist in new entrants into the nuclear-armed arena.[13] Furthermore, in the case of South Asia, he contends that with limited budgets military leaders may be tempted to spend scarce resources on weapons development and thereby fail to develop operational practices that enhance the survivability of their small arsenals.[14]

Focusing his attention on Pakistan's strategic decisionmaking and the India-Pakistan nuclear dyad, Timothy Hoyt questions Sagan's concerns about the Pakistani military's command and control (C^2) of nuclear weapons. He claims that "the Pakistani military's control over nuclear assets, development, and policy represents a theoretically efficient division of labor and a reasonable

---

11. I refer to the Kargil incursion both as a crisis and a war. It counts as a war because it met the standard criterion of 1,000 battle deaths in an interstate conflict. On this subject, see J. David Singer and Paul Diehl, eds., *Measuring the Correlates of War* (Ann Arbor: University of Michigan Press, 1990).

12. The classic statement remains Scott D. Sagan and Kenneth N. Waltz, *The Spread of Nuclear Weapons: A Debate Renewed* (New York: W.W. Norton, 2002).

13. Scott D. Sagan, "The Perils of Proliferation: Organization Theory, Deterrence Theory, and the Spread of Nuclear Weapons," *International Security*, Vol. 18, No. 4 (Spring 1994), pp. 66–107.

14. Scott D. Sagan, "The Perils of Proliferation in South Asia," *Asian Survey*, Vol. 41, No. 3 (November–December 2001), pp. 1064–1086.

organizational solution to the command and control dilemma. It provides for substantial physical security of Pakistan's nuclear arsenal—no matter, given the possibility of unrest and concerns over Islamic militancy—and substantially ensures that the nuclear force will meet the 'always function' test. Within these operational parameters, it is clearly preferable to other possible C^2 options."[15] That said, Hoyt argues that the real problem with achieving stability in South Asia lies in what he refers to as the "strategic myopia" of the military establishment, a proclivity that leads its officers to make poor strategic judgments about a more powerful adversary. Unlike Sagan, whose arguments are largely derived from deductive theory and logic, Hoyt's argument is based on the empirical record of India and Pakistan's previous conflicts.

Other analysts, such as Michael Krepon, have focused on the "stability/instability paradox" to contend that the nuclearization of the region may have rendered it more susceptible to conflict. Following the logic of this paradox, Krepon maintains that the problems of controlling the dangers of escalation have increased the risk of smaller wars. He holds that, because neither India nor Pakistan has a clear appreciation of the other's intentions, each is prone to making serious misjudgments through a process of mutual misperception. In the absence of robust risk-reduction measures, he fears, the two states may become trapped in a spiral of misperception and stumble into full-scale war.[16]

Paul Kapur offers a somewhat different assessment of the relevance of the stability/instability paradox in the South Asian security context. Kapur argues that nuclear weapons, far from inducing stability in the region, have provided Pakistan (the revisionist power) a compelling incentive to provoke India (the status quo power), with the former secure in the knowledge that its possession of nuclear weapons will limit any Indian retaliatory action.[17] Furthermore, he contends that Pakistan's willingness to prod India has grown commensurate with the development and expansion of Pakistan's nuclear arsenal. Although India has exercised a modicum of restraint, he believes that its patience has been sorely tried, and that it has come perilously close to expanding the scope of conflict. Repeated Pakistani provocation may fray India's restraint and prod its decisionmakers to take military action in an attempt to put an end to these

---

15. Timothy D. Hoyt, "Pakistani Nuclear Doctrine and the Dangers of Strategic Myopia," *Asian Survey*, Vol. 41, No. 6 (November–December 2001), pp. 956–977, at p. 976.
16. Michael Krepon, "The Stability-Instability Paradox, Misperception, and Escalation-Control in South Asia," in Rafiq Dossani and Henry S. Rowen, eds., *Prospects for Peace in South Asia* (Stanford, Calif.: Stanford University Press, 2005), chap. 10.
17. Kapur, *Dangerous Deterrent.*

periodic attacks. Such actions, he holds, may lead to full-scale war and to nuclear escalation.

Are the proliferation pessimists correct? Has South Asia become more susceptible to conflict and escalation as a consequence of India's and Pakistan's acquisition of nuclear weapons? Or, contrary to the pessimists' claims, has the region become more secure? To assess the consequences of the overt nuclearization of the region, it is useful to summarize some central propositions about the record of conflict there.

Propositions about Wars and Crises in South Asia

In their first sixty years, India and Pakistan have been involved in four wars (1947–48, 1965, 1971, and 1999), three of which (1947–48, 1965, and 1999)[18] were fought over the disputed state of Jammu and Kashmir.[19] This particular dispute is of such enduring significance because it undergirds the raisons d'être of the two countries. India has deemed it necessary to hold on to this Muslim-majority state as a symbol and assertion of its own secular ideology. Pakistan, meanwhile, which was created as a homeland for the Muslims of South Asia, has had an irredentist claim to the state: for Pakistanis, their very identity remains incomplete without the absorption of Kashmir.[20] Even though the breakup of Pakistan and the creation of Bangladesh in 1971 undercut Pakistan's ideological claim to Kashmir, it has not abandoned its quest to wrest all of Kashmir from India.

Despite the significant stakes involved, all four conflicts, with the possible exception of the 1971 war, involved limited aims. Given the two powers' pau-

---

18. For discussions of the history of wars and crises in the region, see T.V. Paul, ed., *The India-Pakistan Conflict: An Enduring Rivalry* (Cambridge: Cambridge University Press, 2005). For an early treatment, see Russell Brines, *The Indo-Pakistani Conflict* (New York: Pall Mall, 1968).
19. The literature on the Kashmir dispute is voluminous. See, for example, Alastair Lamb, *Kashmir: A Disputed Legacy, 1846–1990* (Hertingfordbury, U.K.: Roxford, 1991); H.V. Hodson, *The Great Divide: Britain, India, Pakistan* (New York: Oxford University Press, 1997); Chandrasekhar Dasgupta, *War and Diplomacy in Kashmir, 1947–48* (New Delhi: Sage, 2002); Jyoti Bhusan Das Gupta, *Jammu and Kashmir* (The Hague: Martinus Nijhoff, 1968); Lord Birdwood, *Two Nations and Kashmir* (London: Robert Hale, 1956); Michael Brecher, *The Struggle for Kashmir* (New York: Oxford University Press, 1953); and Sumit Ganguly, *The Crisis in Kashmir: Portents of War, Hopes of Peace* (New York: Cambridge University Press, 1997).
20. For a discussion of Pakistan's identity, see Stephen P. Cohen, *The Idea of Pakistan* (Washington, D.C.: Brookings Institution Press, 2004). For the ideological basis of Pakistan's claims to Kashmir, see Zulfikar Ali Bhutto, *The Myth of Independence* (New York: Oxford University Press, 1969). For the Indian position on the Kashmir dispute, see Sisir Gupta, *Kashmir: A Study in India-Pakistan Relations* (New Delhi: Asia Publishing House, 1966).

city of firepower, these wars also produced small numbers of casualties, for a variety of intertwined reasons. Moreover, because the principal military commanders on both sides were mostly British trained (as part of their common colonial military heritage), they could anticipate the other's battle tactics and strategies. As a result, none of these wars saw any dramatic tactical or strategic innovations on the battlefield, with the first three wars witnessing mostly set-piece battle tactics. Finally, in all of these conflicts, both sides exercised considerable military restraint, due not only to the limitations of firepower and predictable battle tactics, but also to the willingness of senior military officers to observe informal agreements that hobbled the use of excessive force.[21]

Multiple crises have also characterized Indo-Pakistani relations—several as early as the 1950s.[22] More recently, three crises nearly brought the two states to the brink of war. The first stemmed from Pakistani involvement in an uprising in the Indian state of Punjab and India's response to it through the conduct of a major military exercise, Brasstacks.[23] The second erupted as a consequence of Pakistani support for an ethnoreligious uprising that wracked the Indian-controlled portion of the disputed state of Jammu and Kashmir in December 1989. The third resulted from a series of Pakistani incursions across the Line of Control (the de facto international border in Kashmir) in April–May 1999.

THE BRASSTACKS CRISIS OF 1987

The Brasstacks exercise, the largest in independent India's military history, was the brainchild of Gen. Krishnaswami Sundarji, the chief of staff of the Indian Army. Sundarji was interested in testing some newly acquired command, control, communications, and intelligence capabilities and also in developing the Indian Army's maneuverability and mobility. At the time of the exercise in 1987, significant portions of the Indian military were tied down in a major counterinsurgency operation in the border state of Punjab. Since the early 1980s, that state had been in the grips of a Sikh ethnonationalist insurgency with indigenous origins.[24] The regime of Gen. Mohammed Zia ul-Haq

---

21. For a discussion, see Sumit Ganguly, "Wars without End? The Indo-Pakistani Conflicts," *Annals of the American Academy of Social and Political Science*, No. 541 (September 1995), pp. 167–178.

22. On these crises, see Jyoti Bhusan Das Gupta, *Indo-Pakistani Relations, 1947–1955* (The Hague: Martinus Nijhoff, 1959).

23. The Brasstacks crisis is discussed at length in Kanti P. Bajpai, P.R. Chari, Pervaiz Iqbal Cheema, Stephen P. Cohen, and Sumit Ganguly, *Brasstacks and Beyond: Perception and the Management of Crises in South Asia* (New Delhi: Manohar, 1995).

24. On the origins of the Sikh insurgency in the Punjab, see Mark Tully and Satish Jacob, *Amritsar: Mrs. Gandhi's Last Battle* (Calcutta: Rupa, 1985).

in Pakistan, sensing an opportunity to foment further discord, had quickly become involved in supporting the insurgents.

Accordingly, the exercise was also designed to deliver a clear-cut message to Pakistan that its continued interference in the Punjab was intolerable and that the Indian military, though involved in counterinsurgency operations there, was nevertheless capable of flexing its muscles. As the exercise, which was being conducted in the deserts of Rajasthan along an east-west axis, was about to enter its final phase, the Pakistani military, which was also conducting its own winter military exercises, chose not to return some of its forward-based units to their peacetime positions. Furthermore, neither Indian civilian nor military intelligence could account for the precise location of one of the Pakistani armored units that had been participating in the exercises. These developments caused growing alarm in New Delhi and set off a spiral of mutual misperceptions that contributed to rising tensions between the two countries.

A number of scholars and analysts have claimed that Pakistan delivered a veiled nuclear threat toward the end of the Brasstacks crisis.[25] They also have argued that Pakistan took critical steps toward the acquisition of a nuclear-weapons capability in the aftermath of Brasstacks. This crisis was resolved when the U.S. ambassador in Islamabad and his Soviet counterpart in New Delhi met with key Pakistani and Indian officials to forestall an escalation of the crisis.

THE 1990 CRISIS

The second crisis also had its origins in Pakistani support for an indigenous insurgency, this time in the Indian-controlled portion of the disputed state of Jammu and Kashmir. The insurgency in Kashmir had indigenous origins: it stemmed from the steady erosion of political institutions in the state against a growing backdrop of political mobilization as a consequence of expanding literacy, mass media, and higher education.[26] When the insurgency erupted in December 1990, Pakistan quickly jumped into the fray and over the next several years managed to transform the rebellion into a well-funded, carefully orchestrated extortion racket.[27] The precise scope and dimensions of the

---

25. On this subject, see Devin T. Hagerty, *The Consequences of Nuclear Proliferation: Lessons from South Asia* (Cambridge, Mass.: MIT Press, 1998).
26. For a detailed discussion of the origins of the Kashmir insurgency, see Sumit Ganguly, "Explaining the Kashmir Insurgency: Political Mobilization and Institutional Decay," *International Security*, Vol. 21, No. 2 (Fall 1996), pp. 76–107.
27. On Pakistani involvement in and support for the insurgency, see R.A. Davis, "Kashmir in the Balance," *International Defense Review*, Vol. 24, No. 4 (April 1991), pp. 301–304.

1990 crisis are still shrouded in mystery and doubt.[28] Indian anxieties about Pakistan's behavior were heightened, however, when, toward the end of December 1989, around the time of the outbreak of the Kashmir insurgency, Pakistan completed its largest-ever peacetime military exercise, Zarb-i-Momin. This exercise was clearly a response to Brasstacks and involved seven infantry divisions and one armored division. In the words of the Pakistan Army chief at the time, Gen. Mirza Aslam Beg, the exercise was designed to test a new strategy focused on carrying a future war into India. As he stated, "In the past we were pursuing a defensive policy; now there is a big change since we are shifting to a policy of offensive defense. Should there be a war, the Pakistan Army plans to take the war into India, launching a sizeable offensive on Indian territory."[29]

To the dismay of India's decisionmakers, well after the exercises were completed, the Pakistani forces did not return to their routine peacetime deployments; instead they stayed on near the international border and the Line of Control.[30] Worsening matters, as the uprising continued apace in Kashmir, Pakistani leaders, most notably Prime Minister Benazir Bhutto, traveled to the Pakistani side of the Line of Control on March 13, 1990, where she promised a "thousand-year war" against India.[31] Not surprisingly, Indian Prime Minister Vishwanath Pratap Singh came under enormous public and political pressure to offer a suitable riposte to her statement. Speaking to the Indian parliament, he stated, "I do not wish to sound hawkish but there should be no confusion. Such a misadventure would not be without cost."[32] The war of words continued throughout the spring, as India came to deploy as many as 200,000 troops in Kashmir—both Indian Army units and paramilitary forces—in an effort to stop the Pakistan-supported infiltrators and quell the insurgency.[33]

Even though most Indian and Pakistani armored capabilities were not mobi-

---

28. For one of the better accounts of the crisis, see P.R. Chari, Pervaiz Iqbal Cheema, and Stephen Philip Cohen, *Perception, Politics, and Security in South Asia: The Compound Crisis of 1990* (London: Routledge, 2003).
29. Quoted in Mushahid Husain, "Pakistan, Responding to Change," *Jane's Defense Weekly*, October 14, 1989, p. 779.
30. Gen. V.N. Sharma, interview, "It's All Bluff and Bluster," *Economic Times* (Bombay), May 18, 1993.
31. Raja Asghar, "Bhutto Predicts Victory for Kashmir Independence Campaign," Reuters Library Report, March 13, 1990.
32. Quoted in Moses Manoharan, "Indian Leader Tells Pakistan to Stay Out of Kashmir Uprising," Reuters Library Report, March 13, 1990.
33. See the discussion in Ganguly and Hagerty, *Fearful Symmetry*.

lized and remained in their peacetime deployments, the growing instability within Kashmir and the increasingly bellicose rhetoric from both India and Pakistan caused growing anxiety in Washington. U.S. misgivings about the unfolding crisis stemmed mostly from the knowledge that both sides had made significant strides in their efforts to acquire nuclear weapons. The existence of these incipient nuclear arsenals was of particular concern to policymakers in Washington, given the long history of conflict and discord in the region.

Accordingly, on April 18 the deputy national security adviser, Robert Gates, was dispatched to Islamabad and New Delhi. In Islamabad, Gates categorically informed his Pakistani interlocutors that, in every U.S. war-game scenario involving Indian and Pakistani forces, Pakistan emerged the loser; that Pakistan should not count on U.S. support if a war with India were to ensue; and that it should refrain from supporting terror in Kashmir. In New Delhi, Gates told Prime Minister Singh that the situation in Kashmir was so fraught with tension that any Indian provocation could lead to a spiral of conflict with unforeseen and potentially dangerous consequences. Within two weeks of the Gates visit, the tensions subsided, with both sides making reciprocal concessions. Also, in the aftermath of the Gates mission, India put forward a package of confidence-building measures that became the basis of bilateral talks that helped reduce tensions.[34]

Despite the end of the crisis, the India-Pakistan relationship remained troubled because of the ongoing insurgency in the state of Jammu and Kashmir. Indo-Pakistani relations deteriorated sharply as the insurgency in Kashmir continued to gather force. India, drawing on its experiences with insurgent movements, resorted to a time-honored strategy of using dramatic force against the insurgents while holding out the promise of negotiations and political compromise as long as the insurgents agreed to drop their demands for secession. This strategy had served India well in coping with insurgencies in the northeast and in Punjab, but it proved less effective in Kashmir, where there was a powerful and committed external actor—Pakistan—and where the popular disaffection with the Indian state was widespread. Nevertheless, toward the end of the decade, India had managed to restore a modicum of order (if not law) in the state through an amalgam of political concessions and steady military repression.[35] Furthermore, as India managed to contain the insurgency, global interest in and attention to the conflict started to flag.

---

34. Much of this discussion has been drawn from ibid.
35. Praveen Swami, *The Kargil War* (New Delhi: Leftword, 1999).

THE KARGIL CRISIS OF 1999

The next significant crisis in Indo-Pakistani relations took place in the wake of the Indian and Pakistani nuclear tests of May 1998.[36] This one culminated in a limited war. In the aftermath of the nuclear tests, when faced with considerable international opprobrium, Indian Prime Minister Atal Bihari Vajpayee visited Pakistan while inaugurating a bus service linking the capital cities of the Indian and Pakistani states of Punjab, Amritsar, and Lahore. Subsequently, he signed a number of nuclear confidence-building measures with his Pakistani counterpart, Nawaz Sharif. In a significant symbolic gesture, Vajpayee publicly reaffirmed India's commitment to Pakistan's territorial integrity at the site where the Muslim League, the principal Pakistani nationalist party, had passed its historic resolution calling for the creation of Pakistan in 1940. In light of these developments, the coalition government led by Vajpayee's Bharitiya Janata Party had concluded that relations with Pakistan were improving despite the tensions that followed on the heels of the nuclear tests. Consequently, they chose to lower the state of alertness along the Indo-Pakistani international border as well as along the Line of Control in Kashmir.

The precise motivations underlying the Pakistani incursions across the Line of Control in Kargil remain controversial, despite the emergence of a spate of literature on the subject.[37] Most explanations suggest that Pakistan was motivated to refocus international attention on the Kashmir question.[38] Simultaneously, the Pakistani military was interested in a "fait accompli" strategy,

---

36. For a discussion of the origins of the nuclear tests, see, for example, Raj Chengappa, *Weapons of Peace: The Secret Story of India's Quest to Be a Nuclear Power* (New Delhi: Harper Collins India, 2000). On Pakistan's acquisition of nuclear weapons, see Ashok Kapur, *Pakistan's Nuclear Development* (London: Croom Helm, 1987).

37. There is a paucity of Pakistani literature on the origins of and motivations behind the Kargil crisis. Gen. Pervez Musharraf's memoir, *In the Line of Fire* (New York: Simon and Schuster, 2006), is not especially revealing, as it is both self-exculpatory and disingenuous. In this book he claims that the principal goals of the Kargil incursion were to plug existing gaps along the Line of Control to prevent Indian incursions. The memoir of his Indian counterpart, Gen. Ved Prakash Malik, titled *Kargil: From Surprise to Victory* (New Delhi: HarperCollins India, 2006), is somewhat more forthcoming. It too shifts the bulk of the blame for the intelligence failure onto his civilian counterparts in India. For details of the Indian military operation, see Amarinder Singh, *A Ridge Too Far: War in the Kargil Heights, 1999* (Patiala: Motibagh Palace, 2001). See also Maj. Gen. Ashok Kalyan Verma, *Kargil: Blood on the Snow: Tactical Victory, Strategic Failure* (New Delhi: Manohar, 2002). On various aspects of the conflict, see Jasjit E. Singh, ed., *Kargil, 1999: Pakistan's Fourth War for Kashmir* (New Delhi: Knowledge World, 1999). For the official Indian account of India's intelligence failure and the subsequent conduct of the war, see Kargil Review Committee, *From Surprise to Reckoning: The Kargil Committee Report* (New Delhi: Sage, 2000) [hereinafter *The Kargil Committee Report*].

38. For a crisp summary of Pakistani military and political motivations in launching the Kargil operation, see Prasun K. Sengupta, "Mountain Warfare: The Kargil Experience," *Asian Defence Journal*, Vol. 10 (October 1999), pp. 42–46.

which, if successful, could interdict India's principal supply route to the disputed Siachen Glacier.[39] In pursuit of these goals, the Pakistani military marshaled a substantial body of forces: four independent groups drawn from four infantry battalions and two companies of the highly trained Special Services Group. These units were under the aegis of the Forward Commander Northern Areas and comprised elements of 4 Battalion, the FCNA reserve located in Gilgit, the 6 Northern Light Infantry (NLI) Battalion located in Skardu, the 5 NLI Battalion stationed in Minimarg, and the 3 NLI at Dansam.[40] It is pertinent to mention that Pakistani apologists, most notably Gen. Pervez Musharraf (then chief of the Pakistan Army) have claimed that the Kashmiri mujahideen were responsible for the initial incursions. Only after India began attacking the infiltrators, Musharraf contends, did the NLI become involved. There is little or no evidence to support this assertion.[41]

The first clash occurred between an Indian Army patrol and Pakistani forces on May 5, 1999, in the Kaksar region in the northern reaches of Indian-controlled Kashmir. This patrol had been dispatched to verify information on intrusions that two local residents (and part-time intelligence informants) had provided.[42] The patrol disappeared without a trace. As a consequence of this abrupt disappearance, the commander of the 121 Brigade organized a detailed surveillance and discovered that there were at least 100 intruders in the area. By mid-May, the commander drastically revised his estimate after realizing that as many as 800 enemy personnel were in the region and that important breaches of the Line of Control had taken place in Mushkoh Valley, Kaksar, and Batalik. By the end of the month, the military had again revised its estimates, concluding that significantly more than 800 men had crossed the Line of Control and that those troops had managed to occupy a number of vital strategic salients directly above the road from Kargil to Leh and were now po-

---

39. For a discussion of the concept of a fait accompli strategy, see Alexander L. George and Richard Smoke, *Deterrence in American Foreign Policy: Theory and Practice* (New York: Columbia University Press, 1974). For an Indian perspective on the Siachen Glacier dispute, see Anand K. Verma, "Siachen: An Episode to Remember," *Indian Defence Review*, Vol. 22, No. 3 (August 2007), http://www.indiandefencereview.com/?p=63. For a Pakistani perspective, see Humera Niazi, "The Siachen Glacier: 1984 to 1998," *Defence Journal*, January 1999, http://www.defencejournal.com/jan99/glacier.htm.
40. Sengupta, "Mountain Warfare."
41. The dubiousness of these assertions is forthrightly dealt with in Ashley J. Tellis, C. Christine Fair, and Jamison Jo Medby, *Limited Conflicts under the Nuclear Umbrella: Indian and Pakistani Lessons from the Kargil Crisis* (Santa Monica, Calif.: RAND, 2001).
42. Praveen Swami, deputy editor, *Frontline* (New Delhi), personal communication with author, June 15, 2008.

sitioned to interdict Indian military traffic from Ladakh to Kashmir. Further aerial surveillance revealed that the intruders were well equipped, with snow-mobiles, artillery, and substantial stocks of supplies.[43]

India's initial response was inept, given a paucity of accurate intelligence on Pakistani troop deployments, strength, and capabilities. Consequently, its preliminary assaults on the Pakistanis' well-ensconced positions at higher alti-tudes resulted in substantial Indian casualties. Toward the end of May, the Indian forces realized that without the use of airpower they would not be able to dislodge the Pakistanis and would continue to take massive casualties in frontal assaults. Accordingly, the apex Cabinet Committee on Security decided to send as many as three more brigades into the region and also permitted the use of airpower to dislodge the intruders. Once the requisite permission had been granted, the Indian Air Force carried out its first series of air strikes on May 26. On May 27 the air force launched a second series of strikes specifically directed against Pakistani forces located in Batalik, Turtuk, and Dras.[44] As the Indian forces demonstrated their resolve, on May 31 Pakistan's foreign secre-tary, Shamshad Ahmed, made what most observers have concluded was a veiled nuclear threat. In an interview he stated, "We will not hesitate to use any weapon in our arsenal to defend our territorial integrity."[45]

Subsequent Indian assessments of the Kargil war suggest that this threat was not lost on Indian policymakers. Among other matters, the Indian leader-ship embarked on a concerted effort to formulate a military doctrine that would enable India to respond to Pakistani conventional aggression without risking escalation to the nuclear level. Gen. Ved Prakash Malik, the chief of staff of the Indian Army during the Kargil crisis, played a critical role in trying to formulate such a military doctrine.[46]

It is beyond the scope of this article to provide a detailed account of all the military engagements that were fought during the course of the Kargil conflict. Accordingly, only the key military developments and political turning points during the war are highlighted in the remainder of this section. In the initial

---

43. Further details about the military dimensions of the initial intrusions can be found in Maj. Gen. Ashok Krishna, "The Kargil War," in Krishna and P.R. Chari, eds., *Kargil: The Tables Turned* (New Delhi: Manohar, 2001), pp. 77–138.

44. Manoj Joshi, "The Kargil War: The Fourth Round," in Kanti Bajpai, Afsir Karim, and Amitabh Mattoo, eds., *Kargil and After: Challenges for Indian Policy* (New Delhi: Har-Anand, 2001).

45. "Pakistan May Use Any Weapon," *News* (Islamabad), May 31, 1999.

46. *The Kargil Committee Report.* See also P.R. Chari, Pervaiz Iqbal Cheema, and Stephen P. Cohen, *Four Crises and a Peace Process: American Engagement in South Asia* (Washington, D.C.: Brookings In-stitution Press, 2007); and Malik, *Kargil: From Surprise to Victory.*

stage of the operations, the Indian Army suffered a number of important setbacks despite the use of airpower. One of the most difficult operations involved the capture of the Tololing complex in the Dras sector, where Indian
infantry were asked to make daytime assaults up steep and unforgiving terrain. An initial attempt to capture another important feature, Tiger Hill, met
the same fate. Faced with these setbacks, the Indian military resorted to the
greater use of artillery to soften up Pakistani positions, called for the more
extensive use of airpower (despite the explicit political injunctions against
crossing the Line of Control), and doggedly made progress against the well-
entrenched intruders.[47] By early June the Indian military, in a series of counteroffensive operations—some during daylight and others under the cover of
night—managed to recapture twenty-one positions along the Line of Control.
The air operations proved exceedingly difficult because of Pakistan's substantial surface-to-air missile capabilities, the inability of the principal Indian attack helicopters to operate well at high altitudes, and the rugged terrain,
which enabled the Pakistanis to conceal their surface-to-air missile batteries.[48]
The Pakistani military was equipped with shoulder-fired FIM-92A Stinger and
Anza Mk2 air defense missiles; it also possessed 12.7-millimeter air defense
machine guns.[49] Consequently, it was able to fend off Indian air attacks with
some success.

Between June 14 and 16, the Indian forces captured two critical positions
near Dras and Batalik.[50] The fall of these two positions was of considerable importance because they overlook the principal supply route for the Indian
forces located on the disputed Siachen Glacier. In the wake of these successful
attacks, on June 20 the Indian forces managed to fully reestablish control over
the Batalik region.[51]

Despite these Indian military successes, the hostilities showed few signs of
abating. In an effort to prevent possible escalation of the conflict, the commander in chief of the U.S. Central Command, Gen. Anthony Zinni, visited
Pakistan toward the end of June and bluntly told Prime Minister Sharif to end
military operations.[52] Shortly thereafter, the U.S. deputy assistant secretary of

---

47. Marcus P. Acosta, "The Kargil Conflict: Waging War in the Himalayas," *Small Wars and Insurgencies,* Vol. 18, No. 3 (September 2007), pp. 397–415.
48. Ibid., p. 405.
49. Sengupta, "Mountain Warfare."
50. "India Retakes Two Key Peaks in Kashmir," *Straits Times* (Singapore), June 16, 1999.
51. "India Reports Major Highway Recaptured from Rebels," *New York Times,* June 21, 1999.
52. Farhan Bokhari and Mary Louise Kazmin, "U.S. General Presses Pakistan on Kashmir," *Financial Times,* June 25, 1999.

state, Gibson Lanpher, visited New Delhi, where he apprised Sharif's Indian counterparts about the substance of Zinni's message and counseled restraint on their part. He also informed Indian officials that General Zinni had categorically told the Pakistanis that the United States would not countenance efforts to link their withdrawal from Kargil to the overall Kashmir question.[53] Despite Zinni's firm message, the fighting continued until early July. No doubt surprised by the scope and intensity of the Indian attacks and unable to persuade either the United States or other major powers to back Pakistan, Prime Minister Sharif visited Washington on July 4 in the hope of finding a face-saving solution to the crisis. To his surprise (and to that of his Indian counterparts), the message from President Clinton was unequivocal: the Pakistan Army had to bring about an unconditional withdrawal from Kargil, and the "sanctity of the Line of Control" had to be maintained.[54] Even in the face of this uncompromising message, the Pakistani troops continued to fight. Only on July 9 did Pakistan send an envoy to New Delhi to discuss a possible de-escalation of the crisis. Initially, India expressed little interest in talks, but it later agreed.

On July 12 Prime Minister Sharif gave a nationally televised address where he called for a withdrawal of Pakistan's forces from their mountain redoubts.[55] In his speech, however, he carefully refrained from making any reference to the redeployment of the Pakistani regular forces, maintaining throughout that the mujahideen had scaled and seized the redoubts of their own accord. By July 14 the first group of infiltrators had withdrawn from their positions and ceded ground to the advancing Indian forces. In mid-July, for all practical purposes, the conflict came to a close.

Despite the profound sense of betrayal by the Pakistani regime (and Sharif, in particular), the presence of a jingoistic regime in New Delhi, and the possession of sufficient capabilities for horizontal escalation, Indian policymakers carefully confined the conflict to the Kargil region. They also placed important political constraints on the use of airpower, categorically limiting its employment to the Indian side of the Line of Control. The Indian decision not to ex-

53. C. Raja Mohan, "Pak Must Pull Out Troops," *Hindu,* June 28, 1999.
54. See White House, Office of the Press Secretary, "Joint Statement by President Clinton and Prime Minister Nawaz Sharif of Pakistan," July 4, 1999. For a detailed firsthand account of the negotiations at Blair House, see Bruce Riedel, *American Diplomacy and the 1999 Kargil Summit at Blair House* (Philadelphia: Center for the Advanced Study of India, University of Pennsylvania, 2002).
55. Agencies, "Sharif to India—Let's Talk, Not Waste Time," *Indian Express,* July 13, 1999, http://www.indianexpress.com/res/web/pIe/ie/daily/19990713/ige13071.html.

pand the scope of operations despite grave provocation and the existence of adequate conventional forces appears puzzling.

One seemingly plausible explanation for India's restraint might have been the perceived need to court international public opinion in the aftermath of the nuclear tests. This argument does not withstand scrutiny, however. Given the resentful public mood within the country, an upcoming general election, and the existence of a regime that had few qualms about the use of force to resolve disputes, the inhibitions of global public opinion could not have served as a powerful barrier to the expansion of the conflict. Nor does the swift U.S. intervention provide a sufficiently compelling explanation for the conclusion of the conflict, for the war continued well after U.S. efforts to terminate it. Consequently, even in the absence of incontrovertible public statements, through a process of inference and attribution, one can make a cogent argument that the principal source of Indian restraint was Pakistan's overt possession of a nuclear arsenal. Indian policymakers, cognizant of this new reality, were compelled to exercise suitable restraint for fear of escalation to the nuclear level.

The Road to Operation Parakram

Relations between India and Pakistan remained strained over the next two years, exacerbated by the emergence of a military regime in Pakistan following the October 1999 coup. The situation in Kashmir remained unsettled, as infiltration from Pakistan continued. The event that set in motion renewed tensions came in the wake of a major, if abortive, terrorist attack. On October 1, 2001, a group of insurgents disguised as police officers managed to hijack an official vehicle, load it with explosives, and ram the gate of the well-guarded Jammu and Kashmir State Assembly building in the Indian-controlled portion of Jammu and Kashmir. The ensuing explosion killed twenty-six individuals. Subsequently, all the attackers were killed in a gun battle with Indian security forces. None of the legislators were killed, as they had left the building several hours prior to the attack. A Pakistan-based insurgent group, Jaish-e-Mohammed, claimed responsibility for the attack.[56] This episode constituted the most brazen assault on a governmental body since the onset of the insurgency in Kashmir. Not surprisingly, India lodged a vigorous protest in Islamabad and called on Pakistan to ban the terrorist group. Although con-

---

56. Barry Bearak, "26 Die as Suicide Squad Bombs Kashmir Legislative Building," *New York Times*, October 2, 2001.

demning the attack, Pakistan refused to take such action.[57] In the wake of this incident, no further events of any consequence punctuated Indo-Pakistani relations, even though ties remained extremely strained.

The next terrorist attack, which took place on December 13, 2001, set in motion a chain of events that could have culminated in another war. Assuming that the groups involved in the attack did have its roots in Pakistan, India clearly had sufficient grounds to retaliate militarily against Pakistan. Yet, all India undertook was a significant and protracted exercise in coercive diplomacy, code-named Operation Parakram.[58] What explains India's unwillingness to resort to military action against Pakistan despite a substantial provocation? Three possible explanations suggest themselves. First, India may have lacked the requisite capabilities for a quick, calibrated attack against specific Pakistani targets. Second, deft U.S. diplomacy may have helped stave off an Indian attack. Third, India may have feared that military action could escalate to the nuclear level. In effect, Pakistan's possession of a limited nuclear arsenal acted as a sufficient deterrent to Indian action. To assess the strength of each of these three competing explanations, it is necessary to at least briefly recount the critical set of events that transpired.

On December 13, 2001, a nondescript white Ambassador, a model of car that senior Indian government officials routinely use, drove past the security cordon of the Indian parliament.[59] Within seconds, six armed gunmen emerged from the vehicle and proceeded toward the Central Hall of parliament, which was in session at the time. An unarmed "watch and ward" guard had the presence of mind to quickly close the doors of the Central Hall and sound an alarm shortly after the assailants fired their first shots. A gun battle ensued between the assailants and the security forces assigned to the parliament, leaving all six of the attackers dead.[60] Based on telephone intercepts, Indian authorities claimed that the attackers were all members of Lashkar-e-Taiba and Jaish-e-Mohammed.[61]

57. Celia W. Dugger, "India Wants End to Group in Kashmir Attack," *New York Times*, October 3, 2001.
58. For the classic statement on the subject, see Alexander L. George, *Forceful Persuasion: Coercive Diplomacy as an Alternative to War* (Washington, D.C.: United States Institute of Peace Press, 1991).
59. Joanna Slater, "A Tremor at the Fault Line," *Far Eastern Economic Review,* December 27, 2001–January 3, 2002, pp. 22–23.
60. Celia W. Dugger, "India Recalling Pakistan Envoy over Delhi Raid" *New York Times,* December 22, 2001.
61. For a discussion of Pakistan's involvement with terrorist groups, see Jessica Stern, "Pakistan's Jihad Culture," *Foreign Affairs,* Vol. 79, No. 6 (November/December 2000), pp. 115–126; and Daniel

THE FIRST PHASE

The evolution of this crisis can be divided into two distinct phases. In the immediate aftermath of the attack, the Indian political leadership acted with alacrity. Within a day, the Indian authorities issued a series of demands to Pakistan and also started a process of military mobilization. They called on Pakistan to ban both Lashkar-e-Taiba and Jaish-e-Mohammed, to extradite twenty individuals who India claimed had been involved in terrorist attacks on its soil, and to cease all infiltration into Indian-controlled Kashmir.[62]

On December 18, Indian officials issued a firm warning that India's patience was waning and they expected Pakistan to take action against terrorist groups operating from within its borders.[63] As Pakistani officials equivocated, the United States, on December 20, declared both the Lashkar-e-Taiba and the Jaish-e-Mohammed to be foreign terrorist organizations. In the wake of this declaration, Pakistani authorities froze the assets of the Lashkar-e-Taiba. Nevertheless, to express its unhappiness with Pakistan's limited response, India withdrew its ambassador from Islamabad—a measure it had not resorted to since 1971 when the two countries had gone to war. Faced with ratcheting Indian and U.S. pressure to act against the terrorist groups, General Musharraf's regime arrested fifty militants toward the end of December.[64] India still demanded that Pakistan hand over twenty individuals accused of terrorist attacks on Indian soil, but Pakistan refused.

Faced with what it deemed to be Pakistani intransigence, India continued with its troop buildup and brought seven divisions into attack positions near the Pakistani border.[65] On January 11, in a further attempt to exert pressure on Pakistan, Gen. Sundararajan Padmanabhan, the chief of staff of the Indian Army, in uncharacteristically blunt language stated at a press conference in New Delhi that any country that was "mad enough" to initiate a nuclear strike against India would be "punished severely."[66] Padmanabhan's remarks

Byman, *Deadly Connections: States That Sponsor Terrorism* (Cambridge: Cambridge University Press, 2005).

62. Celia W. Dugger, "Group in Pakistan Is Blamed by India for Suicide Raid," *New York Times*, December 15, 2001.

63. Economist Global Agenda, "Terror in India," *Economist*, December 19, 2001, http://www5.economist.com/agenda/displayStory.cfm?Story_ID=E1_JTSDPQ.

64. John F. Burns, "Pakistan Moves against Groups Named by India," *New York Times*, December 29, 2001.

65. John F. Burns and Celia W. Dugger, "India Builds Up Forces as Bush Urges Calm," *New York Times*, December 30, 2001.

66. Quoted in "We Are Prepared: Army Chief," *Hindu*, January 12, 2002.

were significant because the uniformed military in India rarely, if ever, makes public statements about the higher direction of war.[67]

Against this backdrop of steadily rising tensions and repeated calls from Washington for mutual restraint, Musharraf gave a speech on Pakistani national television on January 12, 2002, where he proclaimed that he would not allow Pakistani territory to be used to carry out terrorist attacks on India or any other foreign country. Still he refused to end Pakistani support for the Kashmiri cause, stating that "Kashmir runs in our blood. No Pakistani can afford to sever links with Kashmir."[68] While welcoming Musharraf's speech, Indian authorities nevertheless insisted that they would withhold judgment until they saw evidence that corroborated his promise.

THE SECOND PHASE

India refused to lower its military alertness throughout January and into early spring, despite U.S. reassurances that progress was being made to curb the support for religious extremism emanating from Pakistan.[69] Admittedly, levels of infiltration across the Line of Control did taper off in the wake of Musharraf's speech. It was difficult, however, to ascertain if such a decline in infiltration could be attributed to Indian military pressure, U.S. diplomatic exhortations, or simply the normal seasonal lull brought on by high levels of snowfall in the Himalayan region. This lull came to an abrupt end on May 14, 2002, when two suicide bombers attacked an Indian military base in Kaluchak, near Jammu, killing thirty-three individuals, mostly the wives and children of Indian Army personnel. Lashkar-e-Taiba initially claimed responsibility for the attack but subsequently denied involvement.[70] The timing of the suicide attack was significant, because it came during a visit to New Delhi by Christina Rocca, the U.S. assistant secretary of state for South Asian affairs. Despite the continuing military confrontation along the Indo-Pakistani border, tensions had eased slightly. This attack, as far as Indian policymakers were concerned, portended one of two possibilities. Either General Musharraf was unwilling or unable to control the jihadis operating from Pakistani territory, or he did not

---

67. Sumit Ganguly, "From Aid to the Civil to the Defense of the Nation: The Army in Contemporary India," *Journal of Asian and African Affairs,* Vol. 26, Nos. 1–2 (1991), pp. 1–12.

68. See "President of Pakistan General Pervez Musharraf's Address to the Nation," Islamabad, January 12, 2002, http://www.millat.com/president/1020200475758AMword%20file.pdf.

69. Todd S. Purdum and Celia W. Dugger, "Powell Now 'Very Encouraged' on Kashmir," *New York Times,* January 19, 2002.

70. Edward Luce and Farhan Bokhari, "Bombers Kill 33 in Kashmir as U.S. Envoy Visits India," *Financial Times,* May 15, 2002.

wish to expend the necessary political capital to rein them in. Consequently, faced with renewed public outrage in India and growing anger within the military, Prime Minister Vajpayee gave a speech to troops deployed along the Indo-Pakistani border where he called for a "decisive fight" against Pakistan. This was no idle threat, because the Indian armed forces were carefully configured along the Indo-Pakistani border to undertake a significant invasion of Pakistan.[71] The message, no doubt, was intended for multiple audiences: Indian, Pakistani, and American. It certainly reached one of its target audiences, for the George W. Bush administration reacted with alacrity. Secretary of State Colin Powell immediately called General Musharraf and reiterated the importance of promptly reining in the terrorists operating in Kashmir. Simultaneously, State Department officials urged Indian officials to eschew military options and to seek a diplomatic resolution of the crisis.

Toward the end of May, war appeared all but imminent. India started to shift critical military assets into position along the border. The Indian Air Force moved several squadrons of fighter aircraft to forward bases; the navy rushed five of its most sophisticated warships from the eastern to the western fleet; and the navy's only operational aircraft carrier, the INS *Viraat*, was removed from dry dock and placed on alert off the port city of Bombay (Mumbai).[72]

These military maneuvers, the bellicose rhetoric from New Delhi, and Islamabad's feckless behavior generated serious concerns in Washington. On May 30, 2002, President Bush sent Secretary of Defense Donald Rumsfeld to the region. Referring to General Musharraf, Rumsfeld publicly stated, "He must stop incursions across the Line of Control. He must do so. He said he would do so. We and others are making it clear to him that he must live up to his word."[73]

Despite Rumsfeld's visit to the region and his explicit warning to Pakistan, tensions continued to mount. Reflecting this heightened possibility of war and perhaps hoping to send a warning to both parties, the United States issued a travel advisory urging all Americans to leave the region. In response, several other key states, most notably the United Kingdom, Germany, and Japan, all issued similar advisories. Simultaneously, Deputy Secretary of Defense

71. "Indian PM Calls for a 'Decisive Fight,'" Reuters, May 22, 2002. For a detailed depiction of the full-scale Indian war plan for early June, see V.K. Sood and Pravin Sawhney, *Operation Parakram: The War Unfinished* (New Delhi: Sage, 2003).
72. Josy Joseph, "The Mood Is for War," *India Abroad*, May 31, 2002, p. 3.
73. Quoted in Elisabeth Bumiller and Thom Shanker, "Bush Presses Pakistan on Kashmir and Orders Rumsfeld to Region," *New York Times*, May 31, 2002.

Paul Wolfowitz met with India's defense minister, George Fernandes, in Singapore in an attempt to defuse tensions. Confronted with these multiple pressures, Pakistan finally changed course. In early June Indian authorities announced that they had detected the first signs that insurgent activities in Kashmir were abating.[74] By mid-June the crisis showed further signs of easing, as truculent statements from both sides drew to a close and further military maneuvers along a tense border ceased. By the end of June, tensions had abated to a degree that India was able to remove its ban on Pakistani overflights of Indian territory and stand down its warships from aggressive patrolling in the Arabian Sea.[75] For all practical purposes, by early July the crisis had ended. India would not withdraw the majority of its forces from the border, however, until October 2002.

SEEKING EXPLANATIONS

Despite the gravity of the provocation, the evidence linking the terrorist groups to the Pakistani state, and the depth of anger in India, why did a regime dominated by a right-wing political party with a history of bellicosity not resort to a military strike against Pakistan? It is tempting to suggest that deft and sustained U.S. engagement or a lack of adequate conventional capabilities compelled India from attacking Pakistan. Yet the evidence for both these arguments, though suggestive, is incomplete. The Indian military mobilization, as argued earlier, started in the wake of the initial terrorist attacks. Toward the beginning of January 2002, Indian military capabilities were largely in place—although admittedly, any element of surprise had been lost and Pakistan had launched a countermobilization. Furthermore, in the aftermath of General Musharraf's January 12, 2002, speech, Indian authorities felt under considerable international (and especially U.S.) pressure to exercise military restraint and enable Pakistani authorities to demonstrate that they were willing to make commensurate changes in their policies. In the wake of General Musharraf's January 12 speech, Pakistani infiltration did subside significantly and no dramatic attacks took place. (Of course, as argued earlier, during this time of year, levels of infiltration naturally decline to a considerable extent because of the effects of seasonal snowfall.)

Nevertheless, when the second attack took place on May 14, Indian forces

---

74. Raymond Bonner, "India Believes Pakistan Restrains Militants," *New York Times,* June 6, 2002.
75. Josy Joseph, "India Removes Overflight Ban on Pakistani Aircraft," *India Abroad,* June 21, 2001, p. 15.

were in place and should have been able to carry out concerted attacks against key targets, especially terrorist training camps in Pakistan. What explains the Indian decision not to act? Once again, a partial explanation can be adduced. Some evidence suggests that India lacked the highly mobile forces equipped with suitable weaponry and night-vision equipment to carry out the type of sharp, quick strikes that would inflict the maximum possible damage on Pakistani-sponsored and -supported training bases.[76] Yet these tactical constraints can only explain India's failure to resort to calibrated, small-scale attacks; they cannot explain why India chose not to resort to a larger war. India clearly had the requisite forces deployed to conduct such a war and a political regime that had successfully defied international public opinion in carrying out nuclear tests. In addition, it had shown the determination to successfully prosecute the Kargil war. Consequently, explanations that rely on the dissuasive powers of timely U.S. diplomacy, or the lack of sufficient military capabilities, while seemingly tempting, nevertheless are not entirely convincing.[77]

The Robustness of Nuclear Deterrence

As the outcomes of the 1999 and 2001–02 crises show, nuclear deterrence is robust in South Asia. Both crises were contained at levels considerably short of full-scale war. That said, as Paul Kapur has argued, Pakistan's acquisition of a nuclear weapons capability may well have emboldened its leadership, secure in the belief that India had no good options to respond. India, in turn, has been grappling with an effort to forge a new military doctrine and strategy to enable it to respond to Pakistani needling while containing the possibilities of conflict escalation, especially to the nuclear level.[78] Whether Indian military planners

---

76. For a discussion of the limitations of Indian capabilities, see Rahul Bedi, "The Military Dynamics," *Frontline* (Chennai), June 21, 2001. See also V. Sudarshan and Ajith Pillai, "Game of Patience," *Outlook* (New Delhi), May 27, 2002, pp. 35–39.
77. It is, of course, possible that another source of Indian restraint stemmed from India's reluctance to launch a military strike against Pakistan because it would have inevitably interfered with and diverted attention from the U.S. military campaign in Afghanistan, reliant as it was on both Pakistani support and the use of its territory and airspace. That said, there is no evidence that this consideration weighed heavily in the strategic calculations of India's decisionmakers. One of the few suggestions in the literature that U.S. misgivings about an Indian attack influenced Indian military calculations is provided in Sood and Sawhney, *Operation Parakram*.
78. On this subject, see Walter Ladwig, "A Cold Start for Hot Wars? An Assessment of the Indian Army's New Limited War Doctrine," *International Security*, Vol. 32, No. 3 (Winter 2007/08), pp. 158–190; and V.R. Raghavan, "Limited War and Nuclear Escalation in South Asia," *Nonproliferation Review*, Vol. 8, No. 3 (Fall–Winter 2001), pp. 1–18.

can fashion such a calibrated strategy to cope with Pakistani probes remains an open question. This article's analysis of the 1999 and 2001–02 crises does suggest, however, that nuclear deterrence in South Asia is far from parlous, contrary to what the critics have suggested. Three specific forms of evidence can be adduced to argue the case for the strength of nuclear deterrence.

First, there is a serious problem of conflation in the arguments of both Hoyt and Kapur. Undeniably, Pakistan's willingness to provoke India has increased commensurate with its steady acquisition of a nuclear arsenal. This period from the late 1980s to the late 1990s, however, also coincided with two parallel developments that equipped Pakistan with the motives, opportunities, and means to meddle in India's internal affairs—particularly in Jammu and Kashmir. The most important change that occurred was the end of the conflict with the Soviet Union, which freed up military resources for use in a new jihad in Kashmir. This jihad, in turn, was made possible by the emergence of an indigenous uprising within the state as a result of Indian political malfeasance.[79] Once the jihadis were organized, trained, armed, and unleashed, it is far from clear whether Pakistan could control the behavior and actions of every resulting jihadist organization.[80] Consequently, although the number of attacks on India did multiply during the 1990s, it is difficult to establish a firm causal connection between the growth of Pakistani boldness and its gradual acquisition of a full-fledged nuclear weapons capability.

Second, India did respond with considerable force once its military planners realized the full scope and extent of the intrusions across the Line of Control. Despite the vigor of this response, India did exhibit restraint. For example, Indian pilots were under strict instructions not to cross the Line of Control in pursuit of their bombing objectives.[81] They adhered to these guidelines even though they left them more vulnerable to Pakistani ground fire.[82] The Indian military exercised such restraint to avoid provoking Pakistani fears of a wider attack into Pakistan-controlled Kashmir and then into Pakistan itself.

Indian restraint was also evident at another level. During the last war in

---

79. Ganguly, "India's Pathway to Pokhran II."
80. For a reasonably comprehensive list of these jihadi groups, see K. Santhanam, Sreedhar, Sudhir Saxena, and Manish, *Jihadis in Jammu and Kashmir: A Portrait Gallery* (New Delhi: Sage, 2003).
81. On this subject, see J.N. Dixit, *India-Pakistan in War and Peace* (New Delhi: Books Today, 2002), p. 55.
82. Midlevel Indian Air Force personnel, interviews by author, Washington, D.C., December 1999. For more evidence, see Jaswant Singh, *A Call to Honour: In Service of Emergent India* (New Delhi: Rupa, 2006).

Kashmir in 1965, within a week of its onset, the Indian Army horizontally escalated with an attack into Pakistani Punjab. In fact, in the Punjab, Indian forces successfully breached the international border and reached the outskirts of the regional capital, Lahore. The Indian military resorted to this strategy under conditions that were not especially propitious for the country. Prime Minister Jawaharlal Nehru, India's first prime minister, had died in late 1964. His successor, Lal Bahadur Shastri, was a relatively unknown politician of uncertain stature and standing, and the Indian military was still recovering from the trauma of the 1962 border war with the People's Republic of China.[83] Finally, because of its role in the Cold War, the Pakistani military was armed with more sophisticated, U.S.-supplied weaponry, including the F-86 Sabre and the F-104 Starfighter aircraft. India, on the other hand, had few supersonic aircraft in its inventory, barring a small number of Soviet-supplied MiG-21s and the indigenously built HF-24.[84] Furthermore, the Indian military remained concerned that China might open a second front along the Himalayan border. Such concerns were not entirely chimerical, because a Sino-Pakistani entente was under way. Despite these limitations, the Indian political leadership responded to Pakistani aggression with vigor and granted the Indian military the necessary authority to expand the scope of the war.

In marked contrast to the politico-military context of 1965, in 1999 India had a self-confident (if belligerent) political leadership and a substantially more powerful military apparatus. Moreover, the country had overcome most of its Nehruvian inhibitions about the use of force to resolve disputes.[85] Furthermore, unlike in 1965, India had at least two reserve strike corps in the Punjab in a state of military readiness and poised to attack across the border if given the political nod.[86] Despite these significant differences and advantages, the Indian political leadership chose to scrupulously limit the scope of the conflict to the Kargil region. As K. Subrahmanyam, a prominent Indian defense analyst and political commentator, wrote in 1993:

---

83. On the Indian military debacle of 1962, see Steven A. Hoffmann, *India and the China Crisis* (Berkeley: University of California Press, 1990).
84. For details about the Indo-Pakistani military balance in 1965, see Brines, *The Indo-Pakistani Conflict*.
85. On the decline of Nehruvian inhibitions about the use of force, see Kanti Bajpai, "India: Modified Structuralism," in Muthiah Alagappa, ed., *Asian Security Practices: Material and Ideational Differences* (Stanford, Calif.: Stanford University Press, 1998). See also Sumit Ganguly, "India's Foreign Policy Grows Up," *World Policy Journal*, Vol. 20, No. 4 (Winter 2003–2004), pp. 41–47.
86. Gen. Ved Prakash Malik, chief of staff of the Indian Army, interview by author, San Francisco, California, November 1999.

The awareness on both sides of a nuclear capability that can enable either country to assemble nuclear weapons at short notice induces mutual caution. This caution is already evident on the part of India. In 1965, when Pakistan carried out its "Operation Gibraltar" and sent in infiltrators, India sent its army across the cease-fire line to destroy the assembly points of the infiltrators. That escalated into a full-scale war. In 1990, when Pakistan once again carried out a massive infiltration of terrorists trained in Pakistan, India tried to deal with the problem on Indian territory and did not send its army into Pakistan-occupied Kashmir.[87]

Subrahmanyam's argument takes on additional significance in light of the overt acquisition of nuclear weapons by both India and Pakistan.

Third, Sagan's assertion about the dominance of the Pakistani military in determining Pakistan's security policies is unquestionably accurate. With the possible exception of the Kargil conflict, however, it is far from clear that the Pakistani military has been the primary force in planning for and precipitating aggressive war against India. The first Kashmir war, without a doubt, had the explicit approval of Pakistan's civilian authorities.[88] Similarly, there is ample evidence that the highly ambitious foreign minister, Zulfikar Ali Bhutto, goaded President Ayub Khan to undertake the 1965 war.[89] Finally, once again Bhutto, as much as the Pakistani military dictator Yahya Khan, was complicit in provoking a war with India in 1971, following the outbreak of a civil war in East Pakistan.[90]

Consequently, even though deductive theories may suggest that military organizations are universally more prone to the use of force and the adoption of offensive military doctrines, an assessment of the empirical evidence from South Asia suggests a more complex reality. Even though the Pakistani military has been risk prone and intransigent toward India, the evidence does not support the proposition that the Pakistani military has been more war prone. Civilian decisionmakers have often played a critical role in urging the military to undertake aggressive actions. Furthermore, in the context of weak demo-

---

87. K. Subrahmanyam, "Capping, Managing, or Eliminating Nuclear Weapons?" in Kanti P. Bajpai and Stephen P. Cohen, eds., *South Asia after the Cold War: International Perspectives* (Boulder, Colo.: Westview, 1993), p. 184.
88. On this subject, see Hodson, *The Great Divide*. See also the rather self-serving account of Maj. Gen. Akbar Khan, *Raiders in Kashmir: The Story of the Kashmir War, 1947–48* (Karachi: Pak Publishers, 1970).
89. Brines, *Indo-Pakistani Conflict*.
90. The best discussion of Pakistani decisionmaking can be found in Richard Sisson and Leo E. Rose, *War and Secession: Pakistan, India, and the Creation of Bangladesh* (Berkeley: University of California Press, 1990).

cratic institutions and with politicians desirous of exploiting an existing culture of populist jingoism, civilian regimes, especially in Pakistan, have demonstrated a substantial propensity to resort to war.[91]

Was the Kargil conflict, then, an important exception to the Pakistani civilian elite's propensity for bellicosity toward India? Was Nawaz Sharif merely the hapless victim of General Musharraf's machinations? The evidence on the subject remains both incomplete and murky. It is incomplete because there are no adequate and dispassionate Pakistani accounts of civil-military relations during the Kargil crisis. It is murky because key individuals who were involved in making the decisions have provided self-serving and utterly contradictory accounts.[92] On the basis of the available evidence, it appears that Sharif had some inkling of the military's plan for making incursions into Kargil. He may not have been fully briefed however, and he may not have adequately comprehended the scope and dimensions of those plans.[93]

What policy implications flow from this analysis? U.S. and multilateral efforts to roll back the Indian and Pakistani nuclear weapons and ballistic missile programs have all proven futile. Neither country in the foreseeable future will willingly dispense with these programs. Under the circumstances, it behooves the United States and other major powers, given Pakistan's parlous political order, to help secure its nuclear arsenal from theft, sabotage, or unauthorized usage. Some information within the public domain suggests that the United States has already undertaken modest efforts toward those ends.[94] Simultaneously, it would be desirable to urge India to adhere to its plans to create a "minimum deterrent capability."[95] Despite some setbacks, the dramat-

---

91. On the war proneness of weak democratic regimes, see Jack L. Snyder and Edward D. Mansfield, "Democratic Transitions, Institutional Strength, and War," *International Organization*, Vol. 56, No. 2 (Spring 2002), pp. 297–337.

92. For a sound assessment of the limited evidence, see Owen Bennett Jones, *Pakistan: Eye of the Storm* (New Haven, Conn.: Yale University Press, 2002).

93. For a thoughtful assessment of the contradictory claims, see Ayaz Amir, "The Ghost That Won't Go Away," *Dawn* (Karachi), July 23, 2004. See also Shaukat Qadir, "An Analysis of the Kargil Conflict, 1999," *Royal United Services Journal*, Vol. 147, No. 2 (April 2002), pp. 24–30. The controversy about the extent of Sharif's knowledge of Musharraf's war plans continues. In an interview (in Urdu) with a private Pakistani television channel, Geo TV, on June 2, 2008, Gen. Jamshed Gulzar Kiyani, the deputy director-general of the Inter-Services Intelligence directorate during the Kargil operation, claimed that Sharif had not been fully briefed on the likely costs and consequences of the operation. The interview is accessible at http://hk.youtube.com/watch?v= WpeaO119CDE&feature=related. (I am grateful to Aqil Shah, a doctoral candidate in the Department of Political Science at Columbia University, for providing me with the electronic link.)

94. David E. Sanger and William J. Broad, "U.S. Secretly Aids Pakistan in Guarding Nuclear Arms," *New York Times*, November 18, 2007.

95. Basrur, *Minimum Deterrence and Indian Nuclear Security*.

ically improved climate in Indo-U.S. relations makes it possible for the United States to hold meaningful discussions with India on a range of strategic issues without provoking the misgivings of India's strategic community about such a dialogue.[96] Finally, to avert further Indo-Pakistani crises over Kashmir, both sides need to be encouraged to continue with the peace process that they embarked on in 2004. Specifically, the United States should urge India to pursue a meaningful political dialogue with disaffected Kashmiris with a view toward bringing them into the political process. Although such a dialogue has been under way for some time, substantive progress has been limited. Washington should also prod the Pakistani government to abandon its reliance on various jihadi groups to prosecute its strategic aims in Kashmir. This issue is of particular significance because these groups may not always remain answerable to their Pakistani sponsors and may carry out acts of violence and terror that could easily destabilize a fraught bilateral relationship.

---

96. Daniel Dombey and Edward Luce, "Ties Expected to Prosper Despite Diplomatic Setback," *Financial Times*, June 11, 2008.

Ten Years of Instability in a Nuclear South Asia

S. Paul Kapur

India's and Pakistan's nuclear tests of May 1998 put to rest years of speculation as to whether the two countries, long suspected of developing covert weapons capabilities, would openly exercise their so-called nuclear option. The dust had hardly settled from the tests, however, when a firestorm of debate erupted over nuclear weapons' regional security implications. Some observers argued that nuclearization would stabilize South Asia by making Indo-Pakistani conflict prohibitively risky. Others maintained that, given India and Pakistan's bitter historical rivalry, as well as the possibility of accident and miscalculation, proliferation would make the subcontinent more dangerous.[1] The tenth anniversary of the tests offers scholars an opportunity to revisit this issue with the benefit of a decade of hindsight. What lessons do the intervening years hold regarding nuclear weapons' impact on South Asian security?

Proliferation optimists claim that nuclear weapons had a beneficial effect during this period, helping to stabilize India and Pakistan's historically volatile relations. Sumit Ganguly and Devin Hagerty, for example, argue that in recent years "the Indian and Pakistani governments, despite compelling incentives to attack one another . . . were dissuaded from doing so by fear that war

S. Paul Kapur is Associate Professor in the Department of National Security Affairs at the U.S. Naval Postgraduate School and a Faculty Affiliate at Stanford University's Center for International Security and Cooperation. He is author of Dangerous Deterrent: Nuclear Weapons Proliferation and Conflict in South Asia (Stanford, Calif.: Stanford University Press, 2007). The views expressed in this article are solely the author's and do not necessarily reflect those of the U.S. Navy, the Department of Defense, or the U.S. government.

For helpful comments and criticism, the author thanks Sumit Ganguly, Cari Costanzo Kapur, Scott Sagan, and International Security's anonymous reviewers. Sahaja Acharya and Laura Thom provided valuable research assistance.

1. For optimistic arguments, see Kenneth N. Waltz, "For Better: Nuclear Weapons Preserve an Imperfect Peace," in Scott D. Sagan and Waltz, The Spread of Nuclear Weapons: A Debate Renewed (New York: W.W. Norton, 2003), p. 117; K. Subrahmanyam, "India and the International Nuclear Order," in D.R. SarDesai and Raju G.C. Thomas, eds., Nuclear India in the Twenty-first Century (New York: Palgrave Macmillan, 2002), p. 83; and John J. Mearsheimer, "Here We Go Again," New York Times, May 17, 1998. For pessimistic arguments, see Scott D. Sagan, "For Worse: Till Death Do Us Part," in Sagan and Waltz, The Spread of Nuclear Weapons, pp. 106–107; P.R. Chari, "Nuclear Restraint, Nuclear Risk Reduction, and the Security-Insecurity Paradox in South Asia," in Michael Krepon and Chris Gagné, eds., The Stability-Instability Paradox: Nuclear Weapons and Brinkmanship in South Asia, Report No. 38 (Washington, D.C.: Henry L. Stimson Center, June 2001), p. 16; and

International Security, Vol. 33, No. 2 (Fall 2008), pp. 71–94
© 2008 by the President and Fellows of Harvard College and the Massachusetts Institute of Technology.

might escalate to the nuclear level."[2] It is true that since 1998 South Asian militarized disputes have not reached the point of nuclear confrontation or full-scale conventional conflict.[3] Nonetheless, I argue that optimistic analyses of proliferation's regional security impact are mistaken. Nuclear weapons had two destabilizing effects on the South Asian security environment. First, nuclear weapons' ability to shield Pakistan against all-out Indian retaliation, and to attract international attention to Pakistan's dispute with India, encouraged aggressive Pakistani behavior. This provoked forceful Indian responses, ranging from large-scale mobilization to limited war.[4] Although the resulting Indo-Pakistani crises did not lead to nuclear or full-scale conventional conflict, such fortunate outcomes were not guaranteed and did not result primarily from nuclear deterrence. Second, these crises have triggered aggressive changes in India's conventional military posture. Such developments may lead to future regional instability.

Below, I examine three phases of Indo-Pakistani relations since the nuclear tests. First, I discuss the period 1998 to 2002. I show that during these years Indo-Pakistani tensions reached levels unseen since the early 1970s, resulting in the 1999 Kargil war as well as a major militarized standoff that stretched from 2001 to 2002. An examination of this period reveals that nuclear weapons facilitated Pakistan's adoption of the low-intensity conflict strategy that triggered these confrontations, and that the crises' eventual resolution resulted primarily from nonnuclear factors such as diplomatic calculations and conventional military constraints. In the article's next section I examine the years 2002 to 2008. I argue that although Indo-Pakistani relations became more stable during this period, the improvements were modest and had little to do with nuclear weapons. Instead, they resulted mainly from changes in the international strategic environment, shifting domestic priorities, and nonnuclear security calculations. In addition, this period saw the emergence of strategic trends that could eventually undermine South Asian security. In the article's subsequent section, I discuss these developments' likely impact on future regional stability. I show that past Indo-Pakistani conflict led the Indians to begin formulat-

Kanti Bajpai, "The Fallacy of an Indian Deterrent," in Amitabh Mattoo, ed., *India's Nuclear Deterrent: Pokhran II and Beyond* (New Delhi: Har-Anand, 1999), pp. 150–188.
2. Sumit Ganguly and Devin T. Hagerty, *Fearful Symmetry: India-Pakistan Crises in the Shadow of Nuclear Weapons* (New Delhi: Oxford University Press, 2005), p. 9.
3. By "full-scale" conventional conflict, I mean a conflict that involves states' regular militaries, crosses official international boundaries, and is great enough to threaten the loser with catastrophic defeat.
4. By "limited" war, I mean a conflict resulting in at least 1,000 battle deaths that involves guerril-

ing a more aggressive conventional military doctrine. This could increase Indo-Pakistani security competition and result in rapid escalation in the event of an actual conflict. Thus nuclear weapons not only destabilized South Asia in the aftermath of the nuclear tests; they may damage the regional security environment in the years to come. In the article's final section, I discuss the implications of my argument.

Nuclear Weapons in South Asia, 1998 to 2002

In 1998 India and Pakistan were enjoying a period of relative stability that had begun in the early 1970s. These years were not wholly tranquil, having been punctuated by periods of considerable tension. For example, a serious disagreement had arisen between the two countries during the mid-1980s over Pakistani support for a Sikh separatist movement in the Indian Punjab.[5] Also, since 1989 India and Pakistan had been at loggerheads over Pakistan's backing of a bloody insurgency in the Indian state of Jammu and Kashmir.[6] Nonetheless, the two countries had not fought a war with each other since 1972. This was the longest period without an Indo-Pakistani war since the two countries gained independence from Great Britain in 1947.[7] Less than a year after the 1998 nuclear tests, however, India and Pakistan were embroiled in their first war in twenty-eight years.

In late 1998, Pakistan Army forces, disguised as local militants, crossed the Line of Control (LoC) dividing Indian from Pakistani Kashmir and seized positions up to 12 kilometers inside Indian territory. The move threatened Indian lines of communication into northern Kashmir. After discovering the incursion in May 1999, India launched a spirited air and ground offensive to oust the intruders. The operation was characterized by intense, close-quarters combat, with Indian infantry and artillery ejecting the Pakistanis from the mountainous terrain peak by peak. Although expanding the war could have facilitated

---

las, proxy forces, or states' regular militaries, but does not cross official international boundaries on a scale sufficient to threaten the loser with catastrophic defeat.

5. On the Sikh insurgency, see Paul Wallace, "Political Violence and Terrorism in India: The Crisis of Identity," in Martha Crenshaw, ed., *Terrorism in Context* (University Park: Penn State University Press, 1995), pp. 352–409.

6. See Sumit Ganguly, *The Crisis in Kashmir: Portents of War, Hopes of Peace* (Cambridge: Cambridge University Press, 1997); and Sumantra Bose, *Kashmir: Roots of Conflict, Paths to Peace* (Cambridge, Mass.: Harvard University Press, 2003).

7. In the twenty-five-year period between independence and the end of the Bangladesh conflict, India and Pakistan fought three wars: in 1948, 1965, and 1971.

their task, the Indians did not cross the LoC, restricting their operations to the Indian side of the boundary. The Pakistanis finally withdrew in mid-July, after Prime Minister Nawaz Sharif traveled to Washington and signed a U.S.-prepared agreement to restore the LoC. More than 1,000 Indian and Pakistani forces died in the Kargil fighting.[8]

What impact did nuclear weapons have on the outbreak of the Kargil conflict? The roots of the Kargil operation date back to the late 1980s, when Pakistan was beginning to acquire a nuclear capacity.[9] Pakistani leaders, long unhappy with the division of Kashmir, had launched two wars for the territory, one in 1948 and another in 1965. Although neither effort was successful, in both cases the Pakistanis managed to fight the Indians to a stalemate. But Pakistan's 1971 defeat in the Bangladesh war, in which India severed East Pakistan from its Western wing, demonstrated that the Pakistanis could no longer confront India without risking catastrophic defeat. After 1971 Pakistan thus stopped challenging India for control of Kashmir.

By the late 1980s, however, Pakistan's strategic situation had changed, enabling it once more to attempt to undermine the Kashmiri status quo. This change resulted from several factors. First, the Kashmir insurgency threatened Indian control of the region.[10] Second, the anti-Soviet Afghan war offered a model that Pakistan could use to exploit the insurgency.[11] Third, Pakistani leaders believed that, with the end of the Cold War, the world community might be more willing to address the Kashmir issue than it had previously been.[12]

Equally important as these factors, however, was Pakistan's acquisition of a nuclear capability, which enabled the Pakistanis to challenge territorial boundaries in Kashmir without fearing catastrophic Indian retaliation. Pakistani

8. See V.P. Malik, *Kargil: From Surprise to Victory* (New Delhi: HarperCollins, 2006); Kargil Review Committee, *From Surprise to Reckoning* (New Delhi: Sage, 2000); Amarinder Singh, *A Ridge Too Far: War in the Kargil Heights, 1999* (New Delhi: Motibagh Palace, 2001); Y.M. Bammi, *Kargil, 1999: The Impregnable Conquered* (Noida, India: Gorkha, 2002); and Ashok Krishna, "The Kargil War," in Krishna and P.R. Chari, eds., *Kargil: The Tables Turned* (New Delhi: Manohar, 2001), pp. 77–138.
9. The period from the late 1980s until 1998 is often referred to as an "opaque" or "de facto" nuclear period. During these years, India and Pakistan did not possess nuclear weapons, but probably could have produced them if necessary. See S. Paul Kapur, *Dangerous Deterrent: Nuclear Weapons Proliferation and Conflict in South Asia* (Stanford, Calif.: Stanford University Press, 2007); and Devin T. Hagerty, *The Consequences of Nuclear Proliferation: Lessons from South Asia* (Cambridge, Mass.: MIT Press, 1998).
10. See Bose, *Kashmir;* and Ganguly, *The Crisis in Kashmir.*
11. Kapur, *Dangerous Deterrent,* p. 104; and Husain Haqqani, "The Role of Islam in Pakistan's Future," *Washington Quarterly,* Vol. 28, No. 1 (Winter 2004/05), p. 90.
12. Kapur, *Dangerous Deterrent,* pp. 104–105.

leaders have openly acknowledged nuclear weapons' emboldening effects. Benazir Bhutto, who served her first term as Pakistani prime minister from 1988 to 1990, stated, "I doubt that the nuclear capability was [originally] done for Kashmir-specific purposes." She admitted, however, that nuclear weapons quickly "came out" as an important tool in that struggle. "The Kashmiris were determined to win their freedom," and the Pakistani government realized that it could now provide extensive support for "a low-scale insurgency" in Kashmir while insulated from a full-scale Indian response. "Islamabad saw its capability as a deterrence to any future war with India," Bhutto asserted, because "a conventional war could turn nuclear." Thus even in the face of substantial Pakistani support for the Kashmir uprising, "India could not have launched a conventional war, because if it did, it would have meant suicide."[13]

Leading Pakistani strategic analysts agree. According to Shireen Mazari of the Institute of Strategic Studies, with nuclear deterrence "each side knows it cannot cross a particular threshold." Thus "limited warfare in Kashmir becomes a viable option."[14] Even proliferation optimists admit that an emerging nuclear capacity enabled the Pakistanis to adopt a more activist Kashmir policy. Ganguly, for example, acknowledges that one of the "compelling reasons" that "emboldened the Pakistani military to aid the insurgency in Kashmir" in the late 1980s was that "they believed that their incipient nuclear capabilities had effectively neutralized whatever conventional military advantages India possessed."[15]

The Kargil operation was originally conceived in this strategic context. Benazir Bhutto claimed that the army presented her with a Kargil-like plan in 1989 and 1996. According to Bhutto, the operation was designed to oust Indian forces from Siachen Glacier in northern Kashmir.[16] The army formulated a plan in which Pakistani and Kashmiri forces would occupy the mountain peaks overlooking the Kargil region. The logic was that "if we scrambled up high enough . . . we could force India to withdraw" by severing its supply lines to Siachen. "To dislodge us," Bhutto recalled, the Indians "would have to resort to conventional war. However, our nuclear capability [gave] the military

13. Benazir Bhutto, interview by author, August 2004.
14. Shireen M. Mazari, interview by author, Islamabad, Pakistan, April 2004; and Shireen M. Mazari, "Kashmir: Looking for Viable Options," *Defence Journal*, Vol. 3, No. 2 (February–March 1999), http://defencejournal.com/feb-mar99/kashmir-viable.htm.
15. Sumit Ganguly, *Conflict Unending: India-Pakistan Tensions since 1947* (New York: Columbia University Press, 2001), p. 92.
16. See V.R. Raghavan, *Siachen: Conflict without End* (New Delhi: Viking, 2002).

confidence that India cannot wage a conventional war against Pakistan." Bhutto claimed that she rejected the proposal because even if it succeeded militarily, Pakistan lacked the political and diplomatic resources to achieve broader strategic success.[17]

Like these early plans, Pakistan's actual Kargil operation was designed primarily to threaten India's position in Siachen Glacier. According to Pakistani President Pervez Musharraf, "Kargil was fundamentally about Kashmir," where the Indians occupy Pakistani territory, "for example at Siachen." "Emotions run very high here" on this issue. "Siachen is barren wasteland, but it belongs to us," he asserted.[18] Jalil Jilani, former director-general for South Asia in Pakistan's ministry of foreign affairs, described Siachen as "perhaps the most important factor" underlying the Kargil operation. "Without Siachen," he argued, "Kargil would not have taken place."[19]

Like the earlier plans, the Kargil operation was facilitated by Pakistan's nuclear capacity. Jilani explained that the nuclear tests increased Pakistani leaders' willingness to challenge India in Kashmir. In the absence of a clear Pakistani nuclear capacity, Jilani argues, "India wouldn't be restrained" in responding to such provocations. An overt Pakistani nuclear capability, however, "brought about deterrence," ensuring that there would be "no major war" between India and Pakistan. In addition, conflict between two openly nuclear states would attract international attention, encouraging outside diplomatic intervention in Kashmir. Thus, as Jilani explained, nuclear weapons played a dual role in Pakistani strategy at Kargil. They "deterred India" from all-out conventional retaliation against Pakistan. And they sent a message to the outside world regarding the seriousness of the Kashmir dispute: "War between nuclear powers is not a picnic. It's a very serious business. One little incident in Kashmir could undermine everything."[20]

---

17. Bhutto, interview by author.
18. President Pervez Musharraf, interview by author, Rawalpindi, Pakistan, April 2004. Note that Musharraf maintained that local mujahideen had executed the Kargil operation, with Pakistan Army forces becoming involved only after India began its counterattack.
19. Jalil Jilani, interview by author, Islamabad, Pakistan, April 2004. Unlike Musharraf, Jilani conceded that Pakistan Army troops had launched the Kargil incursions.
20. Ibid. Pakistan's nuclear capacity was not the only factor that emboldened its leaders to undertake the Kargil operation. The Pakistanis believed that retaking the Kargil heights would be prohibitively difficult for India. And they hoped that the international community would accept the Kargil operation, given Pakistan's perilous position vis-à-vis a conventionally powerful, newly nuclear India. On Pakistani tactical considerations, see Sardar F.S. Lodi, "India's Kargil Operations: An Analysis," *Defence Journal*, Vol. 3, No. 10 (November 1999), pp. 2–3; Shireen M. Mazari, "Re-examining Kargil," *Defence Journal*, Vol. 3, No. 11 (June 2000), pp. 44–46; Javed Nasir, "Calling

Pakistani analysts also note the emboldening impact of an overt nuclear capability on Pakistan's behavior in Kashmir. Mazari argues that "open testing makes a big difference in the robustness of deterrence," further encouraging the outbreak of limited warfare. She states, "While this scenario was prevalent even when there was only a covert nuclear deterrence . . . overt nuclear capabilities . . . further accentuated this situation."[21] Proliferation optimists concede that these effects played a central role in facilitating the Kargil operation. Indeed, Ganguly and Hagerty note that "absent nuclear weapons, Pakistan probably would not have undertaken the Kargil misadventure in the first place."[22]

Pakistani political leaders and strategic analysts, as well as optimistic South Asian security scholars, thus recognize nuclear weapons' emboldening impact on the Pakistanis' behavior in Kashmir and at Kargil. How, then, do scholars make an optimistic case for nuclear weapons' role in the Kargil conflict? Optimists argue that although nuclear weapons facilitated Kargil's outbreak, they also deterred India from crossing the LoC during the fighting, thereby ensuring that the dispute was resolved without resort to full-scale war.[23] Although it is true that Indian leaders' refusal to cross the Line of Control prevented escalation of the Kargil conflict, the best available evidence indicates that Indian policy was not driven primarily by a fear of Pakistani nuclear weapons.

V.P. Malik, Indian Army chief of staff during the Kargil operation, explains that the Indians avoided crossing the Line of Control mainly out of concern for world opinion: "The political leaders felt that India needed to make its case and get international support" for its position in the conflict. The Indian government believed that it could best do so by exercising restraint even in the face of clear Pakistani provocations.[24] G. Parthasarathy, India's high commis-

---

the Indian Army Chief's Bluff," *Defence Journal*, Vol. 3, No. 2 (February–March 1999), p. 25; Mirza Aslam Beg, "Kargil Withdrawal and 'Rogue' Army Image," *Defence Journal*, Vol. 3, No. 8 (September 1999), pp. 8–11; Ayaz Ahmed Khan, "Indian Offensive in the Kargil Sector," *Defence Journal*, Vol. 3, No. 5 (June 1999), pp. 7–8; and Shaukat Qadir, "An Analysis of the Kargil Conflict, 1999," *Royal United Service Institution Journal*, Vol. 147, No. 2 (April 2002), pp. 2–3. On international opinion, see Ganguly, *Conflict Unending*, p. 122; Ashley J. Tellis, C. Christine Fair, and Jamison Jo Medby, *Limited Conflicts under the Nuclear Umbrella: Indian and Pakistani Lessons from the Kargil Crisis* (Santa Monica, Calif.: RAND, 2001), p. 38; Mirza Aslam Beg, "Deterrence, Defence, and Development," *Defence Journal*, Vol. 3, No. 6 (July 1999), pp. 4–6; and Ejaz Haider, *Friday Times* editor, interview by author, Lahore, Pakistan, April 2004.
21. Mazari, interview by author; Mazari, "Kashmir: Looking for Viable Options," p. 64; and Shireen M. Mazari, "Low-Intensity Conflicts: The New War in South Asia," *Defence Journal*, Vol. 3, No. 6 (July 1999), p. 41.
22. Ganguly and Hagerty, *Fearful Symmetry*, p. 191.
23. Rajesh M. Basrur, *Minimum Deterrence and India's Nuclear Security* (Stanford, Calif.: Stanford University Press, 2006), pp. 73–74; and Ganguly and Hagerty, *Fearful Symmetry*, pp. 160–162.
24. V.P. Malik, interview by author, New Delhi, India, April 2004. On India's battle for interna-

sioner to Pakistan during the Kargil conflict, agrees. Indian leaders refrained from crossing the LoC, he explains, because they believed that doing so would yield "political gains with the world community." "We had to get the world to accept that this was Pakistan's fault," he maintains. Staying on its side of the LoC enabled India to "keep the moral high ground."[25]

Despite these concerns, Indian leaders would probably have allowed the military to cross the Line of Control if doing so had proved necessary. According to Malik, the civilian leadership's "overriding political goal . . . was to eject the intruders." The government thus made clear that it would revisit its policy if India's military leaders ever felt the need to cross the LoC. This did not occur because the Indians quickly began winning at Kargil, and by early June were confident of victory. Malik maintains, however, that "if the tactical situation had not gone well, India would have crossed the LoC," regardless of Pakistan's nuclear capacity. Pakistan had just shown that attacks across the Line of Control need not trigger nuclear escalation. Thus the Indians believed that Kargil could also be "done the other way."[26]

Former Indian National Security Adviser Brajesh Mishra offers a similar analysis: "The army never pushed the government to cross the LoC." "If the army had wanted," he argues, "the government would have considered crossing." Mishra maintains that Pakistan's nuclear capacity would not have deterred the cabinet from granting the army's request, because Pakistan would have been unlikely to use nuclear weapons in that scenario. "Pakistan can be finished by a few bombs," Mishra argues. "Anyone with a small degree of sanity," he asserts, "would know that [nuclear war] would have disastrous consequences for Pakistan."[27]

Former Indian Defense Minister George Fernandes supports these claims. According to Fernandes, India did not need to violate the Line of Control. Once the Indian counteroffensive got under way, the government was convinced that "India was in control" and "did not believe that the tactical situation was going to deteriorate." Simultaneously, the Pakistanis were suffering an international backlash, with "the United States . . . pressuring Pakistan" to undo the Kargil incursions.[28]

tional opinion, see also Maleeha Lodhi, "The Kargil Crisis: Anatomy of a Debacle," *Newsline* (Karachi), July 1999, pp. 30–36; Tellis, Fair, and Medby, *Limited Conflicts under the Nuclear Umbrella*, pp. 21–28; and Irfan Husain, "Kargil: The Morning After," *Dawn* (Karachi), April 29, 2000.
25. Gopalaswami Parthasarathy, interviews by author, New Delhi, India, August 2004 and December 2007.
26. Malik, interview by author.
27. Brajesh Mishra, interview by author, New Delhi, India, May 2005.
28. George Fernandes, interview by author, New Delhi, India, August 2004.

Former Prime Minister Atal Bihari Vajpayee concurs with these assessments. "There was no need to cross the LoC," he explains, "because militarily India was successful. But nothing was ruled out. If ground realities had required military operations beyond the LoC, we would have seriously considered it. We never thought atomic weapons would be used, even if we had decided to cross the LoC."[29]

Tactical and diplomatic calculations, then, rather than Pakistani nuclear weapons, were primarily responsible for the Indian refusal to cross the LoC during the Kargil conflict. This does not mean that Pakistan's nuclear capacity was entirely irrelevant to India's decisionmaking. Malik concedes that Pakistani nuclear weapons led the Indians to rule out full-scale conventional war with Pakistan. As he explains, however, nuclear weapons were "not decisive" in India's refusal to violate the LoC, because the Indians did not believe that crossing the line would trigger nuclear escalation.[30] Nuclear weapons thus did have a stabilizing effect on the conduct of the Kargil conflict, but one must not exaggerate their impact. The danger of a Pakistani nuclear response would have prevented India from deliberately launching a full-scale war against Pakistan. Pakistani nuclear deterrence, however, did not prevent India from violating the Line of Control. Indian leaders' decision against crossing the LoC turned mainly on nonnuclear considerations.[31] And, as noted above, Pakistan's nuclear weapons facilitated the outbreak of the Kargil conflict in the first place.

Although India and Pakistan managed to avoid a nuclear or an all-out conventional confrontation at Kargil, such an outcome was hardly a foregone conclusion. Had the Indians not prevailed from behind the LoC, they probably would have crossed the line and escalated the conflict. It is impossible to know where such actions would have led. Although the Indians would not have deliberately threatened Pakistan with catastrophic defeat, the Pakistanis could have perceived rapid Indian conventional gains as an existential threat, particularly if they endangered Pakistan's nuclear command and control capabili-

---

29. Atal Bihari Vajpayee, interview by author, New Delhi, India, June 2006.
30. Malik, interview by author.
31. Although Indian leaders' accounts could be seen as self-serving, it would be equally beneficial for them to claim that they never considered crossing the LoC during the Kargil operation. This would insulate them from the charge that they were deterred from horizontal escalation by Pakistan's nuclear capacity and would help to promote the reputation for restraint that the Indians desire. Also, Indian leaders do not completely dismiss the deterrent effects of Pakistani nuclear weapons; they admit to having ruled out full-scale war during the Kargil conflict because of Pakistan's nuclear capacity. Thus it is likely that if they had been similarly deterred from crossing the LoC, Indian leaders would be willing to acknowledge it.

ties. The Pakistanis could have responded with a large-scale conventional or even a nuclear attack.[32] Kargil's relatively restrained outcome thus belies the conflict's considerable danger.

During the 1998 to 2002 period, South Asia not only experienced its first war in twenty-eight years; between December 2001 and October 2002, it also experienced the largest-ever Indo-Pakistani militarized standoff. The stand-off's size made its potential consequences even greater than those of the Kargil conflict. Because the crisis did not escalate to the level of combat, prolif-eration optimists argue that it demonstrates the stabilizing effects of nuclear weapons on the subcontinent. A close examination, however, reveals that nu-clear weapons had much the same effect on the 2001–02 crisis that they did on Kargil; they helped to facilitate the confrontation and played only a limited role in resolving it.

The 2001–02 crisis occurred in two phases. The first phase began on December 13, 2001, when militants attacked the Indian parliament while it was in session. No members were killed, although several security personnel died in a gun battle with the terrorists. The Indian government determined that two Pakistan-backed militant groups, Lashkar-e-Taiba, and Jaish-e-Mohammed, had carried out the assault. In response, India launched Operation Parakram, mobilizing 500,000 troops along the Line of Control and the international bor-der. The Indians simultaneously demanded that Pakistan surrender twenty criminals believed to be located in Pakistan, renounce terrorism, shut down terrorist training camps in Pakistani territory, and stanch the flow of militant infiltration into Jammu and Kashmir. If Pakistan did not comply, the Indians planned to strike terrorist training camps and seize territory in Pakistani Kashmir. Pakistan responded with large-scale deployments of its own, and soon roughly 1 million troops were facing each other across the LoC and inter-national border.[33]

In January 2002 President Musharraf took two important steps toward de-

32. See S. Paul Kapur, "Nuclear Proliferation, the Kargil Conflict, and South Asian Security," *Secu-rity Studies*, Vol. 13, No. 1 (Autumn 2003), p. 99. Lt. Gen. Khalid Kidwai, director of the Pakistan Army's Strategic Plans Division, specified loss of "a large part of [Pakistani] territory" as grounds for the use of nuclear weapons. See Paolo Cotta-Ramusino and Maurizio Martellini, "Nuclear Safety, Nuclear Stability, and Nuclear Strategy in Pakistan," Laundau Network, http://www.mi.infn.it/~landnet/Doc/pakistan.pdf (updated February 11, 2002).
33. For detailed discussions of the 2001–02 crisis, see V.K. Sood and Pravin Sawhney, *Operation Parakram: The War Unfinished* (New Delhi: Sage, 2003); Polly Nayak and Michael Krepon, "U.S. Cri-sis Management in South Asia's Twin Peaks Crisis," Report No. 57 (Washington, D.C.: Henry L. Stimson Center, September 2006); and Sumit Ganguly and Michael R. Kraig, "The 2001–2002 Indo-Pakistani Crisis: Exposing the Limits of Coercive Diplomacy," *Security Studies*, Vol. 14, No. 2 (Sum-mer 2005).

escalating the initial phase of the crisis. First, he outlawed Lashkar-e-Taiba and Jaish-e-Mohammed. Then, in a nationally televised speech on January 12, he pledged to prevent Pakistani territory from being used to foment terrorism in Kashmir. U.S. Secretary of State Colin Powell, visiting New Delhi after stopping in Islamabad, subsequently assured Indian leaders that Musharraf was working to reduce terrorism, and was actively contemplating the extradition of non-Pakistani suspects on India's list of twenty fugitives.[34] The evident success of India's coercive diplomacy, as well as a loss of strategic surprise and the resulting fear of high casualties, led the Indians not to attack Pakistan in January 2002.[35] Indian forces, however, remained deployed along the LoC and international border.

The second phase of the 2001–02 crisis erupted on May 14, 2002, when terrorists killed thirty-two people at an Indian Army camp at Kaluchak in Jammu.[36] Outraged Indian leaders formulated a military response considerably more ambitious than the plans adopted in January. Now, rather than simply attacking across the LoC, the Indians planned to drive three strike corps from Rajasthan into Pakistan, engaging and destroying Pakistani forces and seizing territory in the Thar Desert. Before the Indians could act, however, the United States once again intervened. In early June, U.S. Deputy Secretary of State Richard Armitage extracted a promise from President Musharraf not just to reduce militant infiltration into Indian Kashmir, but to end infiltration "permanently."[37] Armitage conveyed Musharraf's pledge to Indian officials. According to Brajesh Mishra, Musharraf's promise, U.S. assurances that Musharraf would honor his commitment, and a notable decrease in terrorist infiltration into Indian Kashmir led Indian leaders to conclude that "coercive pressure was working."[38]

---

34. See "President of Pakistan General Pervez Musharraf's Address to the Nation," Islamabad, January 12, 2002, http://www.millat.com/president/1020200475758AMword%20file.pdf; Alan Sipress and Rajiv Chandrasekaran, "Powell 'Encouraged' by India Visit," *Washington Post,* January 19, 2002; Robert Marquand, "Powell Tiptoes Indo-Pak Divide," *Christian Science Monitor,* January 18, 2002; and Susan Milligan, "India-Pakistan Standoff Easing, Powell Says," *Boston Globe,* January 18, 2002.

35. Mishra, interview by author; and Sood and Sawhney, *Operation Parakram,* p. 80.

36. The victims were mostly women and children, the family members of Indian military personnel. See Raj Chengappa and Shishir Gupta, "The Mood to Hit Back," *India Today,* May 27, 2002, pp. 27–30.

37. Celia W. Dugger and Thom Shanker, "India Sees Hope as Pakistan Halts Kashmir Militants," *New York Times,* June 9, 2002.

38. Mishra, interview by author. See also Rahul Bedi and Anton La Guardia, "India Ready for 'Decisive Battle,'" *Daily Telegraph,* May 23, 2002; Fahran Bokhari and Edward Luce, "Western Pressure Brings Easing of Kashmir Tension," *Financial Times,* June 8, 2002; C. Raja Mohan, "Musharraf Vows to Stop Infiltration: Armitage," *Hindu,* June 7, 2002; Sood and Sawhney, *Operation Parakram,* pp. 95,

India ultimately did not strike Pakistan, and Indian forces began withdrawing from the international border and LoC in October. Why did India demobilize without attacking? It did so primarily because top officials viewed the Parakram deployment as having been successful. No further terrorism on the scale of the parliament attack had occurred during the crisis. And the Indians had secured a Pakistani pledge, backed by U.S. promises, to prevent such violence in the future. Vajpayee explains that "America gave us the assurance that something will be done by Pakistan about cross-border terrorism. America gave us a clear assurance. That was an important factor" in the Indian decision to demobilize.[39] Fernandes maintains that India had "no reason to attack." The Indians had "stayed mobilized to make the point that another [terrorist] attack would result in an immediate response. No further attacks happened."[40] According to Mishra, Operation Parakram's "national goal was to curb terrorism emanating from Pakistan. That national goal . . . was achieved."[41] Additional reasons for India's failure to attack Pakistan in mid-2002 were the loss of the element of surprise; concern with the costs of a large-scale Indo-Pakistani conflict, including the possibility of nuclear escalation; and a desire to avoid angering the United States by attacking its key ally in the Afghan war.[42]

What role did nuclear weapons play in defusing the 2001–02 crisis? Proliferation optimists claim that the confrontation's resolution was primarily the result of nuclear deterrence.[43] The truth is more complicated than the optimists suggest, however. Nuclear weapons did not play a major role in dissuading Indian leaders from attacking Pakistan during the first phase of the crisis in January 2002. As noted above, Indian restraint resulted primarily from the belief that India's coercive diplomacy was succeeding against Pakistan, as well as from concern that, in the absence of strategic surprise, the costs of a conventional confrontation with Pakistan would be excessively high.

Pakistan's nuclear capability did play a role in stabilizing the second phase

98–99; "India: Fernandes Says Forward Mobilization of Troops Achieved Objectives," World News Connection, November 21, 2002; and "Government Carrying Out Strategic Relocation of Army," Press Trust of India, November 20, 2002.

39. Vajpayee, interview by author.

40. Fernandes, interview by author.

41. Mishra, interview by author. Note that Pakistan did not return the twenty fugitives that India had earlier demanded.

42. Sood and Sawhney, *Operation Parakram*, pp. 80, 82, 87; V. Sudarshan and Ajith Pillai, "Game of Patience," *Outlook* (Mumbai), May 27, 2002; and retired Indian generals, interviews by author, New Delhi, India, August 2004.

43. See, for example, Ganguly and Hagerty, *Fearful Symmetry*, p. 170; and Basrur, *Minimum Deterrence*, pp. 94–99.

of the crisis, in May and June 2002. The existence of Pakistan's nuclear weapons prevented the Indian government from planning an all-out attack against Pakistan. As former Indian Army Vice Chief of Staff V.K. Sood explains, "India could sever Punjab and Sindh with its conventional forces." He goes on, however, "Pakistan would use nuclear weapons in that scenario." The Indians therefore sought "not to fight for real estate," but rather to "draw Pakistani forces into battle . . . and inflict damage from which Pakistan would take a long time to recover."[44] Thus Pakistan's nuclear weapons did not prevent India from planning for a significant attack against Pakistan proper, but they did ensure that the attack's projected scope would be limited, so as not to threaten Pakistan with catastrophic defeat. In addition, the possibility of nuclear escalation encouraged resolution of the dispute in June and the eventual demobilization of Indian forces, though it was one of several factors contributing to this outcome. As noted above, by exercising restraint the Indians also sought to avoid antagonizing the United States, and incurring high costs in a conventional conflict. And most important, Indian officials believed that their coercive diplomacy had been successful, and that large-scale military pressure on Pakistan was no longer necessary. Thus nuclear weapons' role in limiting the 2001–02 crisis is mixed. In one instance nuclear weapons had little effect, and in another they did help to ameliorate the dispute, though they were not the principal stabilizing factor.

In evaluating nuclear weapons' impact on the 2001–02 crisis, however, one must not overlook their role in fomenting the standoff. The Parakram confrontation resulted from India's large-scale mobilization and associated coercive diplomacy, which in turn was a reaction to an attack on the Indian parliament and an Indian Army installation by Pakistan-backed Kashmiri terrorist groups. The parliament and Kaluchak attacks were part of a broad pattern of Pakistani low-intensity conflict, which, as explained earlier, was promoted by Pakistan's nuclear weapons capacity.[45] Regardless of any stabilizing effects that they may have had later in the 2001–02 dispute, then, nuclear weapons played a central role in instigating the crisis.

---

44. V.K. Sood, interview by author, New Delhi, India, August 2004.
45. This is not to argue that Islamabad was directly involved in the parliament and Kaluchak operations. My point, rather, is that Pakistan nurtured the militant groups behind these and other anti-Indian attacks as part of its strategy of low-intensity conflict in Kashmir. This strategy, in turn, was facilitated by Pakistani nuclear weapons, which insulated Pakistan from all-out Indian retaliation and attracted international attention. Thus the 2001–02 attacks fit a broad pattern of violence stretching back to the late 1980s and were closely linked to Pakistan's nuclear capacity.

Nuclear proliferation thus had a destabilizing effect on South Asia during the period from 1998 to 2002. By encouraging provocative Pakistani behavior and forceful Indian responses, nuclear weapons facilitated the outbreak of the first Indo-Pakistani war in twenty-eight years and the largest-ever South Asian militarized standoff. And although nuclear deterrence did inject a measure of caution into Indian decisionmaking, it was not critical to stabilizing either dispute. Rather, the Kargil war and the 2001–02 crisis failed to escalate primarily as the result of India's concern with international opinion, faith in the success of its coercive diplomacy, and conventional military limitations.

In the next section, I discuss the years 2002 to 2008. This period witnessed an improvement in Indo-Pakistani relations, with a reduction in confrontations and a warming of diplomatic relations between the two countries. Some commentators attribute these developments in part to the pacifying effects of nuclear deterrence. I show, however, that security improvements during this period were modest and that nuclear weapons were not responsible for them. In fact, nuclear weapons triggered strategic developments that could destabilize the subcontinent in the future.

Nuclear Weapons in South Asia, 2002 to 2008

Since the 2001–02 crisis, South Asia has not experienced a large-scale militarized dispute; militant violence in Kashmir has declined; and India and Pakistan have begun a peace dialogue to resolve the Kashmir dispute. Some observers suggest that the pacifying effects of nuclear deterrence have facilitated these changes.[46] Two facts must be kept in mind, however, when evaluating nuclear weapons' role in the recent Indo-Pakistani rapprochement.

First, improvements in Indo-Pakistani relations, though real, have been modest. To reduce tensions in the region, the two sides have adopted a series of confidence-building measures, such as a cross-LoC cease-fire and the restoration of transportation and trade links between Indian and Pakistani Kash-

---

46. See, for example, V.R. Raghavan, "Nuclear Deterrence: An Indian Perspective," presentation at "The Future of Nuclear Deterrence in the North Atlantic Alliance" conference, West Sussex, United Kingdom, October 2006, http://www.delhipolicygroup.com/bulletin26.htm; Lawrence Freedman, "Nuclear Deterrence May Still Have a Role to Play," *Financial Times*, December 1, 2006; Russell J. Leng, "Realpolitik and Learning in the India-Pakistan Rivalry," in T.V. Paul, ed., *The India-Pakistan Conflict: An Enduring Rivalry* (Cambridge: Cambridge University Press, 2005), pp. 126–127; and Praveen Swami, "A War to End a War: The Causes and Outcomes of the 2001–2002 India-Pakistan Crisis," in Sumit Ganguly and S. Paul Kapur, eds., *Nuclear Proliferation in South Asia: Crisis Behaviour and the Bomb* (London: Routledge, 2008).

mir. [47] According to the Indian government, violence in Kashmir has declined; terrorist-related incidents fell by 22 percent from 2004 to 2005, with civilian deaths falling 21 percent and security personnel deaths falling 33 percent. In 2006, terrorist incidents declined an additional 16 percent, killing 30 percent fewer civilians and 20 percent fewer security forces than during the previous year. Despite this progress, the Kashmiri security situation remains tense. One thousand six hundred sixty-seven terrorist incidents occurred in 2006, killing 540 civilians and security personnel. And estimated instances of militant infiltration into Indian territory from Pakistani Kashmir declined only 4 percent from 2005.[48] As a result, hundreds of thousands of Indian security forces remain stationed in Kashmir. According to a senior Indian diplomat closely involved with the Kashmir peace process, "It is difficult to say" how much the Indo-Pakistani security environment has improved. "The Kashmir evidence is mixed," he notes. "Cross-border [militant] traffic reports are not very positive." Meanwhile, the militants have shifted their geographical focus, and are "now coming through Bangladesh with the help of Pakistani agencies. There has been a change in tactics but not a change in attitude."[49] As Indian defense analyst Raj Chengappa puts it, "We are not in a hair-trigger environment anymore. But the situation is still serious."[50]

Second, improvements in Indo-Pakistani relations have not resulted primarily from nuclear deterrence. The Pakistanis reduced their support for anti-Indian militancy for two main reasons. First, in the wake of the terrorist attacks of September 11, 2001, the U.S. government realized that Islamic terrorism was a global problem with direct implications for the United States' own security. The Americans also decided that they needed Pakistan to serve as a leading partner in their new antiterror coalition. Thus, although the United States had previously turned a blind eye toward Pakistani support for militancy in South Asia, it was no longer willing to do so. To serve as an ally in the U.S. antiterrorism effort—thereby avoiding the United States' wrath and enjoying its

47. See Sumit Ganguly, "Will Kashmir Stop India's Rise?" *Foreign Affairs*, Vol. 85, No. 4 (July/August 2006), p. 48; and "India, Pakistan Agree on Opening of New Bus Link, Trade Routes," Press Trust of India, January 18, 2006.
48. Government of India, Ministry of Home Affairs, *Annual Report, 2006–2007*, pp. 6, 143.
49. Senior Indian diplomat, interview by author, New Delhi, India, December 2007.
50. Raj Chengappa, interview by author, New Delhi, India, December 2007. Chengappa is also the managing editor of *India Today*. See also Ganguly, "Will Kashmir Stop India's Rise?" pp. 48–50; Robert G. Wirsing, "Precarious Partnership: Pakistan's Response to U.S. Security Policies," *Asian Affairs: An American Review*, Vol. 30, No. 2 (Summer 2003), p. 74; and Stephen Philip Cohen, "The Jihadist Threat to Pakistan," *Washington Quarterly*, Vol. 26, No. 3 (Summer 2003), p. 14.

financial largesse—the Pakistanis were forced to reduce their support for Islamic insurgents in Kashmir, in some cases going so far as to outlaw militant groups.[51] Second, Pakistani cooperation with the United States alienated Islamic militant organizations, which branded Musharraf a traitor. These groups subsequently turned against the Pakistani government and attempted on multiple occasions to assassinate Musharraf.[52] This led the government to take further measures against the militants, as a matter of self-preservation. Pakistan's reduced support for anti-Indian militancy, then, is not the product of nuclear deterrence. Rather, this policy shift resulted primarily from changes in the international strategic environment after the September 11 terrorist attacks.[53]

The Indians, for their part, have pursued improved relations with Pakistan for two principal reasons, neither of which stems from nuclear deterrence. First, India's main national priority has become continued economic growth, which Indian leaders believe is essential if the country is to reduce poverty, shed its "third-world" status, and join the first rank of nations.[54] Greater prosperity, in turn, has led to rising economic aspirations among the Indian electorate. Indians increasingly expect, as Chengappa puts it, "better jobs, the American dream." Therefore the government seeks "to focus on growth and to keep the peace," rather than squander resources on continued Indo-Pakistani conflict.[55] Second, recent anti-Indian terrorism, such as the 2005 Diwali bomb-

---

51. Pervez Musharraf, *In the Line of Fire: A Memoir* (New York: Free Press, 2006), pp. 201–204; Stephen Philip Cohen, "The Nation and the State of Pakistan," *Washington Quarterly,* Vol. 25, No. 3 (Summer 2002), pp. 115–116; Samina Yasmeen, "Pakistan's Kashmir Policy: Voices of Moderation?" *Contemporary South Asia,* Vol. 12, No. 2 (June 2003), p. 12; Jessie Lloyd and Nathan Nankivell, "India, Pakistan, and the Legacy of September 11," *Cambridge Review of International Affairs,* Vol. 15, No. 2 (July 2002), p. 281; and Wirsing, "Precarious Partnership," pp. 71–72. Since 2002 Pakistan has received $1.9 billion in U.S. security assistance and $2.4 billion in U.S. economic aid. See Richard A. Boucher, *U.S. Foreign Assistance to Pakistan,* testimony before the Senate Committee on Foreign Relations Subcommittee on International Development, Foreign Economic Affairs and International Environmental Protection, 110th Cong., 1st sess., December 6, 2007.
52. Yasmeen, "Pakistan's Kashmir Policy," pp. 12, 15; and Katherine Butler, "Toppling Musharraf: Heat Rises on Pakistani Leader," *Independent,* February 20, 2006. On the assassination attempts, see Musharraf, *In the Line of Fire,* pp. 244–262.
53. Vali Nasr, "Military Rule, Islamism, and Democracy in Pakistan," *Middle East Journal,* Vol. 58, No. 2 (Spring 2004), p. 202.
54. Indian gross domestic product growth jumped from 5.6 percent to 8.4 percent between 1990 and 2005, and is likely to continue above 8 percent in 2008. See S. Paul Kapur and Sumit Ganguly, "The Transformation of U.S.-India Relations: An Explanation for the Rapprochement and Prospects for the Future," *Asian Survey,* Vol. 47, No. 4 (July/August 2007), pp. 648–649.
55. Chengappa, interview by author. See also "India-Pakistan: Understanding the Conflict Dynamics," speech by Foreign Secretary Shivshankar Menon at Jamia Millia Islamia, April 11, 2007; "Pranab for Peace with Pak," *Statesman,* October 26, 2006; and "Terror Threatens S. Asia: Growth Undermined and Health Care and Education Robbed of Funds, Says PM Singh," *Straits Times* (Singapore), August 16, 2006.

ings in New Delhi and the 2006 train bombings in Mumbai, has been less pro-vocative than previous attacks, such as the parliament assault.[56] The Indians therefore have opted for restraint despite ongoing violence. If a provocation on the scale of the parliament attack were to occur, however, India might well launch a major militarized response, regardless of Pakistan's possession of nu-clear weapons.[57] Indeed, Indian leaders continue to believe, as they did during the Kargil conflict and the 2001–02 crisis, that India could engage Pakistan in large-scale conventional combat without starting a nuclear war. Like Pakistan, then, India's pursuit of improved Indo-Pakistani relations has not resulted from nuclear deterrence. Rather, it is the product primarily of shifting domes-tic priorities and nonnuclear strategic calculations.

Although the 2002–08 period has not seen terrorism on the scale of the par-liament attack, Indian strategists, deeply affected by the Parakram experience, are preparing for the possibility of such an occurrence. As I explain below, these preparations may exacerbate regional security-dilemma dynamics, in-creasing the likelihood of conflict. Thus not only have nuclear weapons had lit-tle to do with the current Indo-Pakistani rapprochement; by facilitating past disputes, nuclear weapons have unleashed strategic developments that may destabilize South Asia well into the future.

Nuclear Weapons and Future Instability

As noted above, nuclear weapons facilitated provocative Pakistani behavior in the wake of the 1998 tests, thereby triggering major Indo-Pakistani crises such as the Kargil conflict and the 2001–02 standoff. Significantly, the effect of these

---

56. The Diwali bombings killed approximately 60 people on the eve of a major Hindu religious festival. Indian authorities blamed the attacks on the Pakistan-backed militant group Lashkar-e-Taiba. See Amelia Gentleman, "Delhi Police Say Suspect Was Attack Mastermind," *International Herald Tribune*, November 13, 2005. The Mumbai bombings killed approximately 180 people in railway stations and aboard commuter trains. Indian authorities blamed the Lashkar-e-Taiba and Jaish-e-Mohammed, as well as the Students Islamic Movement of India, for the attacks. See "LeT, JeM, SIMI Helped Execute Terror Plan," *Times of India*, October 1, 2006. Although the Delhi and Mumbai bombings were more deadly, the parliament and Kaluchak attacks were widely viewed as a greater national affront, as they targeted the foremost symbol of the Indian state as well as the family members of Indian military personnel.
57. Senior Indian diplomat closely involved with the Indo-Pakistani peace process, interview by author, December 2007; senior U.S. military officials, interviews by author, New Delhi, India, De-cember 2007 and May 2005; Michael Krepon, "The Meaning of the Mumbai Blasts" (Washington, D.C.: Henry L. Stimson Center, August 7, 2006); Walter Andersen, "The Indo-Pakistani Powder Keg," *Globe and Mail*, July 19, 2006; and John H. Gill, "India and Pakistan: A Shift in the Military Calculus?" in Ashley J. Tellis and Michael Wills, eds., *Strategic Asia, 2005–2006: Military Moderniza-tion in an Era of Uncertainty* (Washington, D.C.: National Bureau of Asian Research, 2005), p. 266.

crises has not been limited to the past; they have had a profound effect on current Indian strategic thinking, inspiring an aggressive shift in India's conventional military posture. This could increase the likelihood of serious Indo-Pakistani conflict in years to come.

India has long enjoyed conventional military superiority over Pakistan.[58] This advantage has been mitigated, however, by India's peacetime deployment of offensive forces deep in the interior of the country, far from the Indo-Pakistani border. As a result, Indian forces were slow to mobilize against the Pakistanis, requiring several weeks before launching a large-scale offensive.[59] This gave Pakistan time to prepare its defenses and ward off any impending Indian attack. It also allowed the international community to bring diplomatic pressure to bear on India's civilian leadership, thereby preventing it from launching military action.

Many Indian military leaders believe that this mobilization problem prevented India from acting decisively during the 2001–02 crisis. By the time Indian forces were prepared to move against Pakistan, the Pakistanis were able to ready their defenses, making a potential Indian attack far more costly. Most important, the Indians' slowness enabled the United States to pressure the Indian government, convincing it to abandon plans to strike Pakistan. Thus, in the words of a prominent Indian defense writer, Operation Parakram demonstrated that India's "mobilization strategy was completely flawed."[60] In addition, the government's restraint caused rancor within the armed forces. Senior officers believed that civilian leaders misused the military, ordering it to undertake a long and costly deployment and then opting for retreat, leaving the Pakistanis unpunished. As a senior U.S. defense official stationed in New Delhi puts it, Indian commanders "were frustrated. . . . They really wanted to go after Pakistan but couldn't."[61]

To prevent a recurrence of Parakram's failures, the Indians began to formulate a new "Cold Start" military doctrine, which will enable India to rapidly

---

58. See Anthony H. Cordesman, *The India-Pakistan Military Balance* (Washington, D.C.: Center for Strategic and International Studies, 2002); Ashley J. Tellis, *Stability in South Asia* (Santa Monica, Calif.: RAND, 1997); and Kapur, *Dangerous Deterrent*, pp. 50–53.
59. Tellis, *Stability in South Asia*, pp. 20–21; and Gurmeet Kanwal, director, Center for Land Warfare Studies, interview by author, New Delhi, India, December 2007.
60. Sundeep Unnithan, assistant editor of *India Today*, interview by author, New Delhi, India, December 2007.
61. Senior U.S. defense official, interview by author, U.S. embassy, New Delhi, India, December 2007. For critical analyses of Parakram, see, for example, Sood and Sawhney, *Operation Parakram*; and Praveen Swami, "Beating the Retreat," *Frontline*, Vol. 19, No. 22 (October 26–November 8, 2002), http://www.frontlineonnet.com/fl1922/stories/20021108007101200.htm.

launch a large-scale attack against Pakistan. The doctrine will augment the offensive capabilities of India's traditionally defensive holding formations located close to the Indo-Pakistani border. It also will eventually shift offensive forces from their current locations in the Indian hinterland to bases closer to Pakistan. Within 72 to 96 hours of a mobilization order, Cold Start would send three to five division-sized integrated battle groups (IBGs) consisting of armor, mechanized infantry, and artillery roughly 20–80 kilometers into Pakistan along the breadth of the Indo-Pakistani border. The IBGs would aggressively engage Pakistani forces and seize a long, shallow swath of Pakistani territory. Cold Start seeks to achieve three goals: to inflict significant attrition on enemy forces; to retain Pakistani territory for use as a postconflict bargaining chip; and, by limiting the depth of Indian incursions, to avoid triggering a Pakistani strategic nuclear response. Indian military planners hope that these doctrinal changes, coupled with India's growing conventional military capabilities,[62] will result in a more nimble force that is able to prevent a repetition of Operation Parakram's shortcomings.[63]

Cold Start is currently in its nascent stages.[64] The doctrine's continued development and implementation, however, will likely have two major ef-

---

62. From 2001 to 2006, the Indian defense budget increased by 60 percent, from $13.81 billion to $22.1 billion. In the coming five years, India is forecast to spend up to $40 billion on weapons procurement, including fighter aircraft, artillery, submarines, and armor. See Jane's World Defense Industry, "JWDI Briefing: India's Defence Industry" (Surrey, U.K.: Jane's Information Group, September 18, 2007); and Heather Timmons and Somini Sengupta, "Building a Modern Arsenal in India," *New York Times*, August 31, 2007. See also Rodney W. Jones, "Conventional Military and Strategic Stability in South Asia," South Asian Strategic Stability Unit, Research Paper, No. 1 (London: South Asian Strategic Stability Institute, March 2005).
63. This brief overview does not purport fully to explain the complexities of India's Cold Start doctrine. It draws on the following sources: interviews by author in New Delhi in December 2007 with several of Cold Start's intellectual architects, including Vijay Oberoi, former army training command director and army vice chief of staff; Arun Sahgal, head of the Center for Strategic Studies and Simulation, United Service Institution of India, and member of Indian National Security Council Task Force on Net Assessment and Simulation; Gurmeet Kanwal, director of the Center for Land Warfare Studies; and senior U.S. defense officials. See also Col. Amarjit Singh, "Strategy and Doctrine: A Case for Convergence," presentation at the Centre for Strategic Studies and Simulation, United Service Institution of India, New Delhi, 2007; Walter C. Ladwig III, "A Cold Start for Hot Wars? An Assessment of the Indian Army's New Limited War Doctrine," *International Security*, Vol. 32, No. 3 (Winter 2007/08), pp. 158–190; Subhash Kapila, "India's New 'Cold Start' War Doctrine Strategically Reviewed: Parts I and II," No. 991 and No. 1013 (Noida, India: South Asia Analysis Group Papers, May 4, 2004, and June 1, 2004); and Tariq M. Ashraf, "Doctrinal Reawakening of the Indian Armed Forces," *Military Review*, November–December 2004, pp. 53–62.
64. Indian planners will have to overcome a number of organizational and resource-related obstacles before they can fully implement Cold Start. See Ladwig, "A Cold Start for Hot Wars?" pp. 159, 175–190.

fects. First, it will probably exacerbate regional security-dilemma dynamics. Pakistan has always been a deeply insecure state, militarily outmatched by India, lacking strategic depth, and suffering from domestic instability. The Pakistanis could previously expect India's lengthy mobilization schedule to mitigate its military advantages. In the future, however, this may not be the case. As a result, Pakistan will have to maintain a higher state of readiness,[65] and will face incentives to offset Indian strategic advances through increased arms racing and asymmetric warfare. Such behavior could trigger aggressive Indian responses, which would further heighten Pakistani insecurity. These dynamics could undermine recent improvements in Indo-Pakistani relations and increase the probability of crises between the two countries.

Second, Indian doctrinal changes increase the likelihood that Indo-Pakistani crises will escalate rapidly, both within the conventional sphere and from the conventional to the nuclear level. In the conventional realm, Cold Start will enable Indian forces to attack Pakistan quickly, pushing an Indo-Pakistani dispute from the level of political crisis to outright conflict before the Indian government can be deterred from launching an offensive. Vijay Oberoi explains that the decision to attack Pakistan would require "a certain amount of political will. But [Cold Start] makes that political will more likely to be there, since now we can mobilize before world opinion comes down on political leaders and prevents them from acting."[66]

In the nuclear realm, India's Cold Start doctrine would likely force Pakistan to rely more heavily on its strategic deterrent. Brig. Gen. Khawar Hanif, Pakistan's defense attaché to the United States, argues that Cold Start will create a "greater justification for Pakistani nuclear weapons" and may increase the danger of nuclear use. "The wider the conventional asymmetry," he maintains, "the lower the nuclear threshold between India and Pakistan. To the extent that India widens the conventional asymmetry through military spending and aggressive doctrinal changes, the nuclear threshold will get lower." Maj. Gen. Muhammad Mustafa Khan, director-general (analysis) of Pakistan's Inter-Services Intelligence agency, similarly argues that Cold Start "is destabilizing; it is meant to circumvent nuclear deterrence and warning time," and "it is entirely Pakistan-specific." "This will force us to undertake countermeasures," he continues, "and if it becomes too threatening we will have to rely on

65. Ashraf, "Doctrinal Reawakening," p. 59.
66. Oberoi, interview by author. See also "Cold Start to New Doctrine," *Times of India*, April 14, 2004.

our nuclear capability."[67] Thus Cold Start may erode the firebreak between conventional and nuclear conflict on the subcontinent.

The Indians reportedly anticipate such an outcome at the tactical level and are preparing to fight through Pakistani battlefield nuclear strikes.[68] Indian strategists dismiss the possibility of a Pakistani nuclear response against India proper, however. Rather, they maintain that India can calibrate its attack, stopping short of Pakistan's strategic nuclear thresholds and waiting for international diplomatic intervention to end the conflict. As Gurmeet Kanwal explains, "We war-game this all the time, and we do not trip their [strategic] red lines." According to Arun Sahgal, Cold Start "will give Pakistan no option but to bring down its nuclear thresholds. But this shouldn't really worry us. We don't think Pakistan will cross the nuclear Rubicon."[69]

Given the uncertainties that would be inherent in a large-scale Indo-Pakistani conflict, however, such a benign outcome is not guaranteed. For example, an unexpectedly rapid and extensive Indian victory, or failure to achieve a quick diplomatic resolution to the conflict, could result in a far more extreme Pakistani response than the Indians currently anticipate. Thus India's planning for a carefully controlled limited war with Pakistan could prove to be overly optimistic. As a senior U.S. defense official familiar with Cold Start worries, the Indians "think that they can fight three or four days, and the international community will stop it. And they believe that they can fight through a nuclear exchange. But there are unintended consequences. Calibrate a conventional war and nuclear exchange with Pakistan? It doesn't work that way."[70]

Significantly, a large-scale Indo-Pakistani crisis could erupt even without a deliberate decision by the Pakistani government to provoke India. The Islamist forces that the Pakistanis have nurtured in recent decades have taken on a life of their own and do not always act at Islamabad's behest. Indeed, they often behave in ways inimical to Pakistani interests, such as launching attacks on Pakistani security forces, government officials, and political figures.[71] If these

---

67. Brig. Gen. Khawar Hanif and Maj. Gen. Muhammad Mustafa Khan, interviews by author, Monterey, California, June 2007. See also Shaukat Qadir, "Cold Start: The Nuclear Side," *Daily Times* (Lahore), May 16, 2004; and Ladwig, "A Cold Start for Hot Wars?" p. 10.
68. Unnithan and senior U.S. defense official, interviews by author; and Kapila, "India's New 'Cold Start' War Doctrine Strategically Reviewed."
69. Kanwal and Sahgal, interviews by author.
70. Senior U.S. defense official, interview by author. See also Ladwig, "A Cold Start for Hot Wars?" pp. 10–14; Gill, "India and Pakistan," p. 266; and Cohen, "The Jihadist Threat to Pakistan," p. 12.
71. Benazir Bhutto's December 2007 assassination is a case in point. See Mark Mazzetti, "C.I.A. Sees Qaeda Link in the Death of Bhutto," *New York Times*, January 19, 2008.

entities were to stage an operation similar to the 2001 parliament attack, India could hold the Pakistani government responsible, whether or not Islamabad was behind the operation.[72] And with a doctrine that would enable rapid mobilization, India's military response could be far more extensive, and more dangerous, than it was during the 2001–02 crisis.

By facilitating the outbreak of serious Indo-Pakistani crises in the past, then, nuclear weapons have inspired strategic developments that will make the outbreak and rapid escalation of regional crises more likely in the future. Thus nuclear weapons proliferation not only destabilized South Asia in the first decade since the 1998 tests; proliferation is also likely to increase dangers on the subcontinent in years to come.

Conclusion

In the first decade after the Indo-Pakistani nuclear tests, South Asia managed to avoid a nuclear or full-scale conventional war. This does not mean, however, that nuclear proliferation has stabilized the region. In fact, nuclear weapons have played an important role in destabilizing the subcontinent. Nuclear proliferation encouraged the outbreak of the first Indo-Pakistani war in twenty-eight years as well as the eruption of South Asia's largest-ever militarized standoff, and played only a minor role in these crises' resolution. It has little to do with the current thaw in Indo-Pakistani relations. And it has triggered strategic developments that could threaten the region's stability well into the future.

Although I have argued in this article against the claims of proliferation optimists, my findings suggest that both optimistic and pessimistic scholars largely ignore one of nuclear weapons proliferation's most pressing dangers. Proliferation optimists downplay proliferation risks by maintaining that the leaders of new nuclear states are neither irrational nor suicidal. Therefore, these scholars argue, new nuclear states will behave responsibly, avoiding overly provocative actions for fear of triggering a devastating response.[73] Pessimists, by contrast, emphasize problems such as organizational pathologies,

---

72. See Yasmeen, "Pakistan's Kashmir Policy," p. 15; Gill, "India and Pakistan," p. 266; and "Jihad and the State of Pakistan," *Friday Times* (Lahore), March 2, 2007. See also Steve Coll, "The Stand-off: How Jihadi Groups Helped Provoke the Twenty-first Century's First Nuclear Crisis," *New Yorker*, February 13, 2006, pp. 126–139.
73. See, for example, Kenneth N. Waltz, "Waltz Responds to Sagan," in Sagan and Waltz, *The Spread of Nuclear Weapons*, pp. 131–132.

arguing that these factors will result in suboptimal decisionmaking and dangerous behavior by new nuclear states.[74]

The decade since the South Asian nuclear tests, however, suggests that a principal risk of nuclear proliferation is not that the leaders of new nuclear states will be irrational or suicidal, or even that organizational and other pathologies will result in suboptimal policy formulation. The danger, rather, is that leaders may weigh their strategic options and reasonably conclude that risky behavior best serves their interests. Nuclear weapons do enable Pakistan, as a conventionally weak, dissatisfied power, to challenge the territorial status quo with less fear of an all-out Indian military response. Ensuing crises do attract international attention potentially useful to the Pakistanis' cause. And forceful retaliation does enable India to defeat specific Pakistani challenges, while offering it a possible means of deterring future Pakistani adventurism. Thus, given their military capabilities and territorial preferences, India's and Pakistan's recent behavior has not been unreasonable. But even if these policies make sense from the two countries' own strategic perspectives, they are nonetheless dangerous, creating a significant risk of catastrophic escalation. Thus nuclear proliferation could have dire consequences even if new nuclear states behave in a largely rational manner.

This finding has implications not just in South Asia but also beyond the region, including for potential proliferators such as Iran. According to the optimists' logic, because the Iranians are neither irrational nor bent on suicide, the international community should not be inordinately fearful of an Iranian nuclear capability. One need not believe that Iranian leaders seek their own country's destruction, however, to worry that Iran's acquisition of nuclear weapons could pose significant dangers. If the Iranians decided to use their nuclear capability in a manner similar to the Pakistanis, they could increase their support for terrorism, or even engage in outright conventional aggression, to challenge objectionable territorial or political arrangements while insulated from large-scale U.S. or Israeli retaliation. Such behavior would not be irrational if a state were committed to destabilizing its adversaries, extending its influence, and undermining the territorial status quo. But it would be extremely dangerous and detrimental to the interests of the international community.[75]

Nuclear optimists such as Barry Posen, "judging from cold war history," ar-

---

74. See, for example, Scott D. Sagan, "Sagan Responds to Waltz," in Sagan and Waltz, *The Spread of Nuclear Weapons*, pp. 157–158.
75. Scott D. Sagan voices similar concerns about a nuclear Iran. They are, however, based more on organizational shortcomings such as weak state control over military, intelligence, and scientific

gue that "while it's possible that Iranian leaders would think this way, it's equally possible that they would be more cautious." Thus, they conclude, the world "can live with a nuclear Iran."[76] Judging from the vantage point of recent South Asian history, however, the situation could be considerably more dangerous than optimistic scholars suggest. If the Iranians assess their strategic interests in a manner similar to the Pakistanis, they are unlikely to behave cautiously upon acquiring nuclear weapons. Instead they will adopt risky policies that have destabilizing effects similar to those in South Asia. As I have argued, although India and Pakistan have so far managed to resolve resulting crises without catastrophe, this outcome has in no way been guaranteed. Nor, unfortunately, will benign outcomes be guaranteed in future confrontations— either in South Asia or among newly nuclear states elsewhere in the world.

establishments than on states' rational calculations of their strategic interest. See Sagan, "How to Keep the Bomb from Iran," *Foreign Affairs*, Vol. 85, No. 5 (September/October 2006), pp. 45–59.
76. Barry R. Posen, "We Can Live with a Nuclear Iran," *New York Times*, February 27, 2006.

Part III:
Giving Up the Bomb?

The Rise and Fall of the South African Bomb

Peter Liberman

South Africa built six nuclear weapons in the 1970s and 1980s and then scrapped them in 1990–91.[1] As one of the few states to produce nuclear weapons and the only one to dismantle an indigenous arsenal, the South African case presents a rare opportunity to study the causes of nuclear acquisition and disarmament. This article examines the political history of the South African bomb and the light it sheds on three general sources of nuclear weapons policy: security incentives, organizational politics, and international pressure along with state sensitivity to such pressure. It is based on published research as well as dozens of interviews with South African nuclear policymakers.

Official South African accounts and some scholarly studies stress the changing security threat to South Africa as the mainspring behind the nuclear weapons program's development and ultimate demise.[2] Although the militarization and dismantlement of the program did coincide with the vicissitudes of threats

Peter Liberman is Associate Professor of Political Science, Queens College, City University of New York.

I am grateful for helpful comments and criticisms on earlier drafts by David Albright, Michael Barletta, Richard Betts, Avner Cohen, Neta Crawford, David Fig, David Fischer, Jeffrey Knopf, Leonard Markovitz, Andrew Marquard, Jeremy Seekings, Etel Solingen, Waldo Stumpf, and James Walsh. Robert Windrem generously shared ideas and documents. Also invaluable have been supporting grants from the Carnegie Corporation of New York, the Smith Richardson Foundation, and the City University of New York PSC-CUNY Research Award Program. Earlier versions of this article were presented at a May 1999 seminar at the Center for International Security and Cooperation at Stanford University, and at the annual meeting of the American Political Science Association, Atlanta, Georgia, September 2–5, 1999.

1. Interview-based studies following the March 1993 disclosure of the program include David Albright, "South Africa and the Affordable Bomb," *Bulletin of the Atomic Scientists*, Vol. 50, No. 4 (July–August 1994), pp. 37–47; Mark Hibbs, "South Africa's Secret Nuclear Program: From a PNE to Deterrent," *Nuclear Fuel*, May 10, 1993, pp. 3–6; Mark Hibbs, "South Africa's Secret Nuclear Program: The Dismantling," *Nuclear Fuel*, May 24, 1993, pp. 9–13; Frank V. Pabian, "South Africa's Nuclear Weapon Program: Lessons for Nonproliferation Policy," *Nonproliferation Review*, Vol. 3, No. 1 (Fall 1995), pp. 1–19; Mitchell Reiss, *Bridled Ambition: Why Countries Constrain Their Nuclear Capabilities* (Washington, D.C.: Woodrow Wilson Center Press, 1995), pp. 7–44; and an article by a South African nuclear energy official who reviewed the documents, Waldo Stumpf, "South Africa's Nuclear Weapons Program: From Deterrence to Dismantlement," *Arms Control Today*, Vol. 25, No. 10 (December–January 1995/96), pp. 3–8.
2. William J. Long and Suzette R. Grillot, "Ideas, Beliefs, and Nuclear Policies: The Cases of South Africa and Ukraine," *Nonproliferation Review*, Vol. 7, No. 1 (Spring 2000), pp. 24–40; T.V. Paul, *Power versus Prudence: Why Nations Forgo Nuclear Weapons* (Montreal: McGill-Queen's University Press, 2000), pp. 113–117; and Bradley A. Thayer, "The Causes of Nuclear Proliferation and the Utility of the Nuclear Nonproliferation Regime," *Security Studies*, Vol. 4, No. 3 (Spring 1995), pp. 494–495.

International Security, Vol. 26, No. 2 (Fall 2001), pp. 45–86
© 2001 by the President and Fellows of Harvard College and the Massachusetts Institute of Technology.

to South Africa, the state did not face the kind of nuclear coercion or conventional invasion threats commonly thought to trigger nuclear weapons programs.[3] International ostracism of South Africa because of its policy of apartheid certainly exacerbated its insecurity, and isolated states are often prime candidates for nuclear acquisition.[4] But South Africa remained militarily predominant in southern Africa, and Soviet or Soviet-backed aggression was a remote possibility. Moreover, nuclear weapons would have provided only a limited remedy to this threat, even had it materialized.[5]

These weaknesses of the security explanation have led some observers to conclude that domestic politics drove South African nuclear weapons policies. One general domestic explanation for nuclear proliferation, derived from organizational politics theory, is that influential science, energy, and armament complexes spur nuclear acquisition.[6] Heads of state are likely to dominate decisionmaking on policies with such dramatic diplomatic, security, and budgetary ramifications. But scientists' rarefied expertise, particularly when combined with internal secrecy over nuclear policies, gives them extraordinary informational advantages in political debates.[7]

The South African nuclear science agency did have a vested interest in a nuclear explosives research program, as did the armaments agency—but not the

3. Benjamin Frankel, "The Brooding Shadow: Systemic Incentives and Nuclear Weapons Proliferation," *Security Studies*, Vol. 2, Nos. 3/4 (Spring/Summer 1993), pp. 37–78; and Thayer, "Causes of Nuclear Proliferation."
4. Richard K. Betts, "Paranoids, Pygmies, Pariahs, and Nonproliferation Revisited," *Security Studies*, Vol. 2, Nos. 3/4 (Spring/Summer 1993), pp. 100–124; Steve Chan, "Incentives for Nuclear Proliferation: The Case of International Pariahs," *Journal of Strategic Studies*, Vol. 3, No. 1 (May 1980), pp. 26–43; and Robert E. Harkavy, "Pariah States and Nuclear Proliferation," *International Organization*, Vol. 35, No. 1 (Winter 1981), pp. 135–163.
5. The insecurity explanation for nuclear acquisition is derived from balance-of-power theory, which also predicts that states will adopt more-or-less rational strategies within their resource and informational constraints. See Barry R. Posen, *The Sources of Military Doctrine: France, Britain, and Germany between the World Wars* (Ithaca, N.Y.: Cornell University Press, 1984), pp. 59–79.
6. Steven Flank, "Exploding the Black Box: The Historical Sociology of Nuclear Proliferation," *Security Studies*, Vol. 3, No. 2 (Winter 1993/94), pp. 259–294; and Peter R. Lavoy, "Nuclear Myths and the Causes of Nuclear Proliferation," *Security Studies*, Vol. 2, Nos. 3/4 (Spring/Summer 1993), pp. 192–212. For theoretical underpinnings, see Morton H. Halperin, *Bureaucratic Politics and Foreign Policy* (Washington, D.C.: Brookings, 1974).
7. Nuclear secrecy (or "opacity") has many possible origins: fear of precipitating arms races or preventive attack, prior bureaucratic turf struggles, and international nonproliferation pressures. Whatever the reason, keeping potential bureaucratic opponents—such as foreign or finance ministries—in the dark about nuclear issues makes it harder, in some cases impossible, for them to mobilize opposition. See Avner Cohen and Benjamin Frankel, "Opaque Nuclear Proliferation," *Journal of Strategic Studies*, Vol. 13, No. 3 (September 1990), pp. 13–43; and Thayer, "Causes of Nuclear Proliferation," pp. 508–517.

military—in weaponization and delivery systems. Their high prestige helped them make their case to Prime Minister B.J. "John" Vorster in an environment of secrecy that minimized dissent. But it is unclear whether he needed much persuading. Defense Minister P.W. Botha's interest in the program and his reliance on an informal military adviser are somewhat inconsistent with an organizational explanation. The decision to dismantle the program, orchestrated by President F.W. de Klerk and supported by nuclear science officials, also runs counter to organizational politics expectations.[8]

A third general source of nuclear weapons policies are international nonsecurity incentives, mediated by states' varied sensitivities to such incentives. The superpowers' initial nuclear monopoly glamorized joining the nuclear club, for example, but later international antiproliferation sanctions and ostracism raised the costs of going nuclear.[9] Even after the advent of the Nuclear Nonproliferation Treaty (NPT) regime, however, some governing elites continued to see reputational, political, and economic rewards in defying international pressure. Etel Solingen has argued that the economic orientation of nuclear "fence-sitters," states that have neither joined the NPT nor overtly joined the nuclear club, colors their sensitivity to international pressure.[10] According to Solingen, economic liberalizers (including politicians and interest groups as well as government agencies) dislike the budgetary burden and po-

---

8. The title of the South African head of government changed from prime minister to president in the 1984 constitution.

9. On nuclear possession norms, see Scott D. Sagan, "Why Do States Build Nuclear Weapons? Three Models in Search of a Bomb," *International Security*, Vol. 21, No. 3 (Winter 1996/97), pp. 73–85. See also Itty Abraham, *The Making of the Indian Atomic Bomb: Science, Secrecy, and the Postcolonial State* (London: Zed, 1998); Stephen M. Meyer, *The Dynamics of Nuclear Proliferation* (Chicago: University of Chicago Press, 1984), pp. 50–55, 72, 91–111; and Thayer, "Causes of Nuclear Proliferation," pp. 468–474. On the application and effectiveness of economic sanctions against proliferators, which have been quite uneven, see Glenn Chafetz, "The Political Psychology of the Nuclear Nonproliferation Regime," *Journal of Politics*, Vol. 57, No. 3 (August 1995), pp. 743–775; Peter Clausen, *Nonproliferation and the National Interest: America's Response to the Spread of Nuclear Weapons* (New York: HarperCollins, 1993); Daniel Morrow and Michael Carriere, "The Economic Impacts of the 1998 Sanctions on India and Pakistan," *Nonproliferation Review*, Vol. 6, No. 4 (Fall 1999), pp. 1–16; and T.V. Paul, "Strengthening the Non-Proliferation Regime: The Role of Coercive Sanctions," *International Journal*, Vol. 51, No. 2 (Spring 1996), pp. 440–465. I bundle normative with economic pressure here because they were applied in parallel to South Africa, and because the political economy theory examined below suggests that state sensitivities to both NPT norms and trade linkages are shaped by common factors.

10. Etel Solingen, "The Political Economy of Nuclear Restraint," *International Security*, Vol. 19, No. 2 (Fall 1994), pp. 126–169. For a broader application of the theory, see Etel Solingen, *Regional Orders at Century's Dawn: Global and Domestic Influences on Grand Strategy* (Princeton, N.J.: Princeton University Press, 1998).

litical influence of state arms and energy complexes. Liberalizers also see nuclear restraint as a means to international approval, aid, and trade. In contrast, nationalist-statist governments more readily flout international norms and risk sanctions because they care less about international finance and trade, because they gain domestic political support from state enterprises, and because they see symbolic political benefits in defying foreign demands.

In the case of South Africa, changes in state sensitivity to international sanctions and norms did correlate roughly with changes in nuclear policy. In the 1970s and 1980s, South Africa was subjected to an escalating battery of nuclear sanctions culminating in near-excommunication from Western nuclear suppliers, markets, and scientific forums. South Africa had considerable nuclear self-sufficiency, however, and what little potential leverage the sanctions had was blunted by their linkage to apartheid until de Klerk resolved to abandon it. De Klerk's 1989 ascent to the presidency also represented a liberalizing departure from the National Party's nationalist-statist ideology, so the case is consistent with Solingen's hypothesis that liberalizers are more acquiescent to NPT pressures than are nationalist-statists.

Although this case study finds important new South African evidence for each of the three general sources of nuclear weapons policy, it does not establish a clear causal priority among the theories. Fragmentary and sometimes conflicting participant recollections and the lack of a documentary record still impede a clear understanding of the roots of the program. In addition, likely causal factors—South Africa's security environment, apartheid policies, and political leadership—changed almost simultaneously, making it difficult to differentiate which matches best the timing of South African policy shifts. But viewing the South African case through the lenses of these three theories highlights new theory-relevant evidence as well as potential avenues for future research that might help solve remaining puzzles.

This article, focused as it is on these three theories, does not attempt to provide a comprehensive history of the South African nuclear weapons program. But I do report here some newly disclosed details that, though not critical to understanding the sources of South African nuclear weapons policy, contribute to the broader historical record. They include details about the delivery system, a video-guided glide bomb, and the nuclear strategy's development and last-resort threat of battlefield use.

I turn first to the South African decision to build nuclear weapons, beginning with a thumbnail overview and then providing more detail relevant to each theory. I repeat this analysis for the demise of the program, and conclude with a summary of my findings and their theoretical and policy relevance.

The Decision to Build Nuclear Weapons

South Africa began its nuclear enrichment and explosives research as civilian programs apparently aimed, at least primarily, at commercial uses. Pinpointing the date and causes of the shift to a weapons program is difficult, due in large part to limited evidence about the leadership's thinking, but also perhaps to the incremental nature of the shift. It is possible that the decision was taken as early as 1974, but clear evidence of the program's militarization appears only in 1977. Because South Africa's threat environment worsened in the mid-1970s, a decision to acquire nuclear weapons before 1975 would be harder to explain as a consequence of military insecurity than a decision to do so afterward. The significance and quickened pace of militarization decisions from 1977 to 1979 is consistent with a security explanation, as are the recollections of the interview subjects most informed about the program, although the limited utility of nuclear deterrence for South Africa's security problems and the lack of a coherent strategy at the time are not.

Organizational politics theory best explains the development of a latent weapons capability in the early 1970s, while South Africa's security environment was still very benign. Strategic incoherence and the timing of the weaponization decision are also consistent with organizational politics, because a secret weapons program was the South African Atomic Energy Board's best justification for continuing nuclear explosives research after international condemnation in 1977 precluded further work on peaceful nuclear explosives (PNEs). The Atomic Energy Board (AEB) had the advantage of tight secrecy in managing internal debate, as well as direct access to the prime minister. But it lacked powerful bureaucratic allies; the military was excluded and uninformed, though its threat inflation may have had an indirect impact on nuclear policy. Less consistent with an organizational explanation is the fact that the decision to build a nuclear arsenal was taken with great interest and control by the political leadership. Although initial strategic analysis was limited, it was performed not by the AEB but by Defense Minister P.W. Botha's personal military adviser, Army Brig. John Huyser, suggesting that the process was driven from above rather than from below.

South Africa faced moderate material and reputational incentives for nuclear restraint in this period. Western pressure against nuclear testing was intense following the August 1977 discovery of the South African test site in the Kalahari Desert, and the 1978 U.S. Nuclear Nonproliferation Act threatened to starve South Africa's nuclear power industry of fuel. The government's nationalist-statist cast might have predisposed it to defiance and self-sufficiency. But more important was the simultaneous international ostracism of South Africa over its apartheid policies, which convinced the South African government that joining the NPT would provide no relief from nuclear sanctions.

DATING THE DECISION

Dating the South African decision to build nuclear bombs remains difficult. Officials involved in the program contend that the initial nuclear explosives research and development program was aimed at commercial PNE applications such as digging harbors and oil storage cavities.[11] In 1971 the minister of mines approved an AEB recommendation made the previous year to develop PNEs.[12] South Africa's large mining industry, the U.S. Plowshares Program (which had been promoting commercial PNE applications globally during the 1960s), and a large Soviet PNE program gave the idea a veneer of commercial and diplomatic viability.[13] Nonetheless, the program was classified secret almost from the very start.

Of course, the South African leadership knew that a successful PNE program would generate a de facto nuclear weapons capability. Its abstention from the NPT, its approval of the program despite the diplomatic and economic drawbacks of PNEs, and its decision to maintain tight secrecy on the program might all seem to suggest that nuclear weapons were always the intended goal. Indeed, the fact that its pilot enrichment plant (the Y-plant, located at the Pelindaba Nuclear Research Center near Pretoria) was designed to

---

11. Interviews with W.L. Grant, Pretoria, January 28, 1999; and André Buys, Pretoria, August 25, 1999. See also Stumpf, "South Africa's Nuclear Weapons Program," p. 4.

12. The AEB's 1970 proposal recommended the development of gun-type, implosion, boosted fission, and thermonuclear PNE designs; paper studies on the last of these were approved later, in 1973. Telephone conversation with David Albright, May 30, 2001.

13. Interview with Buys. On U.S. and other PNE programs, see Trevor Findlay, *Nuclear Dynamite: The Peaceful Nuclear Explosions Fiasco* (Rushcutters Bay: Brassey's Australia, 1990); Paul R. Josephson, *Red Atom: Russia's Nuclear Power Program from Stalin to Today* (New York: W.H. Freeman, 2000), pp. 243–250; and Vladislav Larin and Eugeny Tar, "A Legacy of Contamination: The Soviet Union's Peaceful Nuclear Explosions," *Bulletin of the Atomic Scientists*, Vol. 55, No. 3 (May–June 1999), pp. 18–20.

produce weapons-grade uranium suggests to some observers that Vorster had already decided by 1969 or 1970—when plans for the plant were finalized—to acquire a nuclear deterrent of some kind.[14] Although this endeavor was ostensibly aimed at commercial uranium enrichment, drawing on South Africa's vast uranium ore and cheap coal energy resources, the technology turned out to be too energy-intensive to be competitive.[15] Pretoria's public objection to the NPT at the time—that it wanted to protect its unique enrichment technology from International Atomic Energy Agency (IAEA) inspectors—was an argument also heard from other nonnuclear weapon states in the enrichment business.[16]

The AEB never conducted a cost-effectiveness study for South African PNEs, which would have been advisable for any commercial venture. Keeping a PNE development program secret also did not make much sense from a commercial standpoint, because secrecy would only postpone the diplomatic difficulties that would inevitably arise when the time came to test or utilize a PNE. This was particularly obvious after India's May 1974 supposed PNE test galvanized Western nonproliferation and anti-PNE policies.[17] As argued below, however, South Africa's decision to press ahead secretly despite these liabilities could

---

14. Comments of an anonymous reviewer. According to David Albright, however, the design was also well suited as a technology test bed for commercial enrichment development. Telephone conversation with Albright.

15. Whether this was a foregone conclusion is unclear. On the one hand, a junior scientist's skepti cal internal report on the economic feasibility of enrichment was buried by the AEB, and commercial mining interests had little interest in enrichment. Secondhand anecdote from A. David Rosin, telephone conversation, June 21, 1999; and correspondence with David Fischer, April 5, 2001. For retrospective critiques of commercial potential, see A.A Eberhard, "Policy Options for the Nuclear Industry in South Africa," *Raw Materials Report*, Vol. 10, No. 1 (1994), pp. 24–31; and David Fig, "Apartheid's Nuclear Arsenal: Deviation from Development," in Jacklyn Cock and Penny Mac-Kenzie, eds., *From Defence to Development: Redirecting Military Resources in South Africa* (Ottawa, Ontario: International Development Research Centre, 1998), pp. 163–180. On the other hand, negotiations with West Germany from 1970 to 1976 over uranium enrichment collaboration do suggest the plausibility of commercial potential; David Fig, "Sanctions and the Nuclear Industry," in Neta C. Crawford and Audie Klotz, eds., *How Sanctions Work: Lessons from South Africa* (New York: St. Martin's, 1999), pp. 75–102, especially pp. 81–84; and Barbara Rogers and Zdenek Cervenka, *The Nuclear Axis: Secret Collaboration between West Germany and South Africa* (New York: Times Books, 1978).

16. Interview with Joerg Menzel, former technical adviser to the U.S. ambassador-at-large for nuclear affairs, Washington, D.C., December 16, 1999.

17. Buys explains the secrecy surrounding the PNE program as follows: "We were initially very naive. We did seriously think that this was just an alternative use for nuclear energy. . . . So although we thought everybody's doing it, and its not a big issue, we were still a little bit worried that the reaction if South Africa would do it would be different. So the program was classified top secret right from the first day. . . . But things can change, so we won't stop the program." Interview with Buys.

have been an artifact of the AEB's organizational impulses rather than of a high-level decision to obtain a nuclear arsenal.

Informed South African sources differ on when Prime Minister Vorster decided to build nuclear weapons. In a 1993 speech disclosing the defunct program's existence, de Klerk dated the shift in motivation to "as early as" 1974.[18] W.L. "Wally" Grant, managing director of the Uranium Enrichment Corporation of South Africa (UCOR) from 1971 to 1979, recalls that "Vorster was informed about the bomb potential, but commercial potential was foremost" in 1971, and that "defense people" were not involved until 1975.[19] Waldo Stumpf, who directed a review of the program before it was dismantled, says that there was no evidence of military intent prior to 1977. All that transpired in 1974, as far as he could determine, was that the AEB reported to Vorster that it could construct a nuclear device, and Vorster authorized going ahead and preparing a test site in the Kalahari Desert.[20] André Buys, then a rising scientist on the AEB explosives team, agrees with the 1977 date. He thinks that the defense minister and the military heard about the PNE program only when the AEB requested a remote military firing range in the Kalahari in 1974 to use as a test site. In 1976 or 1977, a few military scientists conducted a feasibility study on nuclear weapon delivery systems, but "there was no instruction out that there was going to be a nuclear weapons program. They were merely asked to look at possibilities."[21] South Africa's procuring of 30 grams of Israeli tritium in 1977, later described in a secret trial as intended for use in nuclear bombs, is another indication of weaponization plans at that time.[22]

The difficulty of dating the decision to build nuclear weapons persists because of a dearth of evidence from the top political leaders, most of whom are either unwilling to discuss the program or have died. It is possible that Vorster

---

18. F.W. de Klerk, "Speech on the Nonproliferation Treaty to a Joint Session of Parliament, March 24, 1993," in *Joint Publications Research Service, Proliferation Issues*, March 29, 1993. J.W. de Villiers, AEB chief executive officer (1979–90), agreed with the 1974 date and was de Klerk's source. Interview with Jeremy Schearer, former South African foreign affairs official, Pretoria, January 28, 1999; and Albright, "South Africa and the Affordable Bomb," p. 43. A Central Intelligence Agency report asserts that "South Africa formally launched a weapons program in 1973," but its evidence for this is unclear. Directorate of Intelligence, U.S. Central Intelligence Agency, *New Information on South Africa's Nuclear Program and South African–Israeli Nuclear and Military Cooperation*, secret document, March 30, 1983, partially released May 7, 1996, http://www.foia.ucia.gov.
19. Interview with Grant.
20. Interview with Waldo Stumpf, Pretoria, January 27, 1999; and Stumpf, "South Africa's Nuclear Weapons Program," p. 4.
21. Interview with Buys.
22. Court of South Africa, Cape Province Division, *The State versus Johann Philip Derk Blaauw*, case no. 270/87, top secret, September 9, 1988, p. 24.

intended to build nuclear bombs from the early 1970s, but kept this to himself until 1977 or so. Another possibility is that he really did not decide to pursue this course until around 1977. Between these is the alternative that Vorster gradually leaned toward acquiring nuclear weapons, perhaps prodded into re-thinking the government's policy by the 1974 Indian test, but did not need to make a formal decision until an international furor erupted over discovery of the Kalahari test site in August 1977.

Soon after the Kalahari episode, Vorster ordered the AEB to cancel the PNE program, to close down the test site, and to develop a secret nuclear deterrent. The AEB requested clarification on what was needed for a deterrent: Some scientists believed that an ability to detonate a nuclear device underground was sufficient, while others maintained that deliverable bombs were required. Defense Minister P.W. Botha then solicited a study from the South African Defense Force (SADF) chief of staff for planning, Army Brig. John Huyser, on whom Botha often relied informally for military advice. Huyser's six to eight-page memorandum discussed three options—secret development, covert disclosure, or overt disclosure—and recommended the last (i.e., openly joining the nuclear club). Botha approved this document in April 1978 with the hand-written proviso that any disclosure should be delayed "until we are ready" and must be approved first by the government.[23] Huyser's memorandum did not specify numbers or types of weapons, which left the AEB still uncertain about whether a demonstration capability was sufficient.[24]

After Botha succeeded Vorster as prime minister in September 1978, he formed a high-level steering committee (the Witvlei, or White Marsh, Committee) on nuclear weapons policy. It included the prime minister; the ministers of defense, foreign affairs, minerals and energy, and finance; and the chiefs of Armscor (the state arms procurement and production agency), the Department of Foreign Affairs, the AEB, and the SADF.[25] In July 1979, the committee recommended building deliverable nuclear weapons to acquire a "credible deterrent capability" and shifting overall responsibility for the program to Armscor.[26]

---

23. Interview and December 10, 1999, correspondence with Buys. The date is from Reiss, *Bridled Ambition*, p. 9.

24. Interview with Buys.

25. Ibid.; and L.J. Van der Westhuizen and J.H. le Roux, *Armscor: A Will to Win* (Bloemfontein: Institute for Contemporary History, University of the Orange Free State, 1997), pp. 174–175. (This Armscor-commissioned history is based on interviews as well as published sources.) Sources differ over whether the committee was formed in early or late 1978 and whether certain officials were on the committee.

26. Reiss, *Bridled Ambition*, p. 9.

THE NUCLEAR ARSENAL AND STRATEGY

The AEB completed its first two nuclear devices in 1978 and 1979, but neither was deliverable by aircraft. The first was dismantled for parts; the second, which was equipped with measurement instrumentation, remained dedicated for an underground test. Armscor completed its first bomber-deliverable weapon in 1982. Further refinements in reliability, safety, and delivery design delayed completion of the next weapon until August 1987, after which production accelerated so that the arsenal stood at six and a half by late 1989.[27] The new weapons were nuclear versions of Armscor's remotely guided H2 glide bomb, allowing greater range and penetrability than ordinary gravity bombs.[28] Armscor also investigated a mobile nuclear intermediate-range ballistic missile option, conducting paper studies on how the bombs might be adapted into warheads for missiles available from a joint Israeli–South African rocket and reconnaissance satellite program. A new weapons plant—Advena Central Laboratories—capable of manufacturing two to three more advanced warheads per year and loading them on missiles, was started in 1987 and completed just before the program ended in 1989.[29] An even longer-range rocket, a potential intercontinental ballistic missile, was on Armscor drawing boards at the time. But apparently the government had not yet authorized the physical development of ballistic missile warheads.[30]

Armscor's public cost estimate for the nuclear weapons program was 680

27. Albright, "South Africa and the Affordable Bomb," pp. 42–45; and Reiss, *Bridled Ambition*, pp. 11–12.
28. Interview and November 1, 1999, correspondence with Buys. The H2 was remotely guided to a target by video from an aircraft, with a range of 60 kilometers; it may have been based on a similar Israeli system. See Ronen Bergman, "Treasons of Conscience," *Ha'aretz* (English ed.), April 7, 2000; and Helmoed-Romer Heitman, "Raptor Dodges the Defences," *Jane's Missiles and Rockets*, July 1, 1998, p. 10.
29. Interviews with D.W. Steyn, minister of minerals and energy (1984–89), Pretoria, April 10, 1999; Buys; and Max Sisulu, deputy chief executive officer of Denel, Pretoria, August 23, 1999. One official says that Armscor unveiled a missile in 1987 that could reach Nairobi, with an accuracy of within 300 yards of the target; interview with W.N. Breytenbach, deputy defense minister (1987–90), Fish Hoek, South Africa, August 18, 1999. See also David Albright, "South Africa's Secret Nuclear Weapons," *ISIS Report*, Vol. 1, No. 4 (May 1994), pp. 15–16; Department for Disarmament Affairs, United Nations, *South Africa's Nuclear-Tipped Ballistic Missile Capability* (New York: United Nations, 1991); Directorate of Intelligence, U.S. Central Intelligence Agency, *Africa Review—South Africa: Igniting a Missile Race?* secret document, December 8, 1989, partially released April 27, 1997, http://www.foia.ucia.gov; Van der Westhuizen and le Roux, *Armscor*, pp. 179–180; and Mark Wade, "RSA," *Encyclopedia Astronautica*, http://www.friends-partners.org/mwade/lvfam/rsa.htm.
30. Correspondence with Buys, December 10, 1999. On the longer-range RSA-4 missile, see Wade, "RSA."

million rand (or about $500 million in early 1980s dollars). But a separate Armscor accounting estimates the total Defence Department cost at under 800 million rand, not including the Minerals and Energy Department's costs.[31] Because the latter would include fissile material costs, which constituted the lion's share of the 680 million figure as well as the PNE research budget, the total program expense may have been double Armscor's original public figure. Although very costly, the program was still easily affordable for the government. South Africa's annual military budgets ran from 2 to 4.5 billion rand, or between 4 and 5 percent of gross national product, from the late 1970s through the 1980s.[32]

Despite the economic and diplomatic stakes involved, the government did not think very thoroughly about nuclear strategy at first. Buys says that Huyser's memorandum "was not very concise and we often . . . had difficulties in interpreting it. There was a lot of argumentation in it that didn't lead to any clear conclusion."[33] Huyser's recommendation for overt disclosure had been overruled by P.W. Botha, at least for the time being, but Huyser personally interpreted Botha's proviso about "when we are ready" as meaning the completion of the first operational nuclear weapons. His memorandum, moreover, left little guidance on contingencies for nuclear disclosures, threats, or use. Buys recalls that he and other scientists worried that "nobody actually sat down and worked out a proper strategy for what they wanted to do with [the bombs]. And if they're in a desperate situation that they could take an irrational decision simply because they haven't got time to really consider."[34]

Because of these concerns, in 1983 Buys—by this time general manager of

31. Armscor fact sheet provided by Buys; and Stumpf, "South Africa's Nuclear Weapons Program," p. 6. Another source mentioning the 800 million rand figure reports that it did include fissile material costs, and that Armscor's weaponization efforts from 1980 to 1990 cost only 145 million rand. Hibbs, "Dismantling," p. 12. According to AEC Chief Waldo Stumpf, the 680 million figure included 85 percent of the Y-plant's capital and running costs (since 15 percent of its capacity was used to fuel the Safari I research reactor) plus Armscor's costs of producing the devices. Overhead costs that "fell through the cracks," he states, were balanced by the uncredited value of the Y-plant for designing the Z-plant built to fuel South Africa's Koeberg nuclear power station, located near Cape Town. Interview and April 25, 2001, correspondence with Stumpf.
32. Robert Scott Jaster, *South Africa's Narrowing Security Options*, Adelphi Paper 159 (London: International Institute for Strategic Studies, 1980), p. 16; U.S. Arms Control and Disarmament Agency, *World Military Expenditures and Arms Transfers, 1987* (Washington, D.C.: Government Printing Office, 1988), p. 76; and *World Military Expenditures and Arms Transfers, 1985–1995* (Washington, D.C.: Government Printing Office, 1996), p. 90.
33. Correspondence with Buys, December 10, 1999.
34. Interview and December 10, 1999, correspondence with Buys.

Armscor's Circle nuclear weapons plant (commissioned in May 1981, 15 kilometers from Pelindaba)—formed and chaired an Armscor working group to develop a more specific nuclear strategy. The group met monthly for a year, conducting war games, reviewing the nuclear strategy literature, and selectively consulting experts, politicians, and even a leading South African theologian. On the key question of how the Soviet Union or the United States might react to South African nuclear disclosures or tests, the working group consulted P.W. Botha, Foreign Minister R.F. "Pik" Botha, and Director-General of Foreign Affairs Brand Fourie. L. Daniel "Niel" Barnard, National Intelligence Service director-general from 1980 to 1990 and one of the only South Africans who had studied nuclear weapons strategy in any depth, was also consulted. But the working group deemed his academic expertise as too focused on great power politics to apply to South Africa's unique needs.[35]

The working group eventually developed a three-phase strategy emphasizing deterrence and diplomatic leverage. As long as the military threat remained remote, the government would remain at phase one—"nuclear ambiguity"—neither acknowledging nor denying a nuclear capability. If Soviet or Soviet-backed forces threatened invasion of South African territory or Namibia (controlled by South Africa since World War I), the government would try the covert disclosure or covert coercion of phase two. This involved acknowledging the capability privately to relatively friendly Western nations, in the hope of eliciting their intervention. "If they expressed doubts about the existence of our nuclear arsenal, we would invite them to send inspectors to view our bombs. If this failed to convince them to intervene on our behalf we would threaten to detonate a nuclear device underground and therefore 'go nuclear.'" If this failed, and the situation deteriorated further, the government would move to phase three, known as the overt disclosure or overt deterrent strategy, which in turn comprised three steps. South Africa would first publicly declare its capability or conduct an unannounced underground test. If this did not work, South Africa would detonate a nuclear bomb 1,000 kilometers south over the ocean. According to Buys, "the last step would then be to threaten to use the nuclear weapons on the battlefield in self-defense."[36]

The strategy did not specify any further steps, and the working-group mem-

---

35. Ibid.
36. Ibid. The Namibian threshold is reported in Pabian, "South Africa's Nuclear Weapon Program," pp. 7–8. Prior official accounts of the strategy did not acknowledge the threat of battlefield use; see Albright, "South Africa and the Affordable Bomb," pp. 8–9; Reiss, *Bridled Ambition*, pp. 15–17; and Stumpf, "South Africa's Nuclear Weapons Program," p. 5. Some sources indicate that the

bers disagreed about fallback options. Buys's view was that "it was better to throw in the towel, and let the Soviet Union take us. The argument was that to actually use the weapon in any way aggressively would have been a suicidal act. The Soviet Union would have every excuse then to actually attack us with nuclear weapons. We were no match for that. Then we would still lose, but we would destroy the country and the people as well. . . . Others would argue differently, they would say fight to the bitter end. . . . But there was no strategy for that."[37]

P.W. Botha reportedly agreed with Buys, at one point admonishing Armscor officials—upon rejecting their proposals in September 1985 to develop implosion and thermonuclear warheads—that "these devices will never be used offensively by South Africa as it would be suicide."[38] Gen. Magnus Malan, SADF chief from 1976 to 1980 and defense minister from 1980 to 1991, says that he doubts whether nuclear weapons would have ever been used except in retaliation for a chemical or nuclear attack on South Africa.[39] But even those who opposed using the weapons offensively argued that advanced delivery systems would enhance the credibility of the bluff to do so.

The three-phase strategy was finally approved in 1986 or 1987, according to Buys. But P.W. Botha does not appear to have been highly committed to it. Buys recalls him saying of the arm-twisting concept, "Fine, you can put that in as a possibility," and Buys acknowledges that the strategy "was perhaps not taken that seriously because . . . people thought we're a long way off."[40] Another official had the impression that the strategy was intended only as a general guideline.[41]

But in late 1986 or 1987, Armscor was instructed to "make sure that the capability to actually execute the strategy is in place," according to Buys.[42] Because phase two required an underground test, this meant reopening the Kalahari test site, closed since 1977. Armscor built a large hangar—disguised as a stor-

three-phase strategy emerged in 1978, though Buys thinks that this is the result of confusion between Huyser's three options and the strategy developed by the working group. Correspondence with Buys, December 10, 1999.

37. Interview with Buys.

38. Correspondence with Stumpf, repeating a story from J.W. de Villiers. P.W. Botha told me that "we said amongst ourselves that for a country like South Africa to use nuclear weapons would be disastrous." Interview, Wilderness, South Africa, April 8, 1999.

39. Interview with Gen. Magnus Malan, SADF chief (1976–80) and defense minister (1980–89), Pretoria, August 27, 1999.

40. Interview and December 10, 1999, correspondence with Buys.

41. Interview with Breytenbach.

42. Interview with Buys. Also giving a 1987 date is Hibbs, "From a PNE to Deterrent," p. 6.

age and training facility—over one of the test shafts, pumped out the water that had collected, and checked it for readiness.[43] Some ministers believe that Armscor or even P.W. Botha himself seriously considered conducting a test at the time.[44]

SECURITY INCENTIVES AND NUCLEAR ARMING

South Africa developed a nuclear weapons option while it was very secure, but political intentions and steps toward actually building nuclear weapons followed closely the emergence of new threats. Yet the danger to the South African homeland of invasion or nuclear blackmail remained remote. More pressing was the threat to South Africa's support of Angolan rebels and its long-standing occupation of Namibia, which lies between Angola and South Africa proper. But the utility of nuclear weapons for meeting these threats, even if they materialized, was borderline considering the diplomatic and security risks as well as the budgetary costs involved.

In the mid-1970s, Pretoria felt increasingly beleaguered by the collapse of Portuguese control over Angola and Mozambique (April 1974), Soviet aid to the Marxist regime in Angola (from March 1975), Cuban intervention in Angola to support the regime against South African–backed rebels (from October 1975), the election of an unsympathetic Carter administration (November 1976), a mandatory United Nations arms embargo (from November 1977), and growing Western pressure to withdraw from Namibia (from 1977).[45] P.W. Botha recalls that the South African nuclear arsenal was developed as

---

43. According to Reiss, the test site activity occurred from June through October 1988. But Buys recalls that the test site activity occurred in 1986 or 1987, and Stumpf also gives a 1987 date. Interview with Buys; Reiss, *Bridled Ambition*, pp. 13–14; and Stumpf, "South Africa's Nuclear Weapons Program," p. 6.

44. Interviews with Pik Botha, Pretoria, April 9, 1999; Malan; Breytenbach; and Grant (repeating a story he heard from J.W. de Villiers). The story was discounted in interviews with Buys; Stumpf; and Gen. Jan Geldenhuys, Pretoria, August 24, 1999.

45. The South African government's threat environment and perceptions in this period are analyzed in David E. Albright, *The USSR and Sub-Saharan Africa in the 1980's* (New York: Praeger, 1983); Chris Alden, *Apartheid's Last Stand: The Rise and Fall of the South African Security State* (New York: St. Martin's, 1996); Richard K. Betts, "A Diplomatic Bomb? South Africa's Nuclear Potential," in Joseph A. Yager, ed., *Nonproliferation and U.S. Foreign Policy* (Washington, D.C.: Brookings, 1980), pp. 283–305; Neta C. Crawford, "The Domestic Sources and Consequences of Aggressive Foreign Policies: The Folly of South Africa's 'Total Strategy,'" Centre for Southern African Studies Working Paper, No. 41 (Bellville, South Africa: Centre for Southern African Studies, University of the Western Cape, 1995). Chester A. Crocker, *High Noon in Southern Africa: Making Peace in a Rough Neighborhood* (New York: W.W. Norton, 1992); Jaster, *South Africa's Narrowing Security Options*; Robert Scott Jaster, *The Defence of White Power: South African Foreign Policy under Pressure* (New York: St. Mar-

a "diplomatic weapon to defend South Africa."[46] According to de Klerk, the weapons were built to provide "a limited nuclear deterrent capability," necessitated by "a Soviet expansionist threat in Southern Africa, as well as prevailing uncertainty concerning the designs of the Warsaw Pact members. The buildup of the Cuban forces in Angola reinforced the perception that a deterrent was necessary—as did South Africa's relative international isolation and the fact that it could not rely on outside assistance, should it be attacked."[47]

Yet throughout the 1970s and 1980s, South Africa faced neither nuclear-armed neighbors nor a foreseeable invasion threat, unlike other proliferators such as Israel, India, and Pakistan or states that held back (if under strong U.S. pressure) from developing a nuclear capability such as Taiwan.[48] The SADF's primary mission was engaging in counterinsurgency near the South African and Namibian borders. Public rhetoric about a threat of Soviet-backed aggression notwithstanding, the Soviet Union lacked logistical support capabilities for deploying large ground forces in southern Africa, and even an improbable 80,000 Soviet airborne, air assault, and naval infantry units in combination with the Cuban forces would have been hard-pressed to defeat the SADF.[49] Gen. Jan Geldenhuys, SADF chief from 1985 to 1990, acknowledges that "invasions were seen as slight possibilities, adventurous transgressions of borders on such small scale that nuclear capability never came into the picture."[50] The chief of military intelligence in the 1970s, Gen. H. de V. du Toit, now recalls, "I don't think we ever thought it was feasible for anyone to attack us from the north."[51] Pik Botha states that "we did not have a clinical, sober analysis of

tin's, 1989); Annette D. Seegers, *The Military in the Making of Modern South Africa* (London: I.B. Tauris, 1996); and Jack E. Spence, *The Soviet Union, the Third World, and Southern Africa*, Bradlow Series No. 5 (Johannesburg: South African Institute of International Affairs, 1988).

46. Interview with P.W. Botha.

47. De Klerk, "Speech on the Nonproliferation Treaty," p. 27. Also interview with Malan; and Stumpf, "South Africa's Nuclear Weapons Program," p. 5.

48. On Taiwan's early ambitions, however, see David Albright and Corey Gay, "Taiwan: Nuclear Nightmare Averted," *Bulletin of the Atomic Scientists*, Vol. 54, No. 1 (January–February 1998), pp. 54–60; and William Burr, *New Archival Evidence on Taiwanese "Nuclear Intentions," 1966–1976*, http://www.gwu.edu/~nsarchiv/NSAEBB/NSAEBB20/.

49. Albright, *USSR and Sub-Saharan Africa*, p. 100; and Directorate of Intelligence, U.S. Central Intelligence Agency, *Trends in South Africa's Nuclear Policies and Programs*, secret document, October 4, 1984, partially released April 27, 1997, http://www.foia.ucia.gov.

50. Interview with Geldenhuys, August 24, 1999.

51. Quoted in Reiss, *Bridled Ambition*, p. 28.

what the Soviet Union could do in Africa," and in fact South African expertise on Soviet foreign and military policy was negligible.[52]

The defeat of Jonas Savimbi's Angolan rebels (Uniao Nacional par a Independência Total de Angola, or UNITA) and an enemy incursion into Namibia were more realistic threats. Since 1975, South Africa had supported UNITA with arms and periodic interventions to deny a southern Angolan sanctuary to Namibian insurgents and to maintain a buffer against the Angolan regime. Emboldened by infusions of Soviet arms and Cuban troops, the Angolan government increased its efforts to crush UNITA starting in September 1985. Deliveries of advanced Soviet aircraft and air defenses, and an infusion of 15,000 more Cuban troops, enabled a Cuban-Angolan offensive between August 1987 and June 1988 to press into southern Angola for the first time. Cuban President Fidel Castro warned at the time that South Africa risked "serious defeat" and hinted at an offensive into Namibia. The offensive was effectively beaten back by the SADF, but the increased casualties and war costs were political liabilities for Pretoria.

Some sources suggest that the decision to reopen the Kalahari test site was motivated by concern about the Angolan situation. Buys recalls that the site was revisited because "for the first time the government started considering the possibility that we might lose the war militarily." The second stage of the nuclear strategy "would come into operation once we were confronted by a serious and escalating military threat. We got close to that in 1987 . . . in Angola."[53] In a private conversation late in 1987, P.W. Botha reportedly quipped to an associate, "Once we set this thing off, the Yanks will come running."[54] Botha's precise motivations and intentions for reopening the test site remain somewhat unclear, but the weight of evidence suggests he was prompted by the escalating Angolan conflict.[55]

---

52. Interview with Pik Botha, April 9, 1999. See also Margot Light and Philip Nel, "South African Research on Soviet Foreign Policy," *Politikon*, Vol. 17, No. 1 (June 1990), pp. 66–72.
53. Interview and December 10, 1999, correspondence with Buys. Botha "acted immediately" to authorize reopening the test site after the Soviet deployment of air defense systems in southern Angola negated Pretoria's air superiority, according to Hibbs, "PNE to Deterrent," p. 6.
54. Interview with Breytenbach.
55. Reiss argues that the satellite-observable activity around the test site was intended as a signal to persuade the superpowers to secure the removal of Cuban troops in an overall Angolan-Namibian settlement. But the undetectable checking of the test shaft beneath the newly constructed shed suggests an attempt to provide an actual option to test, as Buys and Pabian contend. In a more anodyne interpretation, Stumpf suggests that the test preparations were merely the culmination of a strategic planning process unrelated to the Angolan conflict. See Pabian, "South Af-

Another fear was the possibility that the Cubans or Soviets would use chemical, biological, or nuclear weapons against South African troops or soil. As mentioned above, Malan thought that this might be a possibility. Some in military intelligence—though not civilian intelligence—circles even believed UNITA reports that chemical and nuclear weapons had already been deployed in Angola.[56]

Nuclear weapons, however, provided a limited remedy to these threats. Because South Africa could not threaten the Soviet homeland in a nuclear showdown, at least until South Africa could acquire an intercontinental ballistic missile capability many years hence, it could not credibly threaten a nuclear response to invasion or even to tactical nuclear or chemical attack. As South African officials were well aware, actually using nuclear weapons against Cuban or African troops or Soviet naval assets in southern Africa would have been suicidal. The prospect of such a disaster might still have dampened Soviet aggressiveness or invited Western involvement, providing a degree of existential deterrence. But South Africa's well-known uranium enrichment capability and test site by themselves had already accomplished much of this effect. A secret nuclear arsenal added the option of heightening deterrence when unveiled in a crisis. But the Soviet Union might have reacted to South African nuclear saber rattling by deploying its own nuclear weapons to the region or even by attacking South African nuclear installations.[57]

The covert coercion strategy of enticing Western assistance banked on U.S. aversion to the overt spread and use of nuclear weapons. Washington's reaction to the discovery of the Kalahari test site apparently encouraged South African strategists to think that a catalytic strategy might succeed in drawing U.S. support in the event of a future crisis.[58] But a plausible alternative lesson of the Kalahari debacle was that the strategy could well have failed or even backfired. A South African blackmail attempt might have angered London or Washington, discouraging Western assistance rather than prompting it.[59]

---

rica's Nuclear Weapon Program," pp. 8–9; Reiss, *Bridled Ambition*, pp. 13–14; and Stumpf, "South Africa's Nuclear Weapons Program," p. 6.
56. Interviews with Breytenbach; and Niel Barnard, Cape Town, August 18, 1999.
57. South African strategists believed that maintaining absolute secrecy about the existence and location of South Africa's arsenal minimized the latter danger. Interview with Buys.
58. Correspondence with Buys, December 10, 1999.
59. For critiques of the strategy, see Betts, "A Diplomatic Bomb?" pp. 297–302; David Fischer, "South Africa," in Robert Litwak and Mitchell Reiss, eds., *Nuclear Proliferation after the Cold War* (Washington, D.C.: Woodrow Wilson Center Press, 1994), p. 216; Reiss, *Bridled Ambition*, p. 28; and

The scant attention that Pretoria devoted to these questions is inconsistent with a security explanation. Huyser's confusing memorandum remained official policy for several years. The strategy working group gave key policy questions closer scrutiny, and the group sensibly consulted top foreign ministry officials Pik Botha and Brand Fourie about likely foreign reactions to South African nuclear disclosures. "The answer we got from them was very qualified," says Buys. "They said, maybe if we speak to Margaret Thatcher, it might work. Ronald Reagan might also be persuaded. But for the rest, we don't think we would get anywhere."[60] But more detailed staff studies were not conducted. Although the working group's war games appeared to confirm the strategy's viability, the participants were predominantly senior SADF officers and Armscor technocrats, rather than officials or experts more knowledgeable about Soviet and U.S. diplomacy and strategy.

Faith that the strategy would work derived in part from a lesson drawn from the 1973 Yom Kippur War. At a low point early in the war, Israeli warnings to the United States and a nuclear alert may have prompted a U.S. decision to provide Israel with desperately needed munitions. According to Buys, members of the strategy working group "were aware of the alleged use by Israel of its nuclear capability to obtain U.S. assistance during the 1973 war. We had no proof that this was factual. . . . The allegation probably subconsciously influenced our thinking. We argued that if we cannot use a nuclear weapon on the battlefield (as this would have been suicidal), then the only possible way to use it would be to leverage intervention from the Western Powers by threatening to use it. We thought that this might work and the alleged Israel-USA case gave some support to our view."[61] South African political leaders often drew geopolitical comparisons between the two nations.[62] The close Israeli–South

---

Sagan, "Why Do States Build Nuclear Weapons?" p. 70. For a more favorable assessment, see Richard J. Harknett, "Nuclear Weapons and Territorial Integrity in the Post–Cold War World," in Ken R. Dark, ed., *New Studies in Post–Cold War Security* (Brookfield, Vt.: Dartmouth Publishing, 1996), pp. 49–65.

60. Interview with Buys.

61. Correspondence with Buys, December 10, 1999. An anonymous South African defense official also stated in 1993 that the South African strategy was similar to that of Israel, which "used its bomb as a bargaining chip to get concessions from the U.S." Hibbs, "From a PNE to Deterrent," p. 10. On the 1973 episode, see Seymour M. Hersh, *The Samson Option: Israel's Nuclear Arsenal and American Foreign Policy* (New York: Vintage, 1991), pp. 225–231.

62. P.W. Botha repeated his affinity for Israel in an interview. Another potential source of strategic ideas was French Gen. André Beaufre, whose writings on "total strategy" for counterinsurgency warfare strongly influenced SADF and P.W. Botha's thinking. Beaufre also wrote a book on nuclear

African military partnership, which included ministerial visits from 1974 onward, trade in nuclear materials, rocket codevelopment, and possible cooperation on an Israeli nuclear test in 1979, offered ample opportunity for high-level strategic discussions.[63] (One piece of circumstantial evidence that these discussions occurred was that the minister of mines and the Bureau of State Security chief procured tritium from Israel in 1977, against the wishes of the AEB.[64] Because these officials were not well versed in nuclear science, it seems quite likely that they learned of tritium's military utility from their Israeli contacts.) Although South African leaders may have emulated Israeli nuclear policy, geopolitical and diplomatic differences between the two nations ought to have qualified any analogies drawn from Israeli experience.[65]

ORGANIZATIONAL POLITICS AND NUCLEAR ARMING

It appears that Vorster's formal decision to acquire a deterrent in 1977 involved primarily AEB Chairman A.J. "Ampie" Roux and Defense Minister P.W. Botha, with the latter being the most influential.[66] While Vorster reportedly was con-

---

strategy that discussed how small power nuclear arsenals could leverage great power assistance, but Buys says that his working group was not familiar with it. Correspondence with Buys, December 10, 1999. See also André Beaufre, *Deterrence and Strategy*, trans. R.H. Barry (New York: Praeger, 1965), p. 84.

63. Shimon Peres, the chief architect and strategist of Israel's nuclear weapons program, met with Vorster and P.W. Botha in November 1974, and Vorster visited Israel in April 1976. Bergman, "Treasons of Conscience"; William E. Burrows and Robert Windrem, *Critical Mass: The Dangerous Race for Superweapons in a Fragmenting World* (New York: Simon and Schuster, 1994), pp. 448–466; and Hersh, *The Samson Option*, pp. 259–283. Other sources on South African–Israeli military collaboration include James Adams, *The Unnatural Alliance* (London: Quartet, 1984); Benjamin M. Joseph, *Besieged Bedfellows: Israel and the Land of Apartheid* (New York: Greenwood, 1987); U.S. Central Intelligence Agency, *New Information on South Africa's Nuclear Program and South African–Israeli Nuclear and Military Cooperation*. On Peres's role in the Israeli program, see Avner Cohen, *Israel and the Bomb* (New York: Columbia University Press, 1998), pp. 17–21. For a look back at the suspected 1979 test, see David Albright and Corey Gay, "A Flash from the Past," *Bulletin of the Atomic Scientists*, Vol. 53, No. 6 (November–December 1997), pp. 15–17.

64. According to Stumpf, AEB Chief A.J. Roux initially refused to collect the tritium shipment until ordered to do so by Minister of Mines S.P. Botha. Telephone conversation with Waldo Stumpf, June 4, 2001.

65. The South African–Israeli alliance could have influenced South African nuclear policy through nonsecurity mechanisms as well as through strategic learning. For example, Israel's possession of "a bomb in the basement" might have burnished the status appeal of going nuclear to the South African leadership.

66. The roles of Prime Minister Vorster and Roux are emphasized in Donald B. Sole, "The South African Nuclear Case in the Light of Recent Revelations," in James Brown, ed., *New Horizons and Challenges in Arms Control and Verification* (Amsterdam: V.U. University Press, 1994), pp. 71–80, p. 75. But Botha's involvement was clear from his commission of a delivery feasibility study and of Huyser's memorandum (discussed above).

tent to "let the program develop at its own pace," Botha was "singularly fixated on getting nuclear weapons."[67] Hendrik van den Bergh, the head of civilian intelligence, and Minister of Mines S.P. "Fanie" Botha may also have been involved; together they directed clandestine tritium and uranium ore trade with Israel in 1977.[68] It would have been characteristic of Vorster to make such a decision after conferring with only one or two advisers.[69] This would have heightened the influence of these advisers at the expense of those less likely to support the program.

Many South African sources describe Roux as the "driving force" behind the enrichment and PNE programs.[70] According to Buys, the PNE program was initially conceived as a way to retain roughly two dozen nuclear scientists idled by the 1969 cancellation of the Pelinduna nuclear reactor program, as well as to gain prestige for the AEB and the nation by demonstrating advanced technology.[71] The 1971 authorization of initial PNE research by the minister of mines rather than the prime minister reinforces this explanation. Thus the initial pursuit of commercially ill-fated enrichment and PNE programs, which some observers see as evidence of early nuclear weapons ambitions, may instead have been by-products of the AEB's organizational incentives and influence.

Roux had long-standing direct access to the prime minister.[72] Laurence "Louw" Alberts, AEB vice president from 1971 to 1977, recalls Roux saying, "I can ask this government for anything I want and I'll get it."[73] This could reflect

67. This is the assessment of a "well-placed" source quoted by Hibbs, " From a PNE to Deterrent," p. 5. A former foreign affairs director-general surmises that P.W. Botha persuaded Roux to support a nuclear weapons program, because Roux was not particularly interested in military affairs. Interview with Neil van Heerden, Johannesburg, April 6, 1999. Botha's general influence increased in the last years of the Vorster administration, according to Jaster, *Defence of White Power*, p. 80.
68. Supreme Court of South Africa, *State versus Blaauw*, pp. 21–25. Van den Bergh was a close confidant of Vorster's, but van den Bergh did not inform his own staff about the nuclear program; telephone conversation with George Gruwar, former deputy director-general of the Bureau of State Security, August 24, 1999.
69. Jaster, *Defence of White Power*, pp. 25–26.
70. Interview with Grant; correspondence with Stumpf; Reiss, *Bridled Ambition;* and Sole, "South African Nuclear Case," p. 75. See also A.R. Newby-Fraser, *Chain Reaction: Twenty Years of Nuclear Research and Development in South Africa* (Pretoria: Atomic Energy Board, 1979), pp. 36–42, 197.
71. Interviews with Buys; and an Armscor official, Pretoria, August 1999. On the Pelinduna reactor program, see also Newby-Fraser, *Chain Reaction*, pp. 115–125; and Renfrew Christie, *Electricity, Industry, and Class in South Africa* (Albany: State University of New York Press, 1984), p. 182.
72. Correspondence with Stumpf; and interviews with Piet Koornhof, minister of minerals and energy, 1976–79, Cape Town, August 16, 1999; Grant; and S.P. Botha, Pretoria, August 20, 1999.
73. Interview with Laurence Alberts, Pretoria, August 26, 1999.

prior nuclear enthusiasm on Vorster's part, but it could also have been a result of the nuclear scientists' general prestige, their monopoly on nuclear expertise, and the tight secrecy shrouding nuclear explosives research. Buys explains the lack of critical evaluation of the PNE program as a result of "an era which in hindsight we would call the Kingdom of Science, science for its own sake."[74] Alberts likewise recalls the 1960s and 1970s as "golden years" in which the "priest with the white coat had more impact than the priest with the black coat."[75] Piet Koornhof, minister of minerals and energy from 1972 to 1976, recalls that it would have been unthinkable for him and the other politicians to question the scientists' advice on such technical matters.[76]

Secrecy enhanced the AEB's authority in high-level decisionmaking by removing potentially critical voices and analyses. Knowledge of the program remained on a strict need-to-know basis, and need was interpreted very narrowly at all levels of government. The military was informed about the PNE program only when the AEB requested a remote military base in the mid-1970s to prepare a test site. Even General Malan, then SADF chief, says that he was not involved in Vorster's decision to acquire a deterrent.[77] Pik Botha, foreign minister from April 1977 until May 1994, learned of his government's nuclear capability only in August 1977, when the U.S. ambassador demanded an explanation for the Kalahari test site. When Botha asked Vorster if the charges were true, Vorster simply instructed him to say that the program was for peaceful purposes, and left it at that.[78]

The AEB's organizational interests might also have inclined it toward the militarization of the program in 1977 or 1978. Once the 1977 Kalahari imbroglio had forced the cancellation of the PNE program, a secret nuclear weapons program would have provided an alternative raison d'être for continued nuclear explosives work and for operation of the uranium enrichment Y-plant, even if the AEB were to lose control over a militarized program to Armscor.

---

74. Interview with Buys.
75. Interview with Alberts.
76. Interview with Koornhof.
77. Interviews with Gen. H. de V. du Toit, Pretoria, January 27, 1999; Buys; and Malan.
78. Interview with Pik Botha, Pretoria, August 25, 1999. The foreign ministry was kept in the dark about other security matters as well, such as the SADF's 1975 intervention in Angola. Interview with van Heerden; and Alden, *Apartheid's Last Stand.* The weak position of the diplomats also limited their ability to sell their more sanguine view of the Soviet threat, and hence the need for a deterrent in the first place. "We diplomats thought Russian policy was mischief making," says a former South African ambassador, "but the military people believed the total onslaught." Interview with Donald B. Sole, Cape Town, April 7, 1999.

Roux and UCOR Managing Director Grant were both enthusiastic about the program; Grant recalls that "fighting the communists was our job" and wishing that South Africa had gone ahead and tested a device.[79] The scientists working on the explosives program were divided, with some opposed on moral grounds.[80]

P.W. Botha increased the number of ministers, if not their staffs, involved in nuclear weapons policy with the 1978 establishment of the Witvlei Committee mentioned above. But internal secrecy remained a hallmark of the program for its lifetime. The whole cabinet was never officially informed about the nuclear program until after it had been dismantled. Nor was the program ever discussed in the State Security Council, a powerful interdepartmental agency that coordinated internal and external security policy.[81] The military intelligence chief, General du Toit, was informed only in 1977, when asked to provide security for the cold (i.e., without a fissionable core) underground test planned at the Kalahari site. Even General Geldenhuys, the army chief of staff of the early 1980s, was not informed about the program until he became SADF chief in 1985.[82]

Defense Minister P.W. Botha's support for nuclear weapons did not necessarily reflect the military's preferences or role. As mentioned, the military leadership was not involved in the decision to acquire a deterrent, as was also the case in Israel and India.[83] Had it been properly consulted, it probably would have been unenthusiastic. When later asked to help develop delivery systems, according to Buys, "the military was initially rather reluctant to become involved." While the service chiefs were loyal to Malan, who favored the program, the staff officers' reaction was that "this was not invented here. Thanks very much, but we can do without this. In fact, we don't think there is any utility for this, so you carry on on your own." The air force "was in a battle for finances, and they needed fighter aircraft. They were having a hard time in Angola against Soviet aircraft. That was their highest priority, that was in their

---

79. Interview with Grant. He was less politically connected than Roux, but highly respected as a scientist. Buys thinks that Roux was not a driving force in the weaponization decision. Interview with Buys.
80. Interview with Buys.
81. Interviews with Niel Barnard, Cape Town, January 22, 1999; and various former cabinet members.
82. Interviews with du Toit; and Gen. Jan Geldenhuys, Pretoria, January 25, 1999.
83. Cohen, *Israel and the Bomb;* and George Perkovich, *India's Nuclear Bomb: The Impact on Global Proliferation* (Berkeley: University of California Press, 1999).

strategic plan. They'd rather stop the nuclear program and [use the resources to] buy fighter aircraft."[84] Brigadier Huyser did strongly advocate a nuclear weapons program; Buys calls him "the champion of the program" in the late 1970s, even though he "did not get along very well with the civilian scientists." But as the SADF chief of staff for planning, Huyser was not in the normal chain of command.[85] Defense Minister P.W. Botha's use of a maverick for nuclear policy advice indicates the malleability of organizational forces in the South African case.

That said, the SADF may have indirectly and inadvertently fueled the politicians' appetite for nuclear weapons by overselling the Soviet-Cuban threat. In his long-standing role as defense minister (1966–80), P.W. Botha could have absorbed the military's threat perceptions.[86] It remains unclear, however, whether it was the military that impressed upon the politicians the invasion peril or vice versa. Botha promoted the concept of a Soviet-backed "total onslaught" (i.e., an aggressive, multidimensional campaign to install a loyal Marxist regime in Pretoria) from the early 1970s, and as defense minister he could easily have shaped the military's threat assessment process. Moreover, National Party leaders had domestic political incentives for exaggerating the Soviet threat—to stiffen white support for regional intervention, internal repression, and race policy reforms.[87]

Internalization or "blowback" of alarmist propaganda, whatever its origins, could have heightened actual perceptions of the Soviet threat.[88] As South Afri-

---

84. Interview with Buys.

85. Ibid.; and correspondence with Buys, December 10, 1999.

86. Botha continued to favor the military after becoming prime minister in 1978; in fact, he retained the defense portfolio until 1980, when he took the unprecedented step of promoting the SADF chief to defense minister. Botha also tapped military officers for important positions in the strengthened State Security Council and for his own staff. The SADF, however, was always loyal to its civilian overseers. For analyses of the rising influence of the military, see Philip H. Frankel, *Pretoria's Praetorians: Civil-Military Relations in South Africa* (Cambridge: Cambridge University Press, 1984); Deon Geldenhuys, *The Diplomacy of Isolation: South African Foreign Policy Making* (Johannesburg: Macmillan, 1984); Kenneth W. Grundy, *The Militarization of South African Politics* (Bloomington: Indiana University Press, 1986); and Jaster, *Defence of White Power*. Some observers even allege that Botha owed his political ascent in 1978 to the military's leaking of information damaging to his cabinet rivals; cf. Dan O'Meara, *Forty Lost Years: The Apartheid State and the Politics of the National Party, 1948–1994* (Athens: Ohio University Press, 1996), pp. 246–247.

87. Heribert Adam and Hermann Giliomee, *Ethnic Power Mobilized: Can South Africa Change?* (New Haven, Conn.: Yale University Press, 1979), pp. 128–144; Frankel, *Pretoria's Praetorians*; O'Meara, *Forty Lost Years*, p. 266; and Spence, *Soviet Union, the Third World, and Southern Africa*.

88. On blowback, see Jack Snyder, *Myths of Empire: Domestic Politics and International Ambition* (Ithaca, N.Y.: Cornell University Press, 1991).

can diplomat Donald Sole put it, "The concept of a 'total onslaught' by Communist forces, controlled by the Soviet Union, was increasingly being promoted, partly for party political purposes. Indeed the propaganda to this effect was introducing a degree of paranoia among senior military officers and other government personnel."[89] General Geldenhuys, when discussing the implausibility of invasion scenarios, observed that "sometimes states come to believe their own propaganda."[90] This provides an intriguing explanation for South African perceptions of the need for a deterrent, but it is not an organizationally rooted one unless the propaganda originated in the SADF.

The vagueness and incoherence of South Africa's initial nuclear weapons policy (i.e., Huyser's memorandum) is consistent with an explanation stressing the influence of the AEB and Armscor. (Although a lack of strategic planning could also be explained by a policy that sought nuclear weapons as a status symbol, the tight secrecy maintained on the program suggests that this was not a critical goal.) Vorster's lack of foreign policy experience, and the tight circle of advisers he drew upon, shielded the policy from critical examination. The scientists' initiative to form a strategy working group in 1983 would seem a risky organizational move, because securing approval for a new doctrine could expose the entire program to further debate. But Armscor's control over the working group's staffing and operation minimized this hazard. According to Neil van Heerden, director-general of foreign affairs from 1987 to 1992, "The soldiers argued that this was, in effect, a diplomatic instrument, but the diplomats did not have enough access to test that thesis . . . . [and to show that it is wrong and that it] won't be feasible to project this as a diplomatic instrument."[91] Stumpf also stresses Armscor's autonomy, claiming that Armscor's development of advanced delivery systems was permitted by a prime minister mindful of "keeping his scientists happy."[92]

INTERNATIONAL PRESSURE, STATE SENSITIVITY, AND NUCLEAR ARMING
International pressure deterred South Africa from openly testing or declaring its nuclear weapons, but militated only weakly against a "bomb in the basement." Extensive nuclear embargoes and boycotts were imposed on South Af-

---

89. Sole, "South African Nuclear Case," p. 75.
90. Interview with Geldenhuys, August 24, 1999.
91. Interview with van Heerden.
92. Correspondence with Stumpf.

rica from the mid-1970s. But they were not highly costly in economic terms, and they were seen by Pretoria as anti-apartheid bullying rather than as being selectively targeted against the nuclear weapons program. Because apartheid remained nonnegotiable for the South African government until the end of the 1980s, this linkage blunted the sanctions' coercive potential, as did possibly the leadership's nationalist-statist predisposition.

The United States, France, and West Germany halted their considerable trade and collaboration in nuclear energy and science with South Africa in the late 1970s. Although many of the sanctions cited South Africa's refusal to join the NPT or accept IAEA safeguards on the Y-plant, they were also driven by the broader anti-apartheid campaign that gained steam after the 1976 Soweto uprising and massacres and the 1977 prison murder of Steve Biko, leader of the Black Consciousness movement. Anti-apartheid congressional leaders prompted the Ford administration's 1975 cancellation of nuclear fuel deliveries and 1976 withdrawal of power plant bids. South Africa was voted off the IAEA's board of governors in June 1977, yet another proliferator, India, was not.[93] The 1978 U.S. Nuclear Nonproliferation Act banning nuclear cooperation with non-NPT states made no reference to apartheid, but anti-apartheid domestic sentiment would have made it difficult for a U.S. president to restore cooperation with South Africa even had it joined the NPT. The South African government concluded that "Pretoria's accession to the NPT without fundamental political reform at home would not gain South Africa international acceptance" or an end to nuclear sanctions.[94]

Besides injuring South African pride, nuclear sanctions necessitated a scramble for fuel for its nuclear power plants. But this was circumvented, if expensively, by the building of a second enrichment plant (the Z-plant) and a fuel assembly facility to attain nuclear energy self-sufficiency.[95] More compelling were the harsher and more targeted threats against an overt nuclear weapons policy. The August 1977 U.S., French, and West German démarches against South African testing included threats of broken diplomatic relations, trade

---

93. Stumpf, "South Africa's Nuclear Weapons Program," p. 4. On the heightened international anti-apartheid campaign, see Crawford and Klotz, *How Sanctions Work;* and Audie Klotz, *Norms in International Relations: The Struggle against Apartheid* (Ithaca, N.Y.: Cornell University Press, 1995).
94. Stumpf, "South Africa's Nuclear Weapons Program," p. 5. Pretoria's ambassador to the United States from 1977 to 1982 concurred; Donald B. Sole, "The Rise of Nuclear Sanctions against South Africa," *American Review,* Vol. 6, No. 4 (Autumn 1986), p. 4.
95. Fig, "Sanctions and the Nuclear Industry"; Pabian, "South Africa's Nuclear Weapon Program"; and Sole, "Rise of Nuclear Sanctions."

sanctions, and French cancellation of a contract to build the Koeberg nuclear power plants north of Cape Town. Vorster responded by abandoning the test site, promising not to conduct any tests and declaring that South Africa's nuclear research was aimed only at peaceful uses.

Reputational and normative incentives also did not militate heavily against a nuclear capability. Pretoria thought that the nuclear weapon states' NPT advocacy was hypocritical, given their own expanding nuclear arsenals and inconsistent application of sanctions.[96] In confronting international anti-apartheid pressure, some South African officials even saw a nuclear option as a diplomatic shield. When recently asked how South Africa could have used its nuclear arsenal for diplomatic purposes, P.W. Botha replied that it enabled the country "to maintain its self-respect."[97] National Intelligence Service Director-General Niel Barnard, though he says he was not involved in nuclear policy-making, thought that a "psychological deterrent" would command respect and leverage for South Africa.[98] According to Buys, Brigadier Huyser had "grandiose ideas about the 'status' that nuclear weapons would bestow on South Africa."[99] Defying foreign pressure on the nuclear issue might also have garnered domestic political support from white voters fearful of Pretoria yielding to foreign pressure on apartheid.[100] Such thoughts may have been suggested by the strident Western reaction to the discovery of the Kalahari test site, and could help explain the timing of weaponization decisions following that episode.[101] But the decision to keep the program secret suggests that Vorster and P.W. Botha thought that the costs of joining the nuclear club overtly outweighed the benefits, at least in the near term.[102] Stumpf discounts diplomatic leverage arguments, on the grounds that there was no reason to think that South Africa could obtain any quid pro quos for nuclear restraint.[103]

Etel Solingen's theory would predict that South Africa's nationalist-statist government in the 1970s would be rather insensitive to international pressure and would seek domestic and international reputations for toughness. The rul-

---

96. Interview with Barnard, January 22, 1999; and correspondence with Stumpf.
97. Interview with P.W. Botha.
98. Interview with Barnard, January 22, 1999.
99. Correspondence with Buys, December 10, 1999.
100. One British observer speculated in 1987 that "the development of nuclear weapons might provide a much needed moral boost" to the embattled regime. Christopher Coker, *South Africa's Security Dilemmas*, Washington Papers No. 126 (New York: Praeger, 1987), p. 91.
101. Betts, "A Diplomatic Bomb?" pp. 202–203.
102. As one cabinet member puts it, "We knew we were in a minefield." Interview with H.J. "Kobie" Coetsee, deputy defense minister (1978–80), Cape Town, August 16, 1999.
103. Telephone conversation with Stumpf.

ing National Party was predominantly an Afrikaner nationalist party.[104] While its nationalist fervor was ebbing in the 1970s and 1980s, P.W. Botha himself remained "above all else an Afrikaner nationalist and a National Party loyalist whose language and religious faith were of profound importance to him."[105] The National Party also extensively managed the economy to favor Afrikaners through state employment, education, constraints on wages for blacks, protection of unskilled white labor against black competition, and favoritism to Afrikaner capital.[106] It sustained the import-substituting industrialization policy protecting South African consumer goods production since the 1920s, although the economy remained highly dependent on international trade and capital.[107] Pretoria also responded to sanctions by making massive state investments in coal-to-oil conversion, oil stockpiling, nuclear energy, and military industries.[108] The National Party's nationalist-statist orientation thus may have made it more amenable to the expense of nuclear self-sufficiency and further blunted international NPT pressure.

The Decision to Dismantle

Of the nine nations that have built nuclear weapons, South Africa remains the only one to dismantle them (though post-Soviet nuclear inheritors surrendered their arsenals as well). It would be hasty to generalize from this one case, especially one as unique as South Africa, which embarked on political transforma-

---

104. Adam and Giliomee, *Ethnic Power Mobilized;* and O'Meara, *Forty Lost Years.*

105. Robert Schrire, *Adapt or Die: The End of White Politics in South Africa,* South Africa Update Series (New York: Ford Foundation and Foreign Policy Association, 1991), p. 36.

106. By 1970, 27 percent of white workers (predominantly Afrikaners) were employed by the state or its parastatal industries. Merle Lipton and Charles Simkins, "Introduction," in Lipton and Simkins, *State and Market in Post-Apartheid South Africa* (Boulder, Colo.: Westview, 1993), pp. 1–34, p. 6. See also Adam and Giliomee, *Ethnic Power Mobilized,* pp. 145–176; Milton J. Esman, "Ethnic Politics and Economic Power," *Comparative Politics,* Vol. 19, No. 4 (July 1987), pp. 395–418; Merle Lipton, *Capitalism and Apartheid: South Africa, 1910–84* (Totowa, N.J.: Rowman and Allanheld, 1985); and O'Meara, *Forty Lost Years.*

107. Modest trade liberalization occurred in 1972–76, but the government remained highly protectionist and interventionist at the time that it decided to build nuclear weapons. Botha's government favored market reforms more than did Vorster's, but did little more than loosen several racial labor and financial restrictions that had become highly burdensome to industry. Trevor Bell, "Should South Africa Further Liberalise Its Foreign Trade?" in Lipton and Simkins, *State and Market in Post-Apartheid South Africa,* pp. 81–128; Graham A. Davis, *South African Managed Trade Policy: The Wasting of a Mineral Endowment* (Westport, Conn.: Praeger, 1994); and Stephen R. Lewis, Jr., *The Economics of Apartheid* (New York: Council on Foreign Relations Press, 1990).

108. Neta C. Crawford, "Oil Sanctions against Apartheid," in Crawford and Klotz, *How Sanctions Work,* pp. 103–126; and Fig, "Sanctions and the Nuclear Industry."

tion at the same time that it dismantled its nuclear arsenal. But nuclear rollback decisions provide additional evidence for theories normally used to explain nuclear acquisition decisions, on the assumption that the removal of the causes of a policy should lead to its reversal. This assumption, however, needs some qualification. While security theories predict that threats cause arming, they only weakly predict disarmament when threats evaporate. Superfluous military power endangers a state's security only when it saps economic strength or provokes other states to arm. Nuclear rollback is even harder for organizational politics to explain, because the establishment of government programs increases the size and influence of their bureaucratic constituencies. Exogenous changes in the nuclear weapons establishment's political power or interests must be added to any organizational explanation of disarmament.

In the South African case, dismantlement followed improvements in the security environment in key respects: the winding down of the Cold War, the removal of Cuban troops from Angola, and the expectation that democratizing reforms would end South Africa's regional tensions and international isolation. This is consistent with the security model's weak prediction that a decline in threat may lead to disarmament.

Organizational politics expectations are confounded by the program's demise, because agencies that have pushed a program should become only more motivated and better equipped to protect what they have gained. Although the nuclear establishment and military lost influence under F.W. de Klerk, this was because he and his political allies had decided to denuclearize and demilitarize. The role of a high-level, handpicked cabinet committee and the loyalty of the nuclear agency chief who had helped direct the program for nearly a decade also contradict organizational politics expectations.

International pressure to dismantle did not grow dramatically in the late 1980s, but Pretoria's sensitivity to the economic and diplomatic liabilities of the program did. Over the course of the 1980s, the National Party leadership, motivated to a significant extent by the desire to break South Africa out of its isolation, increasingly favored reforming apartheid. De Klerk and other liberalizers felt international pressure more keenly than had P.W. Botha, consistent with Solingen's NPT sensitivity hypothesis, but the leadership's new sensitivity was due primarily to its decision to end apartheid.

SCRAPPING THE WEAPONS PROGRAM

P.W. Botha showed little interest in nuclear disarmament throughout his time in office. In de Klerk's view, the nuclear program was something of a "pet project" for Botha.[109] Botha did reject Armscor proposals for developing (beyond paper studies) advanced nuclear weapon designs in September 1985, citing budgetary constraints and the pointlessness of an offensive capability.[110] He also publicly announced in 1987 that South Africa was ready to discuss NPT accession, but this was probably little more than a ploy to avert South Africa's possible expulsion from the IAEA at the time.[111] There were some discussions in Pretoria among foreign and military department heads in 1987 and 1988 about joining the NPT, but Foreign Affairs Director-General van Heerden says that the group was stacked with military, Armscor, Atomic Energy Corporation (AEC, the renamed AEB), and intelligence officials who supported the program; that it had little authority anyway; and that it may have been just a sop to Foreign Minister Pik Botha. Although the authorization of these discussions might have indicated a tentative step toward reevaluating South Africa's nuclear weapons policy, according to van Heerden, "P.W. never had any truck with the idea of us joining the NPT."[112] The construction of the $10 million Advena Central Laboratories starting in 1987, the 1987 or 1988 reopening of the Kalahari test site, and Botha's reported 1993 view that de Klerk's dismantling policy was "sabotaging the country," all support this assessment.[113]

F.W. de Klerk changed South Africa's nuclear policy soon after becoming president on September 14, 1989. About two weeks later, he formed an ad hoc cabinet committee to consider NPT accession. Chaired by the newly appointed minerals and energy minister, Dawid de Villiers, it also included the foreign minister, defense minister, finance minister, and the newly appointed minister of administration and privatization. An "experts committee" of Armscor, AEC, and SADF officials provided the staff work, with AEC Chairman J.W. de Villiers and his deputy, Waldo Stumpf, serving as liaisons.[114]

According to Stumpf, who attended the first meeting of the ad hoc cabinet committee, de Klerk "informed those present of his decision to normalize the internal political situation of the country and that the nuclear devices would be

109. Interview with F.W. de Klerk, Cape Town, April 7, 1999.
110. Correspondence with Stumpf.
111. Jaster, *Defence of White Power*, p. 168. The nuclear strategy working group had already concluded that "not signing the NPT but expressing our interest in doing so, and then stalling any negotiations, would be in line with our 'strategy of uncertainty.'" Correspondence with Buys, December 10, 1999.
112. Interviews with Barnard, January 22, 1999; and van Heerden. The group included van Heerden, National Intelligence Service Director-General Niel Barnard, AEC Chairman J.W. de Villiers, and Johannes Steyn of Armscor.
113. Interview with a South African official.
114. Correspondence with Dawid de Villiers, September 6, 2000.

a liability in South Africa gaining international acceptance in the process. . . . There was no debate about the decision but rather how it should be implemented and how South Africa should accede to the NPT."[115] De Klerk's intention is also evident in his selection for the committee of only officials—other than Malan—with no loyalty to the nuclear program and a chairman who he knew opposed it. In fact, de Klerk recalls having "had no enthusiasm for this massive spending programme" back in the early 1980s, and having decided to dismantle between his election as National Party leader in February 1989 and his taking over the presidency.[116]

Stumpf presented a dismantlement plan to the ad hoc committee in November, and de Klerk approved it as well as closure of the Y-plant.[117] The Y-plant was shut down by February 1, 1990, and the weapons were dismantled between July 1990 and July 1991. South Africa formally joined the NPT on July 10, 1991, and its safeguards agreement with the IAEA entered into force in September.[118]

MILITARY SECURITY AND NUCLEAR ROLLBACK

The decision to disarm, like the decision to acquire nuclear weapons, followed significant changes in South Africa's threat environment. Although de Klerk's decision to dismantle preceded the unequivocal end of the Cold War, marked to many observers by the November 1989 breach of the Berlin Wall, South Africa's improved security position had become increasingly evident in the year or two prior.[119] In December 1988, protracted U.S.-mediated negotiations resulted in an agreement for the withdrawal of Cuban and South African troops from Angola and for Namibian independence. In 1988 and 1989, Moscow scaled back aid to Angola, Mozambique, and the African National Congress and discouraged the ANC from continued armed struggle and pursuit of a

115. Correspondence with Stumpf. Dawid de Villiers recalls that de Klerk's instructions were more open-ended; correspondence, September 6, 2000; cf. Reiss, *Bridled Ambition*, p. 17.
116. Interview with de Klerk; and F.W. de Klerk, *The Last Trek: A New Beginning* (London: Macmillan, 1998), p. 273. De Klerk knew about the program from his tenure as minerals and energy minister from 1980 to 1982. After suggesting (during brief remarks at a small ribbon-cutting ceremony) that the government use the nuclear capability "for the benefit of *all* South Africans," Buys recalls receiving a scowl from P.W. Botha but a private appreciation from de Klerk. Interview with Buys.
117. Correspondence with Stumpf.
118. Reiss, *Bridled Ambition*, pp. 17–19.
119. Arguing that a pre-November decision undermines a security explanation is Sagan, "Why Do States Build Nuclear Weapons?" p. 70.

radical socialist agenda.[120] Though de Klerk had believed earlier that the "Soviet Union and Cuban allies had established threatening positions in some of our neighboring countries," by the time he became president, his "advisers' threat analysis was that the threat in southern Africa has changed dramatically because of the implosion of Russia as an expansionist world power."[121] De Klerk also expected that his intended political reforms "would help end confrontation with our neighbors in southern Africa and with the international community."[122] Furthermore, "if we're no longer a pariah, then we can . . . rely on allies to help us in whatever threat might rise again."[123] A 40 percent rollback of overall military expenditure between 1989 and 1993 reflected this sea change in threat perception.[124]

Although the timing of South Africa's nuclear dismantlement is consistent with a security explanation, the declining threat was at best a permissive condition for dismantling. A residual nuclear capability would not have endangered South African security, and the budgetary savings from dismantlement were relatively small. South Africa thus did not have strong security incentives to disarm. Nuclear rollback in this case would constitute strong evidence for the security model, as a weak but successful prediction, were there not other plausible explanations for this outcome. But other factors, though not organizational imperatives, do appear to have played important roles.

ORGANIZATIONAL POLITICS AND NUCLEAR ROLLBACK

The dismantlement decision followed a change in the advisers and agencies involved in nuclear policy decisionmaking. Pro-NPT foreign and economic advisers outnumbered military advisers in de Klerk's ad hoc cabinet committee, whereas military and Armscor officials (plus the pronuclear national intelligence chief) had outnumbered van Heerden in the interdepartmental discussions of 1987–88. But it was de Klerk's clear antinuclear preferences that shaped the new constellation of participants, rather than vice versa.

120. Crocker, *High Noon in Southern Africa*, pp. 373–464; Daniel R. Kempton, "New Thinking and Soviet Policy towards South Africa," *Journal of Modern African Studies*, Vol. 28, No. 4 (December 1990), pp. 545–572; and Michael McFaul, "Rethinking the 'Reagan Doctrine' in Angola," *International Security*, Vol. 14, No. 3 (Winter 1989/90), pp. 99–135.
121. Interview with de Klerk; and de Klerk, *Last Trek*, p. 114.
122. De Klerk, *Last Trek*, p. 274.
123. Interview with de Klerk.
124. Peter Batchelor and Susan Willett, *Disarmament and Defence Industrial Adjustment in South Africa* (New York: Oxford University Press, 1998), pp. 67–68.

De Klerk's charge to the ad hoc cabinet committee, his choice of its members, and his own recollections suggest that he had made his mind up to dismantle the program before allowing an internal debate. Contrary to organizational politics expectations, this points to presidential leadership in nuclear policy-making.[125] It is also surprising, from an organizational politics perspective, that the agencies with the most to lose from dismantling did not try harder to stop it, if only by leaking word about the program and its imminent demise.

Foreign Minister Pik Botha describes himself as a long-standing opponent of the nuclear program, though other officials question how early and forcefully he pressed the issue.[126] In the 1980s, says his deputy van Heerden, "we consistently tried to enter that inner circle by saying that this is an area that has considerable international implications and that the diplomatic arm of government should be brought into the picture. But that was at the time of the maximum perception of threat . . . and the soldiers were flying high and those who were in favor of diplomatic measures played second fiddle."[127] Van Heerden portrays Pik Botha as master of "the art of the possible," and describes the foreign minister's approach on the nuclear issue under P.W. Botha as "salami-slicing tactics."[128]

Finance Minister Barend du Plessis also says that he disliked the program, which would be expected given his budgetary and financial responsibilities. In March 1989, he openly questioned South African "economic survival in the face of an internationally organized assault on the economy. . . . The answer for us clearly lies in the full-scale effort to break the isolation imposed on us, by dynamic expansion of our trade with the outside world and a restoration of our creditworthiness by means of the correct economic measures and political progress."[129] Du Plessis still recalls his angst over the budgetary costs of the nuclear enrichment, weapons, and missile programs.[130]

Armscor and UCOR had the greatest stake in keeping the program going.

---

125. Presidential interest often favors clinging to failing policies to avoid admitting error, but sustained secrecy would have minimized the domestic fallout from a policy reversal. At most, organizational politics might explain Botha's stronger preference for military over diplomatic policy instruments, compared to de Klerk. This strains the theory, however, because it had been nearly a decade since Botha had given up the defense portfolio.
126. Interview with Pik Botha, August 25, 1999. Botha's characterization was echoed in an interview with Grant. Skeptical impressions were heard in interviews with Steyn, Malan, and Buys.
127. Interview with van Heerden.
128. Ibid.
129. March 1989 budget speech, quoted in Robert M. Price, *The Apartheid State in Crisis: Political Transformation in South Africa, 1975–1990* (New York: Oxford University Press, 1991), p. 275.
130. Telephone conversation with Barend du Plessis, August 26, 1999.

Armscor tripled the personnel working on the nuclear weapons program in the 1980s, from 100 to 300, and completed the new Advena Central Laboratories in 1989. Armscor had also made a major investment in a missile program, which was partly aimed at providing a nuclear warhead delivery option.[131] These were only two of many projects for Armscor, which in 1989 employed 26,348 (up from 10,590 in 1977) and controlled 2.2 billion rand in assets (up from 1.2 billion in 1977).[132] The provision of substantial resources to Armscor and the AEC to prevent a "brain drain" may have dampened Armscor's objections. But, enlarged by its role in combating international arms embargoes against South Africa, Armscor should have had considerable political resources to defend its turf.

The nuclear science and energy complex had also grown, despite having lost the weapons program to Armscor. The nuclear scientists' prestige had faded along with the global dimming of expectations for nuclear energy. But UCOR had just built an expensive semicommercial uranium enrichment plant (the Z-plant) to fuel the Koeberg power plants. Restoring access to international nuclear suppliers by joining the NPT would turn both enrichment plants into embarrassing white elephants. In fact, AEC employment would drop from about 8,200 to less than 2,000.[133] Yet D.W. Steyn, minerals and energy minister in the mid-1980s, had recommended disarming and joining the NPT sometime around 1987.[134] Seemingly even more inconsistent with organizational politics expectations was AEC Chairman de Villiers's enthusiastic support for de Klerk's disarmament policy.[135]

The military's stake in the nuclear program was less clear-cut. Military attachment to the program is suggested by de Klerk's suspicion that his disarmament policy "was resented in some circles in the military establishment," as

---

131. Albright, "South Africa's Secret Nuclear Weapons," pp. 14–16.

132. Batchelor and Willett, *Disarmament and Defence Industrial Adjustment*, p. 38.

133. John Walmsley, "The South African Nuclear Industry," *Nuclear Engineer,* Vol. 38, No. 4 (July 1997), pp. 99–103, at p. 100.

134. Interview with Steyn.

135. Fig, "Sanctions and the Nuclear Industry," p. 96. De Villiers was never as enthusiastic about the weapons program as his predecessor, Ampie Roux. Interview with Grant; and correspondence with Stumpf. One possible incentive to scrap the bomb, pointed out to me by Andrew Marquard, might have been to shed apartheid-era baggage in order to maintain support for the AEB under future black governments. South African nuclear power officials were also eager to join the NPT, though this would have been more in line with their organizational interests, because South Africa's state-owned electricity utility—Eskom—needed international capital and technology to expand power production and was paying exorbitant prices for the AEB's low-enriched uranium; cf. Mark Hibbs, "Eskom Will Not Order New Reactor before 1992," *Nucleonics Week,* September 6, 1990, p. 14.

well as a senior official's claim that de Klerk rushed to dismantle in order to steamroll the defense establishment during his presidential honeymoon period.[136] But Magnus Malan, defense minister and former SADF chief, thought only that South Africa should hold out for tangible Western concessions in return for joining the NPT.[137] SADF Chief General Geldenhuys agreed, though he had never seen any military utility in the arsenal and anyway was not consulted on de Klerk's decision.[138] The South African air force had gained a significant management role in the nuclear weapons program, which might have raised its enthusiasm about it.[139] But top generals are rumored to have strongly opposed an Armscor push for nuclear testing and to have feared politicians' reckless use of the capability.[140] Whatever the military's attitude, its influence waned under de Klerk. In addition to cutting military spending drastically, he ended the heavy reliance on military officers in political decisionmaking instituted by Botha.[141] Malan himself had never gained his own power base in the National Party and would be sidelined to a minor cabinet post in mid-1991.[142]

INTERNATIONAL PRESSURE, STATE SENSITIVITY, AND NUCLEAR ROLLBACK
After the near-total nuclear isolation of the late 1970s, only a few further Western sanctions were threatened, and no incentives offered, to change South Africa's nuclear policies. Despite this, van Heerden estimates that U.S. lobbying contributed "30 to 60 percent" to the decision to dismantle, once the external threat had receded.[143] This points to changes in Pretoria's sensitivity to pressure rather than to changes in the economic or diplomatic incentives it faced. De Klerk's decision to abandon apartheid opened the door to normalization, a process that could be accelerated (if not initiated) by joining the NPT. Though the apartheid Rubicon distinguishes South Africa from other nuclear fence-sitters, the government's newly liberalizing orientation is consistent

136. De Klerk, *Last Trek*, p. 274; and Hibbs, "Dismantling," p. 10.
137. Interview with Malan.
138. Interview with Geldenhuys, January 25, 1999.
139. Ibid. According to Buys, over time "there was a change in attitude. . . . eventually I managed to get very good cooperation from the [military], particularly on the safety and security aspect." Interview with Buys.
140. Interviews with Grant; and Breytenbach. This story, however, was discounted in an interview with Geldenhuys, August 24, 1999.
141. Seegers, *Military in the Making of Modern South Africa*, pp. 266–268.
142. O'Meara, *Forty Lost Years*, p. 398.
143. Interview with van Heerden; but see Reiss, *Bridled Ambition*, p. 32.

with Solingen's hypothesis about state sensitivity to NPT norms and incentives.

After the Reagan administration relaxed some nuclear-related sanctions in the early 1980s, congressional and public anti-apartheid mobilization led to a tightened ban on nuclear cooperation in 1985 and a complete ban in 1986.[144] Starting in 1986, the United States stepped up attempts to persuade South Africa to join the NPT in a series of confidential meetings between U.S. Ambassador-at-Large for Nuclear Affairs Richard T. Kennedy and Foreign Minister Pik Botha, some with representatives of other NPT depository states. Kennedy told Botha that the Reagan (and later the Bush) administrations would do everything possible to restore commercial and scientific nuclear cooperation after South African NPT accession, but he acknowledged that they could not prevent an anti-apartheid Congress from raising the bar and keeping nuclear sanctions in place.[145] In addition, Kennedy rebuffed Botha's query about whether South Africa might gain broader sanctions relief for joining the NPT, saying that proliferation could not be rewarded with quid pro quos for reversal. Washington and London threatened to escalate anti-apartheid sanctions further in 1989, but did not offer any incentives specifically for NPT accession.[146]

Neither sanctions nor norms appear to have had much impact on P.W. Botha's nuclear policy, although they did lead Minerals and Energy Minister Steyn to recommend joining the NPT to P.W. Botha around 1987.[147] An avalanche of new Western anti-apartheid sanctions in 1985 and 1986, combined with a debt crisis in South Africa, might have put the NPT on the agenda. De Klerk speculates that Botha's 1987 NPT remarks might have reflected an interest in exploring whether the nuclear program could be used as a bargaining chip to relieve economic sanctions.[148]

---

144. Fig, "Sanctions and the Nuclear Industry," pp. 87–89; and Pabian, "South Africa's Nuclear Weapon Program," pp. 6–7.
145. Interviews with van Heerden; Pik Botha, August 25, 1999; and Richard J.K. Stratford, former special assistant to the U.S. ambassador-at-large for nuclear affairs, Washington, D.C., December 13, 1999. On additional nuclear sanctions in the 1980s, see Fig, "Sanctions and the Nuclear Industry," pp. 88–89. The South African government did press the United States for a new peaceful nuclear cooperation agreement soon after signing the NPT. Correspondence with Fred McGoldrick, former U.S. State Department official, May 31, 2001.
146. Paul Rich, "Changing Relations with the United States," in Greg Mills, ed., *From Pariah to Participant: South Africa's Evolving Foreign Relations, 1990–1994* (Johannesburg: South African Institute of International Affairs, 1994), pp. 98–104.
147. Interview with Steyn.
148. Interview with de Klerk.

De Klerk responded differently to the same incentives faced by P.W. Botha. Unlike Botha, de Klerk and much of the National Party leadership were finally reconciled to real power sharing.[149] De Klerk had a conservative track record, but he appears to have experienced an evolutionary conversion culminating in his September 1989 inauguration as president.[150] As soon as reversal of anti-apartheid sanctions became possible, joining the NPT became an attractive strategy for hastening the process, as a way of placating antiproliferation governments and of demonstrating the irrevocability of change to foreign capitals.[151] De Klerk also saw joining the NPT as a means to draw Western support for his preferred domestic settlement (i.e., protected minority rights and private property): "The ANC must somehow or another be moved to the position where they were really negotiating in the true sense of the word. . . . For that I needed to have credibility outside South Africa that I mean what I say, I have a good cause, and I wanted support for my way of doing things."[152] Van Heerden similarly recalls de Klerk's thinking that "if I can get the Americans and others off my back on this [NPT] issue, then there will be more sympathy for the kind of arguments which I will have to put forward on a domestic settlement."[153] De Klerk also believed that economic improvement from a relaxation of sanctions would help "ensure that the constitutional reform takes place in a hopeful, positive economic atmosphere."[154]

The argument was a subtle one and not universally shared in Pretoria. Many officials, including de Klerk's defense minister, minister of justice, deputy defense minister, national intelligence chief, and SADF chief, thought that de

---

149. Sanctions and isolation were important reasons for the change, but probably not the main ones. Black political resistance, apartheid's economic inefficiency, defections of hard-liners from the National Party to the Conservative Party, an eroding white demographic base, Soviet retrenchment (including withdrawal of support for the ANC), and de Klerk's personality all had an impact. Debating the impact of sanctions are Crawford and Klotz, *How Sanctions Work;* and Anton D. Lowenberg and William H. Kaempfer, *The Origins and Demise of South African Apartheid: A Public Choice Analysis* (Ann Arbor: University of Michigan Press, 1998). For fuller explanations of democratization, see Hermann Giliomee, "Democratization in South Africa," *Political Science Quarterly,* Vol. 110, No. 1 (Spring 1995), pp. 83–105; O'Meara, *Forty Lost Years;* Price, *Apartheid State in Crisis;* Timothy D. Sisk, *Democratization in South Africa: The Elusive Social Contract* (Princeton, N.J.: Princeton University Press, 1995); and Patti Waldmeir, *Anatomy of a Miracle: The End of Apartheid and the Birth of the New South Africa* (New York: W.W. Norton, 1997).
150. Allister Sparks, *Tomorrow Is Another Country: The Inside Story of South Africa's Road to Change* (Chicago: University of Chicago Press, 1995), pp. 91–108.
151. Interview with Pik Botha, April 9, 1999.
152. Interview with de Klerk. Also making this point is Giliomee, "Democratization in South Africa."
153. Interview with van Heerden.
154. Interview with de Klerk. Du Plessis also made this argument; Patti Waldmeir, "Born Again into Capitalism," *Financial Times,* June 11, 1990, Survey, p. 2.

Klerk should hold out for a Western quid pro quo for dismantlement. Some of these officials attribute de Klerk's haste to disarm to his being overly hungry for Western approval, though this could reflect their unfamiliarity with the lack of bargaining opportunities evident from the Kennedy-Botha sessions.[155] De Klerk's inner circle believed that conservative nationalists would be even more opposed to disarmament, as removing a pillar of white power, which is one reason they concealed the decision at least until after the March 1992 white referendum on democratization.[156]

Solingen's theory predicts a correspondence between a state's economic orientation, nationalism, and its nuclear policies.[157] Indeed diminishing Afri-kaner-nationalist ideology, accelerated by the 1982 defection of hard-liners to the new Conservative Party and an increasing proportion of English-speaking supporters, may not have only moved the National Party toward political reform but also heightened its receptivity to international pressure.[158] Although its attention was focused almost entirely on the question of political liberalization, the National Party appears to have shifted its economic bearings by 1989 as well. De Klerk was more inclined to free-market policies than his predecessor had been.[159] His government reduced import tariffs and quotas, privatized the national steel corporation, dismantled racial labor restrictions, and liberalized foreign-exchange controls.[160] As mentioned above, both du Plessis and

---

155. Interviews with Barnard, January 22, 1999; Breytenbach; and Coetsee. De Klerk's eagerness, in his own words, to fully "rejoin the international community" does suggest the importance of international norms, to him at least. Interview with de Klerk.

156. Correspondence with Dawid de Villiers, May 16, 2001; and telephone conversation with Stumpf.

157. Political leaders can select policies that advance the coalition's overall interests even in the absence of overt mobilization. Thus the lack of antinuclear mobilization by South African business and other societal liberalizers does not contradict the theory.

158. On declining Afrikaner nationalism in the National Party, see Hermann Giliomee, "*Broedertwis:* Intra-Afrikaner Conflicts in the Transition from Apartheid," *African Affairs*, Vol. 91, No. 364 (July 1992), pp. 339–364.

159. De Klerk, *Last Trek*, pp. 151, 154, 228. On business support for de Klerk and political reform, see Robin Lee, Margaret Sutherland, Mark Phillips, and Anne McLennan, "Speaking or Listening? Observers or Agents of Change? Business and Public Policy: 1989/90," in Lee and Lawrence Schlemmer, eds., *Transition to Democracy: Policy Perspectives, 1991* (Cape Town: Oxford University Press, 1991), pp. 95–126; Louwrens Pretorius, "The Head of Government and Organised Business," in Robert Schrire, ed., *Malan to De Klerk: Leadership in the Apartheid State* (New York: St. Martin's, 1994), pp. 209–244; Giliomee, "Democratization in South Africa"; Jan Hofmeyr, *The Impact of Sanctions on White South Africa*, Part 2, *Whites' Political Attitudes* (Washington, D.C.: Investor Responsibility Research Center, 1990); O'Meara, *Forty Lost Years*; and Annette Strauss, "The 1992 Referendum in South Africa," *Journal of Modern African Studies*, Vol. 31, No. 2 (June 1993), pp. 339–360, especially pp. 348–349.

160. Bell, "Should South Africa Liberalise Its Foreign Trade?"; Trevor Bell, "Trade Policy," in Jonathan Michie and Vishnu Padayachee, eds., *The Political Economy of South Africa's Transition: Policy Perspectives in the Late 1990's* (New York: Dryden, 1997), pp. 71–90; W. Duncan Reekie, "Should

de Klerk were critical of the program's budgetary burden. De Klerk's tapping of three economic liberalizers (Dawid de Villiers, Barend du Plessis, and Willem de Villiers) for the ad hoc NPT committee may have also reflected a view that internationalist economic priorities should influence nuclear policy.[161]

Conclusions

Three general sources of nuclear weapons policy—security incentives, organizational politics, and international pressure and state sensitivity—shed light on the rise and fall of South Africa's nuclear weapons program. Limited evidence makes it impossible to establish which of the theories best explains the case, but viewing the program through these three theoretical prisms reveals some of the strengths and weaknesses of each from development to dismantlement.

Organizational politics best explains the development of a latent nuclear weapons capability in the early 1970s. The AEB's information monopoly and strict secrecy enabled it to obtain authorization directly from the prime minister and the minister of mines for early research on nuclear explosives. At the time, South Africa's security environment was still very benign, and one would expect greater consultations with defense officials had the program been initially designed to be a deterrent. Although a nationalist-statist outlook predisposed the government to favor state-run projects with potential commercial and prestige value, the lack of international NPT pressures at the time made state sensitivity to such pressures moot.

Organizational politics provides a weaker explanation for the decisions to weaponize and especially to dismantle. A high degree of secrecy continued to limit political debate at the time the Vorster government formally opted for a deterrent sometime in late 1977. Aside from the chief of staff of planning, the military was unenthusiastic about going nuclear, so any organizational push

South African Parastatals Be Privatised?" in Lipton and Simkins, *State and Market in Post-Apartheid South Africa,* pp. 129–160; and Waldmeir, "Born Again into Capitalism." Some observers suggest that the ANC persuaded de Klerk in 1990 to slow down privatization, to give a successor democratic government more say over economic policy. As it turned out, the ANC proved more liberal than the National Party.

161. Dawid de Villiers had previously been involved in developing tariff reduction and privatization policy as trade and industry minister, as had du Plessis as minister of finance. Willem "Wim" de Villiers was a former industrialist and leading free marketeer whom de Klerk appointed minister of administration and privatization.

had to come from the AEB and Armscor. But P.W. Botha's involvement in the decision to weaponize, his reliance on a personal military adviser, and his reaffirmation of the weaponization decision after broadening the decision-making process as prime minister all suggest a top-down rather than bottom-up decision.

The decision to dismantle was directed even more decisively by the head of government. Organizational politics would predict that the agencies that had successfully pushed or accepted the program should have become only more motivated and better able to protect it. Although it is true that the armaments and military establishments lost influence under F.W. de Klerk, this was because he had already decided to demilitarize the country. The nuclear agency chief's enthusiasm for disarmament is also inconsistent with organizational predictions.

South Africa's decisions to build nuclear weapons and then to disarm followed changes in the country's security environment. Official recollections emphasize new threats as the primary incentive for building the weapons, and their disappearance as a necessary condition for dismantling them, though security rationalizations could cloak other motives. The main problems with a security explanation are the remote invasion or nuclear blackmail threats to South Africa, the debatable utility of nuclear deterrence and diplomacy in meeting those threats, and a lack of systematic policy analysis supporting the decision to weaponize. These observations suggest either that the insecurity threshold required to trigger nuclear weapons programs is quite low, extending to threats to non-homeland territories (such as Namibia), at least for states that can do so rather cheaply, or that organizational or other factors contributed to the decision.

The decision to dismantle is also consistent with a security explanation, arriving as it did so soon after the Angolan settlement. But the timing of the decision corresponds more closely to de Klerk's political ascent, as does evidence that P.W. Botha would not have so easily relinquished the program. De Klerk and his associates acknowledge that an improved security environment was a precondition for change, though de Klerk also says that he was never keen on the program. Of course, because apartheid was the root of South African insecurity, political reform and declining threat were inseparably intertwined causes of dismantling.

South Africa's nuclear policies were consistent with Solingen's theory that nationalist-statist regimes favor nuclear weapons programs more than do liberalizing ones, at least among nuclear fence-sitters. But there is little evidence from policy participants that the government's statism or liberalism had a major impact on NPT sensitivity, certainly not compared to the apartheid issue. The international nuclear sanctions that had mounted by 1978 were closely linked to apartheid. The government's nationalist-statist ideology may have made more palatable the costly investments required for nuclear energy self-sufficiency. But any South African government committed to apartheid would have seen little material benefit in joining the NPT, and perhaps some in defying it, though tight secrecy precluded any reputational benefits from actually possessing nuclear weapons.

Although international pressure to dismantle (unlike pressure to reform apartheid) did not intensify much further in the late 1980s, Pretoria's sensitivity to the diplomatic liabilities of the program did. The National Party leadership, motivated to a significant extent by the desire to break South Africa out of its isolation, increasingly favored reforming apartheid over the course of the 1980s. De Klerk's decision to engage in fundamental political change opened the door to economic and diplomatic opportunities that could be attained more quickly by joining the NPT. The National Party had grown less nationalistic and more market oriented, which might have disposed the leadership even more to nuclear disarmament, but much less critically than the decision to break with apartheid.

Clearly, the South African case does not provide a critical case study for testing the three theories. Only organizational politics theory's prediction that disarmament will not occur is clearly disconfirmed. Fragmentary and ambiguous evidence (particularly about the weaponization decisions) and the simultaneous changes in South Africa's security environment, diplomatic relations, and domestic politics impede further weighing of causal influences. It seems possible that combinations of factors discussed here were necessary for key decisions. The South African bomb might never have materialized had one or two of the following factors not been present in the late 1970s: a worsened security situation, a nuclear science establishment with a surplus of expertise and shortage of projects, and linkage of nuclear sanctions to apartheid. Likewise, dismantlement might not have occurred had the security environment not improved, or had a stroke not loosened P.W. Botha's grip on power in 1989.

My focus on the three theories in this article is not meant to imply that they provide the only important explanations for the rise and fall of South Africa's nuclear program. P.W. Botha's personality may have had a large impact. As defense minister, prime minister, and then president, he wielded considerable discretion over the small, secret program. Exaggerated fears of the Soviet threat, of whatever origin, facilitated nuclear acquisition. The impact of strategic transmission or emulation, particularly for pariah states thrown together for lack of other allies, is another possible factor, though one unlikely to be admitted for obvious reasons. Also often, but not always, denied is the impact on the disarmament decision of worries about future ANC governments' handling of the capability. Van Heerden acknowledges hearing this argument, that he worried about it as well, and that it "could well have been an element" in de Klerk's thinking.[162] De Klerk, however, says that it "was not a significant factor in our discussions and our decision," because the political settlement was still five years away, and that he "was thinking about the immediate two years ahead, in which the ANC as power-sharers did not figure at all."[163]

The complexity and ambiguity of this case suggest several alternative policies that might have resulted in greater South African nuclear restraint. Most of them are hard to imagine being adopted, however, given other incentives and constraints that U.S. and other policymakers faced at the time. The United States or other powers might have guaranteed South African security in the event of a Soviet-backed invasion or the use of weapons of mass destruction. Public opposition to apartheid made this an improbable option, though Western officials might have done more to convince Pretoria of the improbability of such threats. Negotiating the withdrawal of Cuban troops from Angola was a more pragmatic though difficult effort in this vein, and U.S. officials recognized the potential side benefits of this policy for nonproliferation.[164]

Had the U.S. Plowshares Program not promoted peaceful nuclear explosives so assiduously in the 1960s, the AEB might never have launched a PNE program in 1970, and might have been less eager to go ahead with a weapons program in the late 1970s. Alternatively, though more difficult politically, would

---

162. Interview with van Heerden.
163. Interview with de Klerk. Stumpf told a reporter in 1991 that "the prospect of black-majority rule . . . was a major consideration" in the government's decision to end the strategic emphasis of the program and join the NPT, but now explains that he believed that the weapons would have been an albatross for a Mandela government. Telephone conversation with Stumpf; and Pabian, "South Africa's Nuclear Weapon Program," p. 19. Malan, but neither Pik Botha nor van Heerden, says that he heard U.S. contacts argue against an ANC nuclear inheritance. Interviews with Pik Botha, August 25, 1999; Malan; and van Heerden. On this issue, see also David Albright and Mark Hibbs, "South Africa: The ANC and the Atom Bomb," *Bulletin of the Atomic Scientists*, Vol. 49, No. 3 (May–June 1993), pp. 32–37, at p. 33; and Reiss, *Bridled Ambition*, pp. 20–21.
164. Telephone conversation with Chester Crocker, U.S. assistant secretary of state for Africa (1981–88), February 18, 2000.

have been to actively engage South African scientists in other pursuits. International codevelopment of enrichment facilities in South Africa, on condition of full-scope safeguards, might also have diminished the AEB's interest in weapons research.[165] International collaboration on reactor research might have soaked up AEB personnel idled by the 1969 cancellation of South Africa's indigenous nuclear reactor program. These days, the collapse of fissile material prices and the disrepute of PNEs have undercut programs that might generate bureaucratic momentum for nuclear weapons. But nonproliferation policies should aim to limit the growth of the civilian nuclear fuel and power industries of nonnuclear weapon states, while being mindful that restricting overt civilian programs may divert organizational impulses toward secret military ones.

States have few foreign policy levers to affect the political-economic orientation of governing coalitions of other nations, but they can tailor economic and social pressures to the sensitivities of the target state. One lesson of the South African case is that successful coercion requires a credible commitment to reward compliance. Harsher sanctions—and not merely nuclear ones—could have been imposed, but these too would not have worked without strong commitments to remove them when South Africa joined the NPT. Against nationalist-statist regimes, however, even finely tuned sanctions can backfire, and in the South African case, the political battles over anti-apartheid sanctions in the United States and Europe would have made it difficult to craft such policies anyway.

---

165. Sole, "South African Nuclear Case," p. 74.

Never Say Never Again

Nuclear Reversal Revisited

Ariel E. Levite

A serious gap exists in scholarly understanding of nuclear proliferation. The gap derives from inadequate attention to the phenomena of nuclear reversal and nuclear restraint as well as insufficient awareness of the biases and limitations inherent in the empirical data employed to study proliferation. This article identifies "nuclear hedging" as a national strategy lying between nuclear pursuit and nuclear rollback. An understanding of this strategy can help scholars to explain the nuclear behavior of many states; it can also help to explain why the nightmare proliferation scenarios of the 1960s have not materialized. These insights, in turn, cast new light on several prominent proliferation case studies and the unique role of the United States in combating global proliferation. They have profound implications for engaging current or latent nuclear proliferants, underscoring the centrality of buying time as the key component of a nonproliferation strategy.

The article begins with a brief review of contemporary nuclear proliferation concerns. It then takes stock of the surprisingly large documented universe of nuclear reversal cases and the relevant literature.[1] It proceeds to examine the empirical challenges that bedeviled many of the earlier studies, possibly skewing their theoretical findings. Next, it discusses the features of the nuclear reversal and restraint phenomena and the forces that influence them. In this context, it introduces and illustrates an alternative explanation for the nuclear behavior of many states based on the notion of nuclear hedging. It draws on this notion and other inputs to reassess the role that the United States

At the time this article was written, Ariel E. Levite was a Visiting Fellow at the Center for International Security and Cooperation (CISAC) at Stanford University.

The author is indebted to Sidney Drell, Alexander George, David Holloway, and Scott Sagan for their valuable input and support. Chaim Braun, Barry O'Neill, Jeremi Suri, and other affiliates of CISAC, as well as *International Security*'s anonymous reviewers, provided helpful feedback and suggestions. I also benefited greatly from comments received from several seasoned practitioners. Tracy Williams deserves much credit for her outstanding assistance. Nichole Argo, Jonathan Neril, Gil Reich, and Anca Ruhlen were exceptional in providing archival research; in addition, Megan Hendershott and Karen Stiller offered invaluable editorial assistance. This research was facilitated in part by a research grant from the Ploughshares Foundation.

1. "Annotated Bibliography of Nuclear Reversal," unpublished memo, Center for International Security and Cooperation, Stanford University, June 2002.

International Security, Vol. 27, No. 3 (Winter 2002/03), pp. 59–88
© 2003 by the President and Fellows of Harvard College and the Massachusetts Institute of Technology.

has played in influencing the nuclear behavior of other states. The conclusion explores some of the policy and research implications of the article's findings.

Current Proliferation Concerns

The nuclear proliferation phenomenon has taken many twists and turns over the years, with the pace, direction, and loci of action varying considerably. In the late 1950s and 1960s, it was widely believed that nuclear proliferation beyond the original club of five (i.e., China, France, Great Britain, the Soviet Union, and the United States) was likely to occur before long, and that it would be led mainly by countries in Europe (most prominently Germany, Italy, and Sweden).[2] With the establishment of the nuclear Nonproliferation Treaty (NPT) regime in 1968–70, however, international concern over nuclear proliferation in Europe began to wane, though worries about proliferation in the developing world persisted, with Latin America and South Africa becoming particular sources of anxiety. More recently, South Asia, East Asia, and the Middle East have become the primary foci of concern. In addition, overall confidence in the stability of the nuclear nonproliferation regime has been shaken by developments in the nuclear arena in India and Pakistan, as well as in Iran, Iraq, and North Korea.

These developments have led two observers to suggest that, despite the remarkable success in producing an indefinite extension of the NPT in 1995, the "complex [NPT] regime intended to contain the spread of nuclear technologies is disintegrating."[3] Moreover, the prevailing assumption is that Iran or Iraq (or both) is bound to cross the nuclear weapons threshold before long, while Libya is proceeding along the same path. If this happens, further "horizontal nuclear proliferation" (a spillover effect on other states) is likely to occur both in the Middle East and beyond. A similar process is considered likely if the security

---

2. According to the Harvard Nuclear Study Group, "In 1963 President [John F.] Kennedy envisioned a world in the 1970s with 15–25 nuclear weapon states." See Albert Carnesale, Paul Doty, Stanley Hoffmann, Samuel P. Huntington, Joseph S. Nye Jr., and Scott D. Sagan, *Living with Nuclear Weapons* (Cambridge, Mass.: Harvard University Press, 1983), p. 215. A similarly somber assessment ("The world is fast approaching a point of no return in the prospects of controlling the spread of nuclear weapons.") appeared in a secret U.S. report presented to President Lyndon Johnson in 1965. See the Committee on Nuclear Proliferation, "A Report to the President," January 21, 1965, http://www.gwu.edu/?nsarchiv/NSAEBB/NSAEBB1/nhch7_1.htm (accessed August 15, 2002).

3. Barry M. Blechman and Leo S. Mackay Jr., *Weapons of Mass Destruction: A New Paradigm for a New Century,* Occasional Paper No. 40 (Washington, D.C.: Henry L. Stimson Center, 2000), p. 4.

situation on the Korean Peninsula and the Indian subcontinent continues to deteriorate. These developments have rekindled interest both in identifying the factors that drive nuclear proliferation and in understanding the processes that govern them.[4]

Challenges to the Study of Nuclear Reversal

Most nuclear proliferation studies have focused on proliferation trends, their prospects, and means of dealing with the challenges they pose. A smaller body of research has focused on the motivations for acquiring or renouncing nuclear weapons. Relatively little has been written on nuclear reversal, although this phenomenon has attracted somewhat greater interest in recent years.[5] Nuclear reversal refers to the phenomenon in which states embark on a path leading to nuclear weapons acquisition but subsequently reverse course, though not necessarily abandoning altogether their nuclear ambitions. Using this definition, a preliminary survey suggests that nearly twenty states have chosen the path of nuclear reversal since 1945 (see Table 1).[6]

---

4. For leading works in this genre, see Scott D. Sagan, "Why Do States Build Nuclear Weapons? Three Models in Search of a Bomb," *International Security,* Vol. 21, No. 3 (Winter 1996/97), pp. 54–86; Bradley A. Thayer, "The Causes of Nuclear Proliferation and the Nonproliferation Regime," *Security Studies,* Vol. 4, No. 3 (Spring 1995), pp. 463–519; Benjamin Frankel, "The Brooding Shadow: Systemic Incentives and Nuclear Weapons Proliferation," and Richard K. Betts, "Paranoids, Pygmies, Pariahs, and Nonproliferation Revisited," both in Zachary S. Davis and Benjamin Frankel, eds., *The Proliferation Puzzle: Why Nuclear Weapons Spread (and What Results)* (Portland: Frank Cass, 1993), pp. 37–38 and pp. 100–124, respectively.
5. A study by Harald Muller, using somewhat different criteria, has identified a similar number of nuclear reversal cases. Most of the countries appear in both lists. See Muller, "Nuclear Nonproliferation: A Success Story," paper presented at the Thirteenth Annual Amaldi Conference on Problems of Global Security, Rome, Italy, November 30–December 2, 2000.
6. The most salient work in this area is T.V. Paul, *Power versus Prudence: Why Nations Forgo Nuclear Weapons* (Montreal: McGill-Queen's University Press, 2000). See also Mitchell Reiss, *Bridled Ambitions: Why States Constrain Their Nuclear Capability* (Washington, D.C.: Woodrow Wilson Center Press, 1995); Mitchell Reiss, *Without the Bomb: The Politics of Nuclear Nonproliferation* (New York: Columbia University Press, 1988); James Doyle, "Nuclear Rollback: A New Direction for United States Nuclear Policy?" Ph.D. dissertation, University of Virginia, 1997; Charles Edward Costanzo, "Returning from the Brink: Is There a Theory-Based Explanation for the Attenuation of Horizontal Nuclear Proliferation?" Ph.D. dissertation, University of Alabama, 1998; James Walsh, "Bombs Unbuilt: Power, Ideas, and Institutions in International Politics," Ph.D. dissertation, Massachusetts Institute of Technology, 2000; Barry R. Schneider and William L. Dowdy, eds., *Pulling Back from the Nuclear Brink: Reducing and Countering Nuclear Threats* (London: Frank Cass, 1998); Etel Solingen, "The Political Economy of Nuclear Restraint," *International Security,* Vol. 19, No. 2 (Fall 1994), pp. 126–169; Leonard S. Spector, "Repentant Nuclear Proliferants," *Foreign Policy,* No. 88 (Fall 1992), pp. 3–20; and William C. Potter, *The Politics of Nuclear Renunciation: The Cases of Belarus, Kazakhstan, and Ukraine,* Occasional Paper No. 22 (Washington, D.C.: Henry L. Stimson Center, 1995).

Table 1. Cases of Nuclear Reversal since 1945.

Never Tried (nuclear abstinence)	Tried but Gave Up (nuclear reversal)	Attained but Gave Up[a]	Still Trying	Attained and Maintained
All (?) other states	Argentina	Belarus[b]	Algeria[c]	China
	Australia	Kazakhstan[b]	Iran[d]	France
	Brazil	South Africa	Iraq[d]	Great Britain
	Canada[e]	Ukraine[b]	Libya	India
	Egypt		North Korea[f]	Pakistan
	Germany			Soviet Union/
	Indonesia			Russia
	Italy			United States
	Japan			––––––––––
	Netherlands[c]			Israel[g]
	Norway[c]			
	Romania[c]			
	South Korea[d]			
	Sweden			
	Switzerland			
	Taiwan[d]			
	Yugoslavia[c]			

NOTE: There have been repeated assertions, but no hard publicly available data, that Finland, Greece, Spain, and Turkey may have also had nuclear weapons aspirations. In the absence of evidence to corroborate these assertions, these countries are excluded here from the category of nuclear weapons aspirants.

[a] For the purposes of this study, the states listed in this category are considered as having undergone nuclear reversal.

[b] These states had nuclear weapons deployed on their territory but not under their command. Only Ukraine appears to have had physical possession of Russian nuclear weapons deployed on its soil, although apparently not the codes necessary to launch them.

[c] The determination and intensity with which these states pursued nuclear weapons remain uncertain.

[d] These are states that appear to have sought to acquire nuclear weapons on more than one occasion.

[e] Canada's nuclear weapons–oriented activity began with its participation in the Manhattan Project in the 1940s. Subsequently, it remained principally tied to the U.S. and British programs.

[f] The status of the North Korean nuclear program remains uncertain, although the North Koreans are suspected of having produced one or two nuclear weapons in the mid-1990s. See National Intelligence Council, *Foreign Missile Developments and the Ballistic Missile Threat through 2015: Unclassified Summary of a National Intelligence Estimate* (Washington, D.C.: National Intelligence Council, December 2001). North Korea appears to have subsequently engaged in a clandestine enrichment project, and in late 2002 threatened to reactivate its plutonium production. But these actions apparently have not yielded any additional weapons-grade fissile material. See the Carnegie Endowment Nonproliferation Project's website at http://www.ceip.org/files/nonprolif/default.asp (accessed January 4, 2003).

[g] Israel's nuclear status is unconfirmed.

For all its accomplishments, the literature on nuclear reversal is plagued by a variety of theoretical and methodological problems. Some of these problems are inherent in the very nature of the reversal phenomenon. Consider, for example, the issue of equifinality. Previous studies have been unable to identify the necessary or sufficient conditions for nuclear reversal, in part because different factors and causal paths, none of which is fully understood, can produce it. In the 1980s and 1990s, for example, Libya apparently temporarily scaled back its pursuit of nuclear weapons (though not its nuclear aspirations).[7] Libya's problematic international standing has compounded its inability to find a willing foreign supplier for the finished product or key facilities,[8] while its weak indigenous technological base continues to preclude the development of a strictly domestic program. Nuclear reversals in Argentina and Brazil, on the other hand, are widely attributed to reduced external security threats and domestic regime changes.[9] In Sweden and Switzerland, another factor appears to have been at work—concern over incurring the wrath of hostile nuclear powers.[10] Also in the Swedish case, the implicit extension of the U.S. nuclear umbrella seems to have played an important role.

Previous studies have also had difficulty assessing the influence on nuclear behavior of factors such as sanctions and nonproliferation norms that have a delayed or "nonlinear" impact (i.e., they take effect only after a predetermined threshold is crossed). Nor have they been able to distinguish between factors that lead to nuclear reversal and those that lead toward proliferation. The case of Egypt is illustrative in this regard.

Egypt's interest in developing a nuclear weapons program in the early 1960s is widely attributed to one or more of the following factors: its perception of an evolving Israeli nuclear capability, an inability to defeat Israel using conventional weapons, a desire to lead the Arab world politically and technologically, and strong domestic support for an indigenous nuclear capability. Egypt ultimately decided not to develop a full-fledged nuclear weapons program, how-

---

7. See National Intelligence Council, *Foreign Missile Developments and the Ballistic Missile Threat through 2015: Unclassified Summary of a National Intelligence Estimate* (Washington, D.C.: National Intelligence Council, December 2001).

8. See Joshua Sinai, "Libya's Pursuit of Weapons of Mass Destruction," *Nonproliferation Review*, Vol. 4, No. 3 (Spring/Summer 1997), pp. 92–100; Leonard Spector, *Nuclear Ambitions: The Spread of Nuclear Weapons, 1989–1990* (Boulder, Colo.: Westview, 1990), p. 182; and Director of Central Intelligence, *Unclassified Report to Congress on the Acquisition of Technology Relating to Weapons of Mass Destruction and Advanced Conventional Munitions: 1 January through 30 June 2001* (Washington, D.C.: Central Intelligence Agency, January 2002).

9. See Paul, *Power versus Prudence*, p. 111.

10. Ibid., p. 97.

ever, because its successive leaders (initially President Gamal Abdel Nasser and later Presidents Anwar el-Sadat and Hosni Mubarak) appear to have concluded that it would be neither necessary nor desirable to do so based on three considerations: the magnitude of the technical and economic challenges involved in the development of such a program, Israel's counterproliferation effort against it, and most important, U.S. diplomatic initiatives toward Egypt employing both carrots (including, apparently, reassurances to Egypt that "Israel will not introduce" nuclear weapons into the Middle East) and sticks.[11] Thus, despite military defeats in 1967 and 1973 and the ongoing development of Israel's nuclear activity, Egypt chose not to join the nuclear club.[12]

Another shortcoming in the existing literature is its failure to explore the possibility that the rationale for developing (or for that matter retaining) nuclear weapons may change over time, with new rationales for doing so emerging to replace older ones that have lost some of their luster. As Alexander George has observed, "Once established, policies often acquire momentum that is difficult to control or reverse."[13] The studies have also failed to acknowledge that to bring about nuclear reversal, it is not enough merely to remove a state's original motivations for obtaining nuclear weapons. This explains why Britain, for example, continues to retain its nuclear arsenal, albeit one considerably smaller than it maintained at the height of the Cold War.

Empirical data on proliferation in general and nuclear reversal in particular often are incomplete or otherwise unreliable because of a combination of extraordinary secrecy, intentional cover-up, and deliberate misinformation. Yet the literature manifests little appreciation of the gravity of these data problems.

Even in democratic countries, nuclear weapons programs are typically compartmentalized (i.e., subjected to especially rigid need-to-know arrangements

---

11. For a discussion of the evolution of Egyptian thinking toward the Israeli nuclear option, see Ariel E. Levite and Emily Landau, *In Arab Eyes: Arab Perceptions of Israel's Nuclear Posture* (in Hebrew) (Tel Aviv: Papirus, 1994).

12. See Michael J. Siler, "Explaining Variation in Nuclear Outcomes among Southern States: Bargaining Analysis of U.S. Nonproliferation Policies towards Brazil, Egypt, India, and South Korea," Ph.D. dissertation, University of Southern California, 1992, pp. 63–97. See also Jan Prawitz, *From Nuclear Option to Non-Nuclear Promotion: The Sweden Case*, Research Report No. 20 (Stockholm: Swedish Institute of International Affairs, 1995), pp. 4, 12. According to Prawitz, among the factors that led to Sweden's reversal of its nuclear policy were the emerging taboo on nuclear weapons and the NPT, neither of which was an issue when Sweden began its nuclear program in the early 1990s.

13. Alexander L. George, *Presidential Decisionmaking in Foreign Policy: The Effective Use of Information and Advice* (Boulder, Colo.: Westview, 1980), p. 41.

even within the government) and shrouded in secrecy. This is intended to prevent potentially harmful information from making its way to prospective proliferants, foreign adversaries, and domestic political foes. The concealment of nuclear know-how, installations, personnel, and materials is often still deemed necessary long after a state reverses its nuclear program. This holds even for democracies such as Australia, Norway, and Sweden, all of which have subsequently become champions of nonproliferation. One reason why Sweden, as well as South Korea, Switzerland, and Taiwan, continue to maintain secrecy over their nuclear weapons programs is to leave open the possibility of restarting them, should circumstances change.[14]

But even where the logic of retaining a nuclear option no longer applies, states typically uphold secrecy for fear of the domestic and foreign political fallout that might result from information about past nuclear activities being made public. Of special concern is the potential of such information to undercut a state's stature as an advocate of nonproliferation. It might also be feared that the release of this information could inspire other countries' nuclear pursuits, whether as a model, source of legitimacy for activity, source of nuclear know-how, or basis for diplomatic leverage in nuclear reversal negotiations. For example, the publication of a semiofficial historical account of the Swedish nuclear weapons program and its later abandonment was designed to persuade Ukraine to give up the Russian nuclear weapons in its possession.[15] The publication, however, deliberately omitted reference to any parts of the Swedish program that could enhance Ukraine's bargaining position in nuclear negotiations with the United States and Russia.

The fear that revelations of past activity could be embarrassing or harmful is a reason frequently given by governments, corporations, and individuals that once were involved in nuclear programs for restricting transparency (Britain in the case of Australia, and Germany in the cases of Argentina and Brazil).[16] Some of the reasons behind nuclear reversal might also prove too politically embarrassing or counterproductive to reveal. For example, did South Africa

---

14. On the suspicions aroused by the secrecy surrounding Sweden's nuclear status, see Steve Coll, "Sweden's Quiet Quest: Nuclear Arms Option," *Washington Post*, November 25, 1994, p. A1. Although Prawitz, in *From Nuclear Option to Non-Nuclear Promotion*, rebutted Coll, even he was unable to penetrate fully the secrecy surrounding key aspects of the Swedish nuclear program.
15. See Prawitz, *From Nuclear Option to Non-Nuclear Promotion*.
16. For the most comprehensive discussion of Britain's long-concealed, extensive assistance to the Australian nuclear weapons program, see Wayne Reynolds, *Australia's Bid for the Atomic Bomb* (Melbourne: Melbourne University Press, 2000).

really give up its nuclear weapons because of U.S. concern over what might happen to them when the government was transferred to the black majority? Did Taiwan reverse course in response to intense U.S. pressure motivated by worries over China's likely reaction?

Worse still, data that reach the public domain may have been deliberately manipulated for one of two reasons: (1) to conceal the true nature of a state's nuclear program or to create the impression that the state has an advanced nuclear weapons program, perhaps that it has even reached a "threshold status" (or "standby capability"),[17] in order to deter would-be adversaries or encourage allies to provide greater security assistance;[18] or (2) to coerce allies into abandoning plans for scaling back their current security commitments, as in the cases of Japan, South Korea, and Taiwan.[19]

A reexamination of the data pertaining to the Italian nuclear program illustrates how inadequate awareness of these shortcomings and biases in the data can profoundly distort scholarly understanding of nuclear reversal. It dispels the commonly held belief that Italy's engagement in a nuclear weapons program in the 1950s was guided by a serious desire to acquire nuclear weapons. The Italians deliberately created this perception so they could use it as leverage in bargaining predominantly with the United States. Italy was able to parlay the suspension of its "nuclear weapons program" into greater external security (including nuclear-specific arrangements) as well as political and economic benefits.[20]

---

17. Nuclear "threshold status" is commonly understood to mean possession of the indigenous ability to acquire nuclear weapons within a relatively short time frame, ranging from a few hours to several months. It has much in common with the CIA's definition of "standby capability," which is the "possession as of now of all of the facilities needed to produce nuclear weapons." See Central Intelligence Agency, *Response to NSSM No. 9, Vol. 7: Disarmament and Miscellaneous*, February 20, 1969, p. 4. NSSM is the acronym for National Security Study Memorandum.

18. See, for example, Leopoldo Nuti, "'Me Too, Please': Italy and the Politics of Nuclear Weapons, 1945–1975," *Diplomacy & Statecraft*, Vol. 4, No. 1 (March 1993), pp. 114–148, especially pp. 120–122. Nuti suggests that the trilateral cooperation project created by France, Germany, and Italy in the mid-1950s for military applications of nuclear technology appears to have been intended, at least in part by the Italians, to apply pressure on the United States to disclose information on nuclear weapons to its European allies. Similar logic appears to have guided Gunnar Randers, who promoted transparency of the Norwegian nuclear program in the hope of motivating the United States to assist it. See Astrid Forland, "Norway's Nuclear Odyssey: From Optimistic Proponent to Nonproliferator," *Nonproliferation Review*, Vol. 4, No. 2 (Winter 1997), p. 8.

19. See, for example, Frankel, "The Brooding Shadow," p. 51.

20. Evidence to support such possibilities is difficult to uncover. Pakistan, South Korea, and Taiwan, however, are widely suspected of having used their nuclear programs as leverage in getting the United States to provide them with assistance.

What Constitutes Nuclear Reversal and Restraint?

In this study, I define nuclear reversal as a governmental decision to slow or stop altogether an officially sanctioned nuclear weapons program. At the core of this definition is the distinction between states that have launched (indigenously or with external assistance) a nuclear weapons program and then abandoned it and those that never had such a program in the first place. Nuclear reversal excludes both termination of unauthorized nuclear weapons–related activity within a government and private-sector research and development in a nuclear weapons–related field (e.g., nuclear fuel–cycle technologies) if the latter was not formally pursued as part of an effort either to create a bomb or at least to acquire standby status. As applied here, this definition does include, however, cases in which a governmental decision to acquire the bomb could not be ascertained (e.g., Argentina).

This definition of nuclear reversal is flexible enough to include cases in which neither the initial pursuit of the bomb nor the eventual rollback of the program was reflected in an explicit government decision. The rationale for this is grounded in the characteristics of most nuclear programs. Would-be proliferants rarely make formal decisions to acquire the bomb or for that matter to give it up before they absolutely have to (e.g., before they are on the verge of attaining or eliminating a nuclear capability), if then. National leaderships are usually reluctant to make a formal commitment to acquiring nuclear weapons (even if the intent is clear) until the technical feasibility, affordability, and political (internal as well as external) viability of this undertaking have been ascertained. Such premature decisions are widely seen as politically risky and, perhaps more important, politically and strategically unnecessary, because the absence of such a formal decision does not usually preclude development of a standby capacity to produce nuclear weapons, under the rationale of creating a nuclear "option."[21] Similarly, rollback processes often begin slowly and hesitantly and proceed incrementally. They are rarely if ever cemented until the trade-offs are apparent and the risks of the decision minimized (in part through nuclear hedging).

---

21. Ashok Kapur concurs with this observation in Kapur, "New Nuclear States and the International Nuclear Order," in T.V. Paul, Richard J. Harknett, and James J. Wirtz, eds., *The Absolute Weapon Revisited: Nuclear Arms and the Emerging International Order* (Ann Arbor: University of Michigan Press, 2000), p. 240.

Nuclear restraint is a phenomenon somewhat akin to nuclear reversal, whereby a state undertakes a policy or external commitment (commonly made to the United States) that, at least initially, falls short of nuclear rollback but nonetheless keeps it from proceeding with some prominent nuclear activities.[22] Such restraint typically pertains to refraining from the construction of certain facilities; the production (of certain or all fissionable materials), testing, assembly, or deployment of weapons; or proclamations of nuclear status. Until conducting their nuclear tests in May 1998, both India and Pakistan had adopted several of these measures—as had North Korea in the domains of plutonium production and reprocessing under the terms of its 1994 Agreed Framework with the United States.

What Drives Nuclear Reversal?

Earlier studies have considered a variety of factors in seeking to explain why states decide to roll back their nuclear weapons programs. Common to all is some diminution of the perceived utility of nuclear weapons either because (1) the external security situation of a state improves or alternatives to nuclear weapons emerge that make them unnecessary; (2) a change occurs within the domestic regime and the state's security and/or economic orientation (central planning vs. market economy); or (3) systemic or state-specific incentives, such as new norms, emerge that diminish the appeal of nuclear weapons.[23] Scholars differ in the weight they assign to one factor (or cluster thereof) over others in influencing the reversal decision. They also often disagree over which domestic entity (the military, the scientific community, a political leader or faction, an interest group) was the driving force for or against nuclear weapons acquisition.

T.V. Paul has argued that no single variable can explain nuclear reversal. According to Paul, the one that comes closest is a state's external security environment, which itself is composed of a variety of factors, including the number, scope, intensity, and duration of militarized disputes in which the state is involved. Paul has advanced instead an explanation based on the notion of "prudential realism," according to which states "balance their interests and capabilities so as to minimize the security challenges they pose to others

---

22. Other forms of restraint pertain to a commitment not to help disseminate further nuclear weapons–usable technology, as well as to refrain from first use of nuclear weapons.
23. For a comprehensive review and assessment of these factors, see Paul, *Power versus Prudence*, pp. 3–11.

and in expectation of reciprocal benign behavior in return." Prudential realism distinguishes itself from the worst-case thinking commonly attributed to hard-core realists by replacing it with a "most-probable" threat assessment.[24] Yet even Paul ultimately deemed this rather elaborate construct insufficient to explain certain cases of nuclear reversal, finding it necessary to weave in several additional (and often case-specific) variables to explain actual instances of nuclear reversal.

The nuclear-reversal case studies in this article reaffirm Paul's conclusion that no overarching explanation for nuclear reversal emerges from the literature. It also suggests that there is considerable variation among the characteristics of the reversal processes themselves. This is not surprising given the diversity of the cases in terms of the time frame, type of regime, economic orientation, geostrategic location, and external security environment. In sum, nuclear reversal is typically driven not by one factor but by a combination of factors, the exact combination of which varies between the cases (or clusters thereof) and over time. Moreover, nuclear reversal cannot be fully understood unless both the nuclear hedging phenomenon and the typical characteristics of a reversal process are considered.

NUCLEAR HEDGING

Nuclear hedging refers to a national strategy of maintaining, or at least appearing to maintain, a viable option for the relatively rapid acquisition of nuclear weapons, based on an indigenous technical capacity to produce them within a relatively short time frame ranging from several weeks to a few years. In its most advanced form, nuclear hedging involves nuclear fuel–cycle facilities capable of producing fissionable materials (by way of uranium enrichment and/or plutonium separation), as well as the scientific and engineering expertise both to support them and to package their final product into a nuclear explosive charge. Nuclear hedging is a strategy that may be adopted either during the process of developing a bomb or as part of the rollback process, as a way of retaining the option of restarting a weapons program that has been halted or reversed.[25] Nuclear hedging may explain at least some of the difficulty encountered to date in efforts to understand nuclear reversal. Indeed, some of the

---

24. Ibid., p. 5.
25. In addition to Egypt and Japan, South Korea and Taiwan constitute more recent examples of nuclear hedging. In the South Korea and Taiwan cases, their reprocessing capabilities were at the center of the nuclear-hedging strategies that led both countries into confrontation with their U.S. ally. For a discussion of South Korea's pursuit of complete fuel-cycle technologies, see Jungmin

cases that have been assumed to involve nuclear reversal may on closer examination be cases of nuclear hedging.

Prime Minister Winston Churchill first articulated the essence of nuclear hedging in a November 1951 memorandum to Lord Cherwell, his ministerial adviser on nuclear matters. In the memorandum Churchill wrote, "I have never wished since our decision during the war that England should start the manufacture of atomic bombs. Research, however, must be energetically pursued. We should have the art rather than the article. A large sum of money will have to be provided for this." Churchill had naïvely expected that he could persuade officials in Washington to allocate some U.S. nuclear weapons to Britain in recognition of the latter's significant scientific contribution to the Manhattan Project.[26] After being rebuffed, Britain launched its own nuclear weapons program.

In the Swedish case, after a period of slow decline in the state's commitment to its nuclear program, the government officially eschewed any desire for nuclear weapons in the mid-1960s. But in practice, not much has changed. Research in all the relevant disciplines of bomb making that had originally been launched in the 1950s continued, under the guise of so-called nuclear defense programs carried out by the Swedish National Defense Research Establishment (FOA)—the same lead agency that had been responsible for Sweden's original nuclear weapons development program. This activity would continue long after Sweden joined the NPT in 1968 and became a champion of nonproliferation.[27] In addition, it means that Sweden is a mere two to three years away from acquiring a nuclear capability.[28]

Kang and H.A. Feiveson, "South Korea's Shifting and Controversial Interest in Spent Fuel Reprocessing," *Nonproliferation Review*, Vol. 8, No. 1 (Spring 2001), pp. 70–78. For a discussion of the Taiwan case, see David Albright and Corey Gay, "Taiwan: Nuclear Nightmare Averted," *Bulletin of the Atomic Scientists*, Vol. 54, No. 1 (January/February 1998), pp. 54–60.

26. Quoted in Margaret Gowing, *Independence and Deterrence: Britain and Atomic Energy, 1945–1952*, Vol. 1: *Policy Making* (New York: St. Martin's, 1974), p. 406. Cherwell's reply to Churchill is revealing: "If we are unable to make bombs ourselves and have to rely entirely on the United States army for this vital weapon, we shall sink to the rank of a second-class nation, only permitted to supply auxiliary troops, like the native levies who were allowed small arms but not artillery." Ibid., p. 407. I am indebted to David Holloway for drawing my attention to this correspondence.

27. For prominent accounts of the Swedish nuclear weapons program, see Jan Prawitz, "Non-Nuclear Is Beautiful, or Why and How Sweden Went Non-Nuclear," *Kungl Krigsventenskapsakademiens Handlingar och Tidskrift*, No. 198 (Stockholm: National Defense Research Establishment, June 1994); Reiss, *Without the Bomb*, pp. 37–77; Paul, *Power versus Prudence*, pp. 84–99; Paul M. Cole, *Atomic Bombast: Nuclear Weapons Decision Making in Sweden, 1945–1972*, Occasional Paper No. 26 (Washington, D.C.: Henry L. Stimson Center, 1996); and Wilhelm Agrell, "The Bomb That Never Was: The Rise and Fall of the Swedish Nuclear Weapons Programme," in Nils Peter Gleditsch and Olav Njolstad, eds., *Arms Races: Technological and Political Dynamics* (London: Sage, 1990).

28. See Central Intelligence Agency, *Response to NSSM No. 9*, p. 3.

Japan provides the most salient example of nuclear hedging to date. The Japan case illustrates how a state signatory to the NPT and a champion of nonproliferation and disarmament can legitimately maintain a nuclear fuel–cycle capability and possess huge quantities of weapons-grade fissile material. Moreover, according to an official British government report, Japan "has key bomb-making components, including plutonium and electronic triggers, and has the expertise to go nuclear very quickly."[29] Japan hardly tries to conceal its hedging strategy (though it does seek to keep some of its more specific features out of the public eye). This is evident in repeated statements by senior government officials that, under certain circumstances, Japan could revisit the issue of nuclear weapons acquisition. A statement by former Japanese Prime Minister Morihiro Hosokawa provides one such example: "It is in the interest of the United States, so long as it does not wish to see Japan withdraw from the NPT and develop its own nuclear deterrent, to maintain its alliance with Japan and continue to provide a nuclear umbrella."[30] Despite the long-term Japanese commitment to the "three nuclear principles" announced by Prime Minister Eisaku Sato in 1968 and formalized by the Diet in 1971 (banning the possession, production, or import of nuclear weapons) as well as provisions in the Japanese constitution that preclude the acquisition of a nuclear capability, senior Japanese officials have repeatedly indicated that these principles could be revised.[31] They have also stated that the constitution could be reinterpreted to permit Japanese possession of "defensive nuclear weapons."[32] In fact, the three principles are carefully worded so as to allow the development of a standby

---

29. "Japan May 'Go Nuclear,' Paper Says," *Japan Times*, August 11, 1993, p. 4, cited in Paul, *Power versus Prudence*, p. 51.

30. See Morihiro Hosokawa, "Are U.S. Troops in Japan Needed? Reforming the Alliance," *Foreign Affairs*, Vol. 77, No. 4 (July/August 1998), p. 5. This statement highlights the role that U.S. extended deterrence plays in restraining Japan's nuclear ambitions and reveals Japan's explicit preference for the U.S. nuclear umbrella over the development of an indigenous nuclear capability. It also demonstrates how Japan uses its advanced nuclear bomb–making potential both as leverage against the United States (lest it weaken its security commitment to Japan) and as a hedge should the United States do so. This case also underscores the limitations of the known universe of nuclear reversal cases, because it may include states that have all along pursued security offsets rather than nuclear weapons. See Yuri Kase, "The Costs and Benefits of Japan's Nuclearization: An Insight into the *1968/70 Internal Report*," *Nonproliferation Review*, Vol. 8, No. 2 (Summer 2001), pp. 55–68.

31. For the most recent official formulation of this position, see comments made on May 30, 2002, by a "high-ranking [Japanese] government official," later identified as Chief Cabinet Secretary Yasuo Fukuda, according to which Japan may reconsider its decade-long commitment to the three nuclear principles. See "Japan Official Hints at Review of Nonnuclear Policy," Jiji Press Ticker Service (Tokyo), May 31, 2002; and Howard W. French, " Koizumi Aide Hints at Change to No Nuclear Policy," *New York Times*, June 4, 2002, p. 10.

32. Paul, *Power versus Prudence*, p. 56.

nuclear capability that stops just short of actual weapons production—allowing Japan to remain within a few months of acquiring nuclear weapons. Under these circumstances, it is not surprising that South Korea has long referred to Japan as an "associate member of the nuclear club."[33]

Nuclear hedging appears to have played a critical role in facilitating nuclear reversal in practically every case under examination in this article, especially early in the reversal process. Its influence begins to subside only gradually if at all and only after the reversal process has gained momentum. What is striking about nuclear hedging as a strategy is its elasticity. Hedging does not translate into a uniform formula for action but merely into a general choice of strategic posture. The time frame that a state deems acceptable to acquire nuclear weapons depends, in turn, on three principal factors: (1) how the state defines the desired "nuclear capability" (e.g., the number of weapons it would have to produce, assemble, and deploy); (2) the amount of advance warning it expects to have of adverse developments that might necessitate nuclear weapons acquisition; and (3) its assessment of the risks, opportunities, and costs of stepping up nuclear preparedness, especially in terms of domestic and foreign reaction to its nuclear hedging posture.

The appeal of nuclear hedging goes well beyond the nuclear weapons option that it facilitates politically as well as technically. Its greatest appeal is the "latent" or "virtual" deterrence posture it generates toward nuclear weapons aspirants or potential aggressors,[34] and the leverage it provides in reinforcing a state's coercive diplomacy strategy, particularly against the United States.

A near-explicit endorsement of this logic found expression in a 1998 statement by President Mubarak of Egypt: "If the time comes when we need nuclear weapons, then we will not hesitate. I say if we have to, because this is the last thing we think about. We do not think now of joining the nuclear club." Mubarak then implied that neither technical nor financial barriers held Egypt back from getting nuclear weapons: "Acquiring material for nuclear weapons has become very easy and it can be bought."[35] Mubarak's warning regarding the potential for (re)activation of Egypt's nuclear weapons program was echoed by Nabil Fahmy, Egypt's ambassador to the United States, who linked it

---

33. Ibid., p. 54.
34. Ibid., p. 59.
35. Interview with the London-based newspaper *Al-Hayat*, quoted in "Egypt's Mubarak Says Egypt Can Join Nuclear Club," Reuters, October 5, 1998.

explicitly to weapons of mass destruction (WMD) proliferation trends in the Middle East.[36]

The Japanese and Egyptian cases underscore the complex relationship between the NPT and nuclear hedging. Contrary to widespread perceptions, the NPT appears to have had less to do with walking key states all the way back from nuclear weapons development to nuclear reversal and more to do with encouraging them (at least initially, and for some permanently) to trade nuclear development for nuclear hedging. This has resulted from a combination of flexibility implicit in NPT definitions of proscribed activities, the narrow focus on International Atomic Energy Agency (IAEA) safeguards as the core of its verification regime, and the NPT's provisions allowing members to engage in fuel-cycle activities. Their combined impact has been to convince many nations that it is easier to hedge and even push their nuclear weapons programs forward to a fairly advanced stage while being parties to the NPT. Both Iran and Iraq have been following this path for years, actively pursuing nuclear weapons while being members of the NPT.[37] All of these examples reaffirm Paul's observation that accession to the NPT is no more than a manifestation of a commitment to (rather than a practice of) nuclear nonproliferation, if that.[38]

CHARACTERISTICS OF THE NUCLEAR REVERSAL PROCESS

This analysis suggests that there is considerable variance in the motivations, direction, and pace governing nuclear reversal processes. The direction and speed of reversal are driven by complex motivations (not all of which may be explicit or widely shared among decisionmakers). Yet for all these differences,

36. Fahmy went on to write: "If this proliferation trend continues unabated, it will inevitably trigger a reevaluation on the part of regional states, prompting some to accelerate the development of their already existing WMD programmes, while forcing others to activate programmes that have so far remained dormant." Fahmy, "Special Comment," *Disarmament Forum,* No. 2 (2001), http://www.unog.ch/unidir/1-02-eSpecial_com.pdf (accessed January 4, 2003).
37. For authoritative assessments of the Iranian and Iraqi nuclear pursuits and ambitions, see the semiannual report submitted by the CIA to Congress on January 30, 2002, entitled *Unclassified Report to Congress on the Acquisition of Technology Relating to Weapons of Mass Destruction and Advanced Conventional Munitions, 1 July through 31 December 2001,* at http://www.cia.gov/cia/publications/bian/bian_jan_2003.htm#14 (accessed January 14, 2003), as well as the U.S. Department of Defense's *Proliferation: Threat and Response* (Washington, D.C.: Department of Defense, January 2001), pp. 34–41. A comprehensive account of past Iraqi nuclear pursuits is also provided by the IAEA reports to the UN Security Council. See, for example, IAEA, *Report by the Director General of the International Atomic Energy Agency in Connection with the Panel on Disarmament and Current and Future Ongoing Monitoring and Verification Issues,* GOV/INF/1999/4 (Vienna, Austria: IAEA, February 24, 1999), pp. 17–21.
38. Paul, *Power versus Prudence,* p. 57.

there are some important underlying similarities across the cases. They all seem to reaffirm the CIA's assessment that "political rather than economic and technical factors restrain most of the nations which are capable of developing nuclear weapons from doing so."[39] Economic resource constraints, technical hurdles, organizational behavior and bureaucratic politics, and even regime change appear to have much lesser roles in the overall direction of a state's nuclear weapons program, but they do typically influence its scope, pace, cost, efficiency, and technical parameters. Among the political factors that play a dominant role, external security considerations—however defined by different leaders—stand out as having consistently had a profound impact on states' nuclear choices. Moreover, although a favorable external security outlook appears necessary to bring about nuclear reversal, it rarely if ever appears to be sufficient, by itself, to produce this outcome. This is where the combination of domestic regime change and the availability of external incentives may tilt the balance in one direction or another.

Reversal processes also seem to share one of three characteristics (and often all three). First, nuclear weapons programs typically fizzle out in a gradual and nonlinear way rather than shut down abruptly and completely. South Africa is the sole known exception to this rule due to the unique circumstances of the handover of power to the country's black majority. Second, states contemplating nuclear reversal do not begin with a clearly articulated objective. This may reflect uncertainty over what that goal ought to be, or it may be a tactic to avoid or deflect counterpressures (where a consensus can be forged on the interim step but not necessarily on the desired result). Third, states considering nuclear reversal rarely assume that it is permanent and irreversible.[40] Indeed, the reversal process allows states both in theory and in practice to switch course and restart their nuclear weapons programs should conditions warrant it. This is especially true early in the process, a point that has been underscored by the recent revelations concerning North Korea's nuclear enrichment project.

Because capping, let alone walking back, from a nuclear weapons program is a momentous decision, typically fraught with political risks and surrounded by domestic controversy, governments have a powerful incentive to devise a process that minimizes risks and friction (through hedging) and generates domestic consensus in support of such a decision. This kind of consensus,

---

39. See Central Intelligence Agency, *Response to NSSM No. 9*, p. 1.
40. For a similar conclusion and an elaboration of the conditions that might result in such a reversal, see Paul, *Power versus Prudence*, pp. 147, 154–155.

whether cultivated entirely indigenously or, as is commonly the case, with some external support and (at times) prodding, typically requires the sophisticated use of offsets and incentives. These have to address the security, prestige, and bureaucratic appeal of a nuclear program. One prominent way in which this appears to have been done has been to offset, at least initially, a declining effort in acquiring nuclear weapons with an investment in peaceful nuclear activity, whether for power generation or further research. Notwithstanding any commercial or energy security rationales for building up the civilian nuclear infrastructure, in some of the countries of concern here, such investments— especially in enrichment and reprocessing technology and facilities—were designed at least in part to facilitate hedging at least for a while (Germany) or to this day (Japan and South Korea). For others, the construction of nuclear facilities could also have served to address issues of prestige and employment associated with nuclear activity, as was the case with Egypt and North Korea.[41] Civilian nuclear technology also underscores the important symbolic yet tangible benefits that accrue to a state for forswearing the nuclear option, of which access to modern reactors is tangible proof. Egypt and North Korea are once again cases in point.

The Role of the United States

Earlier sections have noted the importance of nuclear hedging as well as nuclear restraint in explaining the nuclear behavior of specific states. This discussion has also drawn attention to the centrality of these phenomena for shedding light on the process and not merely the outcome of nuclear reversal. These phenomena in turn yield new insights into the influence that the United States has had on the nuclear choices of key states. The United States has played a unique role in helping to move nuclear aspirants away from nuclear pursuits toward more benign behavior, be it nuclear restraint or hedging if not outright nuclear reversal. Toward that end, it has energetically employed a range of techniques since the early days of the Cold War.

The role of the United States in influencing the nuclear choices of a number of states has long been recognized in the literature on nuclear nonproliferation.

---

41. The United States, for example, promised to provide Egypt with a nuclear reactor in return for signing the NPT in 1981. North Korea was promised two light water reactors in return for signing the 1994 Agreed Framework, committing it to several verifiable steps of nuclear capping (freezing the reprocessing of plutonium and allowing inspections of nuclear waste storage sites).

James Doyle has provided the most comprehensive review of the efforts of successive U.S. administrations to stem the tide of nuclear proliferation and encourage would-be proliferants either to restrain or to abandon their programs altogether.[42] Some works have focused on specific initiatives taken by the United States either alone or with other states, the most recent example being the review by Robert Einhorn and Gary Samore, two former senior officials in President Bill Clinton's administration, of the U.S. effort to stem the tide of Russian nuclear assistance to Iran.[43] There is also extensive discussion of the traditional U.S. role in establishing and ultimately consolidating international nuclear nonproliferation norms and institutions and its efforts to persuade particular nuclear aspirants to desist from their pursuit of nuclear weapons.[44]

The nonproliferation literature, however, still lacks a systematic assessment of the vast array of nonproliferation instruments and assets employed by the United States across the cases of nuclear restraint and reversal. This is a glaring omission because the involvement of the United States in this area is unsurpassed in terms of the great quantity and diversity of resources that it has applied to an array of objectives—even if its policies have not always been consistently or coherently applied.

CHARACTERISTICS OF U.S. NONPROLIFERATION ACTIVITIES
U.S. nonproliferation efforts have four distinguishing characteristics, corresponding to the objectives, strategy, scope, and means of U.S. activity. First, the United States has sought to preserve its nuclear hegemony and diminish the appeal of nuclear weapons for others while improving overall international security. Second, although its stated goal in virtually all the cases has been to arrest or roll back nuclear proliferation, the United States has often settled for the more modest objective of nuclear restraint such as capping the production of fissionable material, banning nuclear testing, or preventing the deployment of nuclear capabilities (all of which it has attempted to apply in recent years to the Indian subcontinent). Third, the scope of U.S. efforts has been both global

---

42. For a comprehensive review of U.S. nonproliferation policies and instruments, see Doyle, "Nuclear Rollback," pp. 23–24. In addition to assessing the efficacy of the U.S. efforts generally, Doyle evaluates their influence in five prominent cases of nuclear rollback: Argentina, Brazil, South Africa, Sweden, and Ukraine.
43. Robert J. Einhorn and Gary Samore, "Ending Russian Assistance to Iran's Nuclear Bomb," *Survival*, Vol. 44, No. 2 (Summer 2002), pp. 51–70.
44. Perhaps the most salient study of this genre is McGeorge Bundy's *Danger and Survival: Choices about the Bomb in the First Fifty Years* (New York: Random House, 1988).

and regional, aiming to mold a nonproliferation regime as well as to influence the local and regional conditions (conflicts, stability) that inspire nuclear aspirations and regulate international trade of nuclear materials. Fourth, U.S. nonproliferation efforts have employed many unilateral but also bilateral, trilateral, and multilateral instruments (from dialogues and treaties to supplier regimes); softer measures (norms and rewards) and more coercive ones; and universal as well as case-specific means.

These distinctions are evident in my survey of nuclear reversal and restraint cases. In the security realm, the United States has repeatedly engaged in diplomatic initiatives aimed at settling or at least defusing conflicts that could fuel proliferation. It has also provided nonnuclear security assistance to increase the recipient's confidence that it can address its security concerns without nuclear weapons.[45] This assistance has appeared in the form of conventional arms transfers and other types of military assistance (e.g., training and education and military-to-military ties), as well as security guarantees.

POSITIVE AND NEGATIVE INDUCEMENTS. Security guarantees extended by the United States have varied greatly in scope, degree of formality, and level of commitment. These guarantees have included both positive and negative security assurances,[46] and pertain not only to U.S. conduct but also to the behavior of third countries of particular concern to the country that the United States is trying to dissuade from acquiring nuclear arms (e.g., providing reassurances to Egypt regarding Israeli nuclear behavior). The security assurances that the United States has made concerning its own behavior have ranged from the soft (less explicit and/or binding) variety (extended, for example, to Ukraine) to bilateral and multilateral collective security arrangements (Australia, Japan, the North Atlantic Treaty Organization, and South Korea), which often are reinforced by the presence of U.S. troops. In NATO, these have been accompanied

---

45. See Alexander Kelle, "Nonproliferation Decisions in Italy," paper prepared for the Workshop on Nonproliferation Decisions: Lessons from Lesser-Known Cases, Monterey Institute of International Studies, Monterey, California, August 19–20, 1996, p. 23; and Doyle, "Nuclear Rollback," p. 242. A good illustration of this point is Ukraine's attempts to procure security guarantees from both the United States and Russia in return for surrendering the nuclear weapons on its territory. This effort ultimately won it only modest guarantees. See James E. Goodby, *Europe Undivided: The New Logic of Peace in U.S.-Russian Relations* (Washington, D.C.: United States Institute of Peace, 1998), pp. 80–88. This case also illustrates the importance of most other incentives for securing nuclear reversal, including enhanced prestige and receipt of conventional arms and financial assistance.

46. Positive security assurances are commitments to extend help in the event of a nuclear attack; negative security assurances are reassurances against a first strike by a nuclear power.

by a promise not only to extend the U.S. nuclear umbrella to member states (and deploy nuclear weapons in some of them) but also to share information on these weapons. This has been coupled with some form of guaranteed formal (though, in practice, mostly symbolic other than as veto power) participation in nuclear weapons decisionmaking. In particular, such assurances have involved so-called dual-key arrangements,[47] bringing NATO countries into the process of U.S. nuclear contingency planning and providing them a veto right over certain pertinent scenarios for the employment of nuclear weapons. In the early 1960s, the United States considered (though never implemented) even more dramatic formulations of nuclear sharing, such as the 1960 proposal for the creation of a multilateral nuclear force.

The threat (or promise) of denying (or providing) economic and technological assistance, including the supply of civilian and nuclear weapons technology, has been another tool commonly (and successfully) used by the United States to encourage nuclear nonproliferation.[48] It has targeted suppliers, recipients, and developers of nuclear weapons–related capabilities, with special emphasis on denying the wherewithal to produce fissionable material.

In most cases, the United States has sought to downplay any explicit linkage between nuclear behavior and the provision (or denial) of economic assistance either unilaterally or through financial institutions such as the International Monetary Fund and the World Bank. Exceptions include the Argentinean case, in which the United States was widely suspected of linking external debt refinancing to Argentine nuclear reversal; energy assistance to North Korea by the Korean Peninsula Energy Development Organization; and bilateral and multilateral deals with Belarus, Kazakhstan, and Ukraine in the early to mid-1990s that facilitated the withdrawal of Russian nuclear weapons from their territory.[49] Most often, however, the quid pro quo is not as obvious, which sug-

---

47. Leopoldo Nuti recounts the importance of such arrangements at the time for the Italians, who were wavering between developing an indigenous nuclear weapons capability through participation in a French-German nuclear (including weapons) program and seeking cover and prestige under an Atlantic nuclear umbrella. See Nuti, "'Me Too, Please,'" pp. 120–132.

48. In addition to the more common U.S. offsets in the form of civilian nuclear technology (originally offered in its Atoms for Peace program of 1953), the United States has occasionally resorted to more direct forms of sharing nuclear weapons know-how and technology to induce the acceptance of nuclear restraints by Britain, France, and even China, most prominently in the domain of nuclear testing. For a reference to U.S. assistance to France, see Joseph S. Nye Jr., "New Approaches to Nuclear Proliferation Policy," *Science*, May 29, 1992, p. 1297. For the nature of the assistance, see Nicola Butler, "Sharing Secrets: Nuclear Weapons Information Exchange between France, Great Britain, and the United States," *Bulletin of the Atomic Scientists*, Vol. 53, No. 1 (January/February 1997), pp. 11–12.

49. In these cases, George H.W. Bush's administration and later the Clinton administration agreed to buy their supplies of highly enriched uranium. See Gilbert J. Brown, "From Nuclear Swords to

gests that a similar dynamic has been at work in many additional cases in which the extension of U.S. economic and security aid and/or other forms of U.S. engagement has coincided with nuclear reversal, or at least its formal codification (in the form of accession to a legally binding obligation prohibiting the production or purchase of nuclear weapons), with Argentina, Egypt, and Brazil being just three cases in point. In the Argentinean case, there appears to have been a linkage between the U.S. de-emphasis of the Carter administration's human rights initiative vis-à-vis Argentina and the (successful) U.S. effort to win the support of the military junta to terminate the country's nuclear weapons program.[50]

In 1976 President Gerald Ford's outgoing administration worked out a secret agreement with Brazil in which the latter agreed to annul a 1975 contract it had awarded to Germany for the purchase of reprocessing plants in return for U.S. security guarantees and promises of military sales. When the deal was leaked to the U.S. press by Jimmy Carter's incoming administration, Brazil's president backed out of the agreement and reverted to his earlier pronuclear stance, seriously straining U.S.-Brazil relations. Brazil canceled its mutual defense treaty with the United States and rejected $50 million in military sales credits.[51]

The U.S.-Brazil deal sheds light on the key role of the United States in facilitating nuclear reversal, but it also illustrates the difficulty, in the absence of reliable information on secret deals as well as on the reasoning of the leadership, of establishing causality in nuclear reversal cases. In part, countries such as Brazil may have been thinking about adopting nuclear reversal anyway, and wanted only to extract a U.S. offset or payoff before carrying out that policy.[52]

Nuclear Plowshares," *Washington Post*, September 1, 1992, p. A17; and Thomas W. Lippman, "Two Nuclear Accords Expected: U.S.-Russia Pact Involves Uranium Buy," *Washington Post*, March 21, 1999, p. A25. In addition, Congress passed the so-called Nunn-Lugar Act, which provides economic aid to these former Soviet republics to guarantee that none of them reneges on its promise to abstain from nuclear proliferation. See Theodor Galdi, *The Nunn-Lugar Cooperative Nuclear Threat Reduction Program for Soviet Weapons Dismantlement*, Congressional Research Service, 94-985-F (Washington, D.C.: Government Printing Office, December 6, 1994), pp. 1–6.

50. For a summary of recently declassified official U.S. documents on the policy toward the Argentinean nuclear program, see Paul Richter, "U.S. Feared a Nuclear Argentina," *Los Angeles Times*, August 23, 2002, http://www.latimes.com/news/printedition/front/la-fg-dirty23aug. story?null.

51. For information on the secret agreement, see A. David Rossin, "Plutonium," Stanford University, forthcoming. On the rejected mutual defense treaty and military sales credits, see Graham Hovey, "Carter Writes to Leader of Brazil," *New York Times*, March 31, 1977, p. 2. On the crisis in U.S.-Brazil relations, see, for instance, Hobart Rowen, "U.S. Shifted on Bonn-Brazil Nuclear Deal," *Washington Post*, May 9, 1977, p. A10. See also David Vidal, *New York Times*, Information Bank Abstract, June 14, 1977; and "Why Latin Americans Are Bitter about Carter," *Washington Post*, April 4, 1977, p. 33.

52. The Japanese case is a convincing example of extracting U.S. security guarantees as a condition for nuclear abstinence. Japan has repeatedly made it clear that the United States is a key player in

In addition, it is unclear whether these countries would have been able or willing to eschew nuclear weapons or to circumscribe their nuclear ambitions even if the United States had not responded to their demands. Moreover, there is evidence to suggest that at least some states (presently North Korea, but previously also Italy, Pakistan, South Korea, and Taiwan) may have deliberately moved ahead on the nuclear weapons path, by collecting information, conducting studies, procuring equipment, and constructing facilities, to attract or drive up the value of U.S. rewards offered to them in return for nuclear reversal.[53]

The extensive efforts by U.S. intelligence to track and analyze nuclear proliferation activities are relatively well documented, not in the least in scores of briefings, testimonies, and annual reports provided by the U.S. intelligence community to Congress. There have also been occasional references to some of the more creative and sophisticated means that U.S. intelligence agencies have employed to collect information, from using a civilian reconnaissance plane to fly over the South African nuclear test site in the Kalahari Desert in 1977 to planting an electronic monitoring device disguised as a rock near the Pakistani nuclear enrichment facility at Kahuta in the mid-1990s.[54]

CLANDESTINE TECHNIQUES. Clandestine techniques constitute additional U.S. tools employed to promote nuclear nonproliferation. Although they have been extensively used, and seem to be correlated with cases of nuclear restraint and even reversal, they have been neither well documented in the open literature nor systematically researched. Yet they merit serious consideration because they can help to put in perspective other explanations for the reversal phenomenon.

---

its security (and specifically) nuclear policy, both by emphasizing the importance of the U.S. extended deterrence guarantee and by notifying the United States of a Japanese report investigating the costs and benefits of Japanese nuclearization. See Kase, "The Costs and Benefits of Japan's Nuclearization," especially pp. 56, 60.

53. There is a correlation between two occasions in which the United States announced its intent to scale back its military presence on the Korean Peninsula (by President Richard Nixon in 1970 and President Carter in 1977) and the intensification of South Korea's efforts to develop a nuclear bomb option. In both cases the United States ended up largely reversing course, as did South Korea. See Kang and Feiveson, "South Korea's Shifting and Controversial Interest in Spent Fuel Reprocessing," pp. 71–72. A similar correlation is apparent between U.S. actions and Taiwan's nuclear weapons program, most prominently following the termination of diplomatic relations between the two countries on January 1, 1979. Then it culminated in a renewed U.S. commitment to the security of Taiwan in the form of the 1979 Taiwan Relations Act, public diplomacy to deter Chinese military invasion of the island, and massive conventional arms sales to Taiwan. For the ups and downs of Taiwan's nuclear program, see Albright and Gay, "Taiwan."

54. David Albright, "South Africa and the Affordable Bomb," *Bulletin of the Atomic Scientists*, Vol. 50, No. 4 (July–August 1994), http://www.thebulletin.org/issues/1994/ja94/Albright.html.

One cluster of U.S. clandestine activities to stop or slow foreign nuclear programs involves operations designed to recruit or trap foreign government agents engaged in procuring nuclear-related materials or foreign scientists engaged in nuclear research and development. Taiwan, for example, originally launched a secret nuclear weapons program in 1964 following China's first nuclear test earlier that year.[55] It abandoned the program in 1976 in response to extensive U.S. pressure. Taiwan restarted the program in 1987, however; and in violation of the 1976 agreement, its Institute for Nuclear Energy Research (INER) began construction of a hot cell facility. The United States apparently learned quickly of this development from Col. Chang Hsien-yi, the deputy director of INER and also a confirmed U.S. agent recruited by the CIA in the 1960s.[56] The United States proceeded to demand that Taiwan permanently disband this facility, which it did; Chang and his family were spirited to the United States shortly thereafter.[57]

Occasionally the U.S. government has also resorted to briefing foreign leaders about nuclear activities occurring in their own countries. The purpose has been to warn them that the United States is aware of the nuclear activity and to encourage them to terminate these activities or at least to scale them back. Perhaps the best-known case involves the June 1989 briefing provided by CIA Director William Webster to visiting Pakistani Prime Minister Benazir Bhutto. The briefing was meant to acquaint her with details of Pakistan's nuclear weapons program that the United States suspected were being withheld from her by the Pakistani military—in particular, Pakistan's transgression of its pledge to the United States concerning uranium enrichment. Although the briefing did not provide Bhutto with dramatic details of which she was previously unaware, it did impress her with the scope of U.S. knowledge of Pakistan's nuclear program, create a common base of knowledge between the U.S. government and the Pakistani premier on this delicate issue, and facilitate the establishment of a follow-up agenda for action. As a result of the meeting, Prime Minister Bhutto conceded her willingness to "work on any information or assessment" by the CIA of the Pakistani program.[58]

---

55. Albright and Gay, "Taiwan," p. 55.
56. See Tim Weiner, "How a Spy Left Taiwan in the Cold," *New York Times*, December 20, 1997, p. A7. According to the article, the CIA refused to disclose more information about Colonel Chang.
57. See Albright and Gay, "Taiwan," pp. 59–60.
58. David B. Ottaway, "U.S. Relieves Pakistan of Pledge against Enriching Uranium," *Washington Post*, June 15, 1989, p. A38.

The United States has also used public leaks to try, first, to embarrass governments engaged in clandestine nuclear weapons activities and, second, to galvanize opposition against them within the United States, inside their own country, and internationally. News leaks have dogged nearly all nuclear aspirants at one time or another. On many occasions the source can be traced back to a U.S. origin. Yet even when it is possible to establish a U.S. connection, it is all but impossible to ascertain whether this is part of an officially sanctioned policy or just another aspect of "doing business" in Washington.

There have also been a number of other initiatives designed to press U.S. administrations to take more forceful action.[59] The U.S. Congress, at times to the chagrin of the administration, has pushed some of these initiatives. One case in point is the 1985 Pressler amendment, which expressed concern over Pakistan's nuclear weapons development and required annual certification of its nuclear status as a condition of U.S. assistance. Another is former President Carter's negotiations with North Korea in 1993, which yielded an agreement in 1994 on the capping of the North Korean nuclear program and eventually also inspections of its facilities in return for providing North Korea with heavy fuel and modern nuclear reactors.

Given the tremendous resources at its disposal and its position as global leader, the United States has been able to exert more influence than any other country over nuclear proliferants and would-be proliferants. Its capacity for influence has been reinforced by the willingness of virtually every administration since World War II to employ U.S. clout to promote the cause of nuclear nonproliferation. Behind this willingness has been the belief that such involvement best serves U.S. (and broader) interests—even if Washington's policies were occasionally inconsistent (e.g., Pakistan), misguided (e.g., the Atoms for Peace initiative of Dwight Eisenhower's administration, which sought to provide states with peaceful nuclear technologies as a means of dissuading their pursuit of nuclear weapons), or otherwise uneven (e.g., France and India).

An understanding with the United States is, in fact, a hallmark of many cases of nuclear slowdown or reversal.[60] Lively debates about the impact of in-

---

59. One example is the consistent encouragement, and occasionally even direct financial assistance, provided in recent years by U.S. government agencies (primarily the Department of Energy, the Department of Defense, and the State Department) to bilateral and multilateral Middle East and South Asian track-two security and arms-control talks sponsored by several highly respected U.S. universities (e.g., Columbia, Stanford, and the University of California, Los Angeles) that do work in the field.

60. Some of the best-documented cases in point are those of Israel, North Korea, South Korea, and Taiwan.

digenous nuclear decisions on a country's relations with the United States have occurred within virtually every democratic nuclear aspirant, most prominently India and Israel. This has led Michael Siler to conclude that the actions of the United States can "make the critical difference," especially in dictating the particular course of a nuclear reversal process.[61] There is no evidence to suggest, however, that U.S. influence has ever been a sufficient factor for inducing nuclear reversal.[62]

U.S. INFLUENCE OVER DOMESTIC REGIMES

Some of the domestic calculations and forces affecting countries' nuclear ambitions have remained beyond the sphere of direct U.S. influence. As a result, although the United States has been able to encourage complete nuclear reversal in Europe and Latin America, and most saliently in South Africa, it has had more modest success in Egypt, Israel, Japan, South Korea, and Taiwan and much less success in India, North Korea, and Pakistan. In these cases, it has been able to limit their ambitions to some form of nuclear hedging and in the cases of India and Pakistan only to limited nuclear restraint. As for Iran, Iraq, and Libya, the United States has been unable to alter their nuclear aspirations, but it has been able to retard the progress of their nuclear programs, primarily by hindering access to fissionable materials and their production technologies and facilities.

The nature of domestic regimes is probably the most important factor affecting nuclear ambitions that remains largely outside the sphere of direct U.S. influence. It also provides some of the most fascinating illustrations of the delicate balance between the strength and limits of U.S. influence on foreign nuclear pursuits.

The studies of nuclear reversal and more broadly nuclear nonproliferation have been unable to establish a direct link between the nature of a regime and its nuclear orientation: Both democratic and totalitarian regimes have sought to produce or purchase nuclear weapons. Even changes in regime have not by themselves automatically yielded a reorientation of the state's nuclear pursuits.[63] Thus, even in those rare cases where the United States might be able to

---

61. Siler, "Explaining Variation in Nuclear Outcomes among Southern States," p. 244.
62. Etel Solingen convincingly demonstrates that U.S. "hegemonic protection," for example, has been neither a sufficient nor a necessary condition for nuclear reversal. But her analysis refers merely to the U.S. role in providing security guarantees. See Solingen, "The Political Economy of Nuclear Restraint."
63. The cases of democracies maintaining or renouncing nuclear weapons after pursuing a nuclear program are numerous (e.g., the United States and Australia, respectively). As for totalitarian re-

encourage a regime change, this would not guarantee, by itself, nuclear reversal or restraint. Regime change can create new opportunities for external influence, however, because it can buy precious time and favorably transform the international or regional security environment, thereby diminishing the need for nuclear weapons. Leaders of a new regime might also be less personally or politically committed to pursuing nuclear weapons, or more amenable than their predecessors to external persuasion and inducements to forgo them. U.S. nonproliferation policy toward Argentina and Brazil underscores this dynamic.

The South African case illustrates the interplay between external influence and regime change in the context of nuclear reversal.[64] The 1989 election of F.W. de Klerk as president led to huge changes in South Africa's foreign and domestic policies, facilitating the end of apartheid and improved international acceptance. And with the end of the Cold War, concern over a communist liberation movement poised to overthrow the South African government dissolved. These developments created a domestic climate more favorable to disassembling South Africa's nuclear weapons program, as "in the transformed [South African] security environment, security threats were no longer crucial, and nuclear weapons seemed unnecessary symbols of a bygone era."[65] By themselves, however, these developments did not suffice to bring about nuclear reversal, at least not the rapid and decisive manner in which it came about. Driving this decision was the determination of the outgoing apartheid regime not to pass on to its successors South Africa's nuclear or ballistic missile capability. There is some evidence to suggest that this position was heavily supported by the United States, which feared the consequences of South Africa's long-range ballistic missiles or nuclear weapons falling into the hands of the new South African government led by the African National Congress (and

---

gimes, Libya, Iraq, and North Korea continue to pursue a nuclear option. The issue of regime change is more intriguing and the effect more complex. Although some countries have reversed their nuclear policies after switching from military to civilian and more democratic rule, this change in policy often is directly linked to the more stable security situation accompanying the regime change. See the cases of Argentina and Brazil in Paul, *Power versus Prudence*, p. 111. Also, some states, such as India and Israel, have evolved to become more democratic while maintaining or intensifying their nuclear programs, but the changes in nuclear policy paralleled security changes rather than regime changes. Pakistan is a case in which a military coup could be associated with acceleration of its nuclear program, but security concerns are not the only factor that explains why other nations under military rule do not always seek to acquire nuclear weapons. See ibid., p. 141.

64. See Peter Liberman, "The Rise and Fall of the South African Bomb," *International Security*, Vol. 26, No. 2 (Fall 2001), pp. 45–86.

65. Paul, *Power versus Prudence*, pp. 115, 116.

by extension possibly the communist regimes with which it was allied, such as Cuba[66]) or nationalist white extremist groups.[67]

Regime change might also affect the way security is achieved, creating a preference for either indigenous reliance or alliance guarantees, thereby influencing the requirement for an indigenous nuclear weapons capability or its renunciation. Both Germany and Japan seem to fall into this category.[68] And once again the United States was ready to extend security guarantees to both.

More broadly, regime change may affect a regime's nationalistic tendencies and the preference for autarky or interdependence, economic liberalization or closure to the outside world. Different regimes may assign higher or lower priority to security concerns versus economic or social progress, potentially influencing the course of their nuclear programs. In fact, Etel Solingen has suggested that the openness and economic liberalization associated with democratic governance is the only regime-based explanation for nuclear reversal that has withstood the test of time.[69] Yet even if this is the case (which is not borne out by the absence of nuclear reversal in economically liberalizing India and Israel), it is clear that formidable outside assistance has also been necessary to facilitate economic liberalization.

Conclusion

The widely held fears of the 1960s of a world filled with dozens of nuclear weapons states grew out of a reality in which scores of countries were toying with, and in some cases actually pursuing, nuclear weapons capabilities. This nightmare scenario did not materialize, however, and since the mid-1960s the ranks of the nuclear powers have barely grown beyond the original five. Only India and Pakistan have tested their nuclear devices and proclaimed them-

---

66. See, for example, "S. Africa to Abandon Missile Launching Programme," in Agence France-Presse, June 30, 1993.
67. See David Albright and Mark Hibbs, "South Africa: The ANC and the Atom Bomb," *Bulletin of the Atomic Scientists*, Vol. 49, No. 3 (April 1993), pp. 32–37.
68. Yuri Kase's "The Costs and Benefits of Japan's Nuclearization," pp. 55–68, is particularly insightful on Japan's investigation of the nuclear option as an alternative method for attaining security. Although the investigation was not brought on by a regime change per se, Prime Minister Eisaku Sato and his administration were behind the creation of the report, which was intended to determine if nuclear weapons were a viable option for Japan. The conclusion of the report has a distinct hedging edge, placing great importance on the U.S. umbrella of extended deterrence as a condition for Japan's maintenance of a nonnuclear policy. Ibid., p. 60.
69. Solingen, "The Political Economy of Nuclear Restraint."

selves nuclear powers, while Israel and North Korea are widely suspected of having acquired the wherewithal to produce nuclear weapons.

This article has focused on nuclear reversal as a means of shedding new light on the gap between those expectations and the present reality. Nuclear reversal not only helps to explain why there are far fewer nuclear powers than once anticipated; it also generates fresh insight into the dynamics and patterns of proliferation, the factors that shape them, and the prospects for influencing them. In the process, this research has concluded that much of the success in curbing global nuclear proliferation has been attained by creating a favorable general as well as nation-specific political climate for restraining and even suppressing nuclear ambitions, as well as by converting many states' nuclear aspirations into a posture of nuclear hedging and, in a few other cases, nuclear restraint. Although this combination accounts for the considerable success in reversing proliferation trends, it also contains the seeds of its own undoing, should either of these conditions change for the worse. In fact, recent developments in both Asia and the Middle East attest to the highly precarious nature of the global order, as does the *U.S. National Strategy to Combat Weapons of Mass Destruction* report published in December 2002.

This leads us to consider the critical role that the United States has played in arresting nuclear proliferation. Obviously neither the United States by itself (or for that matter the Soviet Union at its peak) nor any group of powerful nations working together can impose nuclear reversal on a country that is adamantly opposed to it.[70] Nevertheless, the United States has been unique in its ability to create for most nations the favorable political climate necessary to encourage them to forgo the acquisition of nuclear weapons or, failing that, to transition toward nuclear hedging or at a minimum nuclear restraint. The opening for the United States to bring to bear its influence has been created by the acute demand facing virtually all nuclear programs for sustained, high-level domestic political support (to mobilize scarce resources, overcome bureaucratic and technical hurdles, and offset risks).

This study concludes that three factors have thus far combined to produce relative external success in bringing about nuclear reversal, hedging, or at a minimum restraint among the key nuclear aspirants: a change in the domestic

70. As an elaborate CIA analysis put it as early as 1969, "Neither the U.S. nor the USSR, however, could dictate a decision on the NPT to these nations [referring to the five major holdouts, of which three—India, Pakistan, and Israel—remain]. Even if the major powers were willing to employ drastic sanctions, the results might be counterproductive." See Central Intelligence Agency, *Response to NSSM No. 9*, p. 5.

perceptions of the nuclear aspirants of the utility of acquiring nuclear weapons; sustained U.S. encouragement of such perceptions, made possible by tracking, understanding, and ultimately addressing the nuclear aspirant's concerns and requirements; and a conscious U.S.-led effort to complicate the road to nuclear weapons acquisition for those who embark on it. Building a global norm against nuclear proliferation (using scarce resources to reinforce it), establishing comprehensive safeguards on nuclear facilities, developing restraints on the transfer of nuclear technology, and exercising restraint in its nuclear strategy (especially employing its own nuclear arsenal) have all been part of this overall U.S. approach. This approach, however, is currently undergoing profound change that both reflects the fragility of the nuclear nonproliferation regime and might further accelerate its transformation.

The study also yields one more conclusion, namely that time stands out as the most important variable in any effort to bring about nuclear turnaround. The long lead time from the moment a state launches its nuclear program until the capability emerges (typically measured in a decade or more) is what creates the opportunity to influence the program's course from the outside. It leaves room for the emergence of domestic conditions (leadership, political orientation, security situation) as well as external ones that might be either less conducive to the continuation of the nuclear weapons program or more receptive to external inducements to change the state's nuclear course. This underscores Joseph Nye's conclusion that "history shows that buying time to manage destabilizing effects [that motivate nuclear proliferation] is a feasible policy objective" for attaining nuclear reversal.[71]

Even in the easiest cases, however, merely placing obstacles in a state's path to nuclear weapons acquisition cannot attain success. As the case of Pakistan amply demonstrates, external inducements by themselves cannot prevent a determined regime from acquiring a nuclear weapons capability, even at significant cost and risk to itself and its people. Success is within reach only to the extent that foreign influence and domestic conditions converge, and the foreign effort is closely tuned (in terms of both agenda and timing) to the domestic context. External players need to aim at the key factors affecting domestic nuclear choices: the external security environment, the availability of alternative means to deal with the threats that this environment poses or to attain the other goals that the nuclear program is meant to achieve, and the

---

71. See Nye, "New Approaches to Nuclear Proliferation Policy," pp. 1293–1294.

balance between domestic proponents and opponents of nuclear weapons. They ought to seize on those opportunities in the nuclear program's evolution at which the program's proponents are either replaced, weakened, or otherwise undergo some transformation that may make them susceptible to external persuasion to consider at least nuclear restraint.

In closing, two suggestions for future research are in order. First, the concept of nuclear hedging, as well as the observations regarding the data limitations and their implications, should serve as a catalyst for a reexamination of nuclear reversal cases and further refinement of their theoretical findings. Second, it would be useful to broaden the scope of the empirical investigation of reversal processes beyond the nuclear domain, to compare the insights generated to date on nuclear reversal and restraint with similar processes in chemical and biological weapons programs and perhaps also ballistic missiles. The implementation in recent years of the Chemical Weapons Convention may well provide an opportunity and convenient platform for gaining new access into several such cases.

Part IV:
Contemporary Proliferation Challenges

Nuclear Terrorism

Matthew Bunn

A Strategy for Prevention

$\mathbf{O}$n the night of November 8, 2007, two teams of armed men attacked the Pelindaba nuclear facility in South Africa, where hundreds of kilograms of weapons-grade highly enriched uranium (HEU) were stored. One of the teams opened fire on the site security forces, who reportedly fled. The other team of four armed men went through a 10,000-volt security fence, disabled the intrusion detectors so that no alarms sounded—possibly using insider knowledge of the security system—broke into the emergency control center, and shot a worker there in the chest after a brief struggle. The worker at the emergency control center raised an alarm for the first time. These intruders spent forty-five minutes inside the secured perimeter without ever being engaged by site security forces, and then disappeared through the same point in the fence by which they had entered. No one on either team has been caught or identified.[1] The security manager resigned, and some of the guards on duty that night were fired. The South African government has not released important details of its investigation of the attack. Moreover, before the attack, South Africa had refused U.S. offers to remove the HEU at Pelindaba or to help improve security at the facility, and it continues to refuse such offers.[2] Indeed, South Africa has delayed for years es-

Matthew Bunn is Associate Professor of Public Policy at the Harvard Kennedy School; Co–Principal Investigator, Project on Managing the Atom, and Co–Principal Investigator, Energy Research, Development, Demonstration, and Deployment Policy Project at the Belfer Center for Science and International Affairs, John F. Kennedy School of Government, Harvard University.

1. See Scott Pelley, "60 Minutes: Assault on Pelindaba," *CBS News*, November 23, 2008, http://www.cbsnews.com/video/watch/?id+4628643n&tag+related;photovideo. See also Micah Zenko, "A Nuclear Site Is Breached: South African Attack Should Sound Alarms," *Washington Post*, December 20, 2007; Rob Adam, "Security Breach at Necsa," press release, Nuclear Energy Corporation of South Africa, November 13, 2007; Graeme Hosken, "Officer Shot as Gunmen Attack Pelindaba," *Pretoria News*, November 9, 2007; Graeme Hosken, "Two Gangs of Armed Men Breach Pelindaba Nuclear Facility," *Pretoria News*, November 14, 2007; and Joel Avni, Gertrude Makhafola, and Sibongile Mashaba, "Raid on Site Planned," *Sowetan*, November 14, 2007.

2. After the incident, South Africa did invite a team from the International Atomic Energy Agency (IAEA) to review security at the site. That team's report has not been made public; the brief public announcement indicates that the team made a number of recommendations to improve security training and equipment, but it describes the site's preexisting plan for security upgrades as an "appropriate basis" for physical protection there. See International Atomic Energy Agency, "IAEA Experts Complete Visit to Pelindaba Nuclear Facility in South Africa," press release, No. 2008/02, January 25, 2008, http://www.iaea.org/NewsCenter/PressReleases/2008/prn200802.html. Such IAEA teams, however, are largely constrained to reviewing whether security arrangements meet IAEA recommendations, which are considered vague. For a stock of highly enriched uranium (HEU) such as the one in South Africa, the recommendations call for the material to be in a locked room or vault and for a fence with intrusion detectors surrounding the site; the Pelindaba site follows both of these recommendations. In the 2007 incident, however, the fence was breached, and the intrusion detectors disabled without sounding any alarm.

tablishing and implementing a requirement that the site be able to defend against a defined set of potential attacker capabilities, known as a design basis threat (DBT), as recommended by the International Atomic Energy Agency (IAEA). As of the time of the attack, South African security regulations did not yet include a DBT.[3]

Although there is no publicly available evidence that the Pelindaba attackers were after the HEU stored at the facility, this incident is nevertheless a potent reminder that inadequately secured nuclear material is a global problem, not one limited to the former Soviet Union. The Pelindaba break-in leads to one inescapable conclusion: the world urgently needs a global campaign to ensure that every nuclear weapon and every stock of potential nuclear bomb material worldwide is secured against the kinds of threats terrorists and criminals have demonstrated they can pose. But given the South African refusal to accept international cooperation to improve nuclear security or to allow the HEU to be removed, the incident is also a reminder that sustained high-level leadership will be needed to overcome the serious obstacles to sensitive nuclear security cooperation around the world.

President Barack Obama appears to have drawn similar lessons. In his speech in Prague in April 2009, he warned that nuclear terrorism poses "the most immediate and extreme threat to global security," and he pledged to lead "a new international effort to secure all vulnerable nuclear material around the world within four years."[4]

This chapter draws on lessons such as these to offer (1) an assessment of the risk of nuclear terrorism (considering both the bad news and the good news about that risk); (2) a brief review of the progress of programs to reduce that risk; and (3) recommendations for a comprehensive strategy to lessen that risk as much and as quickly as practicable, focusing on security for nuclear weap-

---

3. In its annual report for the period leading up to the break-in, the South African department that oversees the site acknowledged that the goal of "implementation of a revised nuclear security framework" was "0 percent complete," because "Design Basis Threat (DBT) document not yet established." See Department of Minerals and Energy (DME), *Annual Report 2006/2007* (Johannesburg: DME, 2007), p. 69. The subsequent annual report indicates that the DBT was "still to be finalized" at the end of March 2008, almost five months after the Pelindaba assault. Department of Minerals and Energy, *Annual Report 2007/2008* (Johannesburg: DME, 2008), p. 100. It is notable that the annual report of the responsible ministry for the year involving the incident contains no mention of the incident or any subsequent security improvements. Further, it states that spending on security for Pelindaba was cut 12 percent compared to the year prior to the incident (p. 146), although the number of security officers employed by the department overall increased (pp. 204, 208).
4. See Office of the Press Secretary, "Remarks by President Barack Obama," Prague, Czech Republic, April 5, 2009, http://www.whitehouse.gov/the_press_office/Remarks-By-President-Barack-Obama-In-Prague-As-Delivered/.

ons and the materials needed to make them.[5] This chapter addresses only steps to prevent terrorist acquisition and use of a nuclear explosive. It does not cover the many additional steps needed to limit the spread of nuclear weapons to additional states,[6] or the actions that would be required to address the broad range of nonnuclear means by which terrorists might be able to cause catastrophic harm.[7]

It is worth beginning with some distinctions among different types of terrorism that are often grouped under the rubric of "nuclear terrorism." This chapter considers the risk of terrorists acquiring and using a nuclear bomb—either a stolen nuclear weapon or a crude bomb terrorists might manage to make themselves from plutonium or HEU. The use of a nuclear bomb would be among the most difficult types of attack for terrorists to accomplish—but the massive, assured, instantaneous, and comprehensive destruction of life and property that would result may make nuclear weapons a priority for terrorists despite the difficulties. A far easier type of radioactive attack for terrorists to accomplish would be to acquire radioactive material from a hospital or an industrial site and disperse it either with explosives in a so-called dirty bomb or in some other type of radiological dispersal device (RDD). Such a device could produce a disruptive and expensive mess, potentially create public panic, and possibly impose billions of dollars in disruption and cleanup costs.

---

5. This article draws heavily on Matthew Bunn, *Securing the Bomb 2008* (Cambridge, Mass.: Project on Managing the Atom, Belfer Center for Science and International Affairs, Harvard University, November 2008); and Matthew Bunn and Andrew Newman, "Preventing Nuclear Terrorism: An Agenda for the Next President" (Cambridge, Mass.: Project on Managing the Atom, Belfer Center for Science and International Affairs, Harvard University, November 2008), both at http://www.nti.org/securingthebomb. A substantial literature on the danger of nuclear terrorism is available. For one comprehensive (and alarming) look, see Graham Allison, *Nuclear Terrorism: The Ultimate Preventable Catastrophe* (New York: Times Books/Henry Holt, 2004). For a less alarming analysis, see Michael Levi, *On Nuclear Terrorism* (Cambridge, Mass.: Harvard University Press, 2007).
6. For recent compilations of recommended steps to address the broader problem of nuclear nonproliferation, see, for example, Bob Graham, Jim Talent, Graham Allison, Robin Cleveland, Steve Rademaker, Tim Roemer, Wendy Sherman, Henry Sapolski, and Rich Verma, *World at Risk: The Report of the Commission on the Prevention of Weapons of Mass Destruction Proliferation and Terrorism* (New York: Vintage, December 3, 2008), http://www.preventwmd.gov/report; Weapons of Mass Destruction Commission (WMDC), *Weapons of Terror: Freeing the World of Nuclear, Biological, and Chemical Arms* (Stockholm: WMDC, June 1, 2006), http://www.wmdcommission.org/files/Weapons_of_Terror.pdf; and George Perkovich, Jessica T. Matthews, Joseph Cirincione, Rose Gottemoeller, and Jon B. Wolfsthal, *Universal Compliance: A Strategy for Nuclear Security* (Washington, D.C.: Carnegie Endowment for International Peace, March 2005), http://www.carnegieendowment.org/files/UC2.FINAL3.pdf.
7. For an official listing of major terrorist and natural scenarios that could cause catastrophic harm, see U.S. Homeland Security Council, *National Planning Scenarios*, Ver. 20.1 Draft (Washington, D.C.: U.S. Homeland Security Council, April 2005), http://media.washingtonpost.com/wp-srv/nation/nationalsecurity/earlywarning/NationalPlanningScenariosApril2005.pdf.

But it would cause few casualties, and it would not obliterate the heart of a major city as a nuclear bomb would. The use of an RDD is far more likely, but it would be far less devastating than the detonation of a nuclear explosive; when overall risk is judged by the probability of an event multiplied by its consequences, it is my judgment that the overall risk posed by a nuclear bomb is greater, because its consequences would be so extreme. Terrorist sabotage of a major nuclear facility—which could, if successful, have consequences on a scale comparable to the nuclear reactor disaster at Chernobyl in 1986—is intermediate between nuclear weapons and RDDs both in the difficulty of terrorists pulling it off and in the consequences if they managed to do so. These other nuclear and radiological dangers have been addressed elsewhere, and I do not address them further in this chapter.[8]

Nuclear Terrorism Risks: The Bad News

The real risk of nuclear terrorism is inherently uncertain. But the answers to several basic questions help frame the magnitude of the problem.

A DESIRE FOR NUCLEAR WEAPONS
The primary and most fundamental question is whether terrorists want to use nuclear weapons in the first place. For most terrorists, focused on small-scale violence to attain local objectives, the answer is no. But for a small set of terrorists, the answer is clearly yes. Osama bin Laden has called the acquisition of nuclear weapons or other weapons of mass destruction a "religious duty."[9] Al-Qaida operatives have made repeated attempts to buy nuclear material for a nuclear bomb and to recruit nuclear expertise, including the two extremist Pakistani nuclear weapons scientists who met with bin Laden and his close aide, Ayman al-Zawahiri, to discuss nuclear weapons. For years, al-Qaida operatives have repeatedly expressed the desire to inflict a "Hiroshima" on the United States.[10] Before al-Qaida, the Japanese terror cult Aum Shinrikyo also

---

8. For a useful overview of these various types of nuclear terrorism, see Charles D. Ferguson and William C. Potter, with Amy Sands, Leonard S. Spector, and Fred L. Wehling, *The Four Faces of Nuclear Terrorism* (Monterey, Calif.: Center for Nonproliferation Studies, Monterey Institute of International Studies, 2004), http://www.nti.org/c_press/analysis_4faces.pdf. See also Matthew Bunn and Tom Bielefeld, "Reducing Nuclear and Radiological Terrorism Threats," in *Proceedings of the Institute for Nuclear Materials Management, 48th Annual Meeting,* Tucson, Arizona, July 8–12, 2007 (Northbrook, Ill.: INMM, 2007).
9. Rahimullah Yusufzai, "Interview with Bin Laden: World's Most Wanted Terrorist," *ABC News,* 1999, http://www.islamistwatch.org/blogger/localstories/05-06-03/ABCInterview.html.
10. Steve Coll, "What Bin Laden Sees in Hiroshima," *Washington Post,* February 6, 2005.

made a concerted effort to obtain nuclear weapons.[11] With at least two groups going down this path since the early 1990s, the odds are that others will also do so in the future.

As head of intelligence for the U.S. Department of Energy (DOE), Rolf Mowatt-Larssen testified before the U.S. Senate in the spring of 2008 that "Al-Qaida's nuclear intent remains clear," citing, among other things, bin Laden's successful effort in 2003 to convince a radical Saudi cleric to issue a religious ruling, or *fatwa*, authorizing the use of nuclear weapons on American civilians.[12] Mowatt-Larssen warned that the world's efforts to prevent terrorists from gaining the ability "to develop and detonate a nuclear weapon" are likely to be "tested" in "the early years of the 21st century."[13]

THE ABILITY TO BUILD A CRUDE NUCLEAR BOMB

The next question is whether a sophisticated terrorist group could plausibly build a nuclear bomb if it acquired the needed nuclear material. The answer here is also yes. Making at least a crude nuclear bomb might well be within the capabilities of a sophisticated group, though it would be the most technically challenging operation any terrorist group has ever accomplished. One study by the now-defunct congressional Office of Technology Assessment summarized the threat: "A small group of people, none of whom have ever had access to the classified literature, could possibly design and build a crude nuclear explosive device. . . . Only modest machine-shop facilities that could be con-

---

11. For discussion of the al-Qaida and Aum Shinrikyo efforts, see Matthew Bunn and Anthony Wier, with Joshua Friedman, "The Threat: The Demand for Black Market Fissile Material," in *Nuclear Threat Initiative Research Library: Securing the Bomb* (Cambridge, Mass.: Project on Managing the Atom, Belfer Center for Science and International Affairs, Harvard University, updated June 16, 2005), http://www.nti.org/e_research/cnwm/threat/demand.asp; and Sara Daly, John Parachini, and William Rosenau, *Aum Shinrikyo, Al Qaeda, and the Kinshasa Reactor: Implications of Three Case Studies for Combating Nuclear Terrorism* (Santa Monica, Calif.: RAND, 2005), http://www.rand.org/pubs/documented_briefings/2005/RAND_DB458.sum.pdf. For further details on U.S. intelligence on some of al-Qaida's nuclear efforts, see George Tenet, *At the Center of the Storm: My Years at the CIA* (New York: HarperCollins, 2007); and Commission on the Intelligence Capabilities of the United States Regarding Weapons of Mass Destruction, *Report to the President of the United States* (Washington, D.C.: WMD Commission, March 31, 2005), http://www.gpoaccess.gov/wmd/index.html.
12. For an English translation of this fatwa, see Nasir Bin Hamd al-Fahd, "A Treatise on the Legal Status of Using Weapons of Mass Destruction against Infidels," May 2003, http://www.carnegieendowment.org/static/npp/fatwa.pdf. Al-Fahd has since been arrested and has publicly renounced some of his previous rulings, including this one.
13. Rolf Mowatt-Larssen, testimony before the Senate Committee on Homeland Security and Governmental Affairs, 110th Cong., 2d sess., June 15, 2008. Before taking over as head of DOE intelligence, Mowatt-Larssen led the Central Intelligence Agency's efforts to track al-Qaida's weapons of mass destruction programs and chaired an intelligence community–wide working group on nuclear terrorism.

tracted for without arousing suspicion would be required."[14] Indeed, even before the seizure of nuclear-related documents in Afghanistan, which revealed a more substantial al-Qaida nuclear effort than had previously been detected, U.S. intelligence concluded that "fabrication of at least a 'crude' nuclear device was within al-Qa'ida's capabilities, if it could obtain fissile material."[15] Mowatt-Larssen told Congress that an al-Qaida nuclear bomb effort "probably would not require the involvement of more than the number of operatives who carried out 9/11," and it would be "just as compartmented," making it extraordinarily difficult for the intelligence community to detect and stop.[16]

Al-Qaida's nuclear efforts in Afghanistan were disrupted when the Taliban regime was overthrown in December 2001. But al-Qaida has been reconstituting its ability to plan and direct large, complex operations from the tribal areas of Pakistan. Director of National Intelligence Dennis Blair told the Senate in March 2009 that al-Qaida had been significantly weakened by a series of U.S. and allied efforts during 2008, but that "al-Qa'ida and its affiliates and allies remain dangerous and adaptive enemies," still using the tribal areas of Pakistan as a base for planning and coordinating attacks, and likely still plotting attacks on the United States that would be "designed to produce mass casualties, visually dramatic destruction, significant economic aftershocks, and/ or fear among the population." Blair went on to warn that "over the coming years, we will continue to face a substantial threat, including in the U.S. Homeland, from terrorists attempting to acquire biological, chemical, and possibly nuclear weapons and use them to conduct large-scale attacks."[17]

No one knows for sure what the current status of al-Qaida's nuclear effort is—or how much the organization may have learned from past failures that

---

14. Office of Technology Assessment (OTA), *Nuclear Proliferation and Safeguards* (Washington, D.C.: OTA, U.S. Congress, June 1977), http://www.princeton.edu/~ota/disk3/1977/7705/7705.PDF, p. 140. OTA reached this conclusion long before the internet made a great deal of relevant information much more widely available.
15. Commission on the Intelligence Capabilities of the United States Regarding Weapons of Mass Destruction, *Report to the President of the United States,* p. 276.
16. Mowatt-Larssen, testimony before the Senate Committee on Homeland Security and Governmental Affairs. For discussions of official assessments of the complexity of the operation and the number of people required, see Matthew Bunn and Anthony Wier, "Terrorist Nuclear Weapon Construction: How Difficult?" *Annals of the American Academy of Political and Social Science,* Vol. 607 (September 2006), pp. 133–149. For a particular scenario involving a cell of nineteen people working for roughly a year (probably more than is required for some types of crude bomb), see Peter D. Zimmerman and Jeffrey G. Lewis, "The Bomb in the Backyard," *Foreign Policy,* No. 157 (November/December 2006), pp. 32–39.
17. Director of National Intelligence Dennis C. Blair, "Annual Threat Assessment of the U.S. Intelligence Community," testimony before the Senate Committee on Armed Services, 111th Cong., 1st sess., March 10, 2009, http://www.dni.gov/testimonies/20090310_testimony.pdf.

may increase its chance of future success.[18] But if al-Qaida acquires the needed HEU or plutonium, there would be a very real risk that it could put together and deliver a crude but devastating nuclear bomb.

THE ABILITY TO OBTAIN NUCLEAR BOMB MATERIAL

Could a terrorist group plausibly obtain the material needed for a nuclear bomb? Unfortunately, the answer here is also yes. Nuclear weapons or their essential ingredients exist in hundreds of buildings in dozens of countries. Security measures for many of these stocks are excellent, but security for others is appalling, in some cases amounting to no more than a night watchman and a chain-link fence. No specific and binding global standards for how these stockpiles should be secured exist.

The risk of nuclear theft from a particular facility or transport operation depends on the quantity and quality of the material available to be stolen (i.e., its suitability for use in a nuclear bomb), the security measures in place (i.e., what kind of insider and outsider thieves could the security measures protect against, with what probability), and the threats those security measures face (i.e., the probability of different levels of insider or outsider capabilities being brought to bear in a theft attempt). Based on the limited unclassified information available, it appears that the highest risks of nuclear theft today are in Russia, Pakistan, and at HEU-fueled research reactors around the world.[19]

RUSSIA. Nuclear security in Russia and the former Soviet Union has improved dramatically since the early 1990s; at many sites, the difference between the security in place in 2009 and the security in place in the years after the Soviet collapse is like night and day. But Russia has the world's largest stockpiles of nuclear weapons and materials, scattered in the world's largest number of buildings and bunkers; some serious security weaknesses still remain, ranging from poorly trained, sometimes suicidal guards to serious underfunding of nuclear security; and the upgraded security systems must face huge threats, from insider theft conspiracies that are cropping up everywhere in Russia to large-scale outsider attacks. Since the September 11 attacks, terrorist teams have carried out reconnaissance at secret nuclear weapon stor-

---

18. For a discussion of both the possibility that multiple terrorist failures may contribute to eventual success and the difficulty that insular terrorist groups have in changing their approaches (and replacing ineffective experts), see Richard Danzig, "Limitations of Terrorists . . . and Ourselves," presentation at "Pivot Point: New Directions for American Security," Center for a New American Security, Washington, D.C., June 11, 2008.
19. For more a more detailed assessment of the global nuclear security picture, see Bunn, *Securing the Bomb 2008.*

age sites in Russia;[20] a Russian court case revealed that a Russian businessman had been offering $750,000 for stolen weapons-grade plutonium for sale to a foreign client;[21] and the 2004 Beslan school massacre confirmed the terrorists' ability to strike in force, without warning or mercy. As one indicator of the insider threat, in 2006 President Vladimir Putin fired Maj. Gen. Sergey Shlyapuzhnikov, deputy chairman of the section of the Ministry of Internal Affairs responsible for guarding the closed nuclear cities and other closed territories, because (according to the Russian state newspaper), he was helping to organize smuggling in and out of these closed territories—in particular, distributing passes that allowed people and vehicles to go in and out without being checked.[22]

PAKISTAN. Pakistan's nuclear stockpile is small, stored at a small number of sites, and is thought to be heavily guarded, with substantial security upgrades in recent years, implemented in part with U.S. help.[23] In the spring of 2009, both President Obama and Chairman of the Joint Chiefs of Staff Adm. Mike Mullen expressed confidence that Pakistan's nuclear security measures were sufficient to keep its nuclear weapons out of the hands of militants.[24] But

---

20. Lt. Gen. Igor Valynkin, commander of the force that guards Russia's nuclear weapons, reported two incidents of terrorist teams carrying out such reconnaissance. See, for example, "Russia: Terror Groups Scoped Nuke Site," Associated Press, October 25, 2001; and Pavel Koryashkin, "Russian Nuclear Ammunition Depots Well Protected—Official," ITAR-TASS, October 25, 2001. The Russian state newspaper reported these two incidents and two more involving terrorist reconnaissance on warhead transport trains. Vladimir Bogdanov, "Propusk K Beogolovkam Nashli U Terrorista" [A pass to warheads found on a terrorist], *Rossiskaya Gazeta*, November 1, 2002.
21. For a summary of multiple Russian sources on this case, see "Plutonium Con Artists Sentenced in Russian Closed City of Sarov," *NIS Export Control Observer*, November 2003, http:// cns.miis.edu/pubs/nisexcon/pdfs/ob_0311e.pdf. See also "Russian Court Sentences Men for Weapons-Grade Plutonium Scam," trans. BBC Monitoring Service, *RIA Novosti*, October 14, 2003; and "Russia: Criminals Indicted for Selling Mercury as Weapons-Grade Plutonium," trans. U.S. Department of Commerce, *Izvestiya*, October 11, 2003.
22. "The President Issued a Decree to Dismiss Deputy Chairman of the MVD Department in Charge of Law and Order in Closed Territories and Sensitive Sites, Major General Sergey Shlyapuzhnikov," trans. Anatoly Dianov, *Rossiskaya Gazeta*, June 2, 2006. MVD is the Russian acronym for the Ministry of Internal Affairs.
23. The sparse information that is publicly available is summarized in Nathan E. Busch, *No End in Sight: The Continuing Menace of Nuclear Proliferation* (Lexington: University Press of Kentucky, 2004). For a summary of the approaches Pakistan has taken to strengthen security and accounting (and command and control) for its nuclear assets since the A.Q. Khan network was revealed, see Mark Fitzpatrick, ed., *Nuclear Black Markets: Pakistan, A.Q. Khan, and the Rise of Proliferation Networks—A Net Assessment* (London: International Institute for Strategic Studies, 2007), pp. 112–117. See also Mahmud Ali Durrani, "Pakistan's Strategic Thinking and the Role of Nuclear Weapons," Occasional Paper, No. 37 (Albuquerque, N.Mex.: Cooperative Monitoring Center, July 2004), http://www.cmc.sandia.gov/cmc-papers/sand2004-3375p.pdf; and Kenneth N. Luongo and Brig. Gen. Naeem Salik, "Building Confidence in Pakistan's Nuclear Security," *Arms Control Today*, Vol. 37, No. 10 (December 2007). For a useful journalistic account, see, for example, David E. Sanger, "Obama's Worst Pakistan Nightmare," *New York Times Magazine*, January 8, 2009.
24. Office of the Press Secretary, "News Conference by the President," Washington, D.C., April 29, 2009, http://www.whitehouse.gov/the_press_office/News-Conference-by-the-President-4/29/

Pakistani security systems face immense threats, ranging from nuclear insiders (some of whom have a demonstrated willingness to sell practically anything to practically anybody) to armed attack potentially by scores or hundreds of insurgents. In at least two cases, serving Pakistani military personnel working with al-Qaida came within a hair's breadth of assassinating President Pervez Musharraf.[25] If the military officers guarding the president cannot be trusted, how much confidence can the world have in the military officers guarding Pakistan's nuclear weapons?

HEU-FUELED RESEARCH REACTORS. HEU-fueled research reactors typically have comparatively modest stockpiles of material, but they have some of the world's weakest security measures for those stocks. (Ironically, the security measures at Pelindaba are more substantial than they are at many HEU-fueled research reactors around the world.) And it is important to remember that much of the irradiated fuel from research reactors is still HEU, and is not radioactive enough to pose any significant deterrent to theft by suicidal terrorists.[26] Some 130 research reactors around the world still use HEU as their fuel. Many tons of HEU exist at these research reactors.[27] Often this material is in forms that would require some chemical processing to use in a bomb, but any group that could pull off the difficult job of making a nuclear bomb from HEU metal would have a good chance of mastering the simpler job of extracting HEU metal from research reactor fuel.

OTHER RISKS. Russia, Pakistan, and HEU-fueled research reactors are the highest-risk categories, but there are others where the risks are also real. Transport of nuclear weapons and materials is a particular concern; it is the part of the nuclear material life cycle most vulnerable to violent, forcible theft because it is impossible to protect the material with thick walls and many minutes of delay when it is on the road, and transports of both weapons and materials are remarkably frequent.[28] In the end, virtually every country where these materi-

---

2009/; and Adm. Mike Mullen, Department of Defense News Briefing, May 4, 2009, http://www.defenselink.mil/transcripts/transcript.aspx?transcriptid+4413.

25. Pervez Musharraf, *In the Line of Fire: A Memoir* (New York: Free Press, 2006) pp. 245–256.

26. For a discussion of the proliferation threat posed by irradiated HEU fuel, see Matthew Bunn and Anthony Wier, *Securing the Bomb: An Agenda for Action* (Cambridge, Mass.: Project on Managing the Atom, Belfer Center for Science and International Affairs, Harvard University, May 2004), http://www.nti.org/e_research/analysis_cnwmupdate_052404.pdf, pp. 36–37.

27. Throughout this chapter, "tons" refers to metric tons. Each metric ton equals 1,000 kilograms, or slightly more than 2,200 pounds.

28. For a critical review of transport security in France, see, in particular, Ronald E. Timm, *Security Assessment Report for Plutonium Transport in France* (Paris: Greenpeace International, 2005), http://www.greenpeace.fr/stop-plutonium/en/TimmReportV5.pdf. France has reportedly implemented substantial improvements in security for nuclear material transports since Timm's report, however. See U.S. National Nuclear Security Administration official, interviewed by author, May 2009. In France, long-distance transports of large quantities of separated plutonium are a weekly occur-

als exist—including the United States—must do more to ensure that these stocks are protected against the kinds of threats that terrorists and criminals have shown they can pose.

CONFIRMED THEFTS. Theft of HEU and plutonium is not a hypothetical worry; it is an ongoing reality. In February 2006, Russian citizen Oleg Khinsagov was arrested in Georgia (along with three Georgian accomplices) with 79.5 grams of 89 percent enriched HEU, claiming that he had kilograms more available for sale.[29] The IAEA has confirmed eighteen incidents of theft or loss of HEU or separated plutonium.[30] Other incidents are known to have occurred—the thieves were captured, tried, and convicted—yet they have not been confirmed by the states concerned.[31] What we do not know, of course, is how many thefts may have occurred that were undetected; it is a sobering fact

---

rence. David Albright, *Shipments of Weapons-Usable Plutonium in the Commercial Nuclear Industry* (Washington, D.C.: Institute for Science and International Security, January 3, 2007), http://www.isis-online.org/global_stocks/end2003/plutonium_shipments.pdf. In Russia, the U.S. Nunn-Lugar program sponsors warhead shipments from deployment sites back to storage or dismantlement sites, and these shipments alone occur almost weekly. U.S. Department of Defense, *Cooperative Threat Reduction Annual Report to Congress: Fiscal Year 2009* (Washington, D.C.: U.S. Department of Defense, 2008), pp. 2, 14. Tens of tons of HEU are sent in dozens of shipments over thousands of kilometers of rail in Russia every year. U.S. General Accounting Office (GAO), *Nuclear Nonproliferation: Status of Transparency Measures for U.S. Purchase of Russian Highly Enriched Uranium* (Washington, D.C.: GAO, September 1999), http://www.gao.gov/archive/1999/rc99194.pdf. In the United States, the Secure Transportation Asset program of the Department of Energy, which transports both nuclear weapons and weapons-usable nuclear material, carries out roughly 100 shipments every year—approximately two per week. U.S. Department of Energy, *FY 2009 Congressional Budget Request: National Nuclear Security Administration*, DOE/CF-024, Vol. 1 (Washington, D.C.: DOE, February 2008), p. 313.

29. For an especially useful account of this case, see Michael Bronner, "100 Grams (and Counting): Notes from the Nuclear Underworld" (Cambridge, Mass.: Project on Managing the Atom, Belfer Center for Science and International Affairs, Harvard University, June 2008), http://belfercenter.ksg.harvard.edu/publication/18361/100_grams_and_counting.html. (The seized material was roughly 100 grams of uranium oxide, containing 79.5 grams of uranium.) See also Laurence Scott Sheets, "A Smuggler's Story," *Atlantic Monthly*, April 2008, pp. 60–70; and Elena Sokova, William C. Potter, and Cristina Chuen, "Recent Weapons Grade Uranium Smuggling Case: Nuclear Materials Are Still on the Loose," CNS Research Story (Monterey, Calif.: Center for Nonproliferation Studies, Monterey Institute of International Studies, January 26, 2007), http://cns.miis.edu/stories/070126.htm.

30. For the International Atomic Energy Agency's list of incidents confirmed by the states concerned, see "IAEA Illicit Trafficking Database (ITDB)," Fact Sheet (Vienna: IAEA, September 2008), www.iaea.org/NewsCenter/Features/RadSources/PDF/fact_figures2007.pdf. There are eighteen incidents on this list, but three of them appear to involve inadvertent losses rather than thefts. Some incidents previously on the list have been removed: one plutonium incident involved such a small amount of material that it was reclassified as a radioactive source incident, and one incident previously tracked as an HEU case was confirmed to be LEU. Richard Hoskins, IAEA Office of Nuclear Security, personal communication by author, October 2006.

31. Perhaps the best summary of the available data on nuclear and radiological smuggling is "Illicit Trafficking in Radioactive Materials," in Fitzpatrick, *Nuclear Black Markets*, pp. 119–138.

that nearly all of the stolen HEU and plutonium that has been seized over the years had never been missed when it was originally stolen.[32]

The amounts required for a bomb are small. The Nagasaki bomb included some 6 kilograms of plutonium, which would fit in a soda can. A similar HEU bomb would require three times as much.[33] For a simpler but less efficient gun-type design, roughly 50 kilograms of HEU would be needed—an amount that would fit easily into two two-liter bottles. The world's stockpiles of HEU and separated plutonium are enough to make roughly 200,000 nuclear weapons;[34] a tiny fraction of 1 percent of these stockpiles going missing could cause a global catastrophe.

---

32. The U.S. National Intelligence Council continues to assess that "it is likely that undetected smuggling has occurred, and we are concerned about the total amount of material that could have been diverted over the last 15 years." National Intelligence Council, *Annual Report to Congress on the Safety and Security of Russian Nuclear Facilities and Military Forces* (Washington, D.C.: Central Intelligence Agency, April 2006), http://www.fas.org/irp/nic/russia0406.html. Former CIA Director Porter Goss testified to Congress that sufficient material was unaccounted for so he could not provide assurances that enough material for a bomb had not already been stolen. See Goss, "Current and Projected National Security Threats to the United States," testimony before the Senate Select Committee on Intelligence, 109th Cong., 1st sess., February 16, 2005, http://www.fas.org/irp/congress/2005_hr/shrg109-61.pdf. Goss was not saying that the CIA had definite information that enough material for a bomb was missing, only that the accounting uncertainties are so large that it is impossible to tell whether enough material for a bomb is missing or not. The same is true in the United States; some 2 tons of U.S. plutonium, for example, enough for hundreds of nuclear bombs, is officially considered "material unaccounted for." See U.S. Department of Energy, "Plutonium: The First 50 Years: United States Plutonium Production, Acquisition, and Utilization from 1944 through 1994" (Washington, D.C.: DOE, 1996), http://www.fas.org/sgp/othergov/doe/pu50y.html.

33. The Department of Energy has officially declassified the fact that 4 kilograms of plutonium is in principle sufficient to make a nuclear weapon. U.S. Department of Energy, "Restricted Data Declassification Decisions—1946 to the Present (RDD-7)" (Washington, D.C.: DOE, January 2001), http://www.fas.org/sgp/othergov/doe/rdd-7.html. The amount of plutonium in the first nuclear bomb, in the "Trinity" test in New Mexico, was 6.1 kilograms. See Gen. Leslie R. Groves, memorandum to the secretary of war, July 18, 1945, reprinted as appendix P in Martin J. Sherwin, *A World Destroyed: The Atomic Bomb and the Grand Alliance* (New York: Alfred A. Knopf, 1975). The amount of 93 percent HEU metal required for a sphere with no neutron-reflecting material around it to sustain a nuclear chain reaction (known as a bare-sphere critical mass) is roughly three times the comparable amount for weapons-grade plutonium in the crystalline form typically used in nuclear weapons, known as the "delta phase."

34. The world stockpile of separated plutonium is roughly 500 metric tons (roughly half civilian and half military); the world stockpile of HEU is 1,400–2,000 tons (all but a few percent of which is military). See International Panel on Fissile Materials (IPFM), *Global Fissile Material Report 2007* (Princeton, N.J.: IPFM, 2007), http://www.fissilematerials.org/ipfm/site_down/gfmr07.pdf. The separated plutonium total includes both weapons-grade and reactor-grade plutonium. Reactor-grade plutonium is also weapons-usable. For a detailed unclassified official statement on this point, see U.S. Department of Energy, *Nonproliferation and Arms Control Assessment of Weapons-Usable Fissile Material Storage and Excess Plutonium Disposition Alternatives*, DOE/NN-0007 (Washington, D.C.: Office of Arms Control and Nonproliferation, DOE, January 1997), pp. 37–39, http://www.osti.gov/bridge/servlets/purl/425259-CXr7Qn/webviewable/425259.pdf.

NUCLEAR BOMB DELIVERY POTENTIAL

The next question is whether a terrorist group could deliver a bomb to Washington, New York, or other major cities around the world. Here, too, the answer is yes: they probably could. If stolen or built abroad, a nuclear bomb might be delivered to the United States, intact or in ready-to-assemble pieces, by boat or aircraft or truck. The length of the border, the diversity of means of transport, the vast scale of legitimate traffic across national borders, and the ease of shielding the radiation from plutonium or especially from HEU, all operate in favor of the terrorists. Building the overall system of legal infrastructure, intelligence, law enforcement, border and customs forces, and radiation detectors needed to find and recover stolen nuclear weapons or materials, or to interdict these as they cross national borders, is an extraordinarily difficult challenge.[35]

THE CONSEQUENCES OF A TERRORIST NUCLEAR BLAST

What would happen if terrorists set off a nuclear bomb in a U.S. city? Here, the answers are nothing short of terrifying.[36] A bomb with the explosive power of 10,000 tons of TNT (i.e., 10 kilotons, somewhat smaller than the bomb that obliterated Hiroshima), if set off in midtown Manhattan on a typical workday, could kill half a million people and cause roughly $1 trillion in direct economic damage.[37] No capability is yet available to provide medical care for hundreds

---

35. For a useful discussion emphasizing the ease with which terrorists might follow different pathways to deliver their weapon, see Allison, *Nuclear Terrorism*. For a more optimistic view of the potential of these parts of a defensive system, see Levi, *On Nuclear Terrorism*.

36. For an excellent overview of the demands of "the day after" such an attack, see Ashton B. Carter, Michael M. May, and William J. Perry, "The Day After: Action in the 24 Hours Following a Nuclear Blast in an American City" (Cambridge, Mass., and Stanford, Calif.: Preventive Defense Project, Belfer Center for Science and International Affairs, Harvard University and Stanford University, May 31, 2007), http://belfercenter.ksg.harvard.edu/publication/2140/.

37. See Matthew Bunn, Anthony Wier, and John Holdren, *Controlling Nuclear Warheads and Materials: A Report Card and Action Plan* (Cambridge, Mass.: Project on Managing the Atom, Belfer Center for Science and International Affairs, Harvard University, March 2003), pp. 15–19, http://www.nti.org/e_research/cnwm/cnwm.pdf. This was a rough estimate based on a relatively crude analysis. A number of more detailed analyses of the effects of a terrorist nuclear weapon in a U.S. city are available, though a surprising number of them envision either a bomb going off in an area with much lower population density than mid-town Manhattan or the bomb being detonated at night (when the populations at the center of most cities are far lower, but those populations are easier to get information about from the U.S. census). For a recent official government analysis of such an event in Washington D.C., see, for example, U.S. Homeland Security Council, *National Planning Scenarios*. Recent detailed nongovernment analyses include Charles Meade and Roger C. Molander, *Considering the Effects of a Catastrophic Terrorist Attack* (Washington, D.C.: Center for Terrorism and Risk Management Policy, RAND, 2006), http://www.rand.org/pubs/technical_reports/2006/RAND_TR391.pdf; and Ira Helfand, Lachlan Forrow, and Jaya Tiwari, "Nuclear Terrorism," *British Medical Journal*, February 9, 2002, pp. 356–358.

of thousands of burned, injured, and irradiated people in any reasonable period of time.[38] Terrorists—either those who committed the attack or others—would probably claim they had more bombs already hidden in U.S. cities (whether or not they did), and the fear that this might be true could lead to panicked evacuations of major U.S. cities, creating widespread havoc and economic disruption. If the bomb went off in Washington, D.C., large fractions of the federal government would be destroyed, and effective governance of the country would be sorely tested, despite current planning for continuity of government. Given the horror of the attack, fears that more were coming, and the possibility that the essential ingredients of a nuclear bomb could fit in a suitcase, traditional notions of civil liberties and protection against unreasonable search and seizure would likely fall by the wayside. Devastating economic aftershocks would reverberate throughout the country and the world—global effects that in 2005 United Nations Secretary-General Kofi Annan warned would push "tens of millions of people into dire poverty," creating "a second death toll throughout the developing world."[39] The United States and the world would be transformed forever—and not for the better.[40]

Nuclear Terrorism Risks: The Good News

Fortunately, there is good news in this story as well. First, there is no convincing evidence that any terrorist group has yet acquired a nuclear weapon or the materials needed to make one—or that al Qaida has yet to put together expertise that would be needed to make a bomb. Indeed, there is some evidence of confusion and lack of nuclear knowledge among some senior al-Qaida operatives.[41]

---

38. See, for example, Irwin Redlener, "Survival in the Nuclear Gray Zone: Why We Have Not Addressed Response Planning for Nuclear Terrorism—And Why We Must," testimony before the Senate Committee on Homeland Security and Governmental Affairs, 110th Cong., 2d sess., May 15, 2008, http://hsgac.senate.gov/public/_files/051508Redlener.pdf. Redlener is the director of the National Center for Disaster Preparedness at the Mailman School of Public Health at Columbia University.
39. Kofi Annan, "A Global Strategy for Fighting Terrorism," Keynote Address to the Closing Plenary of the International Summit on Democracy, Terrorism, and Security, Madrid, Spain, March 8–11, 2005, http://english.safe-democracy.org/keynotes/a-global-strategy-for-fighting-terrorism.html.
40. For a meditation arguing that such an attack would leave the very notion of the sovereignty of nation-states in tatters, see Stephen D. Krasner, "The Day After," *Foreign Policy*, No. 146 (January/February 2005), pp. 68–70. Former Undersecretary of Defense for Policy Fred Charles Iklé has gone so far as to describe the threat as "annihilation from within." See Iklé, *Annihilation from Within: The Ultimate Threat to Nations* (New York: Columbia University Press, 2006), p. 160.
41. In particular, both Khalid Sheikh Mohammed and Abu Zubaydah are reported to have be-

Second, making and delivering even a crude nuclear bomb would be the most technically challenging and complex operation any terrorist group has ever carried out. There would be many chances for the effort to fail, and the cumulative obstacles may seem daunting even to determined terrorists, leading them to focus more of their efforts on conventional tools of terror—as al-Qaida appears to have done.[42] Both al-Qaida and Aum Shinrikyo appear to have encountered a variety of difficulties, demonstrating that acquiring a nuclear bomb is a huge challenge, even for large, well-financed terrorist groups with ample technical resources.[43]

Third, the overthrow of the Taliban and the disruption of al-Qaida's central command structure certainly reduced al-Qaida's chances of pulling off such a complex operation. That capability may be growing again, however, as al-Qaida reconstitutes in the mountains of Pakistan.[44]

Fourth, there is a real debate even among the community of violent Islamic extremists over the moral legitimacy of the mass slaughter of innocents. One of the founders of al-Qaida, who wrote two of the books that al-Qaida has long relied on for its ideological justification for violent jihad, has written another book, which argues that most forms of terrorism—and particularly indiscriminate killing of bystanders—are forbidden by Islamic law—and that violent jihad is permissible only under rare circumstances. "There is nothing that invokes the anger of God and His wrath like the unwarranted spilling of blood and wrecking of property," he argues.[45] Al-Qaida was sufficiently concerned over this frontal assault by one of its founders that Ayman al-Zawahiri rushed out a 188-page response only two months after the book was released. Moreover, when al-Qaida organized an electronic question-and-answer session with Zawahiri, many of the questions he chose to answer focused on bitter criticisms of al-Qaida's killing of innocent people, and he was at pains to argue that al-Qaida fighters would kill innocents only when doing so was un-

lieved that uranium, which is only weakly radioactive, would be a good material for a dirty bomb—and there have been other al-Qaida operatives arrested for seeking uranium for dirty bombs as well. See discussion and sources in Bunn, Wier, and Friedman, "The Demand for Black Market Fissile Material."

42. For the most comprehensive available account of this argument, see Levi, *On Nuclear Terrorism*.

43. Bunn, Wier, and Friedman, "The Demand for Black Market Fissile Material."

44. See, for example, Office of the Director of National Intelligence, "The Terrorist Threat to the U.S. Homeland," National Intelligence Estimate (Washington, D.C.: U.S. National Intelligence Council, July 2007), http://www.dni.gov/press_releases/20070717_release.pdf.

45. The new book is from Sayyid Imam al-Sharif, sometimes known as "Dr. Fadl," an original member of the al-Qaida ruling council. See Lawrence Wright, "The Rebellion Within: An Al Qaeda Mastermind Questions Terrorism," *New Yorker*, June 2, 2008, p. 46.

avoidable, quoting bin Laden as instructing al-Qaida's fighters to "make sure that their operations targeting the enemies are regulated by the regulations of the Shari'ah and as far as possible from Muslims."[46] A nuclear bomb, of course, is the apotheosis of indiscriminate mass slaughter, making no distinction between the innocent and the guilty, between Muslims and non-Muslims. These dissents are unlikely to convince bin Laden and Zawahiri, but the more the broader community of extreme Islamists comes to view the nuclear level of mass slaughter as a moral crime, the more difficult it is likely to be for al-Qaida to recruit experts to help them build a nuclear bomb.

Fifth, nuclear security is improving. Although a great deal remains to be done, the fact is that at scores of sites in Russia, the former Soviet Union, and elsewhere, security is dramatically better than it was in 1994. Security upgrades were completed at most Russian nuclear warhead and nuclear material sites by the end of 2008. HEU is being removed from sites all around the world, permanently eliminating the risk of nuclear theft at those sites. An alphabet soup of programs and initiatives—Cooperative Threat Reduction (CTR), the Materials Protection, Control, and Accounting (MPC&A) program, the Global Threat Reduction Initiative (GTRI), the Global Initiative to Combat Nuclear Terrorism (GI), the International Atomic Energy Agency's Office of Nuclear Security, the Domestic Nuclear Detection Office (DNDO), and many more—are each making real contributions. There can be no doubt that the United States and the world face a far lower risk of nuclear terrorism today than they would have faced had these efforts never been begun. These programs are excellent investments in U.S. and world security, deserving strong support. Securing the world's stockpiles of nuclear weapons and the materials needed to make them is a big, complex job, but it is a doable one, as the progress already made demonstrates.

Sixth, hostile states are highly unlikely to consciously choose to provide nuclear weapons or the materials needed to make them to terrorist groups. Such a decision would mean transferring the most awesome military power the state has ever acquired to a group over which it has little control, and potentially opening the regime to overwhelming retaliation—a particularly unlikely step for dictators or oligarchs obsessed with controlling their states and maintaining power.[47]

---

46. "The Open Meeting with Shaykh Ayman al-Zawahiri," As-Sahab Media, 1429–2008, April 2, 2008. As-Sahab is al-Qaida's media arm.
47. See, for example, Bunn, Wier, and Holdren, *Controlling Nuclear Warheads and Materials*, pp. 22–23; and Matthew Bunn, "A Mathematical Model of the Risk of Nuclear Terrorism," *Annals of the American Academy of Political and Social Science*, Vol. 607 (September 2006), pp. 103–120.

All of this good news comes with a crucial caveat: "as far as we know." The gaps in the international community's knowledge of al-Qaida's nuclear efforts remain wide. Some intelligence analysts argue that the lack of hard evidence of an extensive current al-Qaida nuclear effort simply reflects al-Qaida's success in compartmentalizing the work and keeping it secret. It is a sobering thought that a nuclear effort might not require a conspiracy larger than the one that perpetrated the September 11 attacks, which succeeded in remaining secret— and that Aum Shinrikyo was simply not on the radar of any of the world's intelligence agencies until after it perpetrated its nerve gas attack in the Tokyo subway.

Nuclear Terrorism: What Is the Probability?

What are the chances of a terrorist nuclear attack? The short answer is that nobody knows. Former Secretary of Defense William Perry and former Assistant Secretary of Defense Graham Allison are among those who have estimated that chance at more than 50 percent over the next ten years.[48] In a 2006 article, I offered a mathematical model that provides a structured, step-by-step way of thinking through the problem. A set of plausible illustrative values for the input parameters resulted in a 29 percent ten-year probability estimate—by coincidence, the same as the median estimate of the ten-year probability of a nuclear attack on the United States in a survey of national security experts by Senator Richard Lugar's office several years ago.[49] Because there are large uncertainties in each of those inputs, however, the real probability could well be either higher or lower. But even if such estimates are too high by a factor of ten, the danger of nuclear terrorism is high enough to significantly increase the yearly risk of death for everyone who lives and works in downtown Washington or midtown Manhattan, where such a strike is most likely to occur.

Even a 1 percent chance of nuclear terrorism over the next ten years would

---

48. See, for example, Allison, *Nuclear Terrorism*. For a report of Perry's estimate, see Nicholas D. Kristof, "An American Hiroshima," *New York Times,* August 11, 2004, http://www.nytimes.com/2004/08/11/opinion/11kris.html.
49. See Bunn, "A Mathematical Model of the Risk of Nuclear Terrorism." The responses to Lugar's queries are in Richard G. Lugar, "The Lugar Survey on Proliferation Threats and Responses" (Washington, D.C.: Office of Senator Lugar, June 2005), http://lugar.senate.gov/reports/NPSurvey.pdf. The question Lugar's survey asked referred to any nuclear attack on the United States, not just a terrorist nuclear attack, but in a separate question a strong majority of respondents concluded that a nuclear attack by a terrorist group was more likely than a nuclear attack by a state.

be enough to justify substantial action to reduce the risk, given the scale of the consequences. No one in their right mind would operate a nuclear power plant upwind of a major city that had a 1 percent chance over ten years of blowing sky-high—the risk would be understood by all to be too great. But that, in effect, is what we are doing—or worse—by managing the world's nuclear stockpiles as we do today. The nuclear security improvements and nuclear material removals that have been accomplished in recent years—along with the disruption of al-Qaida's central command—have reduced the risk. But the danger remains real.

Progress in Strengthening Nuclear Security

Cooperative nuclear security improvement programs sponsored by the United States and others have drastically reduced the challenges posed by some of the world's highest-risk nuclear stockpiles, providing a benefit for U.S. and world security far beyond their cost—and demonstrating what can be done to address these threats. But in many areas, the progress is insufficient to meet President Obama's goal of securing all vulnerable nuclear stockpiles worldwide within four years. To understand what more needs to be done, it is necessary to have at least a rough picture of what has been achieved so far.[50]

As already noted, the progress in Russia and the former Soviet Union—the original focus of cooperative nuclear security efforts—has been particularly substantial, though major issues remain. Security upgrades for most nuclear warhead sites and nuclear material buildings in Russia were completed by the end of 2008, as part of the work plan agreed to after the Bush-Putin nuclear security accord at the 2005 Bratislava summit. Security upgrades had been installed for the small number of sites in the non-Russian states of the former Soviet Union years ago, though U.S. experts were still helping with further upgrades in Belarus as of the spring of 2009 (after long delays resulting from the hostility between the U.S. and Belarussian governments). In Russia, work continues at a few sites where cooperation was agreed to after the initial Bratislava work plan, and there are some nuclear warhead and nuclear material sites that either Russia has refused to open for cooperative work or for which the United States has declined to provide assistance.

With the completion of most of the agreed upgrades, the most important remaining policy questions focus on more intangible, difficult-to-measure fac-

---

50. For a more detailed assessment of the progress of these efforts, see Bunn, *Securing the Bomb 2008*, pp. 17–113.

tors: Are sufficient security measures being put in place, given the scope of the outsider and insider threats in Russia? Will effective security be sustained over time, after U.S. assistance phases out? Will security cultures at all of these sites be strong enough to ensure that the equipment will be used in a way that provides effective security, and guards will not be turning off intrusion detectors or staff propping open security doors? The National Nuclear Security Administration, the Department of Defense, and their Russian counterparts are working to lay out plans for sustaining security measures at each site, and programs to strengthen security culture, but these issues remain major challenges.

Outside the former Soviet Union, many nuclear security improvement efforts are still in their early stages, and significant gaps remain. The United States and other countries have provided assistance to upgrade security for more than three-quarters of the world's HEU-fueled research reactors whose physical protection did not match IAEA recommendations, but only a small fraction of these have been upgraded to levels designed to defeat demonstrated terrorist and criminal threats. The United States has been cooperating with Pakistan on nuclear security in the years since the September 11 attacks, but what precisely has been accomplished continues to be a secret, and grave concerns remain given the immense scale of the insider and outsider threats that exist there. In China, U.S. and Chinese experts jointly upgraded security and accounting measures for one civilian site with HEU years ago, and a broad dialogue is under way regarding a range of security and accounting measures. Yet, it is still unclear how much effect this dialogue has had on improving security for other Chinese facilities, and cooperation related to military stocks (representing more than three-quarters of Chinese weapons-usable nuclear material) has still not been established. Nuclear security cooperation was not included in the U.S.-India nuclear cooperation agreement negotiated during the George W. Bush administration, and India's nuclear officials have resisted any cooperation in the sensitive area of nuclear security. Ensuring that improved nuclear security and accounting arrangements will be sustained for the long term, and that nuclear staff and guards will take security seriously and not cut corners on nuclear security rules—a problem known as "security culture"—is likely to be a serious issue for nuclear security improvements worldwide (as it is in the United States). In particular, as most nuclear facility managers will not invest in expensive security measures unless they are required to do so, strong, well-enforced nuclear security regulations are essential to achieving effective and lasting nuclear security. Such regulations, however, remain dangerously weak in many countries.

The U.S.-led Global Threat Reduction Initiative, established in 2004, has succeeded in accelerating efforts to remove nuclear material from potentially vulnerable sites and to convert research reactors to using low-enriched uranium (LEU) fuel that cannot be used to make a nuclear bomb. GTRI is helping to convert five or six reactors per year to LEU and is moving hundreds of kilograms of HEU each year to secure locations. Moreover, GTRI has expanded the list of reactors that officials hope to convert. But a faster, much more comprehensive effort is still needed. Only a small fraction of the HEU-fueled research reactor sites around the world have had all their HEU removed. Tons of civilian HEU in many countries are not yet targeted for removal. Even with its expanded scope, the conversion effort will leave roughly 40 percent of the world's currently operating HEU-fueled reactors uncovered, and as yet there is no parallel effort to convince the operators and funders of unneeded research reactors to shut them down. More broadly, to achieve President Obama's four-year objective, consolidation efforts must extend far beyond HEU-fueled research reactors, to focus on reducing all sites and transports with nuclear weapons and weapons-usable nuclear material around the world as much as possible.

At the same time, there is no global standard for how secure nuclear weapons or the materials needed to make them should be, which would provide a target for President Obama's four-year campaign. There is a convention on physical protection of nuclear materials, but it sets no specific requirements for nuclear security; in its newly amended version, the convention requires each party to have a rule specifying how secure nuclear materials should be, but it says nothing about what that rule should say.[51] The IAEA physical protection recommendations are somewhat more specific, but still vague: for a large stock of HEU such as the one at Pelindaba, those recommendations call for putting in place a fence with intrusion detectors, but they say nothing about how difficult it should be to penetrate the fence or to bypass the detectors.[52] The United Nations Security Council unanimously passed Resolution 1540, which legally requires all states to provide "appropriate effective" security and accounting for any nuclear weapons or weapons-usable material they may possess—but the essential elements required for a nuclear security and accounting system to be considered "appropriate effective" remain undefined.[53] Fundamentally, none of these documents says anything about the

51. International Atomic Energy Agency, "Amendment to the Convention on the Physical Protection of Nuclear Material" (Vienna: International Atomic Energy Agency, 2005), http://www-pub.iaea.org/MTCD/Meetings/ccpnmdocs/cppnm_proposal.pdf.

52. International Atomic Energy Agency, "The Physical Protection of Nuclear Material and Nuclear Facilities," INFCIRC/225/Rev.4 (corrected) (Vienna: IAEA, 1999), http://www.iaea.or.at/Publications/?Documents/?Infcircs/?1999/infcirc225r4c/rev4_content.html.

53. For a first cut at defining the elements that must be present for a nuclear security and account-

Figure 1. Progress of U.S.-Funded Programs to Secure Nuclear Stockpiles

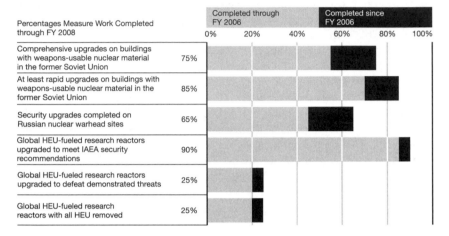

Percentages Measure Work Completed through FY 2008		Completed through FY 2006			Completed since FY 2006		
		0% 20% 40%			60% 80% 100%		
Comprehensive upgrades on buildings with weapons-usable nuclear material in the former Soviet Union	75%						
At least rapid upgrades on buildings with weapons-usable nuclear material in the former Soviet Union	85%						
Security upgrades completed on Russian nuclear warhead sites	65%						
Global HEU-fueled research reactors upgraded to meet IAEA security recommendations	90%						
Global HEU-fueled research reactors upgraded to defeat demonstrated threats	25%						
Global HEU-fueled research reactors with all HEU removed	25%						

SOURCE: Author's estimates
HEU = highly enriched uranium; IAEA = International Atomic Energy Agency

kinds of insider and outsider threats that nuclear weapons and their essential ingredients should be protected against.

Figure 1 provides a summary of several key indicators of the progress of U.S.-funded programs to improve nuclear security, as of the end of fiscal year 2008.[54] As can be seen, the indicators focused on Russia and the former Soviet Union are nearing completion (and have gotten still closer to completion since that time), but only a small fraction of the work covered by the global measures has been completed. Clearly, there is a great deal yet to do if President Obama's four-year objective is to be achieved.

A Comprehensive Strategy for Preventing Nuclear Terrorism

Keeping nuclear weapons and the materials needed to make them out of the hands of terrorists must be a top priority for the Obama administration. To accomplish this goal, the United States will need a comprehensive strategy with

ing system to be considered "appropriate effective," see Matthew Bunn, "'Appropriate Effective' Nuclear Security and Accounting—What Is It?" presentation at the "'Appropriate Effective' Material Accounting and Physical Protection—Joint Global Initiative/UNSCR 1540 Workshop," Nashville, Tennessee, July 18, 2008, http://belfercenter.ksg.harvard.edu/files/bunn-1540-appropriate-effective50.pdf.
54. For the data and discussion behind this figure, see Bunn, *Securing the Bomb 2008*, pp. 90–111.

four key elements (in order of importance in reducing the risk): (1) securing and reducing nuclear stockpiles around the world; (2) countering terrorist nuclear plots; (3) preventing and deterring state transfers of nuclear weapons or materials to terrorists; and (4) interdicting nuclear smuggling.[55]

Success in implementing this strategy will require forging a new sense of global cooperation and commitment to reducing the threat; organizing the government for success; and putting the United States' own house in order— including changing the political environment for nonproliferation by living up to its end of the nonproliferation bargain. The remainder of this chapter provides more specific recommendations for each of these elements.

SECURE AND REDUCE NUCLEAR STOCKPILES

Accomplishing President Obama's objective of ensuring effective and lasting security for all nuclear weapons and materials worldwide within four years will not be easy. The primary obstacles are not technical; in many cases in Russia and elsewhere, comprehensive security and accounting upgrades have been installed in only eighteen to twenty-four months of a decision to do so, even at large and complex sites. Nor will the main obstacles be financial: there are likely to be hundreds of buildings and bunkers requiring security upgrades, and the cost at each is likely to range from hundreds of thousands of dollars to the low tens of millions of dollars. As a result, a level of security that would dramatically reduce today's risk of nuclear theft could be achieved within a few years at a cost in the range of 1 to 2 percent of the roughly $600 billion U.S. defense budget for a single year.[56]

Instead, the primary obstacles to achieving President Obama's objective of nuclear security are political and bureaucratic. Complacency about the threat of nuclear terrorism and the need for further security measures to address it is the foremost obstacle. Interviews and public statements suggest that most policymakers and nuclear managers around the world simply do not believe that nuclear terrorism is a realistic threat. Many believe it would be impossibly difficult for terrorists to acquire a nuclear weapon or the materials needed to make one; others believe it would be impossibly difficult for terrorists to make a bomb if they did obtain the needed materials; others hold both of these beliefs.[57] Many countries see nuclear terrorism, if it is a problem at all, primarily

---

55. For more detail on these recommendations, see ibid., pp. 129–182.
56. For fiscal year 2010, President Obama proposed a defense budget of $663.8 billion, including $130 billion for "contingency operations," primarily in Iraq and Afghanistan. U.S. Department of Defense, "DOD Releases Fiscal 2010 Budget Proposal" (Washington, D.C.: DOD, May 7, 2009).
57. For a particularly extreme statement of the view that nuclear terrorism is not a problem, see John Mueller, "Radioactive Hype," *National Interest*, No. 91 (September/October 2007), pp. 59–65;

as a problem for the United States, not for them. And policymakers, not to mention the managers who have been operating nuclear facilities with a modest level of security for decades without incident, are difficult to convince that major new security measures are needed in a post–September 11 world; many policymakers and nuclear managers see the risk of nuclear theft as something that might happen far away, but not at their facility.

The reality, of course, is that nuclear terrorism is an urgent danger—not just to the United States, but to all countries, as Secretary-General Annan's warning about the devastating global economic effects of such an attack makes clear. As discussed in detail below, making that case, and overcoming complacency, will be the key to success in accomplishing President Obama's four-year objective of improving nuclear security, and it must be a top priority for the Obama administration and for other concerned governments around the world.

Complacency is not the only political obstacle to rapid progress in improving nuclear security—though if political leaders overcome that complacency and become convinced of the urgency of the threat, they will cut through many of the other obstacles. Secrecy is another major barrier. Most countries with nuclear weapons or materials regard the measures they take to protect them as a closely guarded secret, making it difficult for others to assess whether additional steps are needed. U.S. nuclear security cooperation with Pakistan, to take one example, has been substantially hampered by Pakistan's suspicions and unwillingness to let U.S. experts even know where its nuclear sites are, let alone visit them to assess their security. As this example suggests, sovereignty is another important obstacle; many countries regard what they do to protect their nuclear stockpiles as their business and are not interested in having the United States or the IAEA or anyone else tell them that they need to do more. Political disputes pose another problem; as noted earlier, for example, nuclear security cooperation with Belarus has been greatly slowed by the disagreements the United States and the European Union have

or John Mueller, "The Atomic Terrorist: Assessing the Likelihood," January 1, 2008, paper prepared for presentation at the Program on International Security Policy, University of Chicago, January 15, 2008, http://polisci.osu.edu/faculty/jmueller/APSACHGO.PDF. The latter has a more detailed version of the argument and compares believing in a serious nuclear terrorism risk to believing in the "tooth fairy." See also Robin M. Frost, *Nuclear Terrorism after 9/11*, Adelphi Papers, No. 378 (London: International Institute for Strategic Studies, 2005). For replies to some of the myths of the nuclear terrorism skeptics, see Matthew Bunn and Anthony Wier, "Debunking Seven Myths of Nuclear Terrorism and Nuclear Theft," in Bunn and Wier, *Securing the Bomb*; and Anna M. Pluta and Peter D. Zimmerman, "Nuclear Terrorism: A Disheartening Dissent," *Survival*, Vol. 48, No. 2 (Summer 2006), pp. 55–69.

with Alexander Lukashenko's dictatorship. Bureaucratic obstacles—from disputes over taxation and liability issues associated with nuclear security assistance to delays in ministries' reviewing proposed security upgrade contracts—are another critical factor that often constrains the pace of progress.

Overcoming these obstacles will require sustained and intensive leadership from the highest levels of the U.S. government and other governments around the world. Rapid progress will also require a nuanced understanding of the political and bureaucratic situation in each key participating country, including knowledge of who the key players are and what their interests and concerns might be. In some cases, success may require trying to influence bureaucratic arrangements in other countries; for example, to ensure that each regulatory agency responsible for setting and enforcing nuclear security rules has the power, resources, expertise, and independence to do its job. As another example, a research reactor operator whose costs amount to $500,000 a year is likely to fiercely resist new security rules that would cost another $200,000 a year to comply with—but if the arrangement is changed so that the government provides and pays for the extra security, and if the new measures impose few inconveniences on the research reactor staff, the operator may be much more willing to agree to put new security measures in place.

To achieve the four-year goal of nuclear security, President Obama needs to take several steps, outlined below.

LAUNCH A FAST-PACED GLOBAL NUCLEAR SECURITY CAMPAIGN. First, working with other world leaders, President Obama should forge a global campaign to lock down every nuclear weapon and every significant stock of potential nuclear bomb material worldwide, as rapidly as possible. He should make it absolutely clear to countries around the world that this goal is a U.S. priority and that providing effective security for any nuclear stockpiles they may have is essential to good relations with the United States—just as they have long understood that compliance with arms control and nonproliferation obligations is essential.

A one-size-fits-all approach is not likely to work, for the particular issues vary substantially from one country to the next. To make such a global campaign effective, the Obama administration must develop targeted strategies for each key country and for crosscutting issues such as achieving effective global standards for nuclear security or reducing civilian use of weapons-usable materials.

The United States need not pay for or carry out all the security upgrades itself. Much of the effort should concentrate on convincing countries to provide the necessary resources themselves, and to establish their own rules and enforcement procedures; where assistance is required, the United States should work with other donor states to share the burden. In particular, as the states with by far the world's largest nuclear stockpiles (and the only states that exported HEU to large numbers of other countries), the United States and Russia bear a special responsibility and should work together (and, perhaps, with France, the United Kingdom, and other interested donor states) to help countries around the world put effective security measures in place. For a number of countries, working with teams from a country other than the United States might be more politically palatable. For example, China, which has assisted Pakistan's nuclear programs for decades, might be able to work with the Pakistanis on nuclear security upgrades in ways they would never let U.S. experts do.

The Global Initiative to Combat Nuclear Terrorism is a first step toward forging such a campaign. It has been valuable in focusing countries' attention on the issue of nuclear terrorism and building legal infrastructure, capacity for emergency response, law enforcement capabilities, and more. But it has not focused on rapid and substantial security upgrades for nuclear stockpiles, and it demands little of countries to count as partners. A modified approach—centered on locking down all nuclear weapons, plutonium, and HEU to high standards—would be necessary to create the kind of fast-paced nuclear security campaign that is needed.

Such a modified approach might be launched in the lead-up to the Global Summit on Nuclear Security that President Obama has pledged to host by the spring of 2010.[58] The summit, and the diplomatic effort leading up to it, should be structured so that they contribute in concrete ways to rapid and lasting improvements in security for nuclear weapons and materials worldwide. To attend the summit, all countries ought to be asked to make a firm commitment to establish national procedures and rules that ensure that high standards of security will be maintained for all nuclear weapons and weapons-usable materials on their territory, and that they will take other agreed-on steps to reduce the risk of nuclear terrorism. Like the Bush-Putin nuclear security initiative from their 2005 Bratislava summit, the summit should seek to establish an agreed-upon mechanism for following up and reviewing progress. It should also seek to convince each participating country to designate to an official the responsibility for meeting the agreed-on milestones and targets.

---

58. Office of the Press Secretary, "Remarks by President Barack Obama."

Much of the needed global nuclear security campaign can be seen as simply implementation of UN Security Council Resolution 1540's legal requirement for "appropriate effective" nuclear security and accounting. The World Institute for Nuclear Security, launched in the fall of 2008, also can play an important role, allowing operators to exchange best practices and approaches that have worked in achieving rapid and lasting improvements in nuclear security.[59]

To succeed, such an effort must be based not just on donor-recipient relationships but on real partnerships that integrate ideas and resources from countries where upgrades are taking place in ways that also serve their national interests. For countries such as India and Pakistan, it is politically untenable to accept U.S. assistance that is portrayed as necessary because these states are considered unable to adequately control their own nuclear stockpiles. But joining with the major nuclear states in jointly addressing a global problem may be politically appealing. U.S.-Russian relations in particular went into a tailspin after the conflict in Georgia in August 2008, making a real nuclear security partnership with Russia far more difficult to achieve. But with the Obama administration's focused effort to "press the reset button," relations appear to be improving. Whatever the state of U.S.-Russian relations, a nuclear security partnership with Russia remains essential, and the United States and Russia will continue to share overwhelming national interests in keeping nuclear material out of terrorist hands. Such partnerships will have to be based on creative approaches that make it possible to cooperate in upgrading nuclear security without demanding that countries compromise their legitimate nuclear secrets. Specific approaches should be crafted to accommodate each national culture, secrecy system, and set of circumstances.

SEEK TO ENSURE THAT ALL NUCLEAR WEAPONS, PLUTONIUM, AND HEU ARE SECURE. Terrorists will acquire the material to make a nuclear bomb wherever it is easiest to steal. The world cannot afford to let gaps between different programs leave some vulnerable stocks without security upgrades—the goal must be to ensure effective security for all stocks worldwide. Thus far, the United States has programs focused on nuclear security upgrades in Russia, in the states of the former Soviet Union, in Pakistan, and for HEU-fueled research reactors in developing countries—along with a dialogue on nuclear security

---

59. See World Institute for Nuclear Security (WINS), "World Institute for Nuclear Security (WINS) Is Launched in Vienna" (Vienna: WINS, September 29, 2008), http://www.wins.org/content .aspx?id+3.

with China. But no nuclear security cooperation is under way with countries such as India or South Africa. Except for occasional bilateral dialogues, U.S. programs largely ignore stocks in wealthy developed countries, though some of these are also dangerously insecure. Sustained high-level leadership is needed to close these gaps. The Obama administration must develop a four-year plan targeted on ensuring that all nuclear weapons, plutonium, and HEU worldwide have effective and lasting security and accounting measures in place.

EXPAND AND ACCELERATE EFFORTS TO CONSOLIDATE NUCLEAR STOCKPILES. The only way to guarantee that nuclear material will not be stolen from a particular building is to remove the material, so there is nothing left to steal. The fewer the number of locations where these stocks exist, the less will be the chance of one site making security mistakes that adversaries manage to exploit. President Obama should place high priority on working with countries to reduce drastically the number of sites where nuclear weapons and the materials to make them exist, achieving higher security at lower cost. The goal should be to remove all nuclear material from the world's most vulnerable sites and to ensure effective security wherever material must remain, within four years or less—and to eliminate HEU from all civilian sites worldwide within roughly a decade. The effort should go well beyond HEU-fueled research reactors and include the consolidation of nuclear weapons, plutonium, and HEU to the minimum practicable number of sites worldwide. Russia, which has the world's largest number of buildings and bunkers where these weapons and materials exist, and which has so far resisted large-scale consolidation efforts, should be a particular focus.

The Global Threat Reduction Initiative has greatly accelerated the pace at which research reactors are being converted from HEU to LEU fuel, and the pace of removing HEU from these sites to secure locations. But here, too, there are gaps that should be closed. New incentives should be offered so that much of the more than 13 tons of U.S.-origin HEU not covered in current GTRI removal plans will be sent back or otherwise eliminated.[60] A program should be established to give unneeded reactors incentives to shut down (an approach that may be cheaper and quicker than converting reactors to LEU fuel, especially for difficult-to-convert reactors). President Obama should launch new efforts to limit the production, use, and stockpiling of weapons-usable separated civilian plutonium. In addition, he should renew the nearly completed late-

---

60. For discussion, see Bunn, *Securing the Bomb 2008*, pp. 44–54, 105–107.

1990s effort to negotiate a twenty-year U.S.-Russian moratorium on plutonium separation. His action to terminate the George W. Bush administration's efforts to move toward near-term construction of reprocessing plants and fast reactors in the United States is a step in the right direction.

GAIN AGREEMENT ON EFFECTIVE GLOBAL NUCLEAR SECURITY STANDARDS. As nuclear security is only as strong as its weakest link, the world urgently needs effective global nuclear security standards. All nuclear weapons and weapons-usable materials should be protected against the kinds of threats that terrorists and criminals have shown they can pose—at a bare minimum, against two small teams of well-trained, well-armed attackers, possibly with inside help, as occurred at Pelindaba. (In countries where terrorist and criminal groups are especially strong, protection against even more capable threats is needed.) As noted earlier, UN Security Council Resolution 1540 legally requires all countries to provide "appropriate effective" security and accounting for all their nuclear stockpiles. The time has come to build on that requirement by reaching a political-level agreement with other leading states on what the essential elements of appropriate effective security and accounting systems are and then by working to ensure that all states put those essential elements in place.[61] The planned 2010 nuclear security summit is the obvious place to seek such an accord. Ultimately, effective security and accounting for weapons-usable nuclear material should become part of the "price of admission" for doing business in the international nuclear market.

BUILD SUSTAINABILITY AND SECURITY CULTURE. If the upgraded security equipment the United States is helping countries put in place is broken or unused five years after it is installed, U.S. security objectives will not be accomplished. President Obama should step up efforts to gain top-level commitments from Russia and other countries to sustain effective nuclear security for the long term with their own resources. This should include a focused effort to ensure that each country with nuclear weapons, HEU, or plutonium puts in place strong and effectively enforced nuclear security and accounting regulations; as most nuclear managers will not invest in expensive nuclear security measures unless required to do so, effective nuclear security regulation is essential to effective, lasting security. President Obama should also intensify programs to work with countries around the world to build strong security cultures, putting an end to staff propping open security doors for convenience or guards patrolling with no ammunition in their guns.

REDUCE STOCKPILES AND END PRODUCTION. The United States, Russia, and

---

61. See Bunn, "'Appropriate Effective' Nuclear Security and Accounting."

other nuclear weapon states should join in an effort to radically reduce the size, roles, and readiness of their nuclear weapon stockpiles, verifiably dismantling many thousands of nuclear weapons and placing the fissile material they contain in secure, monitored storage until it can be safely and securely destroyed. Such an effort would be an essential first step in fulfilling President Obama's stated goal of "a world without nuclear weapons."[62] Sharp reductions in nuclear stockpiles, if properly managed, would reduce the risks of nuclear theft—and could greatly improve the chances of gaining international support for other nonproliferation steps that could also reduce the long-term dangers of nuclear theft.

To move in this direction, President Obama should launch a joint program with Russia to dramatically reduce total U.S. and Russian stockpiles of nuclear weapons and to place all plutonium and HEU in excess of the amount needed to support these low, agreed warhead stockpiles (and modest stocks for other military uses, such as naval fuel) in secure, monitored, storage-pending disposition. In particular, the United States and Russia should launch another round of reciprocal initiatives, comparable to the Presidential Nuclear Initiatives of 1991–92, in which they would each agree to (1) take several thousand warheads—including all tactical warheads not equipped with modern, difficult-to-bypass electronic locks—and place them in secure, centralized storage; (2) allow reciprocal visits to those storage sites to confirm the presence and the security of these warheads; (3) agree that these warheads will be verifiably dismantled as soon as procedures have been agreed on by both sides to do so without compromising sensitive information; and (4) agree that the nuclear materials from these warheads will similarly be placed in secure, monitored storage after dismantlement. President Obama has already taken another worthwhile step, by reversing the George W. Bush administration's misguided opposition to a verified fissile material cutoff treaty, which has allowed the Conference on Disarmament to agree to begin negotiation of such an accord after many years of delay.[63]

COUNTER TERRORIST NUCLEAR PLOTS

President Obama should work with other countries to build an intense international focus on stopping all the elements of a nuclear plot beyond acquiring the nuclear material—the recruiting, fundraising, equipment purchases, and

---

62. Office of the Press Secretary, "Remarks by President Barack Obama."
63. See Conference on Disarmament, "Draft Decision for the Establishment of a Programme of Work for the 2009 Session," CD/1863, May 19, 2009, http://www.reachingcriticalwill.org/political/cd/papers09/2session/CD1863.pdf.

more that would inevitably be required. Because of the complexity of a nuclear effort, these would offer a bigger and more detectable profile than many other terrorist conspiracies—although, as U.S. intelligence officials have pointed out, the observable "footprint" of a nuclear conspiracy might be no bigger than that of the September 11 plot. The best chances to stop such a plot lie not in exotic new nuclear detection technologies but in a broad counterterrorist effort, ranging from intelligence and other operations used to target high-capability terrorist groups to steps addressing the anti-American hatred that not only makes terrorist recruiting and fundraising easier but also makes it more difficult for other governments to cooperate with the United States. In particular, the United States should work with governments and nongovernment institutions in the Islamic world to build a consensus that slaughter on a nuclear scale is profoundly wrong under Islamic laws and traditions (and those of other faiths)—potentially making it more difficult for those terrorists wanting to pursue nuclear violence to convince the people they need to join their cause.

In addition, President Obama should maintain existing programs aimed at redirecting nuclear weapons scientists to civilian work, but he should reform these to use a broader array of tools and to focus on a broader array of threats, including not only top weapons scientists but also workers with access to nuclear material, guards who could help steal nuclear material, and people who have retired from nuclear facilities but still have critical knowledge.[64] The United States is not likely to have either the access or the resources to carry out this broader mission itself. Instead, it must work closely with partner countries to convince them to take most of the needed actions themselves. President Obama should also work with countries around the world to monitor and stop recruitment attempts at key sites, such as physics and nuclear engineering departments in countries with substantial Islamic extremist communities.

PREVENT AND DETER STATE TRANSFERS

Hostile states are highly unlikely to consciously choose to provide nuclear weapons or the materials needed to make them to terrorist groups, for such

---

64. For a useful discussion of the changed threat environment and its implications for these programs, see Laura Holgate, testimony before the House Subcommittee on Prevention of Nuclear and Biological Attack, Committee on Homeland Security, 109th Cong., 1st sess., May 26, 2005. See also John V. Parachini and David E. Mosher, *Diversion of NBC Weapons Expertise from the FSU: Understanding an Evolving Problem* (Santa Monica, Calif.: RAND, 2005). For additional suggestions for new approaches, see Bunn, Wier, and Holdren, *Controlling Nuclear Warheads and Materials*, pp. 141–146.

a step would risk retaliation that would end their power forever. Nevertheless, the risk of such transfers is not zero—and more states with nuclear weapons would mean more sources from which a nuclear bomb might be stolen. President Obama must engage with North Korea and Iran, and work with other states to put together an international package of carrots and sticks large enough and credible enough to convince these governments that it is in their national interest to verifiably end their nuclear weapons efforts (and, in North Korea's case, to give up the weapons and materials already produced, if that can be achieved). The chances of success in resolving either of these cases appear to be modest—but given the stakes, a major nonproliferation effort focused on these two countries remains justified. At the same time, the global effort to stem the spread of nuclear weapons should be strengthened significantly.[65]

The United States should also put in place the best practicable means for identifying the source of any nuclear attack—including not just nuclear forensics (the science of identifying characteristics of nuclear material and attempting to match them to their source) but also traditional intelligence means. In addition, it should announce that it will treat any terrorist nuclear attack using material consciously provided by a state as an attack by that state and that it will respond accordingly. This should include both increased funding for research and development on nuclear forensics and expanded efforts to put together an international database of material characteristics. Policymakers should understand, however, that nuclear material has no DNA that can provide an absolute match: nuclear forensics will complement other sources of information, but it will rarely make clear where material came from by itself.[66]

INTERDICT NUCLEAR SMUGGLING

Most of the past successes in seizing stolen nuclear material have resulted from conspirators informing on each other and from good police and intelligence work, not from radiation detectors. President Obama should build on these past successes, working with other countries around the world to intensify police and intelligence cooperation focused on stopping nuclear smuggling, including additional sting operations and well-publicized incentives for informers to report on such plots, to make it even more difficult for potential

---

65. For recommendations, see Graham et al., *World at Risk;* and WMDC, *Weapons of Terror.*
66. For discussion, see, for example, Nuclear Forensics Working Group, "Nuclear Forensics: Role, State of the Art, Program Needs" (Washington, D.C.: Panel on Public Affairs, American Physical Society, and Center for Science, Technology, and Security Policy, American Association for the Advancement of Science, February 2008).

nuclear thieves and buyers to come together. The United States should also work with states around the world to ensure that they have (1) units of their national police forces trained and equipped to deal with nuclear smuggling cases, as well as other law enforcement personnel trained to call in those units as needed; (2) effectively enforced laws making any participation in real or attempted theft or smuggling of nuclear weapons or weapons-usable materials, or nuclear terrorism, crimes with penalties comparable to those for murder or treason; and (3) standard operating procedures, routinely exercised, to deal with materials that may be detected or intercepted.

The United States should develop an approach that offers a greater chance of stopping nuclear smugglers at lower cost than the current mandate for 100 percent scanning of all cargo containers. This approach should focus on an integrated system that places as many barriers in the path of intelligent adversaries attempting to smuggle nuclear material into the United States by any pathway as can be accomplished at reasonable cost. (In particular, it is important to understand that neither the detectors now being deployed nor the next-generation Advanced Spectroscopic Portals the Department of Homeland Security has proposed to deploy will have any substantial chance of detecting HEU metal with even modest shielding.) The Proliferation Security Initiative launched in the George W. Bush administration will certainly be one element of such a strategy, but it is likely to be much more effective in stopping transfers of large, readily identifiable items such as centrifuges and ballistic missiles than of nuclear material that can fit in a suitcase.[67]

FORGE GLOBAL COOPERATION AND COMMITMENT

All of the steps described above will require cooperation from dozens of countries around the world. Forging that cooperation must become a central priority for U.S. diplomacy—an item to be addressed with every country with nuclear stockpiles to secure or resources to help, at every opportunity, at every level, until the job is done. A maze of political and bureaucratic obstacles must be overcome—quickly—if the world's most vulnerable nuclear stockpiles are to be secured before terrorists and thieves get to them. Several steps will be critical to overcoming the obstacles to expanded and accelerated progress in reducing the risk.

BUILD THE SENSE OF URGENCY AND COMMITMENT WORLDWIDE. The fundamental key to success in preventing nuclear terrorism is to convince political

67. See, for example, Mark J. Valencia, "The Proliferation Security Initiative: A Glass Half-Full," *Arms Control Today,* Vol. 37 (June 2007), http://www.armscontrol.org/act/2007_06/Valencia.

leaders and nuclear managers around the world that nuclear terrorism is an urgent threat to their countries' security, worthy of a substantial investment of their time and money—something many of them do not believe today. If they come to feel that sense of urgency, they will take the needed actions to prevent nuclear terrorism; if they remain complacent, they will not. Some of the critical work of building this sense of urgency is already being done, especially in the context of the Global Initiative to Combat Nuclear Terrorism. But much more needs to be done, if President Obama's objective of ensuring effective security for all vulnerable nuclear weapons and weapons-usable materials worldwide is to be achieved.

President Obama should work with other countries to take several steps outlined below to build the needed sense of urgency and commitment.

First, upcoming summits and other high-level meetings with key countries should include detailed briefings for both leaders on the nuclear terrorism threat, given jointly by U.S. experts and experts from the country concerned. These joint briefings would outline both the real possibility that terrorists could obtain nuclear material and make a nuclear bomb, the global economic and political effects of a terrorist nuclear attack, and steps that could be taken to reduce the risk. U.S. briefings for U.S. and Russian officials highlighting intelligence on continuing nuclear security vulnerabilities were a critical part of putting together the Bush-Putin Bratislava nuclear security initiative.

Second, it is crucial to convince the intelligence agencies in key countries that nuclear terrorism is an urgent threat and that plausible actions, taken now, could reduce the risk substantially. During the second Bush term, DOE intelligence actively worked with foreign intelligence services both to make this case and to build cooperation against the threat. This effort should be renewed and expanded to include focused efforts by the director of national intelligence, the Central Intelligence Agency, and other U.S. intelligence officials and agencies.

Third, President Obama should direct U.S. intelligence to establish a small operational team that would seek to understand and penetrate the world of nuclear theft and smuggling. In a so-called Armageddon test, the team would be instructed to seek to acquire enough nuclear material for a bomb. Success would dramatically highlight the continuing threat and potentially identify particular weak points and smuggling organizations requiring urgent action. Failure would strongly suggest that terrorist operatives would likely fail as well, increasing confidence that measures to prevent nuclear terrorism were working.[68]

---

68. Both the idea of the "Armageddon Test" and the focus on discussions between intelligence agencies originated with Rolf Mowatt-Larssen, who was head of DOE intelligence in the second

Fourth, building on the exercise program that has begun as part of the Global Initiative to Combat Nuclear Terrorism, the United States and other leading countries should organize a series of exercises with senior policymakers from all of the states with stockpiles of nuclear weapons or weapons-usable nuclear material. These exercises should include scenarios on the possible theft of nuclear material, the possibility that terrorists could construct a crude nuclear bomb if they got enough HEU or plutonium, the difficulty of stopping them once they had the material, and the consequences on all countries of a terrorist nuclear attack.[69] Participating in such a war game can reach officials emotionally in a way that briefings and policy memos cannot.

Fifth, the United States and other countries heading this nuclear security effort should encourage leaders of key states to pick teams of security experts they trust to conduct fast-paced reviews of nuclear security in their countries, assessing whether facilities are adequately protected against a set of clearly defined threats—such as a well-placed insider or two teams of well-armed, well-trained attackers. (In the United States, such fast-paced reviews after major incidents such as September 11 attacks have often revealed a wide range of vulnerabilities that needed to be fixed.)

Sixth, the United States and other leading countries should work with key states around the world to conduct realistic tests of nuclear security systems' ability to defeat either insiders or outsiders. (Failures in such tests can be powerful evidence to senior policymakers that nuclear security needs improvement.)

Seventh, the United States and other key countries should collaborate to create shared databases of unclassified information on past security incidents (both at nuclear sites and at nonnuclear guarded facilities) that offer lessons for policymakers and facility managers to consider in deciding on nuclear security levels and particular threats to defend against. The World Institute for Nuclear Security could be a forum for creating one version of such a threat-incident database. In the case of safety, rather than security, reactors report each safety-related incident to groups such as the Institute of Nuclear Power Operations (the U.S. branch of the World Association of Nuclear Operators). These groups then analyze the incidents and distribute lessons learned about

---

Bush term and previously headed the CIA's post–September 11 efforts to understand and stop al-Qaida's nuclear, chemical, and biological programs. For a public discussion of Mowatt-Larssen's "Armageddon Test" idea, see Ron Suskind, *The Way of the World: A Story of Truth and Hope in an Age of Extremism* (New York: HarperCollins, 2008), pp. 128–129, 244–245, 294–298.

69. The model would be the "Black Dawn" exercise organized by the Center for Strategic and International Studies (and sponsored by the Nuclear Threat Initiative) for key NATO officials. For a description, see "Black Dawn: Scenario-Based Exercise," Brussels, Belgium, May 3, 2004, http://www.csis.org/media/csis/pubs/040503_blackdawn.pdf.

how to prevent similar incidents in the future to each member facility. Finally, they carry out peer reviews to assess how well each facility has implemented the lessons learned.[70]

FULFILL U.S. ARMS REDUCTION OBLIGATIONS. The George W. Bush administration's failed approach to the Nonproliferation Treaty, rejecting all the United States' past commitments to arms reduction progress, soured the atmosphere for cooperation with the nonnuclear-weapons states on a broad range of nonproliferation issues. In international discussions of virtually any step to strengthen the nonproliferation regime—from accepting more intrusive inspections to minimizing civil use of HEU—nonnuclear-weapons states would ask: "But what about disarmament?" President Obama's renewed commitment to negotiated arms reductions—from his declared support for a verified fissile cutoff treaty and ratification of the Comprehensive Test Ban Treaty to his forceful statement of his vision for a world free of nuclear weapons—has transformed the atmosphere. As a result, the Conference on Disarmament has finally been able to agree on a program of work, after years of inaction, and a preparatory committee for the Nonproliferation Treaty Review Conference in 2010 was able to agree on an agenda and approach for that meeting for the first time in many years. These shifts could significantly increase the chances for genuine global support for countering nuclear terrorism.

ORGANIZE TO PREVENT NUCLEAR TERRORISM

Accomplishing President Obama's four-year objective to secure nuclear stockpiles around the world will not be easy. It will require sustained high-level leadership, an effective and comprehensive plan, adequate resources, and the best available information and analysis to support policy.

PUT SOMEONE IN CHARGE. The actions needed to prevent nuclear terrorism cut across multiple cabinet departments and require diplomacy and cooperation in highly sensitive areas with countries around the globe. This work demands sustained effort, day-in and day-out, from the highest levels of the U.S. government—and other governments. The Obama administration must ensure that it has the organizational structure needed to manage and lead these sensitive efforts. At the White House, President Obama has appointed Gary Samore as the coordinator for nuclear, chemical, and biological nonproliferation, arms control, and counterterrorism. But the coordinator's mandate is so broad, and the number of urgent matters in that portfolio so large, that it will

---

70. See Joseph V. Rees, *Hostages of Each Other: The Transformation of Nuclear Safety since Three Mile Island* (Chicago: University of Chicago Press, 1994).

be essential to ensure that there is a senior leader working with Samore who can take full-time responsibility for preventing nuclear terrorism—and ensure that this issue remains on the front burner at the White House every day. President Obama must also act to ensure that each of the key agencies participating in this effort has the organization and leadership needed to succeed. In particular, the National Nuclear Security Administration is implementing the most crucial efforts to secure nuclear materials around the world; if nuclear terrorism is indeed the most urgent threat to global security, this entity must be seen as a central national security agency, with its officials at the same table as officials from the Departments of State and Defense. Once he has put in place an effective structure for U.S. efforts, President Obama should seek to convince Russia and other key countries to do the same.

DEVELOP AND IMPLEMENT A COMPREHENSIVE, PRIORITIZED PLAN. The U.S. government has dozens of programs focused on pieces of the problem of preventing nuclear terrorism, each of which has its own plan for its own piece—and no comprehensive, prioritized plan. There is no systematic mechanism in place for identifying the top priorities or where there may be gaps, overlaps, or inefficiencies. One of the first priorities of the senior official dedicated to preventing nuclear terrorism must be to develop a comprehensive, prioritized, government-wide strategy to reduce the risk of nuclear terrorism—and then to update that plan as new opportunities and obstacles arise. This strategy must link objectives and timelines to programs and resources, and it must define agency roles in executing or supporting the strategy. The senior official charged with leading efforts to prevent nuclear terrorism must hold agencies accountable for delivering outcomes that achieve the strategy. This official would set priorities among competing objectives, seizing opportunities for synergy and eliminating gaps and overlaps. The Obama administration should focus on finding and fixing internal and external obstacles to accelerated and expanded progress.

ASSIGN ADEQUATE RESOURCES. As noted earlier, a level of nuclear security that would greatly reduce the risk of nuclear terrorism can be achieved for a cost tiny by comparison to what nations routinely spend on reducing threats to their military security. Given the huge stakes and the relatively small cost, President Obama and the U.S. Congress should act to ensure that lack of money does not slow or constrain any major effort to keep nuclear weapons and the materials needed to make them out of terrorist hands. In particular, because new opportunities to improve nuclear security sometimes arise unexpectedly, and difficult-to-plan incentives are sometimes required to convince facilities to give up their HEU or convert a research reactor, President Obama should seek, and Congress should provide, an appropriation in the range of $500 million, to be available until expended, that can be spent flexibly on high-priority actions to reduce the risks of nuclear theft as they arise.[71] Such a flexible pool of funds would give the administration the ability to hit the ground running with an expanded and accelerated effort. There should, of course, be notification and full accountability to Congress concerning how this money is spent.

PROVIDE INFORMATION AND ANALYSIS TO SUPPORT POLICY. Good information and analysis on where the greatest risks, opportunities, and obstacles to progress lie will be crucial to preventing nuclear terrorism. President Obama should act to ensure that U.S. and international policies and programs for reducing the risk of nuclear terrorism are informed by the best practicable information, from intelligence, other information collection, and analysis—including independent analysis and suggestions from nongovernment institutions. The highest-leverage area for information collection and analysis is likely to be supporting the design and implementation of programs to improve security for nuclear stockpiles—answering questions that include which sites have particularly large and vulnerable stockpiles, which nuclear facilities have poorly paid staff or corrupt guards, and which research reactors are underutilized, underfunded, and might be convinced to shut down with a modest incentive package. In particular, President Obama should maintain the Nuclear Materials Information Program and ensure that it provides a continuously updated assessment of (1) all the sites and transport links worldwide where the U.S. government believes nuclear weapons or their essential ingredients exist; (2) the quality and quantity of weapons or materials at each of these; (3) the effectiveness of the security and accounting measures in place; and (4) the scale of threats those security measures must address. These factors together can provide an overall assessment of which sites and transport links pose the highest risks of nuclear theft.

PUT THE UNITED STATES' OWN HOUSE IN ORDER
The most urgent nuclear security vulnerabilities are largely outside the United States. But there is much more that can and should be done within the United States as well, as the recent incidents in the U.S. Air Force, noted above, make

---

71. For a discussion of this proposal, and of President Obama's first budget request for threat reduction efforts, see Andrew Newman and Matthew Bunn, "Funding for U.S. Efforts to Improve Controls over Nuclear Weapons, Materials, and Expertise Overseas: A 2009 Update" (Cambridge, Mass.: Project on Managing the Atom, Belfer Center for Science and International Affairs, Harvard University, June 2009), http://belfercenter.ksg.harvard.edu/files/2009_Nuclear_Budget_Final.pdf.

clear. Convincing foreign countries to reduce and consolidate nuclear stock-piles, to put stringent nuclear security measures in place, or to convert their re-search reactors from HEU to LEU fuel will be far more difficult if the United States is not doing the same at home.

FIX U.S. NUCLEAR SECURITY WEAKNESSES. DOE should continue providing funding to convert U.S. research reactors to LEU. Congress should provide funding for DOE to help HEU-fueled research reactors, or research reactors that pose serious sabotage risks, to upgrade security voluntarily. At the same time, Congress should direct the Nuclear Regulatory Commission (NRC) to phase out the exemption from most security rules for HEU that research reac-tors now enjoy, and it should provide funding for DOE to help these reactors pay the costs of effective security.[72] Congress should also insist that the NRC bring its rules for protecting HEU into line with recent studies that make clear that the level of radiation considered "self-protecting" in current NRC stan-dards would pose little deterrent to theft by determined terrorists.[73] In addi-tion, the NRC's requirements for protection of potential nuclear bomb material should be strengthened to bring them roughly in line with DOE's rules for identical material (particularly because the NRC-regulated facilities handling this material are doing so mainly on contract to DOE in any case, so DOE will eventually pay most of the costs of security as it does at its own sites).[74] Congress should also provide incentives to convert HEU medical isotope production to LEU, without in any way interfering with supplies, by imposing a roughly 30 percent user fee on all medical isotopes made with HEU.

---

72. NRC-regulated research reactors are exempted from most of the security requirements that would otherwise apply to any site with HEU, simply because they are research reactors. See U.S. Nuclear Regulatory Commission, "Part 73—Physical Protection of Plants and Materials," in *NRC Regulations: Title 10, Code of Federal Regulations* (Washington, D.C.: U.S. Government Printing Office, 2008), http://www.nrc.gov/reading-rm/doc-collections/cfr/part073/full-text.html.

73. C.W. Coates et al., "Radiation Effects on Personnel Performance Capability and a Summary of Dose Levels for Spent Research Reactor Fuels," in *Proceedings of the 47th Annual Meeting of the Insti-tute for Nuclear Materials Management, Nashville, Tenn., 16–20 July* (Northbrook, Ill.: INMM, 2006). For an earlier examination that reached somewhat similar conclusions, see J.J. Koelling and E.W. Barts, "Special Nuclear Material Self-Protection Criteria Investigation: Phases I and II," LA-9213-MS, NUREG/CR-2492 (Los Alamos, N.Mex.: Los Alamos National Laboratory, January 1982), http://www.sciencemadness.org/lanl1_a/lib-www/la-pubs/00307470.pdf.

74. This distinction is based on government versus private ownership, not on military versus ci-vilian roles. Some of DOE's HEU facilities are entirely civilian, whereas the two large HEU pro-cessing facilities regulated by the NRC, BWX Technologies, and Nuclear Fuel Services do much of their work fabricating fuel for the U.S. nuclear navy. For a discussion of the substantial difference in security levels at DOE and NRC-regulated facilities, and a recommendation for similar levels of security for similar types of material regardless of ownership, see U.S. Government Accountability Office, "Nuclear Security: DOE and NRC Have Different Security Requirements for Protecting Weapons-Grade Material from Terrorist Attacks," GAO-07-1197R (Washington, D.C.: GAO, 2007), http://www.gao.gov/new.items/d071197r.pdf.

Marshaling the funds to help producers convert to LEU would give producers a strong financial incentive to take this step. Because the isotopes are a tiny fraction of the costs of the medical procedures that use them, this would not significantly affect the costs or availability of these life-saving procedures.[75]

PREPARE FOR THE WORST. Finally, no matter what is done to prevent nuclear terrorism, it is essential that the United States be better prepared should such a catastrophe nevertheless occur.[76] Although some steps have been taken to prepare for the ghastly aftermath of a terrorist nuclear attack, a comprehensive plan and approach is needed. The United States needs a rapid ability to assess which people are in the greatest danger and to tell them what they can do to protect themselves. Better capabilities to communicate to everyone when television, radio, and cellphones in the affected area may not be functioning properly are also needed, as are much better public communication plans for the critical minutes and hours after such an attack. The U.S. government needs to do a much better job encouraging and helping people to take simple steps to prepare for an emergency. The United States also needs to enhance its ability—including making use of the military's capabilities—to treat many thousands of injured people. It must also develop more effective plans to keep the government and economy functioning while taking all the steps that will be needed to prevent another attack. (In particular, Congress has not yet acted to put a plan in place for reconstituting itself should most of its members be killed in a nuclear attack.)[77] Many of these steps would help to address any catastrophe, natural or man-made, and would pay off even if efforts to prevent a terrorist nuclear attack succeeded.

Conclusion

Despite nuclear security efforts since 1994, the dangers of nuclear theft and terrorism remain real. Al-Qaida continues to seek nuclear weapons and the materials and expertise to make them, and other groups may do so in the future. Seizures of stolen HEU or plutonium continue to occur. At many sites around the world, weapons-usable nuclear materials are not effectively protected

75. Producing medical isotopes without highly enriched uranium is both technically and economically feasible. See Committee on Medical Isotope Production without Highly Enriched Uranium, National Research Council, *Medical Isotope Production without Highly Enriched Uranium* (Washington, D.C.: National Academy Press, 2009).
76. For an especially useful recent discussion, see Carter, May, and Perry, "The Day After."
77. For a discussion of the importance of such a plan, and specific recommendations, see Continuity of Government Commission, *Preserving Our Institutions: The Continuity of Congress* (Washington, D.C.: American Enterprise Institute and Brookings Institution, May 2003).

against the scale of threats that terrorists and criminals have shown they can pose. Should terrorists ever succeed in acquiring and detonating a nuclear bomb, the global impact would be immense. Nothing is more central to U.S. and world security than ensuring that nuclear weapons and their essential ingredients do not fall into terrorists' hands.

Coping with this danger poses a fundamental challenge. To make progress on the pace and scale that President Obama has envisioned requires surmounting barriers posed by complacency, secrecy, concerns over sovereignty, political disputes, and clashing bureaucratic procedures. These barriers will not be overcome unless President Obama makes the prevention of nuclear terrorism a top priority of U.S. national security policy—not just in words, but in sustained action.

The task, however, is not hopeless. With a sensible strategy, adequate resources, sustained leadership, and partnership with key countries around the world, President Obama can overcome these obstacles and reduce the risk of nuclear terrorism to a small fraction of its present level during his first term. The security of the United States and the world demands no less.

Proliferation Rings

New Challenges to the Nuclear
Nonproliferation Regime

*Chaim Braun and
Christopher F. Chyba*

$\mathbf{T}$he nuclear programs
of the Democratic People's Republic of Korea (DPRK), Iran, and Pakistan provide the most visible manifestations of three broad and interrelated challenges
to the nuclear nonproliferation regime. The first is so-called latent proliferation, in which a country adheres to, or at least for some time maintains a façade
of adhering to, its formal obligations under the Nuclear Nonproliferation
Treaty (NPT) while nevertheless developing the capabilities needed for a nuclear weapons program.[1] That country can then either withdraw from the NPT
and build actual weapons on short notice, or simply stay within the NPT while
maintaining the latent capability for the rapid realization of nuclear weapons
as a hedge against future threats. This was the path followed by the DPRK
with its plutonium program and one that is likely being followed by Iran and
more subtly by others. The second broad challenge is first-tier nuclear proliferation, in which technology or material sold or stolen from private companies
or state nuclear programs assists nonnuclear weapons states in developing illegal nuclear weapons programs and delivery systems.[2] The third challenge—
the focus of this article—is second-tier nuclear proliferation, in which states in

Chaim Braun is a Vice President of Altos Management Partners Inc. and a Science Fellow at the Center for International Security and Cooperation (CISAC) in Stanford University's Institute for International Studies. Christopher F. Chyba is Co-director of CISAC and Associate Professor in Stanford's Department of Geological and Environmental Sciences. He served on the National Security Council staff in the first admin-istration of President William J. Clinton.

The authors are grateful for critiques of an earlier version of this article from George Bunn, Lynn Eden, Rifaat Hussain, George Perkovich, William Potter, Scott Sagan, Todd Sechser, and three anonymous referees. This work was supported in part by grants from the John D. and Catherine T. MacArthur Foundation and by Carnegie Corporation of New York.

1. For a discussion of latent proliferation in the context of Iran, see George Perkovich, "Dealing with Iran's Nuclear Challenge" (Washington, D.C.: Carnegie Endowment for International Peace, April 28, 2003), http://www.ceip.org/files/projects/npp/pdf/Iran/iraniannuclearchallenge.pdf. In January 2004 President Mohammad Khatami of Iran gave public assurances that Iran's nuclear program is peaceful, stated that Iran "vehemently" opposed production of nuclear arms, and de-nied that Iran had received nuclear material from the DPRK. See "Iran Denies Receiving Nuclear Material from North Korea," Agence France-Presse, Davos, Switzerland, January 21, 2004, http://www.spacewar.com/2004/040121200135.i5cph0v8.html.
2. First-tier or primary proliferation may be defined as the spread of nuclear weapons–relevant material from states or private entities within states that are members of the formal nuclear export-ers groups, the Nuclear Exporters Committee (or Zangger Committee) or the Nuclear Suppliers Group. Second-tier suppliers are other states or private entities within states that may be supply-ing nuclear weapons–relevant material on the international market.

International Security, Vol. 29, No. 2 (Fall 2004), pp. 5–49
© 2004 by the President and Fellows of Harvard College and the Massachusetts Institute of Technology.

the developing world with varying technical capabilities trade among themselves to bolster one another's nuclear and strategic weapons efforts.

In the DPRK, Iranian, and Libyan uranium programs, and possibly other national programs, second-tier proliferation centered on Pakistan has exacerbated the threat of latent proliferation. In the Iranian, Libyan, and Pakistani missile programs, and possibly other national programs, missile proliferation activities emanating from the DPRK have further raised the stakes. All three proliferation challenges are interrelated, and the missile and nuclear weapons clandestine supply rings have been intertwined. These issues must be addressed if the nonproliferation regime is to survive. Here we analyze, in light of recent revelations out of Iran, Libya, Malaysia, Pakistan, South Africa, Turkey, and other nations, the dynamics of second-tier proliferation of nuclear technologies, weapons designs, and delivery systems, and their interactions with latent and first-tier proliferation. Second-tier proliferation, in particular, poses a strong challenge to the supply-side approaches that have traditionally been central to the existing nonproliferation regime.

Evidence for the exchange of nuclear weapons–related and missile technologies among several developing countries suggests that we are entering a world in which a growing number of such countries will be able to cut themselves free from the existing nonproliferation regime. We dub these networks of second-tier proliferators "proliferation rings." The full development of such proliferation rings, unless checked, will ultimately render the current export control regimes moot, as developing countries create nuclear-weapons and delivery systems technologies and manufacturing bases of their own, increasingly disconnect from first-tier state or corporate suppliers, and trade among themselves for the capabilities that their individual programs lack. Along the way, technology transfer among proliferating states will also cut the cost of and the period to acquisition of nuclear weapons and missile capabilities, as well as reduce the reaction time of the overall nonproliferation regime.

Concern over second-tier proliferation is hardly new.[3] What is new is that the modalities of the proliferation routes are much more extensive than previ-

---

3. Analyses of second-tier proliferation prior to the 1990s include those in Joseph Pilat and William Potter, eds., *The Nuclear Suppliers and Nonproliferation* (Lexington, Mass.: Lexington Books, 1985); Leonard Spector, with Jacqueline Smith, *Nuclear Ambitions: The Spread of Nuclear Weapons, 1989–1990* (San Francisco, Calif.: Westview, 1990), pp. 29–48; and William Potter, ed., *International Nuclear Trade and Nonproliferation: The Challenge of Emerging Suppliers* (Lexington, Mass.: Lexington Books, 1990).

ously recognized; the spread of technological know-how and manufacturing capabilities is wider than hitherto believed; and such proliferation has undeniably had a major impact on the nuclear weapons and missile programs of several developing countries. In 1990 it was still possible to argue that second-tier suppliers' capabilities were at the lower end of the nuclear export spectrum, and that the export actions these suppliers did undertake were for the most part cautious.[4] Both claims manifestly no longer apply. We now find that proliferation ring members support one another either directly at the state-to-state level or indirectly through once-removed private sector supplier networks. In addition, "rings" of clandestine exchanges of technologies have begun to interact and support one another.

An effective response to the proliferation challenge must address both the supply and demand sides of the problem. Addressing the supply side continues to require limiting the transfer of nuclear weapons–grade material or nuclear weapons technology from first-tier suppliers to potential proliferators, in addition to addressing second-tier proliferation. Addressing the demand side necessitates confronting the balance of factors that states take into consideration when deciding their nuclear-weapons and missile delivery systems policies.[5]

Supply-side action requires increasing the security of nuclear weapons–grade material in the former Soviet Union (FSU) and elsewhere. If continuing efforts in the Cooperative Threat Reduction (CTR) program are successful, and with the expansion of this program to include other poorly protected fissile material, the challenge of nuclear theft and smuggling should recede over time, provided an ongoing commitment of the Group of Eight (G-8) countries,

---

4. See Lewis Dunn, "The Emerging Nuclear Suppliers: Some Guidelines for Policy," in Potter, *International Nuclear Trade and Nonproliferation*, p. 398. Dunn notes the exception of China to his statement that "the emerging suppliers have so far acted relatively cautiously as nuclear exporters."

5. There is an extensive literature on the reasons countries choose to develop nuclear weapons, including Mitchell Reiss, *Bridled Ambition: Why Countries Constrain Their Nuclear Capabilities* (Baltimore, Md.: Johns Hopkins University Press, 1995); Scott D. Sagan, "Why Do States Build Nuclear Weapons? Three Models in Search of a Bomb," *International Security*, Vol. 21, No. 3 (Winter 1996/97), pp. 54–86; George Perkovich, *India's Nuclear Bomb: The Impact on Global Proliferation* (Los Angeles: University of California Press, 1999), pp. 444–468; Peter Liberman, "The Rise and Fall of the South African Bomb," *International Security*, Vol. 26, No. 2 (Fall 2001), pp. 45–86; Ariel Levite, "Never Say Never Again: Nuclear Reversal Revisited," *International Security*, Vol. 27, No. 3 (Winter 2002/03), pp. 59–88; and Kurt M. Campbell, Robert J. Einhorn, and Mitchell B. Reiss, *The Nuclear Tipping Point: Why States Reconsider Their Nuclear Choices* (Washington, D.C.: Brookings, 2004).

the FSU, and other states.[6] In addition to a robust and successful CTR program, the various export control regimes must also be strengthened and deepened.[7] Yet second-tier proliferation may nevertheless increase in scope and sophistication, as members of proliferation rings acquire the resources for, and master the technologies of, weapons manufacture and delivery systems production among themselves. If networks (or rings) of third world nations able to swap nuclear weapons–relevant and missile systems–relevant technologies expand, nonproliferation policies focused on first-tier supply will become less relevant, and demand-side approaches will correspondingly increase in importance.

In addition to the supply-side "push" to proliferation, proliferation "pull" involves a number of demand-side factors. These include regional security and national prestige, requiring responses that go well beyond the NPT itself. Nevertheless, the nonproliferation regime plays an important role in framing the balance of factors that states consider when determining their nuclear weapons policies. As currently structured, however, the regime presents potential proliferators with a skewed set of positive and negative inducements regarding compliance versus noncompliance. If the nuclear nonproliferation regime is to be preserved, a better balance must be struck: one that increases the benefits of adhering to the regime, decreases the negative consequences of adherence, makes clear the negative impact of abandoning the regime, and reassures adherents that the regime protects them against adversaries' nuclear ambitions.

In this article we explore, to the extent possible from sources in the open literature, the interactions among the DPRK, Iranian, Libyan, and Pakistani nuclear technologies, weapons, and missile programs, and discuss the implications of these interactions for the nuclear nonproliferation regime. In this light, we then consider policy options to address second-tier proliferation, beginning with needed incremental improvements to the current regime, an analysis of the more ambitious proposals made in 2003 and 2004 by U.S. President George

---

6. For a review of CTR programs, see Matthew Bunn, Anthony Wier, and John P. Holdren, *Controlling Nuclear Warheads and Materials: A Report Card and Action Plan* (Cambridge, Mass.: Nuclear Threat Initiative and Project on Managing the Atom, Belfer Center for Science and International Affairs, John F. Kennedy School of Government, Harvard University, 2003); for an update, see Matthew Bunn and Anthony Wier, *Securing the Bomb: An Agenda for Action* (Cambridge, Mass.: Nuclear Threat Initiative and Project on Managing the Atom, Belfer Center for Science and International Affairs, John F. Kennedy School of Government, Harvard University, 2004).
7. For a summary and evaluation of export control regimes, see U.S. General Accounting Office (GAO), *Nonproliferation Strategy Needed to Strengthen Multilateral Export Control Regimes* (Washington, D.C.: U.S. GAO, October 2002), http://www.state.gov/documents/organization/14867.pdf.

W. Bush and by Director General Mohamed ElBaradei of the International Atomic Energy Agency (IAEA), as well as further supply-side and demand-side measures.

Intersecting Missile and Uranium Enrichment Rings

Evidence for significant interactions among the DPRK, Iranian, and Pakistani nuclear and missile programs has accumulated in the past several years, and details of links with Libya and other countries have recently also come to light. Any discussion of how the nonproliferation regime might better respond to second-tier proliferation in the future must begin with an understanding, albeit imperfect, of the actions taken by and motivations of the proliferating state and substate actors that have brought the regime to the crisis it currently faces.

THE NORTH KOREAN PLUTONIUM PROGRAM
The North Koreans began reprocessing plutonium in 1989, using their 5 MW(e) graphite-moderated reactor and "radiochemical laboratory"—a medium-size reprocessing plant located at the Yongbyon nuclear center about 100 kilometers north of Pyongyang.[8] The DPRK reactors are thought to be based on the British 1950s' Calder Hall–type reactors that the DPRK built using information available in the technical literature. IAEA inspections of the Yongbyon site in 1992 uncovered the diversion of several kilograms of plutonium following the reprocessing of spent fuel.[9]

The signing of the Agreed Framework between the United States and the

---

8. The abbreviation MW(e) stands for "megawatt electric." A megawatt, or 1 million watts, is a unit of power; 1,000 MW(e) is a typical electrical power output for a large commercial power reactor. MW(e) measures the electrical power output of the plant, as opposed to MW(th), or "megawatt thermal," which measures the plant's thermal power. The plant's thermal output is converted, at an efficiency cost, into electrical power. For terminology and basic reactor physics, see Richard L. Garwin and Georges Charpak, *Megawatts and Megatons: A Turning Point in the Nuclear Age?* (New York: Alfred A. Knopf, 2001).
9. For descriptions of the DPRK plutonium program, see David Albright and Kevin O'Neill, eds., *Solving the North Korean Nuclear Puzzle* (Washington, D.C.: Institute for Science and International Security Press, 2000); Michael M. May, Chaim Braun, George Bunn, Zachary Davis, James Hassberger, Ronald Lehman, Wayne Ruhter, William Sailor, Robert Schock, and Nancy Suski, *Verifying the Agreed Framework*, CGSR-CISAC report (Stanford, Calif.: Center for Global Security Research and Center for International Security and Cooperation, Stanford Institute for International Studies, Stanford University, April 2001), http://cisac.stanford.edu/publications/12020/; and Jonathan Pollack, "The United States, North Korea, and the End of the Agreed Framework," *Naval War College Review*, Vol. 56, No. 3 (Summer 2003), pp. 11–49.

DPRK in October 1994 froze the DPRK's ability to further reprocess the spent fuel from the 5 MW(e) reactor, but not before the DPRK extracted adequate plutonium for at least two nuclear weapons, according to published CIA estimates.[10] Whether the DPRK has successfully manufactured nuclear warheads from this extracted plutonium remains uncertain.[11]

In December 2002 the DPRK withdrew from the NPT, removed the monitoring devices installed by the IAEA on the Yongbyon facilities, and dismissed the IAEA's safeguards inspectors.[12] The DPRK restarted the 5 MW(e) reactor in March 2003 and prepared for the restart of the radiochemical laboratory, facilitated, according to unnamed U.S. officials, by the acquisition of twenty tons of tributylphosphate organic solvent from a Chinese company.[13]

At the time of the signing of the Agreed Framework, the DPRK had a total of 8,000 spent fuel rods that would be subject to IAEA monitoring. Reprocessing this stockpile would provide adequate plutonium for perhaps six additional nuclear warheads.[14] In January 2004 an unofficial U.S. delegation visited the DPRK and saw that the 8,000 rods had been removed from their storage pond; DPRK scientists claimed that these had been entirely reprocessed during a six-month work campaign.[15]

Operation of the 5 MW(e) reactor will produce enough plutonium for one additional weapon per year. Were the DPRK to complete construction of two

---

10. Central Intelligence Agency, *Unclassified Report to Congress on the Acquisition of Technology Related to Weapons of Mass Destruction and Advanced Conventional Munitions, 1 July through 31 December 2001*, http://www.nti.org/e_research/official_docs/cia/cia_cong_wmd.pdf. See also David Albright, "North Korea's Current and Future Plutonium and Nuclear Weapons Stocks," ISIS Issues Brief (Washington, D.C.: Institute for Science and International Security, January 15, 2003).
11. For a discussion of inconsistencies in recent unclassified intelligence assessments of whether the DPRK has produced nuclear warheads from its extracted plutonium, see Pollack, "The United States, North Korea, and the End of the Agreed Framework." A.Q. Khan, a key figure in the Pakistani nuclear program, reportedly told Pakistani authorities that he was shown what he believed to be three nuclear warheads during a visit to the DPRK in 1999. See David E. Sanger, "Pakistani Tells of North Korean Nuclear Devices," *New York Times*, April 13, 2004.
12. IAEA, "Fact Sheet on DPRK Nuclear Safeguards" (Vienna: IAEA, May 2003).
13. See "Allies Discuss N. Korea Nuke Move, *CNN.com*, http://www.cnn.com/2002/WORLD/asiapcf/east/12/22/n.korea.nukes/; and John Pike, "Yongbyon," http://www.globalsecurity.org/wmd/world/dprk/yongbyon.htm.
14. For periodically updated reviews of the DPRK nuclear program, see Larry A. Niksch, "North Korea Nuclear Weapons Program," Congressional Research Service (CRS) Issue Brief for Congress, IB 91141 (Washington, D.C.: CRS, August 23, 2003); and Sharon A. Squassoni, "North Korea's Nuclear Weapons: How Soon an Arsenal?" Congressional Research Service Report for Congress, RS21391 (Washington, D.C.: CRS, February 2, 2004).
15. See Siegfried S. Hecker, "Visit to the Yongbyon Nuclear Scientific Research Center in North Korea," statement before the Senate Committee on Foreign Relations, 108th Cong., 2d sess., January 21, 2004.

other partially built reactors—a 50 MW(e) reactor at Yongbyon and a 200 MW(e) reactor at Taechon—these could produce adequate plutonium for thirty to fifty nuclear weapons per year, depending on North Korea's reprocessing capacity.[16] The January 2004 U.S. delegation reported, however, that the larger Yongbyon reactor seemed to be in a state of extensive disrepair; this might also hold for the Taechon reactor. One of the U.S. fears about the DPRK's weapons stockpile is that, while a few warheads might be held in reserve as an ultimate guarantee of regime survival, a larger number of warheads could be viewed by the regime as sufficient to permit it to conduct nuclear testing or to sell nuclear material (or even warheads) on the black market.[17] Currently it seems most probable, though hardly certain, that the DPRK plutonium-based stockpile will increase at only one warhead per year. The remaining source of uncertainty is the status of the DPRK's clandestine uranium enrichment program.

PAKISTAN AND THE NORTH KOREAN URANIUM ENRICHMENT PROGRAM

The Bush administration stated in October 2002 that the DPRK had acknowledged having a uranium enrichment program.[18] Evidently, subsequent to the

---

16. For the potential rate of accumulation of fissile materials within the DPRK nuclear program, see Henry Sokolski, "Beyond the Agreed Framework: The DPRK's Projected Atomic Bomb Making Capabilities, 2002–2009" (Washington, D.C.: Nonproliferation Education Center, December 3, 2002), http://www.npec-web.org/pages/fissile.htm; and Jon B. Wolfsthal, "Estimates of North Korea's Unchecked Nuclear Weapons Production Potential," write-up (Washington, D.C.: Carnegie Endowment for International Peace, August 2003).

17. According to unnamed U.S. officials, a DPRK delegate to talks with the United States in Beijing in April 2003 threatened (in a corridor conversation outside the meeting) that North Korea might export or test a nuclear weapon. See Glenn Kessler, "N. Korea Says It Has Nuclear Arms: At Talks with U.S. Pyongyang Threatens 'Demonstration' or Export of Weapon," *Washington Post*, April 25, 2003. Two different unnamed officials, however, warned that the North Korean official's words were vague. "No one talked about testing directly, or selling," one official stated. Rather, "there was language about 'taking physical actions.'" Quoted in David E. Sanger, "North Korea Says It Now Possesses Nuclear Arsenal," *New York Times*, April 25, 2003. For an analysis of mistranslations and misunderstandings of North Korean assertions, see Daniel A. Pinkston and Phillip C. Saunders, "Seeing North Korea Clearly," *Survival*, Vol. 45, No. 3 (Autumn 2003), pp. 79–102. See also Marina Malenic, "North Korea Could Give Nuclear Weapons to Terrorist Groups, U.S. Military Officials Warn," NTI Global Security Newswire, April 1, 2004.

18. See Peter Slevin and Karen DeYoung, "N. Korea Admits Having Secret Nuclear Arms; Stunned U.S. Ponders Next Steps," *Washington Post*, October 17, 2002. The DPRK has denied having such a program, however, and a senior Chinese official said in June 2004 that "the U.S. has not presented convincing evidence" that a DPRK uranium program exists. See Joseph Kahn and Susan Chira, "Chinese Official Challenges U.S. Stance on North Korea," *New York Times*, June 9, 2004. See also Paul Kerr, "N. Korea Uranium Enrichment Efforts Shrouded in Mystery," *Arms Control Today*, Vol. 33, No. 4 (May 2003), p. 25; and Dipali Mukhopadhayay and Jon Wolfstahl, "Carnegie Analysis: Ten Questions on North Korea's Uranium Enrichment Program" (Washington, D.C.: Carnegie Endowment for International Peace, January 7, 2003), http://www.ceip.org/files/nonprolif/templates/article.asp?NewsID=3871.

signing of the Agreed Framework, the DPRK decided to accelerate its low-level uranium enrichment research effort into an alternative route to nuclear weapons material acquisition.[19] The DPRK appears to have turned to Pakistan, with its fully developed uranium enrichment program, for help.[20] This apparently led to a missiles-for-enrichment-technology barter deal between Pakistan and the DPRK, a benchmark event in the global proliferation enterprise. According to unnamed Pakistani, Republic of Korea, and U.S. officials, this relationship began as early as 1993 with plans for the Nodong missile provided to Pakistan by the DPRK.[21] In April 1998, Pakistan successfully tested the Ghauri-1 missile, its version of the Nodong. The Pakistani government's lack of hard currency putatively coincided with the DPRK's desire for a uranium route to nuclear weapons, and in that same year the Khan Research Laboratory (KRL) reportedly began to provide Pyongyang with blueprints and components for gas centrifuges for uranium enrichment, compensating for the DPRK's frozen (due to the Agreed Framework) plutonium program. Pakistani officials denied this trade until April 2004, when it made public portions of the confession of Abdul Qadeer (A.Q.) Khan attesting to the transfer of Pakistani enrichment technology to the DPRK. Khan was director of KRL in Kahuta, Pakistan, and leader of the Pakistani uranium centrifuge enrichment program.[22]

---

19. The history of the DPRK's uranium centrifuge program remains poorly understood, although a rough timeline can be pieced together. See Kerr, "N. Korea Uranium Enrichment Efforts Shrouded in Mystery."

20. Central Intelligence Agency, untitled CIA estimate for Congress, November 19, 2002, http://www.fas.org/nuke/guide/dprk/nuke/cia111902.html. See also David E. Sanger and James Dao, "U.S. Says Pakistan Gave Technology to North Korea," *New York Times,* October 17, 2002; and Carla Anne Robbins and Zahid Hussain, "North Korea Had Russian Parts Suppliers," *Wall Street Journal,* October 21, 2002.

21. For accounts of the missiles-for-centrifuges deal, see Gaurav Kampani, "Second Tier Proliferation: The Case of Pakistan and North Korea," *Nonproliferation Review,* Vol. 9, No. 3 (Fall/Winter 2002), pp. 107–116; Mark Hibbs, "CIA Assessment on DPRK Presumes Massive Outside Help on Centrifuges," *Platts Nuclear Fuel,* November 25, 2002, pp. 1, 12–13; International Institute for Strategic Studies, "Pakistan and North Korea: Dangerous Counter-Trades," *IISS Strategic Comments,* Vol. 8, No. 9 (November 2002), pp. 1–2; Daniel A. Pinkston, "When Did WMD Deals between Pyongyang and Islamabad Begin?" (Monterey, Calif.: Center for Nonproliferation Studies, Monterey Institute for International Studies, December 2002); David E. Sanger, "In North Korea and Pakistan, Deep Roots of Nuclear Barter," *New York Times,* November 24, 2003; David E. Sanger "U.S. Widens View of Pakistan Link to Korean Arms," *New York Times,* March 14, 2004; and Christopher Clary, "Dr. Khan's Nuclear WalMart," *Disarmament Diplomacy,* No. 76 (March/April 2004), pp. 31–36. DPRK assistance to the Ghauri program was affirmed by the U.S. National Intelligence Council in December 2001, in *Foreign Missile Developments and the Ballistic Missile Threat through 2015,* http://www.cia.gov/nic/PDF_GIF_otherprod/missilethreat2001.pdf.

22. See David E. Sanger and William J. Broad, "From Rogue Nuclear Programs, Web of Trails Leads to Pakistan," *New York Times,* January 4, 2004; and George Jahn, "AP: Pakistan Knew of Nuclear Black Market," *Washington Times,* March 7, 2004. For reports on Khan's admissions, see David

A.Q. Khan seems to have been the central figure in the DPRK deal. According to Khan's reported testimony, his network provided the DPRK with centrifuge designs based on Pakistani versions of both early- and second-generation centrifuges developed at the Urenco company enrichment plants in Almelo, Netherlands, and Gronau, Germany. Famously, Khan had been employed in the Almelo plant and took design information and listings of component suppliers with him to Pakistan in 1975.[23] Based on that information, the KRL laboratory developed and built two centrifuge models, the P-1 and the more sophisticated and more capable P-2.[24]

By 2001 the DPRK development of centrifuge enrichment capabilities had progressed to the point where the DPRK apparently started shopping for the large-scale supply of machine components required to construct about 4,000 centrifuges. North Korean procurement agents reportedly bought British-manufactured high tensile-strength aluminum tubes from a German company and shipped a consignment of those tubes with freight papers indicating their destination to be the Shenyang Aircraft Corporation in China. The shipment was tracked and halted in Egypt while en route.[25] Were those 4,000 rotor tubings and other centrifuge components obtained by the DPRK, and the enrichment plant completed, it could produce one or two weapons' worth of highly enriched uranium (HEU) per year, depending on the design.[26]

Rhode and David E. Sanger, "Key Pakistani Is Said to Admit Atom Transfers," *New York Times*, February 2, 2004; John Lancaster and Kamran Khan, "Pakistani Scientist Apologizes," *Washington Post*, February 5, 2004; and Peter Edidin, "Dr. Khan Got What He Wanted, and He Explains How," *New York Times*, February 15, 2004.

23. For reviews of Khan's activities, see Douglas Frantz, "Iran Closes In on Ability to Build a Nuclear Bomb," *Los Angeles Times*, August 4, 2003; and Maggie Farley and Bob Drogin, "1 Man, 3 Nations, a World of Peril," *Los Angeles Times*, January 6, 2003.

24. Using Urenco data, the KRL built the P-1 centrifuge, which uses aluminum tubes and has a capacity of 2–3 separative work units (SWUs) per year. By 1995 the KRL had switched to the P-2 centrifuge, which is based on a maraging steel rotor and rated at twice the SWU capacity of the P-1. See David Albright and Corey Hinderstein, "The Centrifuge Connection," *Bulletin of the Atomic Scientists*, Vol. 60, No. 2 (March/April 2004), pp. 61–66.

25. Mark Hibbs, "DPRK Sought Enough Aluminum Tubing in Germany for 4,000 Centrifuges," *Platts Nuclear Fuel*, May 12, 2003, pp. 1, 16–17; Joby Warrick, "U.S. Followed the Aluminum," *Washington Post*, October 18, 2003; and Mark Hibbs, "DPRK Enrichment Not Far Along, Some Intelligence Data Suggest," *Nucleonics Week*, October 24, 2003, pp. 1, 12–14.

26. According to Richard Garwin and Georges Charpak, *Megawatts and Megatons*, p. 59, the gun-type Hiroshima weapon contained about 60 kilograms of HEU. According to Leonard Spector and Jacqueline Smith, *Nuclear Ambitions*, appendix A, more difficult implosion designs require 25 kilograms of HEU, or as little as 15 kilograms or less for increasingly sophisticated designs. According to David Albright and Mark Hibbs, citing an unnamed U.S. official interviewed in 1991, the nuclear warhead design provided to Pakistan by China used about 15 kilograms of HEU. See Albright and Hibbs, "Pakistan's Bomb: Out of the Closet," *Bulletin of the Atomic Scientists*, Vol. 48, No. 4 (July/August 1992), pp. 38–43. It requires about 200 SWUs to make 1 kilogram of HEU. Thus

In this pursuit, as in 1992, the DPRK appears to have underestimated the technical capabilities of the nonproliferation control regime. In 1992 the DPRK seems not to have foreseen that swipes of surfaces by IAEA inspectors in buildings within the Yongbyon complex would provide data on its recent reprocessing activities.[27] In 2001 the DPRK seems to have hoped that it could procure large quantities of dual-use items related to centrifuge manufacturing in the global metal markets without alerting the export control regimes. It was wrong both times, and in that sense the control regimes were effective and performed as designed. In each case, however, the DPRK substantially advanced the technical scope of its proliferation efforts prior to being discovered.

PAKISTAN, EUROPE, LIBYA, AND THE PRIVATE SECTOR PROLIFERATION NETWORK
Libyan President Muammar Qaddafi decided in December 2003 to break with his past proliferation activities, renounce Libya's nuclear and chemical weapons programs, disclose and dismantle them, and forswear missiles that do not conform to 1987 Missile Technology Control Regime (MTCR) guidelines.[28] His decision followed years of negotiations intended to lift sanctions imposed on Libya because of its ties to terrorism and its own proliferation program; a Libyan approach to Britain in March 2003 at the outset of the second Gulf War; and the interdiction in Italy's Taranto Harbor in October 2003 of the German-owned ship BBC *China,* which proved to be carrying the components for several thousand P-2 centrifuges for the Libyan uranium enrichment program.[29]

The revelations flowing from President Qaddafi's decision are remarkable.

---

it will require about 3,000 SWUs to produce one weapon's worth of HEU, or 1,000 to 1,500 P-1 centrifuges operating for one year. For the production capability goal of the DPRK enrichment plant, see Central Intelligence Agency, *Unclassified Report to Congress on the Acquisition of Technology Related to Weapons of Mass Destruction and Advanced Conventional Munitions, 1 January through 30 June 2002,* http://www.fas.org/irp/threat/bian_apr_2003.htm.

27. See May et al., *Verifying the Agreed Framework;* and Albright and O'Neill, *Solving the North Korean Nuclear Puzzle.*

28. Robin Wright and Glenn Kessler, "Analysis—Two Decades of Sanctions, Isolation Wore Down Gaddafi," *Washington Post,* December 20, 2003; and "Iran, Libya, and Pakistan's Nuclear Supermarket," *Disarmament Diplomacy,* No. 75 (January/February 2004), pp. 39–42. Libya's efforts to meet its obligations to the IAEA are given in IAEA Board of Governors, "Implementation of the NPT Safeguards Agreement of the Socialist People's Libyan Arab Jamahiriya," IAEA Report GOV/2004/12, Vienna, Austria, February 20, 2004. See also Paul Kerr, "U.S. Says Libya Implementing WMD Pledge," *Arms Control Today,* Vol. 34, No. 2 (March 2004), pp. 28–29.

29. Stephen Fidler, Mark Huband, and Roula Khalaf, "Comment: Return to the Fold: How Gaddafi Was Persuaded to Give Up His Nuclear Goals," *Financial Times,* January 27, 2004; Ray Takeyeh, statement before the Committee on International Relations, U.S. House of Representatives, 108th Cong., 2d sess., March 10, 2004; and "Qaddafi's Son Says Libya Was Promised Economic, Military Gains for WMD Disarmament," NTI Global Security Newswire, March 10, 2004.

Evidently Pakistan's A.Q. Khan and a few of his senior associates at KRL were at the center of a private sector proliferation network for the clandestine export of centrifuge uranium enrichment technology.[30] Besides the DPRK and Libya, it appears that Iran, Iraq, possibly Syria, and perhaps other countries were approached with offers of nuclear weapons–related deals.[31] The network used a firm, Scomi Precision Engineering, in a third-party country, Malaysia, to manufacture centrifuge components whose ultimate destination was hidden by transshipment through Dubai. The network also reportedly used the Turkish electrical components firm Elektronik Kontrol Aletleri (EKA) to purchase motors and frequency converters for the centrifuges. These components were also shipped on the BBC *China* and were discovered only when the ship docked in Tripoli in March 2004.[32] These transshipments were facilitated by the Dubai-based Sri Lankan businessman Buhary Syed Abu Tahir, the controlling shareholder of Gulf Technical Industries, whom President Bush has described as the "chief financial officer and money launderer" of the Khan network.[33] The network relied on a group of European former colleagues of Khan who worked as

30. See Peter Slevin, John Lancaster, and Kamran Khan, "At Least 7 Nations Tied to Pakistani Nuclear Ring," *Washington Post*, February 8, 2004; William J. Broad, David E. Sanger, and Raymond Bonner, "A Tale of Nuclear Proliferation: How Pakistani Built His Network," *New York Times*, February 12, 2004; and Clary, "Dr. Khan's Nuclear WalMart." For official Malaysian investigation results, see Polis Diraja Malaysia, "Press Release by Inspector General of Police in Relation to Investigation on the Alleged Production of Components for Libya's Uranium Enrichment Programme," February 20, 2004, http://www.rmp.gov.my/rmp03/040220scomi_eng.htm. According to this document, European participants allegedly involved in the Malaysian/Libyan centrifuge efforts included Heinz Mebus and Gotthard Lerch from Germany, Friedrich Tinner and his son Urs Friedrich Tinner from Switzerland, Gunas Jireh and Selim Alguadis from Turkey, and Peter Griffen from the United Kingdom.
31. See David Albright and Corey Hinderstein, "Documents Indicate A.Q. Khan Offered Nuclear Weapons Designs to Iraq in 1990. Did He Approach Other Countries?" ISIS Issue Brief (Washington, D.C.: ISIS, February 4, 2004), http://www.isis-online.org; and Douglas Frantz, "Nuclear Ring May Have Aided Syria," *Los Angeles Times*, June 25, 2004. Possible nuclear links between Pakistan and Saudi Arabia are discussed in Simon Henderson, "Towards a Saudi Nuclear Option: The Saudi-Pakistani Summit," Policy Watch Report No. 750 (Washington, D.C.: Washington Institute for Near East Policy, April 22, 2003); and "Pakistan, Saudi Arabia Reach Secret Nuclear Weapons Deal, Pakistani Source Says," NTI Global Security Newswire, October 21, 2003. An offer of "nuclear power" to Nigeria by a visiting senior Pakistani military officer was asserted, then rescinded. See "Nigerian Military Asserts, Then Denies, Interest in Acquiring Pakistani Nuclear Technology," NTI Global Security Newswire, March 4, 2004.
32. Stephen Fidler and Mark Huband, "Turks and South Africans Helped Libya's Secret Nuclear Arms Project," *Financial Times*, June 10, 2004; and Stephen Fidler, "Turkish Businessman Denies Nuclear Goods Claim," *Financial Times*, June 11, 2004.
33. Quoted in Rohan Sullivan and Patrick McDowell, "AP: Nuclear Financier Has Ties to Malaysia," *TheState.com*, February 18, 2004, http://www.thestate.com/mid/thestate/news/world/7977621.htm; and Raymond Bonner, "Salesman on Nuclear Circuit Casts Blurry Corporate Shadow," *New York Times*, February 18, 2004.

engineers in technology and components supply companies serving Urenco, and later branched out to form their own consulting companies specializing in centrifuge technologies; a South African company was also involved.[34] Even more disturbing, Khan's network evidently sold the design of a workable nuclear weapon to Libya, reportedly offered to provide a design to Iraq in 1990, and possibly made similar offers to other nations.[35]

The support effort for the Libyan nuclear program was likely the most ambitious and elaborate activity undertaken by Khan's network. The Libyan purchases alone are estimated to have netted the network about $100 million; the support for Libya was almost on a turnkey basis, proposing to provide Libya with a workable centrifuge enrichment plant.[36] There is nothing to prevent a European engineering consultant from offering services to a Dubai-based engineering company or a Malaysian precision-equipment manufacturing firm, provided that the end use of the products is sufficiently well disguised to baffle intelligence and export control agencies. But how a collection of private European consultants and equipment suppliers was allowed to continue operating in support of Khan's network over many years is obviously an important inquiry.

---

34. See Michael Wines, "South African Is Charged with Making Nuclear Components," *New York Times*, September 4, 2004; Slevin, Lancaster, and Khan, "At Least 7 Nations Tied to Pakistani Ring"; and Broad, Sanger, and Bonner, "A Tale of Nuclear Proliferation." For estimates of the network's earnings, see David E. Sanger and William J. Broad, "Pakistan's Nuclear Earnings: $100 Million," *New York Times*, March 16, 2004; and Clary, "Dr. Khan's Nuclear WalMart."

35. The warhead is thought to be based on a design tested by the Chinese and later provided to Pakistan in the 1980s. See John Pike, "Pakistan Nuclear Weapons," *GlobalSecurity.com*, http://www.globalsecurity.org/wmd/world/pakistan/nuke.htm. See also William J. Broad, "Libya's A-Bomb Blueprints Reveal New Tie to Pakistan," *New York Times*, February 9, 2004; "Libyan Inspections Find Evidence of Collaboration with Egypt," *World Tribune.com*, March 29, 2004, http://216.26.163.62/2004/me_egypt_03_29.html. The possibility that a package of centrifuge technology, uranium hexafluoride, and nuclear warhead designs was provided by the Pakistani network to the DPRK, citing a CIA assessment, is reported in David E. Sanger, "U.S. Widens View of Pakistan Link to Korean Arms," *New York Times*, March 14, 2004. According to that assessment, a similar package was reportedly sold by Dr. Khan's network to Libya for $60 million.

36. The scope of the Libyan nuclear and chemical programs is discussed in Mark Huband, Roula Khalaf, and Stephen Fidler, "Libya Nuclear Deal Exposes Black Market," *Financial Times*, January 21, 2004; Raymond Bonner and Craig Smith, "Pakistani Said to Have Given Libya Uranium," *New York Times*, February 21, 2004; Judith Miller, "Libya Discloses Production of 23 Tons of Mustard Gas," *New York Times*, March 6, 2004; and George Jahn, "Japan Company Sold Atomic Plant to Libya," *Guardian*, March 12, 2004. Reportedly, in February 2001 the DPRK transferred 1.7 tons of uranium hexafluoride to Libya in support of the uranium centrifuges provided by the Khan network. See David E. Sanger and William J. Broad, "Evidence Is Cited Linking Koreans to Libya Uranium," *New York Times*, May 23, 2004.

IRAN AND PAKISTAN

Iran has been a party to the NPT since 1970, but in 1996 congressional testimony, Director of Central Intelligence John Deutch stated: "We judge that Iran is actively pursuing an indigenous nuclear weapons capability. . . . Specifically, Iran is attempting to develop the capability to produce both plutonium and highly enriched uranium."[37] In August 2002 the media reported the existence of a pilot uranium enrichment centrifuge plant in Natanz; in February 2003 Iran informed the IAEA director general of work on two enrichment facilities at Natanz, a pilot plant nearing completion and a commercial-scale fuel enrichment plant under construction.[38] Iran stated that more than 100 of the 1,000 planned centrifuge casings had been installed at the pilot plant. The commercial enrichment facility was described as being planned to contain more than 50,000 centrifuges, with installation beginning in early 2005.[39] In June 2003 Iran introduced gaseous uranium hexafluoride into the first centrifuge for testing purposes, and in August 2003 a ten-machine small cascade started test operations.[40] Reportedly, a French government document provided to the Nuclear Suppliers Group (NSG) in May 2003 concluded that Iran was concealing a military program within its civilian nuclear program, stating that "Iran appears ready to develop nuclear weapons within a few years."[41] The Iranian foreign ministry has denied that Iran is concealing a nuclear weapons program.[42]

According to unnamed Western intelligence sources cited in January 2003, design information and component parts for the pilot facility were provided to Iran by Pakistan,[43] possibly with support from other states.[44] A.Q. Khan's pri-

37. CIA Director John Deutch, 1996 congressional testimony, quoted in "Iran" (Washington, D.C.: Carnegie Endowment for International Peace, n.d.), http://www.ceip.org/programs/npp/iran.htm.
38. Mohamed ElBaradei, "Implementation of the NPT Safeguards Agreement in the Islamic Republic of Iran," report by the director general to the IAEA board of governors, GOV/2003/40, Vienna, Austria, June 6, 2003, p. 2.
39. Ibid., p. 6.
40. Mohamed ElBaradei, "Implementation of the NPT Safeguards Agreement in the Islamic Republic of Iran," IAEA Report GOV/2003/63, Vienna, Austria, August 26, 2003, p. 7.
41. Reported by Frantz, "Iran Closes In on Ability to Build a Nuclear Bomb."
42. Iranian foreign ministry spokesman Hamid Reza Asefi has called these allegations "poisonous and disdainful rumors" spread by the United States. Quoted in ibid.
43. Mark Hibbs, "Pakistan Believed Design Data Source for Centrifuges to Be Built by Iran," *Platts Nuclear Fuel*, January 20, 2003, pp. 1, 14–16.
44. See Joby Warrick and Glenn Kessler, "Iran's Nuclear Program Speeds Ahead," *Washington Post*, March 10, 2003; and David Albright and Corey Hinderstein, "Furor over Fuel," *Bulletin of the Atomic Scientists*, Vol. 60, No. 3 (May/June 2003), pp. 12–15.

vate sector associate, B.S.A. Tahir, has admitted to selling two containers of surplus Pakistani centrifuge equipment to Iran in 1994 and 1995 for a payment of $3 million.[45] These shipments and other components purchased abroad or manufactured in Iran reportedly allowed the Iranians to assemble 500 operable P-1 centrifuges by 1995.[46]

The Iranian government reported the existence of an enrichment test-bed facility in the Kalaye Electric Company's workshop in February 2003, but it refused permission for environmental sampling at the site until August 2003, when significant modifications to site facilities were noted.[47] IAEA inspectors found traces of HEU at the Natanz plant in June 2003 and in the Kalaye workshop in September 2003. Iranian officials have stated that these traces had been on the equipment when it was purchased from another country, thus denying the production of HEU at the plants but admitting to outside help in their construction.[48] Evidence collected in Iran by the IAEA reportedly implicates Pakistan as a supplier of critical technology and parts,[49] and the IAEA is said to suspect Pakistan as the source of the 90 percent HEU found on some samples.[50] Assistance has allegedly also been obtained from other nations, reportedly including China, the DPRK, and Russia.[51] The IAEA has identified two other Iranian facilities engaged in development work on P-2 centrifuges; in March 2004 the Iranian military acknowledged having produced P-1 type centrifuges in a facility located at the Doshen-Tappen air base near Tehran.[52]

The scope of the P-2 centrifuge program may be larger than the Iranians

---

45. Polis Diraja Malaysia, "Press Release by Inspector General of Police"; and Bonner, "Salesman on Nuclear Circuit Casts Blurry Corporate Shadow."
46. Albright and Hinderstein, "The Centrifuge Connection."
47. ElBaradei, "Implementation of the NPT Safeguards Agreement in the Islamic Republic of Iran," IAEA Report GOV/2003/63, pp. 6–8.
48. Felicity Barringer, "Traces of Enriched Uranium Are Reportedly Found in Iran," *New York Times*, August 27, 2003; and Joby Warrick, "Iran Admits Foreign Help on Nuclear Facility; U.N. Agency's Data Point to Pakistan as the Source," *Washington Post*, August 27, 2003.
49. Warrick, "Iran Admits Foreign Help on Nuclear Facility."
50. Joby Warrick, "Nuclear Program in Iran Tied to Pakistan," *Washington Post*, December 21, 2003; and Craig S. Smith, "Alarm Raised over Quality of Uranium Found in Iran," *New York Times*, March 11, 2004.
51. According to an unnamed non-U.S. intelligence officer and an unnamed former Iranian intelligence officer, the DPRK is providing help to Iran on nuclear warhead design. See Frantz, "Iran Closes In on Ability to Build a Nuclear Bomb." For claims of other nations' participation in the Iranian program, see Glen Kessler, "Group Alleges New Nuclear Site in Iran," *Washington Post*, February 20, 2003; and Leonard S. Spector, "Iran's Secret Quest for the Bomb," *YaleGlobal Online*, May 16, 2003, http://yaleglobal.yale.edu/article.print?id=1624.
52. "IAEA Inspectors Find Centrifuge Equipment at Iranian Air Base," NTI Global Security Newswire, February 19, 2004; and "Iran Talks Quiet in Vienna, but High-Grade Uranium Reportedly Found," NTI Global Security Newswire, March 11, 2004.

originally reported. Iranian representatives have apparently inquired through European middlemen about purchasing "tens of thousands" of magnets for P-2 centrifuges. A centrifuge cascade of this size would be enough to produce several warheads' worth of HEU a year.[53]

Two other enrichment facilities are alleged to have begun operations in 2000 near the villages of Lashkar-Abd and Ramandeh, about 40 kilometers west of Tehran.[54] The Lashkar-Abd site was found by the IAEA to contain an active laser program that could be used for uranium enrichment.[55]

Another element of the Iranian nuclear program is a planned heavy-water reactor and its ancillary facilities in Arak, a city close to Esfahan. Iran declared to the IAEA in May 2003 its intention to build a 40 MW(th) heavy-water moderated and cooled, and natural-uranium fueled, Iran Nuclear Research Reactor (IR-40). The stated purpose of that reactor is radioisotopes production, as well as reactor research development and training.[56] A radioisotopes production facility referred to as the Molybdenum, Iodine, and Xenon facility is currently in operation at the Tehran nuclear research center.[57] There is a heavy-water production plant in Khondab, near the Arak site. A related facility is Iran's fuel-manufacturing plant in Esfahan, which will fabricate the fuel elements for the IR-40 and perhaps ultimately for the Bushehr nuclear power plant; construction began in 2003.[58]

The Iranian nuclear program is technologically broad based, includes redundant facilities, and is well dispersed across many different sites. The latter attribute is a particular advantage of a centrifuge enrichment–based program for any country pursuing a covert capability. In contrast to plutonium production reactors, centrifuge facilities can be built as small-scale distributed facilities that are especially difficult to detect. It is the associated conversion facilities at

53. Louis Charbonneau, "UN Sees Signs of Massive Iran Nuke Plans—Diplomats," Reuters, June 10, 2004; Mohamed ElBaradei, "Implementation of the NPT Safeguards Agreement in the Islamic Republic of Iran," IAEA Report GOV/2004/34, Vienna, Austria, June 1, 2004.
54. Sheryl Gay Stolberg, "Group Says Iran Has 2 Undisclosed Nuclear Laboratories," *New York Times*, May 27, 2003.
55. ElBaradei, "Implementation of the NPT Safeguards," GOV/2003/63, p. 8.
56. "Iran Set to Announce Work on Heavy Water Reactor; Nuclear Inspections Timetable Set," NTI Global Security Newswire, April 9, 2004.
57. ElBaradei, "Implementation of the NPT Safeguards," GOV/2003/40, pp. 5–7.
58. Since a heavy-water reactor operates with natural uranium fuel, plutonium can be produced without a uranium enrichment facility. India and Israel based their nuclear weapons programs on such reactors. A description of the Iranian facilities may be found in ElBaradei, "Implementation of the NPT Safeguards," GOV/2003/40, pp. 5–8; and GOV/2003/71, November 10, 2003, "Heavy Water Reactor Programme" section.

the front and back ends of the enrichment process, required to produce gaseous uranium hexafluoride or metallic uranium, respectively, that are more difficult to conceal.

The IAEA board of governors at its September 2003 annual meeting set a deadline of October 31, 2003, for Iran to provide extensive additional information on its nuclear activities and to suspend all further uranium enrichment–related activities.[59] In October 2003 Iran promised to freeze all uranium enrichment and reprocessing activities, provide full information to the IAEA, and open all requested facilities to IAEA inspectors; in December 2003 it signed the Additional Protocol to the NPT that strengthens IAEA inspection rights.[60] But Iran's compliance was grudging and characterized by attempts to limit the scope of the agreement and threats to cancel it. Indeed, in June 2004 Iran announced that it would resume centrifuge production in response to an IAEA resolution critical of its cooperation with the agency.[61]

MISSILE AND URANIUM PROLIFERATION RINGS

Iran's missile program has also received help from China, the DPRK, and Russia.[62] Additional support has been obtained from companies in Taiwan, Macedonia, and Belarus, according to U.S. Undersecretary of State John Bolton.[63] Israeli sources have claimed that a follow-on missiles-for-centrifuges technical exchange barter deal was struck between Pyongyang and Tehran.[64] Under this putative arrangement, in exchange for Iranian assistance with uranium enrich-

59. Joby Warrick, "Iran Given Deadline to Lay Bare Nuclear Program," *Washington Post*, September 13, 2003.
60. Christine Hauser and Nazila Fathi, "Iran Signs Pact Allowing Inspections of Its Nuclear Sites," *New York Times*, December 18, 2003; and ElBaradei "Implementation of the NPT Safeguards," GOV/2004/11, sec. B.5, p. 10.
61. Dafna Linzer, "Iran Says It Will Renew Nuclear Efforts," *Washington Post*, June 25, 2004.
62. Joseph Cirincione, with Jon Wolfsthal and Miriam Rajkumar, *Deadly Arsenals: Tracking Weapons of Mass Destruction* (Washington, D.C.: Carnegie Endowment for International Peace, 2002), pp. 262–264; Donald H. Rumsfeld, Barry M. Blechman, Lee Butler, Richard L. Garwin, William R. Graham, William Schneider, Larry D. Welch, Paul D. Wolfowitz, and R. James Woolsey, "Executive Summary of the Report of the Commission to Assess the Ballistic Missile Threat to the United States," July 15, 1998, http://www.fas.org/irp/threat/bm-threat.htm.
63. John R. Bolton, "Iran's Continuing Pursuit of Weapons of Mass Destruction," testimony before the U.S. House of Representatives, International Relations Committee, Subcommittee on the Middle East and Central Asia, 108th Cong., 2d sess., June 24, 2004.
64. See Ze'ev Schiff, "North Korea Got Nuclear Know-How from Iran," *Ha'aretz English Edition*, November 21, 2002; and Ze'ev Schiff, "Weapons of Mass Destruction and the Middle East: The View from Israel" (Houston, Tex.: James A. Baker III Institute for Public Policy, Rice University, March 2003).

ment, the DPRK provided Iran with engines for the Nodong missiles (the precursors of the Iranian Shahab-3 missile) and worked out Shahab-3 manufacturing problems in Iran. The Shahab-3 successfully completed its test program in July 2003, and is thought to be able to carry a 1,000-kilogram payload for 1,500 kilometers.[65]

The DPRK has proved willing to sell its missile technologies worldwide. Because the DPRK and its customers are not members of the MTCR, these sales are not in violation of any agreement. The DPRK network of missile sales can be pictured as the hub and spokes of a wheel, with the DPRK at the center. DPRK missile sales to Pakistan and Iran correspond to spokes in this wheel. The DPRK has also sold missiles to Egypt, Iraq, Libya, Syria, and Yemen, and approached other nations.[66] It is a reminder of the importance of export controls to recall that the entire DPRK missile development and export program was initiated in the late 1970s, when the DPRK purchased several Soviet-supplied Scud-B missiles from Egypt and then proceeded to reverse engineer and further develop them.[67]

An analogous group of countries that trade among themselves in uranium centrifuge enrichment technologies appears to have evolved during the 1990s, centered on Pakistan. China was the major historical supporter of the Pakistani nuclear program, putatively providing Pakistan with a complete design of one of its early uranium nuclear warheads; sufficient quantities of HEU for two such weapons; short-range ballistic missiles and construction blueprints; assistance in developing a medium-range missile; support in developing second-generation uranium enrichment centrifuges, including the provision of 5,000 ring magnets in 1994–95; and a 40 MW(th) heavy-water plutonium and tritium production reactor located at Khushab.[68] Smuggling from a number of Western nations, and in particular the acquisition of an entire plant for converting uranium powder to uranium hexafluoride from West Germany between 1977 and

65. Barringer, "Traces of Enriched Uranium Are Reportedly Found in Iran."
66. Cirincione, with Wolfsthal and Rajkumar, *Deadly Arsenals,* pp. 250–251. DPRK offers of missile sales to Myanmar and Nigeria are reported in "Intelligence Officials Suspect North Korean WMD Exports to Myanmar," NTI Global Security Newswire, November 18, 2003; and Nicholas Kralev, "North Korea Offers Nigeria Missile Deal," *Washington Times,* January 29, 2004.
67. Cirincione, with Wolfsthal and Rajkumar, *Deadly Arsenals,* pp. 250–251. See also Federation of American Scientists, Weapons of Mass Destruction—WMD around the World—North Korea Missiles—Hwasong 5/SCUD B, http://www.fas.org/nuke/guide/dprk/missile/hwasong-5.htm.
68. Cirincione, with Wolfsthal and Rajkumar, *Deadly Arsenals,* pp. 148–150, 152, 212–215. China's supply of HEU to Pakistan has been called unconfirmed by one unnamed U.S. official. See Albright and Hibbs, "Pakistan's Bomb."

1980, also played an important role in the development of Pakistan's nuclear program.[69]

Links among these missile and uranium enrichment technology rings accelerate technology transfer within each ring; reduce the total development cost; and if not disrupted, potentially shorten the time period needed for the successful development of the technology. Dating the origin of the DPRK gas centrifuge program is difficult; an unclassified CIA estimate suggests that North Korea began developing this program in 2000 and that its HEU production could be fully operational by mid-decade; this suggests that the DPRK was on course to halve the development time required in other third world states.[70] Pakistan's program, for example, was launched in 1972, was expedited by A.Q. Khan's arrival from the Urenco plant in the Netherlands in 1975, and only in 1985–86 seems to have begun producing HEU.[71] Similarly, foreign assistance has telescoped the timescale for ballistic missile development and production.[72] Obviously, obtaining the blueprints for a working HEU warhead could also greatly reduce the time required to complete a nuclear weapons program. Nuclear and missile proliferation rings could provide a package of uranium enrichment technology, warhead design, and missile delivery system, thereby potentially reducing the time needed to achieve an integrated weapons system. The relationships between the DPRK and Khan networks show the shifting roles that ring members may play, with the DPRK acting on different occasions as a buyer, seller, and supplier to mutual partners.

WHY PROLIFERATE?

Determining the motives that drive nuclear proliferation is difficult, with reasons of national security, national prestige, organizational politics, international pressure, and others all playing a role.[73] Even in the case of the South African nuclear program, where the trajectory of the construction and destruction of its six-warhead nuclear stockpile is known, and dozens of interviews with nuclear policymakers have been undertaken, it is difficult to determine

---

69. Spector and Smith, *Nuclear Ambitions*, p. 91. Uranium hexafluoride is the gaseous form of uranium needed for uranium centrifuge enrichment.
70. See untitled CIA estimate for Congress, November 19, 2002, http://www.fas.org/nuke/guide/dprk/nuke/cia111902.html.
71. Cirincione, with Wolfsthal and Rajkumar, *Deadly Arsenals*, pp. 210–211.
72. Duncan Lennox, "Co-operation Boosts Missile Proliferation," *Jane's Intelligence Review*, January 2002, pp. 39–41; and Rumsfeld et al., "Executive Summary of the Report of the Commission to Assess the Ballistic Missile Threat to the United States."
73. Sagan, "Why Do States Build Nuclear Weapons?"

the relative importance of various motivating factors.[74] Case studies for a number of countries, however, suggest that security concerns provide an especially important motive for pursuing the nuclear option.[75]

Here our concern is more specific: we are interested in measures that could help prevent, and therefore in the motives that might help foster, second-tier proliferation. Why did the Pakistani Khan network provide assistance to the DPRK and, evidently, Iranian, Libyan, and other nuclear programs? What calculations were being made? These questions too are hard to answer; it is difficult enough on the basis of open sources, largely relying on unnamed officials who may be pursuing their own agendas, to sketch what physically has occurred in these exchanges. Going from these already sketchy results to conclusions about motivations is especially challenging. Moreover, the extent to which certain proliferators should be seen as unitary actors is unclear. The authority of successive Pakistani heads of government, for example, has varied vis-à-vis the Pakistani military, intelligence, and nuclear bureaucracies.[76] (Yet cooperation with other nations in centrifuge enrichment has evidently been carried out under three Pakistani governments.) Officials in President Bill Clinton's administration were reportedly concerned "about whether the Pakistani government was sufficiently in control of its nuclear labs and certain nuclear scientists."[77] The rivalry between the KRL and the Pakistani Atomic Energy Commission (PAEC) may also have played a significant role in the nuclear and missile programs' development trajectories in Pakistan.[78] Given the gravity of the Pakistan-DPRK exchanges, however, including decisions regarding the acquisition of particular nuclear-strike systems, it would seem surprising if Khan and the KRL were acting independent of higher authorities, although the effect of the covert nature of the Pakistani nuclear weapons

---

74. Liberman, "The Rise and Fall of the South African Bomb"; and Helen E. Purkitt and Stephen F. Burgess with reply by Peter Liberman, "Correspondence: South Africa's Nuclear Decisions," *International Security*, Vol. 27, No. 1 (Summer 2002), pp. 186–194.
75. See, for example, Liberman, "The Rise and Fall of the South African Bomb"; Perkovich, *India's Nuclear Bomb*, pp. 446–455; and Perkovich, "Dealing with Iran's Nuclear Challenge."
76. For a discussion of this issue during the 1970s and 1980s, see Spector and Smith, *Nuclear Ambitions*, pp. 89–112.
77. Unnamed Clinton administration official, quoted in Dan Stober and Daniel Sneider, "Bush Knew About North Korea's Nuclear Program for More Than a Year," *San Jose Mercury News*, October 25, 2002.
78. Relations between Khan's KRL and the PAEC in the context of the Pakistani weapons program are discussed in Simon Henderson, "Pakistan's Nuclear Proliferation and U.S. Policy," Policy Watch No. 826 (Washington, D.C.: Washington Institute for Near East Policy, January 12, 2004); and Pervez Hoodbhoy, "Pakistan: Inside the Nuclear Closet," *Open Democracy*, March 3, 2004, http://www.opendemocracy.net/debates/article-2-95-1767.jsp.

progam and the role and authority of civilian government remain less clear.[79] Understanding how Khan obtained the warhead design he evidently shared with Libya and possibly others might shed light on these issues, although there are objections to both end-member scenarios—deep Pakistani government involvement and Khan as an independent "rogue actor"—that have been suggested.[80]

Pakistani Prime Minister Zulfikar Ali Bhutto appears to have decided to pursue nuclear weapons development in the year after Pakistan's devastating loss in the 1971 Indo-Pakistani war.[81] Pakistan's relationship with the DPRK may have been driven by a desire to secure appropriate nuclear weapons delivery systems.[82] In the mid-1980s the United States provided forty F-16 aircraft to Pakistan. With appropriate modifications, these aircraft could serve as nuclear delivery vehicles, though unlike ballistic missiles they are vulnerable to air defenses. In 1985, however, the U.S. Congress passed the Pressler amendment to the Foreign Assistance Act, requiring the president to certify annually "that Pakistan does not possess a nuclear explosive device."[83] Presidents Ronald Reagan and George H. W. Bush made these annual certifications to Congress, but with increasing discomfort and caveats in successive years. In 1989 the Soviet army completed its withdrawal from Afghanistan. In October 1990 the Pressler amendment was finally invoked, terminating most military aid to Islamabad, including the transfer of additional F-16s that were on order. In 1989 Pakistan, through PAEC connections, had agreed with China to buy thirty-four solid-fueled M-11 ballistic missiles having a 300-kilometer range with a 500-kilogram payload. By the early 1990s, however, Beijing was under increasing U.S. pressure to comply with the MTCR restrictions on missile transfers,[84] and Pakistan evidently diversified its missile suppliers, apparently

---

79. The hypothesis that Khan was acting on his own is criticized by Kampani, "Second Tier Proliferation"; and in IISS, "Pakistan and North Korea." Kampani also discusses the bureaucratic rivalry between the KRL and the PAEC, and its possible effects. The U.S. State Department determined that DPRK-Pakistani cooperation in missile technology violated the MTCR and imposed sanctions on the KRL and the DPRK's Ch'anggwang Trading Company.

80. Clary, "Dr. Khan's Nuclear WalMart"; and Sharon Squassoni "Closing Pandora's Box: Pakistan's Role in Nuclear Proliferation," *Arms Control Today*, Vol. 34, No. 3 (April 2004), pp. 8–13.

81. Spector and Smith, *Nuclear Ambitions*, p. 90.

82. For details, see ibid., pp. 107–112; Cirincione, with Wolfsthal and Rajkumar, *Deadly Arsenals*, pp. 207–216; Kampani, "Second Tier Proliferation"; and IISS, "Pakistan and North Korea."

83. The texts of the 1985 Pressler amendment, as well as the 1976 Symington and Glenn amendments, are given in the appendices to Richard N. Haass and Morton H. Halperin, *After the Tests: U.S. Policy toward India and Pakistan* (New York: Council on Foreign Relations, 1998).

84. Cirincione, with Wolfsthal and Rajkumar, *Deadly Arsenals*, p. 152; and Dinshaw Mistry, "Beyond the MTCR: Building a Comprehensive Regime to Contain Ballistic Missile Proliferation," *International Security*, Vol. 27, No. 4 (Spring 2003), pp. 119–149.

negotiating the deal with the DPRK for liquid-fueled Nodong missiles having a range of 1,000–1,300 kilometers with a payload of 700–1,000 kilograms. This permitted Pakistan to threaten a much larger set of targets deeper in India than was possible with the M-11. Finally, there has been speculation of cooperation between Pakistan and the DPRK involving the use of DPRK plutonium in the fifth Pakistani nuclear test in May 1998.[85]

Pakistan's decision to share centrifuge enrichment technology with the DPRK may have been driven by a perceived strategic need to acquire a less vulnerable longer-range nuclear warhead delivery system with which to hold Indian targets at risk, as well perhaps as by internal bureaucratic infighting. Pakistan's interests in assisting the Iranian nuclear program would be much harder to understand, although one analyst has speculated that this help may have been a way to reassure Tehran that Islamabad's nuclear capabilities were directed against India or to manage tensions over Afghanistan.[86] In this scenario, the assistance would represent a peculiar kind of negative security assurance. It has also been suggested that Pakistan was attempting either to prevent the emergence of improved Indian-Iranian relations or to foster a common front against the Russian presence in Afghanistan.[87]

Determining the intentions of the DPRK is notoriously daunting, but its motives in the centrifuge-missile exchange with Pakistan would seem easier to discern. The acquisition of uranium centrifuge technology provided the DPRK with an alternative pathway to producing nuclear weapons after its plutonium program had attracted world attention. The deal would have been reached sometime between 1993 and 1997.[88] The DPRK has stated that it will seek a negotiated settlement over its nuclear programs on three conditions: "Firstly, if the U.S. recognizes the DPRK's sovereignty, secondly, if it assures the DPRK of non-aggression and thirdly, if the U.S. does not hinder the economic development of the DPRK."[89] The DPRK nuclear program may serve as either an ultimate guarantor of the regime or as a bargaining chip, but even in the latter role its utility is putatively as a security guarantee.

Iranian leaders' motivations for pursuing nuclear weapons are not easily ac-

85. See David E. Sanger and William J. Broad, "Pakistan May Have Aided North Korea A-Test," *New York Times,* February 27, 2004; and Paul Watson and Mubashir Zaidi, "Death of N. Korean" Woman Offers Clues to Pakistani Nuclear Deals," *Los Angeles Times,* March 1, 2004.
86. Perkovich, "Dealing with Iran's Nuclear Challenge."
87. Sultan Shahin, "Iran, Nukes, and the South Asian Puzzle," *Asia Times,* September 8, 2003.
88. Pinkston, "When Did WMD Deals between Pyongyang and Islamabad Begin?" But see CIA estimate that the DPRK began developing its centrifuge-based enrichment program in 2000. Untitled CIA estimate for Congress, November 19, 2002.
89. DPRK foreign ministry statement, October 25, 2002, http://www.kcna.co.jp/index-e.htm.

cessible to outsiders. It is not even clear who the decisionmakers are, although a small group with little technological or strategic background has been suggested.[90] At least two motives seem to be involved: security concerns vis-à-vis Israel, the United States, and possibly Pakistan (and, in the past, Iraq and the Pakistani-supported Taliban); and nationalism and nationalist-fueled resentment of other nations' perceived hypocrisy on the nuclear issue.[91]

Buttressing the Existing Nonproliferation Regime

The previous section sketched the rise in second-tier proliferation in the form of what we have dubbed "proliferation rings." First-tier proliferation has also played an important role in the establishment of nuclear weapons capabilities among proliferators, including the rings members themselves. We are entering a period, however, in which more states in the developing world will acquire sufficient knowledge and technological and manufacturing capabilities to allow them to disconnect from first-tier suppliers and fill technological gaps in their nuclear and missile programs by trading among themselves. Opportunities for cooperative development and even "latent proliferation by proxy" (one country participating in proliferation ring activities on behalf of another country that wishes to hide its true intentions) will be enhanced. Moreover, increases in secondary proliferation in turn increase the risk of proliferation to terrorist groups.

A critical issue is the extent to which the discovery of second-tier proliferation networks represents the unraveling of a uniquely ambitious set of proliferation relationships that are currently being terminated, or whether such discoveries should instead be thought of as harbingers of what is to come, driven by continuing regional instabilities and abetted by the spread of technological know-how throughout the world. If indeed the nuclear warhead plans revealed in Libya were "copies of copies of copies" as one analyst claims,[92] it

---

90. Perkovich, "Dealing with Iran's Nuclear Challenge."
91. Ibid.; Perkovich assesses the scant evidence available for the different motives fueling Iran's nuclear demand. For a discussion of the utility of Iranian nuclear weapons in meeting its national security needs, see Sharam Chubin, "Iran's Strategic Environment and Nuclear Weapons," in Geoffrey Kemp, ed., *Iran's Nuclear Weapons Options: Issues and Analysis* (Washington, D.C.: Nixon Center, 2001), pp. 17–34. For a discussion of the public debate over nuclear weapons within Iran, see Farideh Farhi, "To Have or Not to Have: Iran's Domestic Debate on Nuclear Options," in ibid., pp. 45–63. See also "Iran's Nuclear Ambitions: Full Steam Ahead?" *IISS Strategic Comments,* Vol. 9, No. 2 (March 2003).
92. Clary, "Dr. Khan's Nuclear WalMart."

would be foolish to think that even rolling up the programs of all the countries known so far to have directly traded with Pakistan would eliminate the possibility that copies of the uranium implosion warhead design are currently floating around the world.[93] The operational answer is clear: the international community must act as if the proliferation rings described here are the shape of the future, while taking steps to increase the chances that history will conclude that these particular rings were a final challenge to nonproliferation due to a few last hard cases. The current networks must be shut down, and measures should be put in place to prevent or detect their rise elsewhere.

In the following sections, we consider various incremental approaches to improving the nonproliferation regime and assess the extent to which they respond to the proliferation rings issue.

COOPERATIVE THREAT REDUCTION

Steps taken to prevent latent, first-tier, or second-tier proliferation will be moot if nuclear weapons or nuclear weapons–usable material may be stolen and directly provided to either a state or terrorist program. To buttress the nuclear nonproliferation regime, therefore, member states must first prevent it from being circumvented through theft and smuggling. The IAEA reportedly traced at least some of the 36 percent–enriched HEU discovered on centrifuges in Iran to Russia.[94] If true, then nuclear smuggling and second-tier proliferation may have already played synergistic roles.

Stealing and smuggling a complete warhead from a state program would seem far more difficult, but cannot be ruled out.[95] Stealing nuclear explosive material in the form of plutonium or HEU is a threat for which there are already anecdotal examples; at least kilogram quantities of HEU (including 90

---

93. For example, the IAEA is reportedly trying to determine whether Egypt may have received the Pakistani nuclear warhead designs from Libya. See "Libyan Inspectors Find Evidence of Collaboration with Egypt," *World Tribune.com,* March 29, 2004.

94. William J. Broad, "Uranium Traveled to Iran Via Russia, Inspectors Find," *New York Times,* February 28, 2004.

95. See Bunn, Wier, and Holdren, *Controlling Nuclear Warheads and Materials,* p. 70. Evaluation of the security of warheads against insider and outsider threats in the Pakistani or Indian programs is more difficult. Pakistani Gen. Khalid Kidwai stated in January 2002 that Pakistani warheads do not have permissive action links (or PALs, devices designed to prevent the explosion of the warhead by an unauthorized user), although the bombs are kept in a disassembled state. See Paolo Cotta-Ramusino and Maurizio Martellini, *Nuclear Safety, Nuclear Stability, and Nuclear Strategy in Pakistan* (Como, Italy: Landau Network, Centro Volta, February 11, 2002), http://lxmi.mi.infn.it/~landnet/Doc/pakistan.pdf. Garwin and Charpak state that PALs on a stolen weapon could eventually be overcome, but this would be challenging for a nonstate group or unsophisticated state program. Garwin and Charpak, *Megawatts and Megatons,* p. 342.

percent HEU, ideal for making the lowest-mass uranium warheads) have been stolen from Russian facilities in the past.[96] By the end of fiscal year 2002, neither comprehensive nor even interim, rapid security upgrades had been completed for 63 percent of the 600 metric tons of vulnerable weapons-usable nuclear material outside of Russian warheads.[97] A terrorist group or unsophisticated state program could conceivably produce a working fission warhead with either stolen weapons-grade plutonium or HEU, but the former would prove extremely challenging because plutonium warheads require spherical explosive compression with precise timing.[98] Assembling a gun-type HEU weapon would be less demanding.[99] If there is a spherical implosion design available to terrorists or proliferators, it would likely be the Chinese/Pakistani uranium-based design, once again indicating that HEU is of the greatest concern.

The first line of defense is therefore to protect and deter against theft, and detect it should it occur. This must be done globally, given that substantial quantities of poorly safeguarded HEU exist outside the FSU.[100] In this context, CTR programs are central. If fully implemented, the June 2002 "10 plus 10 over 10" agreement reached by the G-8 at the Kananaskis summit in Canada should increase available funding, distribute the total funding more equitably (even while committing the United States to do more), and ensure that the G-8 will continue to address this problem throughout the coming decade.[101] If these

---

96. See Lyudmila Zaitseva and Kevin Hand, "Nuclear Smuggling Chains: Suppliers, Intermediaries, and End-Users," *American Behavioral Scientist*, Vol. 46, No. 6 (February 2003), p. 822; and Bunn, Wier, and Holdren, *Controlling Nuclear Warheads and Materials*, app. A.
97. Bunn, Wier, and Holdren, *Controlling Nuclear Warheads and Materials*, p. 66.
98. See Garwin and Charpak, *Megawatts and Megatons*, pp. 347–350.
99. Francesco Calogero, "The Risk of Nuclear Terrorism," paper presented to the Second Pugwash Workshop on Terrorism: Consequences of the War on Terrorism, Como, Italy, October 9–12, 2003, http://www.isodarco.it/courses/andalo04/paper/andalo04-Calogero.pdf.
100. A "global cleanout" campaign of the most vulnerable sites is required, as is the conversion of HEU research reactors worldwide to run on LEU fuel so that the number of sites where HEU can be stolen is minimized. See Bunn, Wier, and Holdren, *Controlling Nuclear Warheads and Materials*, pp. 71–72. The reactor conversion program is discussed in "Reduced Enrichment for Research and Test Reactors," n.d., http://www.nnsa.doe.gov/na-20/rertr.shtml. On May 26, 2004, U.S. Department of Energy Secretary Spencer Abraham during a visit to the IAEA announced the launch of a Global Threat Reduction Initiative to expedite these goals. See http://www.energy.gov/ engine/ content.do?BT_CODE=PR_SPEECHES.
101. The agreement is formally called the Global Partnership against the Spread of Weapons and Materials of Mass Destruction. Under 10 plus 10 over 10, U.S. commitments of $10 billion for nonproliferation cooperation programs with Russia and other former Soviet states will be matched by $10 billion from the other G-8 nations, spread over ten years. See "The G8 Global Partnership against the Spread of Weapons and Materials of Mass Destruction," statement by the Group of Eight leaders, Kananaskis, Canada, June 27, 2002, http://www.state.gov/e/eb/rls/othr/11514

continuing and expanded efforts in CTR are successful, the danger posed by poorly secured fissile material stocks should recede over time, meaning that other measures are not moot.

THE IAEA ADDITIONAL PROTOCOL

Under article 3 of the NPT, the IAEA implements a safeguards and inspections regime intended to ensure that nonnuclear weapons states meet their treaty obligations not to use their nuclear programs to develop nuclear weapons. A measure taken to strengthen the safeguards regime, the so-called Additional Protocol, should make latent proliferation by this route more difficult, and also make it more difficult for countries to build illegal programs through second-tier proliferation.

Starting in 1972, the IAEA safeguards regime under article 3 was codified by IAEA information circular 153 (INFCIRC/153), whose stated goal was the timely detection of the diversion of significant quantities of nuclear material from permitted peaceful nuclear activities to nuclear weapons programs.[102] But monitoring and inspections under INFCIRC/153 were typically applied only to facilities declared by the nation being inspected. By the early 1990s, the cases of the DPRK and Iraq had shown that the INFCIRC/153 safeguards could be sidestepped through the use of covert facilities.[103] Under the INFCIRC/153 oversight regime, IAEA access to undeclared facilities for the purpose of inspections could be refused.[104] More recently, but exemplary of the limitations of INFCIRC/153, Iranian authorities refused to allow IAEA sample collection at two centrifuge enrichment sites.[105]

In reaction to the DPRK and Iraq experiences, in 1993 the IAEA embarked on a two-year project, known as Program 93 + 2, to strengthen the existing safe-

.htm. For analyses of subsequent progress, see Bunn, Wier, and Holdren, *Controlling Nuclear Warheads and Materials*, pp. 54–55.

102. IAEA, "The Structure and Content of Agreements between the Agency and States Required in Connection with the Treaty on the Non-Proliferation of Nuclear Weapons," IAEA Information Circular, INFCIRC/153 (corrected), June 1972.

103. The IAEA did, under INFCIRC/153, request a "special inspection" of the DPRK after its inspectors found reason to believe that a violation may have occurred. The DPRK declined the request. The IAEA reported this to the UN Security Council, precipitating the DPRK's threat to withdraw from the NPT and the Agreed Framework. See IAEA, "The Evolution of IAEA Safeguards," IAEA International Verification Series No. 2 (1998), pp. 21–22.

104. See Ephraim Asculai, *Verification Revisited: The Nuclear Case* (Washington, D.C.: Institute for Science and International Security, 2002), pp. 13–18.

105. "Iran: IAEA Inspectors Turned Away from Nuclear Site, Leave Iran," NTI Global Security Newswire, June 12, 2003; and Craig S. Smith "Iran Postpones a Visit by U.N. Inspectors until April," *New York Times*, March 13, 2004.

guards system. Measures considered were divided into two parts, depending on whether they could be implemented under existing IAEA authority (so-called part 1 measures) or would require additional legal authority (part 2 measures). The additional legal authority for part 2 was provided by the IAEA board of governors in 1997 in the form of an Additional Protocol, INFCIRC/540.[106] As the IAEA explains, "While the chief object of safeguards under INFCIRC/153 is to verify that declared nuclear material was not diverted, the chief object of the new measures under INFCIRC/540 is to obtain assurance that the State has no undeclared activities."[107] Under INFCIRC/540, states are required to make expanded, comprehensive declarations of all their nuclear material and nuclear-related activities; the IAEA may conduct environmental sampling wherever it has access; and the IAEA shall have access to any location to check for undeclared nuclear material or activities.[108] Acceptance of the Additional Protocol by member states is voluntary.[109]

So far, too few states have ratified the Additional Protocol, though steady progress is being made.[110] While eighty-four states plus Euratom had signed the protocol, and fifty-eight had ratified it as of June 2004 (including the United States, which ratified it in April 2004), among Middle East and Persian Gulf states the only signatories were Iran, Jordan, Kuwait, Libya, and Turkey.[111] Indeed, even though every nonnuclear weapons state signatory to the NPT is obliged under article 3 to conclude a safeguards agreement with the IAEA, some states such as Saudi Arabia have not even concluded this basic agreement—to which the Additional Protocol would need to be subsequently added.

States' slowness in ratifying the Additional Protocol goes to the heart of the

---

106. IAEA, "Model Protocol Additional to the Agreement(s) between State(s) and the International Atomic Energy Agency for the Application of Safeguards," IAEA Information Circular, INFCIRC/540 (corrected), September 1997.

107. IAEA, "The Evolution of IAEA Safeguards."

108. For a summary of both part 1 and part 2 provisions, see Ming Shih Lu, "The IAEA Strengthened International Safeguards Systems," Sixth ISODARCO Beijing Seminar on Arms Control, October–November 1998.

109. George Bunn argued that the Additional Protocol could legally have been interpreted to be compulsory for all NPT members; this argument did not prevail. See Bunn, "Inspection for Clandestine Nuclear Activities: Does the Nuclear Non-Proliferation Treaty Provide Legal Authority for the International Atomic Energy Agency's Proposals for Reform?" *Nuclear Law Bulletin*, No. 57 (June 1996), pp. 9–22.

110. For a list of signatories with dates of signature and entry into force, see "Strengthened Safeguards System: Status of Additional Protocols" (as of September 29, 2003), http://www.iaea.org/worldatom/Programmes/Safeguards/sg_protocol.shtml.

111. See Chen Zak, *Iran's Nuclear Policy and the IAEA: An Evaluation of Program 93 + 2* (Washington, D.C.: Washington Institute for Near East Policy, 2002).

bargain of the NPT. The Additional Protocol represents a greater intrusion into a country's sovereignty than does INFCIRC/153. Adherents to the Additional Protocol must provide ten-year fuel-cycle research and development plans to the IAEA, the activities and identities of persons or entities carrying out this R&D, export/import information, and descriptions of facilities. The signatories may also be subject to far more intrusive inspections. All of these are clearly negatives from the point of view of the signatory. What does it gain in return?

This question emphasizes the point that pushing for full adherence to the Additional Protocol must be accompanied by steps to ensure that states view their adherence to the protocol, or indeed to the NPT itself, as worth the price they have to pay. Multilateral demand-side inducements to this end are not necessarily inconsistent with influence the United States or others may unilaterally bring to bear to delay, stop, or roll back a particular state's nuclear program.[112] Increasingly onerous reporting and inspection requirements, as well as the prima facie inequalities of these requirements in comparison to those imposed on the nuclear weapons states (including those outside of the NPT), may be mitigated with appropriate inducements. One important inducement is that the adoption and implementation of the Additional Protocol should make countries less fearful of the nuclear ambitions of their neighbors, which in turn should make them feel more secure. This is the primary argument for the Additional Protocol given by the Bush administration,[113] which claims strong U.S. support for the NPT.[114] In the following discussion, we propose ways of linking the Additional Protocol to other measures to provide further inducements.

Effective implementation of the Additional Protocol faces budgetary obstacles. IAEA member states applied a policy of zero real growth to the IAEA from 1985 to 2003, despite an increase in its responsibilities.[115] The agency's 2004 regular budget was less than $269 million; within this, nuclear verifica-

---

112. A taxonomy of these approaches with historical examples is presented in Levite, "Never Say Never Again," pp. 76–85.
113. Statement by Deputy Assistant Secretary of State Andrew K. Semmel, alternate representative of the United States of America to the Second Session of the Preparatory Committee for the 2005 NPT Review Conference, Geneva, Switzerland, May 5, 2003, http://www.us-mission.ch/press2003/0505IAEASafe.htm.
114. The statement declares, "The United States remains firmly committed to its obligations under the NPT. We are pursuing a number of avenues that promote the goal of nuclear disarmament." Message from U.S. Secretary of State Colin Powell to the 2003 Preparatory Committee Meeting for the 2005 NPT Review Conference, quoted in John S. Wolf, "Remarks to the Second Meeting of the Preparatory Committee," Geneva, Switzerland, April 28, 2003, http://www.state.gov/t/np/rls/rm/20034.htm.
115. IAEA, "How Much Do Safeguards Cost?" n.d., http://www.iaea.org/Publications/Booklets/Safeguards2/part8.html.

tion received about $102 million, the largest single budget category. With U.S. support, the IAEA board of governors accepted a budget increase of $25 million to be phased in from 2004 to 2007.[116] Given the centrality of IAEA safeguards and inspections to the nonproliferation regime, as well as the IAEA's expanding responsibilities, it is extraordinary and self-defeating that the IAEA's budget saw no growth for so long. An underfunded IAEA risks a catch-22 of limited means available to verify safeguards compliance. A robust IAEA should be a high-priority foreign policy objective of the United States.

STRENGTHENING OF EXPORT CONTROL REGIMES

Proliferation rings have benefited from both first- and second-tier proliferation. More robust inspections following broad adoption of the Additional Protocol should help to curtail these routes. Export control regimes are examples of supply-side measures that first-tier nuclear supplier states have adopted. These regimes must be extended to capture second-tier exporters as well. Yet it is also necessary to strengthen controls on first-tier suppliers. Progress in both regards may appear to be in some tension with article 4 of the NPT, which declares the "inalienable right of all the Parties to the Treaty to develop research, production and use of nuclear energy for peaceful purposes without discrimination"; the sentence continues, however, "in conformity with articles I and II of this Treaty." (Under article 1, nuclear weapons state parties agree not to assist nonnuclear weapons state parties in acquiring nuclear weapons; under article 2, nonnuclear weapons states undertake not to receive any assistance in the manufacture of nuclear weapons or seek to build their own.) For this reason, export controls that act to ensure that nuclear weapons technology does not spread are consistent with the NPT.

The export restrictions most relevant to the NPT are those of the NSG and the MTCR.[117] The U.S. General Accounting Office (GAO) has assessed for the U.S. Congress the strengths and weaknesses of these two regimes, along with regimes for chemical and biological weapons (the Australia Group) and conventional weapons (the Wassenaar agreement), which do not so directly concern us here.[118] The GAO recommends a number of commonsense steps that we endorse: (1) improve the completeness and timeliness of members' infor-

---

116. *IAEA Programme and Budget for 2004–2005*, n.d., http://www.iaea.org/About/budget.html. For U.S. support, see Statement by Deputy Assistant Secretary of State Semmel.
117. For the current memberships and guidelines of the NSG and MTCR, see http://www.nuclearsuppliersgroup.org/ and http://www.mtcr.info/english/, respectively.
118. U.S. GAO, *Nonproliferation Strategy Needed to Strengthen Multilateral Export Control Regimes*. See also http://www.australiagroup.net/ and http://www.wassenaar.org/.

mation sharing regarding their export licensing decisions, including denials and approvals of exports; (2) decrease the length of time taken by members to adopt agreed-upon changes to control lists;[119] (3) reconcile differences in how regime members implement agreed-upon controls; and (4) ensure that new members joining regimes have effective export control systems in place at the time they become members.[120]

Item (1) in particular emphasizes how in some cases intelligence related to the actions and, by inference, intentions of some countries of concern could be improved by better capturing and sharing existing information among export control regime members. Some members have never reported any denials of export licenses. The reasons for this have not been evaluated systematically; it is possible that some countries provide "informal denials" to would-be exporters prior to formal applications for export licenses. If these are not reported, other regime members are not necessarily alerted that potential proliferators may be seeking particular items, and a chance to add to a fuller picture of those countries' actions or intentions may be lost.[121]

The MTCR should be considered an integral part of the nuclear non-proliferation regime. First, the text of the MTCR itself recognizes that restrictions on exports of missile technology "is to limit the risks of proliferation of weapons of mass destruction [WMD] (i.e., nuclear, chemical and biological weapons), by controlling transfers that could make a contribution to delivery systems (other than manned aircraft) for such weapons."[122] Ballistic missiles are enabling technologies for WMD. In fact, there is little conventional utility for a 1,500-kilometer range missile in the absence of "smart" targeting ability. Damage effectiveness calculations will favor the quest for nonconventional warheads for such vehicles. Second, the expansion of long-range missile capability is a key psychological driver for the acquisition and expansion of strategic missile defenses; yet missile defenses may serve to spur an increase in offensive delivery vehicles and warheads on the part of some nuclear weapons states. Finally, and as we have seen, missile technology has apparently been a key element in some of the swaps involved in the proliferation of nuclear

119. Ibid. This process can take as long as a year for some members.
120. CIA Director Tenet reported in 2001 that Russia did not have an effective export control system, due to weak enforcement and insufficient penalties for violations. See Central Intelligence Agency, *Unclassified Report to Congress on the Acquisition of Technology Relating to Weapons of Mass Destruction and Advanced Conventional Munitions, 1 January through 30 June 2001.*
121. U.S. General Accounting Office, *Nonproliferation Strategy Needed to Strengthen Multilateral Export Control Regimes.*
122. *Missile Technology Control Regime*, par. 1, http://projects.sipri.se/expcon/mtcrguidelines.htm.

weapons technology. For all these reasons, better control of missile technology should decrease the missile-technology driver of nuclear proliferation.

NECESSARY BUT INSUFFICIENT

While the steps endorsed or advocated so far are important, they represent incremental improvements in the current regime. But there are limits to how far incremental improvements can go, and more ambitious measures will likely need to be implemented. For example, consider improvements in the control of nuclear weapons–relevant exports under the NSG. The roles of the Malaysian firm Scomi Precision Engineering and the Turkish EKA electrical equipment company in producing centrifuge technology for shipment to Libya underscore the need to expand export controls (including controls for dual-use equipment) beyond the first-tier suppliers of the NSG, though the immediate benefits to third world states in adopting dual-use export controls may be unclear.

In some cases, the answer will be to bring additional members into the NSG. Indeed, Estonia, Lithuania, Malta, and the People's Republic of China joined the NSG in May 2004.[123] Some analysts have suggested that the NSG should be globalized, with the body moved away from consensus decisionmaking to majority rule.[124] Widening the NSG, however, could push its decisions toward the lowest common denominator, and it could prove difficult to globalize by majority vote the strengthening of export restrictions, especially for dual-use items. Even the Nuclear Exporters Committee (or Zangger Committee) was bypassed by the NSG in part because of the committee's failure to cover these items.[125] Yet as the Scomi and EKA examples demonstrate, not all exporters of relevant dual-use nuclear equipment are within countries that are members of the Zangger Committee or the NSG. (Malaysia and Turkey are members of neither.) Moreover, effective export controls need to be implemented by all three of the nuclear non-NPT states (i.e., India, Israel, and Pakistan) as well.[126]

---

123. "The NSG—Strengthening the Nuclear Non-proliferation Regime," NSG plenary meeting, Göteborg, Sweden, May 27–28, 2004, http://www.nuclearsuppliersgroup.org/PRESS/2004-05-goteborg.pdf.

124. See, for example, Michael Beck and Seema Gahlaut, "Creating a New Multilateral Export Control Regime," *Arms Control Today*, Vol. 33, No. 4 (April 2003), pp. 12–18.

125. A history of the Nuclear Exporters Committee and the NSG may be found in Leonard S. Spector and Mark G. McDonough, with Evan S. Medeiros, "Appendix D: Nuclear Supplier Organizations," in *Tracking Nuclear Proliferation: A Guide in Maps and Charts* (Washington, D.C.: Carnegie Endowment for International Peace, 1995), pp. 179–183.

126. See Anupam Srivastava and Seema Gahlaut, "Curbing Proliferation from Emerging Suppliers: Export Controls in India and Pakistan," *Arms Control Today*, Vol. 33, No. 9 (September 2003), pp. 12–16.

Bush and ElBaradei Supply-Side Proposals

The incremental approaches to improving the nonproliferation regime just described are important but not sufficient to the challenge posed by proliferation rings. More ambitious proposals were made in 2003–04 by both the Bush administration and the director general of the IAEA.

The heart of the Bush administration's approach to the nonproliferation threat has been to improve enforcement of the supply-side strictures (articles 2 and 3) of the NPT and to close what administration officials see as NPT loopholes that can allow proliferation under the guise of good standing with the treaty (article 4). The administration has not pursued global treaty-based approaches to these ends; rather it has assembled specific coalitions to pursue particular objectives according to mutually agreed criteria for which it would be challenging to gain universal acceptance. In a remarkable move, the administration has also worked through the UN Security Council to impose global nonproliferation measures via resolution. Some of its proposals are substantively similar to recommendations made by Director General ElBaradei, although his proposals are consistent with a global treaty-based approach to these issues. The administration's proposals carry the sense that progress toward the objective takes precedence over allegiance to particular approaches, especially slow ones requiring global consensus.

An important issue is the extent to which these less-than-global supply-side approaches can achieve their objectives in the long term, and whether other approaches could strengthen them or prolong their effectiveness. In the following sections, we present a chronological sketch of the Bush and ElBaradei proposals, then turn to where these proposals fall short and what else could be done.

THE PROLIFERATION SECURITY INITIATIVE

President Bush announced the Proliferation Security Initiative (PSI) in Krakow, Poland, on May 31, 2003.[127] The initiative initially brought together eleven nations to agree to practical steps to interdict shipments of missiles, chemical and biological agents, and nuclear components traveling through their national territories.[128] These countries' formal Statement of Interdiction Princi-

---

127. White House, "Remarks by the President to the People of Poland," Krakow, Poland, May 31, 2003, http://www.whitehouse.gov/news/releases/2003/05/20030531–3.html.
128. The original PSI countries are Australia, France, Germany, Italy, Japan, the Netherlands, Poland, Portugal, Spain, the United Kingdom, and the United States.

ples in September 2003 called on all states to (1) undertake such interdiction measures; (2) streamline procedures for rapid exchange of relevant information; (3) strengthen their national legal authority to accomplish these objectives; and (4) take a series of specific actions in support of interdiction efforts, including not only interdicting craft in their own territory but also to "seriously consider" providing consent to the boarding of a signatory's own flag vessels "by other states."[129] The PSI has expanded to fifteen core members, including Russia; the United States claims that more than sixty other states support the initiative.[130] The United States has also signed boarding agreements with the leading flag states, Liberia and Panama, to allow their vessels to be stopped and searched.[131]

The PSI is a supply-side measure that, unlike traditional export-control suppliers' regimes, directly addresses second-tier as well as first-tier proliferation. The success of the PSI will depend strongly on intelligence; its best-known success claimed by U.S. officials is the interdiction and seizure by German and Italian authorities of centrifuge parts aboard the BBC *China*, the German-owned ship bound for Libya that originated in Malaysia, via Dubai.[132] All the same, the PSI's limitations should be recognized: some high-consequence types of nuclear smuggling could involve small-volume packages that are either transported by means not inspected by the PSI members or that could prove very hard to detect and track; despite U.S. efforts to expand the initiative to include more members, important countries along the transfer routes may choose not to participate; intelligence is imperfect, and timely "actionable" intelligence may be scarce. The PSI is but one supply-side component in what must be a web of measures to counter proliferation, but by speaking directly to second-tier proliferation, it represents an important new step.

129. "Proliferation Security Initiative, Statement of Interdiction Principles," Paris, France, September 4, 2003.
130. The additional adherents are Canada, Norway, and Singapore. See Jofi Joseph, "The Proliferation Security Initiative: Can Interdiction Stop Proliferation?" *Arms Control Today*, Vol. 34, No. 5 (June 2004), pp. 6–13. Russia joined the PSI in May 2004. See George Jahn, "U.S. Welcomes Russia Arms Security Effort," Associated Press, June 1, 2004, http://www.ransac.org/Projects%20and %20Publications/News/Nuclear%20News/2004/612004123906PM.html#1C.
131. Flag states permit foreign-owned ships to operate under their national flag, often for reasons of lower costs or more lenient operating rules. See Wade Boese, "U.S., Panama Agree on Boarding Rules for Ships Suspected of Carrying WMD," *Arms Control Today*, Vol. 34, No. 5 (June 2004), pp. 38–39.
132. See White House, "President Announces New Measures to Counter the Threat of WMD," Fort Lesley J. McNair, National Defense University, Washington, D.C., February 11, 2004, http://www.whitehouse.gov/news/releases/2004/02/20040211-4.html.

DIRECTOR GENERAL ELBARADEI'S PROPOSALS

In October 2003, IAEA Director General ElBaradei called for a new non-proliferation framework "more suited to the threats and realities of the 21st century."[133] Criticizing the behavior of both the nuclear weapons states and the nonnuclear weapons states party to the NPT, ElBaradei focused on the dangers of latent proliferation. The director general made three proposals: (1) limit the production of separated plutonium or HEU to facilities under multilateral control; (2) convert existing HEU facilities to low-enriched uranium and deploy only new systems that are proliferation resistant; and (3) consider multinational approaches to spent fuel and radioactive waste disposal. In addition, he called for renewed attention to the Fissile Material Cutoff Treaty (FMCT). In an editorial published on February 12, 2004, in response to President Bush's speech on related topics, ElBaradei also called for greater adherence to the Additional Protocol, suggested that "no country should be allowed to withdraw" from the NPT, and urged that the export control system be universalized with the enactment of "binding, treaty-based controls."[134] The combination of these measures would make it more difficult for countries to use civilian nuclear capacity acquired under article 4 of the NPT to create a de facto nuclear weapons capability, and then withdraw from the treaty (with only three-months' notice required under the NPT's article 10) to produce them.

With respect to the challenge of proliferation rings, the implementation of ElBaradei's recommendations could increase the difficulty of constructing an illicit program, however supplied, so that the export of nuclear weapons–related material for that end would be discouraged. The dilemma is not so much one of goals as of implementation. A number of ElBaradei's recommendations would have the effect of placing further restrictions on nonnuclear weapons states and even limiting their sovereignty. A global treaty-based approach to these objectives would first have to convince such states that it was in their interest to pursue these objectives. Experience suggests that negotiating a global treaty with tough enforcement measures could take a long time. Alternatively, these objectives could be sought through other means. This has been the approach of the Bush administration.

---

133. Mohamed ElBaradei, "Towards a Safer World," *Economist*, October 16, 2003, pp. 48–50.
134. Mohamed ElBaradei, "Saving Ourselves from Self-Destruction," *New York Times*, February 12, 2004.

PRESIDENT BUSH'S SEVEN PROPOSALS

In his speech at the National Defense University on February 11, 2004, President Bush announced seven proposals "to strengthen the world's efforts to stop the spread of deadly weapons."[135] These are (1) expansion of the PSI; (2) quick passage by the UN Security Council of a U.S. proposal from fall 2003 "requiring all states to criminalize proliferation, enact strict export controls, and secure all sensitive materials within their borders"; (3) broadening of CTR beyond the FSU; (4) NSG denial of enrichment and reprocessing equipment and technologies "to any state that does not already possess full-scale, functioning enrichment and reprocessing plants," while ensuring that states renouncing enrichment and reprocessing have reliable access at reasonable cost to civilian reactor fuel; (5) denial of civilian nuclear reactor–program equipment to states that have not signed the Additional Protocol; (6) creation of a safeguards and verification committee of the IAEA board of governors; and (7) prohibition of membership on this committee or the IAEA board to any state "under investigation for proliferation violations."

These proposals cluster into several groups. Proposals (1) and (2) endeavor to prevent or interdict nuclear weapons–related shipments, and thus speak directly to the proliferation rings issue. Proposal (3) speaks to the primordial need to prevent nuclear theft. Proposals (4) and (5) parallel ElBaradei's suggestions, and if successfully implemented would hamper the ability of countries to pursue illicit nuclear programs, however supplied. Proposals (6) and (7) are less action oriented but would presumably make violations of the NPT more difficult. The proposals are striking for their lack of appeal to universally negotiated approaches. The PSI is a coalition of the willing, and nuclear suppliers' export controls would be improved through the actions of the limited-membership NSG. How to enforce a requirement that only signatories to the Additional Protocol be allowed to import civilian reactor equipment is not specified. The immediately preceding part of the speech, however, leads one to assume that this would be by NSG decision.

SECURITY COUNCIL LAWMAKING

The Bush administration's second proposal, the expansion of export controls to all countries of the world, was to be imposed by vote of the UN Security Council, rather than be the product of a negotiated treaty or agreed reinterpretation

---

135. White House, "President Announces New Measures to Counter the Threat of WMD."

of article 3 of the NPT. President Bush first proposed such a Security Council resolution in his address to the UN General Assembly on September 23, 2003.[136] A draft resolution began circulating in December 2003; subsequent negotiations among the Permanent Five led in March 2004 to a P-5-supported draft resolution that the United States and United Kingdom presented to the ten elected Security Council members. The Security Council adopted Resolution 1540 in April 2004.[137]

There are twelve points listed in Resolution 1540; of these, many "call upon" states to take certain steps, but points (1) through (3) represent Security Council lawmaking, a remarkable new approach to global enforcement of nonproliferation requirements.[138] Point (2) requires states to adopt internal legislation, announcing that the Security Council "decides also that all States . . . shall adopt and enforce appropriate effective laws which prohibit any non-State actor to manufacture, acquire, possess, develop, transport, transfer or use nuclear, chemical or biological weapons and their means of delivery." Point (3) states that the Security Council "decides" that states will "(a) develop and maintain appropriate effective measures to account for and secure" nuclear, chemical, or biological weapons and materials; "(b) develop and maintain appropriate effective physical protection measures; (c) develop and maintain appropriate effective border controls and law enforcement efforts" to prevent illicit trafficking in these materials; and "(d) establish, develop, review and maintain appropriate effective national export and trans-shipment controls over such items, including appropriate laws and regulations to control export, transit, trans-shipment and re-export" of such items along with appropriate penalties for violations. The P-5 have imposed a requirement for supply-side measures against proliferation on every other nation of the world.

Beyond the Bush and ElBaradei Responses

Both President Bush and Director General ElBaradei see the importance of confronting the challenge of latent proliferation, incrementally through the univer-

---

136. White House, "President Bush Addresses United Nations General Assembly," United Nations, New York, September 23, 2003, http://www.whitehouse.gov/news/releases/2003/09/20030923-4.html.
137. UN Security Council Resolution 1540 (2004), http://www.un.org/Docs/sc/unsc_resolutions04.html.
138. We are grateful to George Bunn for emphasizing this aspect of Resolution 1540 in discussions with us.

sal adoption of the Additional Protocol and more radically through limits on HEU production and plutonium reprocessing. Both appeal to supply-side measures to address first- and second-tier proliferation. ElBaradei calls for "treaty-based" universalization of export controls. But as we have argued, universalizing the NSG risks reducing its effectiveness, even as it expands; negotiating a universal regime within the NPT will not directly capture India, Israel, and Pakistan; and negotiating a new universal regime to include all the nations of the UN would be a labor of many years—yet the problem is urgent. Not surprisingly, the Bush administration favors either a Security Council resolution (for export controls) or a coalition of willing states (for the PSI), with neither leading to a new global treaty-based regime.

There is precedent for this approach in the creation of the NSG, largely at the initiative of the United States, subsequent to India's first nuclear test explosion in 1974. But unlike the NSG, which established consensus export controls for participating states, Resolution 1540 requires all nations to adhere to export controls. The resulting tension—global requirements without first reaching global consensus—is evident in the criteria to which the resolution appeals with respect to implementation. Resolution 1540 declares that the Security Council decides that states shall develop and maintain "appropriate" export controls "to prevent the proliferation of nuclear, chemical, or biological weapons and their means of delivery," and that it recognizes the need for "effective national export and trans-shipment controls." But the resolution is silent on whether certain countries are to be prohibited from receiving certain items, and by what criteria.

The PSI bears greater resemblance to the NSG. The September 2003 PSI Statement of Interdiction Principles, for example, declares that PSI members agree to interdict WMD transfer "to and from states and non-state actors of proliferation concern," a phrase that it says "generally refers to those countries or entities that the PSI participants involved establish should be subject to interdiction activities because they are engaged in proliferation."[139] Similarly, in 1994 the NSG agreed that a nuclear supplier should authorize a transfer of trigger list items only when it is satisfied that the transfer would not contribute to nuclear weapons proliferation, recognizing that formal adherence to the NPT may not in itself be a guarantee that a recipient state in fact shares a commitment to nonproliferation.[140] The PSI is more ambitious than the NSG in that

---

139. Proliferation Security Initiative, "Statement of Interdiction Principles," Paris, France, September 4, 2003.
140. INFCIRC/539 (attachment), "The Nuclear Suppliers Group: Its Origins, Role, and Activities," n.d., http://projects.sipri.se/expcon/infcirc_539_1.htm.

PSI countries are pressuring flag carrier states to agree to the boarding of their ships on the high seas. Under the agreements reached with Liberia and Panama, permission will be granted on a case-by-case basis, but failure to respond to a specific request within a two-hour period will be treated as consent to act.[141]

There are three challenges facing the Bush administration proposals. The first two are challenges of effectively universalizing their initiatives. The third concerns the incompleteness of a supply-side response.

UNIVERSALIZATION OF EXPORT CONTROLS AND THE PROLIFERATION SECURITY INITIATIVE

Security Council Resolution 1540 preempts Director General ElBaradei's proposal to universalize export controls. Perhaps the Security Council will ultimately promulgate and update a trigger list of items that would fall under every nation's export controls. This and other steps might come within the purview of the Security Council committee created by Resolution 1540 to report on implementation, should the committee lead to a standing body. But what criteria are to be used for determining which nations are to be trusted as nuclear export recipients? PSI- or NSG-like decisions by a small number of nations will be impossible, unless the Security Council anticipates regularly reaching ad hoc agreement on particular nations that are viewed as unacceptable recipients. Yet every country will have a stake in export controls being effectively implemented by each UN member.

One solution that could be broadly acceptable and useful would be a global requirement that exports can be made only to countries that have concluded Additional Protocol agreements with the IAEA, had these agreements enter into force, and remained in good standing with these commitments. The NSG would continue to exist in addition to this universal export regime, as a first-tier body that could exercise stricter controls that would not have to achieve Security Council approval.

If the Security Council wished to universalize the PSI in a similar fashion, it could also rely on good standing with the Additional Protocol to separate those countries that were "of proliferation concern" from those that were not. The strictest export controls would be applied universally to countries of concern under this definition. The countries of the original PSI, analogously to those of the NSG, could continue to apply their own criteria as well, drawing in part on their own intelligence and suspicions.

---

141. Boese, "U.S., Panama Agree on Boarding Rules for Ships Suspected of Carrying WMD."

THE NEED FOR DEMAND-SIDE STEPS

The PSI and Resolution 1540 suggest that the United States and the P-5 do not view the current situation as one in which the state proliferation dilemma will be solved after a small number of "hard cases" in the world is addressed. Rather, these efforts seek to establish measures with global reach that will, by all appearances, continue indefinitely. This long-term perspective is wise, but it must also be recognized that the technological trajectory of many traditionally nuclear nonsupplier states is such that nuclear weapons–relevant technology will become increasingly available, either by illicit trade within proliferation rings (at least the trade that is not interdicted) or by the creation of indigenous capability. The manufacture of centrifuge-relevant components by Scomi Precision Engineering in Malaysia and EKA in Turkey emphasizes that, even though the PSI may successfully intercept equipment shipments, it will not be effective in interdicting the globalization of technology and know-how. More and more companies and countries will learn to manufacture these components for themselves, especially because most of the required items represent dual-use technologies with legitimate civilian applications. Therefore, in the long run, supply-side steps will not be enough, and demand-side measures must be given greater attention.

In fact, the proposals considered so far all have the effect of tightening the article 2 and article 3 requirements under the NPT for the nonnuclear weapons states. To be fair, they also restrict business opportunities for the nuclear weapons states, an article 1 measure. Nevertheless, for the long-term viability of the NPT, these additional burdens must be balanced by advantages of adherence to the NPT regime. For some states, this will be the advantage, under article 2, of an assurance that similar proliferation restraints are imposed on their neighbors, at times reinforced by positive security assurances from the United States or other countries. However, for those states that suspect their neighbors of having engaged in long-term clandestine or semi-overt nuclear or other so-called WMD acquisition programs,[142] the basic elements of the NPT agreement will not seem to be met. Their adherence to the NPT will entail a degree of uncertainty regarding their long-term security against potentially WMD- armed neighbors.

If the mix of economic benefits expected under article 4 of the NPT, and the security benefits under article 2, are insufficient to compensate for this uncer-

---

142. For a discussion of the confusion and misleading analogies that the use of the blanket term "WMD" encourages, see Christopher F. Chyba, "Toward Biological Security," *Foreign Affairs*, Vol. 81, No. 3 (May/June 2002), pp. 123–127.

tainty, the likelihood of covert defection from the regime will increase. Moreover, to the extent that nations that have successfully proliferated appear to have gained in prestige and security, the more it may seem that defection from the nonproliferation regime, carefully pursued, can bring considerable benefits. In this light, defection is not an irrational decision explained by a nation's "rogue" status, but rather a rational response to an unfavorable balance of incentives and disincentives.

Supply-side measures remain crucial to nonproliferation, but are not sufficient answers to the exchanges of technological know-how that occur within proliferation rings. They will become more difficult to monitor and enforce as the capability to manufacture uranium centrifuges becomes increasingly widespread. Nor will it be easy for supply-side measures to address what occurs on the territory of states with especially weak governments; even the calls in Resolution 1540 for assistance with legal and regulatory infrastructure cannot extend a government's authority into territory it does not de facto control.

Demand-side measures to accompany the new supply-side steps will involve blending, and in some cases strengthening and extending, traditional approaches. Security guarantees and the imposition, or lifting, of economic sanctions will continue to play important roles. These have been deployed in varying ways, and with varying success, in the case of most countries that have been part of the proliferation rings described here. The easing of regional security concerns will also be a crucial objective even as supply-side steps slow a state's ability to develop a nuclear arsenal. All these must be pursued on a case-by-case basis. But a broadly relevant sweetener for many countries could be a program to provide energy support in return for appropriate behavior with respect to weapons development. This would be consistent with, but would expand, the bargain implicit in article 4 of the NPT: that the benefits of nuclear technology be available, under controls, to the nonnuclear weapons states.

AN ESI TO COMPLEMENT THE PSI

A major benefit of the NPT, made explicit in article 4, was supposed to be preferred access to presumed abundant and low-cost nuclear electricity supplies, as also envisioned in President Dwight Eisenhower's Atoms for Peace program of 1953.[143] It has become clear, however, that nuclear power is not a low-cost energy option, but rather a very demanding technology in its construction

---

143. For a description and critique of this program, see Henry Sokolski, *Best of Intentions: America's Campaign against Strategic Weapons Proliferation* (Westport, Conn.: Praeger, 2001), pp. 25–37.

and operation. The hope of utilizing the nuclear energy option for "bootstrapping" a national economy to a higher technical development level, and for raising national standards of living through the supply of low-cost power, has at best only partially been met. And now states are being asked to accept even more intrusive and costly safeguards on their nuclear activities, if not an outright ban on their development of indigenous nuclear fuel–cycle facilities, while in some cases having neighbors that are pursuing, openly or clandestinely, nuclear weapons programs.

The NSG guidelines for nuclear transfers call on suppliers to "encourage" recipients to accept, "as an alternative to national plants," supplier involvement or multinational participation (or possibly both) in their enrichment or reprocessing facilities.[144] The nonproliferation benefits of the resulting transparency are clear; such an approach, however, should be mated with incentives to make the bargain more appealing to recipient countries. A menu of possible energy-related benefits could be clustered under a new Energy Security Initiative (ESI) that would parallel and compensate for the burdens that would be imposed on nonnuclear weapons states by the PSI, the Additional Protocol, and universalized export controls.

In particular, this approach can be tied to fuel-leasing arrangements in which countries with good NPT standing (including with respect to the Additional Protocol) could lease subsidized, lower-cost fuel for their nuclear plants, with the subsidy costs borne by the nuclear weapons or NSG states. Subsidized fuel leasing should be coupled with spent fuel take-back programs and could also, at a later stage, be coupled with the storage of that fuel at regional spent fuel storage facilities to be run by regional organizations and monitored by their own participating members, as well as by the IAEA. Such suggestions have recently been made regarding the DPRK and Iran.[145] Finally, even though article 4 of the NPT speaks exclusively of nuclear energy, consideration should

---

144. Section 6 of the NSG part 1 guidelines reads in part: "If enrichment or reprocessing facilities, equipment or technology are to be transferred, suppliers should encourage recipients to accept, as an alternative to national plants, supplier involvement and/or other appropriate multinational participation in resulting facilities. Suppliers should also promote international (including IAEA) activities concerned with multinational regional fuel cycle centers." See IAEA INFCIRC/254/Rev.6/Part 1 (corrected), "Communications Received from Certain Member States Regarding Guidelines for the Export of Nuclear Material, Equipment, and Technology," May 16, 2003, http://www.nsg-online.org/guide.htm.

145. William J. Perry and Ashton B. Carter, "The Crisis Last Time," *New York Times,* January 19, 2003; Daniel Poneman and Robert Gallucci, "U.S. Should Offer a Better Deal to N. Korea," *Los Angeles Times,* May 24, 2004; and Brent Scowcroft, "A Critical Nuclear Moment," *Washington Post,* June 24, 2004.

be given to expanding its scope to nonnuclear energy alternatives under appropriate commercial terms, as well as to electric transmission grid enhancements, for demonstrable adherence to NPT obligations. Some indications of this approach can be identified in proposals to improve the Iranian oil and gas industries as part of the ultimate solution to Iran's energy supply situation and an acceptable outcome for its nuclear program.[146] A similar approach has been proposed as part of the resolution of the DPRK nuclear standoff, most recently in the six-party talks held in Beijing in June 2004,[147] an approach that in this respect seems to parallel efforts reportedly pursued by the United States and United Kingdom vis-à-vis Libya.[148] The intent of the ESI would be to present an international policy declaration up front, providing a menu of potential incentives to be tailored to the needs of particular countries. In this way the two sides of the NPT bargain would be visibly brought into closer balance.[149]

Cooperation under article 4 need not be limited to energy; indeed the IAEA's Technical Cooperation Program also funds public health and environmental assistance efforts that have a nuclear component.[150] The total 2004 budget for the IAEA technical cooperation program is about $75 million.[151] Further incentives along these lines could be explored as well.

A FISSILE MATERIAL CUTOFF TREATY

Pulling those nuclear weapons states outside of the NPT into a system of constraints on their nuclear programs would have the benefit of increasing the evident equity of the nuclear nonproliferation regime. One way to pursue this approach is through the Fissile Material Cutoff Treaty. The FMCT was sup-

146. For a discussion on Iran's oil and gas reserves and their role vis-à-vis a proposed nuclear power program, see John R. Bolton, "U.S. Efforts to Stop the Spread of Weapons of Mass Destruction," testimony before the U.S. Congress, House International Relations Committee, 107th Cong., 2d sess., June 4, 2003.
147. For a discussion of proposed deals to resolve the DPRK standoff, including energy supply assistance, see Selig S. Harrison, "Turning Point in Korea—New Dangers and New Opportunities for the U.S.," report of the Task Force on U.S. Korean Policy (Chicago: Center for East Asian Studies, University of Chicago, February 2003); and Michael O'Hanlon and Mike Mochizuki, "Towards a Grand Bargain with North Korea," *Washington Quarterly*, Vol. 26, No. 4 (Autumn 2003), pp. 7–18.
148. See, for example, "Qaddafi's Son Says Libya Was Promised Economic, Military Gains for "WMD" Disarmament."
149. Chaim Braun, "Energy Security Initiative (ESI): A New Opportunity to Enhance the Nonproliferation Regime," Center for International Security and Cooperation and Institute for International Studies, Stanford University, August 25, 2004.
150. For example, the sleeping sickness–carrying tsetse fly was eliminated from Zanzibar through the release of radiation-sterilized male flies. See IAEA, "Campaign Launched to Eliminate Tsetse Fly," WorldAtom press release, PR2002/0219, February 2002.
151. *IAEA Programme and Budget for 2004–2005.*

ported by a consensus resolution of the UN General Assembly in 1993, which calls for the negotiation of a "non-discriminatory multilateral and internationally and effectively verifiable treaty banning the production of fissile material for nuclear weapons or other nuclear explosive devices."[152] An FMCT would apply an arms control measure to both the nuclear as well as the nonnuclear weapons states within the NPT. It would also, if it could be globally applied, rein in the nuclear programs of India, Israel, and Pakistan, and thereby begin to reduce the sense that these nations have gained unfair advantages by remaining outside the NPT. The nuclear weapons states promised an FMCT in 1995 as one of the considerations for the indefinite extension of the NPT.[153] At the 2000 NPT Review Conference, one of the "13 steps" related to article 6 obligations agreed upon by consensus was the achievement of an FMCT within five years.[154] Linkage of the FMCT at the Conference on Disarmament in Geneva to the Prevention of an Arms Race in Outer Space initiative delayed progress for years, but there may now be an opportunity to revive the FMCT negotiations.[155]

Were it realized, an FMCT would help in several ways: (1) it would demonstrate further nuclear weapon–state movement under article 6 of the NPT; (2) by putting a cap on Israel's and Pakistan's nuclear weapons material production, it would start to address Iran's security concerns vis-à-vis these two nations; and (3) by placing a cap on India's nuclear weapons material production, it would begin to tackle Pakistan's and even China's security concerns vis-à-vis India. Moreover, the United States has a strong interest in pursuing restraints on the nuclear programs of India, Israel, and Pakistan. For all these reasons, the United States should vigorously pursue an FMCT. In July 2004, however, the Bush administration announced a major shift in U.S. policy to-

---

152. United Nations General Assembly, "Prohibition of the Production of Fissile Materials for Weapons or Other Nuclear Explosive Devices," UNGA 48/75L, December 16, 1993.

153. Paragraph 4(b) of "Principles and Objectives for Nuclear Non-Proliferation and Disarmament," adopted by consensus by the parties to the NPT at the May 1995 extension conference, called for "the immediate commencement and early conclusion of negotiations on a non-discriminatory and universally acceptable convention banning the production of fissile material for nuclear weapons or for other nuclear explosion devices."

154. *2000 Review Conference of the Parties to the Treaty on the Non-Proliferation of Nuclear Weapons: Final Document,* May 2000, par. 15.3. The United States has stated that it "no longer supports all 13 steps." See, for example, U.S. Department of State Fact Sheet Provided to the Second Session of the Preparatory Committee for the 2005 NPT Review Conference, "Article VI of the Non-Proliferation Treaty," May 1, 2003, http://www.state.gov/t/np/rls/fs/20288pf.htm.

155. See "Statement by Mr. Hu Xiaodi, Ambassador for Disarmament Affairs of China, at the Plenary of the 2003 Session of the Conference on Disarmament," Geneva, Switzerland, August 7, 2003, http://www.china-un.ch/eng/53991.html.

ward the FMCT, declaring that it would oppose verification provisions for the treaty.[156]

THE ROLE OF U.S. NUCLEAR WEAPONS POLICY

U.S. nuclear weapons policy has historically played an important role on the demand side of controlling proliferation.[157] For example, the United States has used positive security assurances in the past to convince nonnuclear allies considering nuclear weapons that the protection of the U.S. defense umbrella spared them the need for their own nuclear weapons program. Negative security assurances—reassurances against a nuclear first strike—were originally provided under President Jimmy Carter's administration, but have been weakened by a number of recent Bush administration policy statements. According to excerpts leaked to the press, the Bush administration's 2002 Nuclear Posture Review states that "North Korea, Iraq, Iran, Syria, and Libya are among the countries that could be involved in immediate, potential, or unexpected contingencies." As reported, this statement appears shortly after the same document's assertion that "in setting requirements for nuclear strike capabilities, distinctions can be made among the contingencies for which the United States must be prepared. Contingencies can be categorized as immediate, potential or unexpected."[158] Policy-level statements such as these, along with "axis of evil" rhetoric, may be taken by the DPRK and Iran to mean that they risk nuclear attack by the United States. The United States should instead seek to undermine the security rationale for these states' demand for nuclear weapons, even if certain regional security concerns will nevertheless remain.

Further nuclear policy statements by the Bush administration, such as its December 2002 National Strategy to Combat Weapons of Mass Destruction, its opposition to ratification of the Comprehensive Test Ban Treaty, and its desire to fund research into new-generation nuclear weapons intended for preventive attacks on underground national command centers or biological or chemical weapons bunkers,[159] signal to other nations that nuclear weapons may play a growing, not diminishing, role in U.S. security decisions. They also undermine

156. Dafna Linzer, "U.S. Shifts Stance on Nuclear Treaty," *Washington Post*, July 31, 2004.
157. For a review, see Levite, "Never Say Never Again."
158. For excerpts from the *Nuclear Posture Review*, see *GlobalSecurity.org*, http://www .globalsecurity.org/wmd/library/policy/dod/npr.htm.
159. *National Strategy to Combat Weapons of Mass Destruction*, December 2002, http://www .whitehouse.gov/news/releases/2002/12/WMDStrategy.pdf. See also Carl Hulse and James Dao, "Cold War Long Over, Bush Administration Examines Steps to a Revamped Arsenal," *New York Times*, May 29, 2003.

the impression of progress by the United States to meet its obligations under article 6 of the NPT "to pursue negotiations in good faith on effective measures related to cessation of the nuclear arms race at an early date and to nuclear disarmament," despite the reductions in the size of the U.S. and Russian nuclear arsenals.[160]

In its 2002 National Security Strategy, the Bush administration emphasized that the United States will engage in preventive (which it calls "preemptive") attacks to counter emerging threats.[161] But as the case of the DPRK shows, it is possible for even small third-world nations to deter the United States from military action, either by conventional threats (e.g., artillery aimed at Seoul) or, should they succeed in developing nuclear weapons, nuclear ones. Therefore options for preventive war will remain limited, though not excluded. Moreover, preventive wars will carry very significant costs and unforeseen consequences for the United States. It is exactly to reduce the need or perceived need for such wars that new means of strengthening the nonproliferation regime must be found, and the emergence and expansion of proliferation rings prevented or disrupted.

Conclusion

Latent proliferation and proliferation rings represent two major and broad challenges to the survival of the nuclear nonproliferation regime. Proliferation rings exacerbate the latent proliferation challenge and illustrate the inadequacy of current export controls. The full development of such proliferation rings will ultimately render export control regimes limited to the traditional nuclear suppliers moot, as a set of third world countries (or their substate actors) develop nuclear weapons technology and manufacturing bases, disconnect from first- or second-world suppliers, and trade among themselves for the capabilities that their individual programs lack. Technology transfer among proliferating states could cut the cost and time period to acquisition of nuclear weapons capabilities, and even to deployment of integrated weapons and delivery systems, thus reducing the reaction time available to the overall non-

---

160. The Bush administration asserts that reductions agreed under the Moscow Treaty are strong evidence of its fulfillment of its article 6 obligations. See Wolf, "Remarks to the Second Meeting of the Preparatory Committee."
161. *The National Security Strategy of the United States of America,* September 2002, p. 15.

proliferation regimes. Worse, the possibility that nuclear weapons would be intentionally transferred or lost to terrorist groups cannot be discounted.

Addressing the challenge of proliferation requires action on both the supply and demand sides of the nonproliferation equation. However, a strategy to limit future proliferation rings must rely more strongly on demand-side approaches than nonproliferation regimes have in the past, precisely because of the disconnect they represent from the first and second worlds. The PSI and the Security Council's Resolution 1540 are supply-side steps that speak directly to this problem. But universal implementation of the latter is far from guaranteed, and the former will be increasingly challenged as relevant nuclear know-how and capacity spreads. Therefore, in addition to these supply-side measures, the balance of factors evaluated by states considering proliferation must be shifted back in favor of adherence to the nonproliferation regimes.

While preventive wars against some proliferators may play their role in the future, the United States will likely often find itself strongly deterred from exercising such options except as a last resort, and in the face of high costs. The United States should therefore place an extremely high priority on maintaining the strongest reasonable nonproliferation regimes. But of course no single proposal is a solution. The "silver bullet fallacy," which disdains useful measures that are less than total solutions, must be resisted. Rather, each step must be recognized as but one strand in a web of a multifaceted nonproliferation strategy.

Indeed, the development of proliferation rings and their detachment from traditional nuclear supplier export controls is a reminder that in the long term, any control regime that relies on restricting the diffusion of technology may well fail.[162] One purpose of the existing regimes is therefore to provide the time during which alternative approaches may be found to limit the perceived need for nuclear weapons or other WMD for confronting regional security dilemmas, and to encourage the evolution of governments that do not see WMD programs as useful or wise diversions of their society's resources. U.S. policy, including nuclear weapons policy, should be made with these long-term objectives in constant view.

---

162. Physicist Wolfgang K.H. Panofsky comments, "All new technologies have become dual-use . . . and . . . all new technologies have, in time, spread around the globe." Panofsky, "Nuclear Proliferation Risks, New and Old," *Issues in Science and Technology Online,* Summer 2003, http://www.nap.edu/issues/19.4/panofsky.html.

Ringing in Proliferation

How to Dismantle an Atomic Bomb Network

Alexander H. Montgomery

The nuclear nonproliferation regime has come under attack from a group of academics and policymakers who argue that traditional tools such as export controls, diplomatic pressure, arms control agreements, and threats of economic sanctions are no longer sufficient to battle proliferation. They point to North Korea's reinvigoration of its plutonium program, Iran's apparent progress in developing a nuclear capability, and the breadth of the Abdul Qadeer (A.Q.) Khan network as evidence that the regime is failing.[1] In addition, they claim that proliferation is driven by the inevitable spread of technology from a dense network of suppliers and that certain "rogue" states possess an unflagging determination to acquire nuclear weapons. Consequently, they argue that only extreme measures such as aggressively enforced containment or regime change can slow the addition of several more countries to the nuclear club. This "proliferation determinism," at least in rhetoric, is shared by many prominent members of President George W. Bush's administration and has become the main thrust of U.S. counterproliferation policy.[2] Yet current proliferators are neither as "dead

Alexander H. Montgomery is a postdoctoral fellow at the Center for International Security and Cooperation at Stanford University. Please send comments to ahm@stanfordalumni.org.

The author is grateful for critiques of multiple versions of this article from Paul MacDonald and Todd Sechser; comments from an anonymous reviewer for International Security; suggestions from Chaim Braun, Christopher Chyba, Lynn Eden, Scott Sagan, and Dean Wilkening; and feedback from the participants in the Research Seminar at the Center for International Security and Cooperation, Stanford Institute for International Studies, Stanford University.

1. On proliferation networks in general, see Chaim Braun and Christopher Chyba, "Proliferation Rings: New Challenges to the Nuclear Nonproliferation Regime," *International Security*, Vol. 29, No. 2 (Fall 2004), pp. 5–49. On North Korea, see Jonathan D. Pollack, "The United States, North Korea, and the End of the Agreed Framework," *Naval War Review*, Vol. 56, No. 3 (Summer 2003), pp. 11–49. On Iran, see IAEA (International Atomic Energy Agency) Board of Governors, "Implementation of the NPT Safeguards Agreement in the Islamic Republic of Iran," IAEA report GOV/2004/83 (Vienna: International Atomic Energy Agency, November 15, 2004), http://www.iaea.org/Publications/Documents/Board/2004/gov2004-83_derestrict.pdf. On the A.Q. Khan network, see Gaurav Kampani, "Proliferation Unbound: Nuclear Tales from Pakistan" (Monterey, Calif.: Center for Nonproliferation Studies, Monterey Institute of International Studies, February 23, 2004), http://cns.miis.edu/pubs/week/040223.htm.
2. See, for example, Paul Wolfowitz, "Deputy Secretary Wolfowitz Q&A," International Institute for Strategic Studies, Asia Security Conference, Singapore, May 31, 2003, http://www.defenselink.mil/transcripts/2003/tr20030531-depsecdef0246.html; George W. Bush, "President Announces New Measure to Counter the Threat of Weapons of Mass Destruction (WMD): Remarks by the President on Weapons of Mass Destruction Proliferation," February 11, 2004, http://www.state.gov/t/ac/rls/rm/2004/29291.htm; Condoleezza Rice, "Remarks by National Security

set" on proliferating nor as advanced in their nuclear capabilities as determinists claim.[3] To dismantle the network of existing proliferation programs, the administration should instead move toward a policy of "proliferation pragmatism." This would entail abandoning extreme rhetoric, using a full range of incentives and disincentives aimed at states seeking to acquire a nuclear capability, targeting the hubs of proliferation networks, and engaging in direct talks with the Islamic Republic of Iran and the Democratic Peoples' Republic of Korea (DPRK).

In practice, the Bush administration's nonproliferation policies have been more varied and less aggressive than its rhetoric would suggest. For example, it has been willing to enter talks with North Korea and Libya despite describing both as "rogues." Strong words can be used strategically to convince proliferators that accepting a settlement offer would be better than continuing to hold out. Yet the administration's unyielding rhetoric has placed the United States in a position from which it is difficult to back down;[4] combined with a lack of positive incentives, this stance has convinced proliferators that the United States will not agree to or uphold any settlement short of regime change. Moreover, the administration has not formulated any coherent counterproliferation policies other than regime change and an aggressive form of export control enforcement known as the Proliferation Security Initiative. With respect to two of the key proliferators today—Iran and North Korea—the Bush administration has shown little interest in offering any significant incentives or establishing any clear red lines. Instead, it has relied almost exclusively on China to convince the DPRK to give up its nuclear program and has declined to join the United Kingdom, France, and Germany in talks with Iran.

Proliferation determinists present two arguments. First, dense networks among second-tier proliferators such as Iran, North Korea, and Libya and pri-

Advisor Dr. Condoleezza Rice to the Reagan Lecture," February 26, 2004, http://www.whitehouse.gov/news/releases/2004/02/20040228-1.html; John R. Bolton, "The Bush Administration and Nonproliferation: A New Strategy Emerges," panel 1 of a hearing of the House Committee on International Relations, 108th Cong., 2d sess., March 30, 2004, http://www.state.gov/t/us/rm/31010.htm; and Richard Cheney, "Remarks by the Vice President at Westminster College," April 26, 2004, http://www.whitehouse.gov/news/releases/2004/04/print/20040426-8.html.

3. John R. Bolton, "Preventing Iran from Acquiring Nuclear Weapons," remarks to the Hudson Institute, August 17, 2004, http://www.state.gov/t/us/rm/35281.htm.

4. As Vice President Dick Cheney has argued, "I have been charged by the president with making sure that none of the tyrannies in the world are negotiated with. We don't negotiate with evil; we defeat it." Quoted in Warren P. Strobel, "Administration Struggles to Find Right Approach to N. Talks," *Knight Ridder*, December 20, 2003.

Figure 1. Network Structures and State Intentions Mapped to Nonproliferation Strategies

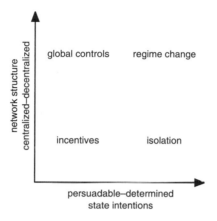

vate agents—including A.Q. Khan and two of his middlemen, Buhary Seyed Abu (B.S.A.) Tahir and Urs Tinner—have rapidly accelerated proliferation and lowered technological barriers.[5] Because these networks are widespread and decentralized, global measures rather than strategies targeted at individual states are necessary to slow these processes. Second, certain rogue states are dead set on proliferating and thus have no interest in bargaining. These two arguments define two variables—network structure and state intentions—encompassing four kinds of states that can be mapped to four different nonproliferation strategies (see Figure 1). Proliferation determinists argue that a number of states (e.g., Iran, North Korea, and formerly Libya) belong in the upper-right quadrant of Figure 1 (regime change); because these regimes are determined to seek nuclear weapons and are connected by effective, decentralized networks, they must be changed.

Both parts of the determinist argument are based on an interpretation of the progress of new proliferators that is at odds with publicly available docu-

---

5. Libya reinvigorated its nuclear program in 1995, then announced its termination in December 2003. On the roles of Tahir and Tinner, see Polis Diraja Malaysia, "Press Release by Inspector General of Police in Relation to Investigation on the Alleged Production of Components for Libya's Uranium Enrichment Programme," Royal Malaysia Police official website, February 20, 2004, http://www.rmp.gov.my/rmp03/040220scomi_eng.htm.

ments. The evidence that decentralized proliferation networks have allowed these proliferators to make great strides is contestable; the evidence that certain types of regimes are dead set on nuclear proliferation and cannot be persuaded to abandon their nuclear programs is even less compelling. Although the source of nuclear knowledge may have shifted from first-tier (advanced industrialized) to second-tier (developing industrial) states, there is no cause for proliferation panic.

In this article I propose an alternative approach—proliferation pragmatism—that rests on two premises. First, nuclear proliferation networks are highly centralized and are much less effective than determinists claim. Second, given sufficient incentives, proliferators can be persuaded to halt or roll back their programs. Consequently, most if not necessarily all states are in the lower-left quadrant of Figure 1; proliferation can be halted or slowed through proper application of country-specific incentives selected from a broad range of options. The presence of second-tier networks is indeed a new problem. Measures to deal with them should be based on an analysis of their structure and the speed of technological development. The hub-and-spoke structure of nuclear weapons and ballistic missile networks—which, I argue, developed in part because of the difficulty of passing on the tacit knowledge required to successfully build and operate these weapons—requires a policy that targets the hubs rather than a policy of systemwide coerced change. Past successes in slowing the spread of nuclear weapons through the use of targeted incentives, rather than demanding regime change, indicate that even the most seemingly determined proliferants can be slowed without resorting to extreme measures.

The two remaining quadrants in Figure 1 (global controls and isolation) differ in their policy prescriptions from pragmatism and determinism. If a proliferation network is decentralized but states that are part of it can be persuaded to halt their programs, global methods (such as those discussed by Chaim Braun and Christopher Chyba) that enhance the bargain of the nonproliferation treaty by providing more incentives and making transfers of nuclear technology more difficult are most appropriate.[6] If the network is centralized but states are determined to develop a nuclear capability, then proliferation can be

---

6. Global methods advocated by Braun and Chyba include universalization of export controls, extension of the Proliferation Security Initative (PSI), an Energy Security Initative to complement the PSI, a Fissile Material Cutoff Treaty, and a policy of nuclear de-emphasis by the United States. Braun and Chyba, "Proliferation Rings."

stopped by threatening to isolate a few key states, similar to the policy of dual containment of Iran and Iraq pursued by President Bill Clinton's administration.[7] Unlike regime change, these prescriptions (especially global controls) are potentially compatible with incentives targeted at specific states, although they will most likely fail if used without incentives.

In the next section, I argue that nuclear proliferation networks have not significantly altered the length of the development cycle of nuclear weapons programs and that regime type has little influence on states' desires to seek such weapons, contrary to the claims of proliferation determinists. I then examine the structure of the proliferation networks and discuss the role of tacit knowledge in shaping those structures and hindering new proliferants. In the third section, I review and critique steps taken to dismantle these networks. I then conclude with recommendations based on past successes.

New Proliferators Are Neither Advanced Nor Determined

Proliferation determinists contend that the inevitable spread of nuclear technology, combined with regimes that are dead set on proliferating, calls for a policy of regime change. Although countries' capabilities and intentions are difficult to ascertain, it is possible to compare particular claims made by determinists with publicly available data and reasonable calculations to demonstrate that the determinist case is far from certain; a policy of regime change requires much better evidence than advocates of determinism have presented. In this section I focus primarily on the cases of North Korea, Iran, and Libya. Because these countries were the primary recipients of nuclear technology from the A.Q. Khan network and have been singled out as by the United States as "rogue" states, these should be easy cases for proliferation determinism. In addition to examining the technological progress of these states, I evaluate the determinists' argument that particular regimes are dead set on proliferating, and find that the available evidence fails to support this assertion.

NUCLEAR NETWORKS: LEAPFROGGING OR FALLING DOWN?
Determinists argue that proliferation networks are ubiquitous, interlinked, and effective. Some even group together proliferation networks and terrorist

---

7. Anthony Lake, "Confronting Backlash States," *Foreign Affairs*, Vol. 73, No. 2 (March/April 1994), pp. 45–55.

networks; for example, President Bush argued in February 2004 that "with deadly technology and expertise going on the market, there's the terrible possibility that terrorists groups [*sic*] could obtain the ultimate weapons they desire most."[8] The same month, National Security Adviser Condoleezza Rice noted, "We now know, however, that there are actually two paths to weapons of mass destruction—secretive and dangerous states that pursue them and shadowy, private networks and individuals who also traffic in these materials, motivated by greed or fanaticism or, perhaps, both."[9] Similarly, Vice President Dick Cheney contended in April 2004 that "our enemy no longer takes the form of a vast empire, but rather a shadowy network of killers, which, joined by outlaw regimes, would seek to impose its will on free nations by terror and intimidation."[10] But how effective are these proliferation networks? Undersecretary of State John Bolton warned in May 2004, "It is clear that the recently revealed proliferation network of A.Q. Khan has done great damage to the global nonproliferation regime and poses a threat to the security of all states gathered here today."[11] Yet the difficulties that the leadership in Pyongyang, Iran, and Libya have encountered in seeking to achieve nuclear capabilities indicate that there are still significant barriers to the development and transfer of technological knowledge.

Although North Korea has received relatively little outside help with its plutonium program, proliferation determinists cite its possession of "up to eight bombs" as a rationale for action, arguing that the leadership in Pyongyang may seek to sell plutonium to third parties.[12] Evidence suggests, however, that North Korea may have much less plutonium than is commonly claimed. In May 1994 the DPRK heightened a crisis it started in 1993 by removing nearly 8,000 fuel rods from its Yongbyon nuclear reactor. In exchange for diplomatic and economic benefits from the United States, the North Koreans agreed to place these rods in sealed canisters under International Atomic Energy Agency (IAEA) supervision; standard calculations estimate that these rods (in addition to the rods that North Korea irradiated before 1989 and may have removed

---

8. Bush, "President Announces New Measure to Counter the Threat of Weapons of Mass Destruction."
9. Rice, "Remarks by National Security Advisor Dr. Condoleezza Rice to the Reagan Lecture."
10. Cheney, "Remarks by the Vice President at Westminster College."
11. John R. Bolton, "Nuclear Suppliers Group Plenary," statement to the 2004 Nuclear Suppliers Group plenary meeting, Göteborg, Sweden, May 27, 2004, http://www.state.gov/t/us/rm/33121.htm.
12. Bill Gertz, "North Korea Seen Readying Its First Nuclear Arms Test," *Washington Times*, April 23, 2005.

and reprocessed) could contain as much as 41.5 kilograms (kg) of plutonium.[13] This calculation, however, assumes a high capacity factor of 80 percent for the reactor between 1989 and 1994.[14] But the North Koreans also placed about 700 broken fuel rods into dry storage, making such a robust reliability unlikely.[15] Multiple shutdowns of North Korea's reactor between 1989 and 1994, possibly caused by mechanical problems rather than regular maintenance, have also been reported.[16] Since the reactor was restarted in early 2003, it has been shut on and off multiple times, indicating that the North Koreans are still experiencing difficulties operating it.[17] Many accounts assume that the North Koreans are understating the amount of plutonium that they have produced; this ignores the significant incentives they have to overstate the amount they may possess as a greater deterrent and for greater leverage.

Since former Los Alamos National Laboratory Director Sigfried Hecker verified in January 2004 that the 8,000 fuel rods were no longer in their cannisters at the Yongbyon facility, most analysts have assumed that they were reprocessed, significantly increasing the potential nuclear material separated by the North Koreans. Yet whether the rods have been reprocessed is unclear.[18]

---

13. According to David Albright, Hans Berkhout, and William Walker, if between 1989 and 1994 the plant was operated 80 percent of the time—a high estimate—it could have produced 33 kg of plutonium in addition to the 9.5 kg still in the rods if only a few rods were extracted in 1989. Albright, Berkhout, and Walker, *Plutonium and Highly Enriched Uranium, 1996: World Inventories, Capabilities, and Policies* (Oxford: Oxford University Press, 1997), pp. 298–299.
14. Capacity factor is equal to the actual energy produced divided by the energy that could have been produced if the reactor was run constantly for the entire time period at 100 percent power.
15. Robert Alvarez, interview with author, Washington, D.C., November 8, 2004; and Robert Alvarez, "North Korea: No Bygones at Yongbyon," *Bulletin of the Atomic Scientists*, Vol. 59, No. 4 (July/August 2003), pp. 38–45. Alvarez was a senior policy adviser in the U.S. Department of Energy who oversaw the canning of the spent fuel rods. Albright, Berkhout, and Walker note the presence of 650 rods in dry storage in addition to the rods extracted from the reactor. See Albright, Berkhout, and Walker, *Plutonium and Highly Enriched Uranium, 1996*, p. 294.
16. Albright, Berkhout, and Walker, *Plutonium and Highly Enriched Uranium, 1996*, p. 298.
17. See, for example, the images at the Institute for Science and International Security of the DPRK nuclear power plant. Corey Hinderstein, "Imagery Brief of Activities at the Yongbyon Site," July 1, 2003, http://www.isis-online.org/publications/dprk/Imagery.pdf. These photos indicate a shutdown sometime between March and June; a second shutdown occurred later that fall. Douglas Jehl, "Shutdown of Nuclear Complex Deepens North Korean Mystery," *New York Times*, September 13, 2003.
18. Hecker avoided arguing that all of the rods had been reprocessed simply by noting that they were no longer in the cooling pond. See Sigfried S. Hecker, "Visit to the Yongbyon Nuclear Scientific Research Center in North Korea," Senate Committee on Foreign Relations, 108th Cong., 2d sess., January 21, 2004, http://foreign.senate.gov/testimony/2004/HeckerTestimony040121 .pdf. Any of three remote-sensing technologies could have detected reprocessing. First, satellite photos could have picked up visible emissions from the reprocessing plant. See Richard R. Paternoster, "Nuclear Weapon Proliferation Indicators and Observables," LA-12430-MS (Los Alamos, N.M.: Los Alamos National Laboratory, December 1992), p. 8. Second, steam from the power plant

But reader problems and reprocessing inefficiencies may have hindered their ability to produce enough plutonium for six to eight weapons. For example, if the reactor ran at a 40 percent capacity factor from 1989 to 1994 consistent with the operating record before the 1989 shutdown and reprocessing losses were 25 percent, North Korea would have a total of about 20 kg of plutonium.[19] Although the standard figure for calculating the amount of plutonium used per weapon is around 5 kg, 6 kg is often used as a more conservative estimate;[20] further the first weapon built by a new proliferator can require up to 8 kg.[21] With the more conservative figure, North Korea would have enough plutonium for only three weapons, not enough to sell or use in a test and still maintain a sufficient deterrent. There is also some question as to whether North Korea has produced nuclear weapons with this material.[22]

Many U.S. officials also raise concerns over North Korea's highly enriched

---

connected to the reprocessing plant could be observed; this was seen briefly in January 2003 but has not been observed since. See David E. Sanger, "U.S. Sees Quick Start of North Korea Nuclear Site," *New York Times*, March 1, 2003. Third, detectors on the border could find Krypton-85 gas emissions; such emissions were reported only once, in July 2003. See Thom Shanker and David E. Sanger, "North Korea Hides New Nuclear Site, Evidence Suggests," *New York Times*, July 20, 2003. While the Central Intelligence Agency and the Defense Intelligence Agency had concluded that North Korea had reprocessed the rods, State Department intelligence was unconvinced as of mid-2004. David E. Sanger and William J. Broad, "Evidence Is Cited Linking Koreans to Libya Uranium," *New York Times*, May 23, 2004. The reprocessing might have been done instead in an unknown underground facility, which could potentially circumvent these detection methods.

19. Alvarez argues that with the large number of broken rods, the capacity factor of the reactor could have been 40 percent. This figure would also be more consistent with the operating record of the reactor before the 1989 shutdown. With 9.5 kg already in the rods, the additional amount of plutonium in the rods would then be about 16.5 kg, for a total of about 26 kg. Alvarez also points out that without skilled knowledge of the PUREX process, the amount of plutonium extracted could be significantly less than assumed. Alvarez, interview with author. The fraction by which this would decrease the amount of plutonium extracted is highly uncertain. One possible indication, however, is the amount of material North Korea itself claimed to have lost in its reprocessing—about 30 percent. See David Albright and Kevin O'Neill, *Solving the North Korean Nuclear Puzzle* (Washington, D.C.: Institute for Science and International Security, 2000), p. 88. The amount of plutonium that North Korea could potentially extract from these rods is therefore probably closer to 20 kg than 42 kg.

20. The Trinity atomic test on July 16, 1945, and the bomb dropped on Nagasaki on August 9, 1945, both used 6 kg or more of plutonium. Richard L. Garwin, "The Future of Nuclear Weapons without Nuclear Testing," *Arms Control Today*, Vol. 27, No. 8 (November/December 1997), pp. 3–12.

21. Albright, Berkhout, and Walker, *Plutonium and Highly Enriched Uranium, 1996*, p. 306.

22. Although the CIA's assessment in 2003 that "North Korea has produced one or two simple fission-type nuclear weapons" is widely cited, the next sentence of the assessment indicates that this conclusion may have been reached using only the vaguest of evidence: "Press reports indicate North Korea has been conducting nuclear weapon–related high explosive tests since the 1980s in order to validate its weapon design(s)." Central Intelligence Agency, "SSCI Questions for the Record: Regarding 11 February 2003 DCI World Wide Threat Briefing," SSCI 2003-3662, Central Intelligence Agency, August 18, 2003, http://www.fas.org/irp/congress/2003_hr/021103qfr-cia.pdf.

uranium (HEU) program. In particular, much has been made of Pyongyang's attempts to acquire parts for its centrifuges in Europe. The Central Intelligence Agency reported in November 2003 that "a shipment of aluminum tubing— enough for 4,000 centrifuge tubes—was halted by German authorities" in April 2003.[23] The shipment in question, however, contained only 214 tubes. If North Korea had received this shipment, these tubes could have been turned into the vacuum housings for 428 centrifuges—enough for only a pilot-sized facility.[24]

The North Koreans seem to be seeking parts for the more advanced P-2 (aka G-2) centrifuge,[25] which operates at higher speeds and requires more sophisticated materials than the simpler P-1 centrifuge. Consequently, this increases the amount of time required to construct a uranium-enrichment facility capable of producing sufficient quantities of nuclear weapons–grade HEU. As one expert has noted, "The North Koreans assumed that their path to HEU would be shortened if they procured the most advanced materials available. Iraq also 'made that mistake.'"[26] Germany's 2003 seizure of the aluminum tubing reveals that the DPRK did not have enough vacuum housings at that time for even a small pilot plant. In addition, it seems unlikely that the North Koreans would have already acquired difficult-to-manufacture maraging steel rotors or other sensitive parts if they could not manufacture the much simpler vacuum housings. Even with a simpler design, they probably would not have progressed to the point of being able to make HEU.[27]

---

23. Central Intelligence Agency Nonproliferation Center, "Unclassified Report to Congress on the Acquisition of Technology Relating to Weapons of Mass Destruction and Advanced Conventional Munitions," January 1–June 30, 2003, http://www.cia.gov/cia/reports/.

24. Joby Warrick, "N. Korea Shops Stealthily for Nuclear Arms Gear; Front Companies Step Up Efforts in European Market," *Washington Post*, August 15, 2003. Assuming 5 separative work units (SWU)/yr. P-2 centrifuges, 428 centrifuges would take nearly two years to produce 20 kg of 93 percent enriched uranium (a standard assumption for a small-implosion nuclear weapon using HEU). But this assumes that no centrifuges break down, which is highly unlikely given the record of North Korea's plutonium program and the difficulties faced by states unfamiliar with centrifuge technology.

25. Mark Hibbs, "Customs Intelligence Data Suggest DPRK Aimed at G-2 Type Centrifuge," *Nuclear Fuel*, May 26, 2003.

26. Quoted in Mark Hibbs, "CIA Assessment on DPRK Presumes Massive Outside Help on Centrifuges," *Nuclear Fuel*, November 25, 2002, p. 1.

27. One "Western centrifuge expert" doubted North Korea's progress, arguing that the suggestion that "the North Koreans could make HEU on a consistent basis with (the CNOR/SNOR design) after, say, five years' time, is pretty unlikely, given all the challenges." Quoted in Mark Hibbs, "DPRK Enrichment Not Far Along, Some Intelligence Data Suggest," *Nucleonics Week*, October 24, 2002, p. 2. The CNOR/SNOR is a simpler aluminum-rotor design similar to the P-1 centrifuge used by Pakistan and distributed by the A.Q. Khan network.

The Libyan nuclear program had been active much longer than the North Korean program, suggesting that even with extensive help, HEU production remains difficult. According to the IAEA, Libyan authorities "made a strategic decision to reinvigorate its nuclear activities" in July 1995. Despite massive assistance from the A.Q. Khan network, including the sale of twenty preassembled P-1 centrifuges, Libya had installed only one 9-machine cascade by April 2002—and never fed any nuclear materials into it. Libya also could not develop the uranium hexafluoride (UF_6) production facilities required to feed the centrifuges.[28] Given that it requires about 1,600 P-1 centrifuges and around 4,500 kg of natural uranium to produce 20 kg of weapons-grade HEU in a year, Libya's program was far from completion.[29] Moreover, the centrifuges that Libya sent to the United States after it gave up its nuclear program lacked rotors.[30]

Iran's nuclear program has also been in existence longer than the North Korean program. Iran's centrifuge enrichment program was established in the mid-1980s. After transient and somewhat dubious successes, Iran has been unable to separate isotopes using lasers since 1994 because of "continuous technical problems." The laser-enrichment equipment Iran received from its foreign suppliers between 1975 and 1998 was for the most part incomplete or never properly functioned; the supposed success of its pre-1994 experiments was measured by the same foreign suppliers who carried out the experiments, lending some doubt as to the veracity of the results.[31] Similarly, since its acquisition of parts for 500 centrifuges (split between two shipments in 1994 and 1996) from the A.Q. Khan network, Iran has made relatively little progress in developing its centrifuge technology. Problems with the bellows required additional shipments in 1997.[32] More than half of the rotors that Iran had assem-

28. IAEA Board of Governors, "Implementation of the NPT Safeguards Agreement of the Socialist People's Libyan Arab Jamahiriya," IAEA report GOV/2004/12 (Vienna: International Atomic Energy Agency, February 20, 2004), http://www.fas.org/nuke/guide/libya/iaea0204.pdf, pp. 4–5.
29. Assuming a natural uranium feed and a 0.3 percent tails assay, 4,000 SWU are required to produce 20 kg of 93 percent enriched HEU from 4,500 kg of natural uranium, enough for a first-generation implosion device. A P-1 centrifuge produces about 2.5 SWU/yr., so 1,600 centrifuges would be required. See Albright, Berkhout, and Walker, *Plutonium and Highly Enriched Uranium, 1996*, p. 469.
30. David E. Sanger and William J. Broad, "As Nuclear Secrets Emerge, More Are Suspected," *New York Times*, December 26, 2004.
31. IAEA Board of Governors, GOV/2004/83, pp. 6, 12–13.
32. Ibid., p. 8. Uranium centrifuges typically have one or more bellows (connectors) between individual stacked segments to prevent the centrifuges from self-destruction when passing through resonance velocities.

bled in the spring of 2004 were unusable.[33] Iran received P-2 designs in 1995 from the A.Q. Khan network, but reportedly did little work on the P-2 centrifuges because of the extensive problems it was already having with the simpler P-1 centrifuge, delaying work on the more advanced design until 2002. The owner of the private company hired to work on the P-2 centrifuges stated that Iran was not capable of manufacturing the P-2's maraging steel rotors, and began work on adapting the design to use a shorter (probably single-rotor) composite carbon tube instead.[34] These time frames are quite close to—or even significantly exceed—the ten to fifteen years that other countries have needed to develop centrifuge programs.[35]

THE IRRELEVANCE OF REGIME TYPE
In addition to arguing that proliferation networks have significantly decreased development times, proliferation determinists contend that particular regimes—referred to variously as "rogue" states, "outlaw" regimes, or members of an "axis of evil"—are inherently prone to proliferation and cannot be deterred or contained, and so must be replaced. In his State of the Union Address on January 29, 2002, President Bush singled out Iran, Iraq, and North Korea as an "axis of evil." Two days later, National Security Adviser Rice identified the same three states.[36] Secretary of State Colin Powell announced the Bush administration's policy of regime change in Iraq in testimony before Congress on February 6, 2002.[37] Discussing Iraq just days before the U.S. invasion on March 20, 2003, Bush stated, "Should we have to go in, our mission is very clear: disarmament. And in order to disarm, it would mean regime change."[38] Although the administration has sought to limit explicit calls for regime change in countries other than Iraq since Powell's testimony, a secret memo by Secretary of Defense Donald Rumsfeld leaked in April 2003 called explicitly

---

33. David Albright and Corey Hinderstein, "Iran: Countdown to Showdown," *Bulletin of the Atomic Scientists*, Vol. 60, No. 6 (November/December 2004), pp. 67–72.
34. IAEA Board of Governors, GOV/2004/83, p. 11.
35. Hibbs, "DPRK Enrichment Not Far Along, Some Intelligence Data Suggest."
36. George W. Bush, "State of the Union Address," January 29, 2002, http://www.whitehouse.gov/stateoftheunion/2002/; and Condoleezza Rice, "Remarks by the National Security Advisor Condoleezza Rice to the Conservative Political Action Conference," Marriott Crystal Gateway, Arlington, Virginia, February 1, 2002, http://www.whitehouse.gov/news/releases/2002/02/20020201-6.html.
37. Todd S. Purdum, "U.S. Weighs Tackling Iraq On Its Own, Powell Says," *New York Times*, February 7, 2002.
38. George W. Bush, "President George Bush Discusses Iraq in National Press Conference," March 6, 2003, http://www.whitehouse.gov/news/releases/2003/03/print/20030306-8.html.

for such change in North Korea.[39] The following month, Deputy Secretary of Defense Paul Wolfowitz demanded "fundamental change" in the DPRK's regime.[40] The investigative journalist Seymour Hersh has reported that the Department of Defense is already conducting covert operations in Iran.[41] Even without an explicit call for regime change, the logic of proliferation determinism—that new proliferants cannot be contained, deterred, or bribed into giving up their nuclear weapon programs—leads to the inevitable conclusion that regime change must occur.

This position is untenable for three reasons. First, there is little or no systematic evidence that regime type is linked to proliferation propensity. Second, proliferation desires have historically varied even while regimes in North Korea and Libya (and Iraq before the 2003 U.S. invasion) remain the same, while in Iran, the 1979 revolution temporarily halted its nuclear program. Third, the direct evidence that contemporary proliferators are dead set on acquiring nuclear weapons does not hold up to scrutiny.

Although authoritarian regimes might be more prone to obtaining nuclear weapons and ballistic missiles than other kinds of states, this is only one factor among many. Surveys of the proliferation literature emphasize security and prestige benefits or organizational pathologies as drivers of nuclear proliferation, rather than domestic political structures or particular leaders.[42] A few studies argue that economic liberalization, not particular leaders, may restrain regimes from developing nuclear weapons.[43] Ironically, because economic growth is also linked to proliferation, the net effect of economic liberalization may be to increase in the likelihood of proliferation. Statistical studies of proliferation between 1945 and 2000 found either a positive correlation between de-

---

39. David Rennie, "Pentagon Calls for Regime Change in North Korea," *Daily Telegraph* (London), April 22, 2003.

40. Wolfowitz, "Deputy Secretary Wolfowitz Q&A."

41. Seymour M. Hersh, "The Coming Wars," *New Yorker*, January 24–31, 2005, http://lexis-nexis.com.

42. See Scott D. Sagan, "Why Do States Build Nuclear Weapons? Three Models in Search of a Bomb," *International Security*, Vol. 21, No. 3 (Winter 1996/97), pp. 54–86; and Tanya Ogilvie-White, "Is There a Theory of Nuclear Proliferation? An Analysis of the Contemporary Debate," *Nonproliferation Review*, Vol. 4, No. 1 (Fall 1996), pp. 43–60.

43. Etel Solingen, "The Political Economy of Nuclear Restraint," *International Security*, Vol. 19, No. 2 (Fall 1994), pp. 126–169; and Etel Solingen, "The Domestic Sources of Nuclear Postures: Influencing Fence-Sitters in the Post–Cold War Era," IGCC Policy Paper PP08 (Irvine, Calif.: Institute on Global Conflict and Cooperation, October 1, 1994), http://repositories.cdlib.org/igcc/PP/PP08.

mocracy and proliferation or no relationship at all. Factors such as diplomatic isolation, economic growth, interstate rivalries, and security threats were much more influential than how democratic or autocratic a regime was.[44] Five of the nine established or suspected nuclear weapons states (France, India, Israel, the United Kingdom, and the United States) are well-established democracies.

Although a particular leader might still make a difference at the margin, none of the cases of contemporary "rogue" state proliferators support the thesis strongly. Bolton has argued that "historically, countries have given up their nuclear weapons programs only at a time of regime change."[45] Yet this argument does not seem to hold for the states singled out as "rogue" regimes. The Iraq Survey Group, constituted by Australia, Britain, and the United States to search for evidence of nonconventional weapons programs after the 2003 Iraq war and removal of Saddam Hussein from power, found "no evidence to suggest concerted [Iraqi] efforts to restart the [nuclear] program" after the 1991 Persian Gulf War.[46] Libya gave up its nuclear, chemical, biological, and long-range missile programs while maintaining the same leader. North Korea's nuclear ambitions have varied while its leaders have been relatively constant; factors other than regime type, such as rapprochement with South Korea and U.S. promises to establish diplomatic and economic ties in exchange for a freeze on North Korea's program, have influenced its decisionmaking at various times. Iran sought nuclear weapons even as a U.S. ally under the shah; the revolution actually led to a cessation of Iran's nuclear ambitions until at least 1985.[47]

44. See Sonali Singh and Christopher R. Way, "The Correlates of Nuclear Proliferation: A Quantitative Test," *Journal of Conflict Resolution*, Vol. 48, No. 6 (December 2004), pp. 859–885; Dong-Joon Jo and Erik Gartzke, "Determinants of Nuclear Weapons Proliferation," November 2003, http://www.columbia.edu/~eg589/pdf/nuke-proliferation-112003.pdf; and Karthika Sasikumar and Christopher R. Way, "Testing Theories of Proliferation: The Lessons from South Asia," paper presented at the Center for International Security and Cooperation–Army War College Conference on South Asia and the Nuclear Future, Stanford, California, June 3–4, 2004.
45. John R. Bolton, "Arms Control and Nonproliferation Issues," press conference, July 21, 2004, http://www.state.gov/t/us/rm/34676.htm.
46. Charles Duelfer, "Key Findings of the Comprehensive Report of the Special Advisor to the DCI on Iraq's WMD," September 30, 2004, http://www.cia.gov/cia/reports/iraq_wmd_2004/Comp_Report_Key_Findings.pdf.
47. On the shah's program, see Anne Hessing Cahn, "Determinants of the Nuclear Option: The Case of Iran," in Onkar S. Marwah and Ann Schulz, eds., *Nuclear Proliferation and the Near-Nuclear Countries* (Cambridge, Mass.: Ballinger, 1975), pp. 185–204. After the revolution in 1979, Iran first constituted its centrifuge program and began construction on the Isfahan nuclear complex in 1985. IAEA Board of Governors, GOV/2004/83, pp. 6, 14.

Much of the argument for regime change comes from a reading of these countries' intentions based on their progress. This is especially true of Iran. Similar to the North Korean case, arguments regarding the rate of Iran's nuclear acquisition are based on worst-case estimates and incomplete information. This is not to suggest that Iran's pursuit of a nuclear capability is solely for civilian purposes, as the Iranian government asserts; rather, advocates of regime change have exaggerated the military capabilities of Iran's nuclear facilities. Moreover, the slow rate of growth of Iran's nuclear program is incompatible with the notion of a regime determined to acquire weapons at any cost.

In an address to the Hudson Institute on August 17, 2004, Bolton made remarks typical of determinist claims regarding Iranian intentions.[48] He emphasizes the potential size of the Iranian pilot facility (1,000 centrifuges) and the planned production facility (50,000 centrifuges). Yet according to the IAEA, the Iranians installed only a 164-machine centrifuge cascade at the pilot plant; as of August 2005, this pilot cascade has not been operated. Uranium was fed into a small test cascade of nineteen machines at the Kalaye Electric Company only in 2002. This represents a substantial lack of progress given the receipt of parts for 500 centrifuges more than ten years earlier.[49] A regime determined to acquire nuclear weapons presumably would have attempted to move more quickly, despite any significant technical difficulties. As noted earlier, Iran has been working on laser enrichment technology even longer—since 1975. Bolton claims that Iran is developing enrichment facilities to produce weapons-grade uranium (containing 90+ percent uranium-235). But the samples acquired by the IAEA from the laser enrichment facility were enriched to just 1 percent; only gram quantities were produced at this level. Moreover, Iran had shut the facility down in response to a lack of progress and interest by May 2003.[50]

Bolton also claims that Iran has an impressive plutonium production program, highlighting the capabilities of its planned 40 megawatt nuclear reactor: "The technical characteristics of this heavy water moderated research reactor are optimal for the production of weapons-grade plutonium." Initial estimates, however, projected that this reactor would not be online until 2014—hardly a crash nuclear weapons program,[51] especially given that Iran has been planning

---

48. Bolton, "Preventing Iran from Acquiring Nuclear Weapons."
49. The centrifuge parts arrived in two shipments: the first in March 1994 and the second in July 1996. IAEA Board of Governors, GOV/2004/83, pp. 6–8.
50. Ibid., pp. 12–14.
51. Ibid., pp. 12–15.

this reactor since the mid-1990s.[52] More recent reports claim that it could be finished more quickly, perhaps by 2009, based on construction times of similar reactors in other countries.[53] An early completion date seems unlikely, however, given Iran's past difficulties in attempting to finish work on its Bushehr reactor, a light-water nuclear power plant originally ordered in 1975 from Germany. Iran's inexperience with nuclear technologies has produced significant delays, despite assistance from Russia; at one point, Iranian contractors had completed only five months of work on Bushehr in twenty-five months.[54] Moreover, merely starting up the reactor would require 80–90 tons of heavy water; as of November 2003, only one of the two heavy-water production lines had been completed. Production of 8 tons per year was supposed to have started in 2004,[55] but as of February 2005, even the first production line had not yet started.[56] Consequently, the reactor will not have a sufficient amount of heavy water until at least 2010.

Bolton also warns that Iran could use the Bushehr reactor to generate plutonium if it pulled out of the Nuclear Nonproliferation Treaty (NPT)—a claim true for any of the seventy countries currently or previously in possession of nuclear research or power reactors, and consequently not a useful measure of a particular regime's desire to proliferate.[57] Moreover, Iran would have to master the necessary reprocessing technology; so far, however, it has succeeded in reprocessing only milligram quantities of plutonium from irradiated targets— a very different technical challenge than reprocessing reactor fuel rods.[58] The Iranians would also have to construct a large-scale reprocessing facility that would be relatively easy to detect. It is also unclear how much knowledge Iran

52. IAEA Board of Governors, "Implementation of the NPT Safeguards Agreement in the Islamic Republic of Iran," IAEA report GOV/2003/63 (Vienna: International Atomic Energy Agency, August 26, 2003), http://www.iaea.org/Publications/Documents/Board/2003/gov2003-63.pdf, p. 9.
53. Jack Boureston and Charles Mahaffey, "Iran Pursues Plans for Heavy Water Reactor," *Jane's Intelligence Review*, November 14, 2003, http://jir.janes.com.
54. Anthony H. Cordesman, "Iran and Nuclear Weapons: A Working Draft" (Washington, D.C.: Center for Strategic and International Studies, February 7, 2000), http://www.csis.org/mideast/reports/irannuclear02072000.PDF, p. 13.
55. IAEA Board of Governors, GOV/2003/75, p. 14.
56. Institute for Science and International Security, "Iran Constructing the 40 MW Heavy Water Reactor at Arak Despite Calls Not to Do So by the European Union and the IAEA Board of Governors," March 4, 2005, http://isis-online.org/publications/iran/arakconstruction.html.
57. Bolton's presentation also includes technical inaccuracies, such as confusing deuterium (D) with heavy water (D_2O).
58. IAEA Board of Governors, GOV/2004/83, p. 17.

can gain from its work on the Bushehr reactor; Russian Minister of Atomic Energy Aleksandr Rumiantsev has claimed that Russian training of Iranian technicians is limited to operation only, without any transfer of knowledge of "actual nuclear technology."[59] Finally, the highly publicized revelation in early 2005 of Iran's small stake in a uranium mine in Namibia was, in the end, old news: Iran had acquired the stake in 1975 under the shah, and its contract does not include rights to the uranium.[60]

In sum, Iran will need years to develop a nuclear weapons capability. If the resuspension of centrifuge manufacturing that began in late November 2004 holds, the acquisition date will continue to be pushed back. Bolton's charge that Iran is "dead set on building nuclear weapons" and is proceeding with an urgency "quite consistent with a desire to produce a nuclear weapon as soon as possible"[61] seems implausible in this light, especially given that U.S. intelligence on Iran has been called into doubt.[62] Even some in the Bush administration estimate that Iran will not have a nuclear capability until sometime in the next decade.[63] Bolton argues that the June 2003 introduction of uranium hexafluoride gas into centrifuges at Iran's pilot plant and the temporary resumption of centrifuge manufacture in July 2004 are inexplicable other than by desire for rapid proliferation.[64] Yet the Iranian leadership has admitted taking these actions primarily to secure a better bargaining position,[65] which seems more plausible given their difficulties with the centrifuges and the considerable length of time before their program reaches completion.

Similar arguments hold for Libya and North Korea. Libya had about thirty people working on its program, far fewer than the thousands usually required for nuclear weapons development. Libya's nuclear activities may have been intended only as a bargaining chip rather than as part of a serious nuclear program; components were collected haphazardly, and development proceeded slowly.[66] After signing the Agreed Framework in 1994, North Korea made a deal with Pakistan to purchase materials and plans for centrifuges in 1997 at

---

59. I thank Sonja Schmid for bringing this to my attention and providing a translation. Aleksandr Rumiantsev, "Interview with the Minister of Atomic Energy," Ekho Moskvy, May 29, 2003.
60. Louis Charbonneau, "Iran in Rio Tinto Link," Reuters, January 31, 2005.
61. Bolton, "Preventing Iran from Acquiring Nuclear Weapons."
62. "U.S. Intelligence on Iran Seen Lacking–Experts," Reuters, February 9, 2005.
63. Nicholas Kralev, "U.S. Doubts Tehran Nukes Are Imminent," *Washington Times*, April 14, 2005.
64. Bolton, "Preventing Iran from Acquiring Nuclear Weapons."
65. Nazila Fathi, "Iran Hints It Sped Up Enriching Uranium as a Ploy," *New York Times*, December 6, 2004.
66. David Crawford, "Libya Was Far From Building Nuclear Bomb; Program Was Haphazard, But Shows How Technology Was Bought Off-the-Shelf," *Wall Street Journal*, February 23, 2004.

the earliest;[67] it embarked on an effort to develop a uranium enrichment program only by late 2000,[68] and started seeking the necessary materials in large quantities in late 2001.[69] Although these dates are ultimately uncertain, the bulk of public evidence does support them: North Korea's multiple efforts to seek parts have all occurred after 2000, with only a single effort to procure frequency converters in 1999.[70] As with Libya and Iran, the North Korean program may be intended as a bargaining chip; some observers argue that Pyongyang's confirmation of its uranium program to U.S. diplomats in October 2002 may have been intended as an offer to put the nuclear issue on the table in exchange for a grand bargain with the United States.[71]

Proliferation Networks: Star Structures and Tacit Knowledge

To justify a policy of regime change, proliferation determinists assume that nuclear technology is spreading rapidly through decentralized networks. Yet proliferation networks, in general, and nuclear proliferation networks, in particular, resemble a star-shaped (aka hub-and-spoke) structure. This structure is a function of the difficulty of transferring tacit knowledge through these networks, thus restricting their growth. This constraint makes these networks vulnerable to a range of counterproliferation measures that target the hub states directly.

THE STRUCTURE OF PROLIFERATION NETWORKS

In their study of "proliferation rings," Braun and Chyba examine second-tier proliferation, in which developing states aid each other in their ballistic missile and nuclear programs.[72] Although these proliferation networks have undercut

---

67. Joseph Bermudez Jr., "Lifting the Lid on Kim's Nuclear Workshop," *Jane's Defense Weekly*, November 27, 2002; and Seymour M. Hersh, "The Cold Test: What the Administration Knew about Pakistan and the North Korean Nuclear Program," *New Yorker*, January 27, 2003, http://jdw.janes.com.

68. Central Intelligence Agency Nonproliferation Center, "Untitled CIA Estimate to Congress," November 19, 2002, http://www.fas.org/nuke/guide/dprk/nuke/cia111902.html.

69. Central Intelligence Agency Nonproliferation Center, "Unclassified Report to Congress on the Acquisition of Technology Relating to Weapons of Mass Destruction and Advanced Conventional Munitions," July 1–December 31, 2001, http://www.cia.gov/cia/reports/.

70. North Korea unsuccessfully sought two frequency converters, used for timing centrifuges, in 1999, then tried again in 2002 and 2003. Part of the 2003 shipment was delivered, but the others were stopped. Mark Hibbs, "Procurement by Iran, DPRK Focuses Attention on 'Catch-All' Controls," *Nucleonics Week*, May 29, 2003.

71. Hibbs, "DPRK Enrichment Not Far Along, Some Intelligence Data Suggest."

72. Braun and Chyba, "Proliferation Rings."

Figure 2. Simple Network Structures

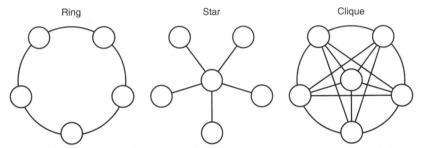

Ring   Star   Clique

NOTE: To isolate all nodes, the center node in the star network can be removed, but many more nodes must be removed from a circle or clique structure.

existing export control measures, they have been less successful than proliferation determinists contend. The optimal strategy to halt the growth of these networks depends on their structure, which can take various forms, including rings or circles (where the connections between nodes—in this case, states—form a circle), stars (where every node is connected through a central hub), or cliques (where all of the nodes are directly connected). Simple examples of these three structures are diagrammed in Figure 2. If the structure is a ring or a clique, then the shutdown of any single node would not unravel the entire network; consequently, global strategies that seek to eliminate all nodes or all connections between nodes might be more effective in dissolving the network than strategies that aim at key connections or nodes. Densely connected, decentralized networks where no single node holds a crucial position in the network are easier in one sense to shut down: connections to additional nodes in the network are easier to discover, although this is balanced by the number of nodes and connections that need to be eliminated to dissolve the network. But if the structure is starlike, then the network is highly centralized; efforts are best concentrated on eliminating the central node and preventing other nodes from becoming hubs.[73]

73. These are ideal types and do not by any means exhaust potential network structures; centralization and density are only two possible network measures. See Stanley Wasserman and Katherine Faust, *Social Network Analysis: Methods and Applications* (Cambridge: Cambridge University Press, 1994).

Existing ballistic missile and nuclear proliferation networks appear to closely resemble stars, in which North Korea and Pakistan are the hubs or central nodes for each network (see Figures 3a and 3b, respectively). No nuclear transactions between the spokes in the nuclear network have been confirmed as of mid-2005.[74] Interestingly, the missile network seems to be closer to a clique than does the nuclear network; however, only Iran and North Korea form hubs.[75] A.Q. Khan delivered plans or parts to Iran, Libya, and North Korea and offered assistance to other countries such as Iraq and possibly Syria. Although the extent of the Pakistani government's knowledge about the nuclear network remains unclear, there is no doubt that A.Q. Khan enjoyed unprecedented operational autonomy; shutting down the network requires convincing the Pakistani government to reestablish bureaucratic control over its program, obtain relevant information from Khan, and stop technology leaks. Consequently, from a policy perspective, Pakistan is the central hub rather than A.Q. Khan himself. Similarly, North Korea forms the center of a missile proliferation network, delivering missile technology to Egypt, Iran, Iraq, Libya, Pakistan, and Syria, among others. Iran forms a smaller hub for missile sales, linking Libya, North Korea, and Syria.

Braun and Chyba also cite other sources of missile technology (e.g., China and Russia), but these nodes are less central and, in any case, less likely to take on a central role if the existing hubs are shut down. Since joining the Missile Technology Control Regime (MTCR) in 1995, Russia has decreased its proliferation of missile technology, although it is still suspected of assisting North Korea and Iran, but at a lower level than before. China agreed to abide by the MTCR and pledged not to assist in the development of nuclear-capable missiles in 2000, then passed related domestic regulations in 2002. Some Chinese companies were still assisting Pakistan and Iran as of 2002, but the Chinese government has made progress in curbing missile technology exports since then, although it has still not become a full member of the MTCR.[76]

---

74. An uncorroborated report alleges that North Korea and Iran have assisted each other since the late 1990s. Louis Charbonneau, "N. Korea Provides Nuclear Aid to Iran–Intel Reports," Reuters, July 6, 2005.
75. Braun and Chyba also argue that China, Russia, Taiwan, Macedonia, and Belarus also assisted Iran. Braun and Chyba, "Proliferation Rings." According to the Nuclear Threat Initiative, China has also given assistance to Iraq, North Korea, Pakistan, Saudi Arabia, and Syria; Russia (or the Soviet Union previously) has also helped Egypt, Iraq, Libya, North Korea, and Syria. See Nuclear Threat Initiative, *Country Profiles,* January 8, 2005, http://www.nti.org/e_research/profiles/.
76. On China's missile exports and dates, see Nuclear Threat Initiative, *Country Profiles.* On its bid

Figure 3a. The Network Structure of Second-Tier Ballistic Missile Proliferation, 1974–2002

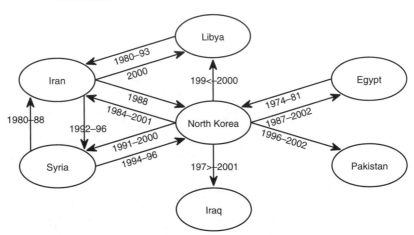

SOURCES: Missile proliferation data are from the Nuclear Threat Initiative, *Country Profiles,* and extend through 2002. Individual and minor incidents were discarded.

NOTE: Only the core second-tier proliferators appear in this figure; other countries that received only limited assistance (e.g., Sudan and Yemen) are excluded. Uncertain dates are marked as < (beginning of decade) or > (end of decade). Minor nodes are excluded; nodes are placed for clarity.

The missile proliferation network shown in Figure 3a exhibits a more dynamic structure than its nuclear counterpart. North Korea received assistance from Egypt from 1974 to 1981, importing Scud missiles that were reverse-engineered by North Korean scientists. In 1988 Iran gave the North Koreans the wreckage of al-Hussein missiles launched by Iraq in the war with Iran. North Korea reciprocated by assisting both Egypt and Iran with their development of ballistic missiles, then later Libya. Syria gave North Korea information on its SS-21 Scarab missiles from 1994 to 1996, and North Korea exported variants of the Scud and Nodong between 1991 and 2000 back to Syria. North Korea also exported Nodong technology to Pakistan, possibly in exchange for nuclear technology, while unconfirmed reports identify exports to Iraq, possibly as recently as 2001. Libya and Syria assisted Iran early in its program by

to join the MTCR, see Wade Boese, "Missile Regime Puts Off China," *Arms Control Today,* Vol. 34, No. 9 (November 2004).

Figure 3b. The Network Structure of Second-Tier Nuclear Proliferation, 1987–2002

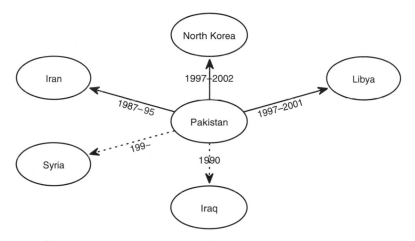

SOURCES: Nuclear proliferation data are from Gaurav Kampani, "Proliferation Unbound: Nuclear Tales from Pakistan" (Monterey, Calif.: Center for Nonproliferation Studies, Monterey Institute of International Studies, February 23, 2004), http://cns.miis.edu/pubs/week/040223.htm.
NOTE: Declined offers of assistance are dotted; uncertain dates are marked as ~ (mid-decade). Minor nodes are excluded; nodes are placed for clarity.

supplying Scud-B missiles; Iran later reciprocated by sharing Scud-C technology with Syria and development assistance with Libya. Missile technology appears to be more transferable than nuclear technology; many of the relationships in Figure 3a involve these reciprocal exchanges.[77] This may in part be a result of the many small technical challenges posed by ballistic missiles, which allows for more decentralization and specialization than does nuclear weapons technology.[78] The density of ties among the participating nodes makes the total shutdown of such networks much more difficult, but it also makes it easier to trace relationships and discover additional nodes in the network.

Evidence that the nuclear proliferation network continues to be centralized was provided in early 2005. In February the U.S. government contended that North Korea had sold uranium hexafluoride to Libya. The "alarming intelli-

---

77. For details on these trades, see Nuclear Threat Initiative, *Country Profiles*.
78. I thank Dean Wilkening for pointing this out.

gence" that North Korea was "actively exporting nuclear material" was deduced "not on a murky intelligence assessment but on hard data."[79] The evidence that led U.S. "government scientists to conclude with near certainty"[80] that the uranium was from North Korea was either from uranium isotopic ratios or from plutonium contaminating the three cylinders of uranium hexafluoride that Libya had received in 2000 and 2001.[81] This would indicate that the network was becoming more decentralized, as nuclear trading was taking place between the separate nodes rather than through the hub. One recently retired Pentagon official described the trade as "huge, because it changes the whole equation with the North. . . . It suggests we don't have time to sit around and wait for the outcome of negotiations."[82] In March the U.S. government disclosed additional evidence regarding large financial transfers from Libya, which the United States claimed implicated North Korea.[83]

Contrary to U.S. claims, the plutonium, uranium, and financial evidence in the Libyan case is far from conclusive. The IAEA had performed similar analyses and found no plutonium traces on the cylinders.[84] The precision of the method used to determine the potential source of uranium has also been called into question, because the isotopic ratio measured (U-234 to U-238) can vary as much as 10 percent.[85] Yet the United States' contention that the uranium must be from North Korea "with a certainty of 90 percent or better" is belied by the admission that the U.S. inspection team had no sample of North Korean uranium.[86] Additionally, these concentrations can differ greatly even within a single mine, making it hard to identify a distinctive fingerprint.[87] The uranium in two of the three cylinders was natural uranium, while the other held depleted uranium; the latter is generally useless for creating either nuclear weapons or

79. Glenn Kessler, "North Korea May Have Sent Libya Nuclear Material, U.S. Tells Allies," *Washington Post*, February 2, 2005.
80. David E. Sanger and William J. Broad, "Tests Said to Tie Deal on Uranium to North Korea," *New York Times*, February 2, 2005.
81. Sanger and Broad reported isotopic ratios; Kessler reported plutonium. Ibid; and Kessler, "North Korea May Have Sent Libya Nuclear Material, U.S. Tells Allies."
82. Quoted in Sanger and Broad, "Tests Said to Tie Deal on Uranium to North Korea."
83. David E. Sanger and William J. Broad, "Using Clues from Libya to Study a Nuclear Mystery," *New York Times*, March 31, 2005.
84. Glenn Kessler and Dafna Linzer, "Nuclear Evidence Could Point to Pakistan," *Washington Post*, February 3, 2005.
85. Steve Fetter, "Nuclear Archaeology: Verifying Declarations of Fissile-Material Production," *Science and Global Security*, Vol. 3, Nos. 3–4 (1993), pp. 237–259.
86. See Sanger and Broad, "Tests Said to Tie Deal on Uranium to North Korea."
87. Jon B. Wolfsthal, "No Good Choices: The Implications of a Nuclear North Korea," House Committee on International Relations, 109th Cong., 1st sess., February 17, 2005.

fuel, while the total extractable weapons-grade uranium content of the former was about 7 kg, far too little for a first-generation nuclear weapon.[88] Given that the North Koreans had not even started attempting to acquire enrichment capabilities in 2000,[89] the depleted uranium is most likely the by-product of Pakistani enrichment. This is additional evidence that the uranium must have at least passed through Pakistan on its way to Libya, consistent with the existing structure of the nuclear network. One of A.Q. Khan's middlemen, B.S.A. Tahir, reported that the cylinders had been flown to Libya aboard a Pakistani airplane in 2001. With respect to the financial evidence, U.S. and foreign officials who had seen the documents in question said that they did not show that payments went directly to North Korea.[90] Nor were the payments necessarily for nuclear materials; they could equally have been for missile transfers.[91] The suppression of information by the United States that Pakistan was the likely intermediary in the deal and the high probability that the container originated in Pakistan upset U.S. allies,[92] because it appeared that the U.S. government was manipulating intelligence information to put pressure on North Korea.[93]

TACIT KNOWLEDGE AND THE SPREAD OF NUCLEAR WEAPONS
Nuclear proliferation networks are more likely to adopt star structures than ring or clique structures in part because nuclear proliferation has greater tacit

---

88. Two of the three cylinders delivered to Libya (one small and one large) contained natural uranium hexafluoride (UF_6); the other small cylinder contained depleted UF_6 at 0.3 percent enrichment. The large one had 1,600 kg of UF_6; the small ones had 25 kg each. Libya received the large cylinder in February 2001 and the small ones in September 2000. See IAEA Board of Governors, *Implementation of the NPT Safeguards Agreement of the Socialist People's Libyan Arab Jamahiriya*, IAEA report GOV/2004/33, International Atomic Energy Agency, May 28, 2004, http://www.fas.org/nuke/guide/libya/iaea0504.pdf, p. 3; and IAEA Board of Governors, *Implementation of the NPT Safeguards Agreement of the Socialist People's Libyan Arab Jamahiriya*, IAEA report GOV/2004/59, International Atomic Energy Agency, August 30, 2004, http://www.fas.org/nuke/guide/libya/iaea0804.pdf, p. 4. Based on a natural uranium percentage of 0.71 percent, this would give a total of 11.6 kg of U-235; assuming a standard tails assay of 0.3 percent and an HEU enrichment of 93 percent, 7.2 kg of HEU could be extracted, about a third of the amount necessary for a small first-generation implosion weapon. Depleted uranium can be put in a blanket around a reactor core to produce plutonium or as a tamper in a nuclear weapon, but it cannot be usefully enriched.
89. Central Intelligence Agency Nonproliferation Center, "Unclassified Report to Congress on the Acquisition of Technology Relating to Weapons of Mass Destruction and Advanced Conventional Munitions," July 1–December 31, 2001.
90. Sanger and Broad, "Using Clues from Libya to Study a Nuclear Mystery."
91. I thank Paul Kerr for pointing this out. See Jeffrey Lewis and Paul Kerr, "A Financial Link in That AQ Khan–North Korea–Libya UF6 Daisy Chain?" April 1, 2005, http://www.armscontrolwonk.com/index.php?id=509.
92. Kessler and Linzer, "Nuclear Evidence Could Point to Pakistan."
93. Dafna Linzer, "U.S. Misled Allies About Nuclear Export: N. Korean Material Landed in Pakistan, Instead of Libya," *Washington Post*, March 20, 2005.

knowledge requirements. Tacit knowledge is knowledge that cannot be formulated in words or symbols, but must be learned through trial and error, potentially under the direct tutelage of someone who has already learned it; nuclear weapons design and production in particular depends heavily on such knowledge. Both Britain and the Soviet Union attempted to replicate the U.S. design from documents that they possessed, yet they had to devote major resources before they proved useful. Every nuclear program has required more time than the three and a half years the Manhattan Project took to build the world's first atomic weapon, despite the transfer of information and even scientists from one program to another.[94] One of the major preoccupations of the U.S. nuclear weapons complex is to retain tacit knowledge in the absence of testing.[95] Ballistic missile development, while also requiring some tacit knowledge,[96] would seem to be easier to transfer. If tacit knowledge was not restricting transfers of nuclear technology, the missile and nuclear networks would have connections between the same states; for example, because Libya and Iran trade missile technology, they would be likely to trade nuclear technology as well. Yet this has happened in only one case, between Pakistan and North Korea.

This constraint structures the proliferation networks. Only the central hub can dispatch experts to train new proliferants in constructing and operating equipment, whereas satellite states might be able to help each other with acquiring equipment but not with providing tacit knowledge. The hub might also have financial incentives to restrict information transfer: for example, selling parts for centrifuges but not instructions on how to build them. Individual satellite nodes are usually likely to form ties (nuclear or not) with each other through their common connections with the hub, thus decreasing chances of a potential dismantlement of the network by eliminating the hub. Such actors—called "structurally equivalent" in network terms—have a propensity to act in similar ways, often forming ties or networks between themselves when direct

94. Donald MacKenzie and Graham Spinardi, "Tacit Knowledge, Weapons Design, and the Uninvention of Nuclear Weapons," *American Journal of Sociology,* Vol. 101, No. 1 (July 1995), pp. 44–99.

95. Alexander H. Montgomery, "Reconstructing Reliability: Confidence in Nuclear Weapons under Science-Based Stockpile Stewardship," master's thesis, University of California, Berkeley, May 1999.

96. Donald MacKenzie, *Inventing Accuracy: A Historical Sociology of Nuclear Missile Guidance* (Cambridge, Mass.: MIT Press, 1993).

competitive pressures are weak.[97] Tacit knowledge requirements, however, help to suppress these ties.

Although some nonstate actors (e.g., Tahir and Tinner) involved in nuclear proliferation networks have been able to individually supply a few parts for centrifuges, they cannot provide the crucial tacit knowledge required to operate them. Parts from the A.Q. Khan network manufactured by the Malaysian company SCOPE were seized en route to Libya in October 2003 by a coalition of Western states. Yet these parts only constituted about 15 percent of the total number of parts for Libya's centrifuges, and none of the most sensitive parts.[98] While decentralized manufacturing may be efficient in some ways, both the lack of a direct connection and an inability to rapidly supply parts and feedback on their performance further hinder nonstate actors from properly supplying parts, let alone providing a complete proliferation solution. Iran, for example, reported that "many difficulties had been encountered as a result of machine crashes attributed to poor quality [imported] components."[99]

Although A.Q. Khan supplied both plans and parts, it appears that without the tacit knowledge required to produce nuclear weapons, the successful development of a nuclear capability requires much trial and error. Indeed, this seems to have been North Korea's problem. As Mark Hibbs has noted, "One official said that some information suggests the DPRK may have 'slavishly followed a recipe' calling for some more advanced components or materials, as called for in the design package provided by its helpers."[100] Although Iran has not fallen into this trap, the numerous problems it has encountered in its program underscore the difficulty of transferring tacit knowledge. The parts that Iran bought on the black market for its centrifuges (outside the A.Q. Khan network) were of highly variable quality; neither the sellers nor the Iranians knew how to judge their quality.[101] Iran is building a yellowcake-to-UF_6 conversion plant at Isfahan based on Chinese blueprints. Yet it has had difficulties produc-

---

97. Competitive pressures or direct negative ties can overcome the tendency of structurally equivalent actors to cooperate unless faced with a greater threat—for example, animosity between Iran and Iraq.

98. David Albright and Corey Hinderstein, "Libya's Gas Centrifuge Procurement: Much Remains Undiscovered," March 1, 2004, http://www.isis-online.org/publications/libya/cent_procure.html.

99. IAEA Board of Governors, GOV/2003/63, p. 7.

100. Hibbs, "CIA Assessment on DPRK Presumes Massive Outside Help on Centrifuges."

101. Mehdi Mohammadi, "Iran Press: Official Interviewed on Nuclear Activities since 1970," BBC Monitoring International Reports, Keyhan (Tehran), translated from Persian, April 28, 2005.

ing high-quality UF$_4$ (uranium tetrafluoride) and converting it into UF$_6$.[102] Although less evidence is available from Libya's program, the lags in time between receiving parts from the A.Q. Khan network and constructing its facilities as well as other difficulties seem to indicate the presence of similar problems. According to one observer, these problems suggest that Libya bought "nuclear technology without actually knowing how it worked."[103]

Yet materials acquisition is only one step in the nuclear weapons acquisition process. Even with a bomb design, many intermediate steps are required to develop a nuclear arsenal. Being able to cast fissile materials and high explosives into the necessary shapes requires extensive experience.[104] As Siegfried Hecker has noted, "The real secrets are in the details of the metallurgy, the manufacturing and the engineering."[105] A.Q. Khan apparently attempted to pass on these secrets, offering "uranium re-conversion and casting capabilities."[106] His success in describing the necessary processes in sufficient detail, however, appears to have been limited. These weapons also require a delivery system; although some of the countries discussed here have advanced ballistic missile programs, miniaturizing, toughening, and fitting a nuclear device that can be used as a nuclear warhead on a missile is not a straightforward task.

The bomb in the design that Libya acquired from the A.Q. Khan network was too large to fit on any of its ballistic missiles[107]—or, indeed, possibly on any missile in development by North Korea or Iran, both of which may have also received copies of the design. Accounts describe the design as "crude" and incomplete.[108] Some sources note that the core device has a mass of about 500 kg;[109] most attribute the design to the fourth Chinese nuclear test in 1966.[110] Yet the total mass of the core device, reentry vehicle, and ballast is much greater; the warhead that most closely fits this description is the one on

---

102. Joseph Cirincione, personal communication, June 3, 2005, from conversations with Western officials and IAEA experts.

103. Quoted in Crawford, "Libya Was Far From Building Nuclear Bomb."

104. MacKenzie and Spinardi, "Tacit Knowledge, Weapons Design, and the Uninvention of Nuclear Weapons."

105. Quoted in William J. Broad and David E. Sanger, "Pakistani's Black Market May Sell Nuclear Secrets," *New York Times*, March 21, 2005.

106. Pierre Goldschmidt, IAEA deputy director-general and head of the Department of Safeguards, "Implementation of Safeguards in the Islamic Republic of Iran," statement to the IAEA Board of Governors, March 1, 2005.

107. Crawford, "Libya Was Far From Building Nuclear Bomb."

108. David E. Sanger, "The Khan Network," paper presented at the Conference on South Asia and the Nuclear Future, Stanford, California, June 4–5, 2004.

109. Albright and Hinderstein, "Iran: Countdown to Showdown."

110. Sanger and Broad, "As Nuclear Secrets Emerge."

the Chinese DF-2A, a 32-ton, 21-meter-long, 1.65-meter-wide missile deployed from 1966 to 1979. This warhead, a 12-kiloton device, weighs 1,290 kg; with a 200 kg reentry vehicle, the total payload would be almost 1,500 kg.[111] By contrast, all of the missiles currently or previously owned or in development by Libya, Iran, and North Korea are designed with a maximum intended payload of at most 1,000 kg.[112] Although range can be traded for payload, whether the warheads are small enough to fit on the missiles is unclear; Scud-based missiles have a diameter of 0.88 meters; the missile with the largest diameter available to these new proliferants—North Korea's Nodong 1—is 1.32 meters wide, 16 meters long, and weighs 16.25 tons, making it a third of a meter narrower and half the mass of the DF-2A.[113] South Korea's National Intelligence Service reported in 2005 that North Korea lacked the technology to put warheads on missiles.[114] Even though other methods could still be used for delivery (e.g., from an aircraft, in a shipping container, or in a truck), they are all considerably less desirable. For example, if Iran wants to deter a state with advanced air defenses such as Israel, a ballistic missile is likely to have far more success; it has significant command and control advantages as well.

Past and Future Counterproliferation Efforts

Numerous strategies for dissuading proliferants and dissolving proliferation networks have been attempted, but few have been successful. Threatening regime change has been minimally effective, and isolating or containing "rogue" states has been counterproductive, coinciding with the growth of networks between them. By contrast, offering benefits that closely mirror some of the core motivations of these states to proliferate has met with some success.

A policy of regime change is unlikely to encourage cooperation and is very likely to convince proliferators that they need nuclear weapons to deter the United States. It is self-defeating: U.S. threats of forcible regime change are

111. John W. Lewis and Hua Di, "China's Ballistic Missile Programs: Technologies, Strategies, Goals," *International Security*, Vol. 17, No. 2 (Fall 1992), pp. 5–40.

112. Daryl Kimball, "Worldwide Ballistic Missile Inventories" (Washington, D.C.: Arms Control Association, May 2002), http://www.armscontrol.org/factsheets/missiles.asp.

113. Joseph Bermudez Jr., "A History of Ballistic Missile Development in the DPRK," Occasional Paper 2 (Monterey, Calif.: Monitoring Proliferation Threats Project, Center for Nonproliferation Studies, Monterey Institute of International Studies, 1999), http://cns.miis.edu/pubs/opapers/op2/op2.pdf, p. 27.

114. Jeong-ho Yun, "North Korea Can't Put Nuke Warheads on Missiles: NIS," *Choson Ilbo* (Seoul), February 15, 2005.

likely to increase the number of states that seek a nuclear capability and bolster existing proliferators' programs as a defensive reaction. North Korea reacted to the invasion of Iraq by claiming that it was reprocessing all of its 8,000
spent fuel rods in late April 2003;[115] then in late August 2003, it threatened to
test a nuclear device.[116] The Bush administration touts Libya's disarmament as
an example of the threat of regime change working, yet this argument does not
hold up under scrutiny. Libya had been attempting to rehabilitate itself for
years, and a final agreement was well in the works before the invasion of Iraq
or the interception of the BBC *China*.[117] Indeed, one Western diplomat suggested that Libya tipped off the United States about the shipment, perhaps as a
good-faith gesture; others have speculated that Libya made the order expect-
ing or intending it to be intercepted to exaggerate the size, worth, and progress
of its nuclear program.[118]

A policy of isolation or containment, such as that applied to Iran and Iraq by
past U.S. administrations, is a strategy that falls short of regime change. Indeed, the threat of isolation itself can be an important bargaining tool. Yet like
economic coercion,[119] threatening isolation is more effective than carrying it
out. The immense efforts made by the United States to isolate and contain Iran
proved successful in delaying completion of the Bushehr nuclear reactor in the
1990s, but this strategy gave Iran no incentive to cooperate and did little to
prevent the transfer of technology from second-tier suppliers.

The practice of isolation can even be counterproductive. Many of the states
in the current second-tier proliferation networks (as well as those in past networks, for example, South Africa and Israel)[120] are isolated from the rest of the
international system, whether through their own choices or through deliberate
policies by the United States and other powerful actors. Isolation has been
identified as a possible correlate of nuclear weapons programs.[121] If "rogue"

---

115. David E. Sanger, "North Korea Says It Now Possesses Nuclear Arsenal," *New York Times*,
April 25, 2003.
116. David E. Sanger and Joseph Kahn, "North Korea Says It May Test an A-Bomb," *New York
Times*, August 29, 2003.
117. Flynt L. Leverett, "Why Libya Gave Up on the Bomb," *New York Times*, January 23, 2004.
118. Crawford, "Libya Was Far From Building Nuclear Bomb"; and Michael Roston, "Polishing
Up the Story on the PSI," *National Interest*, June 9, 2004, http://www.inthenationalinterest.com/
Articles/Vol3Issue23/Vol3Issue23RostonPFV.html.
119. Daniel W. Drezner, "The Hidden Hand of Economic Coercion," *International Organization*, Vol.
57, No. 3 (July 2003), pp. 643–659.
120. David Albright and Mark Hibbs, "South Africa: The ANC and the Atom Bomb," *Bulletin of
the Atomic Scientists*, Vol. 49, No. 3 (April 1993), pp. 32–37.
121. Jo and Gartzke, "Determinants of Nuclear Weapons Proliferation."

states are stopped from connecting with the rest of the world, they will be likely to connect with each other instead—with potentially disastrous consequences. The United States has facilitated connections between isolates by marginalizing them both in its rhetoric and policy and, since Ronald Reagan's administration, grouping them as "rogues," "pariahs," or "outlaws."[122] The Clinton administration slowly moved away from this policy in 1997 after the appointment of Madeleine Albright as secretary of state, who shifted U.S. rhetoric to "states of concern" in June 2000.[123] The Bush administration quickly returned to the "rogue" state rhetoric, then escalated it by referring to Iran, Iraq, and North Korea as members of an "axis of evil."[124] Later, John Bolton expanded the "axis" to include Libya, Syria, and Cuba.[125] This uncompromising rhetoric limits U.S. policy options and places the United States in a difficult negotiating position. The United States and the United Kingdom could not reach an agreement with Libya until the Bush administration complied with a request by high-level British officials to remove Bolton from the U.S. negotiating team; Bolton's unwillingness to compromise was preventing Libya from accepting a deal.[126]

By contrast, diplomatic incentives and economic benefits including aid and suspension of sanctions, have been successful in the past in an unexpected place—North Korea. Given its security relationships, the DPRK might seem to be a "hard case" for using these tools for counterproliferation.[127] Yet two of North Korea's three main demands for eliminating its nuclear program are for the United States to "recognize the DPRK's sovereignty" and to "not hinder [its] economic development."[128] North Korea has consistently responded positively to U.S. diplomatic overtures, economic benefits, and threats of economic

---

122. See Robert S. Litwak, *Rogue States and U.S. Foreign Policy: Containment after the Cold War* (Washington, D.C.: Woodrow Wilson Center Press, 2000); and Robert S. Litwak, "Non-proliferation and the Dilemmas of Regime Change," *Survival*, Vol. 45, No. 4 (Winter 2003), pp. 7–32.

123. Madeleine K. Albright, "Secretary of State Madeleine K. Albright Interview on the Diane Rehm Show, WAMU-FM," June 19, 2000.

124. Bush, "State of the Union Address."

125. John R. Bolton, "Beyond the Axis of Evil: Additional Threats from Weapons of Mass Destruction," remarks to Heritage Foundation, Washington, D.C., May 6, 2002, http://www.state.gov/t/us/rm/9962.htm.

126. Michael Hirsh, "Bolton's British Problem," *Newsweek*, May 2, 2005, http://www.msnbc.msn.com/id/7614769/site/newsweek/.

127. North Korea is unique in the world; it is geographically surrounded by two nuclear powers (Russia and China) and two latent powers (Japan and South Korea), and has U.S. troops are deployed on its border.

128. "Conclusion of Non-aggression Treaty between DPRK and U.S. Called For," Korean Central News Agency, October 24, 2002.

sanctions when deemed credible, and when combined with clear red lines. For example, during the 1993–94 crisis, threats of sanctions were met with North Korean bellicosity. The North Koreans believed that, with its ally China on the Security Council, multilateral sanctions would never pass. Quiet diplomacy combined with a good-faith effort by the United States to negotiate with North Korea convinced China to warn the DPRK on June 10, 1994, that it might not veto sanctions. This threat and a clear delineation by the United States of red lines that would trigger sanctions brought the North Koreans to the bargaining table.[129] Similarly, diplomatic and symbolic gestures by the United States—for example, making joint statements with the DPRK after meetings and replacing its gas-graphite nuclear plants with light-water nuclear reactors rather than with conventional power plants—were key to North Korean concessions during the crisis. These gestures were effective because they allowed North Korea to maintain its status as an equal of the United States and as a nuclear state, albeit not a nuclear weapons state.[130]

The Bush administration should adopt a policy of proliferation pragmatism that balances credible threats of force with promises of benefits to convince the current hubs of North Korea and Pakistan and potential new hubs such as Iran to cooperate. Incentives must be matched with states' underlying motivations for proliferation. Such incentives could include recognition by important states and membership in international organizations as well as economic benefits, including aid and suspension of sanctions.

NORTH KOREA

North Korea should be offered a grand bargain in which its security, economic, and diplomatic concerns are treated as legitimate rather than secondary matters to be resolved after disarmament;[131] the United States has not yet attempted to test North Korea in this way. Convincing the North Koreans that it is not going to be invaded is more likely to prod them into voluntarily giving up their program than is the threat of regime change.

---

129. On China's threat, see Don Oberdorfer, *The Two Koreas: A Contemporary History,* rev. ed. (New York: Basic Books, 2001), p. 320. On establishing clear red lines, see Joel S. Wit, Daniel Poneman, and Robert L. Gallucci, *Going Critical: The First North Korean Nuclear Crisis* (Washington, D.C.: Brookings, 2004).
130. See Alexander H. Montgomery, "A Tale of Two Crises: U.S.-DPRK Nuclear Dynamics," paper presented at the annual conference of the American Political Science Association, Chicago, Illinois, September 2–5, 2004.
131. On this topic, see Michael E. O'Hanlon and Mike Mochizuki, "Toward a Grand Bargain with North Korea," *Washington Quarterly,* Vol. 26, No. 4 (Autumn 2003), pp. 7–18.

The North Korean declaration on February 10, 2005, that it had "manufac-tured nukes for self-defence" seemed to be a new twist in the North Korean crisis.[132] Rather than being an abrogation of the talks, this statement was largely a set of requirements for continuing negotiations, as elaborated by North Korea's representative to the United Nations on February 19.[133] The South Korean government played down the announcement as being short of declaring nuclear weapons–state status.[134]

Although some observers argue against rewarding North Korea or other states for bad behavior for fear of emulation,[135] it is unlikely that any other country would ever aspire to be in North Korea's position, isolated from the rest of the world, dependant on others for basic needs, and desperate enough to attempt to sell its security. Moreover, given the lack of other credible op-tions, making a deal with North Korea is better than threatening regime change or relying on China to pressure it.[136] Six-party talks between China, Japan, North Korea, Russia, South Korea, and the United States began in August 2003 after North Korea withdrew from the NPT and ground to a halt after the third session in June 2004. South Korea's offer in June 2005 to provide electricity to North Korea (despite previous objections from the Bush adminis-tration to including additional inducements) is widely credited with bringing North Korea back to the six-party talks.[137] Others argue that pacts such as the Agreed Framework can be easily violated because covert programs can con-tinue out of view.[138] Yet this argument highlights the problem that countries must ultimately comply willingly with the terms of disarmament—and there-fore inducements must be offered that tackle the fundamental incentives that countries have to proliferate. As U.S. State Department official Paula DeSutter notes, "If we go into this and North Korea has not made such a decision, this is

132. "DPRK Ministry of Foreign Affairs Statement," Korean Central News Agency, February 10, 2005.
133. Chan-ho Kang and Myo-ja Ser, "North's Envoy Lists Conditions," *Joong-Ang Ilbo* (Seoul), Feb-ruary 19, 2005.
134. "North Korea Not Yet a Nuclear Weapons State: Seoul," Reuters, February 13, 2005.
135. Ari Fleischer, press briefing, James S. Brady Press Briefing Room, April 29, 2003, http://www.whitehouse.gov/news/releases/2003/04/20030429-3.html.
136. As Robert Gallucci, the Clinton administration's chief negotiator with the North Koreans during the 1993–94 crisis, put it, "Listen, I'm not interested in teaching other people lessons. I'm interested in the national security of the United States. If that's what you're interested in, are you better off with this deal or without it? You tell me what you're going to do without the deal, and I'll compare that with the deal." Quoted in Scott Stossel, "North Korea: The War Game," *Atlantic Monthly*, July/August 2005, pp. 97–108.
137. Joel Brinkley, "Rice Claims U.S. Role in Korean About-Face," *New York Times*, July 14, 2005.
138. Bolton, "The Bush Administration and Nonproliferation."

going to be like pulling teeth and our confidence at the end may not be what we would like it to be."[139] Unlike North Korea's plutonium program, even a production-scale centrifuge facility would be difficult to detect via technical means. Given the challenges of remote sensing, willing compliance is necessary for disarmament.

Threats of force alone cannot stop North Korea from trading either its missile or nuclear technologies. It is not a member of the MTCR, and its missile exports do not violate any laws; a shipment of Scuds from the DPRK was stopped by Spanish commandos acting on U.S. intelligence in December 2002 but had to be permitted to reach its destination in Yemen.[140] Now that North Korea is no longer a de facto member of the NPT, it is similarly unconstrained to trade in nuclear technology, although recipients that are members of the NPT would be in violation if they accepted nuclear technology for the purpose of pursuing a weapons capability. Yet the North Koreans have been willing to trade both its nuclear and missile programs for recognition, symbolic rewards, and economic assistance.[141] North Korea should be tested to see if it will accept a credibly backed bargain including these three elements.

PAKISTAN

The Bush administration has claimed success in shutting down the A.Q. Khan network that supplied both Pakistan and other proliferators, but its lack of cooperation with the IAEA and an unwillingness to push Pakistan have hampered U.S. efforts.[142] Not only is Pakistan's network continuing to operate, but it may be re-creating parts of it with new middlemen. Joseph Cirincione, director of nonproliferation at the Carnegie Endowment for International Peace, argues, "The network hasn't been shut down. . . . It's just gotten quieter. Perhaps it's gone a little deeper underground."[143] Pakistan continues to seek parts for its nuclear program abroad; Swiss authorities stopped two attempts by the A.Q. Khan network in 2004 to purchase aluminum tubes from Russia for Pakistan's use.[144] The existence of any network of suppliers not within

139. Quoted in Reuben Staines, "Verifying NK Nuke Dismantlement Tough Task: U.S.," *Korea Times* (Seoul), January 31, 2005.
140. Thom Shanker, "If the Scuds Were Going to Iraq," *New York Times*, December 15, 2002.
141. On North Korea's willingness to trade its nuclear program, see Selig S. Harrison, "Inside North Korea: Leaders Open to Ending Nuclear Crisis," *Financial Times* (London), May 4, 2004. On its missile, program, see Oberdorfer, *The Two Koreas*, pp. 439–440.
142. Sanger and Broad, "As Nuclear Secrets Emerge."
143. Quoted in Louis Charbonneau, "Pakistan Reviving Nuclear Black Market, Experts Say," Reuters, March 15, 2005.
144. "Khan's Nuclear Network Still Trying in 2004 to Buy Nuclear Technology: Swiss Report," Associated Press, May 26, 2005.

Pakistan's direct control makes proliferation more likely; suppliers who fill orders for Pakistan's program can fill the same orders for other proliferants. A strong U.S. effort to establish a fissile material cutoff treaty (FMCT) that includes Pakistan would undercut these suppliers; if Pakistan stops producing fissile materials, demand for centrifuge parts will drop significantly.

Although Pakistan is unlikely to roll back either its nuclear or missile programs, the United States and the other members of the MTCR should make it a high priority to ensure that it joins the MTCR and adopts domestic controls on nuclear and missile technologies. Pakistan (as well as India and Israel) should be brought inside the nuclear nonproliferation regime, possibly by relaxing the membership standards for nuclear export control consortia, including the Zangger Committee and the Nuclear Suppliers Group. More information about the extent of the A.Q. Khan network and other potential buyers (as well as the actual recipients) is also needed; the United States should push Pakistan to reveal the identity of the "fourth country" that Khan's network may have supplied or demonstrate that this country is fictional.[145]

IRAN

If the North Korean and Pakistani hubs are effectively shut down, the next logical step would be to turn to nodes that could evolve into new hubs. The advanced state of Iran's missile and nuclear programs, as well as its active participation in both networks, would suggest that it is a likely candidate to take over the central role of spreading nuclear/missile technologies. Indeed, as is shown in Figure 3a, Iran has already formed a mini-hub of missile proliferation between Libya, North Korea, and Syria. The positive response of Iran to potential diplomatic and economic benefits offered by the EU in exchange for the temporary suspension of its uranium enrichment program in November 2004 pending a final agreement is another indication that these tools can be very useful in a context that is normally dominated by security considerations. Suggestions that the United States should continue to play the "bad cop" to Europe's "good cop" with respect to Iran miss the point of the analogy: the good cop is convincing only if he can credibly restrain the bad cop; without a clear signal from the United States that it will accept the outcome of negotia-

---

145. Evidence found in shipping records indicates a possible fourth country beyond North Korea, Iran, and Libya. Barton Gellman and Dafna Linzer, "Unprecedented Peril Forces Tough Calls; President Faces a Multi-front Battle against Threats Known, Unknown," *Washington Post*, October 26, 2004.

tions and not take military action, Iran is unlikely to accept an offer from the EU to restrict its nuclear activities.

The United States should send such a signal—and soon, before Iran gives up on negotiations entirely. President Bush's assertion that "this notion that the United States is getting ready to attack Iran is simply ridiculous" was undermined when he continued: "And having said that, all options are on the table."[146] The minor concessions of airplane parts and support for World Trade Organization membership offered by Secretary of State Rice are insufficient; these gestures appear to be "hawk engagement," where offers over the last year in support of the EU's efforts (promptly rejected by Iran) are made to legitimize coercive action later.[147] Instead, the United States should take seriously the feelers sent out by former Iranian President and head of the influential Expediency Council Hashemi Rafsanjani to open diplomatic channels and deal directly with Iran.[148] The election of Mahmoud Ahmadinejad as president of Iran instead of Rafsanjani in June 2005 should not be used by the United States as a reason to avoid talks. The election does not change Iran's underlying reasons for pursuing nuclear technology, which are intertwined with factors such as international prestige and national pride as much as anything else.[149] As a result, it will be difficult to eliminate Iran's nuclear program completely (just as North Korea required nuclear power reactors in 1994 to save face), but creative applications of technology and diplomacy could produce a lasting compromise that keeps Iran short of the nuclear weapons threshold.

Conclusion

States are neither as determined nor as advanced in their pursuit of nuclear capabilities as proliferation determinists suggest. Part of the reason for this is the difficulty of transmitting tacit knowledge to new proliferators, which restricts the structure of nuclear proliferation networks. Two main implications flow

---

146. Quoted in Elisabeth Bumiller, "Bush Says Europe Should Not Lift China Arms Ban," *New York Times*, February 22, 2005.
147. Victor D. Cha, "Hawk Engagement and Preventive Defense on the Korean Peninsula," *International Security*, Vol. 27, No. 1 (Summer 2002), pp. 40–78.
148. "Region: Tehran Wants U.S. to Open Diplomatic Channel," *Daily Times* (Lahore), March 27, 2005.
149. George Perkovich, "Iran: Nuclear Power as National Pride," *Khaleej Times* (Dubai), March 26, 2005; and Neil MacFarquhar, "Across Iran, Nuclear Power Is a Matter of Pride," *New York Times*, May 29, 2005.

from this analysis. First, existing proliferation networks should be shut down by eliminating the hubs while preventing new ones from emerging. Second, a full range of incentives, instead of the threat of regime change, should be used to convince hub states to stop nuclear transfers.

Both time and diplomatic energy are in short supply, however; the immediate need is to cap and roll back the proliferation of networks created by Pakistan and North Korea and to keep new hubs, such as Iran, from taking their place. Tailored incentives and disincentives must be applied to these states. These policies require both carrots and sticks and need to be broadened beyond security-minded proposals to include diplomatic, symbolic, and economic incentives and disincentives.

This does not mean that policymakers can become proliferation procrastinators and wait until the time is ripe to eliminate these networks. Nor does it mean that they should become proliferation determinists clamoring for regime change and taking drastic steps (e.g., military action against North Korea, Iran, or Pakistan) that could have severe consequences. Policymakers have both the time and the tools to stop these hubs. By acting like proliferation pragmatists, policymakers can dismantle these hubs before they form a network of ties so dense that it will be impossible to pull apart.

Osirak Redux?

Assessing Israeli Capabilities to Destroy Iranian Nuclear Facilities

Whitney Raas and Austin Long

The use of military force to halt or reverse nuclear proliferation is an option that has been much discussed and occasionally exercised. In the 1960s, for example, the United States considered destroying China's nuclear program at an early stage but ultimately decided against it.[1] More recently, the key rationale for the invasion of Iraq in 2003 was the threat posed by Iraq's suspected inventory of weapons of mass destruction (WMD). Although significant evidence of WMD was not found in the Iraq case, the potential utility of military force for counterproliferation remains, particularly in the case of Iran. The possibility of military action against Iranian nuclear facilities has gained prominence in the public discourse, drawing comments from journalists, former military officers, and defense analysts.[2] This makes the Iranian nuclear program a potential test case for military counterproliferation.

Iran's nuclear ambitions have been the subject of serious debate within the international community for more than four years.[3] Media reports have repeatedly discussed the possibility that the United States might attempt a preventive strike against Iran. The United States' ongoing involvement in Iraq, however, may limit U.S. willingness to do so. Israel, in contrast, has more to

Whitney Raas is a Research Analyst at the Center for Naval Analyses in Alexandria, Virginia. She conducted this work while completing graduate studies in nuclear engineering and political science at the Massachusetts Institute of Technology. Austin Long is a doctoral candidate in political science at the Massachusetts Institute of Technology, a member of the MIT Security Studies Program, and Adjunct Researcher at the RAND Corporation.

For helpful comments on previous drafts of this article, the authors wish to thank David Delgado, Brendan Green, Llewelyn Hughes, Colin Jackson, Gordon Kohse, Jon Lindsay, William Norris, Michael Parkyn, Barry Posen, Daryl Press, Joshua Rovner, and two anonymous reviewers.

1. See William Burr and Jeffrey T. Richelson, "Whether to 'Strangle the Baby in the Cradle': The United States and the Chinese Nuclear Program, 1960–64," *International Security*, Vol. 25, No. 3 (Winter 2000/01), pp. 54–99.
2. One widely cited example is Seymour M. Hersh, "The Iran Plans," *New Yorker*, April 17, 2006, pp. 30–37.
3. In 2002 the National Council of Resistance of Iran exposed Tehran's secret nuclear sites at a press conference. "Mullahs' Top Secret Nuclear Sites and WMD Projects Exposed at NCRI Press Conference," *Iran Liberation*, August 19, 2002, pp. 1–4. Since then, repeated International Atomic Energy Agency (IAEA) reports have detailed Iran's nuclear activities. In his 2006 address to the United Nations General Assembly, IAEA Director-General Mohamed ElBaradei stated, "The IAEA continues therefore to be unable to confirm the peaceful nature of Iran's nuclear programme." Quoted in "Statement to the Sixty-first Regular Session of the United Nations General Assembly," New York, October 30, 2006.

International Security, Vol. 31, No. 4 (Spring 2007), pp. 7–33

fear from a nuclear Iran than the United States and may see no choice but to re-sort to force to curtail Iran's capabilities if diplomacy fails.[4]

Israel has repeatedly stated its unequivocal opposition to a nuclear-armed Iran, and much speculation exists about what action the Israelis might take to prevent Iran from developing nuclear weapons.[5] Indeed, multiple reports suggest that Israeli leaders are contemplating a preventive military strike to remove the threat of an Iranian nuclear capability. Such action would not be without precedent: on June 7, 1981, Israel launched one of the most ambitious preventive attacks in modern history. Israeli Air Force (IAF) F-16 and F-15 fighter jets destroyed the Iraqi reactor at Osirak in one of the earliest displays of what has become known as "precision strike." No IAF planes were lost, and despite the political repercussions, the raid was considered a great success.[6]

As Iran's nuclear program moves forward, arguments for preventive action may seem increasingly compelling to the government of Israel. Yet no unclassified net assessment of Israel's current capability to destroy Iranian nuclear facilities exists.[7] The capabilities of the IAF have grown dramatically in the past two decades, but the Iranian facilities are a significantly more challenging target than Osirak.

As an unclassified assessment of military options, this analysis contains a number of assumptions and omissions. First, it relies on public reports regarding Iran's nuclear program, specifically the International Atomic Energy Agency (IAEA) safeguard reports that describe Iran's documented nuclear ac-

---

4. Diplomatic overtures by France, Germany, and the United Kingdom have focused on providing incentives to Iran in exchange for a halt in nuclear conversion and enrichment. These efforts have failed, however, and the UN voted unanimously to impose sanctions on Iran at the end of 2006. Nasser Karimi, "Iran Rebuffs U.N., Vows to Speed Up Uranium Enrichment," *Washington Post*, December 25, 2006.

5. See, for example, Uzi Mahnaimi and Sarah Baxter, "Israel Readies Forces for Strike on Nuclear Iran," *Sunday Times* (London), December 11, 2005, http://www.timesonline.co.uk/article/0,,2089-1920074,00.html; Ian Bruce, "Israelis Plan Pre-emptive Strike on Iran," *Herald* (London), January 10, 2006, http://www.theherald.co.uk/news/53948.html; and Josef Federman, "Israeli Hints at Preparation to Stop Iran," *Washington Post*, January 22, 2006.

6. For details on the 1981 raid, see Rodger W. Claire, *Raid on the Sun: Inside Israel's Secret Campaign That Denied Saddam the Bomb* (New York: Broadway Books, 2004); and Shelomoh Nakdimon, *First Strike: The Exclusive Story of How Israel Foiled Iraq's Attempt to Get the Bomb* (New York: Summit Books, 1987).

7. Some recent works have addressed the possibility of a preventive attack and the potential consequences, but have not presented any actual net assessment of Israeli capabilities against Iranian defenses. Instead, they have simply stated that attacking Iranian facilities would be more difficult than attacking Osirak. See Sammy Salama and Karen Ruster, "A Preemptive Attack on Iranian Nuclear Facilities: Possible Consequences," Center for Nonproliferation Studies Research Story, August 12, 2004, http://cns.miis.edu/pubs/week/040812.htm; and Yiftah Shapir, "Iranian Missiles: The Nature of the Threat," Tel Aviv Note, No. 83 (Tel Aviv: Jaffee Center for Strategic Studies, Tel Aviv University, 2003), http://www.tau.ac.il/jcss/tanotes/TAUnotes83.doc.

tivities. Some observers argue, however, that Iran is likely to have a parallel, covert nuclear program that is as advanced—or possibly more advanced—than the known program monitored by the IAEA. If this is true, a strike against Iran's known facilities would not significantly delay its development of nuclear weapons.[8]

In our view, however, the likelihood that Iran is engaged in a "covert" nuclear program is slim. Given that the known program was not exposed until 2002, a parallel program would, in essence, mean that Iran was developing two covert programs, with all the attendant expense, secrecy, and manpower.[9] Iran probably deliberately concealed its "overt" program with the hope that it would not be discovered. Thus, its large, industrialized facilities, especially those for uranium conversion and enrichment, are likely the primary and most advanced nuclear sites. A disruption of these activities would deal a significant blow to Iran's nuclear ambitions.

Second, this article does not attempt to address all the military scenarios. There are three broad forms that military action could take: a directed strike against Iranian nuclear facilities, a larger strike that included general military targets, or a full-scale invasion with the intent to overthrow the Iranian regime. Because the latter two scenarios are probably not realistic options for Israel, this article concentrates on a military strike directed at Iran's nuclear sites only. In particular, we focus on air power, as the Israelis have purchased significant parts of their air force structure with long-range strikes in mind.

Finally, this article does not take a position as to whether Israel should attempt to destroy Iran's nuclear facilities. The repercussions of such an attack would be significant in terms of diplomatic condemnation and a variety of potential Iranian military responses. The final outcome of diplomatic negotiations over Iran's nuclear program is uncertain, and an attack might only harden Iran's resolve to continue its nuclear program. This article is intended to address the more limited but vitally important question of whether such an attack is even possible, regardless of whether it is a good idea or not.

In addition to providing an assessment of the Iran-Israel scenario, this article provides insight into the more general phenomenon of military counterproliferation, particularly with regard to the use of air power as a counterproliferation tool. As concern over WMD proliferation grows, the use of air power for

---

8. One widely cited example is Graham Allison, "How Good Is American Intelligence on Iran's Bomb?" *YaleGlobal Online,* June 13, 2006, http://yaleglobal.yale.edu/display.article?id=7553.
9. An analogy would be if the United States had simultaneously developed two Manhattan Projects during the early 1940s.

strikes on individual targets may become even more appealing. Indeed, the George W. Bush administration has already made military counterproliferation part of its national strategy.[10] The case of Iran provides a template for the prospects and problems of using air power against targets of interest, especially nuclear-related, hardened, and well-defended targets.

This article seeks to fill this gap in the existing literature by providing a rough net assessment of an Israeli strike on known Iranian nuclear facilities. It does so by updating the Osirak scenario to account for both the improved IAF capabilities and the much tougher Iranian targets. The first section presents an overview of the Osirak raid. The second section describes the nature and location of Iran's nuclear facilities in the context of targeting for the IAF. The third section offers a rough estimate of the "weaponeering" necessary to destroy the target set. The fourth section discusses the forces the IAF and Iran possess relevant to this planned strike. The fifth section evaluates potential attack routes and the likely interaction of Israeli and Iranian forces. The sixth section offers a brief discussion of the likely outcome of an Israeli attack and the implications for military counterproliferation.

The Osirak Strike

The Israeli raid on the Osirak reactor was a calculated risk with no guarantee of success. The government of Prime Minister Menachem Begin was divided on the wisdom of the raid in discussions that began almost immediately after Begin's election in 1977. Begin decided to wait as long as possible before acting. In the meantime, the Mossad, Israel's intelligence agency, took steps to buy additional time. These steps included allegedly sabotaging the reactor cores for Osirak before the French companies that built them could deliver them to Iraq, as well as assassinating Iraqi nuclear officials. At the same time, the IAF began contingency planning for a strike on Osirak.[11] The plan to buy time worked to some degree, but it could not stop the Iraqi nuclear program. In October 1980, the Mossad reported to Prime Minister Begin that the Osirak reactor would be fueled and operational by June 1981. Following an intense debate, the order to strike was given.

---

10. See George W. Bush, *The National Security Strategy of the United States of America* (Washington, D.C.: White House, September 2002), sec. 5, http://www.whitehouse.gov/nsc/nss.html. The 2006 version does not differ on this point. See George W. Bush, *National Security Strategy of the United States of America* (Washington, D.C.: White House, March 2006), http://www.whitehouse.gov/nsc/nss/2006.
11. This summary is drawn principally from Claire, *Raid on the Sun*.

After months of careful preparations, a sixteen-plane strike package of eight F-15s and eight F-16s took off from Etzion air base in the Sinai. The flight profile was low altitude, across the Gulf of Aqaba, southern Jordan, and then across northern Saudi Arabia. The F-16s each carried two Mk-84 2,000 lb. bombs with delayed fuses. These bombs were "dumb," meaning they had no guidance other than that provided by the aircraft dropping them. The F-16s did have onboard targeting systems that would make the dumb bombs fairly accurate, but such accuracy would require that the plane get close to the target.

The strike package arrived near Osirak undetected and at low altitude. The F-16s formed up on predetermined points to begin their bombing runs, while the F-15s set up barrier combat air patrols to intercept Iraqi fighters. At 4 miles from the target, the F-16s climbed to 5,000 feet in order to dive at Osirak and release their bombs. Despite some navigation problems and Iraq air defenses, at least eight of the sixteen bombs released struck the containment dome of the reactor.

The strike package then turned and climbed to high altitude, returning much the way it had come. All sixteen planes successfully returned to Israel after recrossing Jordan. The results of the raid were spectacular. The reactor was totally destroyed, leaving much of the surrounding area undamaged.

Iranian Nuclear Facilities

The Iranians have learned important lessons from the Osirak raid: Iran's nuclear complex is large, carefully concealed, and spread extensively throughout the country, with multiple pathways to a nuclear weapons capability. The Nuclear Nonproliferation Treaty, to which Iran is a signatory, allows states access to peaceful nuclear technologies within certain safeguards and guidelines.[12] Iranian officials have claimed that by 2020, the country's growing population and the expected global demand for oil will require the extensive use of nuclear power to meet Iran's increasing energy needs while still enabling significant petroleum exports.[13] To meet these energy goals, Iran has developed a nuclear power program over the last few decades, including full front-end and back-end nuclear fuel cycle technology.[14]

---

12. *Treaty on the Nonproliferation of Nuclear Weapons,* http://www.un.org/events/npt2005/npttreaty.html, especially art. 4.

13. Reza Aghazadeh, "Iran's Nuclear Policy: Peaceful, Transparent, Independent," presentation by the vice president of Iran, IAEA headquarters, Vienna, Austria, May 6, 2003.

14. The "front end" of the nuclear fuel cycle refers to all activities engaged in prior to placing fuel in a reactor; the "back end" refers to post-irradiation activities. Front-end technology includes ura-

Iran is developing both indigenous uranium enrichment capabilities to produce weapons-grade uranium and a heavy-water plutonium production reactor and associated facilities for reprocessing spent fuel for plutonium separation.[15] Both developments pose proliferation risks, although at present Iran's progress toward enriching uranium appears significantly more advanced than its plutonium production ability. Declared industrial-scale facilities include a light water reactor at Bushehr, uranium mines, uranium conversion and enrichment plants, a fuel fabrication plant, and a heavy-water production facility. Iran is also building heavy water reactors.[16] Smaller, laboratory-scale projects include clandestine plutonium reprocessing and laser enrichment, as well as experiments involving uranium metal.[17] For this study, it is important to distinguish between activities that are low risk for proliferation and those that pose the most serious threat of proliferation. Iran has distributed its many nuclear facilities around the country, which would make it impossible for Israel to destroy the country's entire nuclear infrastructure.[18] To have a reasonable chance of significantly delaying Iranian nuclear efforts, Israel would have to limit the target set to the infrastructure's most critical nodes—that is, those directly involved in the production of fissile material, because without fissile material, no bomb can be produced.

Iran's nuclear complex has three critical nodes for the production of fissile material: a uranium conversion facility in Isfahan, a large uranium enrichment

nium mining, milling, conversion, enrichment, and fuel fabrication, while back-end technology consists of fuel reprocessing and waste management procedures. For more details on the nuclear fuel cycle, see Ronald Allen Knief, *Nuclear Engineering: Theory and Technology of Commercial Nuclear Power*, 2d ed. (New York: Hemisphere, 1992).

15. Weapons-grade uranium is generally quoted as above 93 percent U^{235}. See Owen R. Coté Jr., "A Primer on Fissile Materials and Nuclear Weapon Design," in Graham T. Allison, Coté, Richard A. Falkenrath, and Steven E. Miller, *Avoiding Nuclear Anarchy: Containing the Threat of Loose Russian Nuclear Weapons and Fissile Material* (Cambridge, Mass.: MIT Press, 1996). For information on Iran's plutonium production, see Iran Watch, "Latest Developments in the Nuclear Program in Iran, In Particular on the Plutonium Way," presentation by France, Nuclear Suppliers Group 2003 plenary meeting, Pusan, Republic of Korea, May 19–23, 2003.

16. Unless otherwise noted, the following summary of Iran's nuclear activities has been taken from the following sources: Director-General, IAEA, "Implementation of the NPT Safeguards Agreement in the Islamic Republic of Iran," GOV/2004/11 (Vienna: IAEA, February 24, 2004); Director-General, IAEA, "Implementation of the NPT Safeguards Agreement in the Islamic Republic of Iran," GOV/2003/63 (Vienna: IAEA, August 26, 2003); and Director-General, IAEA, "Implementation of the NPT Safeguards Agreement in the Islamic Republic of Iran," GOV/2003/75 (Vienna: IAEA, November 10, 2003).

17. Andrew Koch and Jeanette Wolf, "Iran's Nuclear Facilities: A Profile" (Monterey, Calif.: Center for International Studies, Monterey Institute of International Studies, 1998), http://cns.miis.edu/pubs/reports/pdfs/iranrpt.pdf.

18. One analyst has identified "more then 400" military targets of interest, although not all are identified as nuclear sites. See Hersh, "The Iran Plans"; and James Fallows, "Will Iran Be Next?" *Atlantic Monthly*, December 2004, pp. 99–110.

facility at Natanz, and a heavy water plant and plutonium production reactors under construction at Arak.[19] In the past, international concerns over Iran's nuclear weapons program centered on Tehran's agreement with Russia to build a light-water civilian reactor complex at Bushehr.[20] But because the Bushehr reactor is not considered crucial to Iran's development of a nuclear weapons capability, we do not include it in the target set.[21] Moreover, even if Israel decided the reactor would be worth attacking, Bushehr is not a hardened target and is on the Persian Gulf coast; thus, submarine-launched cruise missiles could be used rather than an air strike.[22]

Iran's uranium conversion facility (UCF) is the primary chemical facility for Iran's nuclear program. The facility produces uranium hexafluoride (UF_6, the feed gas for uranium centrifuges), uranium dioxide (UO_2) for reactor fuel, and uranium metal.[23] The loss of a domestic supply of UF_6 for enrichment activities, as well as the loss of lines for the conversion of UF_6 back to uranium metal, would greatly reduce Iran's ability to produce enriched uranium for a nuclear weapon in the future. Because the agreement with Russia for fueling the Bushehr reactor requires Russia to provide fuel for the reactor, destruction of the UCF would not immediately affect Iran's ability to supply electric power. It would, however, severely reduce Iran's enrichment and fuel fabrication capabilities by eliminating the primary means of producing UF_6 and UO_2.

Destruction of Iran's UCF would be complicated, however, by activities that have already taken place. Many tons of uranium exist at the UCF in various

19. For a more detailed analysis of Iran's nuclear infrastructure in the context of nuclear weapons development, see Whitney Raas and Austin Long, "Osirak Redux? Assessing Israeli Capabilities to Destroy Iranian Nuclear Facilities" (Cambridge, Mass.: Security Studies Program, Massachusetts Institute of Technology, April 2006).

20. For U.S. concerns over the Bushehr reactor, see Central Intelligence Agency, "Unclassified Report to Congress on the Acquisition of Technology Relating to Weapons of Mass Destruction and Advanced Conventional Munitions, January 1 through June 30, 2002, " http://www.cia.gov/cia/reports/archive/reports_2002.html.

21. Bushehr is not considered essential to Iran's nuclear weapons program for four reasons: the plutonium produced by the reactor is of extremely poor quality for nuclear weapons; fears of unauthorized technology transfer are diminishing as the Bushehr complex nears completion; Iran has signed an agreement to repatriate spent fuel to Russia; and the reactor is heavily monitored by the IAEA with minimal (if any) protest from Iranian officials. For more information, see Harmon W. Hubbard, "Plutonium from Light Water Reactors as Nuclear Weapon Material" (Washington, D.C.: Nonproliferation Policy Education Center, April 2003), http://www.npec-web.org/Essays/2003-04-01Hubbard.pdf.

22. Israel has several Dolphin-class diesel submarines capable of firing Sub Harpoon cruise missiles and potentially Gabriel or Popeye cruise missiles as well. See *Jane's Underwater Warfare Systems* electronic database entry for Dolphin, March 2006.

23. The production of uranium metal actually occurs after the UF_6 has been enriched. The gas, enriched in U^{235}, is returned to the UCF for conversion back to uranium metal.

chemical forms. Destruction of the facility could result in the release of tons of UF_6, UF_4, and other fluorine and uranium products into the atmosphere. In addition to the contamination due to the release of uranium, the presence of fluorine in the atmosphere would almost certainly result in significant production of hydrofluoric acid, a highly corrosive chemical. Presuming that the Israelis are willing to assume the risks inherent in attacking a chemical facility close to a major city like Isfahan, the destruction of the UCF would interrupt the production of UF_6 feed gas for uranium enrichment at Natanz, as well as the preparation of UO_2 fuel for future heavy-water reactors at Arak.

The Natanz facility is the next critical link in the production of enriched uranium. The facility is composed of a pilot fuel enrichment plant and a much larger commercial plant underground, which is awaiting the arrival of thousands of centrifuges. The site is located approximately 200 miles south of Tehran and about 40 miles from the nearest city. To ensure maximum delay of the Iranian nuclear program, Israel would have to wait until the majority of the centrifuges intended for the commercial plant are in place. These thousands of centrifuges represent a massive capital investment that could not easily be replaced. Thus, the optimal time for launching a military strike would be after the centrifuges have been installed but before a large quantity of UF_6 has been introduced. Bombing the empty halls prior to centrifuge emplacement would not significantly damage Iran's nuclear program, as the Iranians could simply place centrifuges in another, potentially unknown facility.

The final fissile material production facility that Israel could target is the heavy water plant and plutonium production reactors under construction at Arak. The heavy water plant is a large facility located in central Iran approximately 150 miles southwest of Tehran. The site itself is about 20 miles from the nearest town.

Iran has only one small research reactor that uses heavy water as coolant, but the Arak heavy water facility will be able to produce more than 16 tons of heavy water per year—much more than is required by this reactor and more than is needed for virtually all civilian applications. Iranian officials have declared their intentions to build heavy water reactors—and, in fact, construction has begun on two such reactors at Arak—that will utilize much of the heavy water produced at this facility.[24] These reactors are scheduled to be completed in 2014.

---

24. It is possible, though not likely, that Iran has built a larger plutonium production reactor that has not been discovered. We judge it unlikely, as reactors are difficult to hide and difficult for Tehran to build without outside assistance.

Heavy water reactors of the kind Iran intends to build pose the greatest plutonium proliferation risk because the plutonium produced by these reactors
would be weapons grade.[25] Iranian officials have told the IAEA that they also
intend to build reprocessing facilities at Arak in order to separate "long-lived
isotopes" from spent fuel burned in future plutonium production reactors at
the site.[26] It is highly likely that the Arak facility could instead be used for the
production of weapons-grade plutonium—the same hot cells could be used to
recover plutonium from spent fuel. Even though construction of the reactor is
only in the initial stages, the Arak facility remains a serious concern, and eliminating the heavy water plant would significantly slow Iran's future ability to
produce plutonium.

Iran's nuclear program contains many more elements, but the three facilities
discussed above are critical for nuclear weapons development. Destruction of
these facilities would have the greatest impact on Tehran's ability to manufacture nuclear weapons—the UCF by denying Iran the ability to make UF_6 for
enrichment, the Natanz facility for enriching uranium, and the Arak heavy
water plant for use in plutonium production system. Of the three, the Arak
heavy water facility is the least important—the plutonium production reactors
at the site are not scheduled for completion for years, and thus the heavy water
produced by the Arak facility will not be necessary until the reactors are completed—while Natanz is the most important site for Iranian production of
fissile material.[27] The destruction of the Natanz facility is critical to impeding
Iran's progress toward nuclearization.

Weaponeering: What Kind of Bombs and How Many?

The IAF has developed substantially better munitions for attacking hardened
targets, such as reactor containment facilities or buried centrifuge plants, than
it used against Osirak in 1981. These improvements come in two forms: enhanced accuracy and enhanced penetration. This makes current munitions
both easier to deliver and more likely to destroy the target.

The acquisition of precision-guided munitions in the 1980s and 1990s
changed the dynamics of IAF bombing. Accurate delivery no longer required

---

25. Plutonium is produced in all uranium-fueled reactors as a natural reaction in the fuel. In other
types of reactors, however, the plutonium produced is non-weapons-grade.
26. Director-General, IAEA, "Implementation of the NPT Safeguards Agreement in the Islamic
Republic of Iran," GOV/2003/63.
27. This of course assumes that there are no other large-scale reactors in the country that could use
heavy water as a moderator to obtain plutonium from spent fuel.

approaching at low altitude and then "popping up" to dive directly at the target as at Osirak. Instead, using both the Global Positioning System (GPS) and laser-guided bombs (LGBs), the IAF can deliver munitions from high altitude with longer standoff range.[28]

For example, the F-16s used against Osirak had a computerized aiming system, which, if the aircraft could make a reasonably steady approach, would give the unguided bombs a circular error probable (CEP) of roughly 8 to 12 meters.[29] In contrast, GPS munitions such as the Joint Direct Attack Munition (JDAM) have a roughly comparable (if not better) accuracy dropped from high altitude and long standoff range (at least 15 kilometers). LGBs have substantially better accuracy, with modern LGBs having a CEP of about 3 meters or less with roughly the same standoff range. Both GPS and LGB munitions have less restrictive "envelopes" than computer-aided bombing, as they can maneuver themselves on target after launch.[30]

Similarly, munitions for attacking hardened targets have been significantly improved since the Osirak raid. These weapons, known as penetrating warheads or "bunker busters," have seen extensive use by the U.S. Air Force. Delivered from high altitude and arriving at steep angles, these munitions can penetrate tens of feet of earth, and even several feet of reinforced concrete.[31]

The IAF arsenal includes a 1,000 lb.–class penetrating bomb known as the PB 500A1.[32] Additionally, Israel has sought to acquire two heavier penetrating warheads from the United States. In September 2004, Israel announced that it would purchase approximately 5,000 precision-guided munitions from the United States, including about 500 equipped with the 2,000 lb.–class BLU-109 penetrating warhead.[33] More recently, Israel has received approval to purchase

---

28. On the benefits of operating at high altitude, see Barry R. Posen, "Command of the Commons: The Military Foundation of U.S. Hegemony," *International Security*, Vol. 28, No. 1 (Summer 2003), pp. 5–46.

29. CEP is the standard measure of accuracy for munitions and is the radius of a circle around the aim point that 50 percent of weapons fired at a target will land within. Computer-aided bombing accuracy is dependent on a number of factors that can generate error. Further, because the bomb is unguided, error propagates with range. The 8 to 12–meter CEP given can be considered near optimal at 2 kilometers. For the theory behind error calculation in computer-aided bombing, see Morris Drells, *Weaponeering: Conventional Weapons System Effectiveness* (Reston, Va.: American Institute for Aeronautics and Astronautics, 2004), pp. 70–93.

30. See *Jane's Air Launched Weapons* electronic database entries for JDAM and Paveway III penetration bombs, November 2006. The envelope is the three dimensional point or area a plane must occupy when the weapon is released in order for it to strike the target.

31. For an overview of penetrating munitions, see Clifford Beal and Bill Sweetman, "Striking Deep: Hardened-Target Attack Options Grow," *Jane's International Defense Review*, Vol. 27, No. 7 (July 1994), pp. 41–44.

32. See *Jane's Air-Launched Weapons* electronic database entry for PB 500A1, February 2007.

33. "American Sale of New Bombs to Israel Sends Message to Iran," *Times* (London), September

100 precision-guided munitions equipped with the 5,000 lb.–class BLU-113 penetrating warhead.[34] After the July 2006 conflict with Hezbollah, delivery of these bombs has apparently been expedited, and they could be rapidly integrated into the IAF.[35]

In addition to precision-guided munitions and bunker busters, Israel maintains two elite special forces units dedicated to assisting with air strikes: one specialized in laser target designation (Sayeret Shaldag/Unit 5101), the other in real-time bomb damage assessment (Unit 5707).[36] These could potentially infiltrate the target zone prior to attack. The presence of one or both units would enable target designation in bad weather. These units could also assess the damage from those weapons that hit their targets and then direct additional munitions to compensate for misses.

Having presented the general outline of IAF capabilities, we now turn to the application of those capabilities to specific targets. Natanz is both the most difficult and most important target to destroy. The main enrichment facility apparently has two large (25,000 to 32,000 square meter) halls located 8 to 23 meters underground and protected by multiple layers of concrete.[37] The combination of large size and hardening makes this a very challenging target.

One method for defeating hardened facilities is to use LGBs targeted on the same aim point but separated slightly in release time to "burrow" into the target, a technique contemplated by the U.S. Air Force in the 1990–91 Persian Gulf War.[38] This takes advantage of the extremely high accuracy of LGBs in combination with a penetrating warhead. The IAF appears to have purchased penetrating LGBs with this technique in mind. Gen. Eitan Ben-Elyahu, former

---

22, 2004. For details, see *Jane's Air-Launched Weapons* electronic database entry for BLU-109. The penetration capability is given as 1.8 to 2.4 meters of concrete, depending on angle of impact.

34. "Pentagon Notifies Congress of Potential 'Bunker Buster' Sale to Israel," *Defense Daily*, April 29, 2005. For details, see *Jane's Air-Launched Weapons* electronic database entry for Paveway III penetration bombs, February 2007. The penetration capability is credited as at least 6 meters of concrete (presumably reinforced concrete) and 30 meters of earth.

35. Tim McGirk, "Israel and the Bombs," *Time*, August 14, 2006.

36. See *Jane's Sentinel Eastern Mediterranean* electronic database entry for IAF, August 2005.

37. See "Natanz," in "Weapons of Mass Destruction," http://www.globalsecurity.org/wmd/world/iran/natanz.htm; and David Albright and Corey Hinderstein, "The Iranian Gas Centrifuge Uranium Enrichment Plant at Natanz: Drawing from Commercial Satellite Images"(Washington, D.C.: Institute for Science and International Security, March 14, 2003, http://www.isis-online.org/publications/iran/natanz03_02.html.

38. See Eliot Cohen, *Gulf War Air Power Survey* (Washington, D.C.: Office of the Secretary of the Air Force, 1993), Vol. 2, pt. 1, pp. 240–241. The U.S. Air Force considered using up to four weapons targeted on each aim point to dig into buried targets. It has been reported to the authors that the technique was successfully used against an underground aircraft storage facility at Podgorica Airfield in Montenegro during Operation Allied Force in 1999, but this cannot be confirmed from unclassified sources.

commander of the IAF and a participant in the Osirak strike, commented on this method of attacking hardened facilities in *Jane's Defence Weekly:* "Even if one bomb would not suffice to penetrate, we could guide other bombs directly to the hole created by the previous ones and eventually destroy any target."[39]

For a heavily hardened target such as Natanz, the BLU-113 would be the most likely weapon to use. One BLU-113 might be sufficient to penetrate the protective earth and concrete over the Natanz facility, but two properly sequenced almost certainly would. The probability of two LGBs aimed at the same point hitting essentially one on top of the other is likely to be about 0.45.[40] Sequencing of the BLU-113s would be necessary for only the upper end of the estimated hardness of the Natanz centrifuge halls. For example, if the facility is protected by 23 meters of concrete and earth, sequencing would be needed only if roughly 2 meters or more of the 23-meter total are concrete. For the lower estimate of 8 meters of concrete and earth cover, one BLU-113 could easily penetrate.

The question then is: How many BLU-113s able to penetrate the centrifuge halls would be needed to ensure destruction? We estimate that the confined blast from three BLU-113s, combined with collapsing ceiling, shrapnel, and incendiary effect, would likely be sufficient to ruin most if not all of the centrifuges present.[41] According to some analysts' estimates, even this might be overkill, as centrifuges in operation are inherently vulnerable to a destructive series of failures from disruptions in the power supply.[42]

The delivery of six pairs of BLU-113s on each hall, for a total of twelve pairs or twenty-four weapons, would give fairly high confidence of achieving this level of damage. With each pair having a 0.45 probability of success, six pairs

---

39. Quoted in Alon Ben-David, "Paveway III Sale to Bolster Israeli Strike Capability," *Jane's Defence Weekly,* May 4, 2005. Note that unlike earlier LGBs, many modern LGBs incorporate inertial navigation and GPS systems; thus, if the laser designation is lost due to dust or smoke from the first bomb, the second bomb will continue toward the designated target with high precision.
40. See appendix for calculations; 0.45 is the midpoint of our estimates, which range from about 0.1 to 0.7 depending on assumptions.
41. Each BLU-113 contains 306 kilograms of Tritonal. Using known TNT blast curves, TNT equivalence value of 1.07 for Tritonal, and the formula for scaled distance $Z = D/W^{1/3}$, we calculate that each BLU-113 detonation would generate 3 pounds per square inch (psi) overpressure at a distance of about 41 meters in a free airburst. Three detonations would cover 50 to 65 percent of the centrifuge hall with this level of peak overpressure, which is sufficient to cause moderate structural damage to wood frame buildings. Vulnerability data are from Department of Defense, *Physical Vulnerability Handbook* (Washington, D.C.: Defense Intelligence Agency, 1974), declassified.
42. Terrence Henry quotes nonproliferation analyst Jon Wolfstahl: "If the [electrical] current powering the magnet fluctuates . . . you can send the centrifuge flying out of its case, careening across the room like a bowling pin, and knocking out the rest of the centrifuge cascades." Henry, "The Covert Option: Can Sabotage and Assassination Stop Iran from Going Nuclear?" *Atlantic Monthly,* December 2005, p. 56.

would give a total probability of about 0.31 of achieving at least three successful penetrations in both halls and a 0.71 probability of at least two penetrations in each hall.[43] In addition to the weapons that actually penetrated the centrifuge halls, all but one or two of the other BLU-113s would be expected to detonate over each hall, possibly collapsing the entire structure. This gives further confidence in the successful destruction of the facility. For greater confidence, the BLU-113 impact points could be targeted by additional BLU-109s, as discussed below. Finally, the above-ground pilot plant at Natanz would have to be destroyed as well. It does not appear to be hardened, so two 2,000 lb. bombs would likely be sufficient. These need not be penetrating warheads.

The next target, the Isfahan UCF, is not buried, though some evidence of tunneling is visible near the complex.[44] Based on photographs and commercial satellite imagery, the facility appears to be rectangular, roughly 180 meters in length with a varying width of 40 meters up to 80 meters.[45] The facility does not appear to be heavily hardened, so penetrating weapons would probably not be required to destroy it. The IAF could choose to use penetrating weapons, however, to pierce the walls and ensure detonation near critical components.

In this case, the smaller BLU-109 would be useful. BLU-109s could easily penetrate, so extremely high accuracy is less important. The facility appears to be roughly 10,000 square meters, so nine BLU-109s would be sufficient to expose the entire facility to sufficient overpressure to rupture chemical storage tanks.[46] The accuracy of LGBs is such that there is a much greater than 0.9 probability of the weapon falling within 10 meters of the aim point. Combined with a reliability of 0.9 for the weapons themselves, targeting the facility with twelve BLU-109s would be more than sufficient to guarantee its destruction.[47]

---

43. By summing the results of the binomial formula for a k of 0, a k of 1, and a k of 2 where $p = 0.45$ and $n = 6$, we can show that the total probability of achieving 0, 1, or 2 successes is 0.44. By subtracting this probability from 1, we arrive at the probability of achieving three or more successes, which is 0.56 per hall. Squaring this probability gives the chance for getting three or more successes in each hall, or 0.44. The same process can be used to determine the probability of at least two successes, which yields 0.84. Squaring this yields a probability for at least two successes in each hall of 0.71.

44. See "Esfahan/Isfahan Technology Center," in "Weapons of Mass Destruction," http://www.globalsecurity.org/wmd/world/iran/esfahan-imagery-tunnel2.htm.

45. This description is based on the imagery at ibid., http://www.globalsecurity.org/wmd/world/iran/esfahan_comp-zonea.htm, as well as photographs in *Jane's Sentinel Eastern Mediterranean* electronic database entry for Israel, October 2005.

46. In a free airburst, the BLU-109's 240 kilograms of Tritonal explosive would produce 10 psi of overpressure, roughly sufficient to rupture storage tanks, at a distance of about 20 meters.

47. As with the centrifuges of Natanz, some analysts believe that the damage threshold for the Isfahan UCF is actually much lower. Henry notes that former CIA officer Reuel Marc Gerecht

The final target, the Arak facility, has two target sets. The first is the heavy-water production plant, and the second is the heavy-water reactor construction site. Neither target is hardened, so they would be relatively simple to destroy.

The central element of the production plant is a set of towers used to manufacture heavy water. There are three main and nine smaller towers in the complex. They are located in two clusters that are approximately 80 meters long and 30 meters wide. Three nonpenetrating 2,000 lb. LGBs, such as the GBU-10 targeted on each cluster, would likely be sufficient to ensure destruction.[48]

The heavy-water reactor construction site consists of an unfinished containment dome and cooling facility. Assuming this incomplete site is worth targeting, four 2,000 lb. weapons should be more than sufficient to destroy it. This brings the total number of weapons needed to have reasonable confidence in destroying all three target sets to twenty-four 5,000 lb. weapons and twenty-four 2,000 lb. weapons.

Israeli and Iranian Forces

In the more than two decades since the Osirak strike, the IAF's deep-strike capability has improved dramatically. An early display of this growing capability was the 1985 IAF strike on the Palestinian Liberation Organization's headquarters in Tunis. This strike required aerial refueling of F-15s and total travel of more than 4,000 kilometers.[49]

The IAF's deep-strike capability remains centered on its F-15s and F-16s. Israel, however, now fields twenty-five of the F-15I Raam and twenty-five or more of the F-16I Soufa, both of which are specially configured for deep strike.[50] The F-15I is the Israeli version of the U.S. F-15E Strike Eagle, an F-15

---

claims that a backpack full of explosives would be sufficient to severely damage the Isfahan facility. Henry, "The Covert Option."

48. The GBU-10's warhead of 428 kilograms of Tritonal would generate 15 psi peak overpressure (sufficient to destroy petroleum fractionating towers, which we use as a proxy) at a distance of about 21 meters; three weapons would ensure that the entire cluster would be covered with this level of overpressure.

49. See Associated Press, "Israel Calls Bombing a Warning to Terrorists," *New York Times*, October 2, 1985.

50. This estimate is based on Israeli acquisitions from Boeing and Lockheed Martin. The first two F-16Is were delivered in February 2004, and the rate of delivery has been roughly two per month since then. Estimates for the total number of F-16Is delivered at the end of 2004 were eighteen to twenty. *Jane's Sentinel Eastern Mediterranean* lists the IAF as having initiated a fifty-aircraft buy in November 2003, which should have been completed by the end of 2005. See "F-16I Sufa (Storm)," Global Security, http://www.globalsecurity.org/military/world/israel/f-16i.htm; *Jane's Sentinel*

modified to optimize its air-to-ground capability. The F-15I is equipped with conformal fuel tanks (CFTs), which when combined with external drop tanks could likely give it an unrefueled combat radius of roughly 1,700 kilometers with a full weapons load.[51] In addition to its bombing capabilities, the F-15I has a built-in electronic countermeasures suite and is very capable in air-to-air combat.

The F-16I is an F-16 Block 52/60 variant produced specifically for Israeli deep-strike requirements. Like the F-15I, it has CFTs to extend its radius of action. The F-16I's exact combat radius is unknown, but is likely to be on the order of 1,700 kilometers with external fuel tanks.[52] Given the Israeli decision to forgo additional F-15I procurement in favor of increased F-16I procurement, its range is presumably not significantly less than the F-15I. The F-16I could deliver two 2,000 lb. bombs while carrying external fuel tanks, and like the F-15I it carries an advanced electronic countermeasures suite while remaining capable in air-to-air combat.

In contrast to the modern systems of the IAF, the Iranian military possesses an odd amalgamation of technologies. Prior to the fall of the shah in 1979, Iran was the United States' premier client state, and as such was well armed with the best technology the United States could provide. Yet following the revolution, much of the Iranian military's technical competence disappeared, as technicians and skilled officers were killed or fled the country. Spare parts for U.S. systems also became difficult to obtain. Subsequently, Iran has sought to upgrade its military technology with purchases from Russia, China, and elsewhere.[53]

This mixture of various systems is readily apparent in Iran's air defense capabilities. While this defense does not appear incredibly effective, it cannot be entirely discounted. The defense comprises three elements: aircraft, surface-to-air missiles (SAMs), and antiaircraft artillery (AAA).

The inventory and capability of the Islamic Republic of Iran Air Force (IRIAF) are qualitatively poor. IRIAF maintenance and training are insufficient to produce an air force capable of competing with a first-class air force such as

---

Eastern Mediterranean electronic database entry for IAF, August 2005; and "Transfers and Licensed Production of Major Conventional Weapons: Imports Sorted by Recipient. Deals with Deliveries or Orders Made in 1994–2004," Stockholm International Peace Research Institute, http://www.sipri.org/contents/armstrad/REG_IMP_ISR_94-04.pdf.

51. For detailed calculations, see appendix.

52. For detailed calculations, see ibid.

53. For a recent overview of Iran's military organization, see Anthony H. Cordesman, "Iran's Developing Military Capabilities," draft paper (Washington, D.C.: Center for Strategic and International Studies, 2004).

the IAF. The IRIAF fields only forty modern MiG-29s; the remainder of its inventory is of 1970s' or earlier vintage. Further, most of the air-to-air missiles that arm the IRIAF fleet are old and of low quality.[54]

The IRIAF, however, would have two substantial advantages against an IAF strike package in Iranian airspace. First, IRIAF aircraft would be operating near their bases and therefore would be less concerned with fuel usage, which is often important in air-to-air combat. Second, the Iranian aircraft could rely heavily on Ground Control Intercept radar to guide them to IAF aircraft. This advantage could allow IRIAF aircraft to begin an engagement from a favorable position (e.g., attacking from behind the IAF aircraft).[55]

Iran's SAM inventory is similar in quality to its aircraft inventory, with the further complication that this inventory is divided between the IRIAF, the Iranian Revolutionary Guards Corps, and the army. The centerpiece of the inventory is the MIM-23B Improved HAWK, which is of early 1970s' vintage. The combination of age and lack of spare parts probably reduces the utility of the Iranian I-HAWKs. Further, Israel also uses the HAWK system and is thus likely to have developed a significant electronic-countermeasures-suite capability against it. Iran's other SAMs are of similar vintage and would have limited utility against first-class air forces.[56] Iran has tried to purchase the advanced Soviet/Russian SA-10 Grumble SAM, but there are no confirmed reports of delivery.[57]

Recent reports indicate that Iran is taking delivery of Soviet/Russian SA-15 Gauntlet SAM systems.[58] This would add a modern low-/medium-altitude mobile SAM with a phased array tracking radar to Iran's arsenal. The maximum engagement range for the system, however, is believed to be 12 kilometers, with a maximum target altitude of 6,000 meters.[59] Because the IAF strike package would likely be flying more than 5,000 meters aboveground and could drop precision-guided munitions from more than 10 kilometers away, it is unlikely that these weapons would present a major risk to the aircraft. In

54. This assessment is derived primarily from ibid., pp. 25–28; *Jane's World Air Forces* electronic database entry for IRIAF, November 2006; *Jane's World Armies* electronic database entry for Iran, October 2006; and "Air Force," in "Military," http://www.globalsecurity.org/military/world/iran/airforce.htm.
55. For an idea of the advantage this type of radar confers, see Marshall Michel III, *Clashes: Air Combat over North Vietnam, 1965–1972* (Annapolis: Naval Institute Press, 1997).
56. See *Jane's Land-based Air Defense* electronic database entry for HAWK, October 2006.
57. See *Jane's Sentinel Gulf States* electronic database entry for Iran, October 2005.
58. See "U.S. Criticizes Russian Sale of Anti-missile Systems to Iran," *Haaretz*, January 16, 2007; and "Tor-M1s to Go to Iran by Year-End," *Jane's Defence Weekly*, October 18, 2006.
59. See *Jane's Land-based Air Defence* electronic database entry for SA-15, October 2006.

contrast, the older I-HAWK is reported to able to engage targets at an altitude of more than 17,000 meters at a range of 40 kilometers.[60] The SA-15 could potentially engage the incoming bombs themselves, but even a modest IAF defense suppression effort would likely minimize this effect.

Finally, Iran possesses a large quantity of AAA. In general, AAA is ineffective at higher altitudes, though it has some advantages over SAM systems. Most notably, AAA can compensate for electronic jamming to some degree by relying on a high volume of fire.

Iran's combined SAM and AAA inventory could provide some defense of key points. Nonetheless, a major weakness remains tying all of these systems together in an effective Integrated Air Defense System (IADS). Without an effective IADS, the Iranian systems would not be fully mutually supporting, which would further limit their capabilities during an aerial attack. Fear of fratricide could also limit the ability of the Iranian air defense to use interceptors and SAMs in the same area.

Possible Attack Routes

The Israelis have three possible attack routes. The first is to fly north over the Mediterranean, refuel from airborne tankers, and then fly east over Turkey to Iran. The second is to fly southeast, skirt Jordan and Saudi Arabia, and then fly northeast across Iraq (essentially the Osirak route), possibly refueling in the air along the way. Alternatively, the Israelis could fly northeast across Jordan and Iraq. Finally, they could fly southeast and then east along the Saudi-Iraqi border to the Persian Gulf and then north, refueling along the way.

The northern route has three main legs. The first is from Israeli air bases to the Turkish border. The likely bases that aircraft would be launched from are Hatzerim (near Beersheba), Hatzor (near Ashdod), and Ramat David (near Haifa).[61] To simplify, we calculate the longest distance to the target set, in this case from Hatzerim. The IAF could reduce this distance by moving planes between bases, though this could provide warning to other countries' intelligence services. The distance from Hatzerim to the Mediterranean is approximately 80 kilometers, and then north to Turkey is approximately 500 kilometers.

---

60. See *Jane's Land-based Air Defence* electronic database entry for HAWK.
61. See "Airfields," in "Military," http://www.globalsecurity.org/military/world/israel/airfield.htm.

The second leg crosses Turkey from west to east, a short distance north of the Syrian border. The route begins east of Adana, passes south of Diyarbakir, and ends at the Iranian border west of Orumiyeh. This is a total distance of about 840 kilometers.

The final leg is southeast across Iran to Arak, Natanz, and Isfahan. We calculate the end point as the distance to the farthest target, in this case Isfahan. The distance from the border near Orumiyeh to Isfahan is approximately 800 kilometers. The total route length is thus roughly 2,220 kilometers.

This route is longer than the estimated unrefueled combat radius of Israel's strike aircraft, but it carries the advantage of aerial refueling over the Mediterranean. Tankers are vulnerable to attack, so being able to refuel over the international waters of the Mediterranean would be a big advantage. Israeli tanker assets are not well documented, but they appear to consist of five to seven KC-707s and four to five KC-130Hs.[62] The KC-130, due to its drogue refueling design, would be unable to refuel F-16s and F-15s without some modification or carrying of special refueling probe-equipped external fuel tanks. The KC-707 can probably deliver roughly 120,000 pounds of jet fuel at a range of 1,000 nautical miles, and can transfer this fuel very quickly.[63] For a strike package of fifty aircraft, the KC-707 fleet could deliver 12,000 to 16,000 pounds of fuel per aircraft at a range of 1,000 nautical miles. As the actual distance to the refueling point would probably be less than 400 nautical miles, there should be more than this amount of fuel available.

By refueling over the Mediterranean, the strike package could maneuver against Iranian air defenses with less concern about fuel. The refueling on the inbound leg of the flight, however, would take place very early (after flying fewer than 600 kilometers), so only a limited amount of fuel could be offloaded to each aircraft before they would be full again. The total distance from Adana to Isfahan is about 1,640 kilometers, very close to the combat radius predicted for the F-15I. This would mean the strike aircraft would probably have to refuel a second time, after leaving Turkish airspace on the return trip. The IAF tankers could wait near the Turkish border to refuel the strike aircraft as they returned to Israel, potentially protected by other IAF aircraft.

---

62. See "Israel—IAF Equipment," in "Military," http://www.globalsecurity.org/military/world/israel/iaf-equipment.htm; and *Jane's World Air Forces* electronic database entry for Israel, October 2006.
63. See Federation of American Scientists, "KC-135 Stratotanker," http://www.fas.org/nuke/guide/usa/bomber/kc-135.htm. The KC 707 has essentially the same airframe as the U.S. KC-135, so we assume they have roughly the same refueling capability.

One disadvantage of this route is that it passes quite close to several Turkish air force bases, including two large ones: Incirlik (near Adana) and Diyarbakir. Turkey's reaction to a potential Israeli incursion is uncertain. Although the Turks would undoubtedly be angry, the central question is whether they would fire on Israeli aircraft. Turkey and Israel have historically enjoyed good military and economic relationships, even if their political rhetoric is sometimes harsh. On the other hand, the current Turkish government of moderate Islamists has to some degree distanced itself from Israel.

Furthermore, this route passes near a number of Iranian air bases: Tabriz, Sharohki (near Hamadan), Kermanshah, Khatami (near Isfahan), and Vahdati (near Dezful).[64] The major bases near Tehran are slightly farther away. This would put the strike package in range of a number of possible intercept squadrons during both ingress and egress.

If the IAF were reluctant to accept the diplomatic problems of flying over Turkey, it could instead cross Syria for most of the east-west leg of this route. It would then have to cross Turkish airspace only briefly near the Iranian border. Syria would almost undoubtedly fire on Israeli aircraft. This route would thus trade significantly higher operational risk for somewhat lower diplomatic costs.

The second route is the most direct route, but it carries major political difficulties. It has one or two main legs, depending on how it is flown. The first leg of option one would be from Ramat David (the farthest from the target) to the Gulf of Aqaba. This is basically the entire length of Israel, so planes might be relocated farther south before the strike. As noted above, however, we assume for simplicity and operational security that all planes launch from home base. The length of this leg would be roughly 360 kilometers. The second leg of option one is from the northern end of the Gulf of Aqaba to the target zone. This leg is extremely long, with the farthest target, Natanz, roughly 1,800 kilometers away. The total distance traveled, 2,160 kilometers, would be scarcely less than that of the northern route. Refueling would be required at some point. The second option, directly across Jordan and Iraq, is shorter. The distance from Hatzerim to Natanz is roughly 1,750 kilometers, which is just over the estimated combat radius of the strike aircraft.

Both options would require cooperation (or at least acquiescence) from the Jordanians and especially the Americans in Iraq. The flight path of option two

---

64. See "Airfields and Bases," in "Military, " http://www.globalsecurity.org/military/world/iran/airfield.htm.

is directly over Jordan and would pass near the capital of Amman and a major air base at Azraq ash Shishan. Each would traverse all of Iraq, and any refueling would likely be over Iraq. It would be all but impossible to accomplish without the notice of the Americans and probably the Jordanians. While any strike against Iran by Israel would be interpreted as having U.S. backing, this option would provide unambiguous evidence of it.

The central route has the advantage of crossing less Iranian airspace than the northern route. It would avoid the base at Tabriz, though the other bases noted above would still be in range. Iranian air defense on the Iraqi border might potentially be on higher alert than along the Turkish border.

The southern route covers perhaps the least well-defended airspace, at least in its initial legs. It is also quite long and poses refueling challenges. It runs west to east across northern Saudi Arabia to the Persian Gulf, then north/northeast into Iran.

The first leg would be the Ramat David to the Gulf of Aqaba route noted above, a distance of 360 kilometers. As with that route, IAF aircraft could be shifted to bases farther south to shorten the distance. From Aqaba the aircraft would cross Saudi Arabia south of the Iraqi border, from the coast near the town of Haql to the Persian Gulf coast near Ras al-Khafji. This is a distance of roughly 1,350 kilometers.

The second leg would cross the Persian Gulf into Iran, and then north to the target zone. The farthest target would be Natanz, a distance of about 700 kilometers. This makes the total route length on the order of 2,410 kilometers, easily the longest route of the three.

The third route poses the same kind of diplomatic challenges as the northern route, as it crosses Saudi airspace and passes near several Saudi air bases. Further, Saudi Arabia has invested significantly in IADS. On paper this appears to be a highly formidable air defense system. Saudi readiness levels are alleged to be very low, however.[65] In addition, much of Saudi Arabia's northern air defense was intended to protect against Iraq, and presumably readiness levels are much lower now that the threat from Saddam Hussein has been removed. In addition, the question would still remain whether the Saudis would fire on Israeli aircraft or simply launch a massive diplomatic protest.

A more serious issue is refueling. The route would be significantly longer than the estimated combat radius of the strike aircraft. The IAF would thus have two options, both dangerous. It could attempt to refuel the strike package

---

65. See Anthony H. Cordesman, *The Military Balance in the Gulf: The Dynamics of Force Development* (Washington, D.C.: Center for Strategic and International Studies, 2005), pp. 131–134.

over Saudi territory, which would be subject to disruption by Saudi forces. Alternatively, it could refuel over the Persian Gulf, which might be less subject to disruption. It would still require flying the tankers across Saudi Arabia, and would also put the tankers in a position to possibly be engaged by IRIAF interceptors over the gulf. The route would pass near several IRIAF bases: Bushehr, Vahdati, Isfahan, and Abadan (a nonmilitary but potentially usable airfield). Shiraz is only slightly farther away.[66]

All of the routes pose significant operational and political risks. From a technical perspective, none are impossible. The remainder of this analysis focuses on Iranian air defenses near the target areas, regardless of the route taken by the IAF's strike package.

The Likely Correlation of Forces

The analysis below assumes that the IAF would attack Iran's nuclear facilities using twenty-five F-15Is and twenty-five F-16Is. The IAF could potentially field a larger strike package, but this would probably tax its refueling capabilities and command and control. This package would probably consist of three smaller packages, one for each of the likely targets.

The interaction of this strike package with Iran's air defenses is highly contingent. In the Osirak strike, IAF aircraft escaped all but the most desultory engagement with AAA around the reactor site. The IAF would probably not be so lucky against Iranian facilities, but Iran's lack of an effective IADS suggests that the level of engagement could potentially be low.

The exact quality and readiness of Iranian equipment is unknown. With moderate reliability and effectiveness in its air defenses, Iran could credibly respond to an IAF incursion. In contrast, if reliability and effectiveness are low, then the IAF could brush aside the Iranian forces with relative ease.

Rather than attempt to map the various contingent outcomes, we look at the number of aircraft that would have to arrive on target to deliver the ordnance noted in the section on weaponeering. From that, we can determine the attrition levels the Iranian air defense would have to generate to prevent the Israeli strikes from being fully successful. We can then make some rough guesses about the likelihood of this occurring.

In the case of Natanz, if each F-15I carried only one BLU-113 (along the centerline) in addition to external fuel tanks and air-to-air missiles, then twenty-

---

66. See "Airfields and Bases," http://www.globalsecurity.org/military/world/iran/airfield.htm.

four F-15Is would have to arrive at the target complex. Note that if the F-15Is carried only one BLU-113 centerline, they could potentially carry additional BLU-109s on the CFT hardpoints. Isfahan and Arak would require fewer aircraft to deliver the requisite ordnance. In the case of Isfahan, six F-16Is would have to arrive at the target complex if each carried two BLU-109s. For Arak, only five F-16Is would have to reach the target.

Iran's air defenses would have to impose significant attrition to cause the IAF mission to fail to deliver the ordnance noted above. The IAF could assign two additional F-16Is (out of twenty-five) loaded with 2,000 lb. bombs to both Arak and Isfahan and then have ten left for defending the strike package. The Iranian air defense would have to down three out of seven assigned to Arak and three out of eight assigned to Isfahan, roughly 40 percent attrition. This would be almost unimaginable given Iranian assets, as even the disastrous U.S. raid on Ploesti in World War II sustained only 32 percent attrition (admittedly out of a much larger total number). More comparably, on the third and worst night of the December 1972 Linebacker II raids on Hanoi, U.S. losses from the first and third wave of B-52s were less than 10 percent, while the total loss that night was slightly more than 6 percent.[67]

The major vulnerability would be attrition in the F-15I force, assuming each carried only one BLU-113. Then, Iran's air defenses would have to impose an attrition rate of only 8 percent (downing two out of twenty-five) to cause the mission to fail to deliver the designated ordnance. This is certainly within the realm of possibility. For example, IAF ground attack aircraft sustained massive attrition in the first days of the 1973 Yom Kippur War, including 8 percent of total fighter strength on the first day. The average daily attrition rate of IAF aircraft in that conflict was only about 3 percent, however.[68]

A potentially more relevant example would be the U.S. raid on Libya in 1986. This strike, code-named El Dorado Canyon, was similar to the proposed IAF strike. It used roughly the same number of aircraft (in this case, twenty-four F-111s) flying very long routes (from England and around France to the Mediterranean). The buildup to El Dorado Canyon in the media was such that the Libyans had at least as much warning as the Iranians could expect. In that

---

67. On Ploesti, see Stephen W. Sears, *Air War against Hitler's Germany* (New York: Harper Row, 1964), p. 74. On Linebacker II, see Alfred Price, *War in the Fourth Dimension: U.S. Electronic Warfare from the Vietnam War to the Present* (Mechanicsburg, Pa.: Stackpole, 2001), p. 120. Both the first and third waves lost three B-52s, out of thirty-three and thirty-nine, respectively. The total sent that night was ninety-nine B-52s, though six were recalled.
68. In a conflict that lasted eighteen days, the IAF lost about 115 fighter-bombers out of a total of 358, for a daily loss rate of 2.5 to 3 percent. See Eliot A. Cohen and John Gooch, *Military Misfortunes: The Anatomy of Failure in War* (New York: Free Press, 1990), pp. 104, 110.

case, only one U.S. aircraft was lost, for an attrition rate of slightly more than 4 percent.[69]

Of course, reliability is an issue with aircraft as well as munitions. If even one F-15I failed to complete the mission due to reliability problems, then the Iranians would have to down only one aircraft. If two failed to function, then the mission would be unable to deliver the designated ordnance without the Iranians even firing a shot. Further, the IRIAF does not have to actually down any IAF aircraft. It must only succeed in engaging the IAF aircraft with sufficient threat to cause them to dump their ordnance in order to maneuver. In Vietnam, this happened with some frequency to U.S. strike aircraft. With the advantage of good Ground Control Intercept radar and SAMs, the IRIAF might achieve similar results.

Yet even if the designated ordnance needed for the total destruction of Natanz were not delivered, the Iranian nuclear program would still be significantly hampered. Even one large bomb detonating in each centrifuge hall would disrupt operations and, if it were operating, would contaminate it with UF_6. Further, to ensure that total destruction is highly likely even with significant attrition in its strike package, the IAF could send additional assets to Natanz, as discussed below.

Finally, Iran's air defense system was only modestly effective against the Iraqi air force during the 1980–88 Iran-Iraq War.[70] This lack of success against what was at best a very poor air force, compounded by the subsequent aging of systems such as the I-HAWK, makes it unlikely that the Iranians would perform effectively against the IAF. This gives additional confidence in mission success.

The IAF could also supplement the F-15I attack on Natanz by assigning F-16Is armed with BLU-109s to attack the BLU-113 aim points. While the BLU-109 is less certain of penetration than the massive BLU-113s, it is still a very capable weapon. Assuming that six F-16Is were assigned to supplement the F-15Is, each could deliver two BLU-109s on each of six BLU-113 aim points. This would result in a greater than 0.8 probability of at least one weapon, BLU-109 or BLU-113, penetrating the Natanz facility.[71] The actual amount of explosive

---

69. See Joseph T. Stanik, *El Dorado Canyon: Reagan's Undeclared War with Qaddafi* (Annapolis: Naval Institute Press, 2002).
70. See Efraim Karsh, "The Iran-Iraq War: A Military Analysis," Adelphi Paper, No. 220 (London: International Institute for Strategic Studies, 1987), p. 40; and Anthony H. Cordesman, *The Iran-Iraq War and Western Security, 1984–1987: Strategic Implications and Policy Options* (London: Jane's, 1987), pp. 114–115, 131, 135.
71. The probability of at least two direct hits on the aim point out of four weapons (two BLU-113s and two BLU-109s) is 0.8, assuming the base case of 0.9 reliability and 0.65 probability of a direct

contained in the BLU-109 and BLU-113 is quite similar, so a high confidence of destruction could be obtained in this manner.

Also, as noted earlier, the F-15Is could carry two BLU-109s, adding more firepower. If each carried one BLU-113 and two BLU-109s, the strike package of twenty-five F-15Is would have twenty-five BLU-113s and fifty BLU-109s. Two of these weapons would be used to destroy the pilot plant, but the rest could be aimed at the underground facility. Even if the Iranian air defense imposed 40 percent attrition (ten aircraft downed), fifteen BLU-113s and thirty BLU-109s would arrive on target, even without supplemental F-16Is. This would allow almost four weapons to be targeted for each of the twelve aim points (six per hall), even without additional F-16Is. This would mean that additional F-16Is could be dedicated to defense suppression and air-to-air roles.

Conclusion

The foregoing assessment is far from definitive in its evaluation of Israel's military capability to destroy Iranian nuclear facilities. It does seem to indicate, however, that the IAF, after years of modernization, now possesses the capability to destroy even well-hardened targets in Iran with some degree of confidence. Leaving open the question of whether an attack is worth the resulting diplomatic consequences and Iranian response, it appears that the Israelis have three possible routes for an air strike against three of the critical nodes of the Iranian nuclear program. Although each of these routes presents political and operational difficulties, this article argues that the IAF could nevertheless attempt to use them.

The operation would appear to be no more risky than Israel's 1981 attack on Iraq's Osirak reactor, and it would provide at least as much benefit in terms of delaying Iranian development of nuclear weapons. This benefit might not be worth the operational risk and political cost. Nonetheless, this analysis demonstrates that Israeli leaders have access to the technical capability to carry out the attack with a reasonable chance of success. The question then becomes one of will and individual calculation.

More generally, this assessment illustrates both the utility and limitations of precision-guided weapons for counterproliferation. Assuming that the intelligence is available to identify targets of interest, precision-guided weapons can fill an important role of destroying the target with increased confidence,

---

hit. Because this does not account for any near misses, it understates the likelihood of success. It also disregards the possibility of the two misses being BLU-113s and the two hits being BLU-109s.

leading to smaller strike packages and lower risk to personnel and equipment. Although limitations still exist, especially in the case of hardened targets, precision-guided weapons have become extremely capable, particularly when strike aircraft are confronted by relatively low-quality air defense. The use of precision strike for counterproliferation should therefore not be discounted lightly.

This analysis, however, highlights the critical nature of target knowledge. In many cases, the means of striking or defending WMD targets may be less important than the ability to locate or hide them. Those seeking to stop proliferation would be advised to invest heavily in intelligence collection and analysis, while proliferators should rely on concealing and dispersing rather than hardening targets.

Additionally, the analysis illustrates that the technical ability to conduct an attack may be overshadowed by the "day after" problem. When Israel struck Osirak, Iraq was involved in a bloody war with Iran that limited its ability to retaliate. With Iraq in chaos, a capable proxy in Lebanon's Hezbollah, and high oil prices, Iran today has a much greater ability to strike back against both Israel and the United States. Although the IAF may be able to destroy known Iranian nuclear facilities (by extension the U.S. Air Force almost certainly can) and significantly delay Iran's nuclear program, Iran's potential responses to such a strike may cause policymakers to reject this option. Despite its potential utility, military counterproliferation must be complemented by political and economic efforts if the spread of nuclear weapons is to be checked.

Appendix: Estimating Aircraft Range and Bomb Sequencing

AIRCRAFT RANGE ESTIMATES
The official ferry range (the range the aircraft can fly one way without refueling) for the F-15E using CFTs and three external fuel tanks is given by the U.S. Air Force as 3,840 kilometers.[1] Other sources suggest that the actual ferry range is in excess of 5,600 kilometers. *Jane's All the World's Aircraft* lists it as 4,445 kilometers. In terms of combat radius,

---

1. For data in the appendix, see John Anderson, *Introduction to Flight*, 5th ed. (Boston: McGraw-Hill, 2005); *Jane's All the World's Aircraft* entry for F-15 and F-16; "F-15E Strike Eagle," http://www.af.mil/factsheets/factsheet.asp?fsID?102; "F-15 Eagle," in "Military," http://www.globalsecurity.org/military/systems/aircraft/f-15-specs.htm; Jaffee Center, "Air Force Equipment," in "Middle East Military Balance," http://www.tau.ac.il/jcss/balance/airf.pdf; "Air Force Equipment F-15E 'Strike' Eagle Long-Range Interdiction Fighter, USA," http://www.airforce-technology.com/projects/f15/; F-15E Strike Eagle, http://www.f-15estrikeeagle.com/weapons/loadouts/oif/oif.htm; "F-16 Fighter Falcon," http://www.af.mil/factsheets/factsheet.asp?fsID=103; "F-16 Fighting Falcon," http://www.globalsecurity.org/military/systems/aircraft/f-16-specs.htm; and "F-16 Fighting Falcon Multi-role Fighter Aircraft, USA," http://www.airforce-technology.com/projects/f16/.

the number most often cited for the F-15E is 1,270 kilometers, which appears to be with CFTs and a full weapons load. The combat radius could be extended by replacing two weapons with external fuel tanks. A simple estimate can be derived from comparing the fuel load with CFTs only (approximately 23,000 pounds) with the fuel load of CFTs plus two 610-gallon external tanks (approximately 31,000 pounds). This ratio is about 1.35, which when multiplied by 1,270 kilometers yields a combat radius of roughly 1,700 kilometers. This estimate also appears to roughly conform to the official ferry range, as with three drop tanks and CFTs the F-15E can carry about 35,300 pounds of fuel, or a ratio of about 1.53. This yields a combat radius of about 1,900 kilometers, or a ferry range of 3,800 kilometers. Ferry range assumes no combat maneuvering, but the official estimate, as noted, is probably highly conservative. Some sources list the combat radius of the F-15E as in excess of 1,800 kilometers, so the 1,700-kilometer estimate is probably conservative as well. Breguet calculations based on unclassified estimates of F-15E performance, a specific fuel consumption of 0.9, a constant velocity of 700 miles per hour, constant coefficient of lift, lift-to-drag ratio of 6.193, and a take-off weight of 80,000 pounds with 30,000 pounds of fuel also produce results in this range (approximately 1,800-kilometer radius), not accounting for weapons release.

The F-16D, which the F-16I is based on, has internal fuel storage of almost 5,900 pounds and an estimated combat radius of 540 kilometers. With the addition of CFTs, one 300-gallon centerline and two 600-gallon external fuel tanks, the F-16I could carry about 19,000 pounds of fuel. Using the simple estimation method above, this is a ratio of 3.22, which would give the F-16I a combat radius of about 1,730 kilometers. As the CFTs have much lower drag than the external fuel tanks, the actual combat radius would probably be higher. At least one source, the Jaffee Center, reports a combat radius of 2,100 kilometers, so this estimate is probably conservative. It appears to be roughly in line with other estimates. Jane's *All the World's Aircraft* lists 1,361 kilometers as the combat radius in a hi-lo-lo-hi profile for the F-16C Block 50 with CFTs, a centerline 300-gallon external fuel tank, and two 370-gallon underwing fuel tanks (roughly 17,100 lbs of fuel), while carrying two 2,000 lb. bombs and two Sidewinder missiles. This estimate is also in line with the official U.S. Air Force ferry range in excess of 3,200 kilometers. This ferry range is with two 600-gallon and two 370-gallon fuel tanks for a total of 18,700 pounds of fuel, a ratio of 3.28. This yields a radius of about 1,770 kilometers and a ferry range of at least 3,540 kilometers.

PENETRATING BOMB SEQUENCING

Bomb sequencing is derived from the formula $P_k = 1 - 0.5^{(LR/CEP)}$, where P_k is the probability of successful landing within the lethal radius (LR) of the target. Additionally, the non-Gaussian distribution of LGBs is represented by the fraction of bombs that exhibit no error (i.e., they directly hit the aim point). The lethal radius is crater size, so there is some probability of a near miss still landing in the crater. In the case of two near misses, the lethal radius is reduced by half; in other words, if the first bomb lands within half the LR of the aim point, then the second bomb will definitely hit within the LR if it too lands within half the LR of the aim point. With these assumptions, there are four probability branches: direct hit-direct hit; direct hit-near miss; near miss-direct hit; and near miss-near miss. These branches have a probability of $(0.65)^2 = 0.42$; $0.65 \times (0.35 \times 0.29) = 0.07$; $(0.35 \times 0.29) \times 0.65 = 0.07$; and $(0.4 \times 0.16)^2 = 0.004$. This yields a cumulative probability of 0.56, which is then multiplied by the cumulative reliability (0.9 × 0.9 = 0.81) to yield a probability of 0.45. The assumption of crater width is based on the 0.37-meter diameter of a GBU-28 combined with the effect of the explosion occurring in the ground, which would rupture the ground surrounding the explosion as well as being vented to some degree out of the entryway of the warhead. This is presumed to create sufficient structural damage to allow the second BLU-113 to penetrate easily if it impacts within a 1.8–3.6 meter radius (10–20 times the diameter of the bomb) of the entry point of the first bomb. This calculation is very sensitive to changes in the parameters, so some variations are presented in Table 1.

Table 1. Variation in Parameters of the BLU-113 Sequenced Penetration

N_{hit}	0.65	0.30	0.50	0.70	0.50	0.15	0.70
N_{nm}	0.35	0.70	0.50	0.30	0.50	0.85	0.30
CEP	6	3	6	2	3	6	3
LR	3	2	3	3	3	3	2
Rel	0.90	0.85	0.90	0.95	0.90	0.90	0.90
Prob	0.45	0.19	0.33	0.70	0.42	0.09	0.53

SOURCES: C.R. Anderegg, *Sierra Hotel: Flying Air Force Fighters in the Decade after Vietnam* (Washington, D.C.: Air Force History and Museums Program, 2001); and Morris Drells, *Weaponeering: Conventional Weapons System Effectiveness* (Reston, Va.: American Institute for Aeronautics and Astronautics, 2004).

N_{hit} = percentage of munitions that directly hit aim point (i.e., non-Gaussian distribution)

N_{nm} = percentage of munitions that exhibit Gaussian distribution of a given CEP

CEP = circular error probable; radius in meters around aim point in which half of Gaussian distributed munitions will fall

LR = lethal radius; in this case, the radius in meters around the impact point of the first BLU-113 that the second must hit within to penetrate the Natanz facility

Rel = reliability; the probability the BLU-113 will function properly

Prob = the cumulative probability of the two BLU-113s functioning and impacting sufficiently close for the second to penetrate the Natanz facility

International Security

The Robert and Renée Belfer Center for
Science and International Affairs
John F. Kennedy School of Government
Harvard University

Many of the articles in this reader were previously published in **International Security,** a quarterly journal sponsored and edited by the Robert and Renée Belfer Center for Science and International Affairs at Harvard University's John F. Kennedy School of Government, and published by MIT Press Journals. To receive journal subscription information or to find out more about other readers in our series, please contact MIT Press Journals at 238 Main Street, suite 500, Cambridge, MA 02142, or on the web at http://mitpress.mit.edu.